Transgender Emergence
Therapeutic Guidelines for Working with Gender-Variant People and Their Families

Transgender Emergence
Therapeutic Guidelines for Working with Gender-Variant People and Their Families

Arlene Istar Lev

Routledge
Taylor & Francis Group
New York   London

The Haworth Clinical Practice Press
An Imprint of The Haworth Press, Inc.
New York • London • Oxford

Published by

The Haworth Clinical Practice Press, an imprint of The Haworth Press, Inc., 10 Alice Street, Binghamton, NY 13904-1580.

TR: 7.30.04

PUBLISHER'S NOTE
Identities and circumstances of individuals discussed in this book have been changed to protect confidentiality. Any resemblance to actual persons, living or dead, is entirely coincidental.

Cover design by Marylouise E. Doyle.

Library of Congress Cataloging-in-Publication Data

Lev, Arlene Istar.
　　Transgender emergence : therapeutic guidelines for working with gender-variant people and their families / Arlene Istar Lev.
　　　　p. cm.
Includes bibilographical references and index.
　　ISBN-13: 978-0-7890-0708-7 (hc. : alk. paper)
　　ISBN-10: 0-7890-0708-8 (hc. : alk. paper)
　　ISBN-13: 978-0-7890-2117-5 (pbk. : alk. paper)
　　ISBN-10: 0-7890-2117-X (pbk. : alk. paper)
　　1. Gender identity disorders. 2. Transsexualism. I. Title.
　　RC560.G45L48 2003
　　616.85'83—dc21

2002156666

This book is dedicated to the transgender community—those who are gender variant and gender defiant and those who love them. This book is especially for Linda, who tried to tell me, and for Rhiannon, who tried to fly.

It is with great respect that I offer this book to my teacher, who reminds me to see God in everyone; this book is but one manifestation of the many lessons I have learned.

ABOUT THE AUTHOR

Arlene Istar Lev, LCSW, CASAC, is a licensed clinical social worker, family therapist, and credentialed alcohol and substance abuse counselor, with twenty years of experience addressing the unique therapeutic needs of lesbian, gay, bisexual, and transgendered people. She is the founder of Choices Counseling and Consulting in Albany, New York, and is on the adjunct faculties of the State University of New York at Albany, School of Social Welfare, and the Vermont College of the Union Institute and University. In addition, Arlene is a board member of the Family Pride Coalition and a contributing editor to *In the Family* magazine.

Arlene's expertise is in issues related to sexual and gender identity, as well as trauma recovery, addictions, adoption, and parenting in alternative families. Arlene works within a feminist family systems and empowerment modality and is trained in numerous psychotherapeutic and psychospiritual arts. She has published in the areas of domestic violence and sexual assault in the LGBT community, and family therapy approaches to working with family members of those who are gender variant.

Arlene is a member of the National Association of Social Workers, the American Psychological Association, the Harry Benjamin International Gender Dysphoria Association, and is an advisory board member of the Lesbian and Gay Family Building Project, Binghamton, New York. She is the former Chair of the National Association of Social Workers (NASW), New York State Chapter, Lesbian and Gay Issues Committee (1986-1994).

Arlene is a frequently sought-after writer and has published in *Transgender Tapestry, And Baby Magazine, In the Family, Alternative Family/Proud Parenting,* and various social work magazines. In addition, she is the author of the forthcoming *The Complete Lesbian and Gay Parenting Guide* (Penguin Press). She maintains an LGBT parenting column and "Dear Ari," an advice column, at <www.ProudParenting.com>. She can be reached through <www.choicesconsulting.com>.

CONTENTS

Foreword

I recently returned from a month in New Zealand, a very civil and pleasant country. The week before returning home, I watched an extraordinary documentary on television called *Georgie Girl.* No, it was not the old English film with Lynn Redgrave but rather the very moving story of Georgina Beyer, a Maori woman who began life as a man. Georgina, after being alienated from her family and culture, worked for years as a sex worker and female impersonator. She has become an openly transsexual woman and has been elected a member of the New Zealand parliament. This courageous, highly articulate, attractive, dignified woman was sent to parliament from a rural, conservative district with her sense of humor intact. I probably don't have it quite right, but in an early speech to Parliament, she said something like, "I used to have a member and now I am a member . . ." and there was a jolly ripple of laughter throughout the halls of government.

A second personal anecdote: A year ago, parents received a letter from the head of my grandson's preschool inviting them to a meeting. It was early December and it seems that one of the teachers was planning to make the social transition from female to male over the Christmas holidays. Included was a letter from the teacher as well, explaining her intentions, the new name she would be taking, and the reasons for her decision. Parents were urged to come to the meeting with questions and any concerns they might have. I attended the meeting with my daughter-in-law. The transsexual teacher was not there, although the other teachers of the two-year-olds did attend, as did the head of school, and two people who had had considerable experience working with transsexual and transgendered persons. The room was filled with parents who, in turn, were filled with questions. Every single comment and question was, in my judgment, appropriate and respectful, mostly having to do with how to answer their two-year-old children's questions, to respond to any confusion they might display, and to discuss how young children learn about gender and what effects this young person's transition from female to male might have on their learning. I left the meeting very moved, having said how courageous I thought the teacher was and how proud and grateful I was to be able to live in a community, and to have my grandson attend a school, that would handle such a potentially controversial issue in such a well-informed, respectful, and positive way. My grandson, for a couple of months, hyphenated his teacher's male and female names to give himself time to get used to the teacher's transition, but by the end of term he too had made the shift from *her* to *him* with no apparent anxiety or confusion. *She* had been and *he* was, before, during, and after, my grandson's favorite teacher.

Isn't this how it should be? Perhaps, though I would wish for far more. How is it that, in the United States, we have only a few women in Congress, and a miniscule number of openly gay, lesbian, or bisexual elected officials? The election of a transsexual former sex worker to public office is not likely to happen in my lifetime. But as Arlene Istar Lev documents in this extraordinary book, we are all participating in or at least witnessing the beginnings of another major civil rights movement—as Ms. Lev terms it, a "gender revolution." On one hand, it is a movement that directly involves a very small percentage of the population; on the other hand, it involves each and every one of us. Why? Because the phenomenon of transsexuality has forced us, more than anything else since the height of the second wave of feminism, to question, to become uncertain about, our deeply bipolar cultural assumptions about gender.

The transgender movement parallels and to some extent overlaps in many ways the lesbian, gay, and bisexual movements. In fact, the "T" in transgenderism has now become an accepted part of the politically correct acronym *LGBT* (lesbian, gay, bisexual, transgender). After decades of simmering, the 1990s brought to the boil a massive shift in the visibility of lesbian and gay people and issues on every cultural level. In popular culture, lesbians and gay men became far more openly identified in film, music, art, and literature. *Ellen, Roseanne, Will & Grace,* and many others led the way, as lesbian and gay became "cool," "chic," "in." Television gave us a heavy dose of talk shows and documentaries. No sitcom or drama worth its salt went without permanent or occasional gay characters, plots, or episodes, as "gayness" became mainstream, part of everyday life. Small but increasing numbers of lesbian and gay people were offered straight roles, and heterosexual stars risked playing gay parts. The very popular Rosie O'Donnell has broken new ground, or at least substantially altered the landscape, not by openly coming out as lesbian but by coming out as a lesbian mother, expanding the public conversation to the level of family.

It is extremely difficult to know how to evaluate this profound shift in LGB visibility, as being cool or chic does not necessarily mean being accepted. As lesbian, gay, and bisexual persons and their allies began to demand access to domestic benefits; to same-sex marriage and civil union; to nondiscrimination in employment, housing, and the military; countermovements also gathered momentum. The 1990s brought us the Hawaii same-sex marriage case and the hastily contrived Defense of Marriage Act. The religious right and the fatherhood and marriage movements marshaled the heavy artillery, the effects most visible in President George W. Bush's recent proposals to link increased welfare benefits with legal, heterosexual marriage. The same-sex marriage movement experienced a ludicrous and severe backlash after the tragedies of September 11, 2001, were blamed on lesbians and gay men, among other "sinners" (though Jerry Falwell, the source of those accusations, did apologize to some extent). The current scandal in the Catholic Church is being blamed on homosexuality, which in turn is being equated with pedophilia. At present, a social and legislative battle over the rights of gay men and lesbians to adopt or foster children is raging in some states. In many parts of the country, nonbiological gay parents still have no claims on children they have helped to rear from infancy or for many years. At the same time, lesbian, gay, and bisexual people find themselves at the center of the debate over the definition of marriage and family, and harassment and violence against lesbian, gay, and bisexual people has become more visible and perhaps even increased.

Concurrently, yet slowly, public conversation has begun to include the hitherto strange, alien, and feared concepts of transsexuality and transgenderism. Again, it is difficult to know where it began, who has been and is leading the way, and when this "revolution" will end or at least reach maturity. While there were no Stonewall riots to mark the shift historically, the movement for transgender rights can point to pioneers such as Christine Jorgensen and Renee Richard, two people who had sex reassignment surgery and allowed their stories to be told throughout the world. As early as the 1970s, rock bands and stars such as Iggy Pop, Queen, David Bowie, Michael Jackson, and Prince began to play with cultural ideas of gender. Drag queens and drag kings, male and female impersonators, including such popular comics as Flip Wilson, for better or worse, became popular sources of entertainment. Humor and music provided stages on which to enact the riddles of gender and tweak society's comfortable dualistic notions. Talk shows, some almost obscenely exploitative and much disparaged, were nevertheless drawing large audiences and providing a forum for lonely transsexuals to tell their stories. Television provided cultural space for a new narrative, turning to transsexuality as the most "far out" cultural trend to be explored. Courageous trans activists such as Leslie Feinberg, Minnie Bruce Pratt, Kate Bornstein, Riki Wilchins, and Pat Califia (now Patrick Califia-Rice), and activist performers such as Kate Clinton, to mention just a few, began to demand our attention. Perhaps even basketball star Dennis Rodman should get some credit for forcing public uneasiness about gender assumptions. A number of powerful films also have undermined cultural stereotypes of gender—such as *The Crying Game, M. Butterfly, Victor/Victoria, Tootsie, The Adventures of Priscilla, Queen of the Desert,* and *Paris Is Burning.* Most recently, the critically acclaimed *Boys Don't Cry,* about the life and death of

Brandon Teena/Teena Brandon, and the HBO special *Normal* have helped raise awareness of the ignorance and violence surrounding transsexuality. Transgenderism and transsexuality, terms I am using interchangeably here, have become important topics in academia too, especially in women's, gender, and cultural studies, as scholars reexamine old ideas and contribute new ones about the meanings of gender and sexuality. Thus the discourse of trans, as Lev demonstrates, has been emerging from many directions for some time.

This discourse is also making its way into the health and human services professions through its educational curriculae and professional organizations, although at a slower pace. *Transgender Emergence* goes a very long way in filling what has been a huge gap in both theory and practice. Very few resources are available to practitioners in psychology, social work, psychiatric nursing, psychiatry, family therapy, and other social/mental health professions. In fact, only in the past few years have various professional organizations undertaken to raise professional consciousness by planning the occasional workshop or lecture led by transgendered people and their helpers, and the professional literature is meager indeed. In many communities, people struggling with gender confusion or discomfort may find no mental health professional with particular knowledge or experience to help rather than harm them, and probably no self-help resources either. In my own fields, social work and family therapy, we have much to try to understand. Arlene Istar Lev's book, with its panoramic yet richly detailed mural of transgenderism, brings this emerging public discourse into the heart of the professions, offering us the chance for a very powerful learning experience.

Lev, always open about her intentions, poses a major challenge to the health and mental health professions from the outset. She sees transgenderism as a normal and potentially healthy variation of human expression. The word "potentially" is used because normality is a social construct, not an individual characteristic or personality, and because she understands the consequences, pain, suffering, and trauma that almost always accompany the trans experience. How can anything be "normal" when the culture makes no space for gender-variant people, when so many of society's professional gatekeepers in the health and mental health professions have limited visions of normalcy and considerable investment in abnormality? In fact, Lev says, DSM-IV's diagnosis of gender identity disorder is the transgendered person's "ticket" into a mandated long and costly line of services, to providing proof that he or she needs and will benefit from hormonal or surgical treatment. So much conspires against the transperson building a narrative of self and self-esteem in a culture that provides little space for gender variance, it is no wonder shame, self-hatred, depression, and other symptoms of despair are often present.

One of the many things I admire about Lev's thinking is her consciousness of the complexity of the trans experience. She is never reductionistic; she is always relational and systemic. She moves from person to context, from context to person; from individual to family and family to individual; from old to young, to partners, to parents, to sources of support in the community. I am amazed at both the breadth and depth of her presentation. As far as I can tell, she ignores nothing. She shines light on transgenderism throughout history and across cultures, deconstructing cultural notions of sex and gender through time and space. Lev recognizes that trans is not just a matter of individual psychology and biology but also about the relationship between the individual and society; it is played out in a powerful political and cultural context. She even puts herself in her mural, making transparent her own political and personal assumptions and the historical/political forces and personal and professional experiences that have helped shape her views.

Although Lev's stance has been more influenced by feminist, constructionist, and systemic thinking rather than psychoanalytic or psychodynamic thinking, she knows thoroughly her ancestors and their legacies, still dominant in the mental health professions, drawing on those sources of knowledge when it seems to help. She gives us a very cogent portrait of theories of biological, developmental, and psychological etiology, theories which, as is the case in lesbian, gay, and bisexual studies, have received far too much attention at the cost of ignoring many other, more fruitful, directions for research. The mysterious and poorly understood relationships between gender and sexuality are thrown open for critical examination, as Lev moves from margin to center and back again, always taking a knowledgeable but critical stance. The reader will find a full discussion of older and current approaches to diagnosis and assessment, a very careful examination of currently preferred standards of care for transpersons, as well as suggestions for working with partners and families of people who are undergoing or have undergone transition.

The child whose gender behaviors and/or identity in formation do not fit prevailing standards for masculine or feminine development is also discussed here, as are the relationships between gender and sexuality in the developing child. Lev also provides an enormously useful chapter on the intersexed individual, that is, the child born with mixed or ambiguous sexual characteristics—an issue which has received increasing attention in recent years, in no small measure due to the experiences of David Reimer whose story is so dramatically documented in Colapinto's book, *As Nature Made Him.* Lev approaches the dilemmas such children and their families face with an empathic eye and an incisive critique of some of the prevailing medical and social "wisdom" that has influenced decision making in this area.

These unbelievably rich, comprehensive travels into the world of transgenderism provide the knowledge and theory foundation on which all good practice rests. Although the book is replete with practice examples and implications, most crucial is that the practitioner/reader of *Transgender Emergence* will be able to enter the life and the context of the transgendered person with new understanding. The practitioner can use that understanding not to make prior assumptions about the experience of any particular person but to ask "good" questions. Much as the anthropologist approaches a "different" or seemingly exotic culture—with a vast reservoir of general knowledge but no specific knowledge or prior judgments about the unique experiences of the particular people he or she will meet along the way—the practitioner here will at the very least have a backpack full of possibilities. That means the practitioner will be able to listen in a new way, to hear things she or he might never have noticed or explored, and to widen the areas of exploration and resources far beyond the closed room of therapy. Lev proposes a highly respectful and collaborative practice, one that locates the individual in a complex world of intimate relationships and social assumptions and accompanies the client as he or she comes to terms with those relationships, questioning the assumptions that are constraining, and reaching for those that are empowering.

I believe that we are all, each and every one of us, multiply gendered. In building our life self-stories, we each perform a uniquely gendered dance choreographed from the available mix of cultural and familial expectations, and rehearsed through our own lived experiences. These expectations are closely aligned with our external sex characteristics at birth, as biology, culture, and even history begin their work long before the moment we actually emerge from our mothers' bodies. From there, most of us are sent down one of two streams, named "male" and "female"; but we have different experiences and are exposed to many influences. Sometimes the social expectation does not fit one's most profoundly felt life experience, often leading to a sense of confusion and self-blame. But some begin to challenge, to test, to demand change in narrow cultural and familial prescriptions for gender and sexuality that do not fit with experience. In spite of the fact that we each have the potential to be uniquely gendered, our biological selves are more or less molded, even forced, by very powerful prescriptions for gender socialization, into two categories—male and female. Woe to us if we happen to be born with obviously mixed sex characteristics. Made possible by medical technology, our bodies must be surgically reshaped so that we can "pass," perhaps as a male with a large enough penis to measure up to some hypothetical social yardstick, perhaps as a female with adequate breasts, micropenis removed, and, for everyone, masculinity or femininity training required to match.

What if one's emerging narrative of self and identity does not match his or her body, but instead feels alien? Right now one faces a future filled with confusion, harassment, and attributions of mental illness—a life at the outer margins of mainstream culture. Many find the ultimate solution in sex reassignment surgery—a long, costly, painful, arduous course of action with uncertain outcomes. Many find themselves profoundly relieved, seamed together in new ways that bring the body and the sense of self into better harmony. My own dream is that we move forward toward recognition that, if gender is a useful social category at all, we need to create space for the many ways to be gendered in this society and to be appreciated and honored for those differences.

Even if you never have a self-identified transgendered client or student or friend, or you think you will not, this extraordinary book belongs in your library. Comprehensive, scholarly, critical, political, contextual, and full of practice wisdom and guidance—Lev's valuable contribution to professional learning nevertheless reads like a novel. It will help you better listen to every person's gender narrative. In fact, it might even make you think about the ways in which you are multiply gendered.

Joan Laird
Professor Emerita
Smith College School for Social Work

Preface

Overview of Transgender Emergence

As the client tells and the worker listens empathically, in the telling and listening, the story gains personal and cultural meaning. This process, particularly with transgendered clients who have been oppressed, marginalized, and silenced, can also be a healing process.

Gary Mallon
Social Services with Transgendered Youth, 1999

This book is informed by an eclectic framework of various theoretical models. It is guided within an ecological social-work model that views people within the context of their environment (Germain and Bloom, 1999). This biopsychosocial model is strengths based and embedded in an understanding of social justice and the role of oppression in human suffering. The therapeutic stance is most influenced by family systems philosophy, particularly a feminist family systems perspective that examines power, structure, and roles within families, especially the meaning of gender. Therapeutic theory is also grounded in a postmodern and social constructionist view of identity development, with a focus on narrative in the self-creation of one's personal life story. The goal of the therapeutic relationship is the empowerment of clients and their families to reauthor their lives in a more meaningful way through the use of attentive, honest, and authentic dialogue.

The clinical and philosophical ideology outlined in this book is based on a belief that transgenderism is a normal and potentially healthy variation of human expression. The working framework outlined here is that nothing is inherently "mentally ill" within transgendered people but rather they are trying to adapt and cope with an untenable culture. The stigma of mental illness could not be associated with gender transgressions unless proper gender expressions were previously imposed. Since they *are* currently imposed, those who are gender variant experience great pain developing an authentic and stable sense of self. It is suggested that the psychotherapist's role is to assist the process of an emerging authentic self, even one that stands outside of socially acceptable gender rules. This means that clinicians must learn to recognize the symptoms of gender dysphoria as developmentally emergent parts of the self.

The first goal for the therapist committed to serving transgendered people and their families is to accept that transgenderism is a normal expression of human potentiality. Therapists and clinicians—people who are trained to work with the vagaries of human pain—are challenged to accept that the symptomatology transgendered people experience is less about their gender variance than it is about the social stigmatization and clinical pathologization of their most sacred expression of self. The emotional pain and dysphoria that gender-variant people express, as well as the apparent life dysfunctions that they exhibit, are part of a developmental process of emerging into a sense of wholeness regarding their gender. *Transgender Emergence* describes a therapeutic empowerment model for the clinical assessment and advocacy of gender-variant people. Transgender emergence is a developmental process whereby gender-variant people examine themselves and their identity, within a context of compassion and empowerment, and progress to an authentic and functional sex- and gender-identity congruence.

Reexamining the therapeutic focus forces the clinical community to re-evaluate some of its cherished philosophies of treatment, including the validity of the diagnosis of gender identity disorder, the surgical treatment of intersexed babies, and the mandated treatment of gender-variant children and adolescents. The role of the therapist as a gatekeeper for the medical system and the use and usefulness of etiological theories and classifications systems will be explored, with a focus on previously neglected populations such as female-to-male transsexuals, intersexed people, and bi-gendered and third-sex identities.

The second goal for the therapist is to place transgenderism within a larger social context that includes an overview of the existence of gender variance throughout history. A biopsychosocial analysis of sexual and gender identity will serve as a foundation for understanding the complexities of gender expression cross-culturally as well as within contemporary Western traditions. This book assumes that gender-variant people are members of larger family and social systems, and that healing from gender dysphoria includes the integration of transgendered people into the wider human community.

Gender variance does not simply live "within" individuals but exists within a larger matrix of relationships, families, and communities. Gender transgressions are not singular experiences that affect only the person in distress. Like the hubs of a wheel, they impact loved ones as well as the community at large. They affect intimate relationships, parenting and sibling relationships, as well as relationships with employers, colleagues, and peers. Therapeutic assessment, intervention, and advocacy in treating gender variance must be utilized within a holistic paradigm that includes spouses, children, and parents, as well as the community. Therapy should focus on the healing of not only individual dysphoria but familial and environmental discomfort as well. The examination of the psychosocial needs of family members should be an integrated part of any treatment strategy. Transgendered people will not be able to resolve their sense of "difference" until their uniqueness is respected, appreciated, and honored within their families and communities. This involves a systems therapy that moves beyond therapeutic interventions into an advocacy-based social work. Gender variance and family stability are never assumed to be mutually exclusive, and families' struggles with transgenderism or intersexed members are seen as part of the developmental, albeit stressful, issues of normative family life-cycle growth and development.

The third goal for therapists is to outline various etiological theories that impact assessment and diagnosis, as well as innovative and possibly iconoclastic treatment strategies to work with gender-dysphoric, gender-variant, transgendered, third-sexed, transsexual, and intersexed people as members of extended family systems. The focus is not on hormonal and surgical treatments, although their importance is acknowledged, but rather on the psychological and developmental processes experienced by gender-variant people and the assessment skills and clinical tools needed to provide compassionate therapeutic counseling.

The book is divided into three parts. Part I examines the Theoretical Understandings of Transgenderism, and sets the stage for defining and understanding the context of gender variance. Chapter 1, "The Transsexual Phenomenon Meets the Transexual Menace," addresses the role of the clinician in treating gender identity issues, including an overview of the history of surgical treatment strategies and evaluation of their success. Critical of the current clinical stance that treatment of gender dysphoria should focus exclusively on the need to diagnose and assess for purposes of medical referrals, the chapter examines the gatekeeping role of clinicians. Suggestions are made to develop a therapeutic standard of care that moves beyond diagnostics into a realm of compassionate, humanistic treatment of the range of psychotherapeutic issues gender-variant people bring to therapy. Clinicians are called on to become gender specialists and transition assistants as they assist clients and families in healing from the dysphoria associated with gender variance.

Chapter 2, "The Legacy: Gender Variance in History," examines the historical, anthropological, and sociological record for examples of what is now named transgenderism. An entire field of studies within itself, it is clear that throughout history and cross-culturally, gender variance has always existed. Manifesting diversely across cultures, treated differently by ruling authorities, and experienced uniquely by individuals, transgendering biological bodies is a distinctly human phenomenon, not a modern medical intervention. Chapter 2 briefly examines a handful of cultural manifestations of gender variance throughout history, including the berdache or Two-Spirit people of North America, the cross-living spiritual experience of the Hijra of Southeast Asia, the cross-gender expressions of both gods and humans within Greco-Roman culture, the treatment of Jeanne d'Arc by Western Christianity, and the Mollies and Tommies of seventeenth- and eighteenth-century European cities. Chapter 2 also examines the sexological theories of late nineteenth-century physicians and social reformers as they tried to understand "sodomites," "hermaphrodites," "transvestites," and others who exhibited sexual and gender "inversions."

Chapter 3, "Deconstructing Sex and Gender: Thinking Outside the Box," examines the four components of sexual identity: natal or biological sex, gender identity, gender-role expression, and sexual orientation. It examines the differences among each of these constructs and how they are connected to one another. Chapter 3 looks at the assumptions created by the social construction of a sex/gender system. The assumption of duality presupposes that sex, gender, gender expression, and sexual orientation are dimorphic—a bipolar system of opposites. This assumption creates an either/or male and female option that "disappears" intersexed people and all gender-variant people, including those who are transsexual, transgendered, cross-dressing, masculine females, or feminine males. It pits men and women against each other by creating them as "opposites," and assumes a heterosexual norm in which homosexual and bisexual people are eternally the "other." The sex/gender system assumes that each component of sexual identity is immutable and unchanging, denying fluidity of gender identity and sexual expression. This model obscures human diversity and creates a system of deviant, pathological, and disordered others that do not fit and therefore need to be "fixed." Understanding the sex/gender system is an essential underpinning to the presenting problems that differently gendered people bring into the therapeutic environment.

Part II, Diagnosis and Assessment, examines the diagnostic and classification systems and etiological theories currently used to examine gender variance. Chapter 4, "Etiologies: Causes and Categories," examines the theoretical perspectives of social constructionism and biological essentialism and the legacy of John Money's sex research. Theoretical models, including knowledge from the biological sciences, psychoanalytic perspectives, cognitive-behavioral and social learning schools, and feminist explanations are all examined for their contributions to the understanding of the etiology of transgenderism. In addition, this chapter explores several perspectives put forth by scientists and researchers on ways to categorize, type, and subtype various forms of gender expression. The limitations of classification systems will be discussed by investigating populations that have been underrepresented.

Chapter 5, "Diagnosis and Transgenderism: The Creation of Pathology," theorizes that the diagnosis of gender identity disorder (GID) is part of a long historical process of labeling and pathologizing sexual and gender differences. The legacy of sexism, racism, homophobia, and erotophobia within psychology and the current *Diagnostic and Statistical Manual of Mental Disorders,* Fourth Edition, Text Revision (DSM-IV-TR), is examined as a tool of social control regarding transgenderism. Despite proclamations of its scientific legitimacy, the DSM-IV-TR is a mixture of clinical assumption and prejudicial judgment, and can be easily misused to hurt gender-variant children. The diagnosis of GID is "the ticket" to medical treatments for adult transsexuals, and the criteria are outdated and exclusionary of many expressions of gender variation. Suggestions for reform are recommended.

Part III, Treatment Issues, examines compassionate, advocacy-based treatment modalities that honor gender diversity and acknowledge the trauma caused by being differently gendered in a gender-dimorphic culture. Chapter 6, "Learning to Listen to Gender Narratives," offers ways to differentially diagnose bona fide mental health disturbances from gender dysphoria and normative reactions to gender oppression. It examines the types of clients who seek therapy to address their gender issues, and what it is they are requesting from their therapist. In addition, it is recommended that the therapist, in moving away from pathologizing diagnoses and assessments based on a gatekeeping strategy, develop a clinical narrative perspective that is focused on the client's own story and respects the client's relationship to his or her unique gender expression.

Chapter 7, "Transgender Emergence: A Developmental Process," outlines a six-stage developmental process that gender-variant people experience while coming to terms with their own gender issues. First, this chapter examines various coming-out processes as some theoreticians have described the lesbian, gay, and bisexual experience of them, and sets the stage for exploring the "emergence" process as it is suggested many gender-variant people experience it. Transgender emergence is described as a normative, albeit often traumatic, trajectory moving from an experience of denial and self-hatred to one of self-respect and gender congruence. The stages are awareness; seeking information and reaching out; disclosure to significant others; exploration—identity and self-labeling; exploration—transition issues, possible body modification; and acceptance and posttransition issues. These stages are not meant to label people, define transgender maturity, or limit anyone to these experiences. The stage model is designed to describe a complex interaction of intrinsic developmental issues and social and interpersonal transactions that are common to many gender-variant people and recognizable for clinicians.

Chapter 8, "Family Emergence," examines the literature on families of gender-variant people, including spouses and children, and discusses its contemporary relevance and the need for more research on this neglected topic. This chapter also outlines the stages that family members, particularly spouses, experience and offers guidelines to gender-variant people for healthy self-disclosure. Also described in this chapter are numerous case studies of the many challenges presented to families of gender-variant people and some of their unique, and sometimes successful, solutions. Finally, this chapter examines the research on children being raised in families with a transgendered parent.

Chapter 9, "Transgendered Children and Youth," examines issues facing children who are gender variant and gender dysphoric, including their relationships with their family and interactions with the medical and social service system. Particular focus is on the issue of parental rights and the treatment modalities created to modify children's behavior. Strategies for treatments have been based on behavioral and psychodynamic theories that pathologize either the family or the child, and the interventions are attempts to "protect" the child from peer ostracism by ensuring that they do not become homosexual and/or transsexual. Alternative treatment modalities are recommended that support families of gender-variant children and encourage advocacy-based education for families, as well as school systems that respect the emergent sexual and gender identities of children and youth.

Chapter 10, "The Treatment of Intersexed People: Time for a New Paradigm," examines the current medical treatment protocols for assigning sex to newborn babies with intersexed conditions and the perceived "psychosocial" emergency that ensues. Discussion includes examining the impact on parents who have an intersexed child, issues facing children and adolescents, as well as adults coming to terms with their medical conditions and the impact of the treatments they have received. The chapter suggests new treatment paradigms that include postponing irreversible medical treatments, therapies designed to assist families in educated decision making, and treatment strategies that address the lifelong identity issues inherent in the lives of intersexed people living within a bipolar sex system.

Many issues are not adequately addressed in this book including those related to hormones and surgery, HIV and AIDS, legal and employment struggles, domestic violence and sexual assault, addictions, posttransition questions, and issues specific to people of color. Numerous concerns are only touched upon and could become entire books themselves, particularly issues involving families, marriage and relationship counseling, the impact of gender variance on children, as well as gender variance manifesting within children. An entire book could be written on the psychospiritual issues revealed through transgender emergence. Much is left to be said.

Some transgendered people will undoubtedly disagree with a basic tenet of this book—that psychotherapy and family therapy can be healing for those who struggle with gender issues. Therapists have often been seen as the enemy of the transgender community, serving as gatekeepers and diagnosticians. This book suggests that therapy within the context of a humane, caring, professional, and clinical context can be profoundly healing. It is, at its root, a sacred process.

Some therapists will likely disagree with another basic tenet of this book—that transgendered people represent natural and healthy expressions of the diversity of humanity and that they suffer extraordinary pain because of repressive institutions. Furthermore, clinicians share in the responsibility for the creation of institutions that have focused more on etiology than on the birth of the human spirit. Psychology is about the study of the soul and psychotherapists must honor the souls of those who have entrusted themselves to their care.

This book is a challenge to both transgendered people seeking support on a journey to authenticity and psychotherapists who have the privilege of bearing witness to their emergence. There is much to be gained from this alliance. On one hand, transgendered people are "seekers" and therapists are trail guides; on the other hand, therapists are serious students of the human condition and transgendered people embody some of humanity's greatest secrets.

Acknowledgments

The writing of this book has been supported by an amazing group of people—academics, scholars, and trans-activists, both within and without the university—many of whom I only know through cyberspace. Special thanks to all my colleagues and friends on transgender-related electronic mailing lists, especially Trans-Academic and Division 44, the Society for the Psychological Study of Lesbian, Gay, and Bisexual Issues of the American Psychological Association. I literally could not have completed this work without your endless resources, ideas, critical thinking, friendship, and deep insightful love of debate.

This book was read in its numerous manifestations by many people who offered valuable critical feedback, resources, endless grammatical corrections, personal and clinical experiences, and cutting-edge theoretical ideas. This list includes Andrea Cookson, P. J. Mears, Reid Vanderburgh, Joanna Andrea Pashdag, Janelle Wielhouwer, Rachel Pollack, Kate Thomas, Randi Kelcher, Kendre Lloyd, Gary Bowen, Jamison Green, Jude Patton, Julie Colwell, Joan Laird, Nina Williams, D. Danaan Weintraub, Maggie Chubb, Cheryl Chase, and Sundance Lev. This book was supported in part by a faculty development grant from the Vermont College of Norwich University (now Union Institute and University) and an individual development award through New York State's United University Professions Professional Development Committee. The staff of the Interlibrary Loan Department and the Dewey Library of the State University of New York at Albany worked hard to locate many difficult-to-find books on sex and gender. Thanks to Nikki for hours of photocopying.

A few people deserve special mention. I am grateful to The Haworth Press for taking a chance with a new author, and especially my editor, Terry Trepper, for his advocacy, support, and trust in my oft-delayed deadline. Despite his sharp editorial eye, I fought him all the way (especially when he thought I overused parentheses)—as any good feminist would. I have been damn lucky to have my words in his tender care. Dallas Denny and the resources of the American Educational Gender Information Service were invaluable, as were Jamison Green and Cheryl Chase (and the ISNA staff), both of whom were incredible sources of information, as well as careful critics. If they tired of my endless questions, they hid it well. Although I am generally not a rule-player, C. Jacob Hale's (1997) "Suggested Rules for Non-Transsexuals Writing About Transsexuals, Transsexuality, Transsexualism, or Trans_____" was an invaluable resource. I appreciate the support shown by Kit Rachlin, Katherine K. Wilson, Laura Markowitz, D. R. Yonkin, and so many others, many of whom took the time to prod me forward and encourage me to continue to write. My colleagues at Choices Counseling and Consulting, especially Jennifer Hescheles and Jennifer Critchley, picked up many loose ends to keep the office running, and were an endless source of encouragement and sushi. I am thankful to Reid Vanderburgh for helping me find the word "emergence," and Julie Shepherd (may her name be a blessing) for the concept of "transition assistant." I am, of course, solely responsible for any weaknesses of the manuscript.

My students' interest in the subject matter always reminded me of its value. Most important, I could not have written this book if it were not for those who trusted me with their stories. I am indebted to you, as much as I am awed by you.

Amazing people emotionally supported me in this work. First are the Jewish therapists who, although they frequently mentioned that I had a lot on my plate, never told me "I" was too much. It turns out I did have too much on my plate. My friends were very kind to me during the past four years, allowing me to have only my work and my family. I promise them more solid attention in the future. In addition to being the wisest people on the planet, the cyber-moms I met online offered hours of diversion and the only social outlet allowed an academic working mother of young children—adult conversation in my pajamas after 11 p.m.

As a clinician I will make an assessment and diagnosis of the fate of this book. I know that members of the transgender community will read this book more thoroughly than members of the professional community for whom it is intended—and will read it with great critical focus. They will devour it and dissect it, and will catch every language inconsistency and political gray area of ambivalence. They will question my motives and intentions, and will challenge each nuance of theory. With soft belly and open heart I welcome their deconstruction. I open myself to the sharp minds of a community coming home to itself. I welcome their refusal to be confined to the language usages I have developed or borrowed. I welcome their sharpened scalpel of political discourse and their informed clinical understanding that often surpasses that of my professional colleagues. They have pushed me to expand and grow into myself, and to name and own myself. Each book, each day, is a stepping-stone on the way to the world we envision.

Being a gender therapist means that I am part of a small cadre of professionals—researchers, clinicians, and theorists—who dedicate their lives to working with transgendered and transsexual people. I beg my colleagues' forgiveness if I have misrepresented their ideas, challenged their most cherished beliefs, or, worst of all, simply misquoted them. My intentions have been honorable, even when my skills have lacked precision. Although my colleagues and I may disagree from time to time, I am proud to be engaged with, and a member of, such a dedicated and brilliant community.

It has been said that the gender revolution is the last great liberation movement of the twentieth century—following in the footsteps of all the great civil rights movements that have molded my life—the black pride movement, the women's liberation movement, the gay and lesbian movement. These movements have changed the face of our world—locally, nationally, and internationally—as well as changed the look of my own face as it looks back at me in the mirror. I am truly a child of these movements, and the life I live is a reflection of all that liberation has made possible. Thanks go to those who make lives of dignity while living on the edge of danger.

It is my hope that the transgendered community continues to grow so this book soon becomes outdated and irrelevant, where the need to critically examine the diagnostic system in reference to gender variance becomes an absurdity. At the close of the nineteenth century the old psychological establishment asked this question: "What do women want?"—a question that today would (hopefully) prompt ridicule. Women wanted, of course, what they still want, what people of color want, what differently abled people want, what queer people of all types want, and what the transgender community is now demanding—to be treated with respect and dignity, to have fair access to a seat on the bus as well as a chair in the conference room. To be treated not as a diagnostic category but as another variation in the infinite forms and styles of human expression.

An amount of frustration exists in trying to acknowledge the contribution of my family, knowing no words can properly thank them for putting up with hours of clickity-clack on the keyboard. From the bottom of my heart I thank my partner who gave me the time to write by caring for our family with dedication and reverence. She brought me plates of food that were left cold, and put up with me crawling into bed as the sun came up and begging her to take our son to preschool. She lives in a house piled with copies of journal articles, overdue library notices, and notes scribbled on small pieces of paper that she dutifully tries to keep free of peanut-butter fingerprints. Since I began this book I watched our older son go from a toddler to a child who still loves cooking, art, and dolls as much as running, playing with cars, and soccer. The arrival of our baby and his months of colic delayed the completion of this book, and now, as I write these words, he waves "bye-bye," enjoying the gender-free, no-pressure bliss of infancy and early toddlerhood in his handsome pink coat. I am blessed to have a family who sustains me.

If they see
breasts and long hair coming
they call it a woman.
If beard and whiskers
they call it a man;
but, look, the Self that hovers in between
is neither man nor woman.

Devara Dasimayya
(Indian devotional saint, tenth century C.E.)

Introduction

> I swear never to be silent whenever and wherever human lives endure suffering and humiliation. We must always take sides. . . . When human dignity is in jeopardy, that place, at that moment, must become the center of the universe.
>
> Elie Wiesel
> Nobel Peace Prize acceptance speech
> December 10, 1986

This is a book about gender and gender transformation. It is a book about transgendered people and those who love them—their spouses, partners, children, parents, and friends. It is written for therapists who counsel gender-variant people and their families, and presents a clinical outline for compassionate and informed psychotherapy and family therapy. This book examines the theoretical and clinical issues concerning transgendered, transsexual, and intersexed people, the relationship of gender identity to sexual identity, and the systemic impact of these issues on family life-span development.

Contemporary society is grappling with understanding gender and cross-gender transgression. Shifting concepts of gender and its impact on social relationships have affected professionals and laypeople alike. The subject of transgenderism is one that produces an array of reactions. Many people find themselves confused and uncomfortable dealing with the idea of transsexualism and "sex-change" surgery. There is an emotional mix of an almost morbid curiosity on one hand and profound revulsion on the other. Transgenderism and transsexuality have been perceived as severe psychopathologies—both perverted and bizarre—which has relegated differently gendered people to the back wards of mental hospitals and red light districts, and has made them fodder for the talk-show circuit.

When issues of transgenderism are raised socially often eyes glance away and conversation suddenly changes, even among people who are quick to tell you they are not judgmental. Rarely do people engage in intellectual inquiry about transgendered issues, although they will often voice unsolicited political or clinical pronouncements about gender-variant people. Cross-gender behavior often invokes a sudden and piercing humor that is intended to hurt. As Randi Ettner and George Brown (1999) wrote, "Even in an age of self-conscious political correctness, it's perfectly acceptable to mock transsexuals" (p. xii). Occasionally people will lower their voices and admit to their own private gender transgressions, ending their disclosure with either brusque humor or a nonchalant disavowal of their confession.

In academic circles, the discourse on gender and transgenderism has created embroiled discussions on the social construction of gender and the power of language in the creation of identity. Scientists hotly debate the issues of biology and the role of biochemicals and brain development in cross-gender behavior. Feminists have expressed concerns regarding what they see as a limited and sexist expression of gender among those seeking "sex changes." They have, in turn, been critiqued by the transgender community for not understanding the deeply personal experience of gender dsyphoria, and what it is to be trapped by not only social expectations of gender but a body that feels alien. Postmodern academic arguments, however, often depersonalize the daily life struggles of those who are intersexed, transgendered, or transsexual. For example, antiracism activists and cross-cultural theorists have brought attention to the lack of academic focus on the diversity of gender expressions already available within communities of color and across cultures. Intersexed activists have criticized queer-studies scholars and transgender activists for using intersexuality to advance their theories regarding the social construction of gender binaries, while ignoring the impact of these binaries on the daily lives and psychologies of intersexed people.

During the past decade people who identify as transgendered, transsexual, or intersexed have come to be a visible political force, a topic of discussion in the public forum, and a consumer market. Television talk shows, mainstream movies, and tell-all biographies have flooded the media. Movies with transgender themes abound and even Disney has contributed by presenting a cross-gender theme in the wonderful though historically inaccurate *Mulan,* whose title character explores the categories and confinements of gender within premodern China. Intended for the under-ten crowd, the movie is replete with raucous cross-dressing humor. Special-interest articles about physicians, attorneys, and college professors who "change sex" are common news stories, often ending with the reporters' amazement that these are competent and articulate professionals, not deranged and confused people. The recent success of the book *As Nature Made Him* (Colapinto, 2000)—the story of a child whose penis was severed during a routine circumcision and his failed medical "transformation" into a girl, which rose to the top of the *New York Times* best-seller list—shows the increased public interest in understanding the relationship of gender, sex, and the human body, as well as the fallibility of sexologists and gender experts.

As transgenderism becomes a part of the popular discourse, transgendered people—and their families—are becoming increasingly aware that they are living within a culture that has ignored, pathologized, and degraded them. Transgendered people have been labeled as narcissistic, histrionic, antisocial, depressed, phobic, obsessive, and, of course, sexually deranged. The inflammatory and derogatory language of clinical assessment often mirrors the descriptions given by talk-show hosts. Transgendered clients are often "treated" using unsubstantiated and outdated etiological theories that incriminate their parents and partners and analyze with surgical precision their sexual fantasies, as well as their morality. Intersexed people are "disappeared" from the human family, the subject considered so shameful that even those living in intersexed bodies are often kept from the truth about their medical conditions.

The transgender movement is shaking the foundations of the mental health system in much the same way that the feminist movement and the gay liberation movement did in the past thirty years. The cultural conditions of judgment and scorn under which transgendered and intersexed people live are mentioned in passing by clinical experts, but the psychological stress of living in a society that has vilified them has not been fully examined within a clinical framework.

Social scientists, therapists, and political activists have begun examining the psychological legacy of racism, classism, sexism, and heterosexism as it is internalized by the oppressed population (see Anzaldua and Keating, 2002; Freire, 1971; Goffman, 1963; Hardy, 1995; hooks, 1996; Moane and Campling, 1999; Moraga and Anzaldua, 1984; Otis and Skinner, 1996; Pharr, 1997), but examining the psychological scars of transgender oppression is still an emerging area. Political organizing and strategizing for increased civil rights and legal protections have recently become the focus for many transgendered and intersexed activists, and the transgender movement has become a turn-of-the-century liberation movement. Following in the tradition and built upon the success of the great liberation movements of the past century—the civil rights and black power movements, the women's liberation movement, and the gay, lesbian, and bisexual movements—the transgender political movement is developing an analysis of transgendered and intersexed people as oppressed minorities.

Examining the psychological legacy of oppression raises pointed questions for the mental health field and the role of clinicians in treating these "disorders."

- Are there gender differences between the sexes that are considered normative, and can it be clinically determined which behaviors are outside of this range?

- In a social milieu that defines gender variance as a perversion, how can a differently gendered person not have clinical symptomatology?
- Is the process of diagnosis creating the social, legal, and psychological problems it is identifying?
- How can a psychiatric diagnosis be internalized as anything but a mental illness?
- Is a psychiatric diagnosis necessary for clinical intervention or client self-actualization?
- What is the role of psychotherapy in the treatment of trauma-based symptoms caused by oppressive social conditions?

Instead of examining transgendered and intersexed people through a lens of disorder and dysfunction, clinicians need to ask what it means to be a healthy, functioning, gender-variant person within an immutable dual-gendered world. If gender variance is a mental health condition, then it, by definition, requires therapeutic intervention. Pathology, however, has never been a useful model for a burgeoning liberation movement.

What does it mean to be a healthy functioning gender-variant person within an immutable dual-gendered world? The mental health problems that are associated with transgenderism may not be etiologically related to the gender variance but caused by the social and political ramifications of being a member of a despised group.

The difficulties that some gender-variant people present within therapy—obsessive cross-dressing, inappropriate acting out, social phobia, impulsivity, depression, anxiety, suicidality, and self-harm behaviors—might be symptoms and sequelae of their social denigration rather than proof of their gender-related mental illness. The problems and shame that intersexed people face might be related more to the secrecy surrounding their medical conditions and the shame of not just being "different" but being considered "wrong" and needing to be "fixed."

Transgenderism is a radical concept that examines the essential nature of biology and gender as well as the social construction of sexuality and culture. Transgenderism, transsexuality, and intersexuality, as normative human variations, challenge fundamental assumptions about sex and gender and shift the basic paradigm of the world as a place occupied by two sexes that are opposite and different from each other to a conception of sex and gender identities as potentially fluid. Transgenderism describes the meeting ground where the social construction of gender intersects with the individual's personal psychological experience of gender, and where biology is not the only determining factor of identity. Transgendered and intersexed people are struggling to define themselves and the parameters of their own lives outside of an illness model.

Terminology that pathologizes gender-variant people has been eliminated from this discussion, except when discussing extant medical theories. Transgenderism, or gender variance, will not be considered a pathology, a disorder, an illness, a disease, a deviance, a manifestation of childhood trauma, a lack of appropriate gender-role modeling in childhood, or caused by a suffocating mother or absent father. It is assumed that gender variance is as natural as any other expression of gender and that etiological theories and psychomedical nosologies serve only to further compound the isolation and social ostracism that is the inheritance of those who are labeled mentally ill.

THE LANGUAGE OF GENDER

Bringing individuals together under a common label is not without consequences.

Gianna E. Israel
Transgender Care, 1997

Agreeing on an inclusive language in which to discuss gender variance is challenging; indeed, finding a language that includes the variety of experiences and expressions emanating from the nascent transgender community is a complex and politically laden project. Limitations are inherent in the current nomenclature, and terminology can be used to constrain discussion as well as illuminate it. Any language used might unintentionally offend someone or might quickly become antiquated and obsolete in this quickly evolving field. However, dialogue is not possible outside of the parameters of language, so choices have been made that will hopefully expand, rather than hinder, this vital conversation and a fertile exchange of ideas. The following discussion refers to language usage regarding gender identity, not sexual orientation (i.e., whether a person is "gay" or "straight").

It has been suggested that the transgender community is "created and manifested through its terminological identification" (Gilbert, 2000), and the process of naming has been essential to identity development. Gender-variant people have been called, and call themselves numerous names. Some of the more common names used today include transsexual, transvestite, transgenderist, and cross-dresser. (See Glossary for definitions of terminology.) Other common terms are transman, transsexual woman, male-to-female (MTF), female-to-male (FTM), bi-gendered, Two Spirit, third sex, gender bender as well as femme, butch, stone butch, and female-bodied man. This list is far from complete.

The term *gender variance* is itself problematic, assuming a difference from the norm when, in reality, there may not actually be a norm that serves as a blueprint. Butler (1990) suggests, "the original identity after which gender fashions itself is an imitation without an origin" (p. 175), in other words there is no baseline normative "male" or "female" nature that serves as template against which everything else is variant. What has been referred to as "maleness" and "femaleness," or masculinity and femininity, are somewhat arbitrary classifications that vary from culture to culture and throughout time. Gender variant, as it is used here, refers to those who diverge from what is most common, usual, or expected; it does not assume, however, that what is normative is necessarily healthier, more functional, or in any way more honorable.

Transgendered is an inclusive term, an umbrella or spectrum concept that includes all people who are gender variant (Green, 1994b). It is a term that was developed within the transgender liberation movement, and this crossroads of clinical and political development offers the widest and most comprehensive language system to include as many gender-variant people as possible. According to Pfäefflin and Coleman (1997), "Transgender is a new term which transcends the restricting and extant categories of gender identity, is more neutral regarding etiology, and encompasses the vast complexity of gender manifestations and identities." Israel and Tarver (1997) noted that the word *transgender* "helps map out a large and nebulous territory in which we can delineate some sharper distinctions" (p. 230). It is, however, admittedly an imperfect term.

Many transsexuals are not comfortable being subsumed under the umbrella of the term *transgendered,* or as one client said, "I'd rather get wet than be under that umbrella." Many transsexuals feel that that their issues are decidedly different from other gender-variant people because of their expressed need to physically alter their bodies surgically and their dependence on the medical professional to assist this process. Transsexuals have been described as

> those who feel that their true gender is at variance with their biological sex . . . who are attempting to "pass" as members of the opposite sex [and] . . . who have either had sex change surgery or are undergoing medical treatment with a view toward changing their sex anatomically. (Shapiro, 1991, p. 249)

Although some transgendered people who are not transsexual may identify with this definition, the term *transgender* also includes a wider diversity of gender variance. Although the desire for physical sex reassignment is a useful gauge to delineate those who identify as transsexuals from other transgendered people, some transsexuals do not have surgery for many reasons, including health problems, financial constraints, complicated family responsibilities, or simply having other current priorities. Whittle (1995) therefore defines transsexuals as "all those people who have lived, or desired to live, a large part of their adult life in the role and dress of that gender group which would be considered to be in opposition to their sex as designated at birth" (p. 38). This takes the focus off genitals and medical technologies and onto the self-identification and daily lives of individuals. Many postoperative transsexuals do not continue to use the term *transsexual*, feeling that this term described their process of transition but not their current identity. They identify simply as a man or woman and want to be accepted in society with the correct gender designation.

Cross-dressers, another subgroup under the term *transgendered*, might also not be comfortable being included within the same rubric as transsexuals. Sometimes it is because those who cross-dress for pleasure or relaxation believe that they are fundamentally different from transsexuals who want to hormonally or surgically change their bodies. Cross-dressers, who are often heterosexual males, are sometimes resistant to any connections, politically or clinically, to issues of homosexuality, which have sometimes been linked to transgendered issues. Unfortunately, these schisms have sometimes been reinforced by the medical profession's emphasis on the differences between these populations, including the assertion that transsexuals exhibit more mental health problems than do "normal" cross-dressers.

At the broadest end of the spectrum, the term *transgendered* includes all gender-variant people, including feminine males and masculine females who might not necessarily consider themselves "differently gendered." It also includes gay and lesbian people who are gender transgressors, e.g., "nelly" men or drag queens and butch lesbians or "he/shes," who might acknowledge their gender difference but not feel aligned with the transgendered movement. Within political communities of lesbian and gay activism there are debates about the usefulness of including, or excluding, transgendered and transsexual issues within these civil rights movements, or even whether transgendered people are welcome at certain social or cultural events. At the most narrow end of the spectrum, the term *transgendered* comprises only those who struggle with issues of potential gender transition and sex reassignment, i.e., transsexuals, as well as some cross-dressers.

Although transsexualism may be uncommon, gender variance is not a rare phenomenon; in its most inclusive aspects, it represents a broad range of humanity. Transgressive gender behavior has been part of the human family as long as there have been expectations regarding human sexual and gender expression. The "naturalness" of a dimorphic and binary system of sex and gender is a construct embedded into the very fabric of our Western cultures. Gender-variant behaviors—labeled transsexualism, transgenderism, and transvestism—have been seen as sexual perversions, mental disorders, and psychopathological behaviors within the psychiatric and helping professions.

The term *transsexual* has been transformed in some political circles as "transexual"—with only one "s"—to distinguish it from the medicalized use of the term *transsexual* (Wilchins, 1997b). The term *trans* is becoming popularized (Feinberg, 1996, 1998) to define the broadest categorization of the gender community, a prefix that has been transformed into a base word. Without ignoring the vast differences in identity and experience within this broad categorization of people and their divergent clinical needs, it is believed that the term *transgendered* encompasses the most comprehensive terminology available to assist psychotherapists in recognizing gender variance or gender diversity in clients.

The terms *male* and *female* refer to one's biological sex, as assigned at birth. Although issues relevant to the clinical needs of intersexed people will be addressed in this book, discussing transgenderism and intersexuality in the same book is not meant to conflate intersexed people with transgendered people. Generally speaking, *intersexed* refers to people who are not easily classified into the established sex divisions because they have the physical sex characteristics, often including ambiguous genitalia, of both males and females. Most have been surgically altered at birth to fit more easily into the male/female binary. Intersexed people and transgendered people have much in common: (1) both groups confound the sex/gender binary; (2) both groups have relationships, often complex ones, with the medical community regarding their treatment needs; and (3) both groups are faced with emotional and cognitive struggles because they exist outside of acceptable norms. Some intersexed people are unhappy with the gender they have been assigned and seek gender reassignment; however, they are officially excluded by a clause in the diagnostic manual from being classified as transsexual. Although most transsexuals are not intersexed, it is common for transsexuals to seek answers to their gender identity confusion by suggesting, or even insisting, that they have a physical condition to explain their dysphoria.

As a general rule, pronouns used throughout this book will reflect the named gender identity of the individual, even when it conflicts with their biological or physiological sex. Since this book addresses clinical concerns for clients dealing with gender issues, many case histories in this book represent people who are unsure of their gender identity and how they wish to be referred to regarding sex and pronouns. Pronoun confusion can sometimes muddy clarity, so decisions to identify people's sex or gender identity in situations where the persons themselves are unclear will be based on their presentation at the time of clinical contact.

However, when people who have clearly identified their gender identity as male or female, pronoun use will reflect this (except when referring to their past). Unfortunately, the medical literature, as well as the media, has often continued to refer to gender-variant people in the pronoun of their birth sex, regardless of their legal gender status, chosen gender identity, or social presentation. The literature has, furthermore, often used the terminology of one's birth sex, e.g., "male transsexual" to refer to male-to-female transsexuals who are living their lives as women and "female transsexuals" to refer to female-to-male transsexuals who are living as men. These individuals will be referred to here as transsexual women or men, transwomen or transmen, or simply women and men. Osborne and Wise (2002) suggested a "split gender identity" for names and pronoun use, which reflects using biologically congruent names for people who are living primarily in their birth sex, and using cross-gender names and pronouns for those who are in the process of transition. They also suggested that for people who are moving back and forth from one sex to another due to struggles with their families' acceptance or work requirements, it is appropriate for the clinician to also change pronouns and names depending on the client's appearance.

Pfäefflin and Junge (1998) suggested that clinicians should reserve words such as "gender dysphoria" and "MTF" or "FTM transsexual," for people before they have sex reassignment surgery. They say therapists should drop "the medical diagnosis as soon as possible and to address patients according to the gender role they live in" (pp. 70-71). This seems to represent a basic respect for individuals, especially those who have demonstrated by the actions of their lives the very importance these words hold to their self-identities.

GENDER DYSPHORIA AND ETIOLOGICAL THEORIES

[C]all me a gender dysphoric if you must, but it's not MY gender I don't like, it's society's idea of what my gender ought to be that bugs me.

Nancy Nangeroni
International Foundation for Gender Education

Gender dysphoria is a clinical term used to describe the symptoms of excessive pain, anguish, agitation, restlessness, and malaise that gender-variant people seeking therapy often express. Fisk (1973) was the first to couple the word *dysphoria,* etymologically derived from the Greek meaning "hard to bear," with the word *gender.* The term is now used throughout the clinical literature to describe the experience of discomfort a person has with his or her physical body and the desire to express the gender attributes associated with the other sex, often including surgical alteration of genitalia and secondary sex characteristics. Steiner (1985a) defined gender dysphoria as "a sense of awkwardness or discomfort in the anatomically congruent role, and the desire to possess the body of the opposite sex, together with the negative affect associated with these ideas, namely anxiety and reactive depression" (pp. 5-6).

Gender dysphoria describes the psychological discomfort experienced with the physiological body and associated gender expectations, as well as a presence of clinical symptomatology associated with emotional difficulties. In a society where cross-gender expression is believed to signal extreme mental illness, experiencing cross-gender feelings can create numerous reactive symptoms in addition to the anxiety and depression that Steiner mentions. These can include dissociation, suicidality, sexual dysfunction, substance abuse, self-mutilation, or even intense hostility toward other differently gendered people. It is rare for someone struggling with gender incongruence not to experience some psychological symptomatology, e.g., insomnia, isolation, dysthymia, anxiety, weight loss or gain, and work or school difficulties.

It is easy to understand how someone experiencing these kinds of symptoms might be perceived as dysfunctional or even emotionally disturbed in the eyes of most mental health specialists. Acceptable gender behavior is profoundly mandated—culturally, religiously, and even economically— and the realization of being relegated to the category of the stigmatized "other" can create extreme discomfort. Niela Miller (1996), a therapist specializing in gender issues, said, "Most of us have grown up in a land that looks upon cross-dressers and transsexuals as psychiatric casualties" (p. xix). It can, however, be argued that the symptomatology associated with gender dysphoria has less to do with issues of gender variance than the dysphoria associated with being "different." Riki Anne Wilchins, a transgendered activist, said that although she has been accused of transgressing the gender system, it is really the gender system that has transgressed her experiences (Wilchins, 1997a).

The term *gender dysphoria* will not be used as a diagnostic label but as a clinical descriptor, a way to articulate the discomfort associated with gender variance within a culture that has rigid gender rules. Gender dysphoria is not a synonym for "transsexual," nor should it be used to describe gender-variant people in general; it is only a useful term when applied to people who are experiencing actual dysphoria. As Israel and Tarver (1997) said, "Once an individual has self-identified transition goals or has established a self-defined transgendered identity, she or he is no longer considered to be gender dysphoric" (p. 8), unless, of course, they are still exhibiting symptoms of gender dysphoria. This is true no matter how unconventionally a person may have resolved their gender issues. There are, of course, many reasons one may experience gender dysphoria, so the term can "effectively describe persons who find their gender statuses hard to bear for substantially social or political reasons, as well as for psychological ones" (Devor, 1997a).

Although theoretical positions vary on the etiology of transgenderism, the clinical and medical literature has been based on the assumption that gender variance is a mental health issue and that most clients who present for treatment are struggling with psychopathology. It has also been assumed that they have numerous sexual dysfunctions and associated paraphilias. As with all cross-sections of humanity, there are of course gender-variant people with mental health issues and unusual or uncommon sexual behaviors. However, to assume that all transgendered people are mentally ill or sexual perverts based on those who seek the services of the mental health system is akin to condemning marriage as unhealthy and pathological based on those clients who come into therapy seeking help for troubled marriages.

It is to be assumed that most clients who reach out for therapeutic services are experiencing some distress. However, it cannot be assumed that gender-dysphoric individuals who seek out psychotherapeutic services are representative of all gender-variant people. It is possible that some transgendered people do not experience any *dysphoria,* but are able to experience their gender differences in an accepting and celebratory way. These people would be less likely to seek out professional counseling, except for a letter of recommendation for hormonal and/or surgical treatment. It is, however, rare for persons to experience their gender identity in conflict with their assigned sex within a society that has rigid gender normative rules, especially before the rise of a transgender liberation movement, and not have this be distressing in some manner.

Gender dysphoria is a natural outcome of living within a culture that has an explicit gender system which associates certain appearances and behaviors with particular gender categories. The mental health field has labeled as pathological all deviations from this rigid system, although it is equally true that the suffering caused by this static system may be what has caused the anguish and dysphoria which has been labeled a mental illness.

Numerous classification systems that categorize gender-variant people have been developed. Clinicians specializing in the field have argued about the nomenclature, but nosological systems generally refer back to the medical model blueprint developed by endocrinologist Harry Benjamin and his observations of his patients in the 1950s. Although attempts have been made to expand this system and changes are constantly made within the diagnostic manuals, certain typographies have remained intact as part of the "known truths" about transsexualism, when in fact these theoretical ideologies are proving to be restrictive of the actual diversity of human gender expression.

The standard schema divides people with gender "disorders" into two groups, displayed on a continuum of severity, ranging from transvestites to "true" transsexuals (see Blanchard and Steiner, 1990; Doctor, 1988; Green and Money, 1969; Lothstein, 1983; Rekers, 1995b; Steiner, 1985a,b; Stoller, 1974; Walters and Ross, 1986; Zucker and Bradley, 1995). These two groups, although having overlapping features, have been seen as dichotomous with salient diagnostic characteristics. When compared to male transvestites, male-to-female transsexuals are assumed to begin cross-dressing at earlier ages, have a less erotic component to their cross-dressing, and dislike their genitals often to the point of being obsessed with removing them. They are also assumed to be homosexual or bisexual (from the perspective of their natal sex) and exhibit numerous comorbid mental health problems. Conversely, transvestites are believed to start cross-dressing during puberty with a strong erotic compulsion to their cross-dressing but without the anatomical dysphoria. They are thought to be more often heterosexual, married with children, and to present less often with severe mental health disturbances. Female transvestites have been declared nonexistent throughout the literature, and female-to-male transsexuals have generally been considered rare, exhibiting few mental health problems, being exclusively homosexual in orientation (from the perspective of their natal sex) and being further along in the transition process when seeking medical services.

Although there may be some general truths to these postulates, they exclude many people struggling with gender identity issues who are not so easily pigeonholed into the categorizations mentioned earlier. The majority of the research has been done on male-to-female transsexuals and male transvestites who have been patients in gender clinics or members of cross-dressing clubs. Perhaps these generalizations best describe individuals who have utilized these services but are not all-inclusive of people with gender-variant experience. Such generalizations have become diagnostic criteria or labels to define potential "kinds" of transgendered people. This is a disservice to the diversity of gender variance that exists and also impacts who is therefore eligible for services. Only recently have these assumptions come under clinical and political scrutiny.

As the movement for transgender liberation grows, more people are coming forth who identify as transgendered and do not fit into any of the previously held criteria, which call into question some of the "hallmarks" of the diagnosis. Examples of gender variance that have been less often described in the literature are described next. Some gender-variant people cross-dress for sexual pleasure and others do so for comfort; some do it for anxiety reduction—and this is true for both males and females. Many people choose to "transition," i.e., live their lives in the gender presentation of the "opposite sex," and others cross-dress for discrete periods of time. Some believe their cross-gender identity to be an "essence"—who they are in the deepest part of their psyche—and experience themselves as being born in the wrong body; some explain it as a "birth defect" that needs to be corrected. Some feel that it is a choice, a preference for how they want to live their lives or how they are most comfortable. Still others feel more fluidity of gender identity and express feeling confined by the restrictions on both genders, choosing to live in a mixed-, dual-, or bi-gendered manner. Some enjoy the performity of gender and blend or mix their gender style as a way to express diverse aspects of themselves. Some enjoy their genitals and are comfortable living in their preferred gender without changing their bodies; others feel profound discomfort with their genitalia or secondary sex characteristics; still others enjoy some body modification without necessarily changing their social presentation; and yet others change their social presentations without changing their bodies. The only way to determine the meaning of each person's experience is through dialogue with him or her, rather than seeking to fit an individual into official classifications systems.

Researchers and clinicians are beginning to recognize areas of transgender expression that had previously been underrecognized. Some examples include: the numbers of female-to-male transsexuals appear to be much higher than historically evident, including those who identify as gay male; the numbers of bi-gender or dual-gender people who do not necessarily want to "cross over" to the other sex but want to live with a more androgynous presentation; and those who desire to live full-time as the opposite sex without any surgical intervention to their genitals. These groups will be briefly explored in the following paragraphs.

The presence of gender-dysphoric females has gone relatively unnoticed and female-to-male transsexualism has been underrepresented in the literature. According to Cromwell (1999) female transgenderism is a complex phenomenon related to the historic invisibility of women's issues in general. For instance, it may have been easier for transgendered females to live in their preferred gender (as compared to transgendered males) in part because there has been a greater range of gender-role and occupational options for females in modern Western society. Females may not experience the same level of stigmatization and social punishment for appropriating masculine clothing and styles as males who wear feminine clothing experience within a patriarchal culture. For that matter, crossing over to the gender of greater social power, although perceived of as a dangerous transgression, may have also been respected and protected within families or communities. In addition, there may be a greater acceptance of masculine or butch presentation within some lesbian communities that enabled certain transgendered females to live within a subculture in which their masculinity was accepted. It is also suggested that transgendered females may not have commonly used the services of traditional gender clinics or cross-dressing clubs and were therefore less likely to be included in the medical and sociological research. Female-to-male transsexuals and female masculinity in general have been invisible to the medical and clinical classifications systems precisely because the way those systems define gender identity "disorders" (i.e., secretive cross-dressing, hatred of genitalia) precludes the experiences of many forms of female-to-male transsexualism and transvestism.

Due to the nature of societal paradigms that view sex and gender as dichotomous, there has been little understanding of people who, despite having "normal" male or female bodies, experience themselves as having both masculine and feminine genders. Not crossing over to the other gender but exhibiting aspects of both men and women, they identify themselves as bi-gendered, dual gendered, or androgynous. They seek medical services to further virilize (or feminize) some of their features, with no intent to pass as the other sex or undergo sex reassignment. Others may identify as members of the other sex and live within the parameters for gender expression of that sex, but not necessarily surgically change their genitalia for reasons of health, money, or personal desire. These newly emerging gender identities confuse the medical model of treatment and raise many questions about treatment as well as the legal ramifications of sex and gender ambiguities.

Intersexed people have also been invisible both socially and clinically. Intersexuality has been assumed a rare condition affecting an insignificant number of people, and those who are intersexed have only recently begun organizing and insisting on adequate medical treatment. Intersexuality refers to a variety of medical and physical conditions impacting people who are not easily classified into the binary of male and female categories. Intersexed people confound the bipolar social categories of male and female in ways similar to transgendered people and have specific clinical issues that have also been neglected by the psychotherapy community.

The reality is that transgenderism, transsexualism, cross-dressing, and intersexuality as they have been defined in the clinical literature do not do justice to the diversity of gender identities and expressions within the lives of gender-variant people. As the political and social movement of transgender and intersex activism expands the definitions of what gender variance is, the clinical community has limited itself to terminology and theories created by the medical establishment. Perhaps there are as many individual words to describe transgender behavior as there are individuals who define and express their own gender variance.

THE FAMILIES OF TRANSGENDERED PEOPLE

Transgendered persons, who wish to live fully their transgendered identity, need forms of family that will support and nourish their existence.

Ken Cooper
Social Services with Transgendered Youth, 1999

People struggling with gender identity issues, and the dysphoria that can accompany them, represent a broad range of human beings. They can be adults as well as children and adolescents. They are biologically born males, biologically born females, and intersexed people. Gender-variant people can be of any age, race, class, ethnicity, cultural, and religious orientation. Gender-variant people can, and do, represent the wide variety of human sexualities, including those who are heterosexual, homosexual, bisexual, and asexual. Gender-variant people are somebody's children and often somebody's parent. They can be somebody's lover, partner, or spouse. As extended family members, friends, colleagues, and neighbors, they represent an aspect of the diversity within the human family.

There has been an absence of clinical focus on transgenderism in general, but this lack is easily eclipsed by the scarcity of professional information on the treatment and support of the families of transgendered individuals, with the possible exception of research on the wives of male cross-dressers. The marriage and family literature is essentially silent on this issue. Sometimes, in long clinical treatises in the medical literature on transsexualism, there will be a few short paragraphs addressing "the wife"—assuming, of course, that most transsexuals are males who are heterosexually married. Historically, clinical advice has consisted of telling the transsexual partners to abandon their families, change their identities, and begin a new life in another city. The underlying assumption was that no wife would remain with her transsexual husband and that transsexualism was detrimental for the children. Transgendered people's professional identities, relationships with children, and emotional bonding with life partners were seen as impossible obstacles in their transition process; something that must be resolved before moving ahead with treatment. "Inevitably," Clemmensen (1990) assured the reader, "the marriage must be dissolved" (p. 130). The wife and children were expected to move on with their lives, as if there had been a familial death.

Little discussion exists in the literature on the needs of the wives, and the possibility of transitioning within supportive families is rarely suggested. Steiner (1990) outlined the assessment process and asked, "Is the married patient, virtually always male, willing to divorce his wife and abandon his children to pursue his cross-gender wishes?" (p. 97), never looking at the situation from the opposite angle and asking whether *the spouse is able to grow and change enough to support her husband's cross-gender "needs."* There is only brief and pathologizing discussion about the partners of female-to-male transsexuals or "same-sex" partners who are dealing with a transitioning spouse. With precious few exceptions, clinical support for parents, children, employers, and friends has been almost nonexistent.

Clinicians who work with transgendered people often receive calls for support from partners and family members. Their pain is visceral and their isolation is overwhelming. Discovering gender dysphoria in a loved one can invite myriad emotions. As with other shame-based issues, there are underlying questions: "Why is this happening to me? Why am I involved with this person?" Wives, husbands, and lovers express concern about themselves: "What is it about me," they ask, "that was *attractive* to this person? Why have I been *attracted* to someone who is a transsexual?" Partners are often caught in an emotional whirlwind over their loved ones' disclosure and wonder if their lives together have been a sham. They may be frightened at what the future will bring. When couples finally come into therapy, they are often on the verge of divorce. Other unresolved issues—similar to those present in all intimate relationships—become entwined in the gender issues. Such couples often have difficulty sorting other marital issues from those that are related to the gender dysphoria. Parents worry about how gender dysphoria will impact their children, and children worry that it is contagious or inheritable.

The literature on transgenderism has elaborated eloquently on the clinical importance of distinguishing between sexual and gender identity (e.g., homosexuality as distinct from transsexualism). Definitions of sexual identity or orientation are based in the concept of there being two types of bodies—male and female—and homosexuality is the name given when two people of the same "sex" are lovers. When people "change sex" they might also be changing the apparent sexual configuration of their relationship (e.g., a gay male couple "becomes" a heterosexual couple, or a heterosexual couple "becomes" a lesbian couple). This change can take place internally within the couple's own perception, or in how they are perceived by the outside world. Being involved with a transsexual can shift the meaning of one's own sexual orientation and cause tremendous interpersonal and marital problems.

These issues have not been discussed in depth in the clinical literature and there is a subtle homophobia that underlies the assumption that families and marriages cannot survive gender transition since marriages have been based on a belief in paired opposites. Moreover, there is not even a glimpse in the psychological literature that having a partner who is transgendered might be fascinating, exciting, or desirable. If transgendered people are considered psychologically ill and maladapted, the subtle assumption is that their partners are also in some manner mentally disturbed. Clinical experience shows that many transgendered people have healthy, long-standing, viable relationships. Indeed, many partners of transgendered people find their spouses not only mentally stable but also sexually appealing. Why does the literature not even recognize the possibility that marriages can withstand the struggles of gender transition, or that a transgendered individual could be romantically attractive?

When children express gender-variant behavior parents inevitably feel uncomfortable and worry whether the behavior is "their fault" or related to their parenting. The literature clearly reinforces this, stating unequivocally that it is indeed their fault. Rekers and Kilgus (1995) wrote, "The main source of gender deviance is found in psychological development . . . and social learning within the family environment" (p. 264). Children expressing "gender-deviant" behaviors—boys in greater numbers than girls—are understood to be suffering from severe psychopathologies (Coates, 1990) and the gender issues have been considered "secondary to more fundamental psychopathology in the child and in his or her family" (Zucker and Bradley, 1995, p. 266).

Although programs have been developed to "treat" these gender-defiant children and often adjunctively their parents, the success of their treatments (based on the elimination or minimization of these behaviors) is unsubstantiated and the ethics are clearly debatable. Embedded in the literature is the assumption that children of gender-variant parents and parents of gender-variant children have psychosocial problems and related gender disturbances themselves, although the research documenting these "truths" is of questionale quality.

Our discomfort with cross-gender behavior and the primacy of appropriate sex roles is nowhere more enforced than when it comes to children who are born with ambiguous or intermediate genitalia. Intersexed children are considered "psychosocial emergencies" and are surgically altered at birth to conform to the best approximation of a male or female child that the medical establishment is currently able to achieve. Families are counseled not to question the child's sex or gender assignment and they are counseled to withhold information from their child so they do not confuse him or her. Often the doctors keep information from the parents thinking this will support the parents' complete belief in the correctness of the surgical alterations. The issues related to parenting an intersexed child—including answering questions regarding "altered" genitalia and fertility, aesthetics, self-image, gender identity, and sexual functioning—are essentially silenced, and the family is left to live with this psychosocial trauma. Counseling strategies and family support services do not exist for these families because any focus on these issues would, the experts say, send a message to these families that their child is not a "normal" boy or girl.

Addressing the needs of the families of transgendered and intersexed people is an unrecognized area of family systems therapy, as well as an underserved population within the gender community. Clinical guidelines for the "treatment" or "management" of transgendered and intersexed people that do not address the issues of their family members in a supportive and systemic manner are inadequate and disrespectful. Clinical guidelines for the management of intersexed children that do not address the impact on the parent who has an intersexed child and the issues of being intersexed for the developing child are a disservice to the psychosocial issues of family development.

That this issue has not come to the attention of family therapists is indicative of the stigma of discussing transgenderism within the clinical community. Throughout this book, family members of transgendered and intersexed people—legal spouses, intimate partners, children, parents, and significant others—are integrated into a holistic paradigm and viewed as a focus for clinical support.

THE NEED FOR TRAINING

There exists a range of personal identifications around woman, man, in-between—we don't even have names or pronouns that reflect that in between place but people certainly live it.

Minnie Bruce Pratt
Sojourner interview, 1996

With the exception of some trained sexologists and a small number of medical doctors and psychotherapists, the majority of clinicians, including social workers, counselors, psychologists, psychiatrists, and physicians, have not received training on the treatment of sex and gender identity or issues involving gender dysphoria and transgenderism. Most psychotherapists are faced with an almost intuitive sense of discomfort when faced with a client who is exhibiting "gender-deviant" behavior or who is expressing gender-dysphoric symptoms. Unaware of the therapeutic needs of trans-gendered and intersexed people, clinicians often reflect back to their clients the same anxiety, depression, isolation, shame, and terror that their clients present to them. At worst, clients have been abandoned and ridiculed at times when they have been most in need of genuine compassion. These pro-nouncements may appear harsh, but clinical experience yields frightening narratives of clients who have been misdiagnosed, mistreated, and mis-guided by uninformed clinicians.

Those who specialize in working with transgendered people are often privy to the bias and judgment of colleagues. Although their training should belay this, helping professionals often discuss gender-variant people with a tone of cynicism and disgust. Transgendered people are perceived by some to be outside the realm of legitimate professional interest, and clinicians who work with transgendered clients are sometimes assumed to be guilty by association, as if they must have a "reason" for working with this unusual population.

There is a dearth of knowledge of sexual and gender identity issues and an erroneous assumption that the numbers of people affected are too small to require any personal continuing education. Those clinicians who have de-cided to pursue professional education regarding transgendered issues will find little information or encouragement in any undergraduate or graduate studies departments. Sometimes transgender issues are discussed within a theoretical context in academia, but rarely within a counseling psychology or social-work curriculum. Sometimes transgenderism is subsumed under "gay and lesbian" training within agencies, but in the few hours set aside there is rarely any time for more than a perfunctory overview of sexual ori-entation issues, let alone gender issues.

If the clinician is proactive and able to donate time and energy to re-search, numerous sources can be cited on the pathology of gender dys-phoria. The majority of the literature about transsexualism involves the proper diagnostic and assessment procedures for sex reassignment surgery (SRS) approval. There is, however, a paucity of theoretical analysis or clini-cal guidelines to assist the psychotherapist in mental health assessment and psychotherapeutic treatment of people struggling with gender variance or gender dysphoria. The clinical literature that exists is often in conflict with the plethora of recent writings emanating from the ever-expanding trans-gendered liberation movement. It appears that political activists are more aware and concerned about the dialogue taking place within the professional community than the clinical experts are cognizant of the issues affecting the real lives of the clients they are "treating." Some physicians and therapists who are transgendered or transsexual have dedicated their professional lives to working within their community and are beginning to bridge this gap.

Although many clinicians are not skilled in sexology or gender identity issues, increasingly transgendered people are requesting services (Wilson, Sharp, and Carr, 1999). The transgendered client often arrives in the office of an untrained therapist and is pathologically diagnosed and "treated," which often consists of serving as the learning fodder for the uninformed, but intensely curious, clinician. Those transgendered clients who come into a therapeutic setting and do not explicitly identify as transgendered are often unrecognized, particularly if they come into therapy for more general concerns, such as family counseling or depression. General clinical assessment almost never includes a thorough assessment of gender identity and expression. Transgendered people who are stable and live happily adjusted lives often do not present for therapy and are considered exceptions to the rule of gender pathology.

Numerous needs assessments surveys have been conducted demonstrating the prevailing need for comprehensive and sensitive services for the transgendered and transsexual communities. Virtually every area of health and human service care is deficient regarding gender-variant people. Studies in San Francisco, California (Transgender Community Health Project, 1999), Boston, Massachusetts (JSI Research and Training Institute, 2000; Marcel, 1998), Washington, DC (Xavier, 2000), and New York City (Valentine, 1998) demonstrate a need to increase services for transgendered and transsexual communities in areas of substance abuse, HIV prevention and treatment, trauma and victimization, as well as basic medical and mental health services. As more clients reach out for services, there is an increased need for basic medical services from sensitive physicians (Wilson, Sharp, and Carr, 1999), informed and educated treatment from counselors (Carroll, Gilroy, and Ryan, 2002; Raj, 2002), and quality services for mental health issues (JSI Research and Training Institute, 2000). A glaring lack of attention to the specific issues faced by transsexual and transgendered people of color remains, although attempts to address these injustices are ongoing (Tarver, 2002; Davis, 1998; Nemoto et al., 1998).

Statistical data and clinical reports show that there is a lack of prevention as well as treatment services for the large numbers of people, adults and youth, who are transgendered and living with HIV/AIDS (Bockting and Kirk, 2001; Bockting, Rosser, and Coleman, 1999; Clements-Nolle et al., 2001; McGowan, 1999; Transgender Community Health Project, 1999; Xavier, 2000), particularly regarding the need for services sensitive to people of color (Nemoto et al., 1998). High numbers of gender-variant people admit to alcohol and other substance abuse and the barriers to receiving adequate treatment are numerous (Finnegan and McNally, 2002; Kreiss and

Patterson, 1997; Lombardi and van Servellen, 2000; Marcel, 1998; Oggins and Eichenbaum, 2002; SAMHSA, 2001; Tayleur, 1994; Transgender Substance Abuse Treatment Policy Group, 1995; Xavier, 2000).

Regardless of one's professional specialization, it is generally expected that all helping professionals have a basic knowledge regarding a variety of mental health issues including normal human development, addictions, psychopathology, and cultural diversity, just to name a few areas. However, many clinicians have not had basic training in sexual and gender identity development, a fundamental part of human life-cycle development. Professional training programs, workshops and seminars, as well as graduate courses and class lectures must be developed by experienced and skilled clinicians to train their colleagues in issues regarding transgenderism. Basic information about gender issues should be available to the nonspecialist clinician so that at the very least proper assessment and referral can be made. Transgendered studies need to become part of all counselor training and in-service programs. Clinicians need to become sensitized to the assessment, treatment, and proper referral for gender-variant people and their families. It is hoped that this book will play a small part in beginning this educational process.

Changes are slowly taking place regarding professional training and more information about transgenderism is becoming available. Some national professional organizations are also beginning to tackle the challenges inherent in creating and providing services to the transgender community. Some examples of these changes include the following:

- *The Healthy People 2010 Companion Document for Lesbian, Gay, Bisexual, and Transgender Health Care* (Gay and Lesbian Medical Association and LGBT health experts, 2001) is an ambitious national agenda for documenting the unmet health needs of the lesbian, gay, bisexual, and transgender community (LGBT) and outlining areas of prevention.
- The American Public Health Association (APHA, 1999) passed a transgender resolution at its 1999 national meeting and devoted an entire issue of its journal to LGBT health care (APHA, 2001), with adequate representation of the "T" (transgender) section (Clements-Nolle et al., 2001; Feinberg, 2001; Lombardi, 2001).
- The National Association of Social Workers (NASW) adopted a policy position on transgender and gender identity issues in 1999. This statement emphatically says that "people of diverse gender expression and identity . . . should be afforded the same respect and rights as those

whose gender identity and expression conform to societal expectations" (NASW, 2000, p. 302).

- The Society for the Psychological Study of Lesbian, Gay, and Bisexual Issues, Division 44 of the American Psychological Association, began a transgender task force in 1999 to address the professional challenges to the implementation of quality mental health services for the transgendered community.
- The Sexuality Information and Education Council of the United States (SIECUS, 1999) devoted an issue of their bimonthly SIECUS Report to transgender concerns.

This is only the beginning of a new era of health care services targeting the unmet needs of transgendered and transsexual people and their families. It is hoped that this book will offer a basic understanding of the field of transgender studies and a usable outline for progressive treatment strategies. This book is designed as a bridge that honors, on one hand, an individual's right to his or her own gender expression and experience and, on the other hand, the burden of being differently gendered and the effect that oppression can have on a person's mental health. Depathologizing transgenderism honors the political, social, and spiritual rights of people to define their own identity, as well as their destiny, without minimizing the psychological legacy of being labeled a "perverted other," and consequently advocates the need for quality, compassionate, and educated clinical services. Naming oneself is basic to self-actualization, and psychotherapists who are asked to bear witness to the exploration process of transgendered people would do best to put down their diagnostic manuals so they can hear the words and descriptions their clients are using to define themselves and the stories clients are telling about their lives.

PART I:
THEORETICAL UNDERSTANDINGS
OF TRANSGENDERISM

Chapter 1

The Transsexual Phenomenon Meets the Transexual Menace

The clinician's phone rings and the woman on the other end is distraught because she just found a suitcase filled with women's clothing and pictures of her husband dressed in the clothes. She is weeping into the telephone, alternating between expressions of compassion, confusion, sadness, and rage.

A lesbian couple who have been lovers for a decade seek counseling because one of the partners has disclosed that she has always felt like a man, and that she feels ready to begin to live as one. Her partner is devastated, caught between loving her partner and not wanting to be lovers with "a man."

A message on the telephone machine says, "I am calling you as a last resort. I know I am a woman," the deep male voice insists. "I don't know whether to be who I am or just kill myself. Please help me."

A mother seeks therapy because she discovers that her fourteen-year-old son has ordered female hormones on the Internet. The family comes into therapy for one session but cancels each following appointment, saying, "Everything is fine now." A year later, her son e-mails the therapist, "What can I do about my facial hair growing in? I have to do something."

Gender-variant people and their families seek professional help for a variety of reasons. They are often in emotional pain and confused, and are seeking understanding and information. At the time of initial contact, people are often "at the end of their rope," expressing suicidality and despair. Sometimes they seek services after a disclosure—or exposure—of the gender issues that have caused chaos in their family life. They enter therapy angry, resentful, and feeling hopeless. Clients often seek out specialists in gender issues after years of conventional psychotherapy, wanting to move ahead in their gender transformation and feeling stymied and trapped by the medical establishment. Questions immediately arise:

- What are the clinical responsibilities for a therapist faced with a client dealing with issues surrounding his or her gender?
- What are the therapeutic guidelines that should be used to assess a client?
- What tools and treatment strategies should a professional helper use to assist the client coping with gender dysphoria?
- What are the guiding theoretical modalities for a social worker, psychologist, or counselor committed to compassionate and empowering therapy?

Looking at the clinical vignettes listed previously, what advice would a therapist have for a woman who has discovered that her husband is a crossdresser? What is the clinical stance for a therapist counseling a couple in which one female partner identifies as a man and the other identifies as a lesbian? What are the guidelines we use to assess whether the despairing male, who "knows" he is a woman, is really a transsexual or simply a delusional person? Finally, what are the ethical implications of working with a gendervariant child who is seeking services and support without his parent's knowledge?

A therapist working with the wife of a cross-dresser as described in the first vignette could find a small amount of research on heterosexual crossdressers and their wives to assist him or her in doing marriage counseling. The research shows that, through a process of educating the wife about cross-dressing and addressing the issues of betrayal and trust, it is possible for the marriage to remain viable. Guidelines also exist to assess the kind of gender dysphoria exhibited by the male in the third vignette and to assist the therapist in delineating gender dysphoria from "other" mental illnesses, outlining the distinctions between cross-dressing, transsexualism, and homosexuality, and examining the eligibility and readiness for medical sexual reassignment. However, if either of these males wants to modify his body through the use of hormones but not "go all the way" with surgical reassignment, the clinical guidelines become muddier and the research base to understand these experiences is not yet available. Gay and lesbian couples managing issues of identity when facing gender transition have few resources available to assist them in their journey. The ethical dilemmas facing therapists working with transgendered youth are complex, and although guidelines to assist clinicians have been recently revised, they are an area of current professional debate.

It is obvious that more research, information, and clinical discussion are needed to address the issues of these previously marginalized populations. It is perhaps less obvious that a reexamination of existing treatment modalities is also in order for some types of gender variance that have already established clinical trajectories. The following vignettes will illustrate some examples of therapeutic treatments that need to be revisited in light of the currently expanding knowledge.

Luz and Felix Garcia were surprised when, after an uncomplicated delivery, their newborn child was quickly removed from the delivery room. After a few tense hours, the physician explained to them that their daughter had some medical complications concerning her genitals that could be addressed surgically. They were assured there would be no further complications and surgical alteration of their child's genitalia was completed within a few days. They received emotional support and postoperative counseling regarding their daughter's medical condition, but they were not informed that their daughter had been born with an intersexed condition and that there were alternatives to surgery.

Alex (nee Alexandria), 13 years old, was referred by the school district, who described her as "very disturbed." The paperwork they sent described her as avoidant, depressed, slovenly dressed, and isolated. She came to the first session accompanied by her parents. Her dress hung awkwardly on her small frame, and her hair was uncombed. Her father spoke to her in a condescending tone, ordering her to talk about "her problem." Alex spoke in a distant voice, avoiding eye contact. Her chart said she was prescribed three pyschotropic medications, and it was obvious she was having difficulty remaining focused. As Alex tried to explain that she felt like she was a boy, her parents cut her off, telling her she was an "idiot." They explained they had brought her to a number of therapists, including one program two hours away. Alex had spent a year in a residential facility for "disturbed children," and she had also been psychiatrically hospitalized three times for suicide attempts. No one had been able to "fix" her, her mother said sadly. Alex looked up with hollow eyes, wondering what her next treatment would be.

Louis seemed an unlikely person to be talking about cross-dressing. He was a large man, with burly hands worn and stained from Louis's fifteen years as a car mechanic. There was very little that could be called feminine about his mannerisms, yet as he talked about his cross-dressing, he grew tender and vulnerable. He confided to me how he'd been hiding his clothes in a box in the attic, and had been secretly dressing when his wife and children were not home. He admitted he did not look all that good in women's clothing, saying, "I know I could never leave the house. Everyone would know that I was a man in a dress." He was terrified that his wife would find out and he would lose his family and children. Louis had seen two other therapists in the past ten years. The first had tried behavior modification techniques, but Louis said, "I failed at all of them." The second clinician recommmended psychoanalysis, and asked Louis whether he could come in to therapy at least twice a week, an expense beyond Louis's budget. With tears in his eyes, Louis said that this was his last hope. He'd heard that there may be a drug he could take that would make his feelings go away.

Spike looked like a young boy, although she was nearly a thirty-year-old female. She wore jeans, work boots, and a very loose shirt. Her hair was very short and mostly covered by a baseball cap. She explained that a friend referred her, although she was not sure she wanted to be in therapy. "I've tried that before," she said, smirking. Spike shared that she had spent two years in counseling nearly a decade earlier with a therapist who thought she dressed like a boy because her father was an alcoholic who had beat her mother and sexually molested Spike and her sisters. "My sister doesn't dress like a boy, even though my father got her too," she said. "I don't want to talk about my father," Spike said. "The only reason I'm here is my friend said you could help me get some kind of medication that would turn me into a boy. I mostly live as a boy anyway, but it would be nice if I could really become one."

The preceding vignettes illustrate the modern "state of the art" of many physicians, psychiatrists, and psychotherapists, and the theoretical models underpinning these clinical strategies are still the therapeutic modalities of choice for many clinicians. Although some trained specialists who work with people dealing with gender identity issues will say that the examples are too critical of helping professionals, many gender specialists are skilled in treating these kinds of cases with compassion and experience. However, the reality is that few helping professionals are actually trained in gender identity concerns and these treatment strategies are more often the norm than the exception.

Utilizing surgical tools, behavior modification techniques, psychoanalytic ideologies, and standardized diagnostic nosologies, clients are "labeled," "repaired," "fixed," "analyzed," and "qualified" within the established framework of institutionalized guidelines. Through extensive psychotherapeutic and analytically based modalities clients are encouraged to explore the unconscious reasons underlying their gender deviance. Behavioralists try to modify improper gender expression by children and youth with the goal of alleviating the anticipated future problems caused by unconventional gender expression. Surgical models attempt to align newborn babies into preestablished normative sex categories, hoping to eliminate later sex or gender confusion, and yet adults who struggle with sex or gender dysphoria, but resist surgical treatments, are refused medical assistance to redefine their gender expression.

The working assumption of the medical model of mental illness is that there is something underlying the "dysfunction" or "disorder" that can be "repaired," "fixed," or "cured." Even contemporary treatment modalities to assist adult transsexuals in sexual reassignment are often based on an expression of resignation and hopelessness that no other options exist. Surgical and hormonal treatments, available for those able to access and afford them, are seen as last resorts after psychotherapeutic models have failed.

The modern treatment of transsexuals is based on a medical model that describes variant gender identity as "disordered" and surgical reassignment is framed as the "cure."

It is undeniable that transsexuals and other transgendered and gender-variant people often experience emotional turmoil and are in need of access to both medical and psychological treatments. However, it is questionable whether models that infer disorder and dysfunction are useful for the self-actualization and empowerment of humans whose basic dilemma involves having a sex or gender identity that does not simply match their physical bodies.

COMPASSIONATE AND CONTROVERSIAL TREATMENT OF TRANSSEXUALS

Transgendered people who choose transsexual treatment, who allow themselves to be medicalized, depend on a system of approval that grants them access to treatment.

Jamison Green
Reclaiming Gender, 1999

Endocrinologist Harry Benjamin (1885-1986) was a pioneer in the compassionate treatment of gender-variant people and was the first modern physician to present the idea that transsexuals could not adjust to their birth sex regardless of the psychotherapeutic intervention aimed at curing them. He encouraged the development of a medical system that would support transsexuals in gender transitioning. Benjamin viewed himself as a maverick and a reformer (Meyerowitz, 2002). Speaking about male-to-female transsexuals, he said,

> Psychotherapy with the aim of curing transsexualism, so that the patient will accept himself as a man . . . is a useless undertaking. . . . Since it is evident, therefore, that the mind of the transsexual cannot be adjusted to the body, it is logical and justifiable to attempt the opposite, to adjust the body to the mind. If such a thought is rejected, we would be faced with therapeutic nihilism. (Benjamin, 1966, p. 116)

This radical idea, that transsexuals could not be "cured," i.e., they could never become comfortable within the gender parameters of their bodies, was the seminal idea from which the modern medical and therapeutic treatment of transsexual people has developed. The idea that intersexed children should not be surgically altered as a "cure" for their sexual ambiguity, or that gender-variant children should not be behaviorally modified as a "cure" for their deviance (defiance?) is just beginning to find advocates now at the beginning of the twenty-first century.

Although, as will be seen, gender variance has always existed historically and cross-culturally, the rise of medical technology and the development of synthetic hormones and surgical procedures to assist males and females in dramatic and effective "sex-changes" brought with it amazing possibilities that shifted the ability of people to physically alter their bodies to conform to their internal experiences. Advances in modern medicine have undeniably been life-saving for many transsexuals. It has been suggested that the emergence of a specific contemporary transsexual identity can be dated to the 1940s when hormones and surgeries first became obtainable, and Hausman has questioned whether the term *transsexual* should even be used "before the advent of surgical and hormonal sex reassignment" (Hausman, 1995, p. 116).

Modern medical sex reassignment treatments were first explored early in the twentieth century. Eugen Steinach first brought public attention to "sex-change" possibilities through his work with animals in 1910 (Meyerowitz, 2002). In 1945, Magnus Hirschfeld described two surgical cases of the 1920s—one a male-to-female transsexual and the other a female-to-male—and, in 1966, Harry Benjamin described the use of hormones in the 1920s to induce breast growth (Pfäefflin and Junge, 1998; Whittle, 1995). As early as 1930, Lili Elbe (born Einar Wegener), a Danish painter, underwent surgical reassignment in Germany (Ebershoff, 2001). In 1965, Pauly (as quoted by King, 1996) cited twenty-eight cases of transsexualism before the 1950s. It was, however, the power of the popular press that brought news of Christine Jorgensen's 1952 "sex change" into the living rooms of middle America and made "transsexualism" part of the contemporary discourse (Bullough and Bullough, 1993; Denny, 1998; Meyerowitz, 1998, 2002). Gender-variant males (and to a lesser extent females) heard for the first time of people actually changing their sex and began to approach the medical establishment for assistance. Reassignment surgeries became the focal points of interest for both medical experts and individuals struggling with gender dysphoria. It is, however, more likely that the advent and availability of synthetic hormones has had the most dramatic impact on the ability of transsexuals to pass undetected in their chosen gender (Bullough and Bullough, 1998). After all, the physical effects of hormones are publicly visible and the surgical alteration of genitals is a private matter.

Although some clinicians are deeply empathetic and regard the use of hormonal and surgical treatments as a necessity for the mental health of transsexual clients, other clinicians and researchers view transsexualism as a pathological disorder that masks mental illnesses. They question whether "transsexualism may be considered iatrogenic, in that advances in surgical technique now permit the realization of fantasies of sexual metamorphosis" (Pauly and Edgerton, 1986, p. 318).

Researchers, academics, policy analysts, feminists, and even transgender activists have expressed a variety of negative opinions on medical and surgical treatments. Billings and Urban (1982) said, "The legitimation, rationalisation and commodification of sex-change operations have produced an identity category—transsexual—for a diverse group of sexual deviants and victims of severe gender role distress" (p. 266). Socarides (1969) said, "Transsexualism represents a wish, not a diagnosis. It is a wish present in transvestites, homosexuals, and schizophrenics with severe sexual conflicts. The issue comes down to whether individuals in these categories of mental illness should be treated surgically for what is basically a severe emotional or mental disorder" (p. 1424). One feminist scholar, critical of transsexual reassignment for "constructing" transsexual identity, said, "Without [surgery's] sovereign intervention, transsexualism would not be a reality. Historically, individuals may have wished to change sex, but until medical science developed the specialties, which in turn created the demand for surgery, sex conversion did not exist" (Raymond, 1979, p. xv). Even transgender activists have voiced criticism about the role of surgical procedures in the modern treatment of transsexuals. MacKenzie (1994) wrote, "The medical promise that sex-reassignment surgery will provide physical characteristics of the 'opposite' sex promotes unrealistic expectations about the physical capabilities of sex-reassignment" (p. 13).

It is perhaps accurate that some transsexuals have unrealistic expectations of the surgical outcomes, regarding appearance as well as its life-changing potentiality. The changes produced by surgery do not, however, "create" transsexuals, as much as it manifests physically a psychic and psychological experience. The anthropological and historical record clearly shows that despite the concerns that transsexualism is iatrogenic and a creation of the modern medical system, rudimentary forms of gender body modification have always existed "throughout history and across cultures" (Cromwell, 1999, p. 98). Stone (1991) said, "Although the term transsexual is of recent origin, the phenomenon is not" (p. 282) and Devor (1997b) said, "The evidence seems clear that there have always been females who felt the need to live their lives as men" (p. 35). Bullough and Bullough (1993), Califia (1997), and Meyerowitz (1998) also give evidence that what is now called transsexualism existed long before the discovery of synthetic sex hormones or the development of advanced genital surgical reconstruction. In reviewing history it is of course hard to know which gender-variant person would have desired hormonal or surgical reassignment had it been available, but as Halberstam (1998a) reminds us, that is perhaps "just as difficult to know today" (p. 97).

During the past forty years, the clinical literature on the therapeutic care of transgendered and transsexual populations has, to a large extent, centered on a discussion of hormonal and surgical bodily transformations. Some areas of scrutiny have included assessing the distinctions between transsexuals and transvestites to determine who was eligible for treatment, and the controversies regarding the success or failure of sex reassignment. As Harry Benjamin's theories were concreted into a "standard reference" for understanding transsexualism, a medical model of gender variance was established, identifying physicians and psychologists as arbiters of who was qualified for surgeries and treatment (Hausman, 1995). Transgendered people who desire hormonal and medical treatment are subject to the medical establishment and its management of their "condition," including being officially diagnosed as a transsexual. Hirschauer (1997) referred to this process over the past half-century as the "medicalization of gender migration."

However, even if the medical profession did not create the transsexual experience, "it is the treatment-seeking behavior of requesting sex reassignment that most often brings the gender disordered [*sic*] individual into contact with the health professional" (Baumbach and Turner, 1992, p. 112). Doctor (1988) said transsexual surgery is "the only major surgical procedure carried out in response to the unremitting demands of the patient" (p. 25).

No doubt many transsexuals are intense, passionate, perhaps even zealous in their desire for surgery. Although it is accurate that transsexuals are often relentless in the pursuit of medical treatments, it is inaccurate to suggest that transsexual surgeries are unique in being carried out solely because of patient demand. Meyerowitz (2002) said those who seek surgery "had what they described as deeply rooted, longstanding, and irrepressible yearnings . . . sometimes with an urgency that bordered on obsession" (p. 130). Many plastic surgeries and reproductive surgeries (vasectomies, tubal ligations, and infertility treatments) are carried out because of the desires of the patient and, sadly, some surgical treatments have been carried out without the permission of the patient (e.g., sterilization of mentally ill and mentally retarded people, sex reassignment surgeries of infants). Transsexual surgeries may, however, be the only surgeries in which clients must be "approved" through a psychological evaluation and the confirming diagnosis of a mental illness in order to receive the treatments they desire.

Since the request for surgical reassignment came to be seen as the hallmark of gender dysphoria (Lothstein, 1979) and, therefore, the eligibility requirement for transsexual treatments, transsexualism became defined by its surgical treatments. This does not infer that transsexualism is a product of the medical model, as much as it is regulated within its specifications. Denny (1998) elucidates this by suggesting that although Christine Jorgensen was the "driving force behind her own sex assignment" (p. 39), the medical experts did not make her into a woman (or, one might add, a transsexual); rather transsexual body modifications become the vehicle for her self-actualization.

The difficulty with the medical model of transsexualism is not that hormonal and surgical possibilities have invented or created a new phenomenon, for transsexualism is no more or less socially constructed than other areas of medicine or other aspects of human identity (King, 1987). The difficulty with the medical model is not that it leaves transsexuals dependent on the medical system, as some feminist writers have suggested (Dobkin, 2000), for many people depend on the medical establishment for treatments to enhance or sustain their lives. The problem is that the medical model has defined and characterized the parameters of the transsexual experience. Bullough and Bullough (1998) suggest that the development of sexual reassignment surgeries did not "empower the client; it simply shifted the power to the team made up of surgeons, psychiatrists, and psychologists" (p. 29). The medical establishment developed diagnostic blueprints that classify and treat transsexualism as a syndrome of gender dysphoria based on genital distress.

The defining trait of transsexualism has been the desire, insistence, and obsession with body modification. It has become institutionalized as the most salient diagnostic criterion. As Stone (1991) said, "The 'wrong body' thesis has delineated the syndrome" (p. 297). Walinder ([1967] 1997) commented that transsexuals "are often convinced that nature has made a mistake in their case, that they really belong to the other sex, that their bodies have developed along the wrong lines. This abhorrence for their own bodies is a consistent feature in transsexualism."

Certainly, many transsexuals experience the severe gender dysphoria that Walinder described, as well as a distress over their sexed genitals. Brown and Rounsley (1996) referred to this as "anatomical dysphoria," and suggested that transsexuals' discomfort is more with their physical bodies, particularly their genitals, rather than a gender identity problem. According to Benjamin (1966) all *true* transsexuals hated their penis and viewed it with disgust. If the penis was seen as a source of pleasure it diagnostically defined the person as a transvestite, not a transsexual, and technically made the patient ineligible for hormonal *and* surgical treatments. However, some people who identify as transsexual do not experience this anatomical dysphoria, and yet these criteria are used to restrict access to hormonal treatments.

Benjamin's focus, as is true for most experts in this field, was male-to-female transsexuals. Until recently FTM transsexuals were considered rare since they did not often apply to gender clinics for surgical treatment and were therefore outside of the medical gaze. Surgical intervention to change one's external genitalia is both more easily, and more successfully, constructed from male to female. This does not, of course, mean that there are more MTF transsexuals. Those born female have had less freedom to live independently, less access to finances, and, perhaps, since the state of the art of female-to-male surgical reassignment is still in its infancy, less willingness to undergo experimental treatments. It is also possible that some female-to-male transgendered/transsexual people do not feel the need to have a penis to feel completely male—especially given the available options. Rachlin's (1999) research on FTMs suggests that, "surgical choices have to do not only with gender identity but also with available resources, technology and individual life circumstances. Restricting the definition of an FTM [i.e., a transsexual] to someone who requests a risky, costly, often technologically inadequate surgery is unrealistic."

Genital surgical options for FTM transition involve operations that are extremely expensive, scarring to the body, and of questionable success (Green, 1994a). Hale (1998) suggested that FTMs view surgical options differently than MTFs. He said that the term *the operation,* which may be a clear reference to the genital surgery for MTFs, should be used cautiously with FTMs "since there is not one and only one operation available . . . as a mechanism of reembodiment" (p. 329). Rachlin (1999) outlined the difficulty with basing transsexual identity on genital dysphoria. She said,

> Attitudes towards GRS [gender reassignment surgery] and one's relationship with one's natural genitals, is frequently part of the diagnostic profile used to determine medical care and legal status for transsexual people. . . . a person who has not had, or does not plan to have, GRS may be denied hormones, surgery (particularly mastectomy or hysterectomy), a legal name or gender change, or ability to legally marry.

For many FTMs, "top surgery" (mastectomy and chest reconstruction) and hormones are of paramount importance for passing. Decisions about "bottom surgery" (genitalia) remain complex, involving financial resources, as well as a risk/benefit analysis of available treatment options.

Genitals remain a focal point for both health care providers and transsexuals precisely because altering them has been the defining characteristic of gender reassignment. Kessler and McKenna (1978) say that when transsexuals focus on having the right genitals they are conforming to cultural expectations. It would certainly be considered pathological if instead they began to "insist on being women with penises or men with vaginas" (p. 123). Maintenance of the social order has, therefore, demanded that transsexualism be defined as a desire for surgical reassignment. Desiring body modification and receiving approval from a therapist, according to Anne Bolin (1988), "provides symbolic and hence 'real' validation for the [MTF] transsexual's pursuit of womanhood . . . supplying an official and dramatic way for people with penises to become people with vaginas, the only proper claimants of the female gender role" (p. 54).

That last clause is significant because recently some transsexuals have, for many reasons, decided against surgical alteration but still desire legal reassignment. They have, essentially, insisted on being men with vaginas and women with penises, raising animosity and terror from both within and without the transgender community. There are legal and medical difficulties that ensue from "allowing" a social identity for men with vaginas and women with penises that makes the difficulty of assessing surgical and hormonal treatment eligibility a very minor issue indeed. However, more people are currently requesting hormonal treatment and surgical alterations without meeting the descriptions for gender identity disorder or transsexualism as outlined in the diagnostic manuals, presenting clinicians and researchers with powerful dilemmas that impact social policy and legal identities.

When Harry Benjamin wrote *The Transsexual Phenomenon* in 1966, he set the stage for a compassionate new treatment for transsexuals with extreme gender and genital dysphoria. However, this model might not be inclusive of all people self-identifying as transsexual within a modern lexicon. The postmodern movement has revised assumptions about the construction and stability of identity development just as the women's movement forced society to reexamine sex and gender roles and assumptions, and the gay liberation movement opened new possibilities for love, romance, and sexual coupling. In a similar manner, the modern transgender liberation movement has unleashed many ways of defining and understanding what has come to be called transsexualism and transgenderism. The title of one grassroots transgender activist organization, the Transexual Menace, refers to the threat that this explosion of new identities has wrought on the established order of the medical model definitions. (The organization's name is reminiscent of the struggle for lesbian inclusion in the women's movement, referred to as the "lavender menace.") At the beginning of the twenty-first century, "the transsexual phenomenon" has met "the transsexual menace," presenting clinicians, physicians, and people dealing with gender variance with a contemporary maelstrom of conflicting ideologies.

Due to the irreversibility of sex reassignment surgery, and the seriousness of surgically operating on someone who might later regret it (Landén et al., 1998; Satterfield, 1988), the medical and psychological research of the past four decades has attempted to identify a "true" or "primary" transsexual to minimize postsurgical regrets in those who were not actually transsexual. Although acknowledging other forms of gender dysphoria, medical treatments were reserved for those who met the stringent criteria of transsexualism. In the past decade it has become obvious to many clinicians, writers, and activists that many people do not easily fit into the categories that have been delineated and yet are seeking medical treatments to redefine their gender presentation (see Bockting, 1997; Bornstein, 1994; Bowell, 1998; Carroll, 1999; Devor, 1989; Cole et al., 2000; Ekins and King, 1999; Feinberg, 1998; Hooley, 1997; McKain, 1996; Nestle, Wilchins, and Howell, 2002; Wilchins, 1997). Carroll (1999) said:

> The mental health field is accustomed to thinking of only two solutions [for gender dysphoria] . . . either changing the identity to match the body (i.e., accepting completely one's given physical gender and gender role) or changing the body to match the identity and adopting completely the identity of the other gender. Increasingly clinicians and transgender individuals themselves are finding that these categories are inadequate to describe the possible resolutions to cross-gender experience. (p. 129)

There is great diversity of people seeking medical treatments who do not identify as transsexual, or who *do* identify as transsexual but do not utilize the word in the same way as the medical community. This heterogeneous group includes heterosexual and homosexual males who cross-dress and desire hormones for feminization but do not desire surgery. Many of these males work as men and live as women the rest of their lives, or perhaps only occasionally cross-dress for eroticism, comfort, or "camp" (i.e., entertainment). Also included are females who seek hormones to virilize their bodies, or perhaps desire breast reduction/chest reconstruction yet still see themselves as females or desire to be seen by others as females. Many have come to define themselves as bi-gendered, mixed gendered, dual gendered, or gender-blended, and seek medical treatments to help accentuate masculine or feminine characteristics. Some see their dual gender as fluid, changing during their life or during the course of a day. Others see their gender as stable and consistent but somewhere in the "middle." Feinberg (1998) suggests that there are "many shades of gender that are not even represented in language yet" (pp. 53-54).

As Bockting (1997) said, "a paradigm shift has occurred signified by an emerging transgender consciousness that challenges the binary conceptualization of gender" (p. 49). Ruth Hubbard (1998) called on scientists who study both physical and social phenomenon to explore this emerging paradigm in science that "stresses fluidity [and] will generate different questions and hence come up with different descriptions and analyses that those derived from the binary view" (p. 53). Breaking down the binary view of "changing sex," i.e., moving from one side of the gender binary to the other, and acknowledging gender as continuum has massive repercussions for the clinical and medical treatment of transsexualism. Gilbert (2000) says, "What we did not consider 25 years ago was the possibility that someone might not want to make a credible gender presentation—might not want to be seen as clearly either male or female," a concept that the psychiatric and medical community is only slowly coming to accept.

There is a need to revise the medical model's therapeutic understanding of transsexualism and transgenderism to one that is more compassionate, inclusive, and accurate. This paradigm shift does not deny or minimize the seminal work of the early experts in this field or the work they did to make hormonal and surgical possibilities available. Nor does this paradigm shift diminish the need for surgeries to be available to those who experience anatomical dysphoria and desire complete sex reassignment. What it can hopefully do is assist clinicians and medical experts to respond to the needs of a broader range of gender-variant people. The paradigm shift is not meant to invalidate the past fifty years of gender treatment. Transsexualism as Harry Benjamin defined it does exist—it is just not the only form of transgenderism that warrants access to medical treatments.

Surgical Statistics, Success, and Controversy

Transsexualism has been considered a rare phenomenon, although gender dysphoria itself may be less rare. Although significant numbers of people identify as transsexual, transgendered, or gender variant, it is, however, difficult to get accurate statistics on a population that is mostly secretive and closeted. It is to be assumed that many people struggle with gender identity issues who never come to the attention of the medical community, and certainly the more closeted the person is, the less likely they are to be included in any statistics—although they may possibly be more in need of psychotherapeutic services. There is no "census" reporting for postoperative transsexuals, and those who have been lucky enough to pass fully in their newly assigned sex often disappear into the mainstream of society. As in discussing all sexual and gender issues, the population that is visible to be counted is only the tip of the proverbial iceberg.

When researchers use statistics to describe transsexual people, we must ask, "Who has been counted in this population? How do we begin to develop accurate statistics; indeed, how do we define who is to be included?" Are transsexuals defined as people who are genitally postoperative or are preoperative people included in the figures? What about nonoperative people, those who chose not to have surgery, are not medically eligible for surgery, or are not financially able to afford surgery yet live full-time in their chosen sex? Are people who receive hormonal treatments counted or only those who have had genital surgery? How can people who are passing ever be counted, particularly those who are exhibiting no obvious distress and do not request medical intervention?

Those who seek treatment in traditional gender clinics are a small proportion of those struggling with gender dysphoria and probably represent a particular subset of gender-variant people, i.e., those seeking medical relief. It would be perhaps easier to count the number of people who have successfully completed sexual reassignment surgery (by examining surgical records) than it would ever be to access the number of people struggling with gender dysphoria. Given the obvious complexity of data collection, the statistics that have been gathered, primarily in European countries, are general estimates of clients requesting and receiving services for SRS. The number of cross-dressers or other differently gendered people has not been well researched. These statistics are gathered through the records of gender clinics that have been established specifically to serve people struggling with gender dysphoria and evaluate their surgical eligibility.

According to the DSM-IV-TR, approximately one per 30,000 adult physiological males and one per 100,000 adult physiological females seek SRS (American Psychiatric Association [APA], 2000, p. 579). These general figures are supported by Meyer-Bahlburg (1985) and research in Sweden (Walinder, [1967] 1997; Walinder, 1971), Germany (Weitze and Osburg, 1996), and England (Hoenig and Kenna, 1974). Australia and New Zealand show an even higher incidence (Ross et al., 1981; Walters, 1997). More people continue to seek treatments over time, and Pauly's estimates of one per 100,000 males and one per 400,000 females are now considered to be very low (Pauly, 1968).

Statistics in the Netherlands, home of one of the most progressive gender clinics, are estimated to be approximately one per 12,000 males and one per 30,000 females (Bakker et al., 1993; Van Kesteren, Gooren, and Megens, 1996). In Singapore, the incidence of transsexualism is also reportedly very high, showing approximately one per 9,000 males and approximately one per 27,000 females (Tsoi, 1988). Most countries do not have clinics specializing in gender issues. For instance, China began to treat transsexualism in the early 1990s (Zhaoji and Chuanmin, 1997) and Japan began to make SRS surgery available in 1998 (Ako, 2001; Kameya and Narita, 2000).

The accuracy or utility of these figures is open to debate, and it has been suggested that they represent figures a few decades old, when transsexualism was even more widely discriminated against than it is today and SRS was harder to obtain. Conway (2001) estimated that approximately 800 to 1,000 MTF surgeries are now performed by a handful of surgeons in the

United States each year and many more Americans go to Europe or Canada for SRS where it is less expensive. She suggests that close to 20,000 surgeries were done in the 1990s and that more than 30,000 males have had SRS since the 1960s. Estimating the number of males in the United States between the ages of eighteen and sixty to be approximately 80,000,000, Conway's figures of one per 2,500 are substantially higher than the official count. (Conway's analysis is methodologically flawed in that she compared the number of surgeries over a forty-year period with the adult male population at a single point in time, rather than with the total adult male population over the same forty-year period. However, methodological flaws are endemic in all of these population studies.) Conway's point, however, should be heeded. Postoperative transsexuals may represent a more significant percentage of the population than has perhaps been recognized. Today many researchers believe that female-to-male transsexuals are as common as male-to-females, although many have only begun to seek medical services in the last few years. These figures represent only those who have *sought services* for gender reassignment. Extrapolating from these figures and including *all* people with significant gender varience—with or without dysphoria—it is obvious that a significant portion of the population is impacted by gender-related issues.

Although gender clinics represent only a small fraction of those dealing with issues related to gender dysphoria, they have been a vital component of transgender care, as well as a source for important research for professionals. Surgeons have responded to the challenge of transsexuals' requests for physical modification by improving surgical techniques with evolving technological advances and offering transsexuals more refined options to remake their bodies in their own images. These clinics have also been criticized for their rigid assessment processes based on research protocols and resulting poor quality of patient care (Denny, 1992). The development of gender clinics serving the transsexual population began with the work of Reed Erickson, a female-to-male transsexual who underwent sex reassignment while under the care of Harry Benjamin in the 1960s (Bullough and Bullough, 1998; Devor, 2000). Erickson was a wealthy man who formed a nonprofit philanthropic foundation called the Erickson Educational Foundation (EEF), which funded the early work of the Harry Benjamin Foundation and the production of educational pamphlets for those seeking services for transsexualism (see Erickson Educational Foundation, 1973).

The EEF also assisted in the organization of the first international conferences on gender dysphoria, which set the groundwork for the formation of the Harry Benjamin International Gender Dysphoria Association (HBIGDA)—a professional organization devoted to the understanding and treatment of gender identity disorders. The EEF was also instrumental in the establishment of the Johns Hopkins Gender Identity Clinic (now defunct), which was developed under the guidance of the controversial and iconoclastic sex researcher John Money and, in 1966, was the site where the first modern surgical sex reassignment in the United States was performed (Bullough and Bullough, 1993).

By the mid-1970s, numerous clinics specialized in gender reassignment. These clinics came under intense negative scrutiny after the release of a report by Meyer and Reter (1979) which questioned the success of SRS for transsexuals. It is interesting to note that John Meyer, a psychiatrist, and Money were both employed by Johns Hopkins at the time this divisive report was released. Janice Raymond (1996) has suggested that Money's colleagues were uncomfortable with his unconventional sexological theories. Regardless of the interpersonal politics involved, Meyer and Reter's (1979) study fueled an extensive debate in the literature regarding the success of gender reassignment surgeries. Meyer and Reter stated that "Sex reassignment surgery confers no objective advantage in terms of social rehabilitation," although they did admit that those who had undergone surgeries stated that it was "subjectively satisfying" (p. 1015).

Following the media exposé of this study, many gender clinics closed down, including, in 1979, the Johns Hopkins Gender Identity Clinic. According to Meyerowitz (2002), Johns Hopkins actually turned away far more potential surgical candidates than it accepted, creating negative feelings in many who were hopeful and then had those hopes deflated. A few other clinics—University of Minnesota and Stanford University—also opened gender clinics and provided assessment and surgical reassignment. There are currently approximately thirty-five to forty clinics specializing in the treatment of gender identity disorder worldwide, according to A. E. S. Webb, former executive director of the Harry Benjamin International Gender Dysphoria Association (HBIGDA) (Schaefer, Wheeler, and Futterweit, 1995), and numerous private physicians who perform gender-related surgeries.

Meyer and Reter's 1979 study seemed to show no long-term improved adjustment for transsexuals that have undergone surgery. Meyer and Reter analyzed a follow-up of fifty transsexual patients who had been seen by the Johns Hopkins Gender Identity Clinic, and the results indicated that sex reassignment did not decrease distress and suicidality, nor did it improve life functioning. Quoted in *The New York Times,* Meyer said that SRS was "not a proper treatment for a psychiatric disorder and it's clear to me that these patients have severe psychological problems that don't go away following surgery" (as quoted in Fleming, Steinman, and Bocknek, 1980, p. 451). However, numerous methodological flaws exist in the study, including self-selected samples, no real measure of adjustment, inadequacies of the outcome criteria and methods to assess the criteria, poor response rates, questionable statistical procedures, and lack of a control group (Abramowitz, 1986; Blanchard and Sheridan, 1990; Doctor, 1988; Fleming, Steinman, and Bocknek, 1980; Green and Fleming, 1990). Doctor (1988) said, "The existing data-base of follow-up research concerning sex reassignment is so incomplete and methodologically flawed that few broad conclusions are warranted" (p. 68).

Despite Doctor's accurate criticism of these follow-up studies and the devastating impact of Meyer and Reter's study, a review of the literature overwhelmingly concludes that surgical reassignment has been successful. From the early outcome studies in the 1960s to more contemporary studies in the 1990s, there have been consistently positive results regarding the satisfaction of patients undergoing surgical reassignment (Green, 2000b). Pauly reported a generally favorable outcome from SRS in 1968, and then, following the Meyer and Reter's report, in 1981 he again reviewed the literature covering eleven follow-up studies on transsexualism and still found generally favorable results (Pauly, 1968, 1981). Money's (1971) early studies showed expressed satisfaction, occupational improvement, lack of criminal behavior, and no increase in psychiatric problems among postoperative SRS patients. According to Blanchard and Sheridan's (1990) and Green and Fleming's (1990) reviews of the literature, the majority of clients who complete SRS are satisfied with the results. Pfäfflin and Junge (1998) reviewed thirty years of literature, including seventy follow-up studies and eight reviews from twelve countries during the years 1961 to 1991, as well as an analysis of their own clinical practice, and concluded "Treatment that includes the whole process of gender reassignment is effective."

Carroll (1999) commented that transsexual individuals who go through structured treatment programs show better psychosocial outcome and fewer regrets, and Walinder, Lundström, and Thuwe (1978), Blanchard and colleagues (1989), and Landén and colleagues (1998) found that those who had surgical regrets did not often fit the strictest criteria for "primary transsexualism." Pfäefflin and Jurge (1998) identified three major causes for role- reversal regrets: (1) poor differential diagnostic procedures, (2) failure to carry out the real-life test, and (3) disappointing surgical outcome. He also acknowledges that many regrets are temporary and are overcome with therapeutic assistance. Ross and Need (1989) found that the psychosocial adjustment of postoperative MTF transsexuals may be related to the adequacy of their surgical results and their ability to successfully pass as females. This was validated by later research (Rakie et al., 1996) which showed that there was an improved quality of life for postoperative MTF and FTM transsexuals, but that those who expressed dissatisfaction were unhappy for reasons related to surgical satisfaction or their ability to successfully pass in their new sex. "Poor support from family" was listed as one of the most salient factors predictive in regrets about SRS (Landén et al., 1998), although, with the exception of the work of Ma (1997) and Chong (1990) in Hong Kong, few programs involve families in their treatment strategies.

How shall clinicians determine which criteria are salient for judging the success of SRS? Shall success be based on few client regrets or personal statements of satisfaction? How about postoperative career improvement and marital stability or psychosocial depression or suicidality? Examining postsurgical functioning is complex because the transition impacts virtually every area of functioning. Doctor (1988) said that external measures such as occupational achievement, marital stability, or educational advancement should be used as measures. These are certainly important variables regarding human fulfillment and were the kinds of indicators Meyer and Reter (1979) used, e.g., employment status, marital and cohabiting success, psychological and legal problems. However, without an analysis of the social and occupational stressors involved in transitioning—the nature of job discrimination, the emotional and financial stress of gender reassignment (without any family therapy to assist transition processes), and the stigma of transsexualism—it hardly seems fair to judge those who change gender for their lack of social, occupational, or marital success. For instance, Blanchard et al. (1989) found that a loss of income for MTFs was significant in their postsurgical regrets, a noteworthy factor since women often make less money than men.

Without examining issues of societal stigma, social, occupational, and marital success are not acceptable criteria to judge satisfaction or success of sex reassignment (Green and Fleming, 1990). It is also ironic that clients are assessed for their relationship success when some clinics have insisted that clients sever their marital relationships before treatments are approved. Carroll (1999) suggested that failure should be judged by significant regret or decline in one or more areas of functioning. By this criterion, reassignment surgeries have been very successful, showing an incidence of regret to be very low (less than 2 percent for male-to-females, and less than 1 percent for female-to-males). Rachlin (2001) said, "Hormonal and/or surgical sex reassignment has proven to be very satisfactory for a select population and Transsexual individuals often benefit greatly from physical and social sex reassignment" (p. 4).

If the success rate is based on client satisfaction, it is expected it would be very high, since those completing the process are a highly selected sample. Receiving surgical reassignment has required extensive evaluation and approval from psychologists, psychiatrists, and surgeons, with most of those requesting services not receiving approval and/or not following through on surgical treatments. If the selection process is strict, then it is assumed that the outcome measures will show success. Walters, Kennedy, and Ross (1986) stated that those who are supportive of surgical options for transsexuals "can increase the likelihood of a favorable outcome . . . by selecting candidates on the basis of their ego strengths and adjustment during the presurgery period" (p. 147). Indeed, clients have traditionally been excluded from approval for exhibiting signs of mental illness, mental retardation, substance abuse, criminality, and assumed postsurgical homosexuality. Clients have also been seen as poor candidates if they lacked positive familial support, did not display significant genital dysmorphia, or could not pass well as a member of the opposite sex.

Another way of judging the success of SRS is to examine the suicide rate for postoperative transsexuals, which is admittedly higher than nonclinical control groups (about 2 percent for male-to-females and 0.5 percent for female-to-males). However, as Carroll (1999) said, there is also a higher risk of suicide for gender-dysphoric people who do not undergo surgery, suggesting that living with gender issues can infer a higher risk of suicide regardless of surgical status. Again, this may well be due to societal transphobia, as well as the incredible stress of transitioning. Doctor (1988) asked,

> How much weight should be given to the subjective, postoperative report by a transsexual that he or she feels better than before, enjoys life more in general, and considers the surgery the most valued step ever taken? Should these more or less self-serving and highly subjective evaluations be accepted as critical criteria for success? (p. 68)

It is suggested that these subjective evaluations should be taken very seriously. How else would any other personal life issue be judged—the success of a marriage, the satisfaction with a home, neighborhood, or job—except by the "subjective" statements of the person who is experiencing it? Irvine (1990) said that "Gender sexologists are disinclined to hear that 'cross-gender behavior,' 'gender transposition,' or 'sexual deviance' can be positive, affirming experiences for those who live them" (p. 239). Researchers continue to interrogate transsexuals to find mental health disturbances or regrets for surgical treatments—and yet the overwhelming feedback is that the majority of people who transition their sex are satisfied that they did it and do not have regrets. Green and Fleming (1990) suggested that postoperative transsexuals do not need to be held to higher levels of psychological functioning than controls, they just need to have "normative" adjustment.

Surgical reassignment of sex is an issue laden with emotionality within the public arena. In a cultural context in which sex is assumed to be immutable, "changing" sex through surgical "mutilation" makes many people squeamish and evokes charges of the "natural order" and "messing with God's creation." Sex reassignment also raises moral, ethical, and legal concerns for physicians and sexologists. It is not surprising that surgical reassignment has been the focus of transsexual self-actualization, medical control, and societal condemnation. Issues are often raised to discredit transsexual treatments that are little more than red herrings. For instance, questions are often raised about the long-term health risks of cross-sex hormonal therapy, despite research showing conclusive evidence that hormonal treatment for gender dysphoria that is provided by a knowledgeable medical expert is an acceptable and safe practice (Asscheman et al., 1989; Van Kesteren et al., 1997). Despite controversies regarding the efficacy of hormonal and surgical treatment protocols for gender-dysphoric people, these treatments have shown long-term success and will undoubtedly continue to remain primary treatments for transsexuals.

Clinicians working with transsexuals and other gender-variant people considering surgical and hormonal treatments will need to examine their own ethical and moral dilemmas in order to work effectively and compassionately with this population. Clients seeking hormonal or surgical treatment must undergo a diagnostic assessment performed by a qualified mental health professional. The Harry Benjamin International Gender Dysphoria Association created standards of care (SOC) for the therapeutic and evaluative process of gender-dysphoric or gender-variant individuals seeking medical treatment. These standards serve as guidelines for both the client seeking treatment and clinician who is completing the evaluation. The standards of care assist in the assessment process of determining "eligibility" for hormonal and surgical treatment, although they clearly state that these are only one possible trajectory for gender dysphoria.

The Harry Benjamin International
Gender Dysphoria Association

Due in part to the early research and writing of Harry Benjamin and the widely publicized case of Christine Jorgensen's transsexual surgery, transsexualism became part of the public discourse in the mid-1960s. It soon became obvious that there was a need for clinical guidelines for the therapeutic and medical needs of transgendered and transsexual clients and the Harry Benjamin International Gender Dysphoria Association initiated the task of developing therapeutic standards of care. Before the development of the first standards of care in 1979, there were no official guidelines for the treatment of transgendered or transsexual people, although physicians did, of course, evaluate their patients for surgical appropriateness. The HBIGDA has remained at the forefront of the evolution of the field of gender dysphoria and the standards of care are updated as knowledge expands (the sixth edition was published in February of 2001). (There are other international standards of care for gender identity issues, which can be found on the Web at <http://www.symposion.com>).

The HBIGDA's standards outline the requirements for both adult and child specialists who work with clients that have gender disorders. These guidelines state that mental health providers can be trained in any credentialing discipline (psychology, social work, psychiatry, nursing, etc.) with at least a master's degree (or equivalent). Providers must have "specialized training and competence . . . in Sexual Disorders (not simply gender identity disorders," receive supervision, and participate in continuing education. In addition, those specializing in child and adolescent care must have knowledge of normal and psychopathological child development (Meyer et al., 2001, p. 12). The SOC outlines five elements of clinical work with clients including: diagnostic assessment, psychotherapy, real-life experience, hormonal therapy, and surgical therapy (Meyer et al., 2001).

The first three elements (diagnostic assessment, psychotherapy, and the real-life experience) fall within the domain of the mental health professional. Only when the clinician assesses the client as eligible and ready to begin gender reassignment, generally based on the success of the client's real-life experience, is the client referred for hormonal and surgical therapies. *Real-life experience* is defined as living in the social role of the opposite sex for one year. It is assumed that this process will "weed out" those people who are not able to successfully live in the opposite gender role before they have irreversible surgical modifications. (The newest guidelines allow female-to-male clients to receive breast surgery early in the treatment process in order to facilitate easier passing as a man.)

In order to receive hormonal or surgical treatment clients must fit the diagnostic criteria for gender identity disorder (see Box 5.3), which is outlined in the DSM-IV-TR (APA, 2000), or the diagnosis of transsexualism, which is outlined in the World Health Organization's (1992) *International Classification of Diseases,* Tenth Revision (ICD-10, see Appendix A). Assessment as defined by the SOC is based on an understanding of gender identity disorder as a mental illness. People who fit the criteria are diagnosed with a mental disorder and are therefore eligible for hormonal or surgical treatments. Those who do not fit the criteria are "protected" from treatment. It is the psychotherapists' responsibility to properly assess clients before they can receive hormonal or surgical care. This is to ensure that clients have resolved any emotional, mental, or comorbid mental health problems before receiving irreversible medical and surgical treatments.

The SOC refer to the process of gender reassignment as "triadic" care, which indicates the three-part process of the real-life experience, hormonal therapy, and surgical treatment. It is interesting to note that the diagnostic assessment—the only part in which the mental health professional is integral to the treatment procedures—is somehow "outside" of the client's transition process, i.e., something that precedes the actual transition.

The HBIGDA standards of care outline ten tasks for which mental health professionals may be responsible (see Box 1.1). It is obvious from reviewing the tasks that the majority are related to diagnosis and referral for hormones and surgery. Guidelines within the SOC for the assessment and treatment for gender-dysphoric people outside of the triadic sequence are vague. The standards include a section on diagnostic nomenclature and one on the mental health professional, which essentially is a review of the diagnostic protocols for diagnosing GID and transsexualism. There is a section on the assessment and treatment of children and adolescents; however, there is no comparable section for adults. There is a section on psychotherapy with adults, and although psychotherapy is also listed as one of the tasks of mental health professionals, the SOC clearly state that, although it can be helpful, psychotherapy is not a requirement for triadic care.

BOX 1.1.
The Ten Tasks of the Mental Health Professional

According to the Harry Benjamin International Gender Dysphoria Association's standards of care, the ten tasks of the mental health professional are

1. to accurately diagnose the individual's gender disorder;
2. to accurately diagnose any comorbid psychiatric conditions and see to their appropriate treatment;
3. to counsel the individual about the range of treatment options and their implications;
4. to engage in psychotherapy;
5. to ascertain eligibility and readiness for hormone and surgical care;
6. to make formal recommendations for medical and surgical colleagues;
7. to document the patient's relevant history in a letter of recommendation;
8. to be a colleague on a team of professionals with interest in gender identity disorders;
9. to educate family members, employers, and institutions about gender identity disorders;
10. to be available for follow-up of previously seen gender patients (Meyer et al., 2001).

However, little has been said about the assessment process itself. No guidelines are given for the evaluation of gender dysphoria and the distinctions between disturbances in biological sex, gender identity, gender-role expression, and sexual orientation are not outlined. No guidelines are offered to assist in the differential diagnoses of gender-related symptoms, including the role of body-dysmorphic disorders, posttraumatic stress reactions, and dissociative processes. In addition, the standards offer no discussion regarding the role of societal repression of gender variance and the impact of homophobia and transphobia on the development of gender dysphoria. Finally, no therapeutic suggestions are offered for working with family members beyond "education." Working effectively with clients struggling with gender dysphoria who do not fit the criteria for GID or do not desire—or cannot choose—triadic treatments is addressed in only one section. This section outlines nonmedical options (e.g., electrolysis, cross-dressing, and breast binding) and some of the processes necessary for integrating gender identity issues (e.g., distinguishing between sexual and gender identity issues).

The HBIGDA's standards of care serve as a useful blueprint for clients expressing transsexualism who meet the diagnostic criteria for GID and are requesting hormonal and/or surgical treatments. The standards are an ambitious attempt on the part of compassionate clinicians to develop guidelines that will support those who need gender reassignment and protect those for whom surgical reassignment is contraindicated. However, the SOC are not guidelines for the psychological evaluation of the continuum of gender dysphorias or the psychotherapeutic treatment of gender-variant people expressing emotional distress and requesting clinical intervention and advocacy. They do not offer therapeutic direction to clinicians working with clients in emotional pain due to gender dysphoria or guidelines to work with families who are struggling with gender variance in a loved one. The SOC have limited value in working with gender-dysphoric people seeking psychotherapeutic services who are not necessarily expressing a desire for medical intervention. Conversely, the SOC also place the psychotherapist in the role of evaluator for gender-reassignment procedures. The theoretical underpinning of the medical model of transsexualism relies on assessment by the mental health provider who is institutionalized as a gatekeeper to the triadic system.

THE MENTAL HEALTH PROFESSIONAL AS GATEKEEPER

[T]rans people had to "pass" the "examinations" of the psycho-"experts," who acted as the gatekeepers to the medical professionals who would provide the hormones and surgery that I knew were essential to not only enhance my life, but in order to keep me alive. As such the psycho-experts became the enemy I had to either persuade to believe me or to defeat (regardless of whether they believed me or not) in order to enter through the gateway.

Stephen Whittle
speech given at the True Spirit Conference
February 20, 2000

Gatekeeping developed initially to ensure the protection of the gender-dysphoric client. There have been documented cases (albeit not many) of clients who have had sex reassignment surgeries and regretted them. Due to other psychological difficulties, previous traumas, mental illnesses, or unresolved sexual identity disturbances, these people underwent expensive and life-altering treatments for which they later felt they had not been properly prepared. Placing therapists between the medical community and the populations requesting services protected these clients from untrained physicians who might not assess them properly or might not have the training to assess them, or even unscrupulous doctors who would use this vulnerable population for their own financial gain.

Gatekeeping also protects the surgeon from litigation, since removing healthy tissue based on the client's explicit desire could present certain legal complications. If a client thinks that he or she was not adequately prepared for the results of the surgery or feels the results promised were not delivered, he or she might have a viable legal case. The assumption is that with the additional step of a therapeutic evaluation, patients have already been screened, assessed, and prepared for treatment before they receive the medical referral.

The consequence for the clinician thrust into this role of gatekeeper is complex. It is the mental health professional's job to assess the client's presenting situation and determine whether the case is therapeutically legitimate according to the current criteria of the SOC, DSM, or ICD. Yet it is also the therapist's job to create a nonjudgmental therapeutic environment that will allow the client to be open, honest, and trusting regarding the psychological issues he or she may be experiencing. The SOC state,

> The establishment of a reliable trusting relationship with the patient is the first step toward successful work as a mental health professional. This is usually accomplished by competent nonjudgmental exploration of the gender issue with the patient during the initial diagnostic evaluation. (Meyer et al., 2001, p. 18)

It is quite difficult to develop an authentic therapeutic relationship with a client when the initial diagnostic evaluation casts the clinician in the role of a gatekeeper who controls access to medical treatments. The client, who may be strongly motivated to pass through the gate, knows that being honest might impede this possibility. Since approval for treatment rests on one's conformity to the diagnostic criteria, there is strong desire on the part of transgendered clients seeking hormonal and surgical treatment to "fit" the outlined criteria. According to the research of Denny and Roberts (1997), nearly 80 percent of the 339 respondents of their survey of transgendered clients were familiar with the clinical standards of care. In her study of fifty-two postoperative male-to-female transsexuals, Walworth (1997) outlined numerous areas in which clients had lied to therapists in order to meet what they thought were the guidelines for transitioning.

Those clients who do not fit the criteria as they are described, yet identify as transgendered or transsexual, are placed in an untenable position: They risk rejection from the mental health professional if they tell the truth about their lives or lie about their experiences to the therapist to receive treatment. The literature mentions this dishonesty as an impediment to treatment—and the SOC discuss the need for collaboration that "prevents stalemates between a therapist who seems needlessly withholding of a recommendation and a patient who seems too profoundly distrusting to freely share thoughts, feelings, events, and relationships" (Meyer et al., 2001). The clients, however, may have good reasons for appearing to be "profoundly distrusting." They may not fit the clinical criteria for a "true transsexual" or the DSM-IV-TR's criteria for GID, or may be involved in sexual behaviors or lifestyle choices that may indeed evoke the clinician's judgment. The client therefore lies to protect his or her interests and avoid being refused requested treatments. It is also sometimes true that clients are misinformed about the SOC, have read older copies of the document, or have received erroneous information via the Internet about the criteria for approval and may be unnecessarily distrustful.

However, whether his or her fears are accurate or not, the client may not be willing to risk being honest. The gatekeeping system places the onus for truth-telling on the client and judges him or her for the conscious confabulation of the truth in order to receive services he or she cannot simply request but must pass an evaluation to receive. The gatekeeping system reinforces a lack of authenticity for the transgendered client, as well as the development of a false relationship between therapist and client.

Transgendered people have begun to question the ethics of this gatekeeping process. Some transgendered activists suggest that the paternalistic tone of protection is ultimately a control tactic dictating who has access to the tools of the medical establishment (Wilchins, 1997; Bornstein 1994).

They argue that anyone can have a nose job or other cosmetic surgeries and that people can dye their hair or pierce their bodies without a "note from their doctor" giving them permission. Interestingly, many common non-transsexual-related cosmetic surgeries are meant to enhance the gender that has already been assigned (e.g., breast augmentation) and do not need therapeutic approval as long as the masculinizing or feminizing trajectory is in the direction of one's biological sex. Many activists believe that there should be no restrictions in their access to medical treatments, often referred to as "hormones (or surgery) on demand." Denny (1993) argued eloquently about the potential dangers of having irreversible and life-altering medical treatments available without any standardized protocols, while recognizing the problems and limitations of the existing SOC.

Activists raise the serious concern that the criteria that has been set forth in the DSM-IV-TR and the ICD-10 do not accurately describe the full spectrum of gender variance experienced in the lives of gender-dysphoric and gender-variant people. Clinicians disagree about how to best categorize gender-variant people. The DSM has changed its labeling system with each new edition, and the major experts in the field—those who have developed and administered gender clinics—differ in how they classify gender disorders. Transgendered people who do not fit the diagnostic criteria as they have been presented have been viewed as gender deviants among the gender deviants and have been left with few clinical options. Denny (1996) asked, "Should medical technologies continue to be available only to a narrowly defined class of persons called transsexuals, with mental health professionals having the responsibility and privilege of deciding who does and does not qualify to receive it?" (p. 44).

The standards of care continue to be evaluated and updated as information in the field expands, and the latest edition outlines increasingly progressive guidelines for the treatment of transgendered youth and FTM transgendered people. Many clients have managed to receive medical services by working with clinicians who do not use the SOC or may not even be familiar with the HBIGDA. Some therapists purposefully do not use the SOC, finding them an inadequate tool. The SOC are, however, a useful schema to assess a client's readiness for life-transforming hormonal and surgical care and can be adapted and individualized for each client's needs. It is often forgotten in the political battles that ensue regarding gatekeeping that the expertise of the clinician to make final decisions based on exceptional cases is undisputed. "The SOC are intended to provide flexible directions for the treatment of persons with gender identity disorders. . . . Individual professionals and organized programs may modify them" (Meyer et al., 2001, p. 3). The standards of care are not legally binding. They are ethical guidelines for the minimum level of care for those presenting with gender dysphoria who request hormonal and surgical treatments—nothing more and nothing less.

It is undeniable that the dual role inherent in practicing psychotherapy while having to serve as a gatekeeper for medical treatments can block the development of a trusting and compassionate relationship between mental health professional and clients seeking services. Many people who come into treatment struggling with gender issues are not seeking hormones or surgery but are seeking compassionate psychotherapy to help them sort out what they are feeling. People struggling with gender dysphoria as well as those who are at peace with their gender variance deserve compassionate therapeutic services that move beyond diagnostics and assessment for approval of medical treatments.

CLINICAL GUIDELINES—THERAPEUTIC STANDARDS OF CARE

I know that with the help of God and those few who believe *as you do* this will be a step into the future understanding of the human race. I wonder where there are *more* who will join us in this struggle.

Christine Jorgensen
in a letter to Harry Benjamin

The guidelines established by the HBIGDA may serve a purpose in assessing clients for hormones and surgery, but a wider range of guidelines needs to be developed to assist mental health professionals in working with the diversity of issues and needs that transgendered clients and their families bring into therapy.

Gender Specialists and Transition Assistants

Setting aside the issues of gatekeeping and pathology, what are the therapeutic needs of transgendered people and their families? What is an appropriate clinically supportive intervention for a heterosexual male who has been secretly cross-dressing and fears his wife will leave him if he tells her? What tools does a psychotherapist use to assist a female client, who has always felt like a man, in processing what coming out as transgendered might mean for her twenty-five-year lesbian relationship? How does a clinician counsel parents whose fifteen-year-old son is being beaten up daily in the schoolyard because he is "girly"? What are useful guidelines for young parents whose five-year-old daughter insists that she is a boy and demands that she wear masculine clothes and be called by a male pronoun? How do we explain bodies and sexuality to a ten-year-old female child with a two-inch clitoris?

The reality is that the psychotherapeutic needs of transgendered and intersexed people, outside of parameters of pathology and "treatment," is an area of study still in its infancy. A handful of books (Ettner, 1996; Ettner and Brown, 1999; Brown and Rounsley, 1996; Miller, 1996; Israel and Tarver, 1997) explore sensitive, humanistic treatment of transgendered people. Most of these authors focused primarily on transsexuals, particularly MTFs, without paying much attention to FTM clients, family members, or the complexities of bi-gendered people's concerns. Another handful of books advocates improved treatment for intersexed children (Dreger, 1999; Kessler, 1998; and Fausto-Sterling, 2000), but these are often read more by sexologists and students of feminist and queer studies than medical doctors and psychotherapists. It is, however, a beginning.

Israel and Tarver (1997) suggested the use of the term *gender specialist,* inferring a certain level of skill and expertise for the clinician working with gender-variant people. Their term connotes the therapist having a repertoire of therapeutic skills that go beyond completing diagnostic assessments and writing evaluation letters for further medical treatments. They recommend that clinicians be familiar with a wide range of psychosocial issues that clients may struggle with, including suicidality, HIV illness, and post-traumatic stress disorder. In their book *Transgender Care* they address the clinical needs of transgendered youth, people who are institutionalized and incarcerated, those who are socioeconomically disadvantaged or living with HIV illness, as well as the specific and often unrecognized needs of people of color—broadening the understanding of the diversity of transgendered people.

A gender specialist must have a greater scope of psychotherapeutic tools for working with gender-variant people than merely the ability to evaluate appropriateness for hormones and surgery (see Box 1.2). Clients struggling with gender dysphoria, families immersed in a process of gender transition, parents coping with intersexed or gender-conflicted teens, and communities needing to integrate transgendered people into school systems and work environments need advocacy and support that is far more complex than mere clinical assessments and medical referrals. Gender specialists need skills to assist clients through the emotional quagmire of evaluating their gender issues and potential transition. A therapeutic stance based in client empowerment encourages clinicians to set aside their own preconceived agendas and to support clients' evaluation of their life situations, making decisions based on educated self-awareness. Gender specialists may work with clients who are struggling with painfully dysphoric feelings regarding their gender.

BOX 1.2.
Guidelines for Gender Specialists Working
with Gender-Variant, Transgendered, and Transsexual Clients

- Therapists working with transgendered clients must have a thorough understanding of gender identity issues, including information on the differences between gender and sexual identity, and the social construction of gender dimorphism. Therapists must be knowledgeable of the current DSM diagnosis of gender identity disorder and the most recent standards of care developed by the Harry Benjamin International Gender Dysphoria Association.
- Therapists must be aware of the issues being raised within the transgender liberation movement regarding the sociopolitical forces in the construction of gender identity and the limitations of a bipolar gender system, as well as the diversity of gender expressions.
- Therapists must have a general knowledge of mental health issues and human development, and training in eclectic psychotherapeutic techniques. Therapists must be able to assess clients for mental illness, as well as addictions and trauma-related symptomatology.
- Therapists must be cognizant of the impact of stress on gender dysphoria and not pathologize the clients' stress-related symptoms. Therapists must have a humanistic perspective that supports the empowerment of client self-identification.
- Therapists should be knowledgeable of issues related to gender identity, sexuality, sexual identity, and gender role development, and be comfortable talking about these issues.
- Therapists should be sensitive to the impact of family-systems concerns, including family of origin and current partners and children, and be able to provide services or referrals for family members.
- Therapists should have resources available for clients, including referrals to endocrinologists and/or psychiatrists, gender clinics, and support groups, as well as recommendations for bibliotherapy and Internet sites.

They are often called on to serve as transition assistants to individuals and their families who are in the process of transitioning.

The concept of a transition assistant removes the stigma of gatekeeping. Instead of playing the role of a tollbooth operator collecting money if the right criteria for entry are met, the transition assistant is able to offer psychotherapeutic support and clinical advocacy. The process of defining one's gender identity, making informed choices given the available options, and deciding to transition is emotionally challenging and creates huge social, vocational, and familial upheavals. In most spiritual traditions one seeks out a guide before undertaking a spiritual quest. The transition assistant is a guide who can help clients and their families negotiate these changes. Guides are prepared for a multitude of circumstances and know the diversity of the terrain. Guides cannot know the inner path of the seeker, but they can often sense when danger is near, know how to prepare shelter in a storm, or lead the seeker to water. Transition assistants are less focused on evaluation and traditional psychotherapy and more concerned with empowering clients and helping them to determine the best path for themselves.

Gender specialists are often called upon to work with three populations that are the focus of this book:

1. Clients exhibiting distress from their gender dysphoria
2. Clients who are transsexual or transgendered and are requesting evaluation and referral for medical treatment
3. The families of the transgendered or intersexed people who need support and advocacy

Gender specialists will be challenged to utilize all of their clinical expertise on human behavior within the developmental life cycle and a wide variety of therapeutic modalities when working with transgendered individuals and their families.

Given the social, political, religious, moral, economic, and familial repercussions of gender-deviant behavior, the fact that people persist in expressing themselves despite public condemnation is a tribute to the strength of the human spirit. The intensity of some transgendered people's desire to transition, which has sometimes been labeled obsessive, can best be reframed as the power of their life force, and their insistence to live true to their own nature. Transgendered clients seek psychotherapy because they are experiencing a crisis of identity and they come seeking their own name.

Chapter 2

The Legacy:
Gender Variance in History

It is not so much that there have always been transgendered people; it's that there have always been cultures that imposed regimes of gender.

Riki Wilchins
Read My Lips, 1997

Naming is an act of power. Names are conferred at birth, names are confirmed at baptisms, names can be changed when one marries. Adam's first act in the world was to name all the creatures. Until recently, the only name gender-variant people had in Western societies were those classified by the sexologists. In the 1990s the term *transgender* was coined to describe a modern social and political experience. It is a grassroots word, a self-naming.

However, transgenderism is not a new phenomenon. It has been well documented throughout human history that individuals have lived cross-gendered from the biological sex in which they were born and outside the parameters of the social roles that were expected of them. Denny (1997) identified thirty ways of expressing and categorizing transgender or cross-gender identities in both Western and non-Western cultures. It is also true that intersexed or hermaphroditic people have always existed, presenting a mixed biological body that was not so easily classified into the existing sex categories and challenging communities to address issues of integrating human difference into social communities. In diverse forms and representations, perceived through the socially constructed lenses of distinct cultures and eras, gender and sex variance have always existed.

Transgenderism is not a new psychological invention or a medical condition, nor is it a recent social or legal dilemma. Gender diversity has a long history, though examining this history presents certain epistemological dilemmas. Studying gender and sexual expression within a historical and anthropological frame depends on reviewing and analyzing documentation across disciplines without a comprehensive and agreed-upon language system. Words are used interchangeably while being defined differently. Concepts explicitly defined in one article are vehemently argued as incorrect or irrelevant in another. Words used in the literature such as *cross-dresser, third sex, hermaphrodite, transsexual,* and even *homosexual* become complicated under etymological scrutiny. For that matter, the simplicity of words such as *male* and *female* do not easily hold up under the postmodern examinations of cultural variation. Words are created within a sociocultural matrix and must be understood contextually as well as phenomenologically.

Gender-variant expression has been analyzed through the lenses of the social sciences—most notably anthropology, history, and sociology. It has been examined by members of diverse religions, including Christian missionaries, modern fundamentalists, leaders of orthodox institutions, and practicing pagan spiritualists. Since the late nineteenth century, hermaphroditism has been classified and dissected by physicians and scientists, and sexual "inversion" has been examined meticulously under a psychoanalytic microscope. In the past few decades, gender-transgressive behavior has been discussed and debated by gay historians and, most recently, by self-identified transgendered and transsexual people, many of whom are scholars in the sciences mentioned earlier. The field of sexology in general, and the study of gender and sexual identity in particular, is fraught with confusing and complex definitions, assumptions, and perspectives that are further complicated by the political challenges levied back and forth by the scholars themselves. Despite the difficulty sorting through the rubble of this fallen Tower of Babel, it is clear that even though language and meaning change, the experiences of transgenderism—though, of course, not the word—have been a universal theme.

This does not mean, however, that the contemporary experience of transgenderism is equivalent in meaning to that of other eras or cultures. How gender identity is perceived in contemporary culture may not be similar to how it was or is seen in the traditional world and may not be comparable from one culture or epoch to another. Cromwell (1999) stated that historically and cross-culturally, "Gender transgressions cannot be equated with contemporary transgendered people because the meaning of 'gender transgression' is also variable and depends upon cultural context" (p. 61). As Gary Bowen said, "I am a very ordinary Native man. My gender variance is solely within the eyes of the dominant culture" (2001, personal communication).

The purpose of this overview is to establish a presence, a visibility, and an "existence" for gender-variant and gender-transgressive people throughout history, to situate their normative presence within the human community. This chapter is meant to serve only as an introduction to the abundant resources available to the student open to investigating the social and political construction of gender and sexuality throughout history and across cultures.

In order to develop a therapeutic model for working with transgendered and intersexed people, it is essential to first understand the universality of sexual and gender-variant expression. This will serve as a counterweight for the pathologizing discourse of the medical model in which transgendered behavior is seen as rare, aberrant, and perverse, and intersexed people as monstrosities that need to be repaired. Although the modern medical establishment has pathologized cross-gender behavior, an overview of the social role of gender-variant people cross-culturally will show that this has not always been so. There are many ways for a culture to respond to gender variance, and it is suggested that the modern clinical method of treating it as a disease is not the most enlightened, civilized, or sophisticated way to incorporate gender-variant people into the human family.

THE HISTORICAL LEGACY

My own transgendered state is a sacred calling given to me by Spirit, not a neurosis discovered by white medicine . . . "transsexual" and "transgendered" are terms that have arisen out of the dominant culture's experience with gender, and are not necessarily reflective of a wide variety of people, cultures, beliefs, and practices related to gender.

Gary Bowen
Trans Liberation, 1998

Gender-variant expression has been documented in a diversity of human cultures including many American Indian and African tribes, Southeast Asian communities, and throughout premodern as well as contemporary European societies. Tales of children born with ambiguous or "mixed" genitalia have been recorded throughout history. What has varied between cultures has been the way sex and gender differences have been explained within each society, the way gender variance has been experienced or expressed, and how gender transgression and sex differences have been addressed within cultures.

Studying the historical legacy regarding gender and sexuality is difficult for a number of reasons. First of all, sexuality is often considered private and privileged information, so it may not be easily accessed. Actual human behavior often differs from prescribed morality and in some cases it might be purposely distorted in order to present an image more consistent with social mores, legal constraints, and familiar expectations. It is difficult to access thorough and complete information about a culture's relationship to gender and sexuality because the information may be deliberately hidden. For instance, utilizing *The New York Times* for research on gay culture in the 1950s would yield a paucity of information—especially since they refused to print the word *gay* until the 1980s. What information did exist on homosexuality was surely couched in terms of deviancy, immorality, and criminal behavior. If researchers based their conclusions about 1950s' gay culture on the mainstream press, they would develop a distorted perspective that did not reflect the vibrancy of homosexual cultures which flourished within a repressive social climate.

Cross-culture study involves the analysis of the observer, who is, by definition, an outsider. Whether researchers are given accurate information, and how much their perspective is distorted by their own preconceptions, ethnocentrism, theoretical values, professional affiliations, or personal goals, is an unknown quantity in the validity of any knowledge gained from historical examination. History is often told through the eyes of the dominant classes, which means that the stories of females, poor people, and people of color are rarely recorded. When they are recorded, they have often been told by judgmental and prejudicial observers. The historical record is steeped in the patriarchal, racist, and heterosexist cultures of the historians themselves, which often gives us as much information about the historians as the actual data they reported.

Many cultures have recognized the existence of more than two genders. These include the Xanith of Islamic Oman, La Guajira of Venezuela and Colombia, and the Acault of Myanmar. Alternative-gendered social positions have also been found among the Maori of New Zealand, shamans of Vietnam and Korea, Zulu of South Africa, Bantu of Angola, Konso of Ethiopia, and the Fanti of Ghana (see Besnier, 1994; Blackwood, 1999; Bullough and Bullough, 1993; Coleman, Colgan, and Gooren, 1992; Feinberg, 1996; Greenberg, 1988; Elliston, 1999; Murray and Roscoe, 1998; Teh, 2001). Thomas (1997) identified five categories of gender within Navajo culture and Cromwell (1999) identified at least seven categories of gender among the Chukchi of Siberia in addition to male and female. Within Islamic tradition, gender is divided into four groups, including hermaphrodites and transsexuals who want to change sex and cross-dressers who do not (Teh, 2001).

Although the majority of research has focused on those born into male bodies, three of the genders of the Chukchi described by Cromwell are for female-bodied people. Roscoe (1998) listed more than forty tribes in which females exhibited some cross-gendered role expression. Elliston (1999) and

Matzner (2001) have described female cross-gendered expression among the Mahu in Tahiti and the Hawaiian Islands, and Blackwood (1999) has studied the Tombois in West Sumatra. In some African tribes "female-husbands" can "become men," carry out all the economic duties, and receive the privileges of men by paying the dowry for a woman, marrying her, and becoming the legal and social father to her children (Murray and Roscoe, 1998; O'Brien, 1977; Oboler, 1980). The majority of these gender differences are not attributed to physical deviations from normative male and female biology, but are social genders defined outside of biological parameters. Labeled and described by anthropologists and historians in various ways, their existence serves as proof of the universality of cross-gender roles, behaviors, and experience and the enduring legacy of cross-cultural gender variance.

The American Indian Two-Spirit Tradition

The most well-researched cross-gendered social role exists in American Indian cultures and has been studied by anthropologists as the berdache tradition. *Berdache* is a linguistically transformed word, originating in Persia *(bardaj)* and utilized in various forms in Italy, Spain, and France. It described male slaves or prostitutes who were forced into passive or subservient homosexual behavior (Williams, 1992; Tafoya and Wirth, 1996). European explorers, colonizers, and missionaries used the label to describe indigenous people who appeared in their ethnocentric worldview to embody a similar social role. It is a less-than-useful word steeped in Eurocentric racism and homophobia.

Historically, Native peoples have had their own terms for the berdache tradition, e.g., *winkte* (Lakota), *nádleehí* (Navaho), *bote* (Crow), *ihamana* (Zuni), and *haxu'xan* (Arapaho) for males, and *hwame* (Mojave) for females. These names connote gender crossovers, or dual-gendered states, roughly translated as "man-woman," or "the one who is constantly changing" (Roscoe, 1998). The term *Two-Spirit,* which will be used here, has been suggested as a contemporary alternative. Tafoya and Wirth (1996) said, "The tribal concept of Two-Spirit describes an individual who has both a male and female spirit. . . . to be a Two-Spirit means one can see in both directions [as a man and as a woman], and therefore understand the world in a more holistic manner" (p. 56). The term is not without problems, since it can be used to describe gay, lesbian, and bisexual Indians, as well as to describe those of "mixed-blood" (Bowen, 1998; Roscoe, 1998), and could serve to further confuse issues of sexuality and gender presentation. However, as with the term *transgender,* it will be used, despite its problems, as a word indigenous to the cultures it represents.

Two-Spirit people are considered a third gender—or in some cases a third and fourth gender—distinguishing between those born male and those born female (Roscoe, 1998). The expression of gender variance has been documented in more than 155 North American tribes and was a salient feature of Indian life (Roscoe, 1998). Though physically Two-Spirit people were not commonly known to be hermaphroditic or intersexed, they are considered to have the social characteristics of both men and women and—consistent with the Indian worldview—they are thought to possess the visions of both sexes (Jacobs, Thomas, and Lang, 1997; Tafoya, 1992; Williams, 1992). Capable of interceding between the physical and spiritual worlds, "the berdache often serve a mediating function between women and men precisely because their character is seen as distinct from either sex" (Bullough and Bullough, 1993, p. 4). Two-Spirit people were often medicine healers and involved with the spiritual leadership of their tribes. Williams (1992) incorrectly identified these medicine healers as "shamans"—technically a word used to describe the spiritual healers from Siberian cultures—but he accurately depicted the overlapping roles of medicine healers and Two-Spirit people. He said, "Shamans are not necessarily berdaches, but because of their spiritual connection, berdaches in many cultures are often considered to be powerful shamans" (p. 35).

The key features of Two-Spirit people were (1) a cross-role specialization in social, productive, and domestic roles; (2) spiritual sanction and associated powers; and (3) gender variation often denoted by cross-dressing behavior. In addition, they most often chose intimate partners with members of their own biological sex (Roscoe, 1994, 1998). The key to understanding the social position of Two-Spirit people is to shift from a Western perception of a dual-gendered system to an understanding that Two-Spirit people occupy a third-gendered position that is distinct and separate from male and female categories. According to Roscoe (1994),

> Berdaches occupied a distinct and autonomous social status on par with the status of men and women. Like male and female genders, the berdache gender entailed a pattern of differences encompassing behavior, temperament, social and economic roles and religious specialization—all dimensions of a gender category. (p. 370)

What is perhaps most important is the belief among many Indian people that Two-Spirit people did not choose their role or status—it was considered their innate nature. As Williams (1992) said, "The idea that someone could freely choose her or his character is as ludicrous to the Zapotecs as the idea that someone could freely choose eye color" (p. 49). Williams quoted Lame Deer, a Lakota shaman, who said, "The Great Spirit made them winktes and we accept them as such . . . to us a man is what nature, or his dreams, make him. We accept him for what he wants to be" (p. 25). It was believed that having a Two-Spirited person in the family guaranteed wealth for the family and was considered a sign of luck. Given the spiritual nature of Native American cultures, being Two-Spirited was seen as a sacred gift and treated with reverence.

The Hijra of India

Indian culture and spirituality is replete with numerous images of cross-gender experience. Within the complex religious and spiritual traditions of Southeast Asia, the Supreme Being is frequently referred to as Shiva, who is often portrayed with his consort Parvarti (or Shakti) blended together as one intersexed figure, known as Ardhanarisvara (Money, 1999). It is believed that maleness and femaleness are simply mirror images of each other, and that gender is an illusion—or maya—that one uses to dress the soul much as one wears clothing to dress the body. Nanda (1994) said,

> The Hindu view that all persons contain within themselves both male and female principles is explicitly expressed in the Tantric sect, in which the Supreme Being is conceptualized as one complete sex, containing male and female sex organs. Hermaphroditism is the ideal. In some of these sects, male transvestism is used as a way of transcending one's own sex, a prerequisite to achieving salvation. (p. 376)

The Indian legends abound with tales of male gods—Vishnu or Krishna—who transform themselves into females. In one story, Vishnu, one of the three most powerful male deities of Hinduism, appears as a beautiful woman named Mohini, who seduces the god Shiva. They mate and produce Harihara, a hermaphroditic god (Bullough and Bullough, 1993; Kinsley, 1987; Nanda, 1994). In the Mahabharata, one of the epic scriptures of India, a king is transformed into a woman and allowed to remain in this body, which he finds more pleasurable (Leach, as cited in Green, 1998a).

In addition to the Hindu gods, the teachers, or gurus, themselves are often found straddling the genders. A great Bengali mystic of the sixteenth century, Chaitanya—who worshipped Krishna and his female consort, Radha—often dressed as both of the lovers to experience the divine love from both experiences (Bullough and Bullough, 1993). The most holy and revered saint Ramakrishna was a devotee of the Great Mother, and worshiped her in the form of Kali Radha or Shakti. He dressed in female clothing as a way to honor her (Bullough and Bullough, 1993; Harding, 1993; Hixon, 1992).

It is an institutionalized part of modern Indian culture for some males to worship the female aspect of the Great Mother by cross-dressing. The Hijra of Bombay belong to a third-gender social role and worship Bachuchara Mata, a form of the Great Mother. Hijra identity is based on their emasculation—either being born hermaphroditic and impotent or undergoing a renunciation of their male virility through voluntary castration. Hijras have often worked as prostitutes and have been sexually involved with natal males (Nanda, 1994). According to Bullough and Bullough (1993),

> Hijras regard themselves as "separate," neither men nor women, although they recognize they were born as men. . . . Hijras dress as women, wear their hair long, pluck their facial hair (they do not shave it), adopt feminine mannerisms, take women's names, and use female kinship terms and a special, feminized vocabulary. They demand to be seated as women in those areas reserved for women, and on one recent occasion they demanded to be counted as women in the census. (p. 9)

Clearly the Hijras occupy a third gender role within their culture, existing somewhere on the continuum of male-female behavior, but outside of the accepted norms of either group. They perceive themselves as "neither man nor woman." They are "not men" because of their impotence and lack of desire for women, and they are not women because they cannot bear children. It is interesting to note that *Hijra* is a masculine noun, although Hijras clearly define themselves through their femininity and inhabit traditional female roles and status (Nanda, 1994).

As Two-Spirit people confuse Western notions of sexual and gender identity, Hijras also confound contemporary understandings of sex and gender. Sadly, but perhaps truthfully, it may be too easy for white, academic, ethnocentric Westerners to dismiss the previous cultural discourses as pertaining to "primitive" tribal people, or those of "backward" third world nations. However, gender-variant people have existed throughout white, "civilized" European culture, and imagery of cross-gendered behavior exists throughout Western history.

Greco-Roman Cultures

Despite the worldwide prevalence of gender-variant behavior, there has been a profound silence regarding how commonplace it has been within Western culture. Greek history, literature, and mythology are replete with stories of cross-dressing. For example, in Sparta it was the custom to shave the head of a bride and dress her in men's clothing, and many artifacts from Greek culture show women wearing false beards. At the festival devoted to Hera at Samos, men donned long white robes that swept the ground and adorned themselves in jewelry. The goddess Ishtar was also worshiped in this manner (Bullough and Bullough, 1993).

The mythology of Ancient Greece tells many tales of intersexed or sex-changing gods and goddesses, as well as godlike heroes, such as Hercules and Achilles, who were known to cross-dress. The shape-shifting god Dionysus was raised as a girl and also later "impersonated" girls. During the ceremonies in celebration of him, men and women cross-dressed. The women, known as *ithiypalloi,* carried large phalluses (Bullough and Bullough, 1993; Feinberg, 1996). In another story, the soothsayer Tiresias, who was born male, was changed into a female for punishment. When he decided he liked being a female, he was then changed back into a male, again as punishment (Green, 1998a). In yet another Greek myth Caenis was transformed from female to male in order to avoid the advances of the god Poseidon, and evoked the outrage of the centaurs for his masculinity (Bullough and Bullough, 1993; Feinberg, 1996).

Amazons, the mythical tribe of women warriors, have been honored by feminists and lesbians alike as strong independent women who rejected male domination. They removed their right breast, supposedly to increase their skills as archers. Pliny the Younger referred to them as "the race of the Androgynae, who combine the two sexes" (Marie Delcourt, as cited in Feinberg, 1996, p, 57). According to the Bulloughs (1993), "In order to defeat the Amazons in battle, the Greek heroes first had to overcome the Amazons' male side through combat and then subdue their female side by having intercourse with them, essentially by rape" (p. 31). Feinberg (1996) questioned whether the myth of the Amazons is not so much the story of women warriors, but actually an example of "transgender resistance" (p. 57), which complements the Bulloughs' thesis that the Amazon myths are symbolic of the threat to the hegemony of Greek patriarchy.

In the Roman courts, cross-dressing was common among members of the royal family, including Caligula and Nero. It is said that Nero, after killing his wife, sought out a lover who looked like her. He found a male slave and transformed him into a woman whom he then married (Green, 1998a). Another emperor, Elagabalus, wore only silk clothing and requested castration so "he could be a true woman" (Bullough and Bullough, 1993, p. 39). The Romans accepted the idea of changing sex as a possibility. As Pliny said, "Transformations of females into males is not an idle story" (as quoted by Bullough and Bullough, 1993, p. 37). Stories of biological hermaphrodites exist, and the word itself is attributed to Hermaphroditos, son of Hermes and

Aphrodite, who became joined with the body of a nymph in Greek mythology.

Stories of gender-variant humans and gods are part of the historical legacy of Western cultures. The meaning of gender variance and how it is interpreted within modern scholarship is open to academic debate, but the presence of these narratives confirms the existence of gender variance in antiquity.

Western Religious Traditions

References to cross-dressing behavior are found in the holy words of most written spiritual traditions. The proscriptions and narrative lore against cross-dressing behavior in the Torah, the Christian Bible, and the Koran speak to the existence, and perhaps the frequency, of such behavior. It has been suggested that scriptural references to cross-dressing were attempts to separate the newly forming religions from the pagan traditions, where cross-gendered behaviors were common and celebrated. As Feinberg (1996) suggested, "The patriarchal fathers wouldn't have felt the need to spell out these edicts if they weren't common practice" (p. 50).

Al-Bukhari, a famous ninth-century commentator on the Koran, devoted an entire section of his writings to "men who wish to resemble women, and women who wish to resemble men" (Bullough and Bullough, 1993, p. 12). Often quoted by religious leaders in both Jewish and Christian traditions is Deuteronomy 22:5, which states, "No male article shall be on a woman, and man shall not wear a woman's garment. Whoever does such practices is revolting to God your Lord" (Kaplan, 1981). Despite the biblical pronouncement, Judaism has historically recognized cross-gender experience. Jewish law lists detailed regulations for people of unclear gender identification, placing certain behaviors and experiences into the accepted "male" categories, others into the "female" categories, and some into neither or both categories (Tosefta Bikkurim 2:3-7).

One of the more dramatic tales of the relationship between cross-dressing behavior and the role of orthodox religion is the story of Jeanne d'Arc, or St. Joan (1412-1431), a Christian patron saint of France. Garber (1992) places Jeanne d'Arc in a long tradition of transvestite female saints, common in the monastic tradition of Christianity. Jeanne d'Arc, however, despite her spiritual convictions and her claim to hearing divine voices, did not choose the path of the monk, but instead the path of the warrior. At the age of nineteen, after winning many victories for the French against the English, she was tried by French ecclesiastics for heretical acts and beliefs. In addition to the accusation that the voices she heard were not God but demons, two of the twelve charges against her dealt with the wearing of male clothes, including spurs and a breastplate. She wore her hair short, refused to marry, and carried a sword and dagger (Bullough and Bullough, 1993; Feinberg, 1996). According to Evans (1978) she was referred to as *homasse,* a derogatory Old French word for a masculine woman. Furthermore, Jeanne d'Arc was believed to have had intimate relationships with women, including La Rousse ("The Red"), with whom she lived, and Catherine de la Rochelle, with whom she admitted to sharing a bed.

Jeanne d'Arc's refusal to wear women's clothes was perceived to be a heretical act. She clearly stated at her trial that she wore male clothing as a religious duty, echoing the spiritual traditions of Two-Spirit people. According to her testimony she said, "For nothing in the world will I swear not to arm myself and put on a man's dress; I must obey the orders of Our Lord" (Evans, 1978, p. 5). During her life, Jeanne d'Arc appears to have been revered as a deity by the local French peasants. She was believed to have magical powers including the power to heal. Her masculine clothing and her armor were worshiped. She was often referred to as "The Maid," and it is believed that she was reared within the older pagan belief systems. Jeanne d'Arc's lifelong friend was Gilles de Rais, who is believed to have been a homosexual (Evans, 1978).

As had been common in non-Western tribal cultures and earlier Greco-Roman cultures there is an association between religious ritual and cross-dressing behavior. With the rise of institutionalized religious orthodoxy, in this case in the form of the Inquisition, the punishment of gender-deviant people became sanctioned and Jeanne d'Arc, known to the Christian world as Saint Joan, was put to death.

Mollies and Tommies—Passing "Women" and Cross-Dressing "Men"

With the increased urbanization and industrialization of modern European and North American cultures, evidence of cross-dressing men and passing women becomes more frequent. In the eighteenth century cross-dressed males gathered in Molly houses and bordellos, where homosexual and cross-dressing men performed mock marriages, play-acted fake births, and engaged in homosexual activities (Bullough and Bullough, 1993; Garber, 1992; Greenberg, 1988; Trumbach, 1994). Although less socially organized than males, females, called Tommies—the root of the word *tomboy*—were also known to cross-dress, often living and passing as men. They married women, worked in male trades, and many lived their lives without detection (Bullough and Bullough, 1993; Cromwell, 1999; Feinberg, 1996; Trumbach, 1994).

The last few decades of scholarship have revealed information about gender-variant people from the fifteenth through twentieth centuries. Intersexed people were of great interest to the medical establishment, who sought them for physical examination and classification purposes, and also wrote medical treatises speculating about their biological origins (Dreger, 1998). Other gender-variant people lived outside of the expected roles of their biological sex and a few examples, described in this section, will suffice to illustrate this rich and complex field of study.

Abbé de Choisy/François de Choisy (1644-1724) was closely linked to the French royal family and was raised as a girl. de Choisy developed deep intimate and sexual attachments with women and adolescent girls and left writings, later published, about his erotic desires to cross-dress (Bullough and Bullough, 1993). A portrait of Edward Hyde, Viscount Cornbury, who served as the governor of New York and New Jersey from 1702 to 1708, hangs today in the New York Historical Society. Hyde is dressed as a woman, although the authenticity of his life as a cross-dresser is still controversial (Bullough and Bullough, 1993; Garber, 1992). Possibly the most notorious gender-variant figure in European history was Chevalier d'Éon (1728-1810), a prominent political diplomat in eighteenth-century France. d'Éon, who lived much of his life in women's clothing, created a huge public scandal, including an official court investigation about his "true" sex. A prolific writer of more than fifteen volumes, it was unclear during d'Éon's life whether he was a man passing as a woman or a woman passing as a man. Havelock Ellis, an early sexologist, was so affected by the story of d'Éon's life that he suggested *eonism* as a clinical term to describe what Magnus Hirschfeld had labeled *transvestism* (Bullough and Bullough, 1993; Kates, 1991; Pauly, 1992).

History reveals the presence of many male cross-dressers who were often prominent, flamboyant, and aristocratic personalities. Female cross-dressers, on the other hand, often lived secretive lives and were "discovered" only after their deaths. In some cases their wives expressed surprise upon learning that their lovers/husbands were female, but whether they were actually unaware, simply avoiding punishment by feigning ignorance, or protecting their partner's honor (or their own) is unknown.

Many of these "passing women" were soldiers, including Hannah Snell/James Grey (1723-1792), who joined the army to find her husband; Flora Sandes (1876-1956), a major of the Siberian army; and American Civil War hero Emma Edmonds/Franklin Thompson (1841-1898). Mary Read (?-1721) and Anne Bonny (1697-?) lived as pirates, and Miranda Barry/James Barry (1795-1865) was a surgeon in the British army. Other cross-dressing females were political figures including Queen Christina/Count Dohna of Sweden (1626-1689), who abdicated her throne to dress in male attire, and Murray Hall (1831-1901), a prominent New York City politician (Bullough and Bullough, 1993; Cromwell, 1999). A well-known example of a passing woman was Mary Frith/Moll Cutpurse (1589-1662), who cross-dressed, lived a life of crime, and may have been physically intersexed (Bullough and Bullough, 1993; Garber, 1992). Moll Cutpurse's story has been source of chapbooks, theatrical productions, and novels since the mid-1600s. One modern fictionalized feminist version defines her as a "swashbuckling heroine" and a lover of women (Galford, 1985).

It is unclear from the historical record how many "passing women" or cross-dressing females were transsexuals or transvestites. Were they dressing for male privilege, or to hide lesbian relationships, or from a need to express their male identity? Historian Alan Bérubé discovered many references to passing women while examining microfilm of old newspapers (Stevens, Freedman, and Bérubé, 1983; The San Francisco Lesbian and Gay History Project, 1989). Louis Sullivan, the founder of the San Francisco support group that later became FTM International—the first organization in the United States for FTM-identified individuals—researched the life of one of Berube's subjects, Jack Bee Garland (Sullivan, 1990a). Jack Bee Garland, also known as Babe Bean (1869-1936), was a well-known newspaper reporter, who lived and worked in Stockton and San Francisco, California. Garland lived full-time as a man, served in the army, appears to have preferred the company of men to women, and until his death few knew that he had been born female.

These examples of cross-dressing people do not, of course, explain or increase one's understanding of gender and sex. They actually serve to amplify the questions of any serious student of gender transgression. Indeed, the eighteenth and nineteenth centuries saw the rise of numerous explanations and theories about cross-gender behavior developed by sexological researchers to describe, codify, and attempt to illuminate the meaning of these "inverted" or "third-sex" people.

MEDICAL SCIENCE AND GENDER VARIANCE

A few years ago . . . sexual inversion was scarcely even a name. It was a loathsome and nameless vice, only to be touched with a pair of tongs, rapidly and with precautions. As it now presents itself, it is a psychological and medico-legal problem so full of interest that we need not fear to face it, so full of grave social actuality that we are bound to face it.

Havelock Ellis
Sexual Inversion, 1897

Sorting through the research conducted by early sex and gender pioneers is a journey into a sort of wonderland. It is a liminal world in which terminology obscures rather than clarifies, and modern concepts of gender, sex, sexual orientation, and sexuality are often conflated. Words such as *hermaphrodite, homosexual, transvestite, eonist, sodomite,* and *sapphist* are used interchangeably. The limits and power of language as a semiotic tool to describe, conflate, define, and confine conceptualizations is nowhere more evident. Sexologists' and theoreticians' attempt to delineate boundaries to classify human diversity succeeded in confusing rather than illuminating the conversation. The modern reader learns as much information about the researchers' views of gender and its transgression as the gender outlaws who were the subjects of their investigation.

The Sexologists—Third Sex and Sexual Inversion

In order to make sense of the sexologists' world it must be understood that in the nineteenth century the relationship between homosexuals and transgendered people was not as clearly delineated as it is today. Homosexual desire was understood to be a kind of gender dysphoria and distinctions were not made between gender and sexual identities. The emerging field of sexology developed under the guidance of physicians, researchers, and social reformers such as Karl Heinrich Ulrichs, Magnus Hirschfeld, Havelock Ellis, and Richard von Krafft-Ebing and their investigation into "types" of sexual deviation was precise and detailed, leading Gayle Rubin to refer to it as a kind of "erotic speciation" (Rubin, 1984, p. 285). They postulated that homosexuals were a third, or intermediate, sex—a male or female who transgressed the proper societal parameters by cross-dressing and behaving as the "other" sex but chose intimate partners of the same biological sex (Hekma, 1994; Kennedy, 1997).

Homosexual desire became "invented" and medicalized (Chauncey, 1982; D'Emilio, 1983; Foucault, 1978; Freedman, 1995; Laqueur, 1990; Plummer, 1981; Weeks, 1981) as it was conflated with gender-variant behavior (Hekma, 1994). Foucault (1978) taught that the concept of homosexuality was "birthed" in the nineteenth century when it was "transposed from the practice of sodomy," which was seen as a "temporary aberration" to an understanding of homosexuals as a separate "species" from heterosexuals (p. 43). Homosexuals became unique humans, with defined temperaments and possibly even particular physiologies.

As Katz (1995) outlined, it was not just homosexuality that was invented, but the term and concept for heterosexuality was also developed. In his words, the terms have "danced in a close dialectical dance" (p. 13). In order for homosexuals to become "the other," heterosexuality had to serve as a "natural" and "normal" counterbalance, a template. Heterosexual behavior, as with homosexual behavior, has, of course, always existed, but the historical social convention of ordering the universe into homosexual and heterosexual persons—different in some fundamental and core manner—did not exist before the sexologists defined the parameters of the discourse. The term *homosexuality* first appeared in the late 1860s and was coined by Karl Maria Kertbeny (a.k.a. Karoly Maria Benkert), but did not come into common usage until the 1890s (Greenberg, 1988).

Homosexuals, as a third sex, were thought to be "inverts"—males who dressed and acted as women and females who dressed and acted as men—and a search began to uncover and understand the biological markings of "inversion" and "third sex" behavior. The term *third sex* was introduced by Karl Ulrichs in the 1860s to describe males who had a "hermaphrodisy of the soul," i.e., a female soul enclosed in a male body (Hekma, 1994; Kennedy, 1997). The concept of third sex depicted an effeminate homosexuality, which he referred to as "Uranism," and believed this to be a congenital condition.

In 1869, Karl Westphal, Berlin's first professor of psychiatry, wrote about those who had "contrary sexual feelings," and in 1877 Richard von Krafft-Ebing wrote about "metamorphosis sexualis paranoia" (Pauly, 1992). Havelock Ellis, an English physician, wrote *Sexual Inversion* in 1897 and described cases of homosexual and transsexual behavior, coining the term *sexoesthetic inversion.* These terms were translated into English as *sexual inversion* (Hekma, 1994). Sexual inversion was believed to be a neurological and psychopathic condition that was hereditary and coexistent with other psychopathologies (Oosterhuis, 1997). In discussing Krafft-Ebing's seminal work, *Psychopathia Sexualis,* Hekma (1994) said, "He assumed that men were attracted to men as if they were women, while women attracted to women should feel like men. . . . Homosexual preference and gender inversion were completely intertwined" (p. 226). Homosexual behavior was so linked to cross-gendered behavior that it was believed people who engaged in sexual relations with inverts, but did not themselves transgress proper societal gender expectations, were not homosexual but merely "perverts" who were seduced by real inverts.

Many of these early sexologists were also advocates of sexual legal reform. Sodomy was a punishable crime in much of Western Europe, and the first homosexual emancipation movement in the late 1800s was based on the idea that inverts and third-sex people were natural and normal human variations. Magnus Hirschfeld, a physician and sexologist, was also the founder of the Scientific Humanitarian Committee, the world's first homosexual rights organization. He lobbied for repeal of Paragraph 175 in Germany, which had made male homosexuality illegal. Hirschfeld coined the terms *transvestiten transsexualism* and *seelischer Transsexualismus* (psychic transsexualism) and described several forms of transvestism and "intermediate sexual types" (Ekins and King, 2001; Steakley, 1997). Havelock Ellis worked closely with Edward Carpenter, a socialist, writer, and homosexual, who advocated sex reform for "intermediate types" in the early 1900s (Greenberg, 1988; Hekma, 1994; Herdt, 1994; Pauly, 1992; Vyras, 1996).

These early sex reformers believed that sexual and gender variances were normal human deviations. Havelock Ellis stated in *Sexual Inversion* that homosexuality was not caused by societal degeneracy but was instead inborn. In 1901 Krafft-Ebing published an article stating that homosexuality was natural, not pathological (Greenberg, 1988; Hekma, 1994). Homosexual inversion was perceived of as natural, in part, because effeminate males who were sexually attracted to other males were regarded as womanlike—especially within working-class urban subcultures (Chauncey, 1994). Krafft-Ebing's work in particular deserves recognition not only because he reframed sexual deviations as a "disease" and not a sin, a crime, or decadence, but "more importantly, because he made it clear that sexuality deserved serious study since it was central to the existence of the individual and society" (Oosterhuis, 1997, p. 73).

Concurrently, physicians in the late nineteenth century entered what Dreger (1998) referred to as the "Age of the Gonads," when hermaphrodites came under the scrutiny of the scientific scalpel. Physiological inversion became a focal point for sexologists and medical specialists in anatomy, who were searching for determinants of the "true sex" of people who were intersexed. People with mixed genitalia became the fascination of "medical men," and the gonads—the existence of female ovaries or male testes—became the final determinants of maleness or femaleness, regardless of one's secondary characteristics or social gender. Inversion, whether it was a transgression of physiology (hermaphroditism), sexual desire (homosexuality), or gender expression (transsexualism or transvestism) became a subject of scientific exploration and exploitation.

In their attempts to categorize and classify gender variant people, the early sexologists left contemporary researchers and clinicians with a complex legacy since the language systems changed from country to country, from epoch to epoch, from scientist to scientist, and from one discipline to another. Modern researchers can learn much about the universality of gender variance and the social construction of gender expression from studying these early theories. They do not, however, give us guidelines on how to think about gender issues within a contemporary context.

The historical, sociological, anthropological, and psychomedical literature on gender variance describes the ubiquitous existence of gender variance. However, these descriptions conceal as much as they reveal. The continuous thread of gender-variant behavior historically and cross-culturally is not difficult to find. However, researchers must avoid the trap of assuming that gender-variant behavior in the historical or clinical record is comparable from one time period to another *or* to the expressions currently manifesting within the postmodern world. Even conditions based on physical or biological "fact" will vary in meaning from one cultural milieu to another. For example, 5-alpha-reductase deficiency (5-ARD) syndrome is an intersexed condition in which the male (XY) body is unable to "read" testosterone due to an enzyme problem and the afflicted child develops what appears to be female genitalia. At puberty, a relatively normal physical masculinization occurs and male hormones virilize the "girl's" body. "Her" penis grows and "she" develops male secondary sex characteristics. This condition is common in the Dominican Republic and in the Sambia culture of New Guinea where a small but consistent percentage of the population are raised to be females who later "become" males. In the Dominican Republic this is called *guevedoche,* which means "penis at twelve," or *machihembra,* which means "first woman, then man." In the Sambia culture the word is *kwolu-aatmwol,* which means, "changing into male thing" (Dreger, 1998; Herdt, 1994; Imperato-McGinley et al., 1979). What is most fascinating is that these children seem to have little difficulty negotiating normative psychosexual struggles. They switch their sex designation and are then reintegrated in their communities with relative ease, confounding much of what would be considered a major psychosexual dilemma within a contemporary Western context.

Although gender-variant behavior is a universal expression, it is always embedded within a cultural matrix that privileges certain experiences and distorts others. King (1993) challenged students of gender studies by asking, "What is the rationale for lumping together the eighteenth-century Mollies, the North American Plains Indian and the modern transvestite? Is it not blind ethnocentrism to simply call all 'objects' transvestism?" (p. 9). It is obvious that the yardstick the missionaries used to understand the berdache was different from how Two-Spirit people were and are seen within their own cultural frame. Cross-dressing as a spiritual calling, as it is expressed by the Hijras as well as by Jeanne d'Arc, does not appear to be a theme within urban settings among the Mollies and Tommies.

It is essential to understand the social context of sex and gender in order to determine the meaning of that expression of gender variance within a particular cultural setting. Modern theoreticians of sex and gender have inherited a legacy from the past century that (1) renders females invisible, (2) conflates homosexual desire with gender transgression, and (3) conflates the concepts of sex and gender.

The Invisibility of Females

Since the 1970s, feminist scholars and activists have recognized the lack of visibility of women's history and experience within recorded history. Scholars often ignore women's issues or contributions and will occasionally defend their bias by stating that information about female lives does not exist. Due to the nature of sexism, women's history has often been hidden and less often documented; however, the feminist movement has birthed a plethora of writing on the role of women historically, sociologically, and politically across racial, ethnic, and class lines.

The invisibility of women's lives was evident during the early gay liberation movement when writings of and about male homosexuals were more visible than comparable writings of and about lesbians (Faraday, 1981). In examining relationships between females, researchers such as Faderman (1981), Rothblum and Brehony (1993), and Smith-Rosenberg (1975) recognized that intimate relationships between women were not necessarily sexual but romantic and committed friendships. Their work raised questions about how to define and label "lesbian" relationships.

In other situations, relationships might be more clearly sexual but less clearly lesbian due to the nature of how gender was expressed. Numerous examples are cited in the literature of females who dressed as men, worked in traditionally male jobs, married women, and were accepted as men within the cultural parameters of their society. As discussed earier, females in premodern and modern Europe often passed as men, and it can be hypothesized that many more gender-variant females lived this way than have been discovered. Weiringa and Blackwood (1999) said, "There are many forms of transgender practices in which females do not conform to the gender roles assigned to members of their anatomical sex" (p. 7).

The female cross-gender person often gained status by occupying a traditionally male role as evidenced by the "manly hearted women" of the North Piegan Blackfoot tribe, whose masculinity raised their social caste. It is possible that gender-variant females have been rendered invisible in part because of their rise to male power. Brown (1989), in her research on premodern Europe, said, "Transvestism struck at the very heart of . . . gender and power relations. By dressing like men, such women were attempting to sever the bonds that held them to the female sphere of the social hierarchy. . . . They were attempting to usurp the functions of men" (p. 73). Shapiro (1991) said, "Those who intentionally move down in the system are more threatening to its values than those who move up" (p. 270), and females who live as men are generally crossing over to a gender of higher social position. However, this can vary in different milieus. For instance, when females of color transition in contemporary culture, they often lose even more social power since men of color in the modern world occupy an underclass social position. There are many instances in which females who lived as men in Western cultures were caught and brutally and criminally punished.

When feminist and gay scholars began to uncover the legacy of females living as men, they labeled the phenomenon "passing women." They theorized that that these females were (1) lesbians or (2) living as men in order to enjoy the increased economic freedom men were permitted (Faderman, 1981, 1991; Katz, 1976). However, many reasons exist for female cross-gender behavior, including convenience, comfort, or simply wanting to move more freely in a male world. Cromwell (1999) referred to females who lived as men for adventure, economic freedom, or male privilege as "transvestic opportunists" (p. 63). The difficulty of assuming that all passing women were protecting lesbian relationships or identities, or attempting to live more freely in a man's world, is that it contributes to the invisibility of female masculinity, transgendered females, and female transsexuals. This invisibility continues through contemporary clinical accounts which state that female cross-dressing is nonexistent and female-to-male transsexualism extremely rare. As Cromwell (1999) pointed out, even the term *passing women* renders those who lived, identified, and experienced themselves as men virtually nonexistent. The term *passing men* might be more accurate. Feminist theories defined lesbianism as an act of resistance to patriarchy (which is certainly one form it has taken) but as Blackwood and Wieringa (1999b) said, "Not all same-sex relationships were acts of resistance" (p. 56). Unfortunately, the historical sexism that feminists have been so critical of was propagated by feminist historians themselves who could only see living as a man to be an act of lesbianism or political survival, not a valid identity construct.

There is no doubt that females have cross-dressed and passed as men in order to live within lesbian partnerships during eras in which female sexuality was denied and lesbianism (sodomy) could have meant death. The question remains, however, whether these passing women were lesbians choosing to pass as men due to homophobia or transsexual men living in relationships that they and their partners identified as heterosexual unions. Cromwell (1999) said, "It is not always possible to make tidy distinctions between FTMs/transmen and butch lesbians; there is much overlap and similarities between the types" (p. 63) and used the term *female-bodied men* to describe this phenomenon.

The existence of gender-variant females who identified and saw themselves as men is currently being reexamined and reclaimed as a part of our history. There are clear examples of passing women who fit a lesbian narrative, such as Mary East/James How (1715-1781), who stopped cross-dressing when her relationship ended. Others who have been relegated to this status but might more easily be identified as "female-bodied men" include Calamity Jane (1852?-1903), Alan Lucill Hart/Alberta Lucille (1890-1962), Little Jo Monaghan (1857-1903), Jack Bee Garland, and Billy Tipton (1914-1989).

Conflation of Homosexual Desire with Gender Transgression

Understanding the difference between sexual orientation (i.e., one's sexual desire for males or females) and gender identity (i.e., one's core identity or expression as a man or woman) is a modern exploration that did not begin until well into the twentieth century. Sexologists, social scientists, feminists, and gay historians have all been guilty of conflating homosexuality with gender variance. Yet sorting out homosexual desire from cross-gender expression is complicated since the two have so often overlapped. Cross-gender behavior has often inferred homosexuality and has therefore served as a social control mechanism to maintain traditional gender polarities. According to Bohan and Russell (1999), "Homosexuality [has often been] regulated by gender-baiting" (p.103).

The sexologists' examination of "inversion" left a linguistic legacy that fails to convey the differences between such concepts as "congenital inverts" and "eonists," "transvestite homosexuals" and "effeminate sodomites," or "hermaphrodites" and "bisexuals." The clinical language that we use today did not evolve until the middle of the twentieth century and it is not always easy to understand historical models within our contemporary knowledge. Categorizing sexual and gender identities using medical terminology might conceal the cultural context of identities, such as homosexual "fairies" within working-class urban cultures in the late 1800s (Chauncey, 1994). In 1949 David O. Cauldwell, a popular pseudoscientific writer of sexology, began using the term *transsexualism* (Meyerowitz, 2002), which he is often cited as originating. Magnus Hirschfeld had, however, differentiated the concept of *transsexualism* from *homosexuality,* and classified the two as distinct syndromes almost twenty-five years earlier. Hirschfeld did not use the term *transvestite* in its modern meaning, but in reference to those who wanted to change sex (Ekins and King, 2001). The term *transsexual* was popularized by Harry Benjamin, an early colleague of Magnus Hirschfeld, who began to publish in the 1960s (Pauly, 1992; Plummer, 1981).

As has been discussed, for the sexologists, females who lived as men were lesbian inverts; to the early feminist and gay scholars, they were oppressed women/lesbians. When feminist and gay academics incorporated the idea of passing women into the chronicle of "women's oppression" as a reaction to homophobia and economic oppression, they effectively "disappeared" the existence of transgendered and transsexual men (Cromwell, 1999). Early historians of homosexuality privileged the same-sex nature of relationships and downplayed the cross-gender expression. For example, Boswell (1980) assumed that homosexual behavior determined a "gay identity" that was unchanging throughout history. Katz (1976), one of the early historians dedicated to documenting a gay history, described the berdache and the passing woman as early gay role models, although he later recognized that these identities were culturally specific. Perhaps in their exuberance for finding "gay ancestors," feminist and gay historians have underplayed questions of gender variance. Gutierrez (1989) has also questioned whether researchers have exaggerated the positive role of the Two-Spirit people within their own cultures, and Tafoya and Wirth (1996) have responded that most likely "attitudes about the Two-Spirit varied widely among Native American cultures: some exalted them, some were indifferent, and some were openly hostile" (p. 56).

Contemporary social scientists, anthropologists, and historians have tried to reexamine these categories with a postmodern understanding of sex and gender, sorting out homosexual desire from transgressive gender behavior (see Duberman, Vincinus, and Chauncey, 1989, for further discussion). Some theorists began recognizing the overlap of sex and gender. For example, Greenberg (1988) classified the berdache within the category of "transgenderal homosexuality," recognizing both the gender and sexuality aspects of this social role. Trumbach (1994) recognized the complexity of the sex and gender relationship when he examined the social roles of the Tommies (or sapphists) and Mollies in eighteenth-century Europe. Halperin (2000) argued that "there is no such thing as a singular or unitary history of male homosexuality" (p. 91), but delineated four different types of same-sex male sexuality evident throughout history and contrasted them with our modern-day concept of homosexuality. Some of these types were also gender variant and others were not.

Since the 1980s, an understanding of the social construction of human culture made it possible to examine the interrelationship of sex, gender, sexuality, and desire and begin to sort out areas of conflation in ways that were not possible for our predecessors. It is clear that sexual orientation and gender expression are two separate components of how people experience and manifest their sexual selves. It is equally clear that they overlap and entwine not only within the study of human sexuality but within human lives (Pauly, 1998).

Conflation of the Concepts of Sex and Gender

Through anthropological and historical study it becomes evident that many different forms of gender expressions and identities are not always linked to one's biological sex. For instance, the term *hermaphrodite* was often used in the seventeenth century to describe effeminate homosexual men (Trumbach, 1994), conflating physical intersex conditions with both sexual desire and sex-role behavior.

How sex and gender are understood within a culture has a tremendous impact on the social construction of sexuality since definitions of homosexual and heterosexual sex are based on definitions of sexed and gendered bodies. The concept of a same-sex relationship assumes that the biological similarity of the partners' bodies is the salient feature of the relationship. In many cultures, the relationship is considered to be homosexual only if the partners express the same gender, regardless of their biological bodies. Lang (1997) said that "a same-sex relationship in many Native American cultures, at least traditionally, is not necessarily at the same time a same-gender relationship" (p. 104), separating the concept of biology from the idea of gender identity.

In some contexts, partners in same-sex relationships are positioned at opposite gender poles, rendering the relationship "heterosexual" since it is based on the gender configurations of the partners. Wesley Thomas (1997), who worked with the Navajo Two-Spirit people, said that "neither a relationship between a female-bodied nádleeh/masculine female and a woman nor a relationship between a male-bodied nádleeh/feminine male and a man are considered a homosexual relationship by traditional Navajo people, although each is termed homosexual in Western culture" (p. 162).

In urban working-class lesbian communities of the 1950s and 1960s there was a "prominence of butch-fem roles . . . and almost all members were exclusively one or the other" (Kennedy and Davis, 1993, p. 5). Although butches were acknowledged as females, their sexuality was mediated through their masculinity. Elliston (1999), who studied the Mahu in Tahiti, said that "same-sex desire always relies on a gender difference" within that cultural setting (p. 239).

It is obvious that sex and gender depict different aspects of human sexuality. Although they are often conflated within modern Western cultures, a same-sex relationship is not equivalent to a "same-gender" relationship. Within certain cultural contexts this can depend less on the biological bodies of the partners than on their gender presentations.

As we deconstruct the history of gender variance it becomes unclear whether those called inverts by the sexologists of the nineteenth century were people who would today be called homosexual or transsexual or how many were actually intersexed. It is equally unclear whether gender-variant people in different epochs were "gay" or not and whether they identified as men, women, or third-sexed people. There can, however, be no doubt that transgendered people—by whatever name we call them—existed, and that what distinguishes them from their cohorts is their gender variance. "The evidence of multiple genders . . . offers support for the theory of social constructionism, which maintains that gender roles, sexualities, and identities are not natural, essential, or universal, but constructed by social processes and discourses" (Roscoe, 1998, p. 5).

The presence of gender-variant people historically and cross-culturally is indisputable. They have been both respected and reviled, subject to high social honor as well as ostracism and annihilation. They have served humankind as shamans and warriors, as priests and prostitutes, as healers and artists, as political leaders, and as child rearers. They have also served as the scapegoats and guinea pigs of religious zeal, political xenophobia, and medical inquisition. Indeed, the transgender experience has been rendered invisible historically, leaving people today to imagine that cross-gendered behavior is a symptom of modern life.

Chapter 3

Deconstructing Sex and Gender: Thinking Outside the Box

[N]o particular understanding of sexual difference historically follows from undisputed facts about the body. . . . The dominant, though by no means universal, view since the eighteenth century has been that there are two stable, incommensurable, opposite sexes and that the political, economic, and cultural lives of men and women, their gender roles, are somehow based on the "facts."

Thomas Laqueur
Making Sex, 1990

It is obvious to any student of history, anthropology, or medical science that gender and its expression have been experienced, described, defined, and treated differently in different epochs. As the inheritors of this legacy of confusing and contradictory language it is necessary to develop a contemporary and comprehensive modern terminology that respects the complexity of gender identity and the different ways that it manifests and is experienced. Gender is a biopsychosocial phenomenon whereby the component parts of self—biological, psychological, and the social construction of culture—intersect and interact in complex ways to create an integrated whole. Many people would also suggest that there is a transpersonal, or spiritual, element to the process of gender identity integration.

FOUR COMPONENTS OF IDENTITY

Gender dichotomies were not only restrictive, they were also constitutive. . . . the gendering of social spheres not only constrained personal freedom, but gender categories also determined what it was possible to know.

Virginia Goldner, 1988

Gender and sex are often used interchangeably and, indeed, we tend to think of them as the same thing. People are as likely to say, "There is a *man*," as they are to say, "There is a *male*," not identifying any salient differences in the terminology used. The word *man* actually refers to the person's gender, whereas the term *male* refers to his sex—the first being a sociological construct and the second being a biophysiological phenomenon. In common discourse we conflate the words *gender* and *sex* and assume them to be equivalent. However, gender is, as Green (1999) said, "a form of communication, a language we use to express and interpret each other socially" (p. 125).

Sexual identity is being used here to describe the complex relationship of biological sex, gender identity, gender-role expression, and sexual orientation. These components of human identity develop and are integrated within a biopsychosocial matrix. *Sexual identity* is not being used in its narrower definition to refer to sexual orientation or preference. These component parts of sexual identity will be outlined in the following sections. The terminology used here borrows from, but is not identical to, other theorists (Coleman, 1987; Diamond, 2002; Money and Erhardt, 1972; Money and Tucker, 1975; Paul, 1993; Shively and De Cecco, 1993). (See Glossary for definitions.)

Biological Sex or Natal Sex

Sex is the physiological makeup of a human being, referred to as the biological or natal sex. Sex is a complex relationship of genetic, hormonal, morphological, chromosomal, gonadal, biochemical, and anatomical determinants that impact the physiology of the body and the sexual differentiation of the brain. Although everyone is assigned a sex at birth, approximately 2 percent of the population are intersexed and do not easily fit into a dimorphic division of two sexes that are "opposite."

The first component of human identity is biological sex. Everyone is assigned a biological sex at birth based on an examination of the visible genitalia. The difference between males and females is initially determined rather simplistically by whether one has an "innie" or "outie." The presence or absence of the phallus is the first, most salient, and often the only variable that determines whether one is a boy or a girl. Biological sex is actually a complex relationship of genetic, hormonal, morphological, chromosomal, gonadal, biochemical, and anatomical determinants that impact the physiology of the body and the sexual differentiation of the brain (Money, 1995; Wilson and Reiner, 1999).

The biological differences between males and females develop at about six weeks into gestation. Before this stage male and female (XY and XX) appear the same, although genetic or chromosomal sexual differences are established at conception. The primitive duct systems are identical until the presence of male hormones triggers the development of male gonads, the differentiation of the duct systems, and the formation of external genitalia. Without the presence of male hormones, the fetus develops female gonads, which has led scientists to label the female development process a "default" system. This means that if the XY fetus does not trigger the correct masculinizing process, it will appear to be female. The gonads produce various hormones that further differentiate male from female and eventually stimulate the development of internal and external genitalia (Money, 1993; Migeon, Wisniewski, and Gearhart, 2001; Carroll and Wolpe, 1996) (see Figure 3.1). Sex, simply, is defined as the bipolar categories of male and female. Intersexuality is a combination, or mixture, of these two poles. *When sex is not easily assigned, the person is referred to as intersexed.*

Gender Identity

Gender is a social construct that divides people into "natural" categories of men and women that are assumed to derive from their physiological male and female bodies. Most people's gender identity is congruent with their assigned sex, but many people experience their gender identity to be discordant with their natal sex. Gender identity is considered a core identity. A person's self-concept of his or her gender (regardless of their biological sex) is called his or her gender identity.

Gender identity is defined as the internal experience of gender, how one experiences his or her own sense of self as a gendered being. Gender identity is experienced as a core identity, a fundamental sense of belonging to one sex or the other (Stoller, 1968b). The sense of being a man or being a woman is an essential attribute of self. Many people would have trouble identifying their sense of "self" outside of the parameters of gender. Nearly everyone has an understanding of themselves as a man or a woman, a boy or a girl.

Gender is a social construct that divides people into "natural" categories of men and women that are thought to derive from their physiological male and female bodies. Gender attributes vary from culture to culture and are arbitrarily imposed. Gender identity is established early in life and is thought to be relatively impervious to change. Children begin to identify their gender

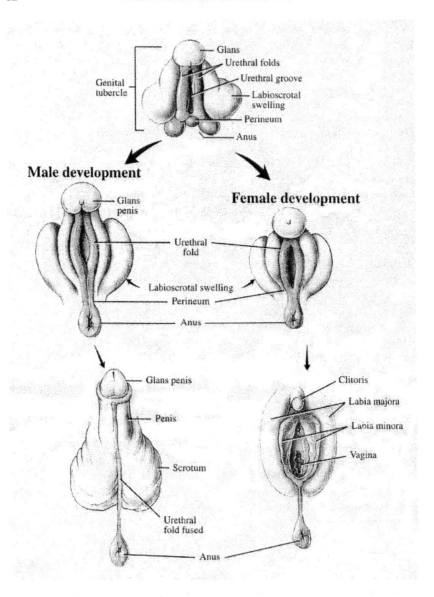

FIGURE 3.1. Development of the male and female external genitalia from the undifferentiated genital tubercle. (*Source:* From Carroll, Janell L. and Wolpe, Paul Root, SEXUALITY AND GENDER IN SOCIETY. Copyright © 1996, by Allyn & Bacon. Reprinted by permission.)

as young as two years old and the sense of gender identity generally stabilizes within the first few years of life. Kohlberg (1966) said that when a child can accurately discriminate males from females and identify his or her own gender status correctly they have reached the stage of "gender constancy"—an essential stage in normative gender development.

For most people their gender identity is congruent with their assigned sex. This means that if they are "male" they experience themselves as "men" and if they are "female" they experience themselves as "women." Bolin (1988) refers to this as the "cultural requirement that women are people with vaginas" (p. 7) and, of course, the opposite is also true—that men are people with penises. People may feel confined by some of the societal assumptions about proper male or female behavior or they may resist certain role restrictions associated with prescribed genders (e.g., men don't cry; women are passive), but most people experience congruence with the label they have been given. They may believe the categories themselves are restrictive but not that they have been wrongly classified.

For other people, however, their gender identity—how they experience themselves in their bodies—is discordant with their natal sex and is in direct conflict with the biological facts of their bodies. Their gender identity is experienced as dysphoric, or dystonic, to their physicality. Transsexuals are people who cross over and are legally reassigned as the "other" sex, and transgendered people live somewhere in the middle of the continuum, either as bi-gender, cross-dressers, or people who move back and forth from one gender expression to the other. Cross-gender behavior is often present from a very young age. This is not to be confused with a psychotic process in which people deny that they have the physiology which they actually have. Transgendered people are aware of the reality of their physical bodies but do not feel that it describes who they really are inside. It is interesting to note that many intersexed people also have stable male or female gender identities, even though their sex classification may be more difficult to ascertain.

A person's self-concept of his or her gender (regardless of biological sex) is called gender identity. Gender and gender identity are "learned and achieved at the interactional level, reified at the cultural level, and institutionally enforced via the family, law, religion, politics, economy, medicine, and the media" (Gagné, Tewksbury, and McGaughey, 1997, p. 478). Kessler and McKenna (1978) said, "The only way to ascertain someone's gender identity is to ask her/him" (p. 9).

When gender identity differs from natal sex, the person is identified as transgendered, often as transsexual.

Gender-Role Expression

Gender role is the expression of masculinity and femininity and has often been referred to as "sex role." Gender roles are thought to be reflections of one's gender identity and are socially dictated and reinforced. It is through gender roles that gender is enacted or "performed" (consciously or unconsciously) and may or may not be related to gender identity or natal sex.

Gender role has commonly been referred to as "sex role," and it is the expression of masculinity or femininity. Gender role is the socialized aspect of gender that is "tied to appearance, behavior, and personality" (Shively and De Cecco, 1993, p. 82). The term *sex role* was originally used by Margaret Mead to describe culturally determined behaviors expected of men and women (Meyerowitz, 2002). Socially dictated and reinforced, gender roles are thought to be a reflection of one's gender identity (which is assumed to describe one's biological sex) but may or may not be related to gender identity or natal sex. Gender roles are how gender is enacted or "performed" (consciously or unconsciously) and are the "public expression of one's gender identity" (Money and Ehrhardt, 1972, p. 4). Money, who first developed the terms *gender role* and *gender identity,* says that they are "two sides of the same coin" (Money and Lehne, 1999, p. 214). He described this as "gender-identity/role" (Money and Ehrhardt, 1972, p. 146).

The acquisition of gender roles is a social process. It is achieved rather than ascribed (Kessler and McKenna, 1978; Lewins, 1995). Gender role is expressed in a variety of ways, including through clothing, mannerisms, grooming or adornment habits, voice inflection, and social interests. It includes:

> public presentations of self in dress and verbal and nonverbal communication; the economic and family roles one plays; . . . the sexual roles one plays and emotions one experiences and displays; and the experiencing of one's body, as it is defined as masculine or feminine in any particular society. (Nanda, 1994, p. 396)

It is undeniable that women and men are, as Blackwood and Wieringa (1999b) said, "situated differently in all cultures" (p. 51) and that social divisions between the sexes exist almost universally. "Gender roles can be defined as the sum of socially designated behavior that differentiates between men and women" (Hamilton and Jensvold, 1992, p. 118). For example, in Western cultures males are expected to be independent, logical, objective, active, competent, and instrumental, while females are assumed to be passive, dependent, emotional, warm, expressive, and nurturant. Studies have shown that when ranked hierarchically gender roles associated with women are considered less mentally healthy and are less valued by both men and women (Broverman et al., 1970; Gilligan, 1982; Hare-Mustin, 1983).

Despite the restrictions on extreme cross-gender expression, gender-role behavior is probably the most flexible of all these variables of identity. Many people express their sense of masculinity or femininity in cross-gender expression without experiencing any discord with their biological sex. For many people there is a range of feminine and masculine behavior that they are comfortable expressing in terms of clothing or mannerisms. One may dress and behave differently playing softball, attending a professional conference, fighting for a seat on the subway, and preparing for a romantic date. Young people are especially flexible about gender-role expression and enjoy stretching approved gender behavior past its approved edges. Bem (1974, 1993) developed a research tool—the Bem Sex Role Inventory (BSRI)—to demonstrate that both men and women have a wide range of traits in both categories. It is possible to view masculine and feminine traits *independently,* instead of on a continuum of opposites (Constantinople, 1973).

Western society has experienced huge upheavals in the rules determining proper male and female gender-role expression in the past forty years. The early women's liberation movement bravely fought against the idea that gendered expectations for men and women are biological givens, arguing instead that they are socially constructed. Issues have ranged from equal pay and access to abortion and birth control to women's right to wear pants in public. This false division of the sexes that emanated from the arbitrary rules of gender was the rallying cry for feminists who have waged a war—a rather successful war—on patriarchal standards. As Newton (2000) said, "Gender categories are learned by all, but 'natural' to none" (p. 170).

When gender role is divergent from social expectations, the person is perceived as a cross-dresser or gender bender, "effeminate" (if male), or butch (if female).

Sexual Orientation

Sexual orientation is the self-perception of one's sexual preference and emotional attraction. Sexual orientation can be directed toward members of the same sex (homosexual), the opposite sex (heterosexual), both sexes (bisexual), or neither sex (nonsexual). Sexuality is experienced through the person's gender identity (regardless of his or her biology).

Sexual orientation is the self-perception of the direction of a person's sexual and/or emotional desire. It describes both sexual preference and emotional attraction. Sexual orientation is less of an internal sense of self and more of an external desire for another person, although certainly sexual orientation becomes integrated as an identity construct. Some people experience their sexual orientation as an unchanging essential part of their nature. Others experience it in a more fluid way. Sexual orientation can be directed toward members of the same sex (homosexual), the opposite sex (heterosexual), both sexes (bisexual), or neither sex (asexual).

Homosexual and heterosexual identity is a modern construction (Chauncey, 1982; D'Emilio, 1983; Freedman, 1995; Foucault, 1978; Halperin, 2000; Plummer, 1981; Weeks, 1981). Although homosexual behavior has always existed, it is only in the modern era that it has been used to define a person's nature or assumed to be an innate part of personhood. Individuals can engage in same-sex behavior and not identify as homosexual. Inversely, individuals can "be" homosexual (i.e., prefer or desire partners of the same sex) and not engage in homosexual behavior. Padgug (1989) said, " 'Homosexual' and 'heterosexual' behavior may be universal; homosexual and heterosexual identity and consciousness are modern realities" (p. 60). Historically, distinctions between people who violated accepted gender roles and people who were sexual with members of their own sex were not clearly delineated (Chauncey, 1982; Greenberg, 1988; Hekma, 1994) and gender-transgressive people were mostly assumed to be homosexual.

Sexual orientation has many component parts, including physical preference, affectional preference, fantasy, and social relationships. It is more than just sexual expression (Klein, 1993). Sexual orientation can refer to sexual behavior, sexual attraction (regardless of behavior), or sense of identity, which may or may not be reflective of behavior or attraction. Sexual orientation is particularly complex in a world where certain sexual expressions (e.g., homosexuality and bisexuality) have been despised and criminally punished. Sexual orientation—the desire for particular categories of sexed or gendered people—may not be the only or best way to describe our sexual desires. Bem (1993) said, that her sexuality "does not mesh with available cultural categories" (p. vii), and Litwoman (1990) discussed feeling forced into a "bisexual" identity since she is attracted to both men and women. Litwoman believed that gender is not the salient aspect of how her desires function.

Due to the societal stigma surrounding homosexual behavior, lesbian, gay, and bisexual people have to "come out" of the assumption that they are heterosexual, not only to others but also to themselves. Although sometimes the terms *sexual orientation* and *sexual preference* are used interchangeably with the term *sexual identity,* they are actually subsets of the broader category of sexual identity. Sometimes the term *sexual identity* is used with pride by people with a homosexual or bisexual orientation to give voice to the idea that their sexuality is not merely a desire but an integrated part of their identity.

When sexual orientation is not heterosexual, it is stigmatized, for homosexuals and bisexuals.

DECONSTRUCTING THE ASSUMPTIONS OF SEXUAL IDENTITY

[T]he category of sex and the naturalized institution of heterosexuality are *constructs,* socially instituted and socially regulated fantasies or "fetishes," not *natural* categories, but *political* ones.

Judith Butler
Gender Trouble, 1990

The four components of sexual identity interact with one another in complex ways and develop and integrate in various patterns. Despite the bipolar divisions of male/female, man/woman, masculine/feminine, and gay/straight, all aspects of human sexuality—physiology, gender identity, gender-role behavior, and sexual identity—have multiple variables and expressions.

As discussed previously, people are assigned to their natal sex category based on visible genitalia. Genitalia are rarely visible publicly so assumptions about male or female sex are actually based on gender-role expression of masculine or feminine features. Gender identity and biological sex is attributed to people based on perceived traits, which are enacted or performed through gender-role expression. Kessler and McKenna (1978) suggest that gender attribution is the foundation for understanding all other components of sexual identity. People use cues to discern whether others are male or female and, in cases of ambiguity, people more easily assume that someone is male, *even when the person has visible female genitalia,* as long as there are enough other masculine cues.

None of these categories offer much information about sexuality itself. Sexual orientation, especially if it is nonnormative heterosexuality, must be achieved through a process of self-discovery and coming out. Sexual orientation may reveal the "love-object choice" of a person, but not whether he or she acts on those desires. The four components do not explore sexual desire, erotic identity, erotic role, or erotic acts (Newton [with Walton], 2000).

The way that societies transform biological attributes into socialized identities—affecting not only reproduction but social power, role characteristics, and the very nature of identity—has been called the sex/gender system (Rubin, 1975). The entire sex/gender system is built on a series of assumptions that are so much a part of our way of thinking we do not realize they are assumptions. The first and most salient of these is the premise of duality.

The Assumption of Duality

It is an assumed truth that humans are divided into two groups, one called male and the other called female. The two groups are considered bipolar opposites, matched parts that fit together as puzzle pieces (see Figure 3.2). This binary division is based on an either/or dichotomy; one is either male or female. Males and females are perceived to be different from each other in scientifically observable ways and across all academic disciples, from the hard sciences such as biology to the soft sciences such as sociology, and even the political sciences such as women's studies. Stone (1991) said,

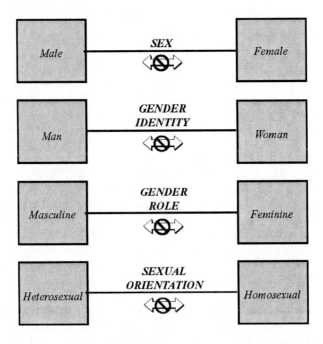

FIGURE 3.2. Sex, gender identity, gender role, and sexual orientation are assumed to be bipolar opposites. This bipolar system renders invisible those who are intersexed, gender variant, androgynous, cross-gendered, and/or bisexual.

"Under the binary phallocratic found myth by which Western bodies and subjects are authorized, only one body per gendered subject is 'right'. All other bodies are wrong" (p. 297).

It is further assumed that men and women are different in personality, desires, behaviors, and interests and that these differences are based on their physiological differences. Masculine and feminine sex-role expressions are assumed to be dichotomous, and people are socialized to be "opposites" that are different and complementary. This duality is then presumed to result in an attraction—as in opposites attract—and places sex and gender identity into a heterosexual male/female structure that is deemed "normal"; everything else is presumed to deviate from this norm. Gayle Rubin (1975) refered to gender as the "socially imposed division of the sexes . . . [that] transform[s] males and females into 'men' and 'women,' each an incomplete half which can only find wholeness when united with the other" (p. 40).

Many difficulties emerge from this paradigm, which will be outlined here and described later. The first problem is that the assumption humans are divided into male and female subspecies determined by genitalia renders people with ambiguous genitalia invisible from the social discourse. Intersexed people, by some estimates to be about 2 percent of the population, are "disappeared" when the only available filing categories are male and female.

Second, this bipolar paradigm socializes men and women to think of themselves as living on different and warring planets—Mars and Venus— and to believe that they are more different from each other than they are similar. Even the nature of research itself, including feminist research, rests in assumptions about male/female differences. Whatever particular differences are being studied, "the range of variation is far greater *among* males or *among* females than *between* the two sexes" (Bleier, 1984, p. 109). Caplan and Caplan (1994) suggested that students of research ask metaquestions about the process of doing research, e.g., "What might be researchers' motives for doing this research?" and "Are certain kinds of bias reflected in the way the research question was asked?" They raised the concern that researchers are "ignoring or downplaying overlap in females' and males' performance or behavior," reminding academics that females and males are far more alike on all variables than they are different (1994, pp. 110-111). As Rothblatt (1995) said, "All of the alleged proofs of sexual dimorphism have suffered from a glaring . . . Achilles' heel—*absolute* differences in men's and women's minds, mental abilities, and psychological natures have never been found" (p. 107). The differences between males and females always privilege males and create an androcentrism that assumes women to be "the other" (Bem, 1993).

Third, the entire system of sexual expression (i.e., sexual orientation or preference) is built on the premise of a bipolar gender system. Assumptions about sexual orientation, even liberal assumptions, are based on the presumption of there being two opposite sexes. A world that is neatly divided into male/female designations also very neatly splits into heterosexual and homosexual people. The possibility of same-sex intimacy exists only as a category when it is compared to opposite-sex intimacy. Sedgwick (1990) said that "without a concept of gender there could be . . . no concept of homo- or heterosexuality" (p. 31). Bisexuality as a paradigm is defined by its middle position between the two available poles. Pharr (1988) said that "homophobia [or, more accurately, heterosexism] . . . is a weapon of sexism," describing the process in which homophobic violence is used to reinforce traditional gender roles (p. 16).

Finally, behaviors that deviate from expected gender requirements are considered clinically diagnosable, rendering cross-gender behavior not just unusual but pathological. Binary sex and gender systems force all people who do not easily fit either polar field—including intersexed, gender-variant, homosexual, bisexual, and transsexual people—into a category of "other" that ultimately stigmatizes them for being different and then pathologizes their uniqueness.

Intersexuality

For most people there is a consistency between their external genitalia, their internal genitalia, their hormones, and their chromosomes and they are easily placed into the available categories of male or female. However, due to the numerous biological variables intervening in the fetal development process it is possible for sexual differentiation to take place atypically. For instance, an irregularity in hormone production, such as an over- or under-exposure to particular hormones or certain genetic conditions, can cause internal or external genitalia to develop outside expected parameters. When external genitals are ambiguous at birth, medical professionals step in to further examine the chromosomes, hormones, and internal genitalia to see if an intersexed condition is present. Of course, no further examination is necessary if the genitals are "normal" looking. Most people have not had their sex scientifically examined, and if they do not have an obvious physiological difference, more subtle intersexed conditions may never be identified.

Intersexed people may have the internal reproductive system of one or both sexes as well as ambiguous or incompletely differentiated external genitalia. People who have the physiological external genitalia of both males and females have been traditionally referred to as hermaphrodites. The Intersex Society of North America (ISNA) said that the word *hermaph-*

rodite is stigmatizing and misleading and a result of scientific theories developed in the Victorian age. They recommended the use of the word *intersex,* a practice that will be followed here.

Intersexuality is found among all populations throughout the world, although with variable frequency. Fausto-Sterling (2000) estimated that when all causes of intersex are considered, approximately 1.7 percent of all births are affected. This is certainly not a small number of people and raises the question of why more people are not aware of the existence of intersexed people. The answer to this question is steeped in biomedical and surgical ethics.

Most intersexed children born in the United States have been surgically altered at birth and assigned to fit into the approved dimorphic sex categories. "People of mixed sex all but disappeared, not because they had become rarer, but because scientific methods classified them out of existence" (Fausto-Sterling, 2000, p. 39). Based on the theories of gender identity development initiated and instituted by John Money (1961; Money and Ehrhardt, 1972; Money, Hampson, and Hampson, 1955a; Money and Tucker, 1975), pediatric endocrinologists and urologists, with the support of the American Academy of Pediatrics (AAP), have routinely recommended surgical "correction" of ambiguous genitalia of intersexed infants (AAP, 1996a,b; Migeon, Berkovitz, and Brown, 1994; Donahoe and Schnitzer, 1996; Federman and Donahoe, 1995; Grumbrach and Conte, 1998).

These surgeries have been justified because of physicians' fears that these babies will develop confused gender identities due to their physical differences. The medical, surgical, and sexological experts have assumed that gender identity emanates as the logical outcome of physiological sex, and that the creation of a morphologically correct body can determine the internal experience of gender. The relationship between natal sex, physiology, and the development of gender identity is far more complex than surgically altering the genitalia of intersexed babies. Crouch (1999) said, "In the West, if one is neither a man nor a woman, then one has no social place or state to occupy" (p. 36).

Despite the lack of follow-up studies on surgically altered intersexed babies, when the AAP released its new guidelines in the summer of 2000, there were no discernible changes in the treatment strategies that had been historically employed. This is despite the tireless efforts of the ISNA under the guidance of Cheryl Chase, despite the publication of numerous accounts by survivors of genital surgeries (Alexander, 1999; Cameron, 1999; Colapinto, 2000; Coventry, 1999; Devore, 1999; Groveman, 1999; Laurent, 1995), and despite the proliferation of clinical research questioning the continuation of "business as usual" (Chase, 1999; Diamond and Sigmundson, 1997a,b; Lewis, 2000). At least the AAP has recognized the movement to reexamine intersex surgical guidelines from an ethical perspective, even if it was only to mention it by discounting it (AAP, 2000).

However, the existence of intersexed people stands as the most direct evidence that biological sex is not simply dimorphic and that calling a baby a "boy" or a "girl" is more of a social decision than a biological one. Simply put, "To be gendered, one must first be sexed, not intersexed" (Crouch, 1999, p. 36).

Sexism and Socialized Differences

Another difficulty with the premise of duality is that it presumes that males and females have different, diametrically opposed psychologies, behaviors, and experiences. The traits of one group are the antithesis of the other, e.g., males are stronger than females and females are more emotionally sensitive than males. However, if we list all gender markers there are none that are, in Kessler and McKenna's (1978) words, *"always and without exception"* true of only one gender (p. 1, italics in original). Many determinants of personality derive from these perceived differences, including career options and clothing choices. In reality, men and women are more like each other than they are different.

Although the feminist movement has taken us far since the 1960s, and no one could deny that the lives of women, individually as well as collectively, have changed in bold and blatant ways, gender-role expectations are still prescribed and restrictive. Although some of the more extreme and rigid boundaries of gendered social expectations have broken down in the past few decades due to the strides of the women's liberation movement, the basic bipolar assumption of male and female differences—based on genitalia and affecting all societal arenas—is mostly intact. Bem (1993) referred to this process of how socialization impacts and reinforces the development of gender appropriate behaviors in children as gender schema theory.

The social rules of gender are based on assumptions about the differences between males and females that are expressed in stereotypic masculine and feminine ways. Most gendered behavior is arbitrary. Although we have grown accustomed to blue for boys and pink for girls, it was only a few generations back that most babies wore white dresses. It is thought that the custom of blue for boys and pink for girls originated in 1929, when a midwife from Bologna, Italy, hung blue and pink ribbons to announce the birth of a child (Giuseppe Vidossi as cited by Belotti, 1975). An early feminist notecard outlined the arbitrary quality of gender polarization by showing two toddlers looking down into their diapers and one saying, "Oh, so that is what determines the difference in our paychecks." Boys are still expected to play with cars and action toys and girls are still expected to play with dolls. A brief viewing of the commercials during Saturday morning cartoons will easily prove this point.

Maintaining distinctions between men and women is a fundamental principle of the sex/gender system, and although it once organized society, it has outlived its functionality. Wittig (1982) felt that feminism itself bought into the "myth of woman," and reified the class of people called women, despite acknowledging that gender attributions were socially created (p. 106). Butler (1990) went so far as to suggest that "there is no gender identity behind the expressions of gender; that identity is performatively constituted by the very 'expressions' that are said to be its result" (p. 33). Transgenderism is so threatening to the status quo precisely because the existence of gender-variant people shows that the boundaries separating men from women are false.

In an interesting historical twist of fate women now have much greater freedom of dress than men do. The social costs are higher for men with only small clothing transgressions. Although men can wear their hair longer or even wear an earring (or two!), it is not unusual for men to be arrested for wearing women's clothing in public. However, female transvestism is no longer a diagnostic concept. Only men can be transvestites because women can wear almost anything they want without social disgrace.

Bisexuality and Homosexuality

Although a dimorphic gender system allows for both same- and opposite-sex relationships, it is inherently a heterosexist one. Homosexuality is allowed as the binary opposite of heterosexuality only to serve as a foil of "otherness," as a way to support the naturalness of heterosexual pairing (Katz, 1995). Rich (1980) analyzed this heterosexual imperative regarding the particulars of women's oppression and referred to it as "compulsory heterosexuality." This is the culturally mandated assumption that women are and will be heterosexual, and despite the rhetoric of sexual "preference," women are socialized into accepting heterosexuality as the only choice.

As stated earlier, the world is presumed to be engineered as a bipolar jigsaw puzzle, with sexually matching parts, which Butler (1990) referred to as "the heterosexualization of desire" (p. 23) (see Figure 3.3). Much of the resistance to the depathologizing of homosexual relationships, clinically and politically, has stemmed from the assumption that gay and lesbian relationships are against this "natural order." If male and female parts are naturally paired then it is reasonable to deduce that any male/male or female/female bonding is unnatural. This renders bisexual people—who probably represent a larger population than either heterosexuals or homosexuals—into a nonexistent category labeled "fence-sitters." Klein (1999) said that bisexu-

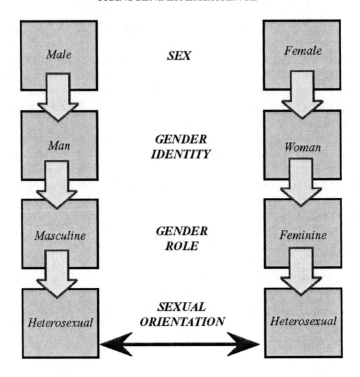

FIGURE 3.3. It is assumed that each of these components lines up and ensures the next.

→ if a person is a male, he is a man;
→ if a person is a man, he is masculine;
→ if a person is a masculine male man, he will be attracted to a feminine female woman;
→ if a person is a female, she is a woman;
→ if a person is a woman, she is feminine;
→ if a person is a feminine female woman, she will be attracted to a masculine male man.

als often have to contend with the myth that "they did not exist, i.e., that they were really gay or straight" (p. 132). Furthermore, since "male" and "female" are a dualistic binary, it creates a false assumption that female homosexuality and male homosexuality are also mirrored opposites (Blackwood and Wieringa, 1999a), a paradigm that not only fails to accurately reflect the gay and lesbian communities in the modern era, it reinforces the invisibility of bisexuals.

It is important to note that historically it was common for gender clinics to insist on a heterosexual postsurgical identity in order to approve a transsexual for surgery. Heterosexism was embedded into the very fabric of gender clinics and even "sex change" theorists could not conceive of "creating" homosexual persons. However, they could justify sex reassignment surgery to a skeptical public if it "fixed" previously homosexual people and made them heterosexual. Devor (1998) said, "Present classification systems are unable to capture adequately the subjective experience of posttransition transsexuals who identify and live as gay men and lesbians" (p. 253). A bipolar sexual system infers and reinforces a heterosexual world.

The Disappearance of Diversity

Another consequence of a dual gender assumption is that it makes invisible much of the diversity of humanity and creates the possibility of certain pathological, deviant, and diagnostic categories. In a dualistic system, certain groups of people simply cannot exist since their existence places them outside of the available categories of definition. Intersexed people, bisexual and homosexual people, and, of course, transgendered and transsexual people have all been rendered invisible or pathologized precisely because they call into question this bipolar system of sex and gender. Butler (1990) said, "Those bodily figures who do not fit into either gender fall outside the human, indeed, constitute the domain of the dehumanized and the abject against which the human itself is constituted" (p. 142).

The Assumption of Immutability

Once upon a time, western European culture thought there was one sex, which of course was male, and females were considered an incomplete and imperfect facsimile (Laqueur, 1990). However, the scientific study of the bipolar nature of human biology fashioned the sex/gender system as we now know it. It is viewed not only as a system of duality but also as an immutable and unchanging facet of human identity. The particulars may vary from era to era or culture to culture, but the basic yin/yang perspective invariably creates an immutable paradigm. Even the concept of the opposite or other sex describes our sense of diametrical distinction, the inability to exist as "both/and." Sex is not something that is considered changeable but is ordained at birth and permanently unalterable. Without this black-and-white division of male and female, our universe would not be divided into opposites that therefore become diametrically opposed (e.g., if men are strong then women are weak). It must also be noted that the very use of the expression "black-and-white" comes from a bipolar and racist paradigm that assumes black and white to be opposites, not variations. It assumes no gray areas at the same time that it assumes no biracial or mixed race people.

The last half of the twentieth century has seen great changes in the social fabric of society as women, and to a lesser extent men, have broken free of many previously prescribed roles. Although men and women have more freedom to move within these role categories, great prohibitions against stepping outside of them or crossing over to the other side of the binary still exist.

Much of the shock exhibited by the birth of an intersexed child, the news of a colleague's transsexual surgery, or the announcement of a heterosexual married friend's lesbianism is related to the belief that sex, gender, and sexual orientation are unchangeable, immutable facets of human nature. Even the gay liberation movement has fostered this belief system by building a civil rights movement based on the idea that homosexuality is innate and unchangeable and therefore natural. Homosexuality becomes socially acceptable when it is defined as inborn and intrinsic. The gay liberation movement, which began as a movement to liberate the homosexual within everyone (Altman, 1971), became politicized as a civil rights struggle for an oppressed minority, a people defined by their inability to change. People are as uncomfortable when a known homosexual has a relationship with someone of the opposite sex as they are when a heterosexual person comes out, in part because it reveals the fluidity and potentiality of sexual desire as natural to all humans.

Assigning a sex to an intersexed infant evokes anxiety precisely because it highlights the arbitrary nature of sex/gender assignment and provokes the fear that the assignment may be incorrect. Transsexuality further highlights the arbitrary categories of sex and gender when a "normally" sexed person reveals that his or her sex/gender assignment is incorrect; the individual is then cast in the role of an outlaw by transgressing these boundaries. Burch (1995) said, "Assignment of gender brings a profound sense of limitation" (p. 292) and stepping outside of the margins that have been assigned highlights the limits of those boundaries.

In reality, all of the categories of sexual identity described earlier have a flexible quality (see Figure 3.4). Each exists on a continuum, which allows for the existence of intersexed, bisexual, and transgendered/transsexual people and a diversity of sexual and gender styles of presentation. "Gender identity," as Bolin (1992) said, "is . . . socially mediated and dynamic rather than fixated and static" (p. 13). In any category people can change their behavior, presentation, or identity and none of these categories represents an immutable entity.

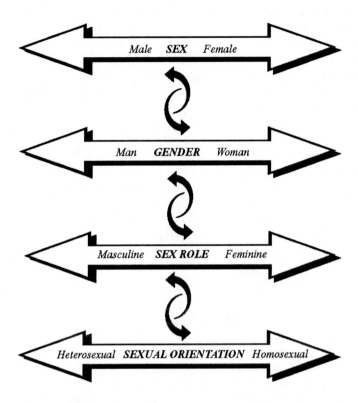

FIGURE 3.4. All components of identity are actually on a continuum. Sex, gender identity, gender-role expression, and sexual orientation are not mutually exclusive (i.e., moving in one direction does not necessarily mean that one cannot also move in the other direction).

If these components are not a binary, then people have flexibility as to where they fit on the continuum and can exist in more than one place at the same time. Intersexed people can, therefore, exist as both male and female simultaneously. This means that men and women do not have to choose between traditional and stereotypically gendered traits but can be androgynous, exhibiting traits of both masculinity and femininity simultaneously. This means options for gender variation exist beyond transsexualism as an act of crossing over from one sex to the other, allowing for a variety of transgendering presentations, including being bi-gendered. Sexual orientation is therefore not "either/or," but allows for bisexual identity, as well as flexible sexual expression throughout the life span.

Fluidity of sex and gender does not mean that any of these components of identity can (or should) be altered from the outside—e.g., gay people should not be "made" into heterosexuals, transsexuals should not be "made" into nontranssexuals, men should not be encouraged to be more virile, nor should women be encouraged to be more ladylike. Nor does it mean that one can simply change by an act of will. However, it does appear that these components can, and do, change for many people. Heterosexuals come-out gay and bisexual, lesbians and gay men can fall in love with someone of the opposite sex, and men and women can, and have, changed their sex assignment to one more congruent for them. Clearly there is fluidity in sexual and gender identity. This fluidity should not be interpreted, however, to infer that outside social forces should attempt to manipulate the sexual or gender identities of people or to minimize the oppression faced by people within certain social categories. The mutability of the component parts of sexual identity can, however, encourage society to broaden its acceptance of diverse experiences of gender and sexual expression.

The Assumption of Biological Determinism

The sex/gender system outlined earlier is presumed to develop naturally, one component part from the other, as if one was a natural outgrowth of the other. Like the Russian folk art of matrushka (nesting dolls), each component of identity is assumed to be secured within the one before it, creating a structure that is both developmental and sequential, determined by natal sex. It is not simply that male and female is a binary system but that "manhood" is an assumed subset of maleness, a natural outgrowth of maleness as it were. Masculinity is then an assumed component of manhood and how manhood is expressed. Each matrushka doll when opened has within it a masculine male man, who is of course heterosexual and attracted to his complementary opposite—a female who expresses womanhood through her femininity. This creates a perfect heterosexual matched unit (see Figure 3.3).

The entire discussion regarding sex and gender is, as Butler (1990) suggested, "always set within the terms of a hegemonic cultural discourse predicated on binary structures that appear as the language of universal rationality" (p. 13). To even begin to question the validity and universality of these concepts makes one appear irrational. To think outside of the box is to step outside of the agreed-upon and known universe. Whittig (1982), placed the known universe into a political perspective when she said, "Masculine/feminine, male/female are the categories which serve to conceal the fact that

social differences always belong to an economic, political, ideological order" (p. 64).

Nowhere is this clearer than examining the discomfort most people have
regarding intersexuality, which blurs the distinction between male and female
and consequently hetero- and homosexuality. As Fausto-Sterling (1993) said,

> Hermaphrodites have unruly bodies. They do not fall into a binary
> classification system . . . inasmuch as hermaphrodites literally em-
> body both sexes, they challenge traditional beliefs about sexual differ-
> ence: they possess the irritating ability to sometimes live as one sex
> and sometimes the other, and they raise the specter of homosexuality.
> (p. 24)

The current social discourse regarding intersexed people challenges our
very notions of a binary system of sexual orientation and desire.

Transgenderism also forces people to step outside of the bipolar division
of male and female and potentially allows not just another option, i.e.,
transitioning from the sex of birth to the gender of experience, but innumer-
able options for how one defines, experiences, and expresses his or her own
gender. In this sense, *transgenderism* is a radical term that tears down one of
the great sacred cows of our time: The division of the species into male and
female. Cromwell (1999) said that "transpeople . . . mix bodies and genders,
have intermediate genders and obfuscate the Western view of two and only
two genders" (p. 99). Transsexuality specifically challenges our way of
thinking because "transsexuals make explicit for us the usually tacit processes of gender attribution" (Shapiro, 1991, p. 257) and shows us not just
how transsexuals acquire a new gender, but how we all create the genders
we express.

The assumption of a binary, immutable developmental sequencing of sex
and gender not only restricts what we know but, to paraphrase Goldner
(1988), actually constrains what is possible to know. In Devor's (1997a)
words, "The dominant gender schema is a matrix of rules which govern the
organization of sex, gender, and sexuality." If the linkages between male/
man/masculinity/heterosexuality are broken, then numerous configurations
of identity, partnership, and expression are potentially birthed.

Gendered Sexuality: The Example of Transgendered Butches

The example of transgender butch identity will be used to illustrate the
complexity, conflation, and deconstruction of various components of sexual
and gender identity. The place where transgender identity meets sexual orientation creates a fascinating quagmire of definitions and identities within a

spectrum of masculine embodiment in females. Corbett (1998) suggested that "there may be forms of gender within homosexuality that contradict and move beyond the conventional categories of masculinity and femininity" (p. 353). The focus here on female masculinities is to counterbalance the historical attention on MTF literature in most major writing on transgenderism.

The relationship between sexual identity and gender identity is complicated, partially because it has been historically linked, for example, in the assumption that inverts were somehow both homosexual and transsexual. It is also complex because it has been conflated within the popular discourse; for example, many people believe that all effeminate males are homosexual. Researchers argue about the development of sexual orientation and gender identities, like the proverbial chicken-and-egg question, searching for which "came first" (Bailey and Zucker, 1995). For instance, Green (1987) proposed that gender identity develops first, influencing gender role and then sexual orientation, and Isay (1987, 1989) suggested the exact opposite developmental sequence—that early sexual preferences affect the development of gender role and identity. Nicolosi (1991) hypothesized that faulty gender identity development in males is caused by poor fathering and impacts the progression of male homosexuality. Freund and Blanchard (1983) questioned whether paternal distance was the *cause* or *effect* of the child's atypical gender expression or it was the early manifestations of the child's sexual orientation. It is possible that cross-gender identity and homoeroticism are both manifestations of the same underlying phenomenon (perhaps prenatal hormones or genetic underpinnings?) or that both are casually unique with neither one impacting the other. Bailey (2003) assumes a biological origin for femininity in males that can manifest as homosexuality or, in the extreme, transsexuality. Although Bailey denies that the search for etiological roots implies a search for a "cure," his descriptive language is seeped in sexist and homophobic commentary. Seeking scientific "truths" for human sexual and gender diversity often ends up emphasizing those that are more unusual, instead of focusing on the unique qualities of all sexual and gender expression. The relationship between sexual orientation and gender identity, whatever its cause, remains a complex one.

Although it may be easy to mark the difference between sexual orientation and gender identity on a chart or grid—clearly "love-object choice," e.g., sexual orientation, is different from internal gender identity—these components of identity are often more difficult to separate in the lives of people. These two separate components of human identity describe different phenomena; however, they often overlap and their relationship can be extremely complex. Social assumptions are often made that gay and lesbian people have cross-gendered identities and that people who are transgendered or transsexuals are gay. This is internalized by people struggling with sexual and/or gender identity issues. It is also true that many people who are gay, lesbian, or bisexual experience confusion about their gender and many people who are gender variant express confusion about their sexual orientation. In reality, gender-variant people can be homosexual, heterosexual, or bisexual and people of all sexual orientations can be transgendered.

It is by examining the gender performativity and expression within the lesbian and gay communities that the multitude of sexual and gender possibilities become highlighted. It is important to note that most gay men and lesbians, despite the stereotypes, present in the expected gender role of their sexed bodies. In other words, their identities as male/man/masculine (or female/woman/feminine) follow through as socially expected. It is their sexual orientation that "switches" categories. When people say that they can always recognize a gay person—referred to within the LGB community as "gaydar"—it is commonly gender variance that they are noting. The majority of LGB people are unrecognizable precisely because their gender is profoundly unremarkable.

It is also true, however, that some gay men and lesbians have always been "gender benders." Within the gay community, feminine males have been referred to as nellies or queens, and within the lesbian community, masculine females have been referred to as butches or dykes. Within certain subcultures of the gay and lesbian community, most notably those that identify as butch/femme, these identities have been an essential and core part of self-identity—not simply a gender-role expression but an expression of actual gender identity (Burana, Roxxie, and Due, 1994; Halberstam, 1998a; Kennedy and Davis, 1993; Munt, 1998; Nestle, 1992). Newton (2000) said, "This masculinity, my masculinity, is not external; it permeates and animates me. Nor is it a masquerade. In my home, when no one is present, I still sit with my legs carelessly flung apart" (p. 199). Furthermore she said, "This gay gender, butch, makes my body recognizable and it alone makes sexual love possible" (p. 197).

The early sexologists were correct in identifying "inverts" as both transvestites and homosexuals, although they were wrong to assume that this was the only form in which homosexuality, or transvestism for that matter, could express itself. Halberstam (1998a) said,

> Inversion as a theory of homosexuality folded gender variance and sexual preference into one economical package and attempted to explain all deviant behavior in terms of a firm and almost intuitive belief in a binary system of sexual stratification in which the stability of the terms "male" and "female" depended on the stability of the homosexual-heterosexual binary. (p. 82)

Cross-gendered identity—masculinity in females or femininity in males—can have many different meanings and experiences and cannot easily be judged on the outside without understanding phenomenologically the experiences of the person. Halberstam (1998a) said,

> There are many histories of bodies that escape and elude medical taxonomies, or bodies that never present themselves to the physician's gaze, or subjects who identify within categories that emerge as a consequence of sexual communities and not in relation to medical or psychosexual research. (p. 161)

Homosexual relationships are often referred to as same sex, signifying the importance of the genitalia of the partners, as well as the similarity of social roles for women-loving women (see Figure 3.5). However, same sex is not the same as same gender. Lesbian couples who identify as butch/femme are often experiencing a same-sex relationship (i.e., they are both females),

Lesbian

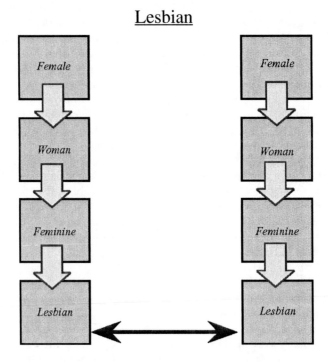

FIGURE 3.5. Attracted to same sex and same gender.

and yet an opposite gender relationship (i.e., they relate in a more man/woman, or masculine/feminine paradigm within female bodies) (see Figure 3.6). Inness and Lloyd (1996) identified four salient aspects of butch identity: she is a masculine woman (though "female" might be a better word here); she is like a man (but she is not one); she adopts an active sexual role; and/or desires femmes. Inness and Lloyd try to uncouple the association of butch with attraction to femmes, describing other partner choices and erotic attractions open to butches. It is also true that not all butches adopt an active sexual role. "Butch" is, to use Rubin's (1992) words, "a category of lesbian gender . . . lesbian vernacular . . . for women who are more comfortable with masculine gender codes, styles, or identities" (p. 467).

Halberstam (1998a) said, "Female masculinity is not simply the opposite of female femininity, nor is it a female version of male masculinity" (p. 29), and attempts to define "what" it is are just beginning. "Butch lesbians," said Cromwell (1999), "have masculine gender identities, but unlike FTMs and transmen, they do not identify as men" (p. 27).

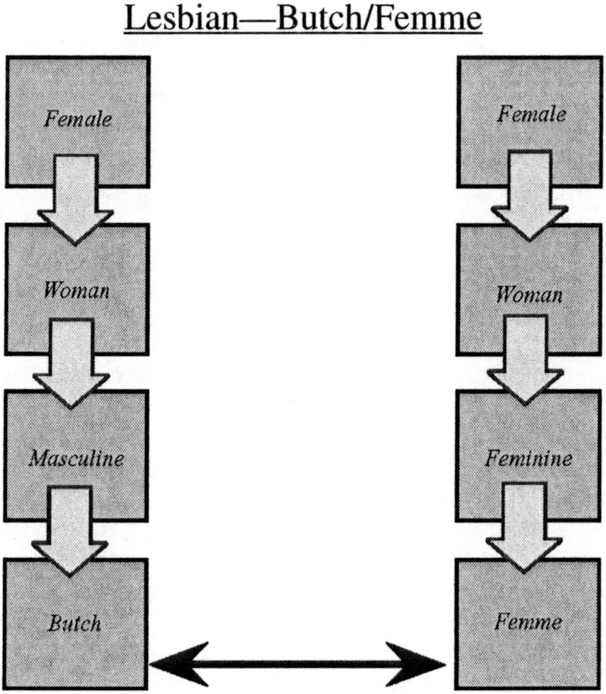

Lesbian—Butch/Femme

FIGURE 3.6. Attracted to same sex and opposite gender role.

Rather than a binary of butch lesbians on one side and FTM/transmen on the other, it is best to see masculine expression as spectrum of behavior and expression involving gender and sexual orientation. Some female-bodied masculine people do not identify as either transsexual or butch lesbians but see themselves as transgendered butches—a category that links the gender identity descriptions of the transsexual paradigm with the historical consciousness of lesbian-butch/femme role dynamics. They express their gender role in typically masculine ways and (to borrow from the masthead of the American Boyz [n.d.] organization) "were labeled female at birth but . . . feel that is not an accurate or complete description of who they are."

Transgendered butches may experience their bodies, sexuality, desires, and identity in many different ways. Some transgendered butches modify their bodies with hormones and/or surgeries and appear as males in public. Others use clothing, hairstyles, and how they move their bodies to connote masculinity. For some, their gender identity is congruent with a female body. Others experience dysphoria in their gender identity. Some transgendered butches identify as lesbian, since they prefer female partners, and others do not see themselves as lesbian because lesbian implies a "woman-to-woman" sexuality, and they do not see themselves as women. Since many have previously identified as lesbians, and are often partnered with women who still do identify as lesbians, they may have strong links to the lesbian community although they do not currently identify as either women or lesbians. Devor (1997a,b) noted that FTMs have often tried to fit themselves into the available social roles, and therefore many identified as lesbians since they were female-bodied and lovers with women, even though the fit was always awkward. Still other transgendered butches do not see themselves as lesbians because they are not sexually interested in other females. They may identify as gay men, although they are technically female bodied.

Eyler and Wright (1997) developed a nine-point gender scale that identifies a continuum of gender identification for genetic females with gender-blended self-perception. Although it is tempting to describe this as a continuum with butch lesbian on one end and female-to-male transsexual on the other (Halberstam, 1998a,b), there are butch lesbians with a strong male identification and transmen who still maintain a sense of themselves as female/woman or lesbian. As Halberstam (1998b) said, "There are many butches . . . [who] pass as men and many transsexuals who present as gender ambiguous, and many bodies that cannot be classified by the options of transsexual and butch" (p. 153). Halberstam warned the reader to avoid creating a "masculine continuum" that assumes butch to be less masculine—or less dysphoric—than transsexual. She said that "gender dysphoria [is not the] exclusive property of transsexual bodies" (Halberstam, 1998a, p. 151) and that more gender dysphoria does not necessarily create a more transsexual identification. Hale (1998) suggested that some butches "might have richer, more solid male or masculine self-identifications than do some [FTMs]" (p. 322) and Bolus (n.d.) said, "FTM identity is not simply the endpoint on the continuum of butch masculinity."

The line where butch/woman identity ends and trans/man identity begins is a territory still being mapped and the heated debate over identity boundaries has been called the "butch/FTM border war." Both FTMs and butches deploy "male signifiers, clothes, hair, mannerisms, and body movements" but they do so with "different motives" within "two different interpretative frames" (Rubin, 1996, p. 194). Rubin explained that "FTMs are men and lesbians are not, no matter how butch they are" (p. 98). He further said that because these borders are "still under construction," when "lesbians and female-to-male transsexuals confront one another they distinguish themselves from the other through a process of disidentification" (p. 98). Some FTMs have rejected their lesbian pasts, which they have come to see as a "mistaken identity" (Halberstam, 1998a, p. 150). For those who clearly experience themselves as transsexual, or as lesbian butches, this process of disidentification is paramount. However, for many transgendered butches it is not so easy to separate these parts of self within their own bodies.

A female couple—one partner appearing masculine (butch) identified and the other appearing more traditionally female—may identify as a lesbian couple, a butch/femme couple, or a heterosexual couple, depending on how gender and sexuality are defined by the couple themselves (see Figure 3.7). Living as a transgendered butch may involve a fluidity of shifting identities in which one passes in the world as a man, but identifies as transgendered among close friends, and yet still sees a gynecologist for routine checkups for his female anatomy. Devor referred to this as "gendered sexuality" (1997b) and explained how one can talk "with accuracy and without contradiction" about a relationship that is homosexual from the perspective of biology yet straight from the perspective of lived identities and social/sexual relationships (pp. xxv-xxvi). Pauly (1998) referred to this as the difference between those who are "homogenderal" and those who are "heterogenderal"—which privileges the importance of gender identity over the genitalia. Pauly (1992) also said that "the important variable is not the genetics of the relationship, but the gender status of two participants" (p. 7).

Of course, gender transitions do not take place in isolation but often impact significant others and their relationship to their own sexual identity. This is illustrated by a conversation that took place between a transgendered butch-identified "guy" who worked and passed in a traditional male job. He was in a long-term partnership that had been lesbian identified before he decided to transition, had chest surgery, and began hormone treatment. One day a co-worker asked him a question about his "wife." He told his co-

Transgendered Butch and Femme

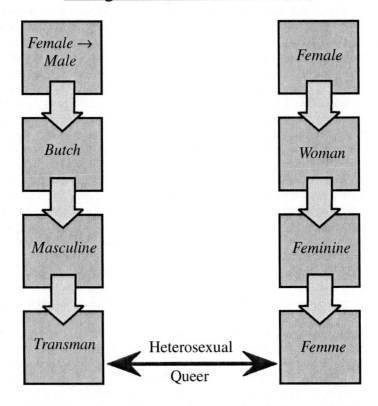

FIGURE 3.7. Attracted to opposite sex and opposite gender role.

worker that he was not legally married and was then asked, "Why not"? After stammering for a minute, struggling to explain his unique situation without revealing himself, he said, "Well, because she's a lesbian." Of course, the co-worker had no idea that the guy had lived most of his life as a "lesbian woman" and still had female genitalia underneath his male appearance. The co-worker was justifiably confused about why a man would partner with a lesbian, although the truth might have confused him even more. The transgendered butch had not changed his sexual orientation (i.e., his sexual desire for women remained constant)—it was his "wife's" sexual identity that was challenged by his transition. How could his wife retain her identity as a "lesbian" when she was partnered with a person who looked like and passed as a "man" in the outside world?

The subject of female masculinity—from butch lesbians and female cross-dressers to fully transitioned female transsexuals (or transmen)—has been historically invisible. Jamison Green (1998) wrote an overview of the history and current experience of female-to-male transsexuals and other female-bodied men and examined the segment of the FTM world that has historical roots in the lesbian-butch paradigm, as well as many other "types" of transmen and masculine females. He is committed to creating a space for "men with female histories" (Green, 2001, p. 62). Gary Bowen (2001, personal communication) said, "When I invented the term 'transman' I deliberately did it to provide a new transsexual term and identity. It was my first attempt to find a word for myself without the baggage of pathology and racism."

Gayle Rubin (1992) said, "Although important discontinuities separate lesbian butch experience and female-to-male experience, there are also significant points of connection . . . the boundaries between the categories of butch and transsexual are permeable" (p. 473). Some transgendered butches enjoy the fluidity of shifting gender identities, and others find this shifting deeply problematic. Each transgendered butch identifies somewhat differently. Many do not see themselves as women, most do not see themselves as men, and others see themselves as both men and women, preferring to identify as bi-gendered or "other" gendered—essentially, a third sex. Transgendered butch, butch lesbian, stone butch, transman (female transsexual), female man, and mandyke are words that attempt to define different experiences for masculinity in females.

Coming to gender congruence in the borderlands can be a complicated process. Dealing with this overlap of sexual and gender identities makes it difficult for clinicians, as well as the people embodying these complex identities, to sort out the meanings and develop a sense of congruence of identity. For those on the outside—e.g., psychotherapists—it may be especially difficult to sort out the gender expressions and meaning for masculine females presenting with gender dysphoria. Is a client with a lesbian past who is struggling with issues related to gender coming out as butch, transgendered, or transsexual? How does she or *he* redefine intimate relationships, comprehend her or *his* history, or define identity. Halberstam (1998a) said the issue of border wars assumes that "masculinity is a limited resource" (p. 144). Perhaps for those born female it has been.

It is not difficult to understand how sexual and gender identity can easily become conflated within the public's eye. Indeed much of the gay rights movement's focus of the past few decades has been to dispel misconceptions that gay people have cross-gender behavior. By and large, this has been successful. When professionals are queried during training sessions as to whether gay men are more "effeminate" than straight men, they immediately denounce that as a stereotype. However, when challenged about this position, and having determined that it is safe to ask difficult questions, professionals will often admit, "Yes, it does seem that many gay men are more effeminate that most heterosexual men. Why is that?"

Obviously, the answer to that question is not simple, but it is true that gender inversion has always been one aspect of the gay community. Although most gay men express and present their gender in a normative male/man/masculine manner and are therefore invisible as gay men, many gay men have gender role expressions that are feminine, and perhaps some have cross-gendered identities. Some cross-gender behavior has served as an entertainment element of the gay community (e.g., drag queens, female impersonators) and other cross-gender presentations have served as a way for cross-gendered individuals to recognize one another in what has been a hostile world. Wearing more feminine colors, wearing an earring, or expressing traditionally feminine mannerisms has served as "in-group" recognition. Gay men jokingly refer to one another as "Mary" or "Blanche," and idolize and imitate glamorous female movie stars such as Bette Davis. Green's (1987) longitudinal study of young "sissy" boys showed that many of these boys grow up to be gay, raising questions about the relationship of sexual and gender identities in early childhood development, including biological underpinnings.

Just as the gay community has denied cross-gender behavior in trying to gain social respect, many transgendered and transsexual people have tried to distance themselves from any association with the gay community. Some of this is, of course, simply homophobia, but it is also an attempt to separate what is actually an issue related to gender rather than sexual desire. In other words, a transsexual may appear to be homosexual, because they are in a same-sex relationship (pretransition), but they experience themselves in an opposite-sex relationship and are therefore heterosexual. The clinical community has continued to confuse this already-complex issue by insisting on utilizing nomenclature that refers to transsexuals as "homosexual" and "heterosexual," basing people's sexual identity on their natal sex, not their chosen gender.

Bockting and Coleman (1992) suggest that each component of sex identity should be assessed separately. The difficulty in this is that each component of identity interacts with other components of identity, creating endless possibilities for expression, and has been limited only by historical social and political parameters. "Gender," as Mitchell (2000) suggested, "is constructed within a relational context" (p. 233). Every descriptor and experience of gender or sexuality is seen through the lens of what is thought possible. Butler (1990) said, "If sexuality is culturally constructed within existing power relations, then the postulation of a normative sexuality that is 'before,' or 'outside,' or 'beyond' power is a cultural impossibility" (p. 40). It is very difficult to be something that has no name: naming calls identity into being. When the only names available that describe one's experience are associated with perversion, it can create a dissonance with one's own embodiment.

At the beginning of the twenty-first century, multiple expressions of sex and gender are better understood and the possibility exists for creating a society that accurately reflects the diversity of humankind. The understanding of these four separate components of identity that overlap and impact one another highlights the need to "dismantle not only androcentricism and biological essentialism, but also gender polarization and compulsory heterosexuality" (Bem, 1993). Rubin (1984) critiqued her own analysis of the sex/gender system and noted that it is not enough to see sex and gender oppression though a lens of feminist thought, but to understand that the sexual system takes place in the context of gender expectations and assumptions of sexual normativity. For example, she said that lesbians are not merely oppressed as women, but also "as queers and perverts" (p. 308). It is not only their biological sex status, or their social gender that is deemed inferior, but also their sexual desire.

When sex is not assumed to be dimorphic, it allows for the existence of intersexed people. When gender is not an assumed matter of binary opposites, it allows for transsexual, androgynous, bi-gendered, butch, nelly, crossdressing, and transgender identities. When sexual orientation is not limited to two choices, bisexuals are given social freedom and homosexuals and heterosexuals are allowed fluidity throughout their lifetimes. Some people fear that if society allows diverse gender expression and variant sexualities to proliferate then people will easily discard genders at will, freely engage in sexchange surgeries, and the institution of marriage will lose its scared and economic value. Halberstam (1998a) disagreed with those concerns. She said transgender discourse "asks only that we recognize the nonmale and nonfemale genders already in circulation and presently under construction" (p. 162). Bem (1995) took this one step further and suggested that instead of eliminating the gender-polarizing lens of Western systems, perhaps we should "begin madly and exuberantly to proliferate ourselves into as many categories of sex/gender/desire as we seem to need" (p. 333).

Mental health providers—social workers, psychologists, and counselors— have a powerful role to play in reexamining what has been considered normative regarding sex and gender identities. Fausto-Sterling (1993) reminded us that, "Scientific and medical understandings of multiple human sexes bring with them both the means to disrupt and the tools to reinforce dominant beliefs about sex and gender" (p. 77). It is a pivotal time for today's clinicians to decide whether to be social control agents or harbingers of social change and social justice.

PART II:
DIAGNOSIS AND ASSESSMENT

Chapter 4

Etiologies: Causes and Categories

In this particular field the evil of ignorance is magnified by our efforts
to suppress that which can never be suppressed, though in the effort of
suppression it may become perverted.

Havelock Ellis, 1897

Searching for the cause of gender-variant behavior has been a preoccupation of the clinical and medical community since sexologists first began presenting case material about inverts in the late nineteenth century. Indeed,
since their goal was to cure or treat gender dysphoria and/or to assist intersex people in achieving complete psychosexual congruity to an assigned
gender, understanding the etiology of gender development and cross-gender
behavior logically became the prevailing focal point of their research. Sexologists, researchers, and clinicians have classified and categorized various
"types" of gender variance according to presentation, severity of dysphoria,
the eroticism of the cross-dressing, and the person's sexual desires. In this
chapter many typologies will be explored that have been developed to assist
in a clinical understanding of gender identity concerns.

ETIOLOGICAL THEORIES: NATURE AND NURTURE— ESSENTIALLY CONSTRUCTED

The search for the etiology of gender-variant behavior has been broad
based and interdisciplinary, including scientific analyses of the human brain
and endocrine system, psychoanalytic forays into sex and gender development, cognitive-behavioral explorations into gender acquisition and social
learning, and feminist discourse on socialization and sex- and gender-based
oppression. These inquiries yield valuable and often fascinating information about human diversity and gender identity, although none has revealed
a unified theory to explain, define, or understand cross-gendered behavior.
Bockting and Coleman (1992) said, "There is no scientific consensus about
a single developmental pathway which leads to gender dysphoria. Determi-

nants of gender dysphoria remain controversial and hypothetical" (p. 113). Various theories will be briefly analyzed in addition to some of the controversies and difficulties inherent in each of them.

The very process of researching and seeking scientific facts about gender identity, and the assumption that there are laws of nature that can be uncovered and revealed as "proof" or "truth," ignores the position of the observer within his or her own social system (Keller, 1985; Caplan and Caplan, 1994). King (1993) said, "Science is not simply discovering . . . [a] phenomenon but is involved in its creation" (p. 3). Nowhere is this truer than in the study of sex and gender, which is replete with assumptions about the "correct" way to be gendered. Bruner (1986), commenting on scientific endeavors, said, "Though they create possible worlds, they leave no place in them for possible alternative personal perspectives on those worlds" (p. 54).

Feminists have long pointed out the androcentric biases inherent in most sciences, particularly those in which researchers try to find biological proof of male/female differences in thinking or personality (Bem, 1993; Bleier, 1984; Carroll, 1998). Kenen (1997) outlined the kind of circular reasoning that often accompanies the search for the etiology of sex and gender differences:

> [S]cientific research on homosexuality does not begin with random populations, but rather with groups of people who are defined as homosexual to begin with (by themselves, by scientists, or both); then, researchers search for a biological (or social) marker common to the group (whether it be a gene, a portion of the brain, or an overbearing mother); finally, if such a marker is found, homosexuality is redefined by the presence of the marker itself. In a curious way, then, each study can be said to reinvent its own object. (p. 197)

Irvine (1990) said, "Ultimately, of course, it is not a question of *whether* politics can infuse sexual science, but of what kind of politics *do* underpin the field" (p. 285). Ekins and King (1998) reminded students of transsexualism that it is not only the characteristics of those who are so labeled that need to be studied, but also "the behaviour of those medical practitioners [and] social workers . . . who, from a sociological point of view, are also part of what transsexualism means in our society" (p. 98).

An ongoing debate regarding the etiology of transgenderism has been over whether there is a biological essentialism of male and female that is transhistorical, transcultural, "natural," and "essential" that exists "independent of our knowledge" (King, 1993, p. 3) or whether social forces mold gender-transgressive—as well as normative—behaviors. Essentialist theory postulates that identities are inherent within human beings (e.g., "I was born gay") and biologically determined. Certainly the study of the brain and endocrine system continue to expand the knowledge base of the human body and its relationship to psychological forces. Some studies suggest that the family co-occurrence of gender dysphoria may be indicative of biological etiology (Green, 2000a). It is undeniable that biology sets a blueprint for sexual and gender expression, yet little is known about how this blueprint develops or is impacted by other variables, particularly environmental, familial, and systemic ones.

Social constructionists (see Gergen, 2000), on the other hand, deconstruct these "other" variables and hypothesize that human identities are social constructs that are not only defined differently but also experienced differently, depending on historical and sociological forces. Biological underpinnings may be influential but do not necessarily determine directionality, and they are always mediated within social milieus; Bem (1993) said a "failure to theorize biology in context" exists (p. 29). Social constructionism moves the debate beyond the question of how gender-variant identities develop and into the realm of analyzing the field in which some gender expressions are perceived of as normal and others rendered deviant.

In the past few decades postmodern scholars have examined the social construction of sexual and gender identities and have theorized that gender and sexuality are created or produced within differing social contexts (Chauncey, 1982; D'Emilio, 1983; Foucault, 1978; Freedman, 1995; Kitzinger, 1987; Laqueur, 1990; Plummer, 1981; Weeks, 1981). The categories of "transsexual" and "transvestite," it is suggested, must be seen within culturally specific contexts that do not simply provide different backgrounds for the same experience, but actually impact the development and manifestation of the phenomenon itself.

There is a tendency to pit biological theories of essentialism against social constructionist theories, although most researchers will concur that both biology and the social environment are dynamic and interactional (De Cecco and Elia, 1993). From the early writing of Freud there was awareness of the limitations of polarizing this argument: "The nature of inversion is explained neither by the hypothesis that it is innate nor by the alternative hypothesis that it is acquired" (Freud [1905] 1962, p. 6). As Udry (2000) said, "Humans form their social structures around gender because males and females have different and biologically influenced behavioral predispositions. Gendered social structure is a universal accommodation to this biological fact" (p. 454).

There has been an assumption that if sex and gender identity is "constructed [then] it is in some sense free, and if it is determined, it is in some sense fixed" (Butler, 1993, p. 94). Socially mediated identities, however, can also be severely restricted, precisely because they are pervasive and universalizing. Social constructionism does not describe a "free" process of picking and choosing identities but describes how the social world defines and limits the actual identities that are possible. As Goldner (1988) said, "The gendering of social spheres not only constrained personal freedom, but gender categories also determined what it was possible to know" (1988, p. 17). As the topic of gender variance becomes a part of the public discourse, academically as well as within popular culture, the definitions, parameters, and language for gender identities expands, allowing humans to "know" even greater possibilities for self-identity.

Unfortunately, clinical paradigms that are biologically driven, as well as those that are based in social constructions of identity development, can be used to pathologize and "cure" gender variance. Irvine (1990) said that a biological explanation based on a medical model "can raise the specter of disease and thus prevention," but "socially mediated factors can also engender responses aimed toward prevention or cure," such as the protection of young children from "deviants" (p. 244). Developing nonpathologizing models for gender variance does not rest in simple etiological explanations that are either biological or sociological in origin, but in the complex web and interconnections between the mind, body, and spirit.

The nature/nurture argument of gender-development theories has been centered in the past few years on the reexamination of the research of John Money. Money (1995) was the first to identify the very concept of gender identity as separate from biological sex. He was an early proponent of sex reassignment surgery (SRS) for transsexuals and was instrumental in opening the first clinic specializing in SRS at Johns Hopkins University. Money believed that the sex a child was reared in was more influential than their biological or genetic sex. He said, "Gender dimorphic patterns of rearing have an extraordinary influence on shaping a child's psychosexual differentiation and the ultimate outcome of a female or male gender identity" (Money and Ehrhardt, 1972, pp. 144-145).

Money and his colleagues at Johns Hopkins theorized that gender identity was somewhat fluid before the age of three years old and encouraged the assignment of sex before the age of eighteen months in cases of intersexed infants or those whose genitals had been damaged. They believed gender identity was not "formed," so the child could be successfully raised in the opposite sex without negative consequences (Money, 1961; Money and Ehrhardt, 1972; Money, Hampson, and Hampson, 1955a,b, 1956, 1957; Money and Tucker, 1975).

In 1966, a case was presented to Money that would become the index case for the surgical alteration of intersexed children for the next thirty years, although the child was not actually intersexed (Colapinto, 1997, 2000; Money, 1975). David (a.k.a. Bruce) Reimer was less than one year old when his penis was accidentally destroyed during a routine circumcision. The case represented a perfect test for Money's theory of gender identity. Since David was an identical twin, his brother offered the scientists a "control case" for comparison. Under Money's guidance, David was surgically reassigned as a girl, and the family was coached on how to raise their twins, a son and their new daughter. For the next two decades this bold experiment, known in the literature as the John/Joan case, was lauded as substantiation for the theory of psychosexual neutrality of infants. Nurture, it was determined, was more powerful than nature.

Milton Diamond, a professor of anatomy and reproductive biology at the University of Hawaii, was skeptical of the research proving psychosexual neutrality and had for many years attempted to challenge Money's claims. It was not, however, easy to dispute someone who was often referred to as the greatest sex researcher of the century. Undaunted, Diamond challenged Money's theories and, as early as 1965 when he was a young graduate student, questioned the role of prenatal hormones in the formation of gender identity and suggested that gender may be hard-wired in the brain (Diamond, 1965). Intersexuals, he said, had psychosexual neutrality precisely because there was an ambiguity not only in the genitalia but also in their brain chemistry or chemical makeup. Despite receiving little recognition for his work, Diamond continued to study and publish his concerns regarding Money's theories and, in the words of Fausto-Sterling (2000), pursued Money "with a determination worthy of Inspector Javert in *Les Misérables*" (p. 69).

Diamond sought to make contact with the clinicians who had followed the case of the "twins" and, in the late 1990s, he connected with Dr. Keith Sigmundson, a psychiatrist with the Canadian Ministry of Health who had treated David during his teenage years when he had lived as a girl. Diamond and Sigmundson began to work in collaboration (Diamond and Sigmundson, 1997b). Sigmundson revealed that, despite Money's claims in the literature regarding David's adaptation to a female gender—i.e., "Her behavior is so normally that of an active little girl" (Money, 1975)—David had never been successful in this role. The case report showed a depressed girl who dressed and acted "like a boy" and was in scholastic as well as emotional trouble. Professionals who presumably knew nothing about the sex-change history noted David's "male" behavior. In fact, the truth was finally revealed that in the late 1970s David had stopped living as a girl, had his breasts removed, and had a penis reconstructed. He was now married and living as a man with his wife and three adopted children. The case that had been presented as proof that gender identity was malleable, if assignment was made early enough in life, and used to justify the early surgical treatment of intersexed babies was finally exposed to be a farce.

Despite Money's claims, it appears that babies—possibly even inter-sexed babies—are not born completely psychosexually neutral but have some underlying biological blueprint that made them "boys" or "girls." However, clearly biology is not the only variable in the development of gender identity, since the majority of transsexuals have normative biologically male or female bodies. It is also true that environmental issues impact cases such as David Reimer's, not the least of which is the secrecy and emotional intensity surrounding the "sex-change" and the coercive attempts at feminization (Hausman, 2000), as well as the parents' unresolved guilt, concerns, and fears for the child.

Money (1998) said, "At each polar extreme, biological determinism and social constructionism run to monomaniacal fanaticism" (p. 299), and indeed Money's beliefs about the power of social construction in the development of gender has made opponents see him as monomaniacal. In all fairness, a thorough reading of Money's research as well as Diamond's over a forty-year period show that both men were aware of the interaction of biology and the environment, nature and nurture (Zucker, 1996a). As societal mores shift back and forth from biological essentialism to social constructionism, these two men have served as cornerstones to what is certainly a complex and fascinating examination of sex and identity. Gender identity is not simply a matter of rearing, and yet it is also not simply a matter of biology. The relationship between biology and social forces appears to be extremely intricate.

Various explanations for transgenderism are briefly outlined in the following sections and it is probably best to examine each of these theoretical positions as one of many elements involved in the development of all gender identities, as well as those that are variant.

Biological Theories

Scientists and researchers have studied the biological etiology of cross-gender experience with interest and precision. They have searched genetic and chromosomal determinants, biochemical and neuro-physiological factors, often linking the etiology of homosexuality and transsexuality to similar processes. They have examined early fetal development including theories of prenatal maternal stress. No abnormalities in chromosomal patterns, gonads or genitals, or sex-steroid levels have been found to be etiological in development of transsexualism (Gooren, 1990). There have been studies over the years linking transsexualism to electroencephalogram (EEG) abnormalities, left-handedness, height in those born male, and polycystic ovarian syndrome in those born female. Other studies have examined family history, comparative twin studies, and prenatal sex hormones (see Ettner and Brown, 1999; Michel, Mormont, and Legros, 2001; Zucker and Bradley, 1995), for a review of these studies).

Newer studies are examining gender identity development and its relationship to hormone-induced cephalic differentiation at critical gestational stages (Dorner et al., 1991). Most recently there has been substantial progress in the studies of neurobiological differences in the structure and function of the brain. These studies have shown that the brains of male-to-female transsexuals exhibit changes in the central part of the bed nucleus of the stria terminalis (BSTc). These somatostatin neuronal sex differences in the BSTc are altered and "crossed" showing a female brain structure in genetically male transsexuals (Kruijver et al., 2000; Zhou et al., 1995).

Even those who believe that cross-gender identity is a product of environmental interactions suspect that biology may play a role in "inducing a vulnerability that then allows the psychosocial factors within the family to exert their effect" (Bradley, 1985, p. 175). Indeed, it is not just researchers who have searched for biological cause, but transsexuals themselves who have expressed hopefulness that finding biological markers would somehow validate what otherwise feels inexplicable. Clients often request chromosomal and hormonal testing. Rarely, however, do these laboratory tests reveal any obvious cross-sex markers.

The biomedical model of sexology has been a predominant paradigm in examining cross-gender identity, leading Irvine (1990) to say, "The creation of the dysfunction called transsexualism represents the epitome of the medicalization of a broader sociopolitical crisis around gender" (p. 265). The difficulty with searching for causes within a medical model is that it is often translated into treatments promising "cures." The mistake may be in assuming that the etiology of transsexuality (and homosexuality) is uni-causal instead of multivariant. As Ross (1986) said, "It may well be that there are different types of gender dysphoria, some with biological contributors, some with familial contributors, and some with primarily psychological and social contributors" (p. 16).

If biological underpinnings are eventually found, which many believe is likely, how will this impact a young civil rights movement's desire for equal citizenship? Bleier (1984) theorizes that biological deterministic thinking in studies of human behavior often "surges at times of political and social upheaval" (p. 5). Biological causation is a double-edged sword offering potentially both a "natural" explanation as well as the possibility for an eradication of the disease, i.e., a final solution to the problem. Clearly, whatever biological influences exist on gender development, they are impacted by psychosocial and environmental determinants, not the least of which is the social value placed on normative versus deviant expressions of gender.

Psychoanalytic Theories

Many psychological theories of gender identity development have their roots in Freudian-based psychoanalytic and object-relations theory. Freud ([1905, 1923, 1925, 1931, 1933] 1962) postulated that infants had a "psychic bisexuality," referring not so much to their ability to be attracted to both sexes, but to their possession of the attributes of both males and females. Very young children do not differentiate themselves as boys or girls and gender identity development—whether a child matured as a boy or girl—depended on socializing influences. Freud theorized that at about three years old, boys became aware that there were people who did not have penises (as they did) and that this evoked a fear of castration. Girls, according to Freud, did not have a sense of their own femaleness until they reached the phallic stage, where they noticed that some people had penises and reacted to this with envy. Mitchell (2000) explains this by saying,

> Women are missing the male organ, so their longing is fantastic and must be renounced. Men are missing passive feelings vis-à-vis other men, which they dread because these feelings are associated with femininity and castration. Men have all the organs they could possibly want; they need to overcome childlike, illusory fears. Women lack the most valued organ; they need to renounce their impossible striving for it. (p. 236)

Critiques of Freud's theory are abundant (see Kleeman, 1971), but it is important to notice that in his theory possession of the penis, as a symbol of masculinity, was essential to male development, and its absence was the main characteristic of female development. Apparently, Freud did not consider that a girl's reaction upon discovering that boys have penises might be one of pity or revulsion, seeing it as an added appendage or growth. Many parents note that boys are equally envious when they realize that girls can carry and birth babies. Penis envy is probably less related to a girl's anatomical deprivation than a desire for the power that a penis represents in a patriarchal world (Chodorow, 1978; Horney, 1967).

According to Freud, gender identity emerges when children identify with their same-sex parent. Since the mother is the first love object for both boys and girls, in order to grow a healthy male identity, boys must learn to separate from their mothers and identify with their fathers. Girls must learn to become like their mothers and desire their fathers. Healthy gender development means cleansing one's self of the "other" gender, which will then culminate in a normative heterosexual identity. Male and female identity, according to this theory, develops in repression of a natural bisexuality. In this view, both homosexuality and transgendered expression are developmental arrests manifesting in cross-gender identification caused by faulty early parenting, particularly mothering. Indeed, feminist analysis has long noted that Freud's theory has not adequately explained "normal heterosexual" women's development since girls do not have to separate from their mothers in the same way that boys do (Chodorow, 1978; Dinnerstein, 1977; Fast, 1984).

Elaborating from this basic theory of gender acquisition, gender disturbances are thought to be the result of difficulties in object relations caused by faulty mother/child relationships (Person and Ovesey, 1976; Stoller, 1966, 1974). In this interpretation, the mother's clothing becomes a transitional object for the cross-dressing male, and female cross-dressing is experienced as a symbolic bonding with the father, especially as a way to identify with his superior power in a patriarchal world. Essentially, gender-variant behavior is seen as related to dominant, overprotective mothers who smother their children and who are usually married to ineffective, distant men. The focus in the literature is on cross-gender-identified boys, with little research on girls. Stoller (1968b), who wrote extensively on transgenderism from a psychoanalytic framework, said,

> The mothers do not permit normal separation to occur, as a result of which the infant cannot adequately tell where his mother ends and he begins. Then . . . [because] he does not have a man present as an object for identification . . . he is . . . left unshielded from *the malignant effect* of his mother's excessive closeness. (p. 102, italics mine)

In Coates, Friedman, and Wolfe's (1991) assessment these mothers are controlling, anxious, and intrusive. They have difficulty separating from their sons, causing them to develop a traumatized attachment-and-separation anxiety.

Mother-blame theories are endemic in psychoanalytic thinking and have impacted virtually all therapeutic modalities since Philip Wylie (1942) coined the term *momism* to label the toxic influence of mothers on their innocent offspring. Mothers have been blamed for everything from alcohol abuse to anorexia, physical health problems, obsessive-compulsive disorder, and aggression. In one study of 125 articles written by mental health professionals for their scholarly journals, it was found that mothers were blamed for seventy-two different kinds of problems in their offspring, ranging from bed-wetting to schizophrenia (Caplan and Hall-McCorquodale, 1985). It should, therefore, not be surprising that they are also blamed for apparent psychosexual disturbances, homosexuality, and gender identity variations.

Feminists have consistently criticized this mother-blame position as an outdated and destructive way to envision family life or parenting (see Caplan and Caplan, 1994; Hare-Mustin, 1991; Hare-Mustin and Broderick, 1979; Luepnitz, 1992; McGoldrick, Anderson, and Walsh, 1991; Silverstein and Rashbaum, 1995; Walters, Carter, and Silverstein, 1992). Women "do not adapt well enough to the baby's needs and, therefore, mothers are blamed for the baby's ego splits and later pathology" (Okun, 1992, p. 39). Prior to the feminist analysis, the literature had not acknowledged the changing role of women in society, the demands placed on mothers, and the privacy and isolation of the nuclear family. Despite nearly forty years of critique, psychoanalytically based theories of transgenderism continue to blame mothers for the development of cross-gender behavior, particularly in sons. A few examples will suffice.

Stoller (1975) blamed gender dysphoria on a "blissful symbiosis" in the mother-son dyad and Person and Ovesey (1984) identified "merger fantasies" and overidentification with the mother. This excessive closeness of the mother-son relationship has been linked to the etiology of homosexuality as well as transsexualism. Bieber et al. (1962) referred to the boys' "extraordinary intimacy with mother," and Saghir and Robins (1973) spoke of the mothers of homosexual men as "overbearing." However, Green's (1987) extensive study on gender-dysphoric boys showed they were separated more frequently from their mothers and for longer duration, and Coates (1990; Coates and Person, 1985) saw a strong connection between mother loss and gender disturbances. Either way, the mothers are to blame for being overinvolved or unavailable.

Many psychotherapists who are not psychoanalysts have been impacted by mother-blame theories. For instance, Zucker and Bradley (1995) said that mothers of gender-dysphoric boys are intimidated by male aggression and encourage femininity as a way to encourage nurturance. Fathers are viewed as passive men who go along with mothers. The mothers are identified as being insecure and temperamentally vulnerable with difficulty managing their affect, which then increases the boys' anxiety. Some theorists have gone so far as to state that the mothers themselves have gender identity conflicts, including cross-dressing experiences and that their mothers were "empty" and deficient, and so they became masculine and bisexual women who then created feminine sons (Stoller, 1968a,b, 1975). This is exemplified in the following analysis by Stoller (1968b):

> [A] strongly bisexual woman, with severe penis envy derived from her father and older brothers, in its turn the result of a sense of emptiness produced by her mother, married an empty man and had a son . . . the boy was (the phallus) of her flesh [and] . . . he was clearly a male and

no longer of her flesh. He was . . . kept as a part of herself, by identification, and treated as an object whom she would feminize. He was his *mother's feminized phallus.* (p. 120, italics mine)

Some theorists blame fathers for causing both homosexuality and transsexuality. The latter is often assumed to be a more serious form of the former (Bailey, 2003; Bieber et al., 1962, Rekers, 1995b; Socarides, 1969, 1982). Nicolosi (1991) said, "The homosexual condition is a developmental problem—and one that often results from early problems between father and son . . . Failure to fully *gender-identify* results in alienation not only from father, but from male peers in childhood" (p. xvi, italics mine). These paternally induced psychopathologies allegedly are caused by a father absence that does not allow the growing boy to bond and identify properly with masculinity. Stoller (1973) said, "I believe that homosexuality can be roughly quantified according to the intensity of transsexual wishes. For males, those with the least transsexual desire are the most masculine. . . . Those who are most feminine (which indicates powerful transsexual wishes) . . . have no heterosexual needs to speak of" (p. 282).

Lothstein (1992) summed up these psychoanalytic theories in saying,

the child's gender identity confusions and inner self structures were molded by the parents in an effort to control their son's body and mind and prohibit him from ever separating and individuating from mother and revealing father's deficiencies as a caregiver, an intimate person, and a male . . . they jointly collaborated . . . to feminize their son [and] they were disappointed with the final product. (p. 102)

Clearly the child in this scenario is a male child. Although many have commented on the excellent "bill of health" most researchers have given females with gender dysphoria, Lothstein disputed this, seeing female-to-male transsexuals as exhibiting serious mental health problems. Stoller (1972) developed a psychoanalytically framed theory regarding the etiology of female-to-male transsexualism, which classically describes a mother, who is psychologically depressed and removed from the family, and a passive father. The "transsexual-to-be" is the daughter who serves as a surrogate husband. Lothstein (1983), who authored the first book focusing on FTM transsexuals, was also psychoanalytically based and believed that gender disorders had their root in preoedipal development. He disputed the "stability" of female-born transsexuals and believed that high numbers of FTMs exhibited severe mental health disturbances and chronic adjustment problems. He thought they had personality disorders and subtle thought disorders caused by dysfunctional and chaotic family patterns that supported and encouraged cross-gender expression.

Of course, psychoanalytic thinking has continued to grow and develop beyond Freud's original theses, and many clinicians today acknowledge the need to incorporate both male and female aspects of self (Fast, 1984; Winnicott, 1966) as well as the need to look at the role of the wider environment in intrapsychic development. However, the literature on the etiology of cross-gender behavior in childhood often relies on outdated and sexist views of gender development, family-induced psychopathology, and psychoanalytic theory itself.

Cognitive-Behavioral and Social Learning Theories

It is clear that many aspects of gender may be linked to socialization, learning, and cognitive processes. All theorists would maintain that the social environment plays an important role in the development of gender roles and that human beings are products of their environment, although the actual impact of how gender develops and is enacted within various social milieus is still unclear. According to Doctor (1988), "It is experience which shapes not only the sexual preferences of a person, but the entire set of complex cognitive determinants that guide behavior" (p. 2).

Kohlberg (1966) did not see children's gender development as emanating from external socialization, but rather from cognitive processes within the child. He identified three cognitive developmental stages. The first stage is called gender identity, in which children around two years old are able to label themselves and others as boys or girls. However, this is based on gendered physical characteristics such as clothing styles, i.e., the child assumes that gender changes if clothing is changed. By three or four years old children enter the second stage, which is called gender stability, and with it comes the understanding that gender remains the same throughout time and that little girls will grow up to be women and not men. Stage three, gender consistency, which children reach at about age five, describes the developmental process whereby children understand that gender remains the same throughout time and situations. For Kohlberg, the way children label and categorize themselves as a boy or girl is central to the organization of their gender identity. Zucker et al. (1999) examined what they called a "development lag" in the development of some children's gender consistency, assuming that the children are "delayed" in accepting their true gender. Zucker and colleagues did not question whether the lag is a conscious resistance to accepting a false identity.

It is easy to understand why a gender-variant person might resist seeing gender as either "stable" or "constant." One could argue that believing that gender is a fundamental and unchanging aspect of self is simply inaccurate, since gender (attributions, behaviors, appearance, and identities) can and do change throughout both time and situations. Gender-variant children who are "failing" to develop according to the normative principles as applied to their genitalia might not be developmentally arrested but actually be expressing their own innate intelligence about their own identity. Studies of sex-category constancy (SCC) in children have shown inconsistent results (Szkrybalo and Ruble, 1999), and numerous variables have been suggested to explain this. None of the suggestions question the phenomenological experience of the children themselves. A gender-variant child would, by definition, not develop gender constancy, for to do so would deny their basic experience of their own identity. Indeed, if gender identity is assumed to start with a child's cognitions, it would be appropriate for a cross-gendered child to "naturally" know his or her core gender identity, even when it did not match his or her sex. Kohlberg (1966) said, "Once the boy has stably categorized himself as a male, he then values positively those objects and acts consistent with his gender identity" (p. 89). This statement could still be accurate if the boy happened to be in a female body.

A main premise of cognitive-behavioral and social learning theorists is that all gender-related behaviors are learned, primarily from role modeling the same-sex parent. Through the process of imitation and role modeling and receiving proper social rewards and punishments, gender behavior becomes reinforced and adopted. Contemporary social learning theorists and cognitive learning specialists believe that same-sex modeling and imitation as well as differential reinforcement are instrumental in the development of normative gender identity (Golombok and Fivush, 1994). These models have assumed that gender identity development is reflective of parental socialization. Feminist theorists have thought that it is not merely parents or even teachers who socialize children into gender polarizations, but the framework of society itself, which Bem (1993) referred to as gender schema. She believed that the very cognitive developmental process in which children engaged was embedded within a socialized gender blueprint.

Doctor (1988) examined the role of sexual scripts in the development and maintenance of erotic cross-dressing. *Sexual scripts* is Gagnon and Simon's (1973) term to explain the social activities that are reproduced to create our sexual selves, a dance of sorts, in which our erotic selves are socialized. Sexual scripts involve cognitive processes and organize erotic ideation and sexual excitement. They become conditioned and reinforcing. In this model, cross-dressers develop sexual scripts involving their feminized selves. The cross-dressing script is reinforced because the cross-dresser experiences a sense of lowered anxiety and sense of relaxation and comfort from cross-dressing.

The majority of treatment modalities to modify cross-gender behavior have originated within these cognitive-behavioral and social learning schools. A person with a gender-variant identity would be viewed through a cognitive social-learning lens as having been poorly socialized and/or developmentally impaired. Rekers and Jurich (1983) said that social-learning variables "have been considered to be the main source of sex-role deviance in childhood and adolescence" (p. 797). Treatment, especially "preventative" treatment for children, has been focused on targeting cross-gender behaviors and extinguishing or punishing those behaviors that are inappropriate (e.g., playing with Barbie dolls for boys) and rewarding "proper" gender behaviors (e.g., playing with makeup for girls). These practices evoke ethical questions about both social learning as well as social control.

Feminist Theory

The early feminist movement found great solace in the ideas of socialization and learning theory at a time when biology was assumed to be destiny and destiny for women meant a severely restricted life. Feminists recognized that in virtually all cultures the roles, tasks, and expectations of male and female behavior have been divided along gender lines and these differences were rule-laden and nonnegotiable. The women's liberation movement called into question the role divisions of male and female, stating that the differences between males and females were culturally determined, not bound by either biology or theology.

Feminism embraced the ideas of social learning theorists and used them as underpinnings to examine the institutionalization of sexism. If gender had been socially constructed, feminist theory postulated, it should be easy to deconstruct it and build a more egalitarian relationship between the sexes. Feminism offered a powerful analysis with which to examine the restrictions of a gendered world and an even more powerful set of tools with which to dismantle a patriarchal power structure that had disempowered women. Despite the great gains of feminism in the past four decades, many feminists soon discovered that it was not so easy to dismantle sexist thinking since it was embedded epistemologically in the very framework of society. Goldner (1988) said,

> It was no longer a matter of demanding equal access to a man's world, but of asking what the world would be like if women had equal access in creating it . . . gender could no longer be conceptualized as simply a bar-

rier to be transcended, because it was itself a metaphysical category, a central organizing principle of knowledge and culture. (pp. 17-18)

Many feminist theoreticians have shown that gender expectations start when children are newborn, and affect how parents, particularly mothers, interact with their infants. Numerous studies have shown that adults actually modify their behaviors toward infants by treating babies perceived to be girls differently than babies who are assumed to be boys (Hoffman, 1977; Leone and Robertson, 1989; Paludi, 1998; Rubin, Provenazano, and Luria, 1974; Seavey, Katz, and Zalk, 1975; Smith and Lloyd, 1978; Stern and Karraker, 1989). Studies show that girl babies are thought to be prettier, softer, and more fragile, and are interacted with more than boy babies are (Wasserman and Lewis, 1985).

Researchers have also examined how society perpetuates stereotypical gender roles in schools (Gilbert and Taylor, 1991), children's stories (Davies, 1989), and how children are dressed (Paoletti, 1987). Studies have shown that boy and girls are given very different toys to play with (Etaugh and Liss, 1992; Miller, 1987; Pomerleau et al., 1990) and that boys' toys involve more spatial skills and girls' toys are directed toward domestic chores (Tracy, 1987). Despite the advances of the feminist movement, a mid-1980s examination of toy catalogs revealed that little has changed over time (Schwartz and Markham, 1985). Thorne (1993) echoed the feminist position on socialization when she said, "Parents dress infant girls in pink and blue, give then gender-differentiated names and toys and expect them to act differently, . . . if boys and girls are different, they are made that way" (p. 2). Fagot el al. (1985) showed how teachers communicated differently to boys and girls and how such differential communication modeled the children's behavior so that one year later they became gender differentiated in traditional gender patterns.

Questioning the dimorphic nature of sex and gender may seem as if it is a natural outgrowth of the feminist movement, but it has actually been a source of deep resistance. The transgender liberation movement has been met with hostility and opposition from the women's movement, when it has been met at all. Irvine (1990) said transsexualism was "one of several barometers that revealed the theoretical tensions within feminism" (p. 269). The feminist movement has not called into question the actual bipolar nature of the sex and gender system; rather it has advocated for egalitarian treatment of all people regardless of their designation. Feminism, although originally committed to deconstructing "natural" definitions of gender, evolved into a movement that has generally accepted a dichotomous sex and gender system, often bordering on an essentialism of "woman" identity at least in a political framework if not a biological one. Feinberg (1998) said,

"Women's oppression can't be effectively fought without incorporating the battle against gender oppression. The two systems of oppression are intricately linked" (p. 17).

However, the premise of two sexes, male and female, is accepted as a given (as evidenced by the near silence in feminist publications addressing issues of intersexuality) and the focus becomes the examination of power imbalances between the two sexes. Within the feminist discourse, transsexualism, particularly male-to-female transsexualism, was seen as an outgrowth of the limitations on male and female behavior. In a nonsexist, liberated world people could act, dress, behave as they wanted to and would not want to "mutilate" or sex-change their bodies, which was interpreted as a kind of "antiwoman" hatred.

Janice Raymond's 1979 book, *The Transsexual Empire: The Making of the She-Male* became the voice of the feminist movement's analysis of transsexualism, but it was a book far more widely read—and critiqued—within the transsexual community than it ever was seminal reading material within radical feminist circles. Deeply transphobic, Raymond's book presented transsexualism as a patriarchal plot that encourages traditional gender roles. She said that transsexualism "constitutes a sociopolitical program that is undercutting the movement to eradicate sex role stereotyping and oppression in the culture" (p. 5). In this model transsexualism is caused by rigid stereotypical gender roles and expectations. The accoutrements of womanhood—those items which define femininity—are seen as reinforcing patriarchal standards for the making of woman according to man's image for those born female as well as those who are (in Raymond's words) "male-to-constructed-females" (p. 27).

Transsexualism, in this view, serves to maintain the gender system by reinforcing the idea that there are two binary groups, male and female, and one can simply move from one to the other. Raymond (1979) said it "only reinforces the society and social norms that produced transsexualism" (p. 18). Germaine Greer (2000), another outspoken feminist who claimed that male-to-female transsexualism reinforces socially mandated gender roles, does not believe that sex reassignment actually turns a biological man into a woman. Feminists do not see transsexualism as a radical political movement for the deconstruction of gender but a perpetuation of the binary system through technological enhancement. Sheila Jeffreys (1997) outlined a "lesbian-feminist perspective" of transsexualism and said that transsexualism is "deeply reactionary, a way of preventing the disruption and elimination of gender roles which lies at the basis of the feminist project" (p. 56). She suggested that sex reassignment surgery is a form of self-mutilation and should be considered a human rights violation. She recommended working toward making SRS illegal as part of the lesbian-feminist agenda. Male cross-dressing, including displays of drag behavior, popular theatrics of the gay male community, were also viewed as disrespectful of women and parodying the worst symbols of women's oppression. Male-to-female transsexuals are viewed as repressed homosexuals (Jeffreys, 1997).

It was not only sex reassignment in natal males that the second wave of feminism was critical of in its birthing of a new understanding of womanhood. It also silenced certain female identities that did not fit the developing vision of women liberation. Butch and femme identities became particularly targeted as mimicry of heterosexual patriarchal images and lesbians were accused of role-playing male and female behavior because it was the only avenue open for them to express lesbian love. Butch lives were explained as choices made within the confines of a sexist culture in which lesbians passed as men for safety or economic security and for the ease it would afford a lesbian couple to live as an apparent heterosexual couple. The male clothing of the butch was not seen as a political statement about women's possibilities but rather as evidence of male-identification. The femme's more traditional clothing and her caretaking of the butch was seen as "buying into" patriarchal ideas of femininity (Jeffreys, 1994; Harne and Miller, 1996).

In order to mobilize as a political movement based in existentialist feminist identity politics, feminism needed to define its parameters. However, in doing so it "simultaneously work[ed] to limit and constrain . . . the very cultural possibilities that feminism is supposed to open up" (Butler, 1990, p. 187). Butches, instead of being viewed as brave and visible homosexuals—a powerful rejection of the limitations of what was possible for women living in a more repressive time—were seen as enemies of the women's liberation movement. According to Rubin (1992), "Butch and femme were brilliantly adapted for building a minority sexual culture out of the tools, materials, and debris of a dominant sexual system" (p. 477). During the early development of lesbian-feminist consciousness, butches and their femme lovers were ousted as upstanding members of a movement that had been built out of the culture that they had created and sustained. Joan Nestle (1981) began the process of reclaiming butch and femme identities and bringing these issues into the lesbian-feminist discourse (see Kennedy and Davis, 1993; Nestle, 1992).

The feminist movement is still struggling to integrate the history of butch/femme identities, the experience of females with masculine gender roles, and the existence of FTM transsexuals within the historical context of lesbian communities. Although the bulk of Raymond's and Jeffreys' hostility toward transgenderism is directed at MTFs, they are also hostile toward butch and FTM identities, viewing them as the ultimate traitors to feminism (Raymond, 1996, p. 218). Cromwell (1999) said, "many FTMs and transmen have lived as, or attempted to live as, lesbians and have found lesbian communities to be relatively tolerant of masculine identities and behaviors" (p. 27). However, this history has yet to be incorporated within the feminist canon. Cromwell (1999) stated, "Feminists should be concerned that male-dominated discourses have made female-to-male transpeople virtually invisible" (p. 9).

Perhaps it was not possible for the nascent lesbian-feminist politics of thirty years ago to analyze the meaning of female cross-dressing expression and male identity within female bodies which invoked the question of whether butches or passing women were actually men. Nestle (1998) addressed this issue when she revisited a story she wrote in the 1980s—a story about a passing woman named Esther with whom she had a brief affair in the 1960s. The story paid homage to Esther's "woman-ness" hidden below her masculine exterior. When Nestle reexamined the story in the 1990s, with far more knowledge of gender, sexuality, and transgenderism, she acknowledged that she wrote a story in the 1980s that lesbian-feminists of that era would embrace. However, the story she wrote does not tell the full truth about Esther and "women" like her. The truth is that Esther lived as a man. Green (2001) examined the process of sorting through lesbian-feminist theory as part of his own embodiment:

> All the theorizing about gender, about male privilege or the moral superiority of women, about the appropriateness of altering one's body ... *would never neutralize the need in me.* I would always be not male and not female, unlike other people who never disturbed the social waters around them, who never thought to question where they fit in. I would also be different from conventionally gendered beings. (p. 62, italics mine)

Of course, "feminist discourse on sex and gender is multifaceted and covers several diverse sites of activism" (Irvine, 1990, p. 136). Despite the resistance in many feminist circles to understanding and embracing transgenderism, the questions raised within both kinds of "gender studies" about the "etiology" and meaning of sex, gender, and gender-role expression and its political ramifications remain remarkably interconnected. In many ways the transgender community has continued the theoretical analysis that was begun within the feminist movement. Green (2001) said, "Gender theory is the triumph of feminism" (p. 59). The questions that feminism brought to the public debate about the meaning of "manhood" and "womanhood" and the limitations in creating a social caste system based on biological bodies are exactly the kinds of questions that are being raised again within the transgender community. There is even a branch of feminism, called transfeminism, dedicated to examining these interlocking issues (Koyama, 1999). Whittle (2000) suggested that perhaps the transgender liberation movement can give back to feminism the very ideas that it originally inherited from feminism. It is a paradox that feminist theory, which is based on a philosophy that "biology is not destiny," would be antagonistic toward the emerging transgender liberation movement, which is the proof of the theory.

Causation and Cure

There is an inherent difficulty with etiological theories. Etiological theories are based on an inherent essentialism of the body (chromosomes or brain chemistry)—or of the body politic (caste affiliations based on gender)—or they are based on a social construction (or deconstruction) of culture (socialization or parental upbringing) consciously or unconsciously, imposed or rejected. Seeking a cause ultimately requires finding a cure. As Whittle (2000) said,

> I do not care whether I was "born this way" or "became this way." The question of the "gay gene" or the "tranny brain" is a potentially frightening route to another eugenics programme to destroy the brilliance of difference in the world, and the sooner we reject these projects the better.

If medical scientists are able to find a cause for transsexualism, transgenderism, or any of the various intersex conditions, will the ultimate goal be to "fix" the defective gene or manipulate the endocrinological soup, to somehow remove the condition? If psychoanalysts are able to determine exactly how gender identity is formed, or rather how it can be controlled to manifest in a particular manner, will families be coerced to develop along those lines? If the cognitive-behavioral building blocks that can actively reward/punish and mold children's gendered preferences, activities, and presentation are discovered, will society impose those through educational and parental mandates? If gendered social roles are finally eliminated so that women and men are treated equally in the eyes of the law, will gendered expressions of masculinity and femininity become taboo so that women and men (whether born female or male) are forced into unisex presentations or risk facing social ostracism?

Perhaps these all seem to be extreme possibilities, but what purposes can the search for "causation" have, except to eliminate what is defined as problematic, reactive, diseased, disordered, pathological, dysfunctional, and politically regressive? If transgenderism, transsexualism, and intersexuality represent a small but consistent part of human diversity, then questions of etiology are not clinical or therapeutic, but teleological and ontological. No matter what causes gender variance—whether it is a naturally occurring biological diversity (or aberration) or a social construction of gender inappropriate parental modeling (or a patriarchally restricted gender system)—the reality is that gender-variant people exist. They are "caused" by the same social and biological conditions within which all of humanity is created. If something exists in nature, it is therefore natural.

The study of gender identity development is a worthwhile pursuit if we stop pathologizing certain experiences and begin examining the diversity of gender expression available. Suchet (1995) suggested that "the goal of gender development should not be the achievement of a single simple, 'gender appropriate' identity, but rather the ability to tolerate the ambiguity and instability that a bigendered self evokes" (p. 52). Although it is interesting to examine those who are exceptions to the general rule of normative development, it is equally interesting to examine the rigid compliance to a sexist dichotomy that most people accept regarding their gender expression. Devor (1997b) said that the etiology of transsexualism is interesting "mostly for what such knowledge can tell us about how society organizes and perpetuates gender and for what we can learn about how our concepts of gender mutate in response to the challenges presented by gender variance" (p. 37).

CATEGORICAL CLASSIFICATIONS: IF THE SHOE DOESN'T FIT—FORCE IT

> People invent categories to feel safe. White people invented black people to give white people identity.
>
> James Baldwin
> *A Dialogue*, 1973

Researchers seeking an understanding of gender variance have not only examined etiological theories, but have also developed classification systems to distinguish various types of transgender expression. When Harry Benjamin first began compiling information on gender-variant people, he was struck by the similarities of the narratives they told. Schaefer and Wheeler (1995) reviewed the archived papers of Benjamin—the case notes of more than 1,500 patients—and said that clients' descriptions of their experiences remain the same in the 1990s as they did when Benjamin began his studies in 1948.

Generally speaking, transsexual clients have been self-diagnosed. They have sought out treatment expressing early onset gender confusion, secretive cross-dressing, a sense of "knowing" that they are really of the other sex, repeated purging of clothes, and intense shame. Despite these similarities, researchers have also noted differences between "types" of gender-variant people, such as the intensity of the gender dysphoria, the quality of mental status, differences in sexual desire, sexual-object choice, and sexual expression.

Dating back to the nineteenth century, when the sexologists began to classify human sexual variations, Krafft-Ebing, for example, identified four types of inborn homosexuality and three learned types (Hekma, 1994). Hirschfeld described ten patterns of transvestic behaviors (Doctor, 1988). More recently, Harry Benjamin (1966) developed a model in which he classified six types or syndromes of gender variance represented on a transvestism-transsexualism continuum. This was the first clear delineation of the distinctions between transvestites and transsexuals, a model that has remained the blueprint of the medical model today. The continuum describes gender-transgressive behavior by the persistence or intensity of cross-dressing behavior and the desire to change one's physiology.

Types and Subtypes

According to the medical model, transvestites and transsexuals represent two types of gender dysphoria and yet also form a continuum between them with more severe gender dysphoria manifesting in a great desire to change sex. Transvestites are generally defined as heterosexual males who have a primarily male gender identity and cross-dress for erotic reasons. Although they enjoy cross-dressing, they express no desire for sex reassignment surgery. They are usually not particularly feminine in childhood and work in traditional male-dominated careers. Erotic cross-dressing was believed to be a hallmark of transvestism, and in those born males, has been used to rule out "true" transsexualism. At the other end of the continuum, transsexuals are identified as people with atypical cross-gender identity development (e.g., sissies or tomboys), lifelong gender dysphoria, hatred of their genitalia, and a persistent desire for sex reassignment surgery. They often appear to be homosexual in sexual orientation, as determined by their natal bodies (postsurgically they will appear heterosexual). This classification paradigm has been used for the past thirty years, but it is promulgated in more contemporary research (see Becker and Kavoussi, 1996; Bentler, 1976; Block and Fisher, 1979; Brown, 1990; Freund, Steiner, and Chan, 1982; Peo, 1988; Michel, Mormont, and Legros, 2001).

Buhrich and McConaghy (1977b) compared these two groups and concluded that "transvestism and transsexualism are separate clinical entities"

(p. 494), despite Benjamin's (1966) assertion that "a sharp and scientific separation of the two syndromes is not possible. . . . We have as yet no objective diagnostic methods at our disposal to differentiate between the two" (p. 35). Most categorical classifications are, however, based on an attempt to delineate between the two groups with precision and accuracy due to the seriousness and irreversible nature of sex-change procedures. As King (1993) said, "Transvestites requesting sex changes were a professional headache" (p. 53). Diagnostic proof of being a "true transsexual" became the admission ticket for medical treatment and fitting the criteria became the obsession for all trans-identified people who desired hormonal or surgical treatments. Baker (as quoted in Buhrich and McConaghy, 1977a) went as far as saying, "A single episode of cross-dressing in association with sexual arousal was regarded as sufficient to exclude the diagnosis of transsexualism" (p. 224).

Many models have been developed to map out classification categories for gender-dysphoric/gender-variant people. Researchers have focused on a few basic areas of clinical features that have consistently appeared to be salient for this population. These have included differences in erotic partner choice (i.e., sexual orientation), presence (or absence) of fetishistic cross-dressing, gender dysphoria beginning at an early age, and the intensity of the desire for body modification. In their attempts to delineate various subtypes, researchers have used language and categories differently, which makes modern day categorizations only slightly less confusing than that of the sexologists a century before. Various specialists have developed their own nosologies and subtypes and highlighted different salient features.

For example, male transsexuals have been further classified into two types, primary and secondary (Person and Ovesey, 1974a,b; Levine and Lothstein, 1981). Unlike primary transsexuals, who have a history of life-long gender dysphoric feelings and cross-dressing behavior, secondary transsexuals do not usually present with histories of childhood gender dysphoria, appear "masculine" in their social presentation, and have a history of sexual pleasure from their cross-dressing. This group seems to almost mature into their transsexualism, outgrowing cross-dressing as a fetishistic behavior. They are perceived as somewhat less stable emotionally, and are more often homosexual after surgery. They have been identified with various mental health problems, including personality disorders, and have been reported to have less successful gender transitions (Walinder, Lundström, and Thuwe, 1978).

Johnson and Hunt (1990) said that the data consistently report that there are two etiological tracks for male transsexuals: one from effeminate homosexuality and the other from heterosexual cross-dressing fetishism. Buhrich and McConaghy (1979) introduced the concept of "marginal transvestism" to identify cross-dressers who do not seem to be fetishists yet exhibit long-standing gender dysphoria, and compared them to "nuclear transvestites." They also did not believe that fetishism should prevent a diagnosis of trans-sexualism, and they concurred with Meyer (1974) that these categorizations created more "ambiguity than clarity" (Buhrich and McConaghy, 1977a). The DSM does not currently acknowledge the concept of secondary trans-sexuals and marginal transvestites, as well as those in the middle of the con-tinuum who are often referred to as transgendered people or transgenderists (although the manual includes a category of GID "not otherwise specified") (Doctor, 1988).

Person and Ovesey (1974a,b; 1984) identified "ordinary" or fetishistic cross-dressers, homosexual cross-dressers, transsexuals, and nonfetishis-tic cross-dressers. Wise and Meyer (1980) examined transvestism from a continuum perspective, recognizing a "border area" in which aging trans-vestites become less fetishistic in their cross-dressing and increasingly more gender dysphoric and likely to request sex reassignment (secondary transsexuals). Roback and Lothstein (1986) concluded that female-to-male transsexuals who transitioned at midlife are less like aging transvestites and more like aging homosexuals, assuming categorical distinctions between those groups. Doorn, Poortinga, and Verschoor (1994) suggested that exam-ining issues of early onset and late onset desire for sex reassignment might be the best way to differentiate these groups. Levine (1993) noted that a his-tory of cross-dressing is a common antecedent for those who request medi-cal treatment. She also noted that cross-dressers represent a diverse group of people, who have in common a "soothing image of themselves as women" (p. 131). Levine minimized the differences between cross-dressers who are heterosexual, homosexual, bisexual, asexual, or paraphilic and said that cross-dressers cross the line into transsexualism when they give up all ves-tiges of male gender-role behavior and work and live full-time as women. Doorn, Poortinga, and Verschoor (1994) suggested that transvestites have both masculine and feminine gender identity subsystems, and that they both are strong enough to seek expression.

Blanchard perhaps more than any other researcher has made classifica-tions of "types" a scientific endeavor, with a particular focus on sexual ori-entation (Blanchard, Clemmensen, and Steiner, 1987). Blanchard (1985) has defined subcategories including transvestite, borderline transsexual, fe-tishistic transsexual, homosexual transsexual, and nonfetishistic transves-tite. In addition to a complex analysis of the differences between homosex-ual and heterosexual types, he also includes bisexuals, analloerotics (those who lack sexual desire directed toward other people), and autogynephilics (those who are sexually aroused by the thought or image of themselves as women) (Blanchard, 1989b, 1990). Blanchard and his colleagues hypothesized that "asexual, bisexual, and heterosexual gender dysphoria are merely variant forms of same disorder" (Blanchard, Clemmensen, and Steiner, 1987, p. 141). Probably Blanchard's most controversial and intriguing contribution to this field has been his concept of autogynephilia.

Blanchard (1989a,b, 1991, 1993a,b) studied autogynephilia extensively and hypothesized that the primary motivation of a subset of what he would call nonhomosexual gender dysphorics fantasize about possessing female anatomy and are erotically excited by the thought or performance of activities that symbolize femininity. He further delineates autogynephilics into three groups: physiologic—those that fantasize about women's physiological abilities such as lactation or menstruation; behavioral—those who fantasize acting or being sexual in a feminine role; and anatomic—those who fantasize about having female body parts (Blanchard, 1991). Bailey (2003), a defender of Blanchard's theories of autogynephilia (1989b, 1991, 1993b), divides transsexualism into distinct paths—homosexual and autogynephilic. Homosexual transsexuals desire to be with men as women, whereas autogynephilic transsexuals are sexually excited by the idea of having a vagina. Linking the transsexuals' goal for sex reassignment to sexual eroticism has caused both relief and rage within the transgender community. Some feel it is an accurate description of their own motivations and desires (Lawrence, 2000), while others feel that it trivializes their gender dysphoria by sexualizing it (Allison, 1998). Still others feel that it is simply bad science (Wilson, 2000). Most disturbing about Bailey's ideas is that when the gay men or transsexuals he meets do not neatly fit into his theories, he assumes they are lying or denying what he has deemed the "truth." Blanchard and Bailey have surely identified patterns that are true for some transsexuals. Why try to fit all transsexuals into this schema?

The typing and subtyping of gender variance etiologically and diagnostically is somewhat complicated and cumbersome and even Blanchard (1993b), a careful categorizer, admitted that these are not necessarily "discrete syndromes." Hausman (1995) said that the researchers exhibit a "kind of classificatory zeal [that] presupposes that the categories described are largely static and are therefore 'discovered' by researchers" (p. 116). The classification systems outlined previously are, at best, contradictory and inconsistent. Different researchers focus on different aspects that they see as significant—for some researchers sexual orientation is a fundamental issue, for others it is fetishism, or mental health status or age of onset—but each comes to the research with a set of assumptions. Gender variance, in actuality, manifests in different ways within human populations and continues to be "rediscovered" and redefined within the parameters of modern life.

Describing "types" of gender-variant people or clustering certain similar traits has its advantages. However, as Irvine (1990) said, "The descriptive terms hardened into diagnostic tools [that] . . . reified the categories into static imperatives" (p. 267). Dreger (1998), in her research on the historical treatment of intersexed people, noted that people create organization systems that "reinforce the system maker's idea of the world" (p. 140). She said that those things deemed important become salient in the classification model and those things that are less important to the classifier fade into the background. The desire to create typology in order to develop carefully delineated categorical distinctions may be one of the obsessive-compulsive qualities of researchers, but often dehumanizes and objectifies the very qualities and persons they are studying.

Certainly the descriptive similarities among unique individuals is important phenomenologically, but it is less clear whether "alleged commonalities of transsexualism [should] . . . become elevated to the level of diagnostic criteria" (Bolin, 1988, p. 53), especially when the diagnostic criteria then becomes the standard for identification and the "proof" for categorical inclusion. Benjamin's classifications still yield basic "truths" about many, if not most, transsexuals seeking treatment. However, there are many self-identified transsexuals who diverge from commonly held assumptions. For example, some transsexuals seem to have erotic experiences while cross-dressing, yet others do not experience the lifelong, intense dysphoria that begins early in childhood. Not all transsexuals experience disgust for their genitalia and some express fear or disinterest regarding surgical and hormonal body modification. It is perhaps interesting to note the various sexual preferences, behaviors, and identities that gender-variant people experience and the correlates between them, but should these variables be the basis for a clinical nosological system?

More recent research disputes some of the long-held "facts" about transsexual and transvestite populations. For instance, Bolin's (1988) research refuted some of the clinical assumptions about transsexuals. They did not have "family histories of dominant mothers and absent fathers, exclusive homosexual orientations, effeminate childhoods, nor did they view their penises as organs of hate and disgust . . . they were not generally hyper-feminine in gender identity or role" (p. xii). In fact, current research shows that transsexuals are aware of the medical criteria regarding transsexual treatment (Denny and Roberts, 1997) and have actually falsified their histories to make their stories match the narratives of "true transsexuals" (Walworth, 1997). Even Harry Benjamin was aware of this pattern, and almost all researchers since have noted it.

Stone (1991) provided an example of this revisionist history when she said that if the original MTF transsexuals who had been approved for treatment did not admit to erotic feelings, then no one else would either. She said, "The prohibition continued postoperatively . . . [and] that no postoperative transsexual would admit to experiencing sexual pleasure through masturbation either. Full membership in the assigned gender was conferred by orgasm, real or faked, accomplished through heterosexual penetration" (p. 292).

Classifying differences and similarities between and among gender-dysphoric, gender-variant, and self-identified transsexuals seeking medical treatment is certainly scientifically useful and sociologically interesting. Using these theoretical classification systems to pigeonhole people into diagnostic categories can limit their medical options while ignoring the social and political realities that impinge on the development of these experiences, raises ethical questions about the clinical utility of behavioral science research (see Figure 4.1).

Identifying the limitations of the evaluative classifications, Levine and Shumaker (1983) reported on a case of a transsexual woman who, by the criteria commonly used today, would be described as a secondary transsexual

FIGURE 4.1. *Hal & Bengie* copyright Jay Hayes-Light. Permission to reprint granted by Dr. Jay Hayes-Light.

and possibly not approved for SRS. However, she had been surgically reassigned and appeared, by her own report as well as that of the researcher, to have "consolidated her feminine gender identity" (p. 247). Ekins and King (1998) discussed the limitations of the medical categories of transvestism and transsexualism and concluded that these categories presume pathology and limit our gaze to "a narrow range of cross-dressing/sex-changing phenomena—those presented to the medical profession" (p. 98).

The Road Less Traveled

Of course, valid reasons exist to develop some parameters for defining treatment since hormonal and surgical treatments are profound and permanent. The need to define "who" is eligible and able to successfully transition becomes a medical and clinical necessity when the risk of regret runs high. Meyer-Bahlburg (1985) referred to the "zone of transition between clinically significant cross-gender behavior and mere statistical deviations from the gender norm" (p. 682), a gray area that sometimes raises questions about diagnostic appropriateness. Approving hormones or surgery for someone who is not really a transsexual, but a homosexual or a transvestite—or mentally ill—can potentially cause immeasurable human suffering, not to mention lawsuits for physicians. Pauly and Edgerton (1986) estimated that 30 to 35 percent of gender-dysphoric people are intensely homophobic gay people. Bockting and Coleman (1992) outlined some of the issues that gender-dysphoric clients present with that are not necessarily indicators of the need to begin medical treatments. These include "a cry for help, an expression of psychological pain stemming from a long history of anxious attachments, generalized anxiety, social phobia, intimacy dysfunction, depression, loneliness and despair" (p. 136).

How does a clinician or a physician determine who is eligible and who is not? What are the signs of "true" transsexualism or "primary" gender identity disorder? For instance, homosexuals who are struggling with deep self-hatred might identify themselves as having a gender identity problem rather than a sexual-orientation conflict, preferring to see themselves as heterosexual transsexuals rather than homosexuals. If gender dysphoria is so intense that the person wants to physically harm their genitals, does that make them too mentally disturbed to give informed consent? If the person does not "despise their genitals," but would simply "prefer" to have them altered, does that make them unsuitable candidates for surgery? If what we know about transsexualism are generalizations, not facts, by what criteria do clinicians approve treatment? Unlike other "lifestyle decisions," transsexuals require medical interventions. They are dependent on the approval of clinical authorities for assistance to live as they choose.

Some transsexual advocates argue for hormones and surgery on "demand" but this position is unacceptable to most medical and clinical professionals. With the exception of certain cosmetic surgeries, surgical and hormonal body modifications to healthy human tissue are unprecedented in the medical profession. Few transsexuals are comfortable having transsexualism seen as merely a "cosmetic" surgery, which appears to minimize the intensity of the dysphoria and the actual "need" for gender reassignment, not to mention making medical and surgical treatments non-insurance reimbursable. Given the mental health considerations of many transgendered people (e.g., feelings of desperation and anguish), as well as the permanency, irreversibility, and intensity of gender transition, some guidelines for evaluation seem necessary.

The standards of care developed by the Harry Benjamin International Gender Dysphoria Association have guided ethical hormonal and surgical care of transsexuals for the past twenty years. However, the information that has directed the development of the SOC has come primarily from approved gender identity clinics and sexological researchers. It is not clear that the type of client who goes to a gender clinic is representative of the diversity of gender variance. Bullough (2000) stated that until recently only two major sources of data on gender-variant people existed, those who went to gender clinics seeking treatment and those who were active in transvestite-type clubs—and even the second type of group did not exist until the 1960s. Two of the most prominent transgendered figures in the media, Christine Jorgensen and Virginia Prince, represent the twin poles of Harry Benjamin's original thesis, as well as the two areas where researchers had focused.

In many ways Christine Jorgensen's story represents the classic male primary transsexual narrative. Many transsexuals have vivid memories of the first time they heard of Christine Jorgensen (Meyerowitz, 2002), and King (1993) shared how people clipped out and saved newspaper and magazine articles about Jorgensen, relieved to find a story "just like mine" (p. 175). Meyerowitz (2002) said, "The Jorgensen story and subsequent news reports brought transgendered people out of the woodwork" (p. 92). One client reported that after she had heard about the support Harry Benjamin had offered Christine Jorgensen, she traveled to the doctor's office and paced in front, afraid to go in. It was another twenty-five years before she was able to begin her own transition.

On the other hand, Virginia Prince represents the classic transvestite narrative. Virginia Prince is founder of the first organizations for heterosexual cross-dressers, including the Hose and Heels Club, the Foundation for Personality Expression (FPE), and Tri-Ess Sorority: the Society for the Second

Self which replaced FPE. She edited *Transvestia* magazine, which started in 1960. Prince downplayed self-eroticism and homosexuality and spoke about cross-dressers as being "femmiphilic" and "transgenderists," and having two selves, i.e., "a girl within" (Bullough and Bullough, 1993, 1997; Prince, 1976; Prince and Bentler, 1972). Prince lives full-time as a woman without surgical assistance.

However, if research has been limited only to those who seek gender clinics and transvestite clubs it is likely that whole populations of people have been rendered invisible. The literature is replete with categorical assumptions about gender diversity. For instance, many researchers have concluded that "[male] transvestites are always heterosexual" (Steiner, 1985c, p. 357), although Bullough and Bullough (1997) have studied male transvestism that is heterosexually oriented.

Block and Fisher (1979), Doctor (1988), Stoller (1982), and Steiner (1985a) stated that transvestism occurs only in males. Blanchard, Clemmensen, and Steiner (1987) said that fetishism "occurs rarely in females" (p. 149), and Stoller (1982) stated that fetishistic cross-dressing in females "is so rare it is almost nonexistent" (p. 99). As recently as 1999, Ettner and Brown said when FTMs cross-dress it is not fetishistic because "male items of clothing possess no erotic properties" (p. 72). "Factual" statements such as these have been disputed. Researchers who perhaps are less familiar with the subculture of sexual and gender expression within the gay and lesbian community overlook the phenomenon of butch lesbians and passing women wearing male attire. The possibility of erotic transvestism in females is ignored, as is the existence of all fetishistic behaviors in females. One reality is that females experience more freedom of dress, which makes their transvestism less noticeable. As Ettner and Brown (1999) said, "Female-to-male transsexuals 'cross-dress,' but this behavior is not remarkable as it does not violate social prohibitions" (p. 72). MacKenzie (1994), however, suggested that, "Although 'masculine' clothes may be in vogue for women, it is an altogether different matter when a woman stuffs a sock in a jock strap to simulate a penis" (p. 89). Indeed the literature on butch identity clearly identifies male clothing as potentially erotic for females who wear it, as well as their lovers, and often serves to emulate traditional male gender in a way that could be described as both "cross-dressing" *and* "fetishistic."

Numerous assumptions have been made about female masculinity, and female-to-male transsexuals have been considered a rare and "homogeneous group" (Steiner, 1985a). The bulk of the research data that has been collected about male-to-female transgendered people—the definitions, categorizations, and classification nomenclature—do not adequately represent the experiences, behaviors, or identities of FTM people. The literature on FTMs until very recently has been sparse. Benjamin (1966) wrote one chapter on the subject that was thirteen pages long and Stoller (1975) wrote one chapter that was twenty-one pages long. Green and Money (1969) included three chapters on FTMs totaling sixty-four pages and Lothstein (1983) completed an entire (rather pathologizing) book. In addition, a handful of professional articles on FTMs exist (Pauly, 1974; Stoller, 1972).

The clinical wisdom has long been that FTM transsexuals (as compared to MTFs) are more emotionally stable, with fewer mental health problems (although Lothstein [1983] disputed this), healthier familial relationships, long-term successful intimate partnerships with women, and a more consolidated cross-gendered identity by the time they seek medical assistance. Research has indicated that they are attracted to feminine women who identify as heterosexual. Blanchard, Clemmensen, and Steiner (1987) said, "Female gender dysphorics, almost without exception, are erotically attracted to members of their own anatomical sex" (p. 140) and Steiner (1985c) determined that, "All transsexual biological females are homosexual in erotic object choice, and all of them wish to have a penis" (p. 353). In reality, the partners of FTMs represent a diversity of sexual orientations. Many female partners are heterosexual women, but many others are lesbian identified (Califia, 1997; Rubin, 1992; Cook-Daniels, 1998; Corbett, 2001). For FTMs that are involved in relationships with women, these relationships appear to be stable regardless of their surgical status (Fleming, MacGowan, and Costos, 1985; Kockott and Fahrner, 1987). Researchers seem surprised that surgery is not a more salient issue in the lives of many FTMs and their partners. Perhaps even more shocking has been the fact that some FTMs have chosen to use their female parts for sexual pleasure or even reproduction (Califia-Rice, 2000; Cromwell, 1999; Lev, in press; More, 1998).

Despite the insistence in the literature that all FTMs are attracted to women, researchers are beginning to report the existence of gay FTMs (Blanchard, Clemmenson, and Steiner, 1987; Coleman and Bockting, 1988; Coleman, Bockting, and Gooren, 1993; Devor, 1998; Rosario, 1996). This is often referred to in the literature as "heterosexual" transsexualism (Dickey and Stephens, 1995) privileging the natal sex, not the gender of presentation, although newer terminology has also emerged such as "transhomosexuality" (Clare and Tully, 1989). According to Sullivan (1990b) the Ingersoll Gender Clinic in Seattle reported that the number of transsexuals who are gay identified seemed to be consistent with homosexuality in the general population.

In the 1990s the number of self-identified female-to-male transsexuals, including gay-identified FTMs, rose dramatically. Are more female-bodied people actually experiencing gender dysphoria or have sociological forces changed to enable them to come forward? It was only with the release of Devor's research in 1997 and Cromwell's work in 1999 that social scientists began to develop an understanding of the complexity and diversity of FTM lives. Devor (1998) revealed the wide diversity in sexual orientations, sexual attraction, and sexual behaviors that FTM's experience, including attractions to women, men, and other transmen. It is important to note that these studies are the work of anthropologists and sociologists, not physicians or clinicians, and only minimal research has been conducted into the lives of transsexual people of color. According to Cromwell (1999) the invisibility of transmen happens on four levels. First, since they were born female and assigned to that sex they are assumed to actually be females. Second, they are rendered invisible because they are seen as pathological (i.e., not quite) women and/or as pathological (i.e., male-identified) lesbians. Third, they are invisible as men, in part because they are able to pass so well. Finally, they are invisible as transmen, since transsexual females are presumed to be rare (pp. 11-12).

If FTMs are more common than researchers have previously believed, why have so few FTMs approached gender clinics? Perhaps fewer FTMs have come into contact with the medical establishment because as females they traditionally have had less access to the financial resources that make transition possible or are cross-living without medical assistance. It is also true that state-of-the-art surgical treatment for FTMs is still rudimentary and many do not consider surgery a viable option (Green, 1994b; Rachlin, 1999). In a fascinating example of not only prejudicial assumptions toward FTMs but also blatant racism, Lothstein and Roback (1984) hypothesized that black "women" do not exhibit gender dysphoria, that they are "inoculated" against it except when they exhibit symptoms of severe mental illnesses such as schizophrenia. They come to this conclusion since their gender clinic sees very few FTMs, and even fewer FTMs of color, and the small sample they have had contact with have mental health problems. They refer to this as a "serendipitous" finding. Many questions might be raised as to why more black female-to-male clients are not seeking services in Lothstein and Roback's clinic—questions about the cost of services, the lack of sensitivity to issues of race and gender identity, as well as the multiple areas of distressful confluence experienced by gender-dysphoric African-American people living with mental health problems. One is tempted to suggest that a person of color would have to be "crazy" to seek treatment with clinicians who actually believe that their lack of presence at a gender clinic indicates their non-existence.

That many people are not visible or do not fit into the established medical model is not actually news although it is interesting in reviewing the literature to see how many articles are actually about the "exceptions." Money and Lamacz (1984) identified a variant gender expression in which males cross-live as women without desiring SRS or sometimes without hormonal treatment. They refer to this with medical terminology, e.g., gynemimesis and gynemimetophilia, although it sounds similar to Prince's description of a "transgenderist." A recent study of more than 1,000 male cross-dressers revealed that, although they describe themselves in similar ways as they did twenty-five years ago, a larger number are interested in living full-time as women and/or beginning hormonal treatment (Doctor and Prince, 1997). Daskalos (1998) recognized transsexuals who change their sexual orientation after transition and Kremer and den Daas (1990) reported the case of a man with what they referred to as "breast dysphoria" who requested hormonal therapy to enlarge his breasts and nipples. He did not identify as transsexual (or, the authors told the reader, homosexual) and did not request any other treatments. Blanchard (1993a) discussed the "she-male" phenomenon—transgendered males who eroticize being women with penises. Many more examples can be given, but these will suffice to show that there are as many forms, types, and expressions of gender variance as perhaps there are gender-variant people.

Blanchard (1989a) made the point that in only one study in his extensive research were people asked how they classified themselves. This is a significant issue and many researchers are beginning to listen to the self-narratives of gender-variant people without necessarily seeking to place them in preconceived classifications, as much as to hear how they explain and understand themselves. One theme that is emerging is a blended sense of gender identity that has been referred to as "bi-genderism," "gender blending," or "gender fluidity." The term *gender blending* was first used by Devor (1989) to refer to females who have "clear female identities and know themselves to be women concurrently with gender presentations that often do not successfully communicate these facts to others" (p. 12). The word has since taken on a broader usage. Ekins and King (1998) said that the word *blending* has two basic meanings—to mix or combine, and to harmonize. Gender blenders are people who "mix" the sense of masculine and feminine rather than "crossing over" to the other side of the binary. Sell (2001) referred to this as "gender intermediacy."

Bornstein (1994) defined this fluidity as the "ability to freely and knowingly become one or many of a limitless number of genders for any length of time, at any rate of change" (p. 52). Gagné, Tewksbury, and McGaughey (1997) said that some transgendered people are "looking for ways to defy categorization based on gender, rather than find a way to fit within the gender system" (p. 482). Newman and Stoller (1973) identified what they referred to as the "bisexual" identity of some MTFs, which referred to their sense of having retained some remnant of their original male identity. It is significant that this was seen as a negative and distressing experience almost thirty-five years ago. It is curious to note how those studied would feel today when having a dual identity has become a social possibility, albeit an unusual one.

Ekins and King (1999) utilized grounded theory to develop a sociologically based model to describe what they call "transgendering." Their model is based in the narrative stories of gender-variant people and the kinds of "gender mobility" they engage in to address their dysphoria. These include:

> *Migrating* body stories involve moving the body from one side of the binary divide to the other on a permanent basis. *Oscillating* body stories are stories of moving backwards and forwards over the gender border, only temporarily resting on one side or the other. *Erasing* body stories are those in which the gender of the person erasing is expunged. *Transcending* body stories tell of moving beyond gender into a third space. (p. 583)

To place their terminology into more familiar language, migrating body stories are best understood as transsexual narratives, and oscillating body stories involve cross-dressing or "transgender" narratives. Erasing and transcending are, however, "newer" models, that involve living outside of a binary gender system. These ideas have been expressed within the transliberation movement by Kate Bornstein (1994), Riki Ann Wilchins (1997), Leslie Feinberg (1998), and Holly Boswell (1991, 1998), among others. Hooley (1997) suggested that these new models represent the "formation of a counter discourse" to the medical paradigm as the "only legitimate or acceptable way of crossing gender" (p. 31). Tauchert (2001) criticized the binary model of "opposites" and suggested that all opposites are actually on a continuum (e.g., day and night also contain dusk and dawn).

Behavioral scientists and clinicians are also beginning to develop alternative models that allow room for gender blending, bi-genderism, and flexible gender-migration patterns. McKain (1996) wrote about mixed-sex people; Cole et al. (2000) presented a transgender model that allows for multiple sexes; and Bockting and Coleman (1992) offered a "comprehensive treatment model that recognizes a wide spectrum of gender identity disorders" (p. 131). More expansive models will allow gender specialists to move out of a gatekeeping model of assessment to a psychotherapeutic relationship that allows for clients' unique narratives within a clinical perspective that is humanistic and empowerment focused.

It is obvious that attempts to examine human sexuality and gender expressions within a medical and psychological framework have been an evolving science with divergent theories and areas of study. Bullough (1999) said, "Perhaps . . . all classification schemes should be regarded as transitional" (p. 115). With only a little more than 100 years of research, the modern study in sex and gender development is a new field with few experts. Since the 1960s research into gender-related issues has expanded, as have medical interventions to assist in gender reassignment. Political issues, including the heightened awareness of human sexuality and concurrent liberation struggles, have impacted contemporary clinical analyses. Feminism has certainly changed gender-role expectations, and the gay liberation movement has depathologized homosexual relationships. As Rubin (1992) suggested, "No system of classification can successfully catalogue the infinite vagaries of human diversity" (p. 473). Perhaps seeking etiologies and cataloging human gender diversity is not the best way to understand gender-variant people or, for those called to work within the helping professions, to serve those who seek services.

Chapter 5

Diagnosis and Transgenderism:
The Creation of Pathology

The history of mental health care is not a success story or a story of progress; it does not follow a straight-line development from grim, torture like activities of early times to benign, enlightened practices of the present.

Leland Bell
Treating the Mentally Ill, 1980

Therapeutic and medical treatment of transgendered and transsexual people is based on the ability to properly diagnose gender-related difficulties. The clinical guidelines of the standards of care adhere to the diagnostic categories of gender identity disorder as outlined in the *Diagnostic and Statistical Manual of Mental Disorders,* Fourth Edition, Text Revision or the medical diagnoses of transsexualism as described in the *International Classification of Diseases,* Tenth Edition (see Appendix A). In order to treat someone for gender issues, we need to be able to accurately recognize gender identity disorders and ascertain transsexualism. It is this very skill that the gender specialist is expected to excel in and for which the SOC were developed.

Diagnostic labeling of gender variance is, however, a controversial and political issue. The therapeutic community and the newly developing political movement of transgender rights are struggling with the usefulness and validity of established diagnostic categories. This is a complex issue and often the discussion of diagnostics among transgender activists takes place outside of the larger context of the history and politics of diagnosing mental illnesses in general. The diagnostic category of GID evokes a discourse about the ability of the diagnostic manual to distinguish between issues of mental health and issues of social control. The sad truth is that the long history of psychiatric diagnoses, particularly regarding issues of sexuality, has been used for social repression, not empowerment or healing. In order to determine the validity of GID as a diagnosis, one must first understand the overall history and construction of diagnoses as tools of social and political control.

THE POWER OF DIAGNOSIS

There is a growing tendency in our society to medicalize problems that are not medical, [and] to find psychopathology where there is only pathos. . . . [The DSM] is the repository of a strange mix of social values, political compromise, scientific evidence, and material for insurance claim forms.

Stuart Kirk and Herb Kutchins
Making Us Crazy, 1997

The *Diagnostic and Statistical Manual of Mental Disorders* (DSM) is the preeminent "bible" of the psychological field, the dominant classification system of psychiatric disorders. The DSM, now in its fourth edition with its most recent revision in 2000, delineates the nosological standard of how mental illness is defined in the Western world. It is mandatory reading in most graduate psychology and social work curriculums.

The DSM is a complex book that has grown from 132 pages in 1952 to its current size of more than 900 pages. It weighs nearly three pounds and its last edition yielded more than one million dollars in revenue for the American Psychiatric Association. It covers more than 300 diagnostic categories, with subtypes and specifiers listed in many areas. Categories are as broad as "Unspecified Mental Disorder (300.9)" to delineated subcategories such as "Alcohol-Induced Psychotic Disorder (291x), with delusions (291.5), or hallucinations (291.3)." A significantly high number of Americans—23 percent of adults and approximately 10 percent of children (Regier et al., 1993; Friedman et al., 1996)—are believed to suffer from a diagnosable mental illness each year.

Gender identity disorder, the official diagnosis for transsexualism, and transvestic fetishism, the official diagnosis for erotic transvestism, are listed within the section on sexual and gender identity disorders. The inclusion of gender identity disorder and transvestic fetishism in a classification of mental disorders is a complex and controversial subject involving the politics of diagnostic systems, and the meaning of mental illness. In order to understand the current controversy regarding these diagnostic categories, it is essential to understand the function and context of DSM diagnoses in a broader context.

The DSM will be examined from three perspectives: (1) the definition of mental illness and the use of statistical normality; (2) the politics of mental illness in relationship to minority groups, including women, people of color, and lesbian, gay, and bisexual people; (3) the context of diagnosing sexual minorities and paraphilic or fetishistic behavior.

The DSM: Diagnosis and Statistics

Diagnostic and classification systems have been widely criticized on many fronts by a number of academics, theoreticians, and social critics (Bartlett, Vasey, and Bukowski, 2000; Eisenberg, 1988; Jensen and Hoagwood, 1997; Kirk and Kutchins, 1997; Szasz, 1970; Wakefield, 1997) yet the DSM remains the essential tool of diagnosis, outlining the boundaries of mental health and illness.

The first area of concern involves the definition of a mental disorder. The DSM (APA, 1994) states, "There is no assumption that each category of mental disorder is a completely discrete entity with absolute boundaries dividing it from other mental disorders or from no mental disorder" (p. xxiii; reprinted with permission from the *Diagnostic and Statistical Manual of Mental Diosorders,* Fourth Edition. Copyright 1994 American Psychiatric Association). Since the boundaries are neither absolute nor discrete, it is possible to diagnose someone with a mental disorder who simply does not have one, to not diagnose someone who does, or to misdiagnose someone who does not quite fit the outlined classification. The boundaries of diagnostic criteria are by definition vague, and decisions of categorical inclusion or exclusion are not based solely on science but on constructs and beliefs. The line between mental illness and mental health function and dysfunction is a judgment call that is at best imperfect. In addition, the definitions are revised every few years, shifting the boundaries of disease and disorder.

The DSM includes a rather long definition of "mental disorder" (see Box 5.1), one that has remained essentially unchanged since it was developed for the DSM-III in 1987, but fails to include a definition of the parameters of mental health. This seems particularly relevant since one of the principles of the DSM is the ability to distinguish between mental health and mental disorders. Wakefield (1997) said, "One cannot identify what has gone wrong (or even whether anything has gone wrong) with the patient's functioning unless one has a good idea of how the patient functions or would function when nothing is going wrong" (p. 634).

Wakefield (1997) said that one purpose of DSM diagnostic criteria is the ability to distinguish true mental disorders from the "vast array of problematic but non-disordered human conditions often referred to as 'problems in living'" (p. 634). Since the DSM does not have a definition for mental health, it cannot distinguish "problems in living" from bona fide mental disorders. "Determining when relatively common experiences such as anxiety or sadness or memory lapses should be considered evidence of some disorder requires setting boundaries that are largely arbitrary, not scientific" (Kirk and Kutchins, 1997, p. 27).

Box 5.1.
Definition of a Mental Disorder

In DSM-IV, each of the mental disorders is conceptualized as a clinically significant behavioral or psychological syndrome or pattern that occurs in an individual and that is associated with present distress (e.g., a painful symptom) or disability (i.e., impairment in one or more important areas of functioning) or with a significantly increased risk of suffering death, pain, disability, or an important loss of freedom. In addition, this syndrome or pattern must not be merely an expectable and culturally sanctioned response to a particular event, for example, the death of a loved one. Whatever its original cause, it must currently be considered a manifestation of a behavioral, psychological, or biological dysfunction in the individual. Neither deviant behavior (e.g., political, religious, or sexual) nor conflicts between the individual and society are mental disorders unless the deviance or conflict is a symptom of a dysfunction in the individual.

Source: APA, 1994, pp. xxi-xxii. Reprinted with permission from the *Diagnostic and Statistical Manual of Mental Disorders,* Fourth Edition. Copyright 1994 American Psychiatric Association.

The DSM stresses that real mental illnesses are located within individuals, not in deviant behaviors that are conflicts between the individual and society. Jensen and Hoagwood (1997) suggested that mental illnesses are never located within individuals, but that "'mental' disorders reside in communities, neighborhoods, and families" (p. 238). The meaning of the word deviance is unclear (Bartlett, Vasey, and Bukowski, 2000) and many DSM diagnoses are related far more to societal functioning than individual distress. Treatment is often pursued not because of the subjective pain of the client, but because their deviant behavior conflicts with societal expectations. This is often true for people diagnosed with addictions, as well as for those living with symptoms of bipolar disorder and schizophrenia—some of whom may indeed experience pain, but this is often determined more by others' assessments than their own subjective corroboration. Brown (1994) said, "The decision to call a cluster of behaviors a mental illness is responsive to many factors that have nothing to do with science but a great deal to do with the feelings, experiences, and epistemologies of those in power and dominance in mental health disciplines" (p. 135).

The authors of the DSM overtly deny that they are creating diagnoses based on prevailing social moral constructs, yet they proceed to diagnose pathology precisely on issues of social acceptability, "normality," and statistical commonness. Since the DSM is a statistical manual, behaviors are judged as abnormal that are uncommon. However, unusual or uncommon conditions—such as high intelligence—can be desirable and not necessarily signs of disorder (K. Wilson, 1998). It is also true that psychopathology can sometimes be an adaptive strategy, reflecting the attempts of the organism to adapt to the broader environmental context (Jensen and Hoagwood, 1997, p. 232).

Holmes and Warelow (1999) pointed out that the term *disorder* reveals "psychiatry's covert social control function, and its aspirations to eliminate behaviour which challenges or disrupts social norms" (p. 169). Statistical data was originally compiled toward the end of the nineteenth century with the intention that it could serve as the underpinning of social policy decisions (Grobs, 1991). Deciding which behavior is "disordered," "abnormal," or "dysfunctional"—especially without any particular guidelines to determine "ordered," "normal," or "functional"—is inherently a political act of judging the acceptability of human behaviors based to some extent on their frequency and commonness.

Critics of the DSM have questioned the value of using statistical infrequency as "evidence" of mental disorders. Szasz's (1970) critique of the psychiatric community suggested that deviations from behavioral norms were not illnesses in the same way that medical or biological deviations might be, and that diagnoses were essentially an excuse for social control. He said, "We call people physically ill when their bodily functions violate certain norms; similarly we call people mentally ill when their personal conduct violates certain ethical, political and social norms" (p. 4). Foucault (1978, 1990), the French philosopher and historian, believed that mental illnesses were constructed in order to justify the power and control of the medical establishment. He referred to this societal tendency to quantify and pathologize as "normalization." Fausto-Sterling (2000) examined how normalization impacted the development of surgical "correction" of intersexed infants. She said that when we "help the normal take precedence over the natural" we create a "populational biopolitics" (p. 8).

Statistics have not only been used to prove deviance but also to normalize behaviors that were once considered deviant. One of the primary political strategies for removal of the diagnosis of homosexuality from the DSM in 1973 (Bayer, 1981; Kirk and Kutchins, 1997) was the "proof" that homosexual behavior is common and therefore a "normal" human behavior. The gay civil rights movement went from a small, "deviant" social group to a massive political movement in part through a strategy of promoting itself as a large constituency of American life. The oft-quoted estimate that 10 percent of all people are homosexual became the basis for the political slogans "we are everywhere" and "come out, come out, wherever you are." The 10 percent estimate is a conflation of various categories of Alfred Kinsey's

(1948) research data on American sexuality. The value of a demographic estimate that is a half-century old and predates the entire gay and lesbian liberation movement is dubious. Although reliable modern statistics for the numbers of gay, lesbian, and bisexual people could be valuable information of social demography, attributing any statistical significance to Kinsey's data is absurd. However, the prevailing thinking suggested that if there were more gay people than had previously been recognized, then homosexuality must de facto be "normal"—for what is common is assumed normal, and what is statistically rare is often considered pathological.

Another difficulty with classification systems is the need for statistical reliability, i.e., the diagnostic categories must be able to be used by many clinicians across disciplines. This means that a diagnosis of depression, for example, should be given to the same patient when assessed by different clinicians. If one clinician thinks the person has depression, but another thinks the person has post-traumatic stress disorder, and yet a third diagnoses the person with avoidant personality disorder, the diagnosis would be considered unreliable. Despite numerous public statements about the increased reliability of the DSM-IV, "There is still not a single major study showing that the DSM (any version) is routinely used with a high reliability by regular mental health clinicians. Nor is there any credible evidence that any version of the manual has greatly increased its reliability" (Kirk and Kutchins, 1997, p. 53). Approval for transsexual surgeries is dependent on the reliability of diagnosis of gender identity disorder and the ability for the diagnosis to be used in a similar manner by various clinicians.

Finally, the DSM has come under intense scrutiny for becoming merely a tool of the managed care systems. The bottom line, in an era of the bottom dollar, is that to receive treatment utilizing third-party reimbursement there must be medical necessity. The dividing line between a medically necessary treatment for depression, anxiety, or gender identity disorder—and one that is not medically necessary—is clearly a judgment call. The question of medical necessity is a critical issue for members of the transgendered community, many of whom feel that they require surgeries to live in harmony with themselves, but these surgeries are often considered to be "elective" by the insurance companies. Although the DSM was never intended to be a tool for the managed health care system, it is undeniable that its use as a reimbursement determinant has become one of its primary functions.

Michael First, text and criteria editor for the DSM-IV, said that the "DSM is a labelling system that is inherently superficial, and it is a convenient fiction to suppose that patients' problems can be broken down into discrete categories [since] we don't understand the etiology of mental illness" (quoted in Wylie, 1995, p. 26). Wylie asked, "How did a manual of frequently hypothetical and unproven categories gain such political, cultural, and financial sway . . . ?" (p. 26). Indeed, questions abound in examining the DSM as a tool of diagnosis and treatment; and when considering its power over those living with gender variance, it wields a frightening control over their lives.

The DSM: Racism, Sexism, and Heterosexism

That the DSM is a flawed document should not be surprising to anyone who understands the complexity of scientific study applied to the vagaries of human behavior. However, the level of blatant social control embedded in the nosological system can be shocking to those who think of psychological diagnosis as a scientific endeavor. The DSM has a long history of labeling problematic political issues as pathological illnesses. The field of psychology has developed within a system that has been racist, sexist, and heterosexist, and remains transphobic. The following examples are illustrative, but far from complete. They serve to illuminate the political nature of diagnostic categories within the past century and are offered to demonstrate the need to critically examine the current biases of the diagnostic system regarding gender variance.

Racism. Diagnostic classifications and statistical analyses have been used to create and defend racist public policy throughout the history of the modern mental health system. Diagnostic manuals that predate the DSM have a long history of what would now be considered blatantly racist ideologies; contemporary manuals may be subtler but not necessarily less racist. "Defenders of slavery, proponents of racial segregation, and advocates for the exclusion of more recent immigrants have consistently attempted to justify oppression by inventing new mental illnesses and by reporting abnormally high rates of insanity to minority groups" (Kutchins and Kirk, 1997, p. 200).

Benjamin Rush, known as the father of American psychiatry, believed that African skin was dark because of a medical illness related to leprosy, an interesting, albeit negative, piece of Rush's historical legacy, conveniently left out of many books about his contributions to medicine. He also believed that people who had a fervent commitment to mass participation in democracy suffered from a mental illness called anarchia (Carter and McGoldrick, 1999; Kutchins and Kirk, 1997; Bell, 1980). Samuel Cartwright, a southern physician, identified drapetomania as a mental illness—its primary symptom was the urge of African slaves to escape slavery. He also identified dysaethesia aethiopica, which described the way slaves destroyed property on the plantation, were disobedient, talked back, fought with their masters, and refused to work. Cartwright's treatment recommendations included "whipping the devil out of them" (Kirk and Kutchins, 1997, p. 210).

Statistical evidence was used to support the continuation of slavery in the United States. In the nineteenth century, early statistical census reports gathered evidence that more blacks were insane in free states than in slave states. In fact, this research was so poorly compiled that one town of thirty-one black people identified eighty-eight mentally ill blacks (Bell, 1980). The census, however, was so well received that John C. Calhoun, who was later to become vice president and at the time of the following statement was a senator, said, "Here is the proof of the necessity of slavery. The African is incapable of self-care and sinks into lunacy under the burden of freedom" (Kutchins and Kirk, 1997, p. 205).

At the end of the nineteenth century, as questions regarding the emancipation of slaves had come to a political head, (white) scientists searched for some way to validate the division of the races. Groups were divided into "races," not just people with different skin tones. Many believed that racial differences were measurable based on biological differences. Within a climate of social Darwinism, human beings were ranked—or to be more precise men were ranked—in a hierarchical fashion in which white men were considered superior and black men were considered to be more animal than human. As white men defended their perceived hereditary advantage on scientific grounds, the lack of "evolutionary advancement" (Bell, 1980, p. 64) of blacks was justified by describing them simultaneously as less likely to be mentally ill because they were simply not intelligent enough and more likely to suffer from specific mental illnesses.

Racism, disguised as science, was levied not only on the African slave population but also on newly immigrating Europeans, mostly peasants coming to this country without education. These immigrants, particularly the Irish, were thought to be more prone to mental illness, criminality, and other forms of social deviance. They were thought to be "inferior biological stock who caused both pauperism and insanity" (Bell, 1980, p. 33). Italians, Slavs, and Jews were believed to suffer from serious mental illnesses based on their biological heredity that was said to "degenerate" with each successive generation. These "facts" were used as the underpinning of legal and political sanctions, such as restrictions on immigration, antimiscegenation laws to restrict marriages between races, and sterilization laws to stop the spread of insanity (Bem, 1993). By 1931, approximately 20,000 people had been sterilized in thirty states under laws that permitted the sterilization of criminals, as well as "any institutionalized insane, idiotic, imbecile or feebleminded person" (Bell, 1980, p. 71).

There are numerous examples of racist thinking dressed up as scientific evidence up to the current day, as evidenced by the popularity of the book *The Bell Curve* (Herrnstein and Murray, 1994), which "proved" the inferiority of black people's intellectual functioning. Loring and Powell (1988) examined the responses of 488 psychiatrists who were asked to assess case studies of both black and white patients. Clinicians ascribed more violence, suspiciousness, and dangerousness to black clients although, unknown to them, the case studies were the same as for white clients. Jones (1982) found that white therapists generally rated their black clients as more psychologically impaired than black therapists did. Evidence shows that blacks and Hispanics are more often diagnosed with schizophrenia than are whites (Wade, 1993), which may be related to class, or even classism, but might have to do with the perspectives of those who are diagnosing.

The psychological study of race is a bizarre compilation of the misuse of statistics, mythology, and assumptions. Understanding the face of racist science throughout the eighteenth and nineteenth centuries makes Hitler's eugenics philosophy and belief in the superiority of the Aryan race seem "less like the aberrant rantings of a mad man and more like the direct result of a century of scientific and political thought" (Kirk and Kutchins, 1997, p. 214).

Sexism. Unfortunately, the treatment of women in the mental health system has been no better than the treatment of people of color and other ethnic minorities, although sexism in clinical treatment has been brought more directly into public awareness in the past thirty years than has racism. From the early physicians and philosophers who raised "The Women's Question"—"what do women want?"—in the late nineteenth century, sexism has been built into the framework of the diagnostic nosology.

Just as medical diagnoses were used to reinforce racism, so were they used to maintain the status quo between the separate gendered worlds of men and women. In 1897, *The New York Times* published an article by the Reverend Charles Parkhurst who accused women of a disease called "andromania" which was described as "a passionate aping" of "everything mannish" (as quoted in Katz, 1995, p. 89). The fear, of course, was that women would win the right to vote, which would, according to Katz (1995), make them change physically and psychically and pass along pathologies to their children.

Women have been diagnosed and treated for a variety of illnesses thought to be particular to women, including neurasthenia, nervous prostration, dyspepsia, and hysteria, which was believed to be related to the wandering of the uterus within women's bodies (Ehrenreich and English, 1973, 1978; Geller and Harris, 1994). It was believed that hysteria was related to women's reproductive capacities and was the cause of all their mental health problems. The "theory of the ovary" was based in the idea that the ovaries directed women's entire psychology and that emotional problems were related to ovarian diseases. Women were medically charged with "eating like a ploughman, masturbation, attempted suicide, erotic tendencies, persecution mania [and] simple 'cussedness' " (Barker-Benfield, 1972, as quoted by Ehrenreich and English, 1978, p. 111).

Freud believed that these "hysterical" women had been abused by their fathers (who were often his medical colleagues), although he later rebutted his own theory when his colleagues threatened to destroy his reputation (Masson, 1984). We now recognize many of these symptoms as post-traumatic stress disorder and that Freud's initial assessment was most likely accurate. Note that some of these "symptoms" were normal behaviors, such as having erotic tendencies, which were pathologized by an institutionalized sexism that assumed women were not, or should not be, sexual. Women were also treated for these mental health problems with a variety of interventions specified for them, including institutionalization in mental asylums, clitoridectomies, hysterectomies, removal of ovaries, leeches applied to the labia, and forced rest cures (Ehrenreich and English, 1978; Geller and Harris, 1994).

The early feminist movement revealed the treatment of women within the psychiatric community with groundbreaking exposés such as Chesler's (1972) *Women and Madness,* and Ehrenreich and English's (1973) *Complaints and Disorders: The Sexual Politics of Sickness.* These books, as with the books that would follow on domestic violence and sexual assault (Brownmiller, 1975; Martin, 1989; Schechter, 1982; Walker, 1984), showed how women had repeatedly been the victims of a mental health system and psychiatric diagnoses that blamed them for the oppressive social conditions in which they lived. Studies emerged which showed that women were treated with more psychotropic medications, reported more psychosomatic symptomology, and were thought to have more psychological difficulties than men (see Mowbray, Lanir, and Hulce, 1985, for an overview of these studies). The very nature of a woman was thought to be unhealthy and inherently symptomatic. If women acted the way they were supposed to they were labeled less mentally healthy than men, and if they behaved more like men they were likewise assumed to have mental health problems (Broverman et al., 1970).

Psychological theories of women's development became an obvious site of examination as feminist thinking evolved in the 1970s and 1980s. Through the work of Miller (1976), Dinnerstein (1977), Chodorow (1978), Gilligan (1982), and Hare-Mustin (1983) a new psychology of women began to develop. A theory of feminist therapy began to evolve that was based on a depathologizing of mental health diagnoses, coupled with deconstructing the ways that DSM diagnoses further oppressed women. L. S. Brown (1994) said,

> Of all the relics of mainstream psychotherapy, diagnosis is the one that has seemed most distant from feminist realities and most grounded in

the problematic parameters of dominant culture. Diagnosis contradicts a political analysis, because it locates the problems in the individual, thereby privatizing both the distress and its implied solutions, and defines the distress as illness, moving the locus of analysis from context to person. (p. 125)

Caplan (1995) outlined the sexism not only in the diagnoses that are currently in the DSM but also the sexism inherent in the process of evaluating the diagnoses that become a part of the nosology of the DSM. She described the details regarding the inclusion in the DSM of the diagnostic category of premenstrual dysphoric disorder (a more severe medicalized description of premenstrual syndrome or PMS). Despite evidence from prominent feminist researchers that there is no empirical basis for the category, and that it carries social and political danger for women, it is now included as a subset that needs "further study." A diagnostic category called self-defeating personality disorder (formerly called masochistic personality disorder) was removed from the DSM after political pressure discredited the American Psychiatric Association's committee process. The committee, however, never stated that the diagnosis was incorrect as a mental illness, only that they had ceased its inclusion.

Although feminist theory has challenged the hegemony of sexism within the dominant diagnostic community, the system as it stands is still replete with sexist ideology. Within recent years, debates about diagnostic inclusion and usage have been waged regarding borderline personality disorder and dissociative identity disorder. These diagnoses are disproportionately seen in women who are victims of trauma and routinely treated with psychopharmacological treatments without any analysis of how the social conditions in which women live propagate their psychological distress (Caplan, 1995; Herman, 1992; Kutchins and Kirk, 1997).

Heterosexism. Examining the history of racism and sexism in the DSM is essential as a frame for understanding the power of diagnostic systems and the role of social control in the development of a science. However, studying the diagnosis of homosexuality is integral to the study of transgenderism, for the two phenomena have been linked historically, legally, and psychologically. Homosexuality, long considered a psychopathology, was removed from the DSM in 1973 (Bayer, 1981), and its removal clearly illustrates the role of politics in the definitions of diagnostic categories. According to Bartlett, Vasey, and Bukowski (2000) the definition of a mental disorder was first developed in reaction to the controversy over removing homosexuality from the DSM.

As was outlined in Chapter 2, the nineteenth century saw the development of the study of human sexuality, and many of the concepts that were then invented and defined are still included in the DSM's section on sexual paraphilias today, including transvestitism, fetishism, and sadomasochism (Hekma, 1994). Foucault (1978) referred to this process of examining human sexuality under the microscope of mental health as the "psychiatrization of perversions" (p. 147).

Homosexuality appeared in the DSM-I under the label of sociopathic personality disturbance, placing it in the rubric of diagnoses that we currently label as personality (or characterological) disorders. Although the organization of the DSM was vastly different in 1952, personality disorders are now Axis II diagnoses, which are thought to be enduring, pervasive, and inflexible personality traits that are resistant to permanent change (this section also once included addictive behaviors). There was no defining characteristic of homosexuality, which was classified under the heading Sexual Deviation (APA, 1952, p. 38).

In 1968, the DSM-II further developed the section on sexual deviations, and listed homosexuality along with other paraphilias including fetishism, pedophilia, and transvestitism. These were considered nonpsychotic mental disorders (APA, 1968, p. 44). Bayer (1981) noted that,

> Despite the existence of a very well developed homophile movement at the time the DSM-II was issued, homosexual activists appear to have been unconcerned with its publication. Two years later the classification of homosexuality in the Manual was to become the central focus of the Gay Liberation movement's attack on psychiatry. (p. 40)

The growth of the homophile movement, and later the gay and lesbian liberation movement (see D'Emilio, 1983; Duberman, 1993), created a new politic, an emerging sense of political protest, and the focus of societal change rested on removing the diagnosis of homosexuality from the DSM.

Evelyn Hooker researched the first nonclinical sample of homosexual men in 1969, and she discovered that this population did not exhibit the mental health issues that had been attributed to them (D'Emilio, 1983). She found that many of her subjects were satisfied with their sexual orientations, showed no significant psychopathology, and were functioning well socially and occupationally. Hooker's research played an instrumental role in the eventual removal of homosexuality from the DSM. A number of other reasons for homosexuality's removal from the DSM included a changing belief that even if the etiology of homosexuality was caused by a mental illness, the consequence or outcome was not in itself disturbed. It was determined that the condition failed to meet the DSM's criteria for distress, disability, and causing an inherent disadvantage (APA, 1980; Stoller et al., 1973).

Although it is often stated that homosexuality was officially removed from the DSM in 1973 (actually the seventh printing of the DSM-II), in reality the category was replaced in the DSM-III with a somewhat less noxious diagnosis—ego-dystonic homosexuality. Dystonic refers to the subjective experience of unhappiness and is contrasted with syntonic behavior or one's comfort with same-sex desires. The DSM-III clearly stated that this diagnosis should be used only when there is a "sustained pattern of homosexual arousal that the individual explicitly states has been unwanted and a persistent source of distress" (APA, 1980, p. 282). It also states that "distress resulting from a conflict between a homosexual and society should not be classified here" (APA, 1980, p. 282). The DSM fails to provide guidelines on how to distinguish between ego-dystonic homosexuality that involves conflicts with society and that which does not.

It soon became clear to the DSM's authors that many homosexuals living in a homophobic and heterosexist culture suffer terribly from low self-esteem, sexual identity confusion, and the general internalization of being a stigmatized minority. Ego-dystonic homosexuality was removed in the DSM-III-R (Revised Edition) because, "It suggested to some that homosexuality itself was considered a disorder . . . [and] almost all people who are homosexual first go through a phase in which their homosexuality is ego-dystonic" (APA, 1987, p. 426).

Most clinicians today, including clinicians specializing in working with LGBT clients, believe that homosexuality has been completely removed from the DSM. However, a residual category for homosexuality still remains in the DSM-IV-TRC, under the category of Sexual Disorders Not Otherwise Specified (NOS). This category includes three items, the last of which is, "Persistent and marked distress about sexual orientation" (APA, 2000, p. 582). Although written in a deceptively neutral manner, it is clear that this category is not intended for heterosexuals who are distressed about their sexual orientation and seeking treatment to "become" gay. If a clinician still believes that homosexuality is pathological—and there are ongoing efforts to reinstitute the diagnoses of homosexuality in the DSM (Socarides, 1999; Nicolosi, 1991)—there are numerous ways to diagnose and treat homosexuals utilizing the extant classifications systems. Sexual Disorder NOS is one, and the other is through the diagnosis of gender identity disorder.

The DSM and Sexual Deviations

Gender identity disorder is classified in the section of the DSM called Sexual and Gender Identity Disorders, which outlines three general groups of sexual and gender-related difficulties: sexual dysfunctions, paraphilias, and gender identity disorders. The subsection on sexual dysfunctions involves difficulties with sexual performativity (e.g., orgasmic difficulties and male erectile problems) that are often accompanied by intrapsychic distress and interpersonal difficulties. The subsection on gender identity disorders will be delineated in the following discussion. The subsection on paraphilias outlines sexual deviations and will be the focus of this discussion.

An understanding of the subsection on paraphilias is essential to understanding the DSM's position on sexual and gender variation, since transvestic fetishism (i.e., erotic cross-dressing) is classified as a paraphilia. The term *paraphilia* was developed by Wilhelm Stekel in the 1930s to replace *perversions* (Bullough, 2000), and came from *para* (beyond, abnormal, altered, or incorrect) and *philia* (to like, to love, to have an attraction or tendency toward). Money (1998) defined *paraphilia* as "love beyond the usual." The DSM-IV-TR defines paraphilias as "recurrent, intense sexually arousing fantasies, sexual urges, or behaviors involving 1) nonhuman objects, 2) the suffering or humiliation of oneself or one's partner, 3) children or other nonconsenting persons" (APA, 2000, p. 566). The DSM gives no definition for normal human sexual behavior; it does, however, develop a complex nosology for deviant sexual practices.

The focus in the following discussion is on sexual pathology that (1) is uncommon, (2) is nonconsensual and often illegal, and (3) causes clinically significant distress or impairment. The purpose in deconstructing the subsection on paraphilias is not to deny that many unusual sexual behaviors can be harmful to self or others, nor that sexual compulsive behaviors do not warrant clinical attention. Some paraphilias are dangerous, pathological, or nonconsensual and necessitate legal sanction. However, as John Money (1998) said, "No absolute criterion standard exists by which to separate paraphilia as a personal, harmless, and playful eccentricity from paraphilia as a social nuisance or a noxiously morbid or lethal syndrome" (p. 144). Paraphilias, as they are now classified in the DSM, include many human sexual variations. Some of these are illegal; others are nonconsensual; and all of which are somewhat unusual, statistically speaking—with little distinction made between disordered behavior and sexual "play" between consenting adults. This lumping together of issues of minority sexuality with criminality and mental illness is a great flaw in the design of the DSM for the treatment of people with sexual disorders as well as the civil liberties of adults with uncommon, albeit "kinky," sexual expressions. Pathologizing human sexuality will deter those who need treatment from reaching out to the clinical community and perpetuate the illusion that those who are mandated into treatment for inappropriate, compulsive, violent, or nonconsensual behaviors are representative of the communities of people who practice minority sexualities.

Rare and unusual behaviors. Little systematic or comprehensive research on human sexual behavior has been conducted, and funding for sexuality research has not been readily available. It is important to realize how little actual information we have on human sexuality, especially on human sexual variations. The most well-known sex research is that of Kinsey (1948, 1953), but Kinsey's research is already outdated. It is interesting to note that his book on male sexuality sold out within weeks of its publication to a primarily lay audience, despite it being a scholarly book written for professionals (D'Emilio, 1983). This may be indicative of the interest the public had in human *sexual behavior,* a term Kinsey coined to describe a range of erotic practices, regardless of the social and moral climate of the times. Perhaps people were seeking confirmation from the research that they were not alone in their sexual desires.

Kinsey (1948, 1953) studied the erotic lives of 10,000 people and exploded many myths about human sexuality. He maintained an "ideological posture of extraordinary tolerance for the diversity he had discovered in his data on sexuality" (Bayer, 1981, p. 45). His research clearly profiled how common it was for American men and women to engage in numerous "deviant" sexual behaviors, including masturbation, premarital sex, adultery, and homosexuality. It is not surprising that the first transsexual patient Harry Benjamin saw was through a referral from Kinsey.

It is extremely difficult to ascertain information on sexual behaviors in general, and people rarely admit to behaviors that are stigmatized and diagnosable. The DSM-IV-TR states that although "paraphilias are rarely diagnosed in general clinical facilities, the large commercial market in paraphilic pornography and paraphernalia suggests that its prevalence in the community is likely to be higher" (APA, 2000, p. 568). If the majority of people who engage in paraphilias are not seen in clinical populations, then are assessments about the mental health of people who practice these sexual behaviors being made based on clinical samples of people with other mental health problems? Furthermore, is it possible that people engaging in paraphilic behavior who are not exhibiting "clinically significant distress or impairment" do not seek out mental health services because they do not need them?

The DSM-IV-TR states that females are "almost never" (APA, 2000, p. 568) diagnosed with paraphilias (the male to female ratio suggested is 20:1). Since male paraphiliacs commonly engage in many of these sexual behaviors with other persons, the assumption must be that such acts are either all homosexually oriented or that women are being forced to engage in these behaviors against their will. Certainly, evidence suggests that some gay men engage in paraphilic behavior and that women are victimized by forced sexual activity, paraphilic and otherwise, in high numbers. However, it is also possible that women are consensually engaging in the same paraphilic behaviors as men but are less often diagnosed, which raises questions about how the gender of the participant affects the application of diagnostic labels. Can it be that prejudices about women's sexuality affect the assumptions researchers bring to their studies, the kinds of questions clinicians inquire about, and the concerns women themselves bring into therapy?

The numbers of people interested in paraphilic activity—women as well as men—has become increasingly more apparent with the growth of the Internet. It is no accident that the Internet has become a "gathering place" for sexual minority people who often feel safer discussing vulnerable issues within a communication network in which people are nameless and faceless. Web sites dedicated to issues of kinky sexuality are numerous, with hundreds of thousands of visitors each month. Clearly, the DSM's pathologizing of certain sexual proclivities has not stopped people from exploring these interests. What was previously thought to be "rare and unusual" sexuality may be fairly common.

Consensuality. Many of the disorders in the paraphilias section of the DSM involve a nonconsenting partner (e.g., pedophilia, frotteurism, exhibitionism, and voyeurism) who is "used" in some manner by the perpetrator. The issue of consent is a primary issue defining many paraphilias. However, instead of focusing on the question of consent and the issues involved in forced sexual contact with an unwilling partner, the DSM focuses on the erotic behavior itself. A primary difficulty with the paraphilia section of the DSM is that the issues of eroticism, sexual desire, and consensual sexuality are conflated with issues of forced sex, legality, and social control.

For example, the diagnosis of pedophilia is defined as "sexual activity with a prepubescent child" (APA, 2000, p. 571) and since children are not considered able—legally or psychologically—to consent to sexual expression with an adult, why is the pedophile's sexual interest the focal point of investigation, instead of the forced sexual behavior? The DSM does not diagnose rape as a psychopathology, and acts of sexual assault and violence are not explained as being about sex or sexuality. Feminist theory explains these behaviors as driven by power and control enacted within a sexual arena (Brownmiller, 1975). If pedophilia is an erotic sexual disorder, then rape should also be an erotic sexual disorder, since both clearly involve sex. Sexual assault, however, is not a psychological diagnosis—it is a criminal offense. In the case of pedophilia, it is not simply the perpetrator's eroticism that is the problem. It is his (commonly male) *behavior* that is illegal.

Other paraphilic disorders, e.g., frotteurism, exhibitionism, and voyeurism, involve sexual behaviors such as "rubbing against" another human and desiring to exhibit and/or view other human bodies that involve nonconsenting partners. Again, the "pathology" is not the desire or the eroticism. It is the nonconsensual nature of the sexual expression. The desires themselves are common, normative sexual experiences. What could be healthier than being sexually aroused by looking/being looked at and "rubbing"? Indeed, capitalizing on these basic human desires is the basis for huge consumer marketing strategies in the fashion industry, the cosmetic industry, and the media. Even Freud, in his exploration of sexual "perversions," admitted that such behaviors were "rarely absent from the sexual life of healthy people." He said that it was not the *"content"* of the unusual sexuality that defined it as a perversion but the "exclusivity and fixation" that made them pathological (Freud, [1905] 1962, p. 27).

What is pathological about these disorders is that these behaviors are nonconsensual, which also makes them illegal. Perhaps a section in the DSM involving nonconsensual sexual exploitation and abuse would be more appropriate than conflating inappropriate sexual behavior with consensual sex acts explored for sexual pleasure. However, does perpetrating a sexual crime mean that the person has a mental illness? Why are these issues being diagnosed in a clinical classification system? Perhaps they would be better dealt with in the criminal justice system.

The DSM-IV-TR does not offer a context for viewing many of these sexual behaviors as consensual, although it does suggest that paraphilias must be **"distinguished from the nonpathological use of sexual fantasies, behaviors, objects as stimulus for sexual excitement"** (APA, 2000, p. 568). The challenge here is that the DSM does not define "nonpathological." The diagnostic sections on sadism and masochism illustrate this dilemma. According to the DSM-IV-TR, sadistic and masochistic (S/M) behaviors must be "real, not simulated" (APA, 2000, pp. 572-574), but it does not define what this means. Many people engage in S/M sex, that is "simulated" in the sense that it is theatrically choreographed, but it is also "real" in the sense that the sensations are authentic. The context of the clause "real, not simulated" perhaps refers to consensuality, but the lack of specificity leaves this diagnostic category open to arbitrary use and potential misuse by clinicians who do not believe consensual sadomasochistic behavior is possible. If the writers of the DSM understand that consensual sadistic or masochistic sexual behaviors are acceptable (which the previous quote seems to suggest), then it is not the erotic nature of the sexuality that is pathological but the lack of consent that is problematic. Practitioners of S/M sexual activity define S/M by its consensual nature (Thompson, 1991). Nonconsenting sadism and masochism is nothing less than sexual assault, which is a criminal act and not a sexual behavior. Again, the DSM conflates issues of pathology with questions about forensics.

Furthermore, the DSM labels behavior "sexual sadism" that seems to have little to do with either sex or sadism. For example, the DSM-IV-TR mentions that a sexual sadist might take a job driving an ambulance in order to be near his or her desired stimulus (APA, 2000, p. 567)! If a person took a job driving an ambulance because he or she found it sexually stimulating, this might indeed be indicative of a mental health problem. However, labeling it "sexual sadism" does not help us to clarify or understand the issue. The focus in the DSM is on the erotic nature of certain behaviors instead of the obsessive, delusional, or aggressive behavior of perpetrators.

It is also interesting to note how the DSM dissects sexual behaviors into "parts" that are then pathologically analyzed. If there is a diagnosis for frotteurism—defined as "touching and rubbing against a nonconsenting person" (APA, 2000, p. 570)—perhaps there should also be a diagnosis (with more clinical words, of course) for other common inappropriate sexual behaviors such as "looking up skirts" or "whistling, flirting, or provocative staring in public." Why is only frotteurism officially considered a "diagnosis"?

Finally, the DSM's definition of paraphilias includes not just behaviors but "sexually arousing fantasies, [and] sexual urges," although the latest revision states that clinical significance for certain paraphilias is defined by the person acting on his or her urges or experiencing interpersonal difficulties (APA, 2000, p. 566). Can someone be diagnosed with a mental illness because of his or her sexual fantasy life or because a partner is uncomfortable with his or her sexual interests? The vagueness of this subsection, coupled with a lack of discussion on the parameters of healthy "normal" human sexual expression, leave these diagnostic categories open to misuse by clinicians who are struggling with issues of morality and religiosity.

Clinically significant distress. To meet the diagnostic criteria for a paraphilia an individual must experience "clinically significant distress and impairment in social, occupational, or other important areas of functioning" (APA, 2000, p. 566), although it is clearly stated in the DSM-IV-TR that "many individuals with these disorders assert that the behavior causes them no distress and their only problem is social dysfunction as a result of the reactions of others to their behaviors" (APA, 2000, p. 567). If erotic deviance is a problem only if distress and social dysfunction result, then people without distress or social dysfunction should not be labeled pathological.

However, according to the DSM, distress includes legal complications and impairment in social functioning. This is an interesting dilemma since the legal complications and social problems are often directly related to the pathological nature of the diagnosis. In other words, since a person can be arrested for engaging in nonnormative sex in certain locales, a person can then fit the criteria for a psychiatric diagnosis by being arrested since he or she now has legal and social problems associated with the paraphilia. In circular logic, people are diagnosed as mentally ill for having distress about a sexual expression that has been defined as deviant, and the distress itself solidifies the justifications for the diagnosis. If paraphilias that are consensual were legal, and if they were not labeled as psychiatric diagnoses, then people might not have emotional, legal, or social distress regarding them.

Remember that the DSM-IV-TR clearly asserts, "Neither deviant behavior (e.g., political, religious, or sexual) nor conflicts between the individual and society are mental disorders" (APA, 2000, p. xxxi), so distinguishing between distress that is within a person and distress that is socially induced is paramount. Merely having one's erotic desires labeled as pathological creates shame, and the shame in turn causes the distress that is then defined as the diagnostic hallmark of the disorder! Ego-dystonic homosexuality used to be classified in the DSM's section on paraphilia until it was understood that the ego-dystonic emotions and behaviors that many gay, lesbian, and bisexual people experience, particularly when first coming out, are the costs of being associated with a stigmatized minority. The DSM no longer reinforces the internalized shame by using the effects of the stigma as proof that gay, lesbian, and bisexual people are mentally ill. However, the DSM still labels other issues of sexual diversity "paraphilias" and misunderstands the shame that people experience to be proof of their mental illness.

Sexual behaviors can have an obsessive quality and some people experience recurrent and pervasive fantasies about commonly practiced sexual behaviors that can cause severe distress or dysfunction. Sexuality disturbances can cause severe anxiety and can become sexually compulsive or even impulsive. A person who is obsessed with sexual thoughts—whether they are common sexual practices such as masturbation or less common sexual behaviors such as sexual masochism—must be clinically treated for his or her obsessive thoughts as well as potentially impulsive behaviors. However, it is not the erotic stimuli or the sexual desires that is pathological—it is the obsessive, compulsive, and violent nature of the behavior. Again, why is the focus on the psychosexual phenomenon instead of the dysfunctional behavior?

The DSM: Social Science or Social Control?

Although a discussion of the paraphilias may seem to be tangential to gender identity issues, the paraphilia subsection of the DSM includes the diagnosis of erotic transvestitism. Questions of disorder, diagnoses, political classifications, and professional erotophobia are at the crux of any discussion on assessment and treatment issues of this paraphilia. Is erotic cross-dressing behavior a mental disorder and an indication of psychopathology? If so, why is it considered a fetish only when exhibited by heterosexual males? If someone who cross-dresses experiences compulsions to cross-dress or distress regarding these desires, should the identified problem be his or her compulsion, anxiety, or the clothes that he or she is wearing? This would be like referring to agoraphobia—the fear of leaving one's house—as "paranoid house disorder," and the treatment resting on changing the living quarters from a colonial to a ranch. Clearly this diagnostic category—and probably all gender-related diagnoses of the DSM—needs to be reexamined in light of contemporary knowledge of sexuality and sexual deviations.

In reviewing the history of diagnostic classification systems, it is revealed that labeling dysfunction has been neither benign nor scientific. The influence of religious morality and legalistic social control is evident, which is not surprising given that these institutions have historically governed sexual mores. In a scientific and secular culture, the diagnostic manual is not the place for value-laden sexual morality. Indeed, an investigation of the treatment of people of color, ethnic minorities, women, lesbian, gay, and bisexual people, as well as other sexual minorities under the guise of mental health and diagnosis, is an exposé of racist, sexist, heterosexist, and erotophobic thinking masquerading as science.

The invention of classification systems to label sexual deviations occurred during the mid to late 1800s, the same era that racial classifications were being scientifically formulated. Somerville (2000) said, "It was not merely a historical coincidence that the classification of bodies as either 'homosexual' or 'heterosexual' emerged at the same time that the United States was aggressively constructing and policing the boundary of 'black' and 'white' bodies" (p. 3). Racial science postulated that homosexuals had many of the same characteristics that "primitive" races had (as compared to the more "advanced" European ones), including "degeneracy, . . . regression, and hypersexuality" (Terry, 1999, p. 36). Carter (1997) outlined how the theory of "decadence" impacted the belief that homosexuality was unnatural and inferior to heterosexuality, commenting that it was believed homosexuals were "racially immature people who had developed neither the psychic nor the physical capacity to separate males from females as firmly as a civilized adult could have done" (p. 164).

Alfred Binet, co-creator of the Binet-Simon intelligence test, was also the inventor of the sexual category of "fetishism" (Hekma, 1994, p. 223). These seemingly disparate concepts are both used as tools to hierarchically rank and classify people. In an era when many groups of politically disenfranchised people were demanding equal rights as citizens, "the science of physical difference was often invoked to invalidate claims for social and political emancipation" (Fausto-Sterling, 2000, p. 39). Wilchins (1997b) jested that American Psychiatric Association has its own disorder, which she calls "GenderPathoPhilia," defined as "(1) an obsessive fear or need to pathologize any kind of gender behavior that makes you feel uncomfortable; (2) a dread disease that strikes nine out of ten American psychiatrists" (p. 225). This raises interesting questions about exactly "whose" behavior is obsessive.

Bringing justice to the diagnostic system regarding ethnic and racial differences, gender differences, and sexual identities and behaviors has been, and continues to be, an uphill battle. As long as normative human differences are defined as pathological, people will remain covert about their involvement, exhibit symptomatology related to their shame, and, when discovered, will become stigmatized and held up as examples of human aberration. Kinsey (1948) suggested that if there were not social constraints against homosexuality it would be more commonplace, and history has born the truth of this. Perhaps the same is true for paraphilias and gender variance as well. As long as psychology continues to condemn people for their sexual and gender differences, they will continue to manifest mental health problems related not to their differences but to their being labeled pathological.

The process of removing homosexuality from the DSM is a story rarely told, of how a diagnosed mentally ill minority took charge of its own destiny through personal empowerment and political advocacy, and claimed its right to human citizenship. This history can serve as a model for transgendered people. It is also true that many of the early gay liberationists, particularly the heroes of the Stonewall rebellion, were gender-variant people themselves. For homosexuals in the late 1960s there was the "realization that one was collectively oppressed rather than individually disturbed" (Plummer, 1981, p. 25), a realization that began to dawn on gender-variant people in the 1990s.

If homosexuality had not been removed from the DSM in 1973, it is unlikely that public discussions of gays in the military, domestic partner benefits, or gay adoption would be part of the public policy debate. Throwing off the yoke and stigma of abnormality allowed not only for the psychological growth of self-esteem on the part of gay, lesbian, and bisexual people but also for legal and political transformations that would never have been granted to a "mentally ill" population. The great bravery shown by the small handful of out, white, gay male clinicians and activists who first confronted the medical and psychological establishment in a much more homophobic era has never been fully acknowledged or appreciated by their inheritors. One cannot help but wonder: if they had not taken the risks they did, and if this diagnosis had remained on the books, what opposition we would face in having it removed today?

Today, the absurdity of many of the sexist, racist, and heterosexist diagnoses discussed earlier probably appear as obvious as political prejudices dressed up as medical science. It is too easy to ignore these prejudices of the past, however, and to refuse to see how the belief systems that birthed these situations still exist today. Blaming ignorant men of past eras who lived by absurd stereotypes and mistaken conventions may ease their inheritors of professional shame, but in an effort to separate themselves from these theories clinicians may fail to recognize the mythologies of the present.

Homosexuals were the first group of sexual "deviants" who organized to have their erotic identities depathologized. As Rubin (1984) said, "Sexualities keep marching out of the Diagnostic and Statistical Manual and on to the pages of social history" (p. 287). The remainder of this chapter examines how gender has been pathologized, both as a fetish and as a sexual disorder, and the controversies involved in removing these diagnoses from the DSM.

GENDER AS PATHOLOGICAL DIAGNOSIS

The master's tools will never dismantle the master's house.

Audre Lorde
The Transformation of Silence into Language and Action, 1984

Outlining the history of biases in the scientific formulation of mental health diagnoses sets the stage, it is hoped, for a reevaluation and deconstruction of the gender identity disorders and the paraphilic diagnosis of transvestic fetishism. As has been stated, the standards of care for transgendered and transsexual people depend on proper "diagnosis." It stands to reason that if the diagnostic system is flawed, then assessment and treatment concerns will be negatively affected.

Transvestic Fetishism

Transvestic fetishism is located in the paraphilia section of the DSM-IV-TR's chapter on sexual and gender identity disorders. The diagnostic criteria for transvestic fetishism are listed in Box 5.2. In some ways, these criteria are simple and direct, compared to the complex classifications in other sections of the DSM. In order to evaluate this diagnosis, one must understand both fetishism and transvestism. Etiologically, there is a distinction between transvestism and transsexualism, with transvestism considered a less serious disorder than transsexualism. Transvestism involves cross-

---

Box 5.2.

Diagnostic Criteria for 302.3 Transvestic Fetishism

A. Over a period of at least 6 months, in a heterosexual male, recurrent intense sexually arousing fantasies, sexual urges, or behaviors involving cross-dressing.

B. The fantasies, sexual urges, or behaviors cause clinically significant distress or impairment in social, occupational, or other important areas of functioning.

Specify if:

With Gender Dysphoria: if the person has persistent discomfort with gender role or identity

Source: APA, 1994, p. 531. Reprinted with permission from the *Diagnostic and Statistical Manual of Mental Disorders,* Fourth Edition. Copyright 1994 American Psychiatric Association.

---

dressing behavior but does not commonly involve conflicts in one's core gender identity. Transvestites cross-dress for pleasure or relaxation and often have an opposite sex persona, but are thought to have less gender dysphoria or desire for surgical reassignment (Peo, 1988). Many in the transgendered community consider the term *transvestite* a clinical invention and prefer the term *cross-dresser.*

Fetishism is defined as "an object or bodily part whose real or fantasied presence is psychologically necessary for sexual gratification and that is an object of fixation to the extent that it may interfere with complete sexual expression" (Merriam-Webster, 2000). Usually this erotic attraction is directed toward nonliving objects such as clothing or certain textures (e.g., silk, leather, and rubber) that enhance sexuality. Fetishes are usually intensely arousing and required or are strongly preferred for sexual excitement. The question of whether fetishes "interfere" with or "enhance" complete sexual expression depends on the definition of "complete." Does completion infer heterosexual intercourse, orgasm, or human intimacy? One bisexual woman noted that from her vantage point both heterosexuals and homosexuals appear to be "genderfetishists," limiting the "complete" range of their sexual expression (Litwoman, 1990). Indeed, prototypical heterosexual sex often involves a near-obsessive fixation on certain body parts (e.g., breasts) and even body types (e.g., slender), but these are considered socially normative desires and not pathological. However, a fixation on, say, feet or fat women would, of course, infer a "fetish."

It is interesting to note that another definition of fetish is "an object (such as a small stone carving of an animal) believed to have magical power to protect or aid its owner" (Merriam-Webster, 2000). This raises interesting questions about the nature of the intense "obsessive" quality of certain sexual objects and the transcendent and even "spiritual" power these objects may convey to the owner.

Transvestic fetishism is the erotic experience of cross-dressing behavior, and the diagnosis is explicitly to be used when there is "clinically significant distress or impairment in social, occupational, or other important areas of functioning" (APA, 2000, p. 575). If a person cross-dresses without any clinical distress or impairment, or if he or she cross-dresses for nonerotic purposes, he or she cannot be diagnosed with this mental disorder. It is not the eroticism of the behavior but the presence of clinical distress and impairment that metamorphosizes transvestism into a disorder. However, due to the stigma associated with cross-dressing behavior, distress may develop if the person is "caught" cross-dressing, with social and occupational ramifications following close behind. Cross-dressing, if discovered, can interfere with marital relations, as well as occupational stability, and may have legal ramifications in certain locales.

The DSM-IV-TR states that transvestic fetishism "has been described only in heterosexual males" (APA, 2000, p. 574), which raises some interesting questions. Is cross-dressing "normal" when homosexual or bisexual men have fantasies or sexual urges to cross-dress? Are females who cross-dress exhibiting signs of mental health, but heterosexual males exhibiting signs of mental illness? Can it be that heterosexual males are held to a different standard of behavior than females and homosexual males? It is considered aberrant behavior for heterosexual men to wear women's clothing, and it is considered bizarre for them to become turned on by doing so. Sexism assures that heterosexual men who wear women's clothing will experience distress in the form of social, occupational, and even legal problems, especially if they are caught with "their pants down." Wilson (1997) said, "The criterion serves to enforce a stricter standard of conformity for males than females. Its dual standard not only reflects the disparate positions that men and women hold in American society, but *promotes* them" (p. 5, italics mine). The implication, as Wilson explained, is that males who want to emulate females—the inferior and more despised sex—are exhibiting a mental disorder, but females who desire to emulate male power in their dress are mentally healthy.

Most sexologists assume that when females cross-dress it is not erotic. For instance, Ettner and Brown (1999) said, "male items of clothing possess no erotic properties" (p. 72). This is not, however, accurate. Many females experience eroticism wearing male clothing, and erotic cross-dressing is not limited to heterosexuals. Bullough and Bullough's (1997) research showed "a significant variation in sexual orientation among people who cross-dress" (p. 10) and erotic cross-dressing behavior exists within both the lesbian and gay male communities. However, heterosexual males who cross-dress experience social ostracism, raising many questions about the social control purposes of gendered clothing.

The values underlying the diagnosis of transvestic fetishism are more about sexist values and conflicts between individuals and society than they are about sexual disorders or human distress. This violates the definition of a mental disorder outlined in the DSM. Like the disorders of the past that reflected the social mores of the times (e.g., anarchia, drapetomania, hysteria, homosexuality), transvestic fetishism is a normal human behavior transformed into a mental illness. Transvestic fetishism might be statistically uncommon; it might cause distress if the person fears getting caught; it might create dysfunction if the person believes that he or she has a mental problem; it might cause marital problems depending on the spouse's sexual proclivities; it might interfere with the enactment of other sexual behaviors; it might be concurrent with gender dysphoria; it might be erotically pleasing; it might present emotional confusion and introspection for the participant. It is not, however, a mental illness, a disease, or a dysfunction, unless, of course, it is obsessive or nonconsensual. Transvestic fetishism is a sexual behavior, variant perhaps, but merely an erotic sexual inclination, one that causes no inherent harm. Therefore it should not be listed in a manual of mental disorders.

Gender Identity Disorder

The development of the diagnostic category for transsexualism was an important step toward legitimizing gender dysphoria as a valid mental health concern. The formal recognition of gender identity disorders affirmed them "as conditions worthy of evaluation and treatment" and acknowledged sex reassignment surgeries "as a legitimate treatment and not an elective or cosmetic surgery" (Pauly, 1992, p. 3). Medical treatment for transsexuals became available because a diagnostic category existed that supported the intractability of cross-gender experience, although clinicians have argued about the correct terminology. Fisk (1973) advocated "gender dysphoria," the ICD uses "transsexualism," the DSM uses "gender identity disorder," and Di Ceglie (1998) recommended "atypical gender identity disorganization" (p. 9).

Schaefer, Wheeler, and Futterweit (1995) outlined seven diagnostic criteria that have historically defined transsexualism:

1. Individual has felt prolonged discomfort with anatomic sex.
2. Individual has experience living in the opposite-sex role.
3. Individual is determined to undergo surgical restructuring of genitals.
4. Individual selects procedures to physically alter sexual characteristics to simulate those of the other gender.
5. Gender identity disorder appears to be permanent and constant over time . . .
6. Individual has no intersex or genetic abnormality [sic].
7. Gender identity disorder is independent of, if not caused by, any other mental disorder. (p. 2022)

The inclusion of GID in the DSM has not been without its controversies. Interestingly, the development of a diagnosis for transsexuality coincided with the removal of homosexuality from the DSM (Whittle, 1993). As outlined earlier, the removal of homosexuality was the result of an organized political campaign to depathologize sexual orientation diversity. However, concurrent with this reevaluation of previously held notions about homosexuality, transsexuality was created as an appropriate category of pathology. According to Wilson (1997), "American psychiatric perceptions of transgendered people are remarkably parallel to those for gay and lesbian people before the declassification of homosexuality as a mental disorder in 1973" (p. 15). Furthermore, GID may be used to diagnose gender-variant homosexuals, especially youth, continuing the pathologization of lesbian, gay, and bisexual people under a new diagnostic category (Rottnek, 1999; Scholinski, 1997).

Since its inception in the DSM, GID has been through a number of clinical revisions, and the current diagnostic criterion continues to be examined for omissions and limitations (Bower, 2001). Transsexualism was included in the DSM in 1980 as a separate nosological category but was later assimilated into the larger section on sexual and gender identity disorders (Bradley and Zucker, 1997; Michel, Mormont, and Legros, 2001). *Transsexuality* was defined in the DSM-III as a "Sense of discomfort and inappropriateness about one's anatomic sex; Wish to be rid of one's own genitals and to live as a member of the other sex; . . . continuous (not limited to periods of stress) for at least two years; [with an] Absence of physical or genetic abnormality, [and] Not due to another mental disorder, such as Schizophrenia" (APA, 1980, pp. 263-264). Transsexualism was further subclassified with a fifth digit code by sexual identity styles (e.g., asexual, homosexual, heterosexual, or unspecified). A separate category was also developed for children who were gender variant—gender identity disorder of childhood.

A number of difficulties emerged with this classification. First, it established a linkage between the desire for sex reassignment surgeries with transsexualism. Since a diagnosis of transsexualism is necessary for any hormonal treatments or reassignment surgeries, and erotic cross-dressing may preclude this diagnosis, transsexuals may lie to clinicians about their libidinous feelings when cross-dressed (Walworth, 1997). Some transsexuals might maximize their gender and genital dysphoria in order to conform to official guidelines and receive the treatments they desire.

Second, the subtyping according to sexual orientation was extremely confusing since biological sex was used as a point of reference, privileging natal sex over self-identified gender identity, which negates not only the experience of the person but also the entire significance and intention of his or her transformation. This created huge terminology and communication difficulties that are still evident when sorting through the literature (Pauly, 1992).

Finally, the DSM diagnosis of gender identity disorder of childhood had accurately identified the early manifestations of gender dysphoria and gender variance in many young children. Unfortunately this set the stage for the "management" of these children through clinics intended to "fix" their inappropriate gender behavior, rendering invisible those whose gender issues did not surface in early childhood (i.e., "late onset" or "secondary" transsexuals). This category was later subsumed into the general category of GID.

The DSM-III-R was the first diagnostic manual to describe gender identity disturbances that were not transsexualism under a subclassification referred to as "nontranssexual type." Unfortunately, this subclassification was removed in later editions. Gender-variant people who do not wish to "be rid of" their own genitals were relegated to a "non" category; they could not be classified as transsexuals and therefore became ineligible to access certain treatment strategies available only to "true transsexuals."

The DSM-IV classified gender identity disorders in the section on psychosexual disorders, creating new criteria for diagnosis (see Box 5.3). Unlike the previous edition, the criteria for children, adolescents, and adults are classified together, but there are separate diagnostic codes for children (Bradley and Zucker, 1997). Specifiers are required for "sexually mature individuals," to describe their sexual attractions (p. 582). There are four choices—sexual attraction to males, females, both, or neither—and it is stated that those who are attracted to "neither" often have schizoid traits. Furthermore, gender-variant females are assumed to be almost exclusively attracted to females (i.e., they are pretransition lesbians), although excep-

Box 5.3.
Diagnostic Criteria for Gender Identity Disorder

A. A strong and persistent cross-gender identification (not merely a desire for any perceived cultural advantages of being the other sex).

In children, the disturbance is manifested by four (or more) of the following:

  (1) repeatedly stated desire to be, or insistence that he or she is, the other sex
  (2) in boys, preference for cross-dressing or simulating female attire; in girls, insistence on wearing only stereotypical masculine clothing
  (3) strong and persistent preferences for cross-sex roles in make-believe play or persistent fantasies of being the other sex
  (4) intense desire to participate in the stereotypical games and pastimes of the other sex
  (5) strong preference for playmates of the other sex

In adolescents and adults, the disturbance is manifested by symptoms such as a stated desire to be the other sex, desire to live or be treated as the other sex, or the conviction that he or she has the typical feelings and reactions of the other sex.

B. Persistent discomfort with his or her sex or sense of inappropriateness in the gender role of that sex.

In children, the disturbance is manifested in any one of the following: in boys, assertion that his penis or testes are disgusting or will disappear or assertion that it would be better to not have a penis, or aversion toward rough-and-tumble play and rejection of male stereotypical toys, games, and activities; in girls, rejection of urinating in a sitting position, assertion that she has or will grow a penis, or assertion that she does not want to grow breasts or menstruate, or marked aversion toward normative feminine clothing.
In adolescents and adults, the disturbance is manifested by symptoms such as preoccupation with getting rid of primary and secondary sex characteristics (e.g., request for hormones, surgery, or other procedures to physically alter sexual characteristics to simulate the other sex) or belief that he or she was born the wrong sex.

C. The disturbance is not concurrent with a physical intersex condition.

D. The disturbance causes clinically significant distress or impairment in social, occupational, or other important areas of functioning.

Source: APA, 1994, pp. 537-538. Reprinted with permission from the *Diagnostic and Statistical Manual of Mental Disorders,* Fourth Edition. Copyright 1994 American Psychiatric Association.

tions are noted (p. 578). The classification of sexual orientation continues to be a controversial issue.

The current DSM criteria are now used primarily for diagnosing two distinct groups of people. The first group—gender-variant children and adolescents—are treated for their gender-inappropriate behavior and cross-gender identification. The second group—self-identified transgendered and transsexual people—depend on the diagnosis. It is essential to assist them in receiving the medical, hormonal, and surgical treatments they desire. The usefulness and difficulties of diagnosing each of these populations is outlined as follows.

Gender-Variant Children and Adolescents

Treating gender-variant children and youth for gender inappropriate behavior is controversial, raising questions about the sexist social control of children and their inability to consent to treatment. An examination of the diagnostic criteria indicates a reliance on socially determined assumptions about proper behavior for boy/girl behavior. The focus is on cross-dressing behavior, cross-sex roles in fantasy play, a desire to play games that have been assigned to the other sex, and a desire for opposite sex friends. The DSM-IV uses the word *stereotypical,* recognizing its own biases, but, by its inclusion of these behaviors in a diagnostic manual, reinforces the maintenance of a "correct" boy/girl division in play, fantasies, and dress.

Sexism is ubiquitous in this section of the DSM-IV-TR, despite the caveat that cross-gendered behavior cannot be "merely a desire for any perceived cultural advantages of being the other sex" (APA, 2000, p. 581). There are no indications or guidelines on how to assess for the distinction between social nonconformity and intrapsychic illness. The differences between a child's desire to "be" the other sex or to have the perceived privileges of that sex are left unexplored. There are cultural advantages (and disadvantages) to each of the gender categories and the bipolar division of gender restricts access to the "other." For boys, who may desire quieter play (not rough-and-tumble) or enjoy playing with dolls, or for girls, who are athletic and prefer games assigned to boys, the cultural advantages afforded the other sex can surely be appealing.

Despite more than forty years of an active feminist movement, and strong attempts to deconstruct stereotypical clothing and game choices, the DSM still pathologizes differently gendered behavior. The DSM assumes that boys and girls are different and should wear different clothes, enjoy different kinds of games, engage in different kinds of play, and have friends of the same sex. That these culturally variable, sexist assumptions about gendered behavior—what Green (1987) refers to as "cultural artifacts" and "whims of tradition" (p. 259)—should be placed in a diagnostic manual and used as a yardstick for mental health and illness, is (i.e., should be) of serious professional concern.

There are major problems with using the diagnosis of GID for gender-variant children. First, the DSM-IV uses blatantly sexist criteria for defining gender identity disorder, which pathologizes all nonconforming gender-variant children, while doing little to actually identify children struggling with gender dysphoria (Menvielle, 1998; Richardson, 1996, 1999). The DSM-IV stated that mental disorders cannot be "conflicts between the individual and society" (pp. xxxi-xxxii), yet gender appropriate behavior in children is obviously a topic of conflictual public policy debate.

The loosening of rigid gender roles might be viewed as a sign of healthy social change, not psychiatric illness. Many boys dislike rough-and-tumble play and many girls have a marked aversion to feminine clothing, without struggling with their gender identities. Some children might avoid traditional role-oriented behavior and its restrictions as a way to live fuller, more meaningful lives. The little girl who insists she will never marry because she wants to be an explorer is stepping out of culturally assigned roles. She is correct in believing that it will be more difficult to reach her goals if she is in a conventional marriage and becomes a mother.

The majority of children diagnosed with GID are young boys. Given that the societal sex-role restrictions on young males are more extensive than those for females, it raises questions about the need to maintain male privilege and status. Boys are punished (i.e., treated) for gender-deviant behavior, whereas girls' behavior is tolerated and often rewarded, as long as their behavior stays within certain, less confining, guidelines. The language of the DSM reflects this, since boys need only to "prefer" girl's clothing, but girls must "insist" on boy's clothing to meet the diagnostic criteria. The DSM's implicit approval of sex-role divisions does not merely reflect social values but reinforces them.

In addition, retrospective studies have shown that gender-variant boys often grow up to be homosexual, not transsexual (Bailey and Zucker, 1995; Green, 1987; Zuger, 1984), meaning that it might not be "gender" identity dysphoria that is being identified but early manifestations of sexual orientation diversity (Isay, 1997b; Menvielle, 1998). This raises a red flag about the treatment of potentially prehomosexual children in a psychiatric system that supposedly does not identify homosexuality as a disorder. Lawrence Mass (as quoted in Minter, 1999) suggested, "American Psychiatry is . . . engaged in a long, subtle process of reconceptualizing homosexuality as a mental illness with another name—the 'gender identity disorder of childhood'" (p. 12). The American Public Health Association (APHA) recognized that, "Gender

Identity Disorder within the DSM-IV is misused by some healthcare professionals to treat pre-homosexual and pre-transsexual children and adolescents so as to promote their development into nontranssexual, heterosexual adults" (APHA, 1999, p. 35).

Finally, and perhaps most significantly, because the wording is so vague and obviously sexist, it does not assist clinicians in actually serving young children in despair about their gender identity or expression. It is questionable whether the diagnosis as it currently stands is able to adequately identify young children—boys as well as girls—who are struggling with gender dysphoria, and whether they can be differentiated from gender-atypical children who are not in distress (Bartlett, Vasey, and Bukowski, 2000; Richardson, 1996, 1999).

Transsexual and Transgendered Adults
Seeking Treatment

For adults who are gender variant and seeking medical assistance, the diagnosis of GID is their "admission ticket" to hormonal and surgical treatments. The diagnostic label of GID is the official proof that one is a transsexual and therefore eligible for medical assistance. Without meeting the criteria described in the DSM or convincing a physician to step outside the established guidelines, they are unable to receive medical services.

As the issue of civil rights for transgendered people becomes part of the public discourse, the question of whether it is appropriate to have a diagnosis for transsexualism or GID—indeed whether it is appropriate to view transgenderism *as* a disorder—has become a complex discussion involving both the clinical/medical community and the burgeoning transgender political movement (Califia, 1997; O'Keefe, 1999; Wilson, 1998). Both sides—those who are opposed to the diagnosis and those who wish to retain it—feel that the question of diagnosis is pivotal to the discussion.

The medical model of diagnoses is built on a two-gender system, which is limited to people who have "a stated desire to be the other sex, frequently passing as the other sex, desire to live or be treated as the other sex, or [have] the conviction that he or she has the typical feelings and reactions of the other sex" (APA, 2000, p. 581). Although these experiences are common among many transsexual people, it does not, as has been shown, describe the experience of all transsexuals, and certainly not all transgender people. Some gender-variant females wish to masculinize without necessarily transitioning to the other sex, and some gender-variant males desire hormones to be more feminine but do not desire SRS. Strict adherence to the guidelines makes such individuals ineligible for medical treatment.

This creates a clinical situation in which clients often lie to therapists in order to receive treatment. Transgendered people are usually well read about gender issues, having devoured clinical literature more thoroughly than have most therapists. According to the research of Denny and Roberts (1997), nearly 80 percent of the 339 respondents to their survey of transgendered clients were familiar with the clinical standards of care. Walworth (1997) outlined in her study of fifty-two postoperative male-to-female transsexuals numerous areas in which clients had lied to therapists in order to meet what they thought were the guidelines for transitioning.

Advocates of the removal of GID clearly state that GID does not meet the definition of a mental disorder since no pathology is present, and some clinicians concur that no evidence of comorbid pathology exists (Carroll, 1999; Schaefer, Wheeler, and Futterweit, 1995). Activists say that as long as transgendered and transsexual people are diagnosed within a mental health manual, questions of civil liberties in areas of unemployment, child custody, and forensics will remain biased. They feel that the diagnosis of GID is based on a rigid, inflexible, and sexist view of gender that is dualistic and bipolar and that the removal of GID becomes a political necessity. Conover (2002) voiced these concerns when she said, "Psychological and psychiatric 'helpers' who operate out of sickness theories about transgender people do not draw their mandate from science but rather from a defense of current cultural traditions. They wrap themselves in the mantle of science to justify the professional status, their control, and their fees" (p. 149). From an activist's perspective, the professional community represents a kind of "evil empire," and the trangender community are freedom fighters. Wilchins (1997a), a powerful opponent of the GID label, said, "I intend to fight for my political freedom. I will not be told that I am mentally ill. I will not be told that I am disabled. I will not live within the confines of a mental diagnosis which is a lie" (p. 44).

Many transgendered people fear removing GID will eliminate any possibility of insurance reimbursement for treatments related to gender issues, although at this time insurance companies in the United States rarely cover these treatments. As Wilson (1997) said, "psychiatric classification remains the sole justification of medical necessity that is recognized by surgeons and endocrinologists who perform sexual reassignment procedures. Lacking a psychiatric diagnosis of transsexualism, or an alternative physiological diagnosis, such procedures might be less available to transsexuals" (p. 2). Despite Wilson's mild language, it would be more accurate to say that medical procedures could be completely withdrawn from transsexuals without the DSM diagnosis. As O'Hartigan (1997) said, "Provision of healthcare is dependent upon a need for treatment; and where there is no pathology, there is no need" (p. 46). In addition, many transsexuals are comfortable with the medical model and feel it is an accurate description of their dysphoria. Some transsexuals commonly refer to being born with a "birth defect" that needs to be "fixed." As Nelson (1998) said, "Pathologization is not altogether without benefit to those labeled 'sick'" (p. 222).

Although it has been suggested that there are many similarities between the homosexual and transgender communities' struggles for civil rights, transgendered people depend on the medical field in a way that LGB people do not (Wilson, 1998). As Hausman (1995) said, "The difference between homosexual and transvestic activities and their transsexual counterparts, however, is that the former attempted (and continue to attempt) to throw off medical regulation, while transsexuals needed medical regulation and therefore sought to obtain (and manage) it" (p. 131).

Although it is true that transgendered people—particularly transsexuals—"need" the medical profession, the diagnostic system as it is currently organized might be creating more problems than it is offering solutions. The diagnostic process currently insists that a client must be diagnosed mentally ill in order to be approved for treatment, yet he or she has to be sane enough to understand the consequences of the treatments. Whittle (1995) quoted one transsexual who described this catch-22 as follows: "If you are distressed enough to qualify for surgery, your mental reasoning has been impaired to the point where you probably cannot give informed consent. But if you are not that distressed, you will not be offered the surgery to which you are able to consent" (p. 2).

The medical model is built on client "dysphoria," although professionals working with this population know that many arrive in treatment having found a solution to their distress, i.e., transition. It has been suggested that people do not need psychiatric permission to have cosmetic surgeries. Wilchins (1997) jested that we do not diagnose people who desire nose jobs with "Rhino-Identity Disorder" (p. 191). Even Stoller (1975), who does not usually hesitate to utilize the language of pathology when discussing sexual variations, in a discussion about the removal of homosexuality from the DSM said, "Diagnoses that fail to describe succinctly and accurately [should] be removed" (p. 206).

Pauly believed that GID should remain in the DSM because gender disorders are less common than homosexuality, and thus are less likely to be a simple variation of the human condition, relying on statistical frequency as the determining factor. He also noted the significant incidence of mood disorders and Axis II pathology in many gender-variant people, although he does not acknowledge that such incidence may be related more to the stigma of cross-gender behavior than the gender identity disturbance itself. Finally, Pauly (1990) is concerned about the loss of insurance reimbursement for treatment and the availability of money for continued research (p. 10). This is echoed by the Harry Benjamin International Gender Dysphoria Association standards of care, which state, "The use of a formal diagnosis is often important in offering relief, providing health insurance coverage, and guiding research to provide more effective future treatments" (Meyer et al., 2001).

Zucker has consistently defended the DSM's diagnosis of GID and repeatedly refuted criticisms levied at the current diagnostic criteria (Bradley and Zucker, 1998; Zucker, 1999a,b). Zucker and his colleagues treat children with gender dysphoria, and they appear to have an honest concern and compassion for these children and their families. They are not motivated, as are other proponents of GID, by religious ideation or political conservatism. They simply believe that gender-atypical expression in childhood leads to transsexual actualization in adulthood and that these represent pathological mental illnesses.

The HBIGDA is careful to advise against using this diagnosis to harm transgendered people. "The designation of gender identity disorders as mental disorders is not a license for stigmatization, or for the deprivation of gender patients' civil rights" (Meyer et al., 2001). This raises the question of whether it is possible to protect civil liberties for gender-variant people, or to develop such liberties if gender-variant people's identities are based on receiving psychopathological diagnoses.

Reform of the GID diagnosis is necessary or the basic civil liberties for transgendered and transsexual people will remain elusive. Reform incorporates a broad range of challenges, including depathologizing cross-gender experience; recognizing transsexual trajectories that are based in mental health, not distress or dysfunction; broadening the eligibility for medical referral to include those with nontranssexual, gender-variant experiences; eliminating blatant heterosexism and sexism from the diagnostic criteria; and curtailing the use of GID to treat homosexuality and gender variance in children and youth (Wilson and Lev, 2003). The task ahead is to reform GID without eliminating clinical and medical treatments for transgendered and transsexual people.

One suggestion for reform involves removing GID from the DSM and using the diagnosis of *transsexualism* (in an updated and revised form), already described in the ICD-10 (see Appendix A), for medical treatments and reimbursement. Utilizing a diagnosis from a manual of physical ailments would validate the need for medical treatment without inferring a mental health diagnosis, e.g., gender transition would become an insurance-reimbursable medical condition similar to pregnancy. Wilson (2002) recommends reexamining the use of *gender dysphoria,* which focuses the psychiatric diagnosis on issues of distress rather than the gender differences, for DSM inclusion. She says, "The very name, Gender Identity Disorder, suggests that cross-gender identity is itself disordered or deficient." Unlike the diagnosis of *ego-dystonic homosexuality,* the dysphoria or dystonia in the case of gender-related issues is not related to external approval, but internal, anatomical discomfort. Cantor (2002) recommends utilizing the diagnosis of *identity problem* (313.82) listed in the DSM, which would move the focus off the gender aspects and onto the identity issues that are paramount in sex reassignment. It is, however, questionable whether codes in this section— Additional Conditions that May be the Focus of Clinical Attention—would be insurance reimbursable. An alternate possibility would be the DSM diagnosis of *adjustment disorder,* which recognizes the stress of transition without pathologizing gender variance.

Clearly the issue of diagnosis and GID reform will be one of the most salient challenges impacting transgendered people in the decades to come.

Cromwell (1999) spoke eloquently from the spirit of the growing movement for transgendered liberation when he said, "Although a wrong body discourse may lead to a cure for some, it also constructs gender diversity as pathology and not everyone wants to be cured" (p. 121). Halberstam (1998a) echoed this when she said,

> The human potential for incredibly precise classifications has been demonstrated in multiple areas; why then do we settle for a paucity of classifications when it comes to gender? . . . there are many ways to depathologize gender variance and to account for the multiple genders that we already produce and sustain. (p. 27)

As has been shown, the DSM has a long history of diagnosing oppressed people with mental disorders. Nelson (1998) suggested, "Medicine's nosology . . . ought to consider not only the biology but also the political and social character of 'diseases'" (p. 227). Civil liberties have only been granted to oppressed people when they have insisted upon them and when they have proven themselves competent to utilize them. In order to receive medical treatment, transgendered and transsexual people must prove themselves "disordered." In order to be granted civil rights, transgendered and transsexual people must prove themselves mentally sane. It is incumbent on the mental health field not to place people in this double bind. Approval for treatment must depend not on being mentally ill but on being mentally sound enough to make empowered and healthy decisions regarding one's body and life.

PART III:
TREATMENT ISSUES

Chapter 6

Learning to Listen to Gender Narratives

People often say that this or that person has not yet found himself. But the self is not something that one finds; it is something one creates.

Thomas Szasz
The Second Sin, 1973

Redefining transgender expression and transsexual experience as normative manifestations of human diversity requires a severing of the associations of cross-gender identity with mental illness. As Raj (2002) said, "The traditional psychological paradigm is starting to shift from a transphobic to a positive one." However, the legacy of pathologizing etiologies has left clinicians with few theoretical guidelines with which to assist gender-variant people who are struggling with the ramifications of living within a rigidly gendered culture or the internalized shame that manifests as gender dysphoria. The development of an advocacy-based treatment modality, including clinical assessment tools and intervention strategies, must be grounded with respect for the diversity of human gender expression. This treatment philosophy holds three tenets:

- Everyone has a right to his or her own gender expression.
- Everyone has a right to make informed and educated decisions about his or her own body and gender expression.
- Everyone has the right to access medical, therapeutic, and technological services to gain the information and knowledge necessary to make informed and educated decisions about his or her own body and life.

This model redefines the nature of the gatekeeping relationship as one based in advocacy, education, and support. It allows clients to examine, interrogate, and evaluate their gender identity and expression, within their own etiological frameworks and definitions of meaning. Based on an ecological model that is strength based and empowerment focused, it allows clients the right to educated self-determination. The purpose of therapy is not for a clinician to evaluate clients to determine whether they have gender identity disorder or to determine how to "cure" their illness. This does not dilute the more traditional therapeutic role of assisting clients in self-evaluation or insight-based clinical work; rather, it refocuses the work from the therapist as an "evaluator" to a collaborative effort in which both client and therapist are engaged in supporting the client's authentic identity development. As Vanderburgh (2001) said, "The client is the only one who can make decisions about core identity issues" (p. 20). The goal of therapy is to assist the client in greater self-knowledge so he or she can make informed decisions about his or her gender expression, self-identity, body configuration, and ultimate direction of his or her life.

An empowerment model does not simply support a "surgery-on-demand" position, nor does it mean that everyone who has a desire to remove or alter body parts should have his or her request honored by surgeons. Surgeons would be foolish to not require some kind of clinical assessment of a client's mental health before performing invasive and irreversible surgical procedures. Since surgeons are not experts in psychosocial mental health assessment, it seems reasonable that those who are trained in recognizing serious mental health disturbances should be asked to make this assessment before surgery can be scheduled. Certainly, if a surgeon is willing to risk dissatisfied consumers of services—and their potential lawsuits—it should be their legal right to do so, and there are physicians worldwide who forgo the need for any psychological assessment before sex reassignment surgeries. It is, however, reasonable to assume that most reputable surgeons would want to know that their patients have worked through all (or at least many) of the emotional issues necessary to embark on a life-changing (and often life-saving) sex reassignment. Consumers themselves might be concerned about the motivations of a surgeon who has no guidelines for evaluating patients besides their ability to pay for services.

Green (2000b) said, "It is difficult to identify another psychiatric or medical condition in which the patient makes the diagnosis and prescribes the treatment," therefore, it has been a challenge for clinicians to know which clients demanding surgery should be accommodated. Attempts to delineate "true" transsexuals from confused cross-dressers and repressed homosexuals has been an area of ongoing research. Age of onset of gender dysphoria, substance abuse, marital status, comorbid mental health problems, level of anatomical dysphoria, criminality, assumed postsurgical homosexuality, psychoanalytic assessments of childhood issues, ability to successfully pass, and threats of suicide as a valid determiner of the "seriousness" of the applicant have all been fodder for the psychological assessment process utilized to approve transsexuals for medical treatments. Ability to successfully pass would more likely mean acceptance. Heterosexual marriage and unwillingness or inability to conform to standard sex-role conventions would more likely mean rejection. The Stanford clinic, according to Meyerowitz (2002), had a grooming clinic to assist surgical patients in proper presentation. Determining which criteria are clinically useful and valid versus those that are steeped in conventional sexist (and heterosexist) assumptions and social control tactics is an ongoing discussion involving researchers, policymakers, psychologists, social workers, grassroots activists, medical professionals, ethicists, and the legal system.

In this fairly new and evolving field, much has changed and even more will continue to change over the next decades while experts debate paradoxical dilemmas regarding client care. Insurance companies, for instance, refuse to cover services that are not "medically necessary." Determining that they are medically necessary may mean maintaining a mental health diagnosis that interferes with other civil liberties. Changing legal paperwork regarding sex designation—birth certificates, names changes, driver's licenses, passports, and marriage licenses—creates potential judicial minefields regarding issues of same-sex marriage, "fathers" giving birth to their children, and whether one's legal status should depend on surgical sex completion or the social gender one presents on a daily basis. Legal and policy-related issues often depend, for better or worse, on the decisions made by psychological boards and research committees. For instance, the ability to legally change one's name to one of the opposite sex often depends on an affidavit written by a mental health expert stating that the person has been living in the other sex and has begun—or is approved for—hormonal and surgical treatment. However, if a person identifies as bi-gendered with no intention of "living in the other sex," can she or he be legally supported in a name change? Issues that have little to do with psychotherapy do have an impact on psychotherapy as a field and are also impacted by decisions made by professional organizations of affiliated psychotherapists.

The Harry Benjamin International Gender Dysphoria Association continues to reexamine and modify their standards of care to reflect changes in clinical thinking. Postoperative heterosexual orientation is no longer a determining factor in approving clients for medical treatments; nor is the ability to successfully pass. (This does not mean that a particular therapist, clinic, or gender team might not still utilize these factors.) Clinicians debate in the literature whether age of onset of gender-dysphoric symptoms is relevant for successful transition and how to properly assess those with comorbid mental health conditions. In its most recent edition, the standards allow for transsexuals who are born female to be approved for breast reduction/ chest reconstruction and hormonal treatment *before* beginning the "real-life experience," since success at living as a man without these treatments would be significantly compromised. The new standards of care also outline guidelines for earlier treatment of adolescents. Therapeutic treatment of gender-variant people within a nonpathologizing model is uncharted territory and raises ethical issues about the treatment of those who are underage as well as those who exhibit mental health problems. Although the SOC are clear in stating that the presence of psychiatric comorbidities "does not necessarily preclude hormonal or surgical treatment" (Meyer et al., 2001, p.13), clinicians might still struggle with determining whether a mentally retarded person or a person with a history of schizophrenia or traumatic abuse is able to give informed consent to have gender reassignment. Ettner (1996) asked, "Can a crazy person legitimately request surgical reassignment or is this a delusion that will lead to post-surgical regret and possible suicide?" (p. 50).

Although every person has a "right" to his or her own gender expression, this model does not infer that every person has the same capacity for decision making or the ability to understand the necessary information to make educated decisions about his or her body. For instance, a three-year-old child may experience gender dysphoria and might even be able to articulate gender dissonance and cross-gender identity. This does not assume that a three-year-old is able to make informed medical decisions or understand the social implications of cross-gender appearance. Similarly, many people with mental illnesses exhibit gender dysphoria and cross-gendered behavior who may not be good "candidates" for SRS, indeed might be harmed by the emotional issues evoked by the surgical treatments. Determining mental competence is an essential skill for mental health experts specializing in gender issues. The literature on transgenderism and transsexualism is replete with examples of the mental health issues that gender-variant people experience, raising serious questions about their competency and ability to make educated and informed decisions. Attempts to deconstruct the meaning behind these mental illnesses and ways to utilize a strengths-based advocacy model with those who suffer from mental health problems will be analyzed in the following sections.

MENTAL HEALTH ISSUES AND TRANSGENDERISM

The voice on the phone is halting and measured when I return the phone call requesting an appointment. "I can't believe I'm actually calling you. I need to talk with someone. I'm very afraid. I've never told anyone before, but I need to talk about gender issues."

One does not need to be a competent or skilled clinician to determine that the person who left this message is in deep emotional pain. Potential clients often leave repeated messages like this, sometimes for years on end, with no callback number. When clients attend therapy, they are often frightened and overwhelmed and exhibit many apparent symptoms of mental disturbance, including anxiety, panic attacks, obsessive-compulsive disorder, depression, manic episodes, impulsive behavior, eating disturbances, sleep disorders, sexual paraphilias, as well as marital problems, histories of childhood trauma, and chronic unemployment. The list of mental health disturbances that gender-variant people are thought to suffer from is exhaustive. Almost all writers discuss this population in terms of "illness," "pathology," "disorder," "condition," and "problem" and identify clients as demanding, manipulative, controlling, coercive, and paranoid. Gender-variant people are identified as impulsive, depressed, isolated, withdrawn, anxious, thought-disordered, and suffering from narcissistic, schizoid, and borderline personality features. They are perceived as immature and egocentric with profound dependency conflicts, although natal males are almost always seen as more disturbed than natal females (with the exception of Lothstein, 1983, who views females as equally disturbed). This is true in almost any article or book that addresses the clinical needs of this population, including those written by supportive clinicians who have committed their lives to advocating for the therapeutic and medical treatments that enable transsexuals to live in their chosen gender expression. A few examples will suffice.

According to Person and Ovesey (1976), who believed that cross-dressers did not suffer from the same mental health problems as transsexuals, "transvestites, as a group, are invariably anhedonic and experience feelings of loneliness and emptiness" (p. 231). In 1984 they identified two groups of homosexual cross-dressers: "passive-effeminate homosexuals with hysterical personalities and hyperaggressive effeminate homosexuals with narcissistic personalities ('drag queens')" (p. 170). Holtzman et al. (1961) talked about transgendered people expressing "anxiety, hostility, and pathognomonic verbalizations" (p. 290) as well as rigid and compulsive features. Sperber (1973) said that those with gender dysphoria have borderline personality issues and Gosselin and Wilson (1980) identified "clear evidence of introversion and high neuroticism compared with normal males" (p. 104). Hartmann, Becker, and Rueffer-Hesse's (1997) preliminary results "indicate significant psychopathological aspects and narcissistic dysregulation in most of [their] gender dysphoric patients."

Steiner (1985b) identified "narcissistic personality, borderline personality organization, and antisocial personality" (p. 335) as frequently associated with transsexualism. Meyer (1974) noted similar psychopathology in addition to schizoid features, depression, anxiety, suicidality, and even homicidal tendencies. Hoenig, Kenna, and Youd (1970, as quoted in Langevin, 1985) indicated that 70 percent of transsexuals have additional psychiatric diagnosis, although only 13 percent are psychotic. Hartmann, Becker, and Rueffer-Hesse (1997) identified "significant narcissistic pathology," and

Levine and Lothstein (1981) have written extensively about comorbid psychopathology. Lothstein (1983) in particular finds FTMs to have primitive defense structures related to their borderline personality disorder, including "denial, projection, projective identification, splitting, omnipotence and devaluation" (p. 237). Bockting and Coleman (1992), who developed a very progressive model for treatment, found that "many clients suffer from a variety of Axis I disorders (most commonly anxiety and depression), as well as Axis II personality disorders" (p. 136). Psychology and social work textbooks used in graduate programs reiterate this view of trangendered people as mentally ill (McConaghy, 1997; Money and Lehne, 1999; Zucker, 2000). None of these books mention another view or perspective outside of a psychopathological one.

Certainly, these expert clinicians are skilled at diagnoses and able to accurately identify psychopathologic conditions. The need for diagnostic assessment and differential diagnosis is paramount, for gender identity disturbances can mask more serious mental health problems or may be a less significant part of a pervasive psychopathology. Brown (1990) outlined various diagnoses that may include gender dysphoria, including body dysmorphic disorder, malingering, and schizophrenia with gender-identity disturbance. Clearly clients exhibiting what he calls "homophobic homosexuality" are not good candidates for medical treatments.

The difficulty lies not in professional assessment processes or diagnostic competency, but rather in the perspective that assumes psychopathology in all gender-variant people without understanding the context for their difficulties. When Evelyn Hooker studied the first *nonclinical* sample of homosexual men in 1969, she discovered that this population did not exhibit the mental health issues that had been attributed to them in previous studies of clinical samples of homosexuals (D'Emilio, 1983). Similarly, most studies of transsexual and gender-variant people are composed of those who seek services from clinicians, the very people who are most likely to be experiencing dystonia and dysphoria, and those most desperate for services. However, unlike homosexual men, transgendered and transsexual people who desire body modification *must* seek out services to live authentically and, paradoxically, the very criteria which make them eligible for these services also determine that they have mental health issues. For example, the need to prove that one is transsexual has historically depended on one's distress in his or her body and hatred of his or her genitals to the point of expressing suicidality and self-harm behaviors. These same behaviors lead clinicians to label such clients as borderline, obsessive, depressed, and impulsive.

That some gender-variant people exhibit these symptoms is indisputable; however, it is necessary to make a clinical distinction between mental disorders that are independent of gender issues and those that are the symptoms and sequelae of living with daily social denigration. Ego-dsytonic homosexuality was removed from the DSM when it became evident that most homosexuals struggled with their identity due to the homophobia of the social world, not because of an intrinsic psychological disturbance. Similarly, most gender-variant people suffer from deep internal struggles with their gendered and sexual selves given the societal nature of transphobia and the internal conflicts that develop trying to live contrary to their natures in a dimorphic culture. Sadly, the clinical community has often reinforced these struggles, rather than alleviated them. Wilson (1997) said, "The psychiatric interpretations of inherent transgender pathology serves to attribute *the consequences of prejudice* to its victims, neglecting the true cause of distress" (p. 7, italics mine), i.e., the daily assaults on the human dignity of transgendered people. The impact of transphobia on the mental health of transgendered people has been rarely acknowledged and even less frequently addressed, with few researchers even mentioning its influence.

This is not to deny that there are gender-variant people with bona fide mental health issues which are etiologically separate from their transgender issues, even if they are interwoven into their daily lives as transgendered people. Smith (1988) examined the relationship between psychopathology and homosexuality and diagrammatically described the relationship. He showed how homosexuality, when it was considered an illness, was included in a larger set of all psychopathologies, disallowing any homosexuality that was not considered psychopathological. However, utilizing a Venn diagram, Smith showed how homosexuals with psychopathologies were a small subset of all those with mental health problems and allowed for homosexuality—actually the majority of homosexuals—without psychopathological symptomatology (see Figure 6.1). This model has been adapted to the language and concepts used in this book in Figure 6.2.

In Diagram 1 in Figure 6.2 it is assumed that gender variance (under the labels gender identity disorder and transsexualism) is, by its nature, a psychopathology, denying the possibility of gender variance that is not a psychological disturbance. In Diagram 2, the two circles once again overlap, showing that most people with psychopathological diagnoses are not gender variant, and those who are gender variant are not all suffering from psychological disorders.

Despite research efforts seeking to find psychosocial disturbances in the transgender population, some researchers have found that transgendered people do not exhibit more mental health problems than other people, and most studies on female-to-male transsexuals have commented on their mental health. Bentler and Prince (1970) found "no gross differences detected between the transvestites and controls on neurotic or psychotic scales" (p. 435). Holtzman et al. (1961) commented on the "generally well-organized

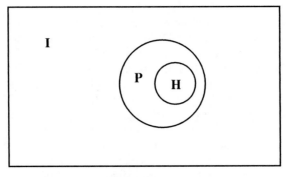

DIAGRAM 1
I = Set of all individuals
P = Set of all psychopathological individuals
H = Set of homosexually adjusted individuals

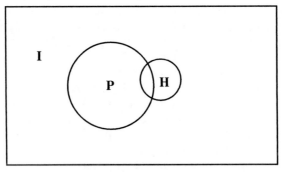

DIAGRAM 2
I = Set of all individuals
P = Set of all psychopathological individuals
H = Set of homosexually adjusted individuals

FIGURE 6.1. Venn diagrams depicting conceptions of homosexuality (adapted from Smith, 1988).

and intellectually adequate thought processes" (p. 290) of the gender-variant people they studied. Brown, Wise, and Costa (1995, as cited in Carroll, 1999) looked at personality characteristics of nonclinical gender-variant people as compared to a nonclinical control group and found no significant differences. Haraldsen and Dahl (2000) conducted a comparison study of transsexual patients with those who have personality disorders, as well as healthy adults, and discovered that transsexuals showed a low level of

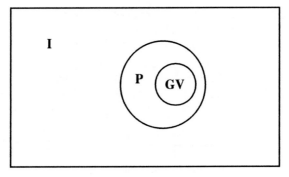

DIAGRAM 1
I = Set of all individuals
P = Set of all psychopathological individuals
GV = Set of gender-variant individuals

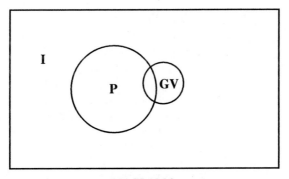

DIAGRAM 2
I = Set of all individuals
P = Set of all psychopathological individuals
GV = Set of gender-variant individuals

FIGURE 6.2. Venn diagrams depicting conceptions of gender-variant individuals (adapted from Smith, 1988).

psychopathology. Micah et al. (2000) utilized the MMPI-2 and found a low level of psychopathology for those labeled *transsexuals,* and a moderate to severe level in nearly 50 percent of those diagnosed with the outdated label of *gender identity disorder of adolescence and adulthood, nontranssexual type* (GIDAANT). They did not find evidence for personality disturbances. Cohen-Kettenis and van Goozen (1997, 2002) studied adolescents seeking SRS, and showed a low level of mental health problems. Schaefer, Wheeler, and Futterweit (1995) state that "there is no evidence of frequent occurrence of co-morbidity" (p. 2027), and Carroll (1999) said, "Individuals with transgender experiences do not necessarily exhibit higher levels of mental disorders than the nonclinical population" (p. 135). Of course, no psychological tests differentiate gender-variant people from those who are not gender variant. As Rachlin (2001) said, "there is no reliable diagnostic test that a doctor might prescribe to assess the appropriateness of such a patient for surgery."

When children and youth exhibit gender identity issues, researchers have documented high levels of psychoemotional problems. It is important, however, to note the referral source. For example, when Di Ceglie et al. (2002) analyzed the data of 124 children and adolescents referred for treatment of gender-related disturbances in London in the 1990s, they found a high incidence of antisocial behaviors, depression, anxiety, and family-related difficulties, as well as, for the boys, a high level of harrassment/persecution. However, nearly 50 percent of the children and youth had been referred by a psychiatrist and/or mental health specialist, which raises serious questions about whether their psychological disturbances were caused by other mental health issues. Even more noteworthy is that many children had self-harm/self-injurious behaviors, as well as inappropriately sexualized behaviors, which are often indicative of sexual abuse (Herman, 1992; Miller, 1995). In addition, a high incidence of both physical and mental health problems occurred in family members. Di Ceglie et al. (2002) noted that, "It is possible that the presence of a gender identity disorder may lead to other problems in the course of development, or other problems might contribute to the development of the gender identity disorder." It is also possible that children and youth in more functional families, who do not themselves exhibit mental health issues, find other ways to cope with their gender issues, and therefore remain under the radar of specialized gender clinics. In addition, this data highlights the need for clinicians to pay special attention to how gender-variant children and youth are treated within their own families and schools, and to protect them from potential abuse.

Stating that most transgendered people are not mentally ill does not mean that some transgendered people may not live with mental illnesses. According to the research of Cole et al. (1997), less than 10 percent of a study of 435 primary transsexuals showed a history of mental illness. Figure 6.2 describes an overlap of these two groups, showing that although some gender-variant people are indeed mentally ill, most do not exhibit psychopathologies. Axis I and Axis II diagnoses can manifest in two ways in working with gender-variant people. They can manifest as symptomatology or sequelae to the difficulties of living as a transgendered person in a dimorphic and transphobic social world or they can be present as a mental illness separate from the gender issues. Furthermore, it is important when working with people with active mental illnesses to examine how gender issues and mental illnesses have become entwined in the etiology, treatment, or self-understanding of mental illness. Has the person's cross-dressing been blamed on his or her mental illness? Do they view their cross-gender desires as causing their depression? Have they been treated with medications to eliminate the obsessive quality of the cross-dressing? Sorting out these distinctions can involve a complex assessment process. The following two frameworks can assist clinicians in determining the distinctions between mental health issues that are manifestations of gender dysphoria and those that arise independent of gender identity development.

When Mental Illnesses Are Not Mental Illnesses— *Traumatic Sequelae and Psychospiritual Growth*

One useful theoretical model to examine the relationship between mental health symptoms and gender variance is the psychosocial processes of coping with trauma. The role of post-traumatic stress disorder—first identified in war veterans and later in survivors of sexual abuse—has been described in the etiology of many mental health problems (Bass and Davis, 1988; Briere, 1989; Herman, 1992; van der Kolk, McFarlane, and Weisaeth, 1996), although it has not yet been applied to the psychosocial development of gender-variant people. Symptomatology of PTSD can include insomnia, isolation, depression, high anxiety, dissociation, suicidality, sexual dysfunction, substance abuse, mood instability, self-mutilation, weight loss or gain, and work or school difficulties, all symptomatology commonly seen in gender-variant people. Sometimes the symptomatology will be so overwhelming that the personal narrative about gender might be subsumed into this symptomatology, and the therapist will see the gender as just one more manifestation of dysfunction instead of the core issue that clarifies the maladaptive patterns.

Herman (1992) suggested that trauma survivors experience a "dialectic of trauma"—labile moods that alternate from expressively frozen to intensely dramatic emotionality, as the client relives his or her trauma and dissociates from it. She said, "People who have survived atrocities often tell their stories in a highly emotional, contradictory, and fragmented manner which undermines their credibility . . . the story of the traumatic event surfaces not as a verbal narrative but as a symptom" (p. 1). PTSD is a common sequela to traumatic events, although when examining lifelong gender dysphoria there is often no discernible traumatic *event* to focus on, but rather a series of smaller experiences that have culminated in years of denying one's essential sense of self. The fear of social punishment for transgressing social norms and the long-standing presentation of a false self can also *create* numerous mental health problems. The high incidence of mental illness among transgendered people noted in the literature might better be understood as reactive symptomatology and posttraumatic sequelae. It is literally *crazy-making* to live a false self.

Smith (1988) described some of the intrapsychic and psychosocial factors that contribute to psychopathology in homosexually oriented persons. Substituting "transsexualism" for "homosexuality," it is easy to see the similarities. Smith outlined the impact of "social stigmatization, including overt disapproval of lifestyles, lack of protection against discrimination in housing, employment, and association, and in many jurisdictions, criminal sanctions against it . . . it is therefore not surprising that those individuals with immature or maladaptive coping styles become psychologically wounded by the constant application of this stigmatizing process" (p. 61).

Identifying some gender-variant people as survivors of PTSD is not another way to pathologize them (after all, PTSD is just another mental health diagnosis in the DSM). It is a way of understanding the etiology of their mental health symptoms without holding transsexualism, gender variance, or psychopathic parenting as the cause. Much of the symptomatology seen in some gender-variant individuals—especially those seeking therapeutic services explicitly for gender dysphoria—mimics the emotional and behavioral symptoms displayed in those seeking services to address histories of childhood sexual abuse, recent violent and abusive traumas, as well as "homosexual panic" (see Baptiste, 1990). Understanding the context of the etiology does not eradicate the symptomatology. It offers direction for treatment of the trauma and recognition of the gender variance separate from the trauma associated with living in a rigidly gendered culture. The following vignette describes a client who sought services for his gender dysphoria and exhibited signs of numerous mental health disturbances. Addressing his gender dysphoria within a larger social context of oppression and environmental assaults on his personhood allowed for the alleviation of his symptoms over the course of psychotherapy.

Nelson paced the waiting room, his eyes darting back and forth. When invited to sit down in my office, he sat on the edge of the seat, alternating between direct, penetrating eye contact and avoidant, flittering glances around the room. He spoke rapidly, often contradicting himself, as he narrated a long story involving a troubled childhood, time in prison, abuse by police officers, three failed marriages, numerous health problems, and chronic unemployment. Throughout his life Nelson has secretly cross-dressed. He was once caught by friends and publicly humiliated. The one time he ventured out of the house dressed as a woman, he was arrested for "prostitution," beaten, and sexually assaulted by the police.

Nelson was suicidal and desperate. He identified his gender issues as his mental "sickness" and viewed them as "intruders" into his life. He described his desire to be female as if he was being taken over by an alien force.

It took Nelson years of hard work in psychotherapy to feel comfortable with himself as a gender-variant person. With the assistance of short-term psychotropic medications, attendance at a cross-dressing support group, contact with an electronic mailing list for transgendered people, and months of grieving over how his female persona had been trivialized, abused, and shamed throughout his childhood and adolescence, Nelson was able to begin to come to terms with his gender variance. His demeanor grew calmer and more focused. He expressed less anxiety, laughed more frequently, began to make friends both within and outside of the gender community, and began to allow his female self a fuller range of expression by going out socially. This was a difficult and painful journey, but despite Nelson's obvious psychosocial and environmental difficulties upon beginning therapy, he was not "mentally ill." Nelson suffered, and suffer he did, from gender dysphoria that was induced by internalized transphobia.

One example from the literature will explore how the issues of trauma have been conflated with mental illness processes. Stoller (1973), who gifted this field with many in-depth analyses of his own clinical process—a vulnerability that is admirable—described the psychoanalytic therapy of a gender-dysphoric female client. He referred to this client as Mrs. G, an interesting choice of language for this masculine female, given that she might best be described as a butch lesbian (or perhaps bisexual, as she is not exclusively homosexual) or perhaps, in a different era, as a transman, but in either case she would probably not identify with her brief marital history as a way to describe herself. Mrs. G is described as "psychotic"—which, indeed, she well may have been—but she is also a survivor of trauma, which is not addressed in Stoller's examination. Stoller offered detailed descriptions of their therapy sessions, including a chapter called "Mrs. G's Penis," which reviews sessions focusing on the penis Mrs. G claims she has hidden inside her body. Although this does sound "psychotic," it is not an uncommon experience for transsexuals and other gender-dysphoric people to "think" or "believe" that their true sex is somehow hidden in their bodies and they are often able to describe these "psychic parts" in vivid detail. A brief overview of the erotic literature written by many mentally sound transmen, masculine females, and their partners will bear this out.

According to Stoller (1973), Mrs. G "*permitted* herself to be used by men" (p. 278, italics mine), "had intercourse with so many men" (p. 70), and tried to kill men because of her "heterosexual despair" (p. 280), which Stoller believed to be at the root of homosexuality. Stoller also mentions that by the age of eight Mrs. G had been routinely sexually abused by a grandfather, two uncles, and several strangers (Stoller refers to this as "having sex"), and at age eleven or twelve she was sexually abused by a baby-sitter, a professional photographer who forced her to make a sexual movie with another woman. Stoller said Mrs. G "not only wanted to be up against her mother's body: she also craved her father. This must have been why she was, in fact, so often the victim of infamous assaults by men" (p. 278). Stoller seems to blame Mrs. G for the horrible victimization she endured as a young child, as if something in her psychology had somehow invited these assaults. He seems to have little insight, despite years of analysis with Mrs. G, that her history of trauma, and the fact that she is a Mexican-American female living in poverty (a fact Stoller mentioned parenthetically on page 275) *might* have some impact on her life, her mental health, and her relationship to her gender identity. Sadly, trauma is a fact of life for many gender-variant people and is often increased if the person is stigmatized for other reasons, particularly class, racial, or ethnic oppression. In addition to the abuse often inflicted by well-meaning parents, gender-variant people are commonly the victims of sexual and bias-related violence (Courvant and Cooke-Daniels, 1998; Lev and Lev, 1999; Xavier, 2000). According to the Transgender Community Health Project (1999), 59 percent of the participants in their study reported a history of forced sex or rape. The literature on PTSD outlines the symptomatology that presents itself in trauma survivors, which looks incredibly similar to the diagnoses that are comorbidly seen in gender-dysphoric people.

Another useful model to examine the relationship of gender variance and mental illness is the concept of "spiritual emergence" (Grof and Grof, 1990), which is described as a state of "profound psychological transformation" that may include intense emotions, nonordinary states of consciousness, sensory changes, unusual thoughts, as well as various physical manifestations (p. 31). People experiencing spiritual emergence often appear psychotic, having dramatic shifts in awareness and manifesting many symptoms found in the DSM (Lukoff, Lu, and Turner, 1992). Grof and Grof (1990) described spiritual emergence as a normative spiritual experience, which is recognized in most non-Western cultures but has no equivalent in Western society, forcing many people into a spiritual emergency, a psychospiritual crisis. They outlined numerous ways to distinguish spiritual emergence from mental illnesses.

It is interesting to note that in one study of self-identified third-gender people (people who identify as neither men nor women), 93 percent reported having experienced transcendent spiritual events and/or having unusual "paranormal" abilities. More than 50 percent had these experiences repeatedly or very profoundly (Sell, 2001). In many spiritual traditions, a sense of a "calling" exists—a sense that one does not choose to be a healer, shaman, priest, or medicine man or woman but is called to this work. This resonates with the determination and passionate commitment with which many gender-variant people embrace their gender odyssey and is reminiscent of Jeanne d'Arc's refusal to put down her military career or end her cross-dressing because she was obeying "the orders of Our Lord."

Although transgendered people who are seeking services for gender dysphoria often describe their experiences in profoundly spiritual and religious language, there has been little focus in the clinical literature on the meaning of transgenderism as a spiritual experience. Clinicians have assumed that the symptomatology that transgendered people express during therapy has been present their whole lives, perhaps downplaying the intense explosion of emotionality that has brought them to seek services at a given time. Would clinicians diagnose the behaviors of a woman in the throes of labor as indicative of her mental status? Perhaps the importance of the timing of transgendered people seeking therapy has been minimized, and too much focus has been placed on the symptomatology they present at this time of revelation and spiritual emergence.

When Mental Illnesses and Gender Dysphoria Coexist

Of course, some gender-variant people exhibit signs of mental health disturbances that began previous to, or concurrently with, the gender issues they are presenting, and these Axis I and Axis II diagnoses must be acknowledged and treated.

Given the high statistics for substance abuse in the general population and the even higher statistics within the LGB community (Finnegan and McNally, 2002; Kus, 1995; Ratner, 1993), it seems probable that substance abuse and addictions are prevalent problems within the transgendered population as well (Kreiss and Patterson, 1997; Lombardi and van Servellen, 2000; SAMHSA, 2001; Tayleur, 1994; Xavier, 2000). In one study, 27 percent of those seeking services for gender issues reported alcohol abuse and 23 percent reported drug abuse (Valentine, 1998). One client, with an extensive and life-threatening history of alcohol and substance abuse and chronic relapse, was shuffled around for years, from treatment center to treatment center, where he was prohibited from not only cross-dressing but also from discussing any issues related to his gender dysphoria or his drunken homosexual escapades. It was thought that this would distract from his focus on treatment. His providers were obviously extremely uncomfortable with his gender and sexuality issues and admitted they thought his desire to cross-dress would "vanish" if he engaged in treatment and remained sober. Each time he left long-term treatment facilities for life on the "outside," he would try to address the gender issues. However, he lacked the intensive support to which he had become accustomed, and while he was trying to stay sober *and* address the added stress of facing his gender issues, he continued to relapse. This case exemplifies the need for comprehensive training of all mental health counselors, including those specializing in substance abuse treatment.

Substance abuse is only one of many mental health disturbances that can coexist with gender identity issues and present numerous ethical dilemmas for the psychotherapist. The following case describes a client with long-standing severe mental illness who also expressed lifelong gender dysphoria.

Terry (MTF) was not initially sure why she came to therapy except that her friends at the cross-dressing club had recommended it. Terry was forty years old and had suffered from debilitating depression and panic attacks for which she was medicated at a local mental health clinic. She had been diagnosed as having bipolar disorder with episodic mania, which at least one counselor thought was more likely to be schizophrenia or schizoaffective disorder. Terry was obviously thought-disordered, leaping from one discussion to another. She had a very flat affect, avoided eye contact, and had bizarre communication patterns that involved repeating what the clinician had just said and reviewing and reiterating her medication dosage schedule. Her dress was slovenly and her hygiene left much to be desired. She also expressed a lifelong gender disturbance, secretive cross-dressing without masturbation, and a desire to be a female, as well as verbalized clearly her interest in hormone therapy, although she was unaware of how to procure it.

Terry's presentation as a female was as slovenly as her presentation had been as a male. However, she was able to respond to all of the clinician's recommendations regarding appropriate dress as she accomplished her real-life experience. After an extensive evaluation period; case-conferencing with her physician, psychiatrist, and mental health counselor; collateral reports from her mother, neighbor, priest, and employer; as well as a second-opinion letter from another gender therapist, it was confirmed that Terry met all the diagnostic criteria for GID and was referred to an endocrinologist to begin a low dose of female hormones. It was thought best to move slowly and cautiously with Terry, since it was not known how hormones would impact her psychosocial functioning or her other medications. Low-dose cross-sex hormones, in addition to making only minor changes in a person's physiology, can also alleviate anxiety for some gender-variant people.

The endocrinologist was hesitant to prescribe hormones given the extensive history of mental illness, so he referred Terry to a psychologist for testing and to another psychiatrist for a second opinion (both of whom admitted to having no experience working with people with gender dysphoria). These consultations were paid for out of pocket by the client, who lived on social services. Terry was then rejected as a good candidate for hormone therapy, since she was labeled "chronically and severely depressed"—with no acknowledgment of how her evaluation process (over two years in duration) had become intensely *depressing*.

After her rejection, Terry began ordering hormones over the Internet, which she adapted well to, although her physician refused to continue monitoring her since he did not support her hormonal use. After six months on hormones, Terry had a breakdown. The treatment team blamed this on her hormone use although Terry had being having episodic breakdowns for twenty years. The clinicians involved in this case were concerned that hormones would harm this vulnerable and mentally ill client. She therefore received an extensive evaluative process that increased her symptoms and left her without access to medical management. Given the severe mental health issues Terry lives with, she exhibited incredibly skilled coping in dealing with the repeated rejections from the medical establishment, as well as adaptive functioning in her ability to find an alternative way to procure the hormones (albeit not one that should be supported clinically). A low-dose medically monitored treatment protocol and a supportive clinical team would have "protected" this client far more than the invasive and repetitive psychological testing and ultimate refusal of competent medical care, which resulted in having no medical monitoring for her hormone treatment. Her mental status did not improve on hormones. Terry suffered from the same mental health problems she did before beginning hormones and, sadly, will probably continue to struggle with them with or without quality medical treatment for her gender dysphoria. The question of a successful real-life experience must be evaluated within context of the client's quality of life and functionality *before* treatment. Clients should not be held to a higher standard of success than their pretransition norm. This case exemplifies the need for flexible treatment protocols designed by a team of gender specialists across a wide diversity of disciplines.

Terry's mental health issues, although impacting her gender issues, were probably not causally related to them. Sometimes gender dysphoria, trauma, and mental illness are linked in an etiological way, as described in the following case:

Micah, a female-to-male transsexual, was severely and violently sexually abused as a child by his father because he refused to look and dress as a girl. The abuse began when Micah was a small child and continued until his late teens. In his first year of college, he suffered a massive breakdown for which he was hospitalized. He continued to exhibit mental health problems for the next twenty years, spending as long as two- to three-year intervals in psychiatric hospitals, much of which he does not remember due to dissociation. He attempted suicide numerous times and repeatedly self-mutilated, trying to remove his breasts. He also struggled with severe bulimia and associated physical problems. Micah passed easily as a male without hormonal assistance, although he was referred to as "she" throughout his psychiatric treatments. During the years he was under psychiatric care, neither his trauma history nor his gender issues were addressed. The extensive charting (shipped from the psychiatric hospital, upon request, in boxes) repeatedly stated that he needed to be stabilized before addressing his trauma issues or gender dysphoria. During these twenty years, Micah completed two master's degrees and had maintained a ten-year relationship with a woman. Finally, at his girlfriend's insistence, Micah became involved in a group for sexual abuse survivors. Micah's group therapist understood the need for specialized gender counseling, and with the help of his therapy team, Micah began to heal from the effects of his childhood abuse and was able to begin living full-time as a man.

Many of Micah's mental health issues stemmed from the intense and brutal abuse by his father. Since his father's abuse was directly related to Micah's gender expression, it correlated with how he felt about himself as a gendered person. It was also seen as causal by psychotherapists, who wanted to treat his mental illnesses in the hopes it would cure his gender issues. Micah suffered severe dissociation and splitting, and continues to work on integrating his split parts. He identified feeling "right" as a man, was unwavering in his commitment to his transition, and felt that the hormonal treatments increased his energy, stamina, and emotional well-being, although he continued to struggle with depression, self-mutilation, dissociation, and self-esteem issues throughout his transition process. Mental health issues are not simply resolved by addressing gender issues, any more than they are likely to be alleviated by attempting to ignore them. Issues related to dissociative identity disorder need particular attention due to the complications involved with different parts of the self vying for dominance (Saks, 1998; Schwartz, 1988). Seil (1997) suggested that dissociation might explain the historic distinction in the literature between primary and secondary transsexuals. He postulated that secondary transsexualism might best be seen as a dissociative reaction to ego-dystonic transsexualism. Eating disorders and body dysmorphia also need to be evaluated carefully, for some clients become obsessed with modifying their bodies, and their gender disturbances might be related to other, more complex, issues of depersonalization and disembodiment (see Fernández-Aranda et al., 2000 for a case report on a transsexual client with anorexia nervosa).

Some people exhibit gender-related issues as part of other mental health disorders and may not be best served by SRS treatment, but rather need a thorough assessment of their mental status and treatment for their mental illness. Cohen-Kettenis and Gooren (1999) suggested that

> Transsexuals with severe concurring psychopathology or belonging to the nonhomosexual or late-onset group should not all be rejected for SRS, but these individuals do need a much more thorough diagnostic procedure, an adjusted (hormone) treatment policy, and more therapeutic support before it is decided that SRS is a viable treatment option. (p. 328)

To summarize, gender-variant people often exhibit mental health symptomatology, which is really sequela to living in a gender binary in which they do not fit. Sometimes they have bona fide mental health problems, some that are independent of the gender issues and others that are etiologically entwined with them. Therapists providing services to gender-variant people need to be able to recognize mental health disturbances and offer appropriate treatments for them. However, mental health problems should not be determining factors in providing medical treatments for gender issues, nor should the assessment process to determine eligibility and readiness be so lengthy, costly, or emotionally stressful as to cause more problems than it solves. As Carroll (1999) said, "It is possible that an individual with a history of depression or psychiatric hospitalizations would continue to experience these problems postoperatively, but still be considered better off after reassignment" (p. 133). People with mental health problems need clinicians who can be advocates and who can assist them in coping with what may prove to be a difficult transition process. When clients have difficulties with the transition process, such difficulties should not be blamed on the clients' inappropriateness as candidates but rather on the availability and quality of supports the clinical community provides to those who live with chronic mental health issues.

CLIENTS SEEKING THERAPY

> There is a power differential in the therapy context, and it is one that cannot be erased, regardless of how committed we are to egalitarian practices. . . . If we believe that we can arrive at some point at which we can interact with those people who seek our help in a way that is to-

tally outside of any power relationships, then we are treading on dangerous ground.

Michael White
Re-Authoring Lives, 1985

Not all clients expressing gender variance or even gender dysphoria present with similar issues or desire the same "solutions." Baumbach and Turner (1992) compared three clinical cases of gender dysphoria in females to illustrate various ways that clients present in therapy. Their comparison highlighted the distinctions between one client manifesting gender-dysphoric symptoms, another with a fantasized solution to change gender, and a third with an actual request for reassignment. It is essential for the clinician to understand why a client is seeking services, which may determine the direction of counseling.

People seeking services for gender-related issues fall into three broad categories: (1) clients who are struggling with gender-dysphoric feelings; (2) clients who are expressing gender variance and seeking letters of referral for medical treatment; and (3) clients who are presenting with family-related issues. This last category includes the gender-variant person as well as his or her loved ones who seek treatment because they are struggling with their significant other's gender issues.

Clients Struggling with Gender-Dysphoric Feelings

This first group is generally composed of people who have been dealing with gender confusion since early childhood and are seeking "help." Less commonly, people in this group are coping with gender issues that have surfaced in adulthood with a tremendous urgency. People in this category are classically referred to in the literature as gender dysphoric, i.e., their gender differences are causing them tremendous distress and they come to therapy wanting relief. Often shame ridden and emotionally distressed, they are rarely informed about transgenderism beyond daytime talk shows and sometimes believe that their behaviors and feelings mark them as mentally ill. Sometimes they are well read on the issues, which only increases their fears of being mentally ill. They are explicitly seeking therapeutic "expertise," either wanting to be diagnosed as a way to label and understand their pain or to be found outside of the diagnostic criteria which they hope would free them from a condition that plagues and obsesses them. They are requesting amelioration for their pain and are seeking a "cure," either to be "fixed" from their internal confusion or to be diagnosed with a mental illness that will explain it.

Therapeutic contact may be the individual's first attempt to deal with a gender issue that has been troubling him or her for decades. The phone call may represent the culmination of years of emotional desperation. When making first contact with a therapist, these clients are often frightened and their behavior can border on paranoid. They are concerned about who might see them entering or leaving the office and are often unwilling to utilize their insurance plans. The level of terror and shame regarding transgenderism for some individuals cannot be minimized. They might seek specialized gender services, but sometimes they are not aware that such services exist or that they would be necessary. They may assume the therapist has more information about gender identity issues than she or he does and/or may attend therapy for months and even years afraid to bring up the topic. Many clients share that they had been involved in long-term therapy but were unsure how to broach the subject and, since it is rarely asked as part of an intake assessment, it simply never "came up."

Jon Waterhouse entered therapy seeking to understand his lifelong compulsion to dress in women's clothing and his desire to live as a woman, for which he felt shame ridden. His psychiatrist began to examine issues from Jon's early childhood, focusing on his mother's preference for his older sister and the extreme sibling rivalry he had with a younger brother. The emotional scars of Jon's childhood became the explanation for his gender dysphoria and cross-dressing behavior and it was clinically assumed that once he worked through these issues his need to cross-dress would be resolved and he would comfortably live as a man. It was never suggested to Jon that cross-dressing was a common behavior that some men found enjoyable and that it was disputable whether the healing of childhood issues would end the cross-dressing behavior. It was never suggested that other males also desired to live as women and had successfully done so with medical assistance. No attempts were made to connect Jon with educational materials to learn more about cross-gender expression or social organizations to meet others who were like him. The focus was curing his gender dysphoria by healing his childhood wounds.

Psychotherapy is often used as an excuse to explore causation rather than future options. It is certainly appropriate for Jon to explore salient issues from his childhood, as well as the lessons he learned from his family regarding gender. However, it is also a therapist's job to educate clients about alternative explanations for gender dysphoria outside of an ego-psychology model, and to assist them in making social and self-help connections to others who also experience gender variance.

Most clients struggling with gender dysphoria are explicitly seeking a therapist to engage in psychotherapy. Psychotherapy, although not a requirement for gender transition, can be a useful tool for sorting out issues related to gender identity. According to the HBIGDA standards of care,

> Psychotherapy often provides education about a range of options not previously seriously considered by the patient. It emphasizes the need to set realistic life goals for work and relationships, and it seeks to define and alleviate the patient's conflicts that may have undermined a stable lifestyle. . . . Ideally, the clinician's work is with the whole of the person's complexity. The goals of therapy are to help the person to live more comfortably within a gender identity and to deal effectively with non-gender issues. (Meyer et al., 2001, p. 18)

Psychotherapy can be useful for transgendered, transsexual, gender-non-conforming, and gender-dysphoric clients at many stages of life. Psychotherapy can alleviate or investigate feelings of shame (Anderson, 1998; Bradshaw, 1988); examine the context, meaning, or roots of gender dysphoria; discuss possibilities for managing gender expression or the impact of transitioning on family, career, and personal integrity; explore various life options, including those that are related to gender as well as those that are independent of it; or cope with posttransition issues. The psychotherapy process can be helpful in withdrawing from living a false life and awakening to an authentic self, as evidenced by the following case.

I loved when my parents were away when I was young, and later when my wife and kids would leave town. I would plan what I would wear and how I would dress. I had this sense that Simone could finally come out. As I dressed, and put on makeup, I would feel as if a part of me that was sleeping would come to life. Sometimes it was incredibly erotic, and other times just relaxing and comfortable, but it was always joyful, like welcoming an old friend home. As I began to stop ignoring this part of me, Simone began to demand more attention—a life of her own. I began to realize how much Robert was really my costume. Simone had always been my most honest sense of myself, my real self, but I had been sending Robert out into the world instead. He is really false, but it was he who everybody said I should be.

Clients seeking psychotherapy for gender dysphoria are an eclectic group. Sometimes they present in an ingratiating manner, pleased that someone will discuss their issues respectfully. Other times they are highly symptomatic, presenting with panic attacks and insomnia. They may be naive about the consequences of transitioning, viewing it as a cure-all for other psychological issues. Steiner (1990) warned, "You should be prepared to see individuals who many present physically looking somewhat bizarre, either flamboyantly or inappropriately dressed, or looking like a man in 'drag'" (1990, p. 96). One client arrived for a 9 a.m. appointment wearing a fancy evening dress and a theatrical wig of long locks that cascaded to the floor. Often clients have no experience going out of their houses dressed as their favored gender and have no framework to judge how successful they are in passing. Sometimes they are exploring long-suppressed fantasies and may not have suitable discrimination regarding appropriateness. It may be necessary to focus on safety issues or utilize fashion magazines to help them develop more fitting female attire. Sometimes clients are highly logical, seeking medical treatises or scientific facts to explain, support, or fix their gender dysphoria. Such clients need tremendous amounts of support and can be emotionally fragile. They need a therapist who is able to offer compassion, education, and resources as the clients explore the gender needs and future options, as well as assess for other mental health difficulties.

Psychotherapy is about an internal process of transformation. Gender therapy is not simply about surgery or hormones or even transition. It is not really about "becoming" something as much as it is about allowing the false parts of self to recede so that an authentic self can emerge.

Clients Seeking Medical Treatments

The second group of clients who seek therapy for gender issues is composed of people who identify themselves as transgendered or transsexual and have specifically sought the services of a gender specialist as source of referral and case management (Anderson, 1998). They are self-identified transsexuals or transgendered people who are seeking to begin or continue a transition process and, in order to be approved for hormonal treatment and surgery, must have referral letters from clinical psychotherapists. Brown and Rounsley (1996) referred to this population as "knowing patients," since they come into therapy knowing exactly what they are seeking. Many of these clients fit the diagnostic criteria precisely as it is outlined in the DSM. However, others who define themselves as transgendered do not fit the DSM's criteria.

Sam Levine sought therapy in order to obtain a referral for hormone therapy. Sam, a biological female, appeared extremely masculine, often "passing" as a man, although she lived and worked as a woman. Sam was currently single, had always been involved with women, but says that she had always seen herself more as a heterosexual man than as a lesbian. She wanted to start testosterone treatments, which she had read about on the Internet, so she could virilize her appearance. She said that she was tired of the ambivalence of looking more like a man than a woman, but still being referred to as a "she." Having very small breasts, she had no desire for breast reduction or chest surgery, nor was she seeking genital alteration. Sam appeared socially and occupationally adjusted and was not seeking psychotherapy. She simply wanted a referral for hormone therapy and assistance finding an attorney who could advise her how to change her legal identity. Sam's therapist refused to write referral letters without an extensive six-month evaluation. After completing the evaluation her therapist turned her down as not meeting the standard established criteria for hormonal therapy.

Sam is an articulate, highly motivated, and mature client who is surely capable of making decisions in *his* life regarding his gender presentation. Although Sam did not meet the criteria of a classic transsexual, Sam was able to find a sensitive and flexible gender therapist who helped him move through transition without requiring traditional psychotherapy. Sam's transition was successful professionally, emotionally, and within the context of his intimate relationship and family of origin. In his case, the rigidity of the therapeutic guidelines created unnecessary obstacles and additional stress, rather than serving to ameliorate Sam's painful dilemma.

Self-identified transgendered people are often able to speak articulately about their gender issues and are often less closeted and more knowledgeable about transgenderism than those seeking therapy explicitly for gender dysphoria. They are able to express concerns about their future, are sometimes in less emotional pain, and are often clearer about their gender identity. They are usually well read about gender issues, having reviewed clinical literature more thoroughly than most therapists. According to the research of Denny and Roberts (1997) nearly 80 percent of the 339 respondents of their survey of transgendered clients were familiar with the HBIGDA's standards of care. It is questionable whether a study of 339 *clinicians* would reveal such a high level of awareness.

In many cases such clients are not interested in therapeutic counseling but need to go through a gatekeeper to access the various medical interventions available. The SOC require an evaluation. They do not, however, require psychotherapy. The SOC clearly state, "Not every adult gender patient requires psychotherapy in order to proceed with hormone therapy, the real-life experience, hormones, or surgery" (Meyer et al., 2001, p. 1988). Nonetheless, it is common "transsexual folklore" (to use Bolin's words) for clients to feel "mandated" to psychotherapy and state knowledge of requirements that do not currently exist. However, most gender clinics have stringent requirements for evaluation purposes. Petersen and Dickey's (1995) comparative study of gender clinics showed that 74 percent adhered to more conservative policies than recommended in the HBIGDA's standards of care, including withholding hormonal treatment for six months or longer after having determined that the client fits the diagnostic criteria for GID.

Since many clients in this category are frustrated with the medical system's control over their lives and are struggling with the internal pressure of their own identity issues and desire to transition, they can often present in a way that alienates professionals. Clients may see therapists as obstacles blocking them from hormonal therapy and they often view therapy as a hoop to jump through. Clients are unable to envision the therapeutic relationship as a vehicle of support (Denny and Miller, 1994; Vitale, 1996). Developing an honest therapeutic relationship with an educated client who is trying to "use" the clinician to obtain approval letters can be challenging. Clients are often terrified of the therapist's power to diagnose them and/or may be furious that they need a diagnosis in order to receive the medical care they desire. For many clients, having to be "diagnosed" to actualize themselves is frustrating or even humiliating. Bowen (1998) said, "I accepted the label 'transsexual' in order to obtain access to the hormones and chest surgery necessary to manifest my spirit in the material world" (p. 63). However, *transsexual* was never a term Bowen identified with or respected.

One reason relatively few professionals commit their time to trying to help gender-dysphoric persons is that many find the experience very frustrating and the clients belligerent, demanding, and almost always impatient. Green (2000b) discussed one gender identity clinic that was "besieged by patient complaints." Steiner (1990) said,

> gender dysphoric patients as a group can be difficult to manage. They can be manipulative, demanding, and narcissistic . . . you will be overwhelmed by patients who insist that they are transsexual and demand immediate surgical sex reassignment. You must be prepared to withstand onslaughts on your interests in transsexuals as people, to be accused of dragging your feet, and to withstand transsexuals' demands to know why you have not surgically reassigned them yesterday. (pp. 95-96)

Bolin (1988) offered some insight into this negative view of the client/ therapist relationship. She said

> I have noticed generalized animosity toward the psychiatric profession indicative of an inherent imbalance in power between mental health caretakers and transsexuals . . . many of the professionals' claims that transsexuals are resistant to counseling may be viewed in this light . . . power weighs heavy on the side of the caretaker . . . the evaluation is at the crux of the unequal power relationship. (p. 52)

Developing a healing and trusting relationship that starts from the premise of power and exclusion is a challenge and the need to reframe the role of gatekeeper with one that is more conducive to a therapeutic alliance is the first priority. These clients are often desperately in need of an advocate and are less often in need of a therapist. They need a gender specialist who is also a transition assistant. The clinician must delicately balance his or her multiple roles as "gatekeeper" and develop a team approach to working with the client. Transgendered people are often fighting, literally, for their lives in a world that does not see them as they are. The therapeutic relationship can be the first place where they can put down their sword and shield and simply experience acceptance.

Clients Presenting with Family-Related Issues

The third group of clients reaching out for services includes family members and those who are struggling with issues in their intimate and familial relationships. Often couples will reach out to a therapist after a transgendered person has come out and the family is thrown into turmoil coping with the ramifications. Transgendered people, who may be comfortable with their own transition process or even involved in their own individual counseling, will sometimes seek assistance in coming out to a partner or spouse or request specific marital/couple counseling. In some instances, clients contact therapists because spouses desire separation, which clients are hoping to avert.

Partners, spouses, and parents often seek services on their own, in search of information, education, or a place to vent their fears and anguish. Often transgendered people, in the throws of their own transition process, are unavailable as supports or are selfishly overfocused on their own issues. They may not be aware of the intensity in which these issues are impacting their loved ones. Children are often thrown into confusion over a disclosure and, especially if the parents are in crisis, it will leave them frightened. Spouses will often seek services for their children, denying their own need for self-care. Other family members, including siblings, in-laws, and aging parents, also seek gender specialists for help understanding their loved one (see Lesser, 1999, for one therapist's work using self-psychology with the parent of an adult transsexual).

Therapists need to acknowledge the seriousness of family disruption as well as work to help the family normalize it. Families move through normative developmental stages throughout the life span, and as Carter and McGoldrick (1999) wrote, "Stress is often greatest at transition points from one stage to another in the developmental process as families rebalance, redefine, and realign their relationships" (p. 7). For many families, transgenderism is so far off their sense of "normal" that it is difficult for them to see it as an issue of stress or life span development. However, reframing the discussion away from pathology in this way can be very helpful. Analogies to the shock of other crises such as unwanted medical diagnoses (e.g., cancer) can be helpful to engage the compassion of family members and also can be a validation of the intensity of their emotionality. However, these approaches must be used very cautiously so the transgendered person is not labeled as being "ill." Working together with the whole family, to help them adjust to what is surely a crisis in family life, can assist family members in coming to terms with gender issues in a conscious, proactive, and empathic manner.

Intimates are not always affected in a negative way. Occasionally partners are supportive, but rarely is the support consistent and they often vacillate between emotions that are hostile, furious, sad, accepting, and resigned. The way a partner experiences transgenderism will also impact the transgendered person's own acceptance. For instance, the man who cross-dresses and whose wife accepts it—or finds it erotically stimulating—will probably not exhibit the same level of dissonance as someone whose wife is disgusted by the behavior. A female-to-male transsexual who chooses to have breast removal/chest reconstruction and begin hormonal therapy with the approval and consent of a female lover will transition with greater ease than in cases in which the lover resists being involved with a transsexual man. Although some families deal with transition issues easily, most couples struggle with transgender transitions, especially those who are seeking out therapeutic help.

TRANSGENDER NARRATIVES

> It is the life-plot rather than actual somatic sex change that symptomizes the transsexual. . . . In order to achieve the diagnosis necessary to access the medical technology to change sex, one must recount a transsexual narrative; the subject is necessarily a transsexual before changing sex.
>
> Jay Prosser
> *Second Skins,* 1998

The relationship between gender-variant, particularly transsexual, people and the medical establishment is complex and problematic due to the numerous role confusions demanded of the therapeutic community. Therapists and clinicians who work within the "gender community" are a small cadre of professionals, dispersed internationally, and include those with a wide variety of professional trainings, including psychiatrists, psychologists, social workers, educators, and researchers. Some work in gender clinics that have established protocols for assessment and diagnosis, while others are independent practitioners, often isolated in their work and having few colleagues to confer with about gender issues. Gender specialists are a unique and compassionate group of practitioners who are motivated by concern and kindness toward a population that has been sorely neglected, choosing to work in a professional venue in which there is little interest or respect.

Gender specialists are, however, also gatekeepers for the medical profession. They are the final checkpoint before referrals can be made for medical treatments. Therapists need to "diagnose" and "assess" clients for "eligibility" and "readiness" for hormonal treatments, having as their resources the criteria of the *Diagnostic and Statistical Manual of Mental Disorders,* the guidelines of the Harry Benjamin International Gender Dysphoria Association, and, of course, their clients' stories. As Billings and Urban (1982) said, "Since transsexualism is initially self-diagnosed and because there are no organic indications of the 'disease', physicians are dependent upon the accuracy and honesty of patients' statements for diagnosis" (p. 108).

Indeed, our entire understanding about gender variance has been gleaned from the stories told to therapists and physicians. Oosterhuis (1997) said that the earliest reports on transgenderism from von Krafft-Ebing's extensive case studies and collected autobiographies "furnished psychiatrists with the life stories and experiences upon which medical interpretations were grounded" (p. 83). Our definitions of transsexuals, which set the parameters for approval of medical treatments, are based on clinical accounts, recorded by sexologists, particularly Harry Benjamin and Magnus Hirschfeld, and other early medical advocates of transsexuals. These textbook accounts helped determine who was a bona fide transsexual and became the criteria against which all other gender-variant persons who desired medical treatments were compared and judged. However, as Plummer (1995) said, "The research stories of hundreds of sexological studies conducted over the past few decades are not mere reflections of our sexual lives, but *play an active role in their construction*" (p. 12, italics mine).

Numerous writers have recognized the similarity of the stories that transsexuals tell, reflecting with amazement how closely they resembled Harry Benjamin's initial cases. Stone (1991) wryly commented that "the reason the candidates' behavioral profiles matched Benjamin's so well was that the candidates, too, had read Benjamin's book, which was passed from hand to hand within the transsexual community, and they were only too happy to provide the behavior that led to acceptance for surgery" (p. 291). Approval for hormonal and surgical treatments *depends* on telling the right story and since "reputable clinics treated only 'textbook' cases of transsexualism, patients desiring surgery, for whatever personal reasons, had no other recourse but to meet this evaluation standard" (Billings and Urban, 1982, p. 109). Steiner (1990), for instance, warned clinicians that the "patient's story may have been 'influenced' by a transsexual friend and 'coached' as to what they think you, the examiner, want to hear [and] . . . the patient's self-report is influenced by his or her readings in the medical or scientific literature on transsexualism" (p. 97). Walker (1981, as cited in Petersen and Dickey, 1995) identified thirty-five cases in which clients had fabricated their life histories.

Those seeking sex reassignment medical treatments know that they will be approved only if they present certain "truths" about their lives, so regardless of their own personal stories they study Harry Benjamin's cases, or in the modern age of the Internet, go online to read the criteria for approval, and construct a story to bring to a clinician. Educated about the diagnostic protocols—or sometimes misinformed about them—clients narrate their story for therapists and attempt to conform to the stereotypes that research states a "true transsexual" should display. Billings and Urban (1982) referred to this as "the con" (p. 109), and Plummer (1995) said that this con game is about "learning to tell the best story to fit the part [because it is only by] incorporating the 'textbook accounts' into their life that they can become eligible for transsexual surgery" (p. 42). Hausman (1995) said, "In a context where telling the right story may confer legitimacy upon one's demand and the wrong story can foil one's chances for sex change, the autobiographies of those transsexuals who have successfully maneuvered within the strict protocols of the gender clinics constitute guidebooks of no mean proportions" (p. 143).

This "transsexual narrative" as the basis for diagnosis and treatment contains certain basic criteria without which one cannot be called a "transsexual." These criteria include nonerotic cross-dressing and cross-gender behavior, interests, and expression starting at a young age, disgust regarding genitalia and secondary sex characteristics with a desire to change or remove them, and an ability to "pass" the real-life test which includes full-time living in the new gender, often including paid employment or full-time school attendance and proof of legal paperwork changes. Recent research shows that whether or not clients meet these guidelines, they are aware of their existence and will comply with them by lying instead of telling the truth and risking medical rejection (see Figure 6.3). Bolin (1988), in her research, found that "transsexuals feel that they cannot reveal information at odds with caretaker impressions without suffering adverse consequences. They freely admit lying to their caretakers" (p. 63). Walworth (1997) outlined in her study of fifty-two postoperative male-to-female transsexuals numerous areas in which clients had lied to therapists in order to meet what they thought were the guidelines for transitioning.

FIGURE 6.3. *Hal & Bengie* copyright Jay Hayes-Light. Permission to reprint granted by Dr. Jay Hayes-Light.

Lying, for clients born male, has included denying their sexual arousal to wearing women's clothing, denying their sexual attraction to women (i.e., postoperative lesbianism), lowering the age of onset of their cross-dressing behavior, and denying any sexual pleasure from their male genitalia. They also denied substance use and suicidal ideation (Walworth, 1997). It is unknown how many FTMs have hidden their gay identities from researchers and clinicians at gender clinics, who had already rendered gay transmen nonexistent. Lewins (1995) referred to this as "game-playing" and discussed how clients are "afraid to declare their true feelings and behavior" (p. 94). One of the transsexual women he interviewed offered the advice that one should not talk about lesbianism, feminism, or anal sex because it might affect approval for surgery. Wilchins (1997) said that since she was "determined to be a 'successful' transsexual, [she] . . . worked earnestly at being straight, at developing the proper attraction to men" (p. 177). Unfortunately, she was unable to succeed. Clients not only lie to therapists about these issues, but, as Lawrence (2000) said, sometimes also doubted themselves, questioning whether they were "really" transsexual if their experiences were different than the standard blueprint. She said, "They had imagined they were unique in experiencing autogynephilic arousal . . . [and] had been unwilling to disclose their feelings to caregivers."

It is easy to accuse such clients of "conning" and "game-playing," but the nature of the system as it has been developed "requires" the person who desires medical treatments to have a consistent autobiography. Indeed, it is necessary for the "authorization" of medical approval (Prosser, 1998). Prosser (1998) said that "autobiography is transsexuality's proffered symptom" (p. 104), and that it is the "patient's position to confess, [and] the professional's—half priest holding the key to the patient's salvation, half detective decoding the clinical narrative—to listen, to take note—and precisely to police the subject's access to technology" (p. 111). How can anything resembling psychotherapy take place within this kind of system?

The transsexual narrative as it is outlined is not inaccurate—it is simply not inclusive. Stories such as those told to Harry Benjamin are real. Transsexuals who fit those descriptors exist and have been the people best served by the established medical paradigms (and consequently are resistant to proposed changes). When Christine Jorgensen's story became a media sensation it paved the way for people who identified with her to seek similar treatments. It also created a narrative with which many people could identify. White and Epston (1990) said,

> in striving to make sense of life, persons face the task of arranging their experiences of events in sequences across time in such a way as to arrive at a coherent account of themselves and the world around them. Specific experiences of events of the past and present, and those that are predicted to occur in the future, must be connected in a lineal sequence to develop this account. (p. 10)

Narrative and autobiography are intrinsic to human life. Most people are able to respond to basic identifying questions about who they are, such as their place of birth, ethnic identity, age, marital status, and place of employment. It is considered a tragedy when someone has amnesia and cannot remember who he or she is, or, when due to external circumstances such as war, people are unable to access the files that record these "facts" of their lives. Adoptees often spend their lives searching for remnants of their history because their narrative feels incomplete without knowing the origins of their story. Gergen and Gergen (1986) said, "The most essential ingredient of narrative accounting (or storytelling) is its capability to structure events in such a way that they demonstrate, first, a connectedness or coherence, and second, a sense of movement or direction through time" (p. 25). This creates "directionality" among events that would otherwise be isolated and unintelligible (Gergen and Gergen, 1984, p. 174). Events become ordered and organized, and the life story—all human life stories—is structured and linear, describing and making sense within a particular worldview of the events that are experienced.

Narrative, in this sense, is "an organizing principle for human action" (Sarbin, 1986, p. 9). Epston, White, and Murray (1992) said, "Stories enable persons to link aspects of their experiences through the dimensions of time" (p. 97). Human beings attempt to understand their lives by imposing "structure on the flow of experience" (p. 97). Fivush (1994) reminded us, "We are all authors of our own autobiographies" (p. 136).

Indeed, the transsexual narrative that astute "listeners" such as von Krafft-Ebing, Magnus Hirschfeld, and Harry Benjamin have handed down is a marvelous testament to the persistent lifelong anatomical dissonance and intense desire to change not only appearance and presentation but genital configuration that many gender-variant people experience. With advances in technology those who have lived this narrative can actualize their desires. The transsexual narrative as it has been developed contains all the important rules for constructing an intelligible story (Gergen, 1994). These stories show a temporal ordering of events (e.g., cross-gender identity since early childhood, persistent desire to be the opposite sex), causal linkings (e.g., continued desires throughout adolescence and early adulthood), demarcation signs (e.g., childhood cross-dressing, lack of genital pleasure in adult sexuality), and a "valued endpoint" (reassignment surgery). These stories and the similarities between them are "real." They are not made up or invented, but born of the very stuff from which human lives are made.

However, and this is a big "however," stories are not simply mirrored reflections of our lives—they are "historically constructed and negotiated in communities of persons and within the context of social structures and institutions" (White, 1993, pp. 36-37). Stories can only be created by that which is known, that which is possible, or that which can be imagined. Bruner (1987) asked whether autobiographies should be seen not as records of what happened but as "a continuing interpretation and reinterpretation of . . . experience?" (p. 12). The stories that were developed to justify sex-change surgery in the 1950s and 1960s, following the discovery of sex hormones and the invention and sophistication of genital surgeries, have a certain order, structure, and "valued endpoint," precisely because that was the endpoint that was newly available.

All life stories are created with certain parts being highlighted as particularly salient. No one has *one* life story; all people have multiple stories, of which certain selected narratives are chosen for different purposes (Gergen and Gergen, 1984). When a recovering alcoholic in Alcoholics Anonymous tells his or her life story, the story may highlight events that are associated with drinking and downplay events that involve, say, voluntary charitable efforts. When a woman reveals a medical history, she will probably not talk about the important books she has read. When reporting a robbery to a police officer, one does not talk about the house paint options that are available at the department store. People will tell a different narrative of their lives if they are asked, for instance, about their sexual frequency versus their parenting styles, even though the threads of these aspects of their lives are interwoven, take place within the same life frame, and exist concurrently (as all new parents who are attempting to rekindle a romance only to be interrupted by a crying baby know). It is not simply that all people have multiple stories but also that stories happen simultaneously. All autobiographies are, in this sense, selective. Certain "facts" are emphasized and others diminish in importance.

Transsexuality is a story that has been told in a particular way, and the collected medical narratives have served as guideposts. Like most people, transsexuals have a need to make sense of their lives, to find order, coherence, and generate a valued endpoint. The selected narrative must, of course, fit the basic design of their lives (e.g., a person who never drinks will not be able to create an "alcoholic narrative"), but it must also structure the ordering of life events to give it meaning and enhance some lucid goal (e.g., an alcoholic who can admit he or she has a drinking problem is offered an endpoint of sobriety). Jerome Bruner (1994) asked, "Could there be any human activity in which the drive to reduce cognitive dissonance is so great as in the domain of 'telling about your life'?" (p. 46). This is, of course, no less true for transsexuals. Perhaps, due to the uniqueness of transsexual narratives, transsexuals are the harbingers of the power and profundity of what it means to face the challenge of making sense of one's life narrative. Prosser (1998) said, "Transsexuality is always a narrative work, a transformation of the body that requires the remolding of the life into a particular narrative shape" (p. 4).

Transsexuals are, of course, not alone in creating the stories of their lives. All human beings engage in myth building. McAdams (1993) said, "The making of a personal myth is a psychosocial quest. . . . Defining the self through myth may be seen as an ongoing act of psychological and social *responsibility*" (p. 35). Myth here is not a synonym for fairy tale, falsehood, or illusion but more akin to the ability to originate and inspire legendary archetypes. Creating something valuable and worthy out of our lives is a hero's journey of epic proportions. It is not make-believe as much as it is growing out to one's edges, the acts of becoming fully human.

Of course, some people are better storytellers than others. Many people literally see their life events as the fodder for "story," while others merely see these events as mundane and not worthy of attention. From the literary "classics" of Ernest Hemingway, William Faulkner, or Charles Dickens to the feminist classics of Charlotte Perkins Gilman, Virginia Woolf, or Tillie Olsen; from the black writers of life narratives and "biomythographies"—Zora Neale Hurston, James Baldwin, and Audre Lorde to the prolific nature accounts of Henry David Thoreau and John Muir, or even the humorous true-to-life parenting stories of Erma Bombeck—storytellers reveal in stark, raw color the deep truths of everyday life. They make our lives real. For some who live the transgender experience their lives are sad, confusing non-stories—explained only by pathology and despair. For others the transgender experience has been a hero's journey of adventure and magic, not only an alteration of the body but also a transfomational life passage.

Many stories reveal a moment of insight, of realization—a sense of time standing still, when the main character reaches a turning point or experiences an epiphany. It can be as simple as Dillard's (1974) spiritual experience noticing the light shining through the leaves of a tree—what she calls *seeing* the "tree of light"—or as complex as Wright's (1966) character Bigger Thomas's terror when he realizes the price he will pay for the murder of a white woman. McAdams (1993) said, "Our personal myth develops in periodic episodes that punctuate the relative equilibrium of the rest of our adult life" (p. 109). Life can never be the same after this moment of revelation. One client said, "I didn't know anything about gender or transsexualism until I read this Web page, and suddenly my whole life made sense—just like that, in one moment."

More commonly stories are woven slowly into sense from nonsense, into form and structure from chaos. Indeed, the genre of coming-out stories for lesbian, gay, and bisexual people often fits this paradigm. Plummer (1995) said that coming-out stories "show the speaker moving out of this world of shadows, secrecy, and silence—where feelings and pains had to be kept to oneself and where tremendous guilt, shame, and hidden pathology was omnipresent—into a world which is more positive, public and supportive" (p. 50). Coming-out stories reveal a "narrative plot" that is "driven by acute suffering, the need to break a silence" followed by the actual coming-out experience, coming home to oneself. Plummer (1995) said, "These are always stories of significant transformation" (p. 50).

Coming-out stories have been shared in the lesbian, gay, and bisexual communities for years, a symbolic sitting around the fire pit and retelling one's emergence from one's own shadows. The first kiss, the first moment of recognition, the first visit to a gay bar—these experiences become a shared "knowing" instead of a shameful secret. Coming-out stories have also been popular within the emerging transgender community. Califia (1997) identified the autobiographical accounts of male-to-female transsexuals as the "first wave" of the modern transgender movement, and stated that it was often through reading that transgendered and transsexual people discovered that they were not alone. The autobiographies of Christine Jorgensen (Benjamin, 1967), Jan Morris (1974), Renee Richards (1983), and Deidre McCloskey (2000) were and are read and reread by MTF transsexuals seeking a reflection for their internal experience. An Internet search will reveal literally thousands of personal coming-out stories on transgender themes.

It has been harder for female-to-male transgender people, whose stories have been less often told, to find these reflections. When Leslie Feinberg's (1993) book *Stone Butch Blues* was first published, it was immediately read and passed around among butch, stone-butch, FTM, and transgendered lesbians who were excited to finally find a narrative with which they could relate. Members of one support group shared that the book so powerfully affected them that they each remembered exactly where they were when first reading this book, the physical location was a window frame surrounding the experience—the book's effect on their lives was transformative. Historical biography has also helped transgendered people experience a sense of their place in the unfolding of the human story. Figures such as Jeanne d'Arc, or anthropological accounts of Two-Spirit people, serve as role models and heroes, literally mythic legends, to admire and emulate. These spiritual ancestors serve to reintegrate cross-gender expression back into the historical legacy in which transgendered people have been accepted and respected.

Bohan and Russell (1999) explained the power of narrative and myth building. They said, "Each person's coming to her or his identity involves creating narratives about who she or he is. This is far more than a matter of making up stories, and it implies neither truth nor the absence thereof" (p. 19). Although creating narratives is a universal process of becoming a self, few are privileged to feel the power of transformation in the way that transsexuals can. Bohan and Russell said that narrative identity development is "dynamic" (signifying potency and strength), "reiterative" (it repeats itself over and again throughout the life span), and "generative" (being both fertile and productive). Narrative and story building are living processes. Mears (2001) said, "It was not . . . until I began to tell my story, that I could see my true self for the first time. It is in the telling of our narratives that we put meaning into our own life story . . . other stories helped me to shape my own" (pp. 3-4).

The power of narrative is indisputable. However, due to the historical privileging of a particular transsexual narrative as *the* narrative within the medical taxonomy—or the most recent addition of the "autogynephilia narrative" as *the* alternative plot—transsexual discourse has become a linear path that has virtually eliminated the possibility of other gender journeys. The invisibility of alternative transgender pathways led Conway (1998) in her exploration of autobiography to say, "It's probably necessary to believe in essential maleness and femaleness to have a transsexual experience . . . transsexual life stories can't be told in any but essentialist terms" (p. 150). Nothing could, of course, be farther than the truth and Nakamura (1997) explored various alternative transgendered-narrative tropes. Although some transsexual narratives emanate from an essentialist perspective ("I was born in the wrong body"), equally intriguing transsexual narratives reflect the complexity of socially constructed, gender-fluid, and gender-oscillating identities.

The process of telling the story of one's life can take place only within a framework of available stories. One cannot simply "be" gay in a culture that has no word for homosexuality or any visible expression of same-sex behavior. This is not to say that a person could not engage in homosexual behavior; rather, the meaning ascribed to that behavior is defined within a cultural matrix. Life stories must have a developmental trajectory, i.e., they always start in infancy and they cannot start in adolescence. Bruner (1994) said "The story form affects the organization of experience just as surely as it affects memory recall" (pp. 47-48). It becomes impossible to have a "history" of an experience when the experience does not yet have a "story form" or a defining language. Often people revisit and restructure their pasts to make sense of them based on adult information (deMonteflores and Schultz, 1978).

Until recently, the only story that has been available for transsexuals—the track of "true transsexualism"—has reflected the lives of a limited number of transgendered people. It is still a useful framework and can serve as an entry point to discuss a broader diversity of transgender subjectivity (Brown, 2001). Newer narratives have developed in the past ten years, but they have not yet been incorporated into the medical canon. Since only the official narrative has been privileged, people who do not easily fit it have either felt unrepresented or have tried to mold themselves to fit the only legitimized framework. All people live their lives within the stories that they have learned to tell about themselves. To a large extent the only possible stories are the ones that already exist. If a story plot that reflected their experiences did not exist, it may have been impossible for them to narrate their own story.

THERAPIST AS MIDWIFE: THE BIRTH OF STORY

Oppressed people resist by identifying themselves as subjects, by defining their reality, shaping their new identity, naming their history, telling their story.

bell hooks
Talking Back, 1989

Gender-variant people reaching out for therapeutic help are seeking information about themselves. They are living with numerous internal experiences, often since early childhood, regarding a dissonance with their gender identity, their gender role, their sense of masculinity or femininity, their genitalia or secondary sex characteristics, and/or how they are perceived in public or private as a gendered person. Bruner (1987) said, "The story of one's own life is, of course, a privileged but troubled narrative in the sense that it is reflective: the narrator and the central figure in the narrative are the same" (p. 13). Therefore, clients seek therapy not only because they want information and answers (they could just go to the library or Internet for that) but because they also want to "talk." They are seeking a dialogic relationship, someone outside of themselves to tell their story to who can listen and reflect it back to them.

Freire (1971) said, "Dialogue is the encounter between [human beings], mediated by the world, in order to name the world" (p. 76). The therapeutic encounter is an opportunity for a conversation to take place in which clients can "hear" themselves into existence. The therapist serves as a mirror, as a foil, and as a compatriot on the client's internal journey. Anderson and Goolishian (1992) said, "Telling one's story is a re-presentation of experience; it is constructing history in the present" (p. 37). White and Epston (1990) saw the role of the therapist not merely as a listener, but as an audience, and an interactive one at that. They said,

> in the act of witnessing the performance of a new story, the audience contributes to the writing of new meanings; that has real effects on the audience's interaction with the story's subject. . . . When the subject of the story 'reads' the audience's experience of the new performance . . . he or she engages in revisions and extensions of the new story. (p. 17)

The process of constructing a life narrative is never a solitary experience. Narratives and life stories take place within communities of shared experiences, as part of the social discourse. Becoming a man or woman is always a social process. As Simone de Beauvoir (1953) said, "One is not born a woman, but rather becomes one" (p. 249). This is no different for transsexuals. "Clients unveil the story of their lives in conjunction with a specific reader/therapist, therefore the therapist is always a co-author of the story that is unfolding" (Lax, 1992, p.73). Coming out transgendered or emerging transsexual is an inherently social process (unlike becoming gay, which can remain hidden from public view) and involves both micro and macro components (Lewins, 1995). The therapist helps the client externalize the problem (White, 1995; White and Epston, 1990) so it is no longer experienced as being inside the transsexual person as a psychological problem, but rather a problem to be managed within the social arena. Gergen (1991) said,

> the patient develops with the psychiatrist a form of narrative or constructed truth as opposed to a historical truth, and it is the narrative truth that largely determines the outcome of treatment. In the therapeutic setting and beyond, we find autobiography is anything but autonomous; it is more properly sociobiography. (p. 164)

Sadly, most clinicians have not recognized their role in the unfolding of the client's story. Instead, they have seen themselves as objective observers. Few therapists have been able to examine their own internal processes for what transsexual and intersex narratives evoke within *them* (see Quinodoz, 1998; Williams, 2002, for a psychoanalytic self-examination of a countertransferential experience with clients). For therapists who feel uncomfortable thinking that they are "cocreating" a transsexual narrative, it is important to realize that therapists, especially those who have worked with transsexuals in a more traditional model, have always cocreated gender narratives. For many years it was considered part of therapeutic treatment to encourage clients in transition to cut off all ties with their past and consciously reconstruct a false history in their new gender.

Stone (1991) said, "The highest purpose of the transsexual is to erase him/herself, to fade into the 'normal' population as soon as possible. Part of this process is known as constructing a plausible history—learning to lie effectively about one's past" (p. 296). Following this strategy, clients needed to prepare answers for questions such as, "What kind of games did you play when you were a little girl?", which would deflect any awareness from the fact that they had never actually *been* little girls. This treatment strategy encouraged clients to move to new cities, end marriages, sever longtime friendships, and develop an entirely new social system in their newly emerged gender. "We are not supposed to want attention as transsexuals . . . in order to be a good—or successful—transsexual person, one is not supposed to be a transsexual person at all" (Green, 1999, p. 120). Bornstein (1994) said, "Transsexuality is the only condition for which the therapy is to lie" (p. 62). Indeed, transsexual treatment may be the only treatment strategy that taught people to actively lie about their histories in order to create a healthy future. Scheman (1999) synthesized the ideas of transsexual activists by saying,

> the only way to be a "certified" transsexual is to deny that you are one, that is, to convince the doctors (and agree to try to convince the rest of the world) that you are and always have been what you clearly are not, namely simply and straightforwardly a woman (or a man). Since you cannot have a history that is congruent with such an identity, you are left without a past. (p. 75)

Using a narrative model is not about creating histories or inventing life stories. It is about allowing clients struggling with gender identity issues to tell their own stories in their own words. It is an evocative process in which the therapist is the midwife, assisting in the birthing, offering encouragment and support but essentially witnessing the client's own birthing process. The goal is to assist the client in finding significance and purpose in the life he or she has lived, developing organization and structure in which to make sense of it, and to determine direction and goals for his or her future. "Using the narrative metaphor leads us to think about people's lives as stories and to work with them to experience their life stories in ways that are meaningful and fulfilling" (Freedman and Coombs, 1996, p.1). Brown (2001) suggested that examining the trauma issues, as well as the healing processes, is a useful model for hearing the narratives of intersexed people.

There are many useful tools for working with gender-variant clients in a narrative manner. Ideally it is best to avoid all stigmatizing and medical terminology. The term *transsexual* has often been a "medical category [that] . . . becomes [a client's] identity" (Irvine, 1990, p. 266). Try to help clients find words of their own to describe themselves, which will often change over time because the exploration process of transgender emergence is often "adolescent," in that many identities become possible, feasible, and are tried on to see if they fit. Even the process of using the word *transgender* is often a frightening experience for a client. Sometimes it is the key experience of a session, simply saying the word. One client, a young transsexual woman who insisted she was intersexed (e.g., her gender variance was biologically natural for her) and *not* transsexual said, "I am looking for Internet sites on hair removal. You know, male-to-female transsexual sites, because that *is what I am, you know.*" For her, owning the term *transsexual* not as a medical term but as a means to find a like-minded community, was an act of empowerment. She said, "Did you hear that? I finally called myself a transsexual."

It is also preferable to refer to clients in the gender pronouns and names that they identify, regardless of their actual presentation. For some clients it is the first time they have disclosed their cross-gender name to someone else, the first time they have heard it spoken out loud. Some clients will try different names and others will seek confirmation that they have chosen a "good" name. Even for clients that decide not to transition, use of opposite sex pronouns can be a profound experience in assisting them in understanding whether their gender desires are only fantasy or something more salient. If a client presents in a way that leaves the clinician unclear as to gender identity, ask him or her to clarify it!

Carroll (1999) identified four common outcomes of psychological treatment: unresolved outcome; acceptance of biological gender and role; engaging in the cross-gender role on an intermittent or part-time basis; and adopting the other gender role full-time. It is important that the therapist not be invested in which outcome a particular client finds best suited to his or her life. Carroll does not acknowledge the possibility of mixed-role position as another resolution. Bockting and Coleman (1992), however, acknowledged this possibility. They said, "A unique aspect of our treatment model is that it allows for individuals to identify as neither man nor woman, but as someone whose identity transcends the culturally sanctioned dichotomy" (p. 144). They also discussed how difficult it can be for a client to live between genders in a bipolar social world. They offered a case example of a client who felt neither male nor female and experimented with living in a mixed gender presentation, but found that it provoked confusion for others. She/he discovered that "playing a woman" was, in contemporary society, what worked best even though the internal experience of her/his own gender identity was still mixed.

Schaefer, Wheeler, and Futterweit (1995) identified a number of therapeutic goals for working with transgendered clients. These include clients understanding that their gender identity is not a disease or illness, that there is no cure, and that being transgendered is not their fault. They also remind clients that "the inner expression of the condition and its various intensities will emerge and reemerge throughout their life" (p. 2030). Finally, they say that clients have an obligation and responsibility regarding the gender variance, which is "to learn reasonable and secure ways of living their [lives]" including "how to make a living and how to make a relationship" (p. 2030).

In addition to individual, marital/couple, and family therapy, group therapy is often a useful modality for working with transgendered clients (Miller, 1996; Stermac et al., 1991). The benefits of group treatments include being with like-minded others and experiencing a sense of universality to individual concerns (Yalom, 1995). Clients try on new identities and explore their abilities to pass in their chosen gender. Often they are able to challenge one another regarding issues of denial or shame within a group setting that might appear more confrontational in a one-on-one meeting. The following exchange took place within a group for MTF transgendered people. They were discussing the relationship between their masculine and feminine selves, and in a respectful manner expressed many divergent views:

BETTY: There is only one *me*. In my work life I dress as a man, and mostly at home I dress as a man, and people think they are talking to Bill, but I know that I am always Betty, and those people that can handle that I let them know too. I wish I could dress the way Betty is most comfortable, but it makes my wife uneasy and I'm not ready to deal with my boss, so Betty presents as Bill, but she's always Betty.

SANDRA: I am who I am, and I am both male and female. It doesn't matter what I'm wearing—how feminine or masculine I am—I am always a trans person. I'm not trying to pass as anything.

MARTHA: I don't care who knows that there is a male body underneath my dress; it makes them crazy that I look so good, and I love confusing them.

KATIE: Passing is very important to me. I would hate to have anyone know that I once lived as a man. I work very hard at it.

One of the therapist's responsibilities is to interview clients and determine their appropriateness for medical treatments. This involves a psychosocial assessment process and writing a letter to medical providers determining diagnosis and eligibility (see Appendix C). Even if the therapist rejects a gatekeeper role and is more interested in the person's emergent developmental identity formation, he or she is still responsible for gathering certain information and establishing that medical treatments are appropriate for a particular client. Although therapists should not simply refuse someone for medical referral who does not fit the outdated diagnostic criteria, they are mandated to carefully assess potential candidates. What kinds of assessment criteria should a therapist utilize? What kinds of stories would prohibit a medical referral? Box 6.1 includes three salient criteria for making a psychosocial assessment for a medical referral for transgender or transsexual treatments.

According to the HBIGDA's standards of care, clients must meet the following eligibility requirements to begin hormonal treatment: They must be at least eighteen years of age; knowledgeable of the medical limitations, social benefits, and risks of hormones; and must have either a documented real-life experience of at least three months prior to the administration of

---

BOX 6.1.
Guidelines for Psychosocial Assessment for Medical Referral

- Does the client experience a discomfort with his or her assigned sex and express a desire to feminize or virilize his or her body? Has this desire been of long-standing duration, i.e., not transient or spontaneous?
- Does the client understand the various options available for gender modification? Does the client comprehend what hormonal and/or surgical treatments will *and will not* do? Does the client have a realistic appraisal of the impact of various treatments physically, socially, vocationally, and within intimate familial relationships?
- Is the client mentally, cognitively, and emotionally capable of making an informed decision that will permanently alter his or her body and social relationships? Does the client have any serious mental health problems that are likely to interfere with his or her ability to adjust to a life in a new gender or with the process of transition? Is this being addressed clinically?

---

hormones or a period of psychotherapy of a duration specified by the mental health professional after the initial evaluation (usually a minimum of three months). It is important to note that exceptions to these criteria are included in the SOC. For example, although the age criterion is eighteen years old, guidelines to begin hormonal treatment for adolescents are outlined within the SOC. Although the SOC suggest three months of psychotherapy following the evaluation period, these guidelines are not—as is often assumed— "rules" for referrals, since psychotherapy itself is only a recommendation.

Some controversy exists regarding the use of hormone therapy before the real-life experience. The SOC clearly state, "In selected circumstances, it can be acceptable to provide hormones to patients who have not fulfilled [all the criteria] . . . for example, to facilitate the provision of monitored therapy using hormones of known quality, as an alternative to black-market or unsupervised hormone use" (Meyer et al., 2001, p. 20). Schaefer, Wheeler, and Futterweit (1995) and O'Keefe (1999) suggested that beginning hormones before the real-life experience can sometimes be beneficial. For example, some clients may work in jobs in which it is not feasible to transition at work, yet they desire hormonal changes. One client began hormone treatment and lived as a female except during work hours. She knew that she would lose her job if she transitioned yet did not want to wait until her retirement to start cross living. She viewed herself as a "cross-dresser" at work. The most important evaluative process for the clinician is to thoroughly explore whether the client understands the effects of hormones (Cohen-Kettenis and Gooren, 1992) and is prepared, psychologically and physically, to face the impact of gender transition. It is also important to assess whether the client is able to take hormones responsibly, follow through on medical recommendations, and maintain routine medical checkups.

The transgender emergence model described in the next chapter is a way to conceptualize the psychological and developmental processes that transgendered and transsexual people experience. It is not meant to replace the real-life experience, as much as it situates the experience within a social and developmental framework. The RLE has often been referred to as the real-life "test" and has been viewed as an obstacle course that people who desire to transition need to "pass." Indeed, it has often been enforced in ways that involve a series of legal maneuvers and petty rules that have little to do with successful gender transition (see Clemmensen, 1990). Viewing the transgender experience as a developmental process makes the RLE not so much a test that one passes or fails but an experiential containment field in which one explores the parameters of gender possibilities. It is not based on the therapist's criteria of how transition should progress (divorcing one's wife, changing one's name, "passing" successfully) as much as the client's personal, evolutionary emergence into an integrated identity.

The pain transgendered people experience is not based solely on the transgender experience but also how this experience is constrained socially, politically, and clinically. Clients are not always able to recognize the degree and extent to which they have internalized negative messages about their gender variance or the pervasive impact it has had on every level of their lives. If the social world allowed for greater flexibility of gender expression, the pain that transgendered and intersexed people experience would be less extreme. If gender-variant experience was celebrated, it is likely that transgender experience would not be so easily quantifiable, since it would resemble a normative, developmental process of developing an authentic self. In other words, if gender were not prescribed and assumed, then everyone would need to examine his or her own experience of gender and this exploratory process would be universal and normative. The process that transsexuals experience of wanting to change their outward appearance to match their inner sense of self—though certainly psychologically and physically challenging—might be accomplished with minimal social and emotional turmoil if the cultural environment did not pathologize the process.

Living in this bipolar culture, where gender and sex have been linked in the public and professional mind, and where transgendered behavior is proscribed and transgressions are punished, it is inevitable that a person who is transsexual, transgendered, intersexed, or differently gendered will experience some dysphoria and distress coming to terms with his or her authentic self. A knowledgeable and compassionate gender therapist can assist in an active depathologizing of the emotional vortex of gender variance, gender exploration, and gender transition, and can, through the process of dialogue and empowerment, support the person in authentic reauthoring of his or her life experiences.

Chapter 7

Transgender Emergence:
A Developmental Process

Bodies are very unstable foundations on which to build identities.

Riki Wilchins
InYourFace News interview, August 18, 1999

Transgendered people often live in a confusing and painful internal world where their perceived sense of self is at dissonance with the societal norms surrounding them. They have learned to hide not only from others but also from themselves. This process of developing an authentic self for transgendered people means they must move through an experience of *emergence*—of realizing, discovering, identifying, or naming their gender identities.

COMING OUT

The process of transgender emergence resembles the coming out that has been described in the literature on gay and lesbian identity development. "Coming out" is an expression developed within the lesbian and gay liberation movement and is now used within mainstream culture to describe any personal disclosure, usually one that has some stigma attached to it. Although people today will often say that they are coming out as alcoholics, incest survivors, or even members of a religious community, coming out initially referred specifically to disclosures about sexual orientation, particularly homosexuality. Coming out can be used to describe the experience of admitting something to oneself (e.g., "When did you first realize that you were gay?") and coming out can mean the first time you chose to disclose something to another person. Coming out is a lifelong venture. It never ends because there are always people who do not yet know (Cohen and Savin-Williams, 1996).

The concept of coming out infers that one is "inside" of something, usually metaphorically described as a closet, that they must come out "of" or come out "from." Coming out is based on the assumption that one has an identity that others have placed on them. When people come out as sexual abuse survivors or alcoholics, they are coming out of the assumption that they are not victims of sexual abuse or alcohol abusers and are admitting that they indeed are members of those groups. Despite research showing a high incidence of sexual abuse and alcoholism in the general population (Russell, 1986; Finklehor, 1979; NIAAA, 1994) the public assumption that these are rare occurrences remains. One must "come out" to be included in a stigmatized category or people just assume that they are not members of that category.

Coming out as gay is based on the social assumption that everyone is heterosexual until proven otherwise. A clinician can ask a gay client, "When did you first come out?" and the client can respond by discussing the process that he or she went through to identify, accept, and disclose their sexual identity. Yet a clinician does not commonly ask heterosexual clients, "When did you first come out as heterosexual?" The question sounds absurd because heterosexuality is assumed. Heterosexuals simply do not have to come out because everyone is believed to be heterosexual. When gay people come out they are coming out of the heterosexist assumption that they *are* heterosexual. Coming out is a useful concept only within a society that defines and prescribes a normative direction for sexual desire, i.e., people could not come out as gay unless everyone is assumed to be straight. These normative assumptions serve to isolate people who are different, and deMonteflores (1993) identified various strategies that lesbian and gay people utilize to manage this sense of "difference." Coming out—whether for alcoholics, incest survivors, homosexuals, bisexuals, or transsexuals—is the first step in identity development, and labeling oneself with this new identity is a necessary part of exploring this new identity. In Alcoholics Anonymous this process is formalized with the introduction, "My name is _____ and *I am* an alcoholic" (emphasis mine).

The coming-out process for gay, lesbian, and bisexual people has been well documented. To begin to understand the process of transgender emergence, the process of sexual identity development will be examined first because it can serve as a general blueprint to describe the process of gender identity acceptance. Coming out gay and emerging transgendered are, however, not completely analogous processes, but gender identity emergence follows a similar trajectory as coming out gay and carries within it related psychosocial consequences. The term *sexual identity* is used here to signify the "owning" or "claiming" of a gay, lesbian, or bisexual orientation, and identifying with it "who" the person is, not simply whether he or she behaves homosexually.

Various models for the coming-out process for lesbians and gays have been delineated (Cass, 1979; Coleman, 1981, 1982; Hanley-Hackenbruck, 1988; Sophie, 1985/1986; Troiden, 1993). The models describe the process of internalizing a positive self-image of an identity that is socially stigmatized. Despite a difference in nomenclature, these models (see Figure 7.1) show the person moving through a series of developmental stages from an early awareness and confusion about sexual identity to a mature integration and synthesis of sexual identity within the larger construct of one's identity, emphasizing milestone events and developmental tasks.

People do not necessarily move through the stages in order, and certainly people do so at different paces. Some people begin their coming-out process in their early teens, while others do not begin to examine their sexual identity until well past middle age. Cass (1998), an originator of one of the models presented, stressed in her later work that these models are a "Western phenomenon," not a universal truth or cross-cultural experience. It is accurate that many clients, mired in their own cultural assumptions, experience their own sexual and gender identities in a teleological and developmental schema, but it is important for practitioners to remember that all human identities are impacted by the construction of particular cultural and social perspectives. These coming-out stage models represent processes particular to the ways that social identities are structured in dominant Western cultures.

The models for coming out lesbian and gay have not adequately described the experience of bisexual women and men (Blumstein and Schwartz,

Lesbian and Gay Identity Formation

Cass (1979)	Coleman (1982)	Sophie (1985/1986)	Hanley-Hacken-bruck (1988)	Troiden (1993)
Identity confusion	Pre–coming out	First awareness	Prohibition	Sensitization
Identity comparison	Coming out	Testing and exploration	Ambivalence/practicing or compulsion/exploration	Identity confusion
Identity tolerance	Exploration	Identity acceptance	Consolidation/integration	Identity assumption
Identity acceptance	First relationship	Identity integration		Commitment
Identity pride	Integration			
Identity synthesis				

FIGURE 7.1. Comparison of coming-out stages for sexual identity development.

1993; Klein, 1993; Klein et al., 1985; Markowitz, 1995). Bisexuality was often seen as a stage in coming out gay or lesbian until bisexual development as an authentic and complete identity was established. Since bisexual identity can be fluid, modifications of the coming-out stages have been made in examining identity development in bisexual people (Weinberg, Williams, and Pryor, 1994). Bisexuals often struggle with finding a label to properly describe their sexuality (since the binary of heterosexual and homosexual does not quite fit), and they also seem to maintain a greater flexibility and potential changeability in their sexual behavior, expression, and identity. Bisexuals may be "integrated" in their identity and yet still experience shifts in sexuality or self-labeling throughout their life span (see Figure 7.2). In other words, the flexibility and potential fluidity of the sex of their romantic partners is not a sign of disturbance but a hallmark of bisexual identity. It is possible that gay, lesbian, and heterosexual identity development are also inherently flexible and fluid outside of a binary system.

Although sexual and gender identity are clearly two different aspects of self, there are some similarities in coming out homosexual or bisexual and emerging transgendered or transsexual. For gays, lesbians, and bisexuals, as well as transgendered and transsexual people, there is, first of all, a need to come to terms with socially despised aspects of self. However, emerging transgendered is not the same as coming out lesbian, gay or bisexual, and the need for a separate schema to map out the developmental stages of coming to terms with a transgender identity is essential.

Bolin (1988, 1992), an anthropologist, described the process in which transsexuals transition from one sex to the other as a rite of passage akin to traditional tribal rituals that formalized movement from one stage or status into another. She identified a three-phase process referred to as separation, transition, and incorporation. Bolin described the process whereby males with gender dysphoria "became" women, by moving through a process of first labeling themselves transsexual then experiencing themselves as fully female—a process that describes gender transition. She said,

> Whether consciously or unconsciously, caregivers have chosen a term that is the symbolic equivalent of birth. Transition is a medical term associated with childbirth. It refers to the period of maximal cervical expansion prior to the actual birth of the child. Correspondingly, transition for transsexuals is the period prior to their final rebirth, when they become at last complete females, both socially and physically. They return once more to the setting of their first birth, the hospital, where medical professionals, who first declared that "it's a boy," now declare them female. (Bolin, 1992, p. 27)

| Initial confusion |
| Finding and applying the label |
| Settling into an identity |
| Continued uncertainty |

FIGURE 7.2. Bisexual identity development (Weinberg, Williams, and Pryor, 1994).

Although not all transgendered people "transition" from one sex to another, all move through a psychological, sociological, and perhaps a spiritual process of coming to terms with their variant gender identity. Unlike gay, lesbian, and bisexual people who have the option to remain closeted if they choose about their desires, their behaviors, and even their lifestyles, transgendered and transsexual people who do modify their bodies must engage in a transaction process with others who will witness and react to these visible body changes.

Lewins (1995), in his research on male-to-female transsexuals, recognized six stages to "becoming a woman." He labeled them (1) abiding anxiety, (2) discovery, (3) purging and delay, (4) acceptance, (5) surgical reassignment, and (6) invisibility. Lewins' model describes the classic transsexual trajectory, including complete surgical transition and the "purging" behavior so often seen in transgendered people, as well as a final resolution that includes "going stealth" about one's transsexual history. Rachlin (1997) also examined a six-stage transition process, emphasizing the importance of the relationship between client and psychotherapist in moving through the stages of: (1) distress and confusion, (2) self-definition, (3) identifying options, (4) acting to make changes, (5) coping with the consequences of transition, and (6) moving on with a life in which gender identity is not a central issue. Transgender emergence follows a similar stage pattern but includes a wider range of transgender identities and pathways to resolution.

Developing a gender identity is a normative process that everyone experiences, but for gender-variant people the process is distorted by social expectations and repression. Butler (1990) said, "Precisely because certain kinds of 'gender identities' fail to conform to those norms of cultural intelligibility, they appear only as developmental failures or logical impossibilities from within that domain" (p. 24). The emergence process described in the following section is normative within a culture that allows only dimorphic gender expressions. It describes an adaptive process that is necessary within a confining social system. Although many similarities exist in the process of gender identity integration that intersexed people experience and many of the stages are more relevant for gender-variant children and adolescents, this chapter addresses the transgender emergence as transgendered and transsexual adults experience it.

TRANSGENDER EMERGENCE

Emergence involves a complex interaction of intrinsic developmental issues and social and interpersonal transactions. These stages are assumed to be developmental, meaning most people move through them in order and resolution of one stage is necessary in order to integrate it and move on to the next. It is not assumed that every single person will experience this process exactly as it is delineated. As in all developmental stage models, it is understood that people move back and forth and often revisit earlier stages as part of their normative evolution. The process of emergence is impacted by many variables including racial, ethnic, and cultural differences regarding gender; class access to money and the ability to procure therapeutic or medical treatment; mental health issues that are unrelated or only peripherally related to gender identity; age; marital status; religious upbringing; and current spiritual identification. Emergence is also influenced by the place of residence and the values of the society and culture a person is born into (e.g., urban versus rural, North American versus the Middle Eastern). Individual experience and variation affect all of these stages.

These stages are not meant to "label" people, define transgender maturity, or limit anyone to these experiences. They are meant to outline a general trajectory of experiences for transgendered and transsexual men and women who are coming to terms with gender variance at the beginning of the twenty-first century, and moving from an experience of denial and self-hatred to one of self-respect and gender congruence. It also best describes those who present themselves to a clinician seeking help for their transgenderism. It is assumed that some people do not experience a "crisis" in their gender identity and perhaps move through these stages without any therapeutic assistance. Emergence as a transgendered person is formulated here as a six-stage process (see Box 7.1).

Stage One: Awareness

> You're neither unnatural, nor abominable, nor mad; you're as much a part of what people call nature as anyone else; only you're unexplained as yet . . .

Radclyffe Hall
The Well of Loneliness, 1928

BOX 7.1.
States of Emergence

1. *Awareness*—In the first stage, gender-variant people are often in great distress. The therapeutic task is the normalization of the experiences involved in emerging transgendered.
2. *Seeking information/reaching out*—In the second stage, gender-variant people seek to gain education and support about transgenderism. The therapeutic task is to facilitate linkages and encourage outreach.
3. *Disclosure to significant others*—The third stage involves the disclosure of transgenderism to significant others—spouses, partners, family members, and friends. The therapeutic task involves supporting the transgendered person's integration in the family system.
4. *Exploration: Identity and self-labeling*—The fourth stage involves the exploration of various (transgender) identities. The therapeutic task is to support the articulation and comfort with one's gendered identity.
5. *Exploration: Transition issues/possible body modification*—The fifth stage involves exploring options for transition regarding identity, presentation, and body modification. The therapeutic task is the resolution of the decisions and advocacy toward their manifestation.
6. *Integration: Acceptance and post-transition issues*—In the sixth stage the gender-variant person is able to integrate and synthesize (transgender) identity. The therapeutic task is to support adaptation to transition-related issues.

The first stage of emergence as a transgendered person is *awareness*. Awareness is the coming into consciousness of the internal sense of feeling different and the realization that indeed one may *be* different. For many transgendered people the awareness of gender differences goes back to early childhood. One mother described being in the supermarket with her three-year-old son when someone stopped them and said, "What a sweet little girl." When she tried to correct the person, her son said, "No, Mama, you know I am really a girl." Stories like this abound, of the early recognition of gender identity difference (by self and often by others), and the frustration of living in a world that does not see or cannot support one's authentic identity. Indeed the emergence process for differently gendered people involves facing and defying societal and familial expectations of gender-appropriate behavior.

Often transgendered people have a long history of cross-dressing behavior or opposite-sex fantasies going back to early childhood, which they sometimes cope with through intense denial and avoidance. It has been assumed that transsexuals always identify their cross-gendered identity in childhood. Indeed, this has been one of the hallmarks of the diagnosis. However, personal narratives and clinical experience do not bear this out. Some transgendered and transsexual people do not begin to express unease with their birth gender until puberty or adulthood when the pressure to perform within culturally prescribed rules becomes concretized.

For most people, awareness of their gender incongruity is experienced as a *gender dysphoria,* a profound discomfort with their birth sex and confusion over what it means. The length of time the person has been aware of his or her gender issues, the intensity of which he or she has repressed these feelings, the depth of sense of shame and isolation and social/religious/ cultural background will all impact how a person experiences the awareness stage of his or her emergence process. Some people experience awareness of their gender variance for many years without it becoming excessively disturbing. Generally in Stage One, gender discomfort comes into consciousness or increases in a way that is psychically and emotionally dysphoric.

Most transgendered people have been aware of their gender variance for a long time before beginning to face it. Sometimes beginning therapy is the culmination of years of trying to suppress the issue. Many transgendered people have tried various ways to cure themselves, utilizing religion, marriage, aversion therapy, and other behavior modification techniques. Other transgendered people have allowed themselves a certain degree of freedom to express themselves, wearing androgynous clothing or cross-dressing at home, for instance, and have coped with their gender dysphoria by trying to limit and control it. Often they have moved back and forth from periods of experimenting to periods of suppression, including purging clothing. Some transgendered people have socialized within communities where their cross-dressing was more normalized. For other transgendered people, their awareness of their gender dysphoria has remained hidden completely, dissociated from conscious memory.

When transgenderism comes to the surface of conscious awareness, or intensifies and can no longer be suppressed or denied, a floodgate of emotions is often thrown open. The shock of gender dysphoria surfaces like the intensity of sexual abuse or other traumatic events that have been buried under daily consciousness. The force of gender-variance awareness can rise up like a tidal wave, threatening the entire foundation of one's life and identity. Hanley-Hackenbruck (1988), in discussing the coming-out process for lesbians and gay men, said, "The shock occurs when the person suddenly discovers or finally admits belonging to this stigmatized group, but he or she cannot believe that the negative stereotypes could possibly apply to herself or himself" (p. 22).

People are thrown into what Bass and Davis (1988) described in their work with survivors of child sexual abuse as an *emergency stage.* Gender dysphoria is rarely repressed the way sexual abuse memories can be; however, gender identity issues are often suppressed and denied and can surface with great intensity. Coming into awareness of transgendered feelings, and the overwhelming terror associated with it, cannot be underestimated. Admitting these feelings or experiencing a sudden increase in the intensity of them can be overpowering. The sense of powerlessness, terror, and non-stop crisis is a common experience in this stage of awareness and the world is experienced as a place that is unfathomable, inconsistent, and unstable. The search for solid ground becomes desperate. People often feel as if they are losing their minds.

Early stages of awareness of transgenderism can be analogous to shaking a full seltzer bottle and then opening it. The seltzer will shoot out of the bottle with great force. Metaphorically, gender issues are also experienced as having this kind of force because they have been kept hidden and bottled up. People often confuse this initial explosion of emotion to be indicative of what their lives will be like when they emerge as a transgendered person, i.e., they are confusing the emergence process itself with the experience of *being* transgendered. Seltzer, when not shaken, is actually rather benign. Being transgendered does not necessarily condemn one to a life of turmoil, although emerging transgendered can create chaos and upheaval. As addicts often confuse the withdrawal process from an addictive substance with the actual experience of living a sober life, clients often confuse the initial process of becoming aware of their gender dysphoria with their identity as a transgendered person.

Clients often present in therapy at this stage, appearing anxious and overwhelmed, exhibiting many signs and symptoms of mental health disturbances. Symptomatology presents in the early stages of awareness as insomnia, isolation, distancing from family and friends, depression, weight loss or gain, and work or school difficulties. It can also include high anxiety, dissociation, suicidality, sexual dysfunction, substance abuse, self-mutilation, or even intense reaction formation expressed through acting out against other differently gendered people. Rita, a transgendered woman, described the awareness stage as follows:

As I became aware of how false my life had always been, it became harder and harder to live it. I became depressed at work and withdrawn at home. I began to feel anger at my body, which had started to disgust me. I had many "accidents" that year, breaking bones twice and burning myself badly. I was not consciously trying to hurt myself, but looking back I can see how my carelessness was a form of rage at myself. I became so jealous of my teenage daughter, who was maturing into an attractive woman, living an adolescence that I could never have. I became completely sexually dysfunctional with my wife, who thought it was because she had gained weight. I had no one to talk to, and sometimes I would roam the streets at night contemplating desperate ways to end my life.

Not all gender-variant people at the awareness stage react with the intensity that Rita did. Some transgendered people experience the awareness stage with great joy and a sense of release. This is especially true for people who do not exhibit any classic gender dysphoria in their youth, but as adults with access to transgender information became interested in the possibilities of gender transformation and physical body modifications. They too experience an emergence process, although it is perhaps not as emotionally terrifying. Their first awareness can be experienced as more euphoric than dysphoric, and as a celebration of the freedom to explore their gender expression. It is possible that as transgenderism comes out of the proverbial closet, more people will be able to traverse this stage gracefully, as it is, for instance, often easier for gay people to come out now than it was twenty years ago.

Certainly those who have never suppressed their gender issues may not come into a sense of "awareness," since they have always been aware. What may shift is the need to address these issues. Sometimes a discernible event forces gender issues into the position of central focus, such as the death of a parent or the end of a marriage. Other times, clients present with a simple statement such as, "It is time." These people may move quickly and painlessly through the first three stages and begin a process of labeling and developing an identity construct that works for them.

The majority of transgendered and transsexual people seeking counseling for gender dysphoria present in the awareness stage and are in great emotional pain. For some transgendered people, traversing this stage is excruciating, and not all survive. Some clients exhibit an almost psychotic presentation due to the intensity of their fear and shame. However, as Smith (1988) said in discussing the impact of homophobia on the human development of gays and lesbians, "What is notable is the resiliency of the human spirit in the face of such adversity and the strength of character attained by so many survivors" (p. 61). Given the stress of presenting a false self for most of one's life, the high level of mental health and functional behavior seen in the majority of transgendered people attests to the strength and coping skills of many of these individuals.

Therapeutic Goal

The first therapeutic goal of the awareness stage is normalizing gender identity issues. This involves letting clients know that "normal," average people from all walks of life have feelings of gender dysphoria or gender variance. Clients often feel shame and struggle with self-hatred. They often express suicidal ideation, high levels of anxiety, and obsessive-compulsive behavior. Sometimes they are depressed and barely functioning in their work or home lives. Their relationships are often in turmoil. Occasionally they engage in dangerous or unhealthy behaviors. Frequently they are isolated and feel as if they are the "only person in the world" to feel this way. They may arrive skeptical about therapy, over- or undermedicated, and/or severely depressed. In the extreme, they may appear somewhat thought-disordered and paranoid. The clinician's duty is not to further pathologize the client, but to help him or her to see the connection between gender issues and stress levels and symptoms.

The clinician must create a "holding environment" (see Winnicott, 1957), a safe space for repressed emotions and forbidden thoughts to emerge. This holding environment is a kind of "container" (Bass and Davis, 1988) that allows traumatic issues to surface. Issues of confidentiality are paramount, as is the client's commitment to his or her own physical safety. The therapist's relaxed comfort regarding gender issues and referencing of others who are transgendered through examples and stories can ease the sense of shame and isolation for clients. The therapist brings with him or her an immense power of authority, and modeling acceptance, kindness, and ease can help assuage the intensity of dysphoria. "Surely," the person in the awareness stage is thinking, "if the therapist doesn't think I'm mentally ill, maybe— just maybe—I'm really okay."

It is equally important for the therapist not to have an agenda as to the outcome or meaning of the client's experiences. Common wisdom within the transgendered community as well as among professional advocates is that the awareness and intensification of gender issues indicates the need to pursue complete transition. Transition is often presumed by the client to preclude a continuation of a marriage or a "normal" family life and these fears can intensify the client's emotional conflict and actually create marital disturbances. Gender therapists advocating for the needs of transgendered clients often unwittingly promote this sense of intensity by assuming there is only one outcome available for the client—complete gender transition— or framing the discussion within a polar field, i.e., either the client will or will not transition. Accommodation or compromise positions between the poles are often unexplored.

The awareness stage is not the time to make decisions about transitioning. The therapist's role at this stage is to create a safe environment for the client to explore all of his or her thoughts and ideas, perhaps including transitioning, but not to interpret meanings or determine therapeutic direction. It is also important to recognize and honor the client's need and desire to maintain his or her family stability and offer reassurance that this is possible.

Given the relative newness of the transgender liberation movement, the lack of available information on transgender identity, the intensity of social stigma, and the deep sense of shame experienced by most people in early stages of awareness, the majority of people in this first stage of identity formation remain closeted, hidden, and isolated. Transgendered people in the awareness stage possibly outnumber all other transgendered people. Certainly they represent the majority of transgendered people seeking clinical support, especially outside of established gender clinics. Since this stage of emergence is so fraught with symptomatology and emotional pain, it is no wonder that therapists have labeled transgendered people as "mentally ill."

As public awareness grows and clinical advocacy increases, more people will begin to come into awareness of their own gender issues. It is possible that more people are struggling with gender identity than is yet apparent, particularly when the discussion is broadened outside of the transsexual need for complete sex reassignment. Herman (1992), discussing the surfacing of traumatic memories, said, "Clinicians know the privileged moment of insight when repressed ideas, feelings, and memories surface into consciousness. These moments occur in the history of societies as well as in the history of individuals" (p. 2). This is an important insight, as we are living in times when it is not just individuals who are developing awareness of their gender difference, but also society as a whole is reexamining the limitations of the existing binary gender system. Certainly this represents an interesting feedback loop. As more people emerge transgendered, the greater the social awareness of the issue. Concurrently, the greater the social awareness of transgenderism, the more likely it is that more people will experience individual moments of awareness. It is also hoped that as more people successfully move through the developmental stages of emergence, the stigma of mental illness will fade and the reality of stress and trauma will be recognized for what it is.

Stage Two: Seeking Information/Reaching Out

> It is not difference which immobilizes us, but silence. And there are so many silences to be broken.
>
> Audre Lorde
> *The Transformation of Silence into Language and Action,* 1984

Stage Two of emerging transgendered is about beginning a journey. Whereas the awareness stage was about the surfacing of memories and the internal focus of the awareness of personal identity, Stage Two begins a movement outside of oneself. The transgendered person is beginning to say out loud, "I *am* transgendered (or transsexual, or whatever word he or she uses to describe himself or herself). This is who I am." This stage involves coming out not just to oneself, but coming out to other people. Transgendered people begin seeking information about transgenderism and reaching out to find others like themselves. This stage is usually easier to traverse and significantly less traumatizing for transgendered people than Stage One. Unlike Stage One, which is often overwhelming and exhausting, Stage Two is more emotionally exhilarating and transformative.

Seeking Information

Seeking information about gender identity issues has become easier in recent years than it ever was before. This is, in part, because of the greater social awareness of the issue, as well as an increase in the number of professionals who are educated about gender identity. However, the main reason for the increase in information about transgenderism can be attributed to two sources—the burgeoning transgender liberation movement and the technological explosion of the Internet.

Historically (and the similarity here with the gay liberation movement is undeniable), transgendered people have often had few resources for information about themselves outside of prejudicial and outdated medical textbooks that outline their illness and discuss them as objects. In the past decade information about transgenderism has gone from a trickle to a full stream, including personal narratives, medical and clinical treatment issues, political essays, and social theories regarding gender. Although this is true in books and magazines, in a large measure the increase in transgender information is due to the advent of the personal computer and the World Wide Web. As one woman recently said at a conference, "If you are dealing with gender issues, you *must* get online—you will find a home there."

The Internet has become the source of information for everything from medical and surgical techniques, to advice on *passing,* to support for significant others, to socializing and dating, as well as academic and philosophical discourse on gender. Rachlin's (1999) research showed that FTM-identified clients "rated contact with other FTMs and information from within the FTM community as the most important factors influencing their decision of whether and what type of surgery to pursue" and that a significant amount of this contact had taken place on the Internet. Some people enter the awareness stage *after* learning about transgenderism through the Internet. They begin exploring these issues as detached and somewhat amused observers and eventually come to recognize themselves in their reading. In these cases the information leads to the awareness.

In Stage Two of the emergence process, transgendered people begin to explore current knowledge about transgender identity and they seek narratives about their lives. Prosser (1998) documented the power of narrative as a transformative tool in claiming a transgender identity. As more literature becomes available, people are devouring this information, seeking identification with the authors. Clients often come to sessions clutching books under their arms, inquiring as to whether the therapist has read a particular book. They want to know whether their own personal narrative is familiar to the clinician. After years of isolation, they are seeking, and have sometimes found, a story that resembles their own.

Transgendered clients are not only well read on the autobiographical accounts surfacing on the Internet and in bookstores, they are also connoisseurs of the medical textbooks that have defined their lives. As new books have emerged that have countered the medical hegemony of transgender issues, they have been bought, read, discussed, disputed, and analyzed. Their tattered pages have been passed from hand to hand, serving as an almost underground resource for a community seeking to define itself. Information abounds on the Internet, satisfying a variety of needs. In addition to narratives and medical literature, there is also a plethora of information on the social costs of transitioning, civil rights organizing, tips for more effective passing, and educational and academic pursuits. Clients in Stage Two often spend hours reading literature and Web pages. One client would bring in volumes of material that he had downloaded from the Internet, anxious for his therapist to learn about everything he had been reading.

Political theory regarding the oppression of transgendered people is a particularly fertile area of exploration for many clients. Transgendered people respond to this material in a variety of ways. After years of feeling shamed for their gender expression, some are relieved and excited to find people who are proud and also angry about the treatment of transgendered people. Others recoil from political organizing, feeling as if participation will expose them and bring greater punishment from society. Some disbelieve that society will ever grant social justice to transgendered people and others dedicate their lives to ensuring that transgendered people will someday be assured legal rights. Sometimes people who lean toward conservative politics distance themselves from transgender organizing and civil rights issues, which they perceive to be too left-wing. Many clients are, at first, uncomfortable with associating with political issues, particularly clients who have benefited from their race, gender, or class privileges and for whom emerging transgendered is their first experience being perceived of as an "other" in society.

Amassing information is essential to the client emerging as transgendered and is the first step in the development of a fully integrated identity. Transgendered clients are often better informed and more knowledgeable than many therapists and physicians and are often able to challenge experts in the field. There are many benefits to working with clients who are educated about their own "diagnosis." They are often able to engage in deep clinical and philosophical discussions about gender and society, and can have insight into their own childhood and sexuality. They are often grateful for the opportunity to discuss these issues, allowing a respectful and working relationship to develop with the clinician. However, there are drawbacks to this self-education. In an age of information, there is room for misinformation. Some clients have misunderstood clinical textbooks or have faulty information about the requirements for transition. Afraid of being refused the treatment they perhaps desperately want, they will often lie to fit into a rigid definition they read on the Internet. Assisting clients in accessing accurate information, recognizing that others like themselves exist, and developing an understanding of being part of a wider community is one of the rewards of Stage Two.

Reaching Out

Transgendered people also begin to reach out to others in Stage Two. The fear of being "found out" for transgendered people cannot be minimized. Many transgendered people have never told anyone about their cross-dressing or desires. Reaching out is the single most difficult task of their lives. Sometimes the therapist is the first person to whom they disclose.

Some reach out by calling, or attending, a transgender support group. More of these social supports are available now than ever before and many people travel great distances to meet people like themselves. They are often afraid, wondering what the social rules are in this new environment ("Should I go dressed or not?"). Sometimes these experiences are a great relief ("I finally found people just like me") but other times these meetings are disappointing. People sometimes feel "different" or out of place at the meeting. If the majority of the group members are older, or younger, or all of the "opposite" sex, there can be a sense of estrangement that can further feelings of isolation. They are often confronted with their worst fears about "who" they are (and how they are perceived within society) as they face their own internalized *transphobia* through their negative feelings toward one another. One client complained that a group was comprised only of transsexuals and was not made for transvestites such as him. Another client complained about the same group. She said that it was nothing but "men in dresses" and not for "real women" such as her. Finding people to identify with can be difficult, and simply finding other transgendered people does not necessarily decrease one's sense of isolation and aloneness.

For those who have access to the Internet, the online transgender network has become a haven of sorts where people can socialize in chat rooms and join e-mail groups. For many transgendered people who have lived their whole lives feeling isolated and alone, finding this expansive network is akin to being "over the rainbow." This is especially true for people who have other issues of minority identity that make them feel different—e.g., age, race, or disability. One can find specialized groups for transgendered teens, Jewish transgendered people, transgendered people of color, and diverse discussion lists for medical issues, political issues, and fashion needs.

For many people, connecting with others who have similar stories—not just reading a narrative in a book, but actually talking with people who are like them—is an extraordinary relief. Certainly, the anonymity of the Internet provides a mask to be both "out" and "in" at the same time, what Denny (1997) referred to as "virtual gender" (p. 39). People can change their identity or log off without any need for social exchange, and yet also explore a whole world without the fear of "getting caught," except of course by others who can access their computer and follow the history trail of their whereabouts. The benefit of being online is the ability to be "stealthy" and explore being in a new gender without worrying about issues of passing. You can truly "appear to be" who you say you are online.

> I never thought that anybody else felt the way that I did. I mean, I knew that there were people called "transsexuals" and I knew they could have some "operation," but I wasn't sure what, if anything, that had to do with me. I just knew that everyone thought I was a girl, but I knew I've always been a guy. The first time I entered a transgender chat room, I wasn't even sure what that was. I listened to these guys talking about wanting to have a man's body, I heard them talking about their body parts as if they were male, and something began to shift inside of me. I realized for the first time that I could make myself in my own image. I could become who I knew myself to be.

Despite the benefits of human connection, some clients will refuse to meet or socialize with other transgendered people. Others will express defensive projection, verbalizing an intense hostility toward other transgendered people and not wanting to identify with "them." There are also clients who are very uncomfortable with the "technological revolution" of the Internet and resist being involved with it. This can be a difficult challenge for gender therapists, who see the value that community can play in healing much of the shame and isolation clients feel. Some clients who have lived with an awareness of their transgenderism for many years—living double lives or cross-dressing in private—resist moving into this stage. They are often depressed and unmotivated and see their gender issues as a burden that they must bear alone. They do not see any release in transitioning or any hope for human connectedness. Gently assisting these clients in moving out of their isolation and into a community can be a moving and worthwhile experience.

As transgendered people begin to identify with others, they often reexamine their own experiences and histories. This process has been referred to in the gay and lesbian coming-out literature as "restructuring the past" (deMonteflores and Schultz, 1978). The literature within the LGB community is replete with stories of childhood experiences that can now be reexamined and reclaimed. Transgendered people experience the sudden surfacing of repressed memories of cross-dressing, secret opposite-sex names, or stories written and games played in the "role" of the other sex. What were once acts of shame (e.g., getting caught cross-dressing, refusing to wear a dress, insisting that one had a penis or breasts) are revisited as acts of defiance and pride.

Transgendered people are each unique and their experiences and timing need to be respected. One client attended a transgender gathering and came home relaxed and at peace with herself after years of resisting this kind of involvement. Another client, however, attended a similar conference and came home anxious and disturbed. She complained that the environment made her feel forced to transition. Premature socializing (or too much information) can increase the anxiety symptoms of Stage One or the pressure of coming out to others in Stage Three. However, the power of a community cannot be minimized. Gagné, Tewksbury, and McGaughey (1997) said, "Entering into a community of supportive others allow[s] for an exploration and resolution of identity" (p. 504).

On the other hand, sometimes people leap into what Niela Miller (1996) calls "genderland" with a vengeance—assimilating information and making new friends with vigor and speed. They embrace their new identity and their new community completely and thoroughly, separating themselves from their previous lives. They often cut off old friends and family, change their name and dress, insist on beginning hormone therapy immediately, and forge ahead with intensity and single-mindedness. The peer pressure supporting this within some transgender communities can be very powerful. A concern, especially for young people, is failing to understand the implications of their choices and forging ahead without preparation. One man announced that he was transitioning two weeks after first discovering the word *transgender.* It is easy to imagine the therapist's reluctance to support this transition without further exploration of the client's issues.

This is an exciting stage for clients, as well as a rewarding stage for therapists. Clients are often excited and come in each week with new information and experiences to share. Growth and expansion are the dominant themes as the client moves into a more solid sense of identity.

The Therapeutic Goal

The therapeutic goal of this stage involves assisting the client in gaining accurate education about transgenderism and reaching out for support from the transgender network. To be able to effectively assist clients, therapists must themselves be educated about transgenderism. This includes having access to books and magazines (that they have already read) and making them available for clients to borrow. The therapist must also be knowledge-able about the Internet and have a list of Web sites that clients can access to assist them in their "research." Therapists must also be prepared to do some immediate "homework" when clients find a new Web site or book that has a dramatic impact on their emergence process.

One of the most difficult challenges for the therapist is in assisting the client to pace their emergence process. For some clients this involves exposing them to information to which they may be a bit resistant. This is never about "forcing" or "pushing" a client. Some transgendered people who are de-pressed and feel hopeless have developed an almost "learned helplessness" (Seligman, 1972) regarding their gender dysphoria. One client said, "I don't know why I have to live with this. Why can't I just 'change'?" When it is suggested that he could "just change," he resists eye contact and sinks lower into his seat. It is not about overt fear. It is the disbelief that anything positive can come from his "condition."

More commonly though, clients are likely to enter this stage expressing all the glee of elementary school children at the day's end. They are finally released from what has felt like a prison. For the first time they have hope and a sense of freedom. They are like a coiled spring, ready to pop. In their exhilaration and excitement, some do not think clearly about jobs, careers, spouses and children, and sometimes take risks that may entail grave conse-quences. Fathers may begin cross-dressing at home and in front of their chil-dren, who are confused and frightened. Husbands may begin discussing hormone therapy with wives who are still bitter and angry over the disclo-sure. Some people agree to meet strangers from a chat room without ade-quate thought to their own safety. Other people make plans to have surgery without an assessment of the doctor's skills, only looking at cost. Clients seek out black market hormones, trying to circumvent the medical system, potentially endangering their health.

The desire to move forward for some clients is very intense. The internal pressures of long-term repression, plus the intensity of a near-obsessive pull to transition can create a kind of pressure cooker that can feel and be explosive. Some clients will interpret the therapist's attempts to pace the emergence process as a stalling tactic, especially if they do not see the therapist as an advocate but rather as gatekeeper. In some situations a low dose of hormones at this juncture can serve to "medicate" the client's anxiety as well as redirect the focus of therapy away from the hormones and onto other more salient issues. Steiner (1985a) suggested this can be particularly helpful with older transvestic male clients who are unable to transition due to marital commitments. However, low-dose hormones can be a useful treatment strategy with other populations of transgendered clients as well. The HBIGDA's standards of care state, "Hormone therapy can provide significant comfort to gender patients who do not wish to cross live or undergo surgery, or who are unable to do so. In some patients, hormone therapy alone may provide sufficient symptomatic relief to obviate the need for cross living or surgery" (Meyer et al., 2001). Be aware that even at low doses some changes can become permanent—breast growth for males, deeper voice for females.

The clinician's role during this stage is to stabilize the emergence process and help the client to examine and reexamine the choices she or he is making, and the effects it will have on her or his life. In some cases this involves couple counseling with a spouse or partner. It can also involve family work with children to help them understand and adjust to this situation. In almost all situations it involves some exploration of work, career, and finances. Transitioning at work will have greater success if done carefully and in methodological steps.

It is best at this stage for the client to gather information and make connections without necessarily making decisions about his or her future. It is, however, challenging for most transgendered people to slow down when they see all new options opening up for them and are excited about moving forward. Assisting clients in moving forward carefully and deliberately, instead of impulsively, will help them transition with the greatest ease and the least chaos. Pacing at this stage can affect the success of the transition process, but it is no small task to convince clients of this.

Stage Two is when transgendered people learn more about themselves and their identity and reach out to meet other transgendered people. It can be an exciting time. Working with clients to help them move through these stages with some gentleness and ease can be rewarding. It is the therapist's task to maintain a supportive role in clients' lives while they venture out into the unknown.

Stage Three: Disclosure to Significant Others

> Perhaps the most significant mental health and social support issue
> faced by transgendered individuals revolves around the disclosure of
> one's transgendered status and needs to others.

> Gianna Israel and Donald E. Tarver
> *Transgender Care,* 1997

The process of self-disclosure to intimate others is often frightening, and
many transgendered people cope with this by avoidance. It is also true that
family members are often hostile and punitive toward the transgendered
person who risks disclosure. The intensity of emotions on both sides of the
equation only highlights the importance of these relationships. Fear and
avoidance are the flip side of anger and resistance. People want their families to be safe and remain consistent, and gender issues can often shake the
foundation of the basic notions of intimacy, security, and stability.

Transgendered people are placed in a classic double bind (Bateson et al.,
1952). They have become aware of an essential part of themselves and have
begun to normalize it through their process of gathering information and
connecting with others who are also dealing with gender issues. A part of
them, long hidden and denied, is finally coming out, and they want to share
it with others whom they love and are close with. Yet they are also aware of
the impact this will have on their loved ones. They are fearful, and rightfully
so, that others may not be as enthusiastic as they are. Sometimes due to their
concern of losing their partners and families they try to suppress their transgender feelings, which, in turn, increases their confusion. The pressure
within to come out and the (perceived) pressure outside to stay in, cause an
emotional quagmire. It is precisely their intimacy with significant others
that pushes them to want to disclose and it is this very intimacy that they risk
losing by disclosing. Clients often vacillate between strong emotions to
fully transition and equally strong emotions to "stop this whole process."

At this stage most people have already begun to break their isolation. Perhaps they have already disclosed to a therapist and begun to reach out to
other transgendered people, either online or through support groups. They
might have told a supportive friend or spouse. Some transgendered people
have already talked with significant others and occasionally they begin a
clinical process at their insistence or with their support. Sometimes spouses
have known since early in the relationship, but the disclosure at this juncture
might be revealing that the gender issue is more involved than they initially
thought it was. For many transgendered people, this stage represents the
most painful and difficult passage of their entire emergence process.

Sometimes clients do not have the luxury of self-disclosure and are found out. Transgendered clients are sometimes discovered by a parent, a spouse, or even exposed by the police, and they actually experience a Stage Three disclosure before fully experiencing Stage One awareness and certainly before having access to Stage Two resources.

Disclosing to significant others and family members is almost always a terrifying prospect for the transgendered person. They fear rejection and abandonment from those who are most important to them. Parents are afraid to admit to their transgendered identity, believing they will be cast out from their families and lose custody of their children, which, unfortunately, is a possible outcome. The thought of disclosing to family members almost universally increases the transgendered person's anxiety and fear.

Sometimes the act of disclosure is experienced as an enormous release of tension, and, regardless of the response, is viewed with relief. However, the disclosure itself will often evoke an array of emotional reactions from significant others that can overwhelm the transgendered person. Caught in this transactional feedback loop, the gender-variant client often experiences an increase in symptomatology, including feeling anxious, depressed, or suicidal, and behaving in dangerous, unpredictable ways. They desperately want to please their loved ones, but also need to honor themselves. This double bind evokes much of the emotionality of Stage One but is fortified with the knowledge and support of Stage Two.

Family of Origin

For the adult transgendered person, coming out to family members is often frightening and sometimes avoided until well into transition. One client did not tell his mother that he had started taking male hormones, although when they spoke on the phone his mother kept asking if "she" had a cold because of the deepening of his voice. Another client had completely transitioned and came out to her family by arriving home, after a five-year absence, as a woman. The parents of a thirty-five-year-old son came into therapy when they found out that their son, an esteemed professor at an Ivy League college, was picked up by the police dressed as a woman.

Disclosure to family of origin will obviously be influenced by the previous relationship of the client to the family. In families that have a long history of conflict, abuse, addictions, or abandonment, the client rarely expects support, although sometimes it is especially painful to experience their disinterest and ambivalence when finding the courage to disclose. Sometimes transgenderism is seen as the "final straw" of this painful relationship for the transgendered person and/or his or her family members and serves to sever all familial contact. Although this is an obviously painful resolution, it often feels as if it is a healthy one for the transgendered person, who can now move away from unhealthy family dynamics and potential further abuse.

If the family was unaware of any history of gender-dysphoric behavior the disclosure can be shocking and can sometimes be followed by a bitter and hostile reaction. This is especially true in fundamentalist families or families with strict cultural, religious, or moral codes of behavior. For many people the concept of someone "changing sex" is considered so abhorrent that they cannot resolve this dilemma without assuming mental illness or "evil" on the part of the transgendered person.

More commonly, the family is aware of the gender issues, but has coped with them through denial, avoidance, and silence. Bringing this conversation into the family discourse can be met with a range of emotional reactions from anger to support, and the family's ambivalence is often presented in a labile, changeable, and inconsistent manner. One day family members may be interested and kind, the next day hostile and judgmental. This can, of course, increase the transgendered person's sense of instability and symptomatology (e.g., anxiety, depression). Although amusing to the whole family in retrospect, one mother of an adult child stood up and pounded her fist on the table saying, "I forbid it"—as if she could still control her "baby's" choices in a matter such as this. Families of origin rarely have a vote in what their adult children decide to do with their bodies, but not having a vote doesn't mitigate the emotional confusion of having a child (or sibling) "change" sex. Nickel-Dubin (1998) reported on a father who said that his hardest moment was when his "daughter" had her breasts removed because this made the decision irreversible. The father also discussed his confusion having his daughter enter the men's room behind him. These moments punctuate the changes in a family's life.

In rare cases, this disclosure can serve as an "aha" for family members who have been aware of the gender dysphoria and feel relieved that it is finally coming to the surface and being addressed. Often this response comes from family members the client least expects support from, e.g., a grandparent or a sibling who has distanced from the family.

Significant Others: Spouses and Partners

Coming out to partners and spouses presents a range of potential conflicts. In rare instances, the partner is completely unaware of the gender issues. When the couple has been together for many years, the shock of this disclosure can be devastating. It is to be expected that partners will experience a range of emotions, including hurt, fear, and betrayal. The marriage or relationship is thrown into a crisis, not unlike the kinds of emotional challenges experienced with an infidelity, a physical or mental illness, infertility, or the death of a child. Spouses are distrustful and feel deceived and they usually have little outside support to assist them in managing these issues. The partner will experience a process that parallels, but is not the same as, the transgendered person's process. The emotional process they experience is itself an emergence experience.

More commonly, family members have known about the gender differences for many years. Perhaps a male spouse has been a cross-dresser for many years and cross-dressing may have been incorporated into the couple's erotic lives. Perhaps a heterosexual female partner has been perceived as "strong" or "tomboyish" or a lesbian partner as "butch" or "dykey." Heterosexual male partners may have been viewed as "sensitive" or "gentle" or even prided themselves on being nontraditional men. Gay male partners may have taken pride in an identity as "nelly" or referred to themselves as a "queen." The gender-bending behavior of their partners and spouses may have been comfortable or uncomfortable. Some will admit to finding it attractive. However, experiencing an increase in gender dysphoric feelings or shift in behavioral or lifestyle needs is rarely met with enthusiasm and is more often perceived as a betrayal.

Partners are often at very different stages of acceptance than their transgendered or transsexual spouses. Family members usually experience a sense of shock and are in an "emergency stage" of their own just as the transgendered person is beginning to feel a need to move forward with their transition. It is emotionally overwhelming to realize that one's spouse is transgendered and it immediately brings up concerns and questions about one's *own* identity. The spouse or partner may ask: "Why is this happening to *me?*" or "What is it about me that made me pick a transsexual for a partner?" or "What does this mean about my sexuality?" or "Was I not good enough or not attractive enough?" They may also ask some version of, "What will the neighbors think?"

This is further exasperated by the often obsessive and near-narcissistic behavior of the transgendered person at this stage of his or her own emergence process. Having repressed this essential sense of self for so long, the disclosure stage is often experienced as a final hurdle, and now that his or her spouse or partner knows, the person is ready to move full-speed ahead (the need to emerge causes tremendous internal pressure). Transgendered people who are in an emergence process can appear impulsive and compulsive. They are often depressed with bouts of hyperactivity. They can be inappropriate and may be prone to lying about their whereabouts as well as their purchases. Sometimes they start to take hormones or begin electrolysis treatments without their partners' knowledge. Some transgendered people come out in impulsive anger, while others carefully plan the disclosure for months or even years. Some cover up their fears by pretending the reaction does not matter to them, while others overwhelm their partners with shame and guilt. It has been suggested by some spouses that their partners' behavior is reminiscent of adolescent behavior, and indeed the emerging self *is* most often developmentally adolescent-like.

Gender issues need to be seen within the context of other normative developmental concerns and family issues that can impact couple relationships. The marriage needs to become a safe context to examine these issues, so that gender issues can become just another difficulty that the family must face and integrate. If children are involved, concerns about the children can produce a protective and antagonistic reaction. Spouses are often reluctant to support transition solely because of their fears of how it will impact the children. Some transgendered people choose not to move ahead with any transition process in order to avoid trauma to their children.

> I did an informal investigation of all the people at The Clubhouse. Every one of the men who told their wives about their female selves and who had young families had been divorced. Every man there who waited to disclose until the children were grown up had wives who were supportive. I asked Natalie, one of the cross-dressers' wives who comes to The Clubhouse with her husband, if she would've stayed with him when the kids were younger. She said, "Absolutely not!" That was all I needed to hear. I will not risk losing my wife, or the kids, or going through a divorce. I will keep my femme self a secret until our youngest goes to college.

Concerns about the children's gender identity development become paramount, and fear that children will be ostracized and stigmatized in school often override the transgendered person's own emotional issues. The flip side of this are transgendered persons who seem oblivious to the impact of their transition on their children. Often angry at the courts or their spouses, they feel "oppressed" by the clinical concern regarding their children's adaptation and respond with apparent insensitivity to their children's developmental needs. Children's adaptation to transition will follow the trajectory of their parents. The more skill and acceptance the parents exhibit, the easier the transition will be for the children.

The Therapeutic Goal

Stage Three involves not only assisting the transgendered client in disclosing gender issues to significant others, but also integrating the partner's issues and concerns into the transgendered person's process. The transgendered person is often so focused on his or her own transition process, *or* so guilty about "forcing" this issue on their loved ones, that they are unable to be compassionate toward family members. The technique of pacing described in Stage Two becomes even more crucial once disclosure to partners is made. The significant others of transgendered people may initially be unwilling participants on this journey. They are often many steps or stages behind the transgendered person and are expected to "run and catch up." Sometimes partners and spouses appear to be accepting of the information, and have little negative reaction. Transgendered clients need to be aware that the initial reaction may not, in fact probably is not, reflective of their family's entire emotional experience.

Therapists working with couples at this stage can err therapeutically in two directions. They can "side" with the nontransgendered spouse or they can "side" with the transitioning spouse. Most therapists who are not knowledgeable about transgenderism, and who assume it is an illness, will—consciously or unconsciously—assist the spouse in a self-healing and self-protective strategy that ultimately leads to distancing from the relationship. Conversely, therapists who are gender specialists are often minimally sensitive or even cognizant of the issues faced by the spouse. Sometimes a few sessions of marriage counseling are completed, but often the clinician is obviously aligned with the transgendered person, and the spouse is invited in to session in order to be "educated." The spouse can perceive this to be indoctrination, and the issues she or he raises may not be seriously addressed as valid family issues. Therapists often approve hormones or body-modification surgeries without proper counseling for the partner. The family's commitment to one another and their history together is given a back seat to the importance of the transgenderism. Family members often refuse to work with gender therapists because they fear that their issues will not be respected. Good therapeutic intervention requires addressing both partners with equal regard—balancing the needs of the transgendered person's internal pressure to transition with the spouse's need to process the meaning of transgenderism in his or her life.

Even in the healthiest of families the disclosure of transgenderism can be emotionally unbalancing. Under the best of circumstances it will generally take some time for family members to accept and understand. The therapist working with transgendered people in intimate, committed partnerships must be skilled in family system dynamics and prepared to address the issues of family members in addition to the issues of their transgendered clients.

Stage Four: Exploring Identity and Transition

> [Transsexuals] . . . must decide whether to live with their contradictory
> body; or to adjust them to agree with their heart.

Lou Sullivan
*Information for the Female to Male Cross Dresser
and Transsexual,* 1990

In Stage Four, transgendered people begin to explore the meaning of their transgenderism and search for a label or identity that best explains who they are. The key issue in this stage is the acceptance and resolution of their gender dysphoria and a developing comfort with their gender identity. They are no longer talking about "what" is wrong with them or obsessed with familial or social approval but are engaged in a self-reflective process of authenticity. This is the stage in which transgendered people come to terms with a great truth about *who* they are.

Clients in this stage become aware of the diversity of labels that they can use to define themselves and begin to see there is not one way to "be" transgendered. This can grant them a sense of near breathtaking relief. This stage can be far less emotional and intense than the previous stages, although some might see it as the calm before the storm. At times it is highly philosophical and even metaphysical, as clients examine deep issues of meaning and ask universal questions such as, "Who am I?" "What is the purpose of my life?" and "Who am I living for?" Questions about the meaning of gender surface and issues of social convention and whether hormonal therapies are "natural" become paramount. Childhood is often revisited with painful memories and intimate relationships are reexamined regarding future options. They are no longer fighting their gender issues and the dysphoria starts to ebb. They know themselves to be transgendered, possibly transsexual, and are growing comfortable with this identity.

Stage Four is about exploration of roles, clothing, and mannerisms in ways that are exciting but can also be frightening. Transgendered people may start to explore more cross-dressing and experiment more frequently with "outings," risking more exposure. In what is often a bold move, more outward signs of masculinity or femininity begin to appear. Transgendered females experiment with appearing more masculine, even when they are still living and identifying as women. They may cut their hair shorter or style it in a more traditionally male way. Since the social rules for females are less restrictive than for males, many transgendered females already dress very masculine. The changes at this stage are often more subtle but involve ceasing to wear any feminine apparel and changing how they carry themselves.

By this stage, many transgendered women have had a long history of owning opposite-sex clothing and accoutrements, but may have never worn them publicly. Now they begin wearing more feminine clothing and jewelry. Some dress in exclusively women's clothing, although the clothes may at first be more androgynous styles bought in the women's department. They begin to experiment with "outings," which can be trips to the mall or out to dinner with a supportive friend. In addition to the feeling of freedom they experience being out, they are also scanning for potential problems. They often struggle with being mistaken for effeminate gay men if they dress subtly or outward violence if they dress more brazenly.

Transgendered people are extremely cognizant of the subtleties of gendered mannerism and often utilize therapy to discuss these nuances. Facial or hand gestures, sitting postures, and use of voice are experimented with and tested for accuracy. As clients grow more comfortable with themselves and their natures, they also develop a comfortable "style," a way of dressing that fits them. One male cross-dresser described how she dresses in women's clothes at home, and men's clothes at work. She said, "It used to be much more erotic when it was more forbidden, but now it just feels normal. The other day I found myself going out to the store to pick up some milk, and didn't even stop to see what gender I was presenting as; I just picked up my purse and went out."

That might appear to be an unremarkable thing—to just pick up one's purse and go out—but for those struggling with gender identity concerns and issues of passing, it is an act that represents tremendous integration and identity consolidation. Passing means "blending in and becoming unnoticeable and unremarkable as either a man or a woman" (Cromwell, 1999, p. 39) and is usually experienced as a major accomplishment. Many clients live in fear of being "read," or recognized as someone who is cross-dressed. Lewins (1995) noted that "becoming a woman" is a social process that involves building confidence and competence. The more one "does gender" the more confidence one has. He also noted that the less the person worries about passing, the more relaxed they become, and therefore the more successful they are.

In Stage Four, transgendered people begin to explore their future options for transition, its impact on loved ones, and their future vocational and financial needs. Many people decide not to take hormones or transition full-time, although they may consider these options. Sometimes people want to take low doses of hormones to assist them in great body congruence, yet they do not desire to transition or live full-time in the other sex. It is important not to attribute a hierarchy to the emergence process, and sometimes people feel pressure from within the transgendered community to "move ahead," when they are unsure whether this is what they want or what is best for them.

When I first came to therapy I wasn't sure if I was a really confused lesbian or a transsexual. I knew I could never consider taking hormones or changing my physical body, and I had no idea who I wanted to have sex with, let alone who would have sex with me. Being in therapy gave me the permission I needed to dress the way I wanted and to present myself in the world in a more masculine manner. Thankfully I am small breasted. I had my name changed to a man's name, and now I am just comfortable walking through the world with my male self, and knowing that I can have sex with women or men, and that I am OK. I don't know if I will ever choose to start hormones, and I am pretty sure I would never have surgery, but today I am just happy to be myself.

Ideally the process of negotiating transition possibilities takes place with the knowledge of family members and with their support. Issues of the differing needs of partners must be negotiated, and management of the impact of the stress must be carefully monitored. Work-related problems often begin to surface at this stage, and the excitement about beginning to transition is often thwarted by the reality of job loss, as few employers will tolerate an obviously transgendered employee and even fewer companies offer protection for transitioning workers.

Transgendered women (MTF) often dress outside the home for the first time on a visit to the therapist or will use the therapist's bathroom as an opportunity to change their clothes. They are seeking approval from the therapist and openly request advice on dressing and passing. Often, electrolysis is begun at this stage, which is often a time-consuming, expensive, and painful endeavor. Facial hair needs to grow in for a few days before the treatments, so they may look more male and "scruffy" for a few days, followed by days where their skin is red and puffy.

For some clients the journey to this fourth stage is laborious and exhausting. Some lose many things dear to them in this emergence process, and not all are well equipped to cope effectively with the resulting emotional pain. The internalized hatred and confusion about their gender identity or the disappointment and criticisms of family and friends can easily overwhelm the client. The consequences for exploring gender transition can be devastating. This might mean final rejection from their family of origin, or ending a relationship with a beloved partner who cannot accept or live with the transition. For others it may mean rejection by their children or even the legal loss of custody. It can mean forced career changes or associated financial losses (Miller, 1996).

This can be the most dangerous stage for clients and many exhibit depression and suicidal ideation or begin abusing substances. Some transgendered people at this stage do not take proper precautions for their safety. This is especially common for MTF clients who are often unaware of the daily hazards of living as women within a sexist society. They are often resistant to listening to the potential danger of either being perceived of as a woman or being seen as a man dressed as a woman. They sometimes scoff at the idea of violence against women or hate crimes against "queers," placing themselves in potentially hostile situations. At times they become belligerent toward others who recognize them as cross-dressers, almost baiting them.

Other transgendered people are hypervigilant about potential dangers and are so scared that they are unable to go out. Bias-related violence is a frightening reality (Courant and Cooke-Daniels, 1998; Lev and Lev, 1999) and Smith documented the number of violent deaths of people who are, or are thought to be, transgendered or transsexual on her Web site <http://www.gender.org/remember/>. Sometimes carrying a letter from a therapist that explains their situation can serve to alleviate clients' fears, although functionally it may not do much to protect them from violence. If a police officer stops them, the letter may prevent their being detained, but it will obviously not protect them from hate crimes.

Some clients first come into therapy at this stage of emergence. Essentially having worked through their issues regarding their gender outside of a clinical context, they are informed about resources, educated about gender transition, and "out" to family and friends. They come into therapy having already decided to begin hormone treatment as a way to resolve their gender dysphoria and are not experiencing any obvious distress about their decisions. They request referrals for hormones and cannot move further within the gatekeeping system without therapeutic approval. Some clients are very angry about having to go through an assessment process and are therefore very "resistant" clients. However, it is not only the client that is angry but potentially the clinician who is uncomfortable with the client's demands. Block and Fisher (1979) said, "Their demands for quick agreement with the desired diagnosis and referral to surgery may anger us as we experience it as an invasion of our professional prerogatives or an insult to our status as experts" (p. 118). In many cases, the assessment process is easily completed, and from the information gathered from collaterals, it is clear that the person fits the documented criteria for gender identity disorder and has no contraindications for hormonal treatment. Following the guidelines established in the HBIGDA's standards of care, a clinician may complete an assessment and refer the client on for medical treatment. Follow-up with these clients can be useful since transition can bring emotional upheaval and clients should always be informed of the therapist's availability if problems arise.

The Therapeutic Goal

The therapeutic goal for Stage Four is to assist the client in their exploration of various transgender identities and the resolution of a sense of authentic self as a cross-gendered person. The transgendered client is beginning to self-label and explore different options for their future. The more space transgendered people have to examine their feelings, behaviors, fantasies, and desires, the "gentler" the emergence process will be and the greater likelihood they have of finding a presentation and definition that best fits their needs.

The therapist in this stage must be a good listener and will often discover that there are far more ways to experience gender than they had ever dreamed possible. Witnessing the power of transformation can fill the therapist with wonder and awe, and indeed the therapist *is* a witness to this process. Often the client who entered therapy in Stage One anxious, possibly suicidal without discernible self-esteem, will begin to blossom in this stage. The therapist must maintain an attitude of openness and advocacy for the client in this process, assisting them in examining the many options available to them, and understanding the potential consequences of their choices. Referring to clients with their chosen names and proper pronouns is essential, although sometimes their presentation might appear to be in direct conflict with the language used.

Client advocacy at this stage is fundamental. Sometimes spouses begin divorce procedures, threatening to take full custody of children. Often jobs are in jeopardy due to the changes in gender presentation or, in some cases, the fallout of the behaviors of the past developmental processes have left legal complications. Clients often utilize therapists as fashion consultants, asking for advice on clothing, and arrive for therapy seeking approval for new haircuts or clothing styles. Therapists might be needed to intervene with school systems and work environments. Continuing family therapy is an excellent idea but this is often an expensive stage for clients due to the cost of electrolysis, job insecurities, change in living arrangements, and preparation for future surgeries or career changes. Therapy can be a financial luxury during this process, which is unfortunate because it is a time when therapy can be particularly useful. This is an exciting stage in transgender development, filled with hope and transformation.

Stage Five: Exploring Transition and Possible Body Modification

> I could achieve my personal goal of adulthood. This means that I have
> chosen to change my appearance . . . it does not mean that my gender

is socially—or even medically—constructed. My gender has not changed; I have simply made its message clear.

Jamison Green
Unseen Genders, 2001

The fifth stage of emergence is a time of consolidating gender presentation and making decisions about body modification. This stage continues the exploration of the previous stage, but for some people involves beginning hormones, preparing for surgeries, and completing electrolysis. Not all transgendered people choose to make body modifications, but most explore the possibility. Discussions about transsexualism dominate the therapeutic process, while clients explore hormonal and surgical options, and begin to realistically examine the impact that transitioning can have on their marriages, families, and occupational choices. Clients often begin electrolysis, hormones, and the "real-life experience." Questions of passing become paramount. For many transsexuals desiring to live full time in an opposite gender presentation and wanting to fully pass, the stage of living "in between" during the transition process is the most painful time of all.

Since the hallmark of gender identity disorder is a "preoccupation with getting rid of primary and secondary sex characteristics (e.g., request for hormones, surgery, or other procedures to physically alter sexual characteristics to simulate the other sex)" (APA, 1994, pp. 537-538) clinicians and clients place great emphasis on the desire to modify one's body. A client who expresses no desire—or a transient desire—for body modification, cannot technically receive the label of "transsexual" and has historically been ineligible for any hormonal or surgical treatments. This makes it especially difficult for clients to discuss their fears and anxieties about hormonal treatments, particularly when they are concerned that any hesitancy they express will later be used to withhold treatments.

The medical establishment has historically been very reluctant to offer hormonal and/or surgical assistance, unless the client was willing to "go all the way." Transitioning to the "other" sex was acceptable, however, virilizing or feminizing one's body to a mixed-gender presentation, or presenting as the other gender without completing genital surgery, was considered heretical. Transgendered people have often felt stuck between two untenable realities—living in bodies that felt dissonant or having a full sex change. Middle-ground positions were not seen as options. One client who said that she wanted to keep her breasts but begin male hormones was called "a freak" by her therapist. Clients who are comfortable being called by either pronoun are often counseled to choose one or the other. Clients are encouraged to not use gender-neutral names but choose strongly gendered names.

It is now becoming obvious that there are more forms of gender variance that respond well to medical treatments than transsexualism.

Some transgendered people live between genders as compromise positions. Due to a partner's resistance to body modifications, or job-related issues, people have negotiated "solutions" that are workable concessions. Some may live double lives in which they are able to cross-live in one part of their lives, but not another. Some maintain this double life indefinitely. For example, a person may work at a high-paying career as a man, but live the rest of her life as a woman in another city. One client, who identified as transsexual, chose to remain in a rather feminine-presented male body because his wife stated that she would leave him if he medically modified his body.

Other transgendered people, however, take pride in being between genders. They enjoy switching back and forth. This is especially common among transgendered youth and people who have chosen to live more alternative, or bohemian lives, and reside in parts of the country where one can secure a livelihood while living in an unconventional manner. In addition, some females may want to virilize their bodies and some men might want to feminize their bodies with the help of hormonal therapy, and yet not transition out of their birth sex. The fluidity of gender presentation makes them comfortable and allows them to explore both their masculinity and their femininity.

Some transgendered people are resistant to taking hormones because they want to preserve their singing voice or are concerned about altering their sexual response or adversely affecting their health. One client, who is a herbal healer, would not consider taking male hormones, but was able to research alternative herbal choices. The impact of these natural androgens was less dramatic than synthetic ones but was enough to satisfy his needs for hormonal support without compromising his values. It is possible to have an integrated and solid gender consolidation that does not easily fit in male/female boxes. People must not be forced to "choose" if their nature tells them to take a middle path.

There are also people who have chosen to have certain procedures, even though they were comfortable living in a middle-position, because they felt it was too stressful to live in the "real" world. Bockting and Coleman (1992) reported the case of a "gender-neutral" client, who chose to live as a woman because living in the middle proved too stressful. In a world where gender is polarized, living in the middle can be disorienting for others even though it is comfortable for the person.

Some transmen and transgendered women choose to live in the opposite gender role without securing genital, or "lower," surgeries. There are numerous reasons for this. For some it is simply not feasible financially. One client resisted genital surgery because of his fear that he would lose sexual feelings. Others explained that their genitals are "just not that big a deal" to their identity as the other sex, a position that contradicts the medical field's definition of transsexuals as people who hate their genitals and want them removed. Religious prohibitions can impact decision making. In Islamic tradition, genital surgery impacts burial rituals, complicating family acceptance (Teh, 2001). Sometimes clients struggle with feeling guilty about this, as if they "should" want surgery or perhaps, they fear, they are not "real."

Others do not feel secure with the medical procedures as they are currently available. This is commonly true for FTMs. Phalloplasty surgery is more technically complex than surgical techniques for MTFs, is less researched, and far more expensive. Some transmen have been disappointed postoperatively in the results. Alternatively many transmen have chosen testosterone treatment, which can enlarge the clitoris, and metoidioplasty, which can release the clitoris from the pubis, leaving a small, but functioning penis. Commonly, FTMs are choosing to live as men without normative male genitalia (Rachlin, 1999; Cromwell, 1999). There have, of course, always been men who have small penises and secure male identities. Garfinkel (as described in Kessler and McKenna, 1978) distinguished between the possession of a penis as biological event and as a cultural assumption. A person who lives as a man and appears as a man, is assumed to be a man (i.e., a person with penis) based on attributed symbols, regardless of his actual anatomy. Since manhood has in many ways been defined by the presence of a phallus, this can sometimes present identity conflicts for the transman, as well as difficulties in sexual relationships.

Beginning hormonal therapy or preparing for surgeries needs to be clinically paced, so the client is making the best decisions possible given their financial resources and the medical options available. It is important to study surgical options, to discuss them with medical providers, and most of all, to talk with other transgendered people in order to find the best providers with the most satisfied consumers. Utilization of the Internet is essential. Many physicians have Web sites and even post pictures of their surgical results. Finances are also a consideration and need to be addressed as part of the clinical preparation. Exploration of hormones and surgeries can be a time-consuming process.

When I first began this process and admitted to myself that I was a transsexual, I just wanted to move ahead as fast as I could. I hated having to have an assessment, and then waiting weeks for an appointment with that damned endocrinologist. I felt you were all blocking me, and it made me feel powerless and very angry. I've realized that it was not you I was angry at; I was angry at all those years that I stayed in an unhappy marriage so that I wouldn't lose my kids—and I wound up losing them anyway. I was angry that I allowed myself to have so much shame with my gender issues that I was known everywhere as a blatant homophobe. By the time I began these hormones, I knew who I was, and what was right with me. I do not have shame anymore, and I feel ready to just live my life.

Many clients have fears about seeing an endocrinologist for the first time. They assume that they have to present in a certain manner to be approved for hormones, and it is important that the therapist have a close working relationship with the physician to assuage clients' fears in a realistic way. Some endocrinologists are excessively intrusive into transsexuals' psychological motivations, and clients may need clinical support and advocacy in coping with the physician's invasive or judgmental manner. Monitoring the client carefully after beginning hormones is very important. Hormonal treatment can make dramatic changes for clients, both in how they look and how they feel. Most of these changes are positive, including an immediate sense of well-being that may be more psychological than physiological. FTMs often experience an increase in sexual interest and a greater sense of well-being. They do not necessarily exhibit higher aggression (Cohen-Kettenis and Gooren, 1992), although an increase in aggression should be carefully monitored. MTF clients often experience a decreased interest in sex, as well as orgasmic difficulties and problems sustaining erections. They also experience a lessening of tension and a sense of greater relaxation (Cohen-Kettenis and Gooren, 1992). As clients begin to take hormones and live in their new gender identities, they often "grow into" their new identity, and like the proverbial snake shedding their skin, it is difficult to remember who they were before since the new skin fits so well. Remember, this is not really the birth of new gender identity, but the revealing of what has always been hidden.

For some clients, reactions are less than positive. Some transgendered women say they become emotionally weepy and frightened. Some transmen describe becoming overly aggressive and sexually voracious. Sometimes a "tweaking" of the dosage by the endocrinologist can help. Other times it is simply a matter of acclimating to the dramatic power of hormonal treatment. The physical changes can be dramatic for transmen, especially for those who have small breasts or have already had breast reduction/chest surgeries. Once a beard is grown, few people will question whether the transman is male. For both men and women, the emotional freedom of being on hormones, regardless of the actual physical changes, is a great relief. Clients who are struggling with comorbid mental health issues can sometimes begin to decompensate after beginning hormonal treatments and need to be carefully monitored.

By this stage, most clients have had some experience living crossgendered, although it might be solely in their homes or within the safety of transgendered support groups. They have had experience coming out to others and have coped with both positive and negative reactions. Most clients in this stage have made basic decisions about the trajectory of their gender transition and are already receiving some treatment (electrolysis, chest surgery, hormonal treatment) and are exploring a full-time cross-gender role. Those who choose to have genital surgeries have begun to research their options and examine their finances for feasibility.

For those who intend on living full-time in the opposite sex, the "real-life test" begins. The real-life experience—often referred to as the real-life test—was designed by John Money as a way to ensure that transsexuals understood the everyday realities of living as the opposite gender (Money, 1978, as cited in Bockting and Coleman, 1992). As clients begin to negotiate the real-life experience, they often feel as if they are indeed being tested. Although many questions are raised by the role of gatekeeper in enforcing the real-life test, this process is often a wake-up call for clients to begin to understand the real-life costs of changing gender. Although it has been recommended that the real-life test precede hormone treatment, both transgendered women and transmen are able to more successfully pass after hormone therapy has begun (Schaefer, Wheeler, and Futterweit, 1995). Once body modifications begin, transgendered people are forced out of the closet—a critical difference between coming out gay and emerging transgendered. During the transition process transgendered people are caught living "in the middle" and this can present certain legal as well as work-related difficulties.

Each client's situation is unique and needs to be treated that way. Sometimes clients will begin a treatment process, such as hormones, and change their mind. One client had nearly transitioned to living full-time, and then decided to revert back to his original gender, although this is rare. Another client could not risk going out cross-dressed because she was a minister, but began hormones years before she was able to leave her profession and live full-time. Another client lived nearly full-time for five years, except for her work life. Since she had a good job, she was not willing to risk her livelihood. She was also concerned about the effects the hormones would have on her physical ability to do her job. The HBIGDA's standards of care offer guidelines but are very clear about the need for sound therapeutic judgment in utilizing the guidelines in a flexible manner.

Clients often look for positive feedback on their presentation. They show off their bodily changes and boast about their new breasts or hair growth. For transgendered people who are interested in complete transitioning, concerns about passing begin to arise and the question of whether they will pass can become all-consuming. Issues of passing can become the nucleus of their therapeutic work. Both feminist and medical literature have been critical of how rigid transsexuals are in their gender conceptions, appearing to mimic sexist roles, and producing caricatures of masculinity and femininity. However, much of this is reinforced, if not directly created, by the medical sexologists who have judged transsexuals' authenticity on their ability to pass. Gender clinics essentially became "grooming clinics," teaching clients how to behave within proper cultural mandates for appropriate gender expression (Stone, 1991).

For FTMs, passing is often more easily accomplished, particularly for small-breasted females. For those who desire to fully pass as men, the Internet offers advice on how to appear masculine, but not "butch" (i.e., stereotypically lesbian). Taking testosterone will produce a lower voice and facial hair and even those who are small in stature often pass easily. Kessler and McKenna's (1978) research showed that male "cues" are powerful in determining our attribution of gender. People more easily ignore or justify female body signifiers when obvious male signifiers are present (e.g., facial hair). Breast binding is common and looser clothing can mask more feminine curves. Some FTMs, especially during transition, look more like teenage boys rather than men, which can also be disconcerting. Some transgendered women (MTFs) who are of small stature are also able to pass. To enhance their ability to pass, many use "props" that are available on the Internet or in specialty magazines to round out their hips or fill out their bust line. Some transgendered women enjoy using these and some are frustrated to have to be "fake" in order to look real. Electrolysis becomes an important goal during this stage (permanently removing a five-o'clock shadow can help with a feminine presentation). Numerous surgical options can reduce the size of the Adam's apple, shorten the broader forehead of most males, or soften the shape of the jaw to create a more feminine look. Although these cosmetic surgeries may seem extreme, as well as quite expensive and therefore not accessible for everyone, they can often make a profound difference in the ability of an MTF to pass. For the client for whom passing is essential, either for their own comfort or due to their desire to be passable in the workplace, these cosmetic surgeries should not be trivialized. Billings and Urban (1982), however, expressed concern that transsexuals "are in danger of becoming surgical junkies as they strive for an idealized sexuality via surgical commodities" (p. 113). It is important to remind MTFs that the desire for the perfect body is an age-old, and often unattainable, feminine pursuit. A more feminist awareness of body acceptance may be an important therapeutic focus. For some clients the pursuit of passing becomes nearly obsessive.

I began to notice how small my hands were and realized that everyone would know those were not male hands. I began to hide my hands, and keep them in my pocket all the time. Afraid that my voice would give me away, I noticed that I stopped talking to people, always shifting my eyes. I lived in fear that I would be "caught," and was thrilled whenever someone called me "he" or "sir." Even after I had chest surgery and had been on hormones for a while, I began to take more T [testosterone] than prescribed. I was walking through the world with quite a chip on my shoulder, thinking this was very male. Then a friend reminded me: I wanted to be recognized as a guy, not a "prick." I didn't need to take on every ugly characteristic that males had been assigned. I finally began to develop more ease with my body and remembered that I could be a "gentle-man." I began to trust that no one was going to think I was a woman with my thick beard. I finally began to relax.

Some transsexuals need to accept that they cannot pass well and will be seen as "transsexuals" regardless of their presentation (Bockting and Coleman, 1992). Some are quite comfortable with this and others are profoundly uncomfortable. Transgendered women often have difficulty passing as women since biological males are often tall, with larger hands, and distinctive features such as square jaws, facial hair, baldness, and prominent Adam's apples. As one client said, "I have to accept that I can either live my life as a 'man,' or as a 'man in a dress,' but I will never pass as a woman. I need to accept that I am a 'tranny,' and that is what I will always be no matter how I dress or live." Although the client made this remark flippantly, the pain beneath this statement is quite apparent.

Historically, some gender clinics would not approve people for transition unless they were able to pass well, as it was assumed that passing well was an important determinant for a successful postoperative future. Transsexuals were expected to "disappear" back into the mainstream of modern life as men and women. Although some transsexuals prefer this transition route, many transsexuals—those who can pass as well as those who are less likely to pass—are choosing to be out and open about their gender transition. Whittle (1999) said that transgendered people "have always been programmed to pass and hence disappear. . . . [If they don't pass, they are] punished for [their] . . . failure to become real" (p. 7). Stone (1991) said that passing has meant "constructing plausible histories" and being accepted as a "natural" member of the other gender (p. 296). By identifying as a "woman of transsexual experience" or "a transgendered man," some people are retaining their sense of self as transsexuals.

The Therapeutic Goal

In this stage of transition, the psychotherapist is truly a transition assistant. The therapist monitors the client's progress and offers support through the transition. It is not the clinician's job to have an agenda about proper social presentation or the choices of the transgendered person, although it is his or her job to validate the diversity of choices available and make sure the client is aware of the implications of his or her choices.

Clinically speaking, it can be a difficult transition for the therapist, since clients often change their minds and choices and the therapist can feel "one step behind." It is essential for the therapist to work through his or her own issues and resistance about client choice regarding "elective" surgical techniques and gender-reassignment surgeries. If the therapist remains judgmental, or is unable to discuss the details of the surgery and feels "disgusted" by these processes, he or she will not be able to help the client. Therapists should not assume that clients should utilize medical treatments or that they "must" follow up with surgery if clients begin hormone therapy.

Clients will often need referral letters to begin hormonal treatment or surgical procedures. They will need therapists who are able to assist them in negotiating the medical and judicial systems as they begin a process of physical and legal "sex change." It is also essential that family therapy (with partners and children) continue during this stage of transition. Transgendered clients change rapidly at this stage, physically as well as mentally, and most family members are struggling with some loss of the person they once knew. Remaining an advocate for all members of the family and assisting in communication and openness, particularly in areas of sexuality, is necessary for successful transition.

Stage Six: Integration and Pride

> The wood does not change the fire into itself, but the fire changes the wood into itself.

> Meister Eckhardt
> Christian mystic, 1260-1329

It may seem strange to begin discussion of this last stage with a quote from a mystic. However, the process of gender transition, like all powerful and shamanic acts, is mystical and transformational. Stage Six is the stage of synthesis, in which transgendered persons are able to fully integrate themselves into their new identity. Ideally, they do not deny their previous selves and their dysphoria has been mitigated. Lewins (1995), a sociologist who writes about transsexualism, recounted his personal process of coming to terms with his son's reassignment as a woman and his family's struggle with how to preserve memories of their son before his transition. Lewins said both the family and the transsexual person must resolve the present and incorporate the past. This can include discussing what pronouns to use when referring to the past or how to deal with childhood family photos.

Schaefer, Wheeler, and Futterweit (1995) suggested that transsexuals be encouraged "never to totally discard the memories of living in the original natal role," since this is a vital aspect to integrating one's whole identity.

Of course, many paths toward integration exist. Some transsexuals chose to live "stealthily" and others choose to be more "out" about their history or current transgendered status. In Lewins' (1995) stage model the final stage of what he calls "becoming a woman" is "invisibility." In this model it is assumed that all transsexual women want to "disappear" as transsexuals and become invisible as people who once lived as men. This is certainly true for many fully transitioned people, who desire to pass and do not want to be recognized on the streets. However, it is unfair to identify this as a stage of completion into "womanhood," since many transsexuals, men and women, are not willing or interested in becoming invisible.

Although some transsexuals choose to "disappear" and not have any involvement with the transgender community after their transition, more recently many fully transitioned people have chosen to maintain contact and involvement in transgender civil rights issues. Part of the integration stage for those active in political struggle is finding a balance between their righteous anger at the social violence toward transgendered people and not allowing their anger to envelop them. This does not mean that they are not committed to progressive change; indeed people in this stage are often those most capable of advocating for political and legal changes. Suzette, a client, described it this way:

I come from a wealthy family. I was their golden child, who reaped all the rewards of their wealth—private schools, summers in Europe, and eventually law school. I mean, nobody gets out of law school without debt, except me, of course. Transsexuality simply does not happen in families like mine, so I stayed deep in the closet. When I first began reading about trans issues, I was surprised to learn about trans political organizing. I discovered there was actually a legal group advocating for transsexuals, and I thought that was laughable. *Right,* I thought, *a bunch of social derelicts demanding legal protection.* But something happened as I began to really accept my own transsexualism. I guess I became angry. I would read these horrible accounts of trans people losing custody of their children or being fired from their jobs, and I began to see myself as a member of an oppressed minority. I knew I had to do something. I guess I became one of those people I used to think were so crazy. It doesn't seem crazy to me anymore to use my power as an attorney to represent people like myself who are being discriminated against. Now, I have become one of those people who thinks the world can change.

It is important that the various choices people make for their lives after transition are not viewed in a hierarchal manner—different people for various reasons utilize different strategies. Clinically, the only salient concerns are the comfort the person has with his or her own life choices and his or her ability to manage situations of potential exposure when they arise. Transgendered people in this stage do not experience shame about being transsexual or transgendered and are comfortable with their transition choices. Many transsexuals have fully transitioned and moved away from an "identity" as transsexual. They are living fully as men or women and gender issues are an irrelevant part of their lives. However, this does not mean that all transgendered peopled are living full-time in the opposite sex, nor does it mean that how they are living will not change at some point in the future. It means that they have found some resolution to their gender dysphoria and have made satisfying adjustments to living in a gender-polarized system. Similar to the stage model presented at the beginning of this chapter for bisexuals, transgender emergence allows for "continued uncertainty" and fluidity as part of the integration stage. The experience of comfort and pride in their journey is most evident in this stage.

Whatever words or labels people use to define themselves—transsexual, transgendered, cross-dresser, transman, transwoman, butch, drag queens, drag kings, bi-gendered, queer, or simply men or women—they have become comfortable with who they are and where they stand in the transgender continuum. They have synthesized a key element of their identity— their gender identity—into the greater whole of who they are (artist, parent, business owner, chef, accountant, attorney, etc.). The development of their gender identity—a process that was stifled a long time ago by a society that could not allow for difference—has finally caught up with the rest of their development.

Some transsexuals at this stage have completed reassignment surgeries. Others are still saving money or have decided against having genital surgeries. In the beginning of this journey some transsexuals focused exclusively on "getting the surgery," as if surgery validated their gender transition, and have seen this through to completion. In the integration stage, most transsexuals, including those who are postsurgical, accept that "the surgery" is neither the end all or be all of their identity. Although they may choose surgery, their gender identity does not depend on their genitalia, but on who they know themselves to be.

Bolin (1988, 1992, 1997), in her research on MTFs, commented on the developmental process of transsexual transitioning as a rite of passage. She said, "The transgender rite of passage was rich with ritual and symbolic metaphors of becoming, of transformation, and of the death of a man and the birth of a woman" (Bolin, 1988, p. 15). She described a reversing of the ordering of birth and adolescence, in which the person first goes through adolescence as a preparation for their birth. It is as if the person first recognizes a transsexual identity, and by allowing that to emerge over time "the primary transsexual identity assumes an increasingly subordinate position, and the female subidentity becomes crystallized into a primary identity" (Bolin, 1988, p. 99). Through interaction with their social environment, and being seen and accepted as women, their self-esteem as women is enhanced as they are increasingly accepted into a female social sphere. Although transsexual men and women have very different social and political experiences, a similar rite of passage is applicable for transmen.

The Therapeutic Goal

Transition, particularly surgical completion, often has meant the end of therapeutic treatment (except for follow-up studies for research). It is true that an explicit need for therapeutic intervention regarding gender issues at this stage of transition rarely exists. Gender identity is usually well consolidated by Stage Six, and some clients drift away from the therapeutic relationship, for it serves as a reminder of their transition.

However, the period following gender transition can be an emotional landmine for many people. Certainly relieved to finally have their physical and social lives integrated, clients may still be coping with issues of grief as they recount the losses associated with their transitions. It is recommended that clinicians consider continuing therapeutic support past actual surgical dates and supporting people through what might be a difficult time of reorientation and integration (Schaefer et al., 2000; Walters, Kennedy, and Ross, 1986). Clients may experience a post-transition depression or disappointment that transition may not have solved all their problems. One MTF client suddenly went back to dressing as a man following her surgery. This lasted two months and then abruptly stopped. She resumed living as a woman. Years later she is still unsure why she did that. Sometimes clients in this stage need assistance educating family members, require an expert witness to maintain custody of their children, or an advocate to retain their employment status or housing situation. In addition, clients may need therapy to deal with the myriad other life issues that they bring into therapy. It is essential for clients to know that they can always return to therapy to address any issues that surface.

Emergence is presented here as a normative, developmental process. Adults who have been robbed of their gender identity exploration due to a repression of cross-gender dysphoria or identity will need to move through these developmental stages. They can come through this emotional process into an integrated sense of self. Transgendered people who have synthesized their gender identity into their larger self-identity can make excellent gender clinicians themselves.

Chapter 8

Family Emergence

Through the transgression of loving someone who is differently gendered . . . it is possible for someone who does not appear to be a gender outlaw to become one.

Pat (now Patrick) Califia
Sex Changes, 1997

Clinical issues affecting families of gender-variant people have received little attention in the medical literature. Transgendered people have too often been viewed as people without families, or, sadly, as though their families are disposable. Transitioning, especially as it is viewed within the medical model, too often has been framed as an either/or option—to transition *or* to remain part of their families. One clinician, a colleague, said, "I encouraged him to cross-dress secretly until he was really ready to leave his wife and live as a woman"—as if a separation was inevitable when the client disclosed his gender issues and living with secrets was healthy for a marriage. Attempts to receive clinical treatment for family issues are often thwarted by insurance companies that not only will not cover "gender identity" issues, but also will not cover therapy for family members coping with the impact of those issues. One insurance company refused to reimburse the wife of a male transsexual. They said, "It is not *her* problem."

Searching thorough the literature will yield a paucity of clinical advice to assist couples and families to survive the impact of gender dysphoria or gender reassignment. Clinically, little guidance is available on how to work with partners, spouses, children, and other family members. Interestingly enough, the marital and family therapy literature is almost completely silent on this issue, which is especially surprising given the extensive discourse in the last decade on the role of both gender and ethnicity in families (McGoldrick, 1998; McGoldrick, Anderson, and Walsh, 1991; McGoldrick, Giordano, and Pearce, 1996), as well as the growing fields of lesbian and gay family studies and life span development studies (Benkov, 1994; Bozett and Sussman, 1990; D'Augelli and Patterson, 1995; Laird and Green, 1996; Cohen and Savin-Williams, 1996; Slater, 1995). Although gender roles and

271

power, ethnic and cultural diversity, and alternative family dynamics have been analyzed within a family systems frame, *trans*genderism has been virtually ignored. Mallon (1999) commented on the lack of professional writing on transgenderism in the mainstream social work journals. Indeed, a thorough search of the social work literature revealed few articles (see Chong, 1990; Cullen, 1997; Gainor, 2000; Oles, 1977; Peo, 1988; Wicks, 1977). One author discussed utilizing structural family therapy with transsexuals (Ma, 1997). The question of how gender and sexuality are mediated *within* same-sex families has barely been addressed, assuming that same-sex relationships do not confront issues of gender diversity (Laird, 1999; Loulan, 1990).

The research available, mostly published in journals specializing in "sexuality" issues, has focused on the "wives" of cross-dressers—who are referred to in the literature as "transvestites"—and, to a lesser extent, on the wives of male-to-female transsexuals. The nonclinical literature has also been sparse, and since so few more contemporary books exist, Prince's (1967) classic advice book, *The Transvestite and His Wife,* still circulates today. Although brief discussions appear in the literature regarding the partners of gender-variant females, minimal clinical information is available on parenting issues for transgender parents or parents raising transgendered children. The literature has been virtually silent regarding heterosexual men whose wives choose to transition or gay men whose male partners begin to live as women and it has been assumed that few of these relationships have survived. (For a man whose wife is transgendered, the husband would be faced with not only the loss of his "wife," but also the homophobia of now being involved with a man. It is a rare man in this patriarchal culture that would embrace that challenge.) Although stability of relationships is often used as a criterion to determine postsurgical success, there is virtually no discussion in the literature on how to weather the storm of gender transition and its impact on marital issues or sexuality. Very little hope is given in the literature that a relationship with a gender-variant partner could be functional or fulfilling.

PARTNERS, SPOUSES, AND SIGNIFICANT OTHERS

When an individual solves the problem of self-expression through transsexualism, new problems are created on medical, legal, and moral grounds for other members of society.

David E. Grimm

Steiner (1985c) warned clinicians who work with clients with gender dis-orders that they "will *occasionally* have to *deal with* the partners of patients" (p. 351, italics mine). She did not suggest that it is a clinician's responsibil-ity to *deal with* the entire family, despite the presumption that cross-gender expression is always disruptive and conflictual for the family. Steiner (1985c) continued, "Marital therapy is generally unsuccessful because the transves-titic spouse will not relinquish his [sic] cross-dressing behavior" (p. 358). It seems obvious that marital therapy is bound to fail if the cessation of cross-dressing behavior is deemed necessary for the marriage therapy's success.

The most frequently studied family members in the literature are the wives of transvestites, whose husbands were in treatment or were them-selves seeking treatment (they were assumed to have psychosexual and mental health problems). Stoller (1967b) classified women who marry or become lovers with transvestites in three categories: malicious male-haters, succorers, and symbiotes. He explained that male-haters dress their sons in girls' clothing and are angry, competitive, and degrading toward men. Succorers overindulge their husbands and convert them to cross-dressing and behaving as women and the symbiotics are compulsively drawn to cross-dress their sons in girls' clothing, are bisexual, homosexual, sexually "neuter," or present with a "boyish femininity" (p. 90). These women are de-scribed as competitive, angry, and "inadequate" women who have not only chosen these presumably dysfunctional relationships but may be causally responsible for the cross-dressing behavior of both their husbands and their sons.

Research has further shown that the wives of transvestites experienced difficulties with self-esteem (Feinbloom, 1976), although Weinberg and Bullough's (1988) research show that women with high self-esteem rate their marriages to cross-dressers as "happier" and tend to find benefits of being married to cross-dressers. Steiner (1985c), reporting on the research of Wise, Dupkin, and Meyer, said that wives of transvestites had experi-enced troubled childhoods with "poor parenting and with multiple losses, and resultant poor self-esteem. Consequently, and because their depend-ency needs were met being involved with a cross-dresser, they sacrificed their own sense of self-worth and desire to engage in mutually satisfying re-lationship by marrying a transvestite" (p. 358). Wise (1985) said, "transves-tites' mates often need a masochistic and dependent relationship for their emotional homeostasis . . . [and have] psychological conflicts that promote the desire to stay with such men" (p. 299). Wise recommended a careful evaluation of these wives for various psychiatric problems, including affec-tive disorders, borderline personality disorder, and "acute masochistic themes" (p. 297). In other words, these are deeply troubled women, perhaps harbor-ing severe psychopathologies, or maybe they are codependents, unable to leave their unsatisfying relationships because of their own emotional deficits. Indeed, the assumption is that these relationships are, by their very nature, unsatisfactory.

Other researchers have examined nonclinical samples of wives of transvestites and have not found the same problems with self-esteem (G. R. Brown, 1994; Doctor, 1988), although Brown and Collier (1989) commented on the level of "acceptable suffering" these wives endured and thought that the "partnerships were often maintained by intense denial and sacrifice of their personal sense of self in order to avoid even the possibility of separation and/or divorce" (p. 77). Familiarity with feminist literature might lead researchers to the conclusion that "sacrifice of personal self" is commonly correlated with being a "wife," with or without a cross-dressing husband.

All of the research to date has been conducted on small samples. Doctor's (1988) study included thrity-five wives or partners. Even the larger samples are still relatively small. For example, G. R. Brown's (1994) study included 106 women and Weinberg and Bullough's (1988) study included 70 women who may not be representative of the wives of cross-dressers. Brown and Collier (1989) found a significant percentage of "obesity" among this population, as did Wise, Dupkin, and Meyer (1981). G. R. Brown (1994) found that a high percentage of the wives had no children (44 percent) as did Talamini (1982) (41 percent) and Doctor (1988) (41 percent)—although the importance or meaning of this information is unclear.

The demographic information gathered about these wives raises interesting questions about what the researchers are seeking. In addition to questions about weight and parental status, G. R. Brown (1994) questioned their history of lesbian experiences, substance use, and sibling order in their families of origin. It is unclear what information these correlates yield. What does it mean if firstborn children are more likely to marry a cross-dresser? What are the inferences being made about wives of cross-dressers by noting that some of them are fatter than other women? Are researchers suggesting that these women chose to be child-free because of the cross-dressing? Brown explained the potential meaning of some of these correlations, e.g., higher levels of substance abuse might indicate lower self-esteem. He also said that firstborn children may be more "neurotic," and therefore seek out mates who are more tender or soothing, inferring (without any other information) that this might be the relational pattern between a cross-dresser and "his" spouse. He did not, however, explain the purpose of the question regarding previous lesbian experiences, but the underlying assumption of the question seems to be that females with a history of lesbian relationships might be more likely to be attracted to (or *attractive* to?) a cross-dressing male—an interesting, but unsubstantiated, speculation.

Given the small sample studied and the speculative quality of the correlations, it is unclear how to utilize the information yielded from these studies. Many alternative explanations for these demographics have not been explored by researchers that may have far more to do with sampling methodology than any pertinent details about the women. For instance, it is possible that women who are partnered with cross-dressers and who do not have children (or whose children are grown) are more likely to attend cross-dressing functions, seek therapy, respond to questionnaires, and participate in research than those who are busy parenting small children. It is also worth noting that this research has been conducted almost exclusively with white, middle-class women, with the bulk of the women gleaned from clinical samples or through their husband's involvement in cross-dressing clubs, limiting the potential universality of the information.

One area of research has focused on comparing the wives' levels of acceptance toward their cross-dressing spouses. Defining "acceptance" is complicated and it is easily assumed that wives who attend cross-dressing functions, or clubs, are more accepting than those who would refuse to attend. Certainly those who attend receive support from other wives, as well as much positive feedback from cross-dressing members whose wives are unwilling to attend (Talamini, 1982). G. R. Brown's research (1994), however, showed not "acceptance" but a high level of discomfort, confusion, and anger in many wives who nonetheless attended social activities with their cross-dressing spouses, particularly among newcomers.

Differences among those wives who are "high acceptors" and those who are "low acceptors" (G. R. Brown, 1994) or "rejectors" (Brown and Collier, 1989) have shown that finding out a husband is a cross-dresser after marriage or commitment was associated with significant difficulties accepting or even tolerating the cross-dressing (Brown and Collier, 1989; Weinberg and Bullough, 1988; Talamini, 1982). Weinberg and Bullough (1988) found the longer a woman had been married to a cross-dresser, the more negative her feelings were about her husband's cross-dressing—although this also correlates with women who found out later in the marriage about the cross-dressing. G. R. Brown (1994) said that these "issues of betrayal and lost trust . . . were major obstacles to intimacy" (p. 527). This research reinforces the need to assist cross-dressing or gender-dysphoric males to disclose earlier in their relationships and to develop strategies to assist families who are dealing with later disclosure and the betrayal and trust issues that inevitably follow. Weinberg and Bullough (1988) commented on how wives and husbands collaborate to manage the stigma of cross-dressing, and how their success in this endeavor may impact wives' acceptance and therefore satisfaction in the marriage. It is interesting to speculate how disclosure and "coming out"—as much of the lesbian and gay community has done in the past thirty years—would impact the satisfaction of these marriages.

Low acceptors also said that their husbands were self-centered and narcissistic, which they defined as their husbands' excessive self-admiration and purchasing clothing and accessories with little thought to the families' financial needs (Doctor, 1988). The narcissistic self-obsession can be recognized as part of the normative emergence process for a transgendered person who has repressed or hidden these issues for many years. Describing this as "normative," however, does not alleviate the impact of this behavior on spouses or families and the need to clinically address how to manage coming-out issues and maintaining responsibility to one's family. In one study, wives stated that they had little sexual arousal toward their partners' cross-dressing (Doctor, 1988), although in Weinberg and Bullough's (1988) research 43 percent of the women said they had had sex with their husbands while he was dressed, many stating that they had "tolerated" it. The impact on intimacy and sexuality of cross-dressing is an underaddressed issue in the literature. Clearly the sexuality issues that develop within a heterosexual marriage when a male partner identifies as a cross-dresser will need to be the focus of clinical attention.

It is important to note that, despite struggling with predictable issues, relationships between cross-dressing males and their female wives have shown relative stability, longevity, as well as happiness (G. R. Brown, 1994; Weinberg and Bullough, 1988; Doctor, 1988; Peo, 1988). Although a few wives considered divorce or separation (Brown and Collier, 1989; Wise, 1985), "One is struck by the tenacity and longevity of these unconventional relationships" (G. R. Brown, 1994, p. 528). Doctor (1988) said, "They seem to be an unremarkable group of women . . . unusual only in the sense that they unexpectedly found themselves in a marriage with a transvestite husband" (p. 193).

A discrete difference between cross-dressers and transsexuals is assumed by most researchers and only longitudinal studies would reveal whether the self-identity of the male cross-dresser, his gender dysphoria, and/or desire for medical treatments increased or changed over time, and how that impacted the stability of his marriage. Even fewer studies of the partners of male-to-female transsexuals have been conducted. One study (Gurvich, 1991) showed that when married wives discovered their husband's transsexualism, "their perceptions of their relationships changed drastically after disclosure." The women experienced a wide array of feelings including abandonment, rejection, shock, disbelief, anger, betrayal, depression, anxiety, confusion, low self-esteem, sexual difficulties, and numerous physical health problems. These findings are similar to what wives of cross-dressers have experienced, although perhaps these wives have even more intense reactions. When a husband reveals gender issues, the impact on intimate heterosexual partnerships and the reverberations throughout the entire family system are considerable.

Another study compared the welfare of transsexual patients who had partners with those who did not. Those with partners "received significantly more ratings by psychiatrists of being stable in their general social adjustment" (Huxley, Kenna, and Brandon, 1981a, p. 138). Huxley, Kenna, and Brandon (1981b) concluded that the reason these relationships work, however, is because the couples share a "delusion-like or overvalued idea" that the transsexual is of the other sex (p. 149), an idea that the researchers clearly do not share. Blanchard (1990) also noted that female partners of FTMs report that they perceive their mates as "a man without a penis" (p. 82), which could be viewed as representing a spouse's support of their partner, as well as their shared resonance regarding his "correct" gender identity and expression. It is, however, viewed as indicative of pathology—a shared "delusion." Researchers rigidly follow a medical model that links psychopathology and transsexualism. They can only explain marital commitment through this lens, despite the higher level of functioning of the transgendered partner who remains in a loving family.

Historically, gender specialists have viewed marriage as "a contraindication to cross-sex surgery" (Randell, 1971, p. 57). Certainly, there can be conflict for the transgendered person between the need to address gender dysphoria through transition and the desire to remain with a partner. Being married or in a committed relationship can impact the decision-making process for someone dealing with gender dysphoria. Marriage can even be a purging mechanism (Anderson, 1998)—choosing to marry or make a relationship commitment, either heterosexually or homosexually, can be a way to avoid dealing with one's transsexualism. Married or partnered transgendered people often delay addressing their gender issues or postpone dealing with reassignment because of concerns regarding rejection by spouses or fears of losing custody of their children (Lewins, 1995).

However, this conflict is also reinforced by gender programs and gender specialists who place transgendered people in an untenable dilemma: To live authentically *or* remain in a loving commitment partnership. This dilemma is not merely theoretical, but embedded in the guidelines of many treatment programs. The guidelines of one program stated, "Any patient who has been legally married must provide proof of divorce to protect the surgeon and the referring physicians from possible lawsuits from alienated spouses" (Clemmensen, 1990, p. 124). This rule effectively eliminates any legal complications for the clinics that might develop when two "same-sex" partners who want to remain together are still legally married.

Some gender specialists seem surprised that transgendered people would want to remain in their marriage. Steiner (1990) said, "One also encounters married men who believe that their wives would consent to live with them as lesbian lovers after sex reassignment . . . and who are unhappy when we inform them that we would not, in any case, approve surgery for a legally married man" (p. 102). The idea that a wife might also choose the option of living with her former husband "as" a lesbian lover, instead of losing the relationship completely, seems outside of the clinicians' imagination. Blanchard (1990) referred to this dilemma as "the frustrating conflict between his desire to live as a woman and his reluctance to *abandon* his wife, children, or career" (p. 58), without noting that the client's frustration is iatrogenically created within the existing programmatic guidelines. The choice of language also reinforces the either/or proposition that underlies this treatment philosophy. According to this model, choosing to transition not only means divorcing one's spouse, but "abandoning" him or her, severing contact with children, and even leaving one's professional livelihood. It is actually far more likely that the nontransitioning partner will abandon the transgendered spouse, that the courts will sever custody rights to the children, and that the employer will fire the worker, yet the choice of language used infers the responsibility for these losses rests with the transgendered person. The transphobia of these institutions means that families are not provided with resources or support to manage this existential life-cycle process.

In all fairness, this treatment philosophy is based on an older model that assumed that transsexuals would have the most successful transition if they left their marriages and started new lives. Although some transsexuals still choose to do this, it is less often the expectations of gender clinics. When transsexuals present with grief and sadness about leaving a partner, having already lost a spouse, or the fear of losing children in a custody battle, it has often been viewed as a sign that they are not ready to transition—i.e., not ready to "move on"—instead of a healthy, normal reaction to a major life change. Interestingly, the impact of this loss of family for the transsexual person is not factored into research studies of the "success" of SRS, except to note the "instability" of their relationships. Spouses and families have been viewed as appendages more easily removed than transsexuals' unwanted body parts.

Although transsexual men (FTMs) and their relationships have been studied less frequently, the literature has often noted the longevity and stability of relationships between FTMs and their female partners (Fleming, MacGowan, and Costos, 1985; Kockott and Fahrner, 1987; Lothstein, 1983; Pauly, 1974; Steiner and Bernstein, 1981; Steiner, 1985c) and that partner involvement implies positive outcome for transition (Blanchard and Steiner, 1983). However, the underlying tone of many researchers barely hides their judgment of both transmen and their partners, i.e., even their compliments are pathologizing. For instance, Pauly (1974) commented that the partners do not appear to be "grossly psychotic, particularly unusual, or inappropriate in any way, save [for their] capacity to understand and tolerate an extraordinary situation. Possibly this belies the underlying passivity, dependence, or homosexual propensity of the partners of female transsexuals" (p. 504). The last clause regarding the homosexuality of the partners of FTMs is indicative of how these partnerships are viewed by some clinicians as "really" homosexual, although it is often not how partners see themselves. Steiner and Bernstein (1981) were bewildered by the stable, long-term relationships between FTMs and their female partners. They speculated "on the reasons why a normal biological female would choice a 'penis-less man' as a partner" (p. 178).

Blanchard (1990) said, "The type of partner desired by these transsexual women *[sic]* is a feminine woman with no history of homosexual relationships" (p. 82). It is accurate that many transmen identify as heterosexual men involved with heterosexual women. However, it is also true that some FTMs once had strongly integrated lesbian identities before transition (Devor 1997a,b), and that their lesbian lovers are not only faced with the issues of their partners' transition, but needing to come to terms with their own sexual identities now that their partners identify and present in the world as a man. For many lesbians, being perceived as heterosexual, and being involved sexually with a man, is deeply troubling to their sense of identity. Califia (1997) referred to this as an "undocumented state of crisis" (p. 216). Clinicians have often assumed that female partners of transmen would welcome the transition and embrace being in an apparently heterosexual relationship. This shows an ignorance of lesbianism, both as a sexual identity and as a political community, as well as a heterosexist assumption by the researchers that a heterosexual life would naturally be desired.

Partners and spouses often feel emotionally abandoned while their loved ones sort out painful issues related to their gender identity. Faced with issues of betrayal, supporting partners who are often in great distress, fear of social ostracism, concerns for their children, and an unknown future, partners and spouses often wind up being neglected by their preoccupied partner and neglecting themselves. Focusing on the concerns of the spouse must become an important area of clinical concern for those interested in transgendered health care and marital and family therapy.

DEVELOPMENTAL STAGES FOR FAMILY MEMBERS

Loneliness, and the inability to find partners, is one of the best-kept secrets in the transcommunity. . . . Transbodies are the cracks in the gender sidewalk. When we find partners, they must be willing to negotiate the ambiguity of the terrain.

Riki Wilchins
Read My Lips, 1997

Just as transgendered and transsexual people move through a developmental process of emergence, of coming out and coming into their authentic selves, the family members of gender-variant people also experience developmental processes. Although there are many ways to label these stages, their course is fairly uniform. Kelley (1991) said that these stages are "as predictable as those steps described by Kübler-Ross in her work on death and dying" (p. 126). Rosenfeld and Emerson (1998) and Ellis and Eriksen (2001) utilized Kübler-Ross's stage model to show how families cope with a transgendered member. As most developmental theorists have noted, although developmental stage processes are expectable and predicable, they are rarely linear. They often resemble "a kaleidoscopic journey in which individuals react and respond independent of one another and in different stages, depending on the circumstances" (Cole et al., 2000, p. 185).

The family emergence model (see Box 8.1) depicts the developmental processes of the whole family system, and is viewed within a life-cycle framework, describing the impact spouses, parents, and children experience when a family member—husband, wife, partner, child, or parent—is facing their own transgender emergence. Family emergence involves a complex interaction of developmental and interpersonal transactions. It is an adaptive process, one that family members are often unwilling participants in, and in which they may feel somewhat like hostages on another person's journey. An important distinction exists between engaging in one's own transgender emergence because there is an inner pull to live more authentically and being "forced" to cope with another person's emergent transgender feelings. Family members often express resistance, avoidance, and denial about even beginning the process. It is important to remember, however, that not every family member will experience transgender emergence as a "crisis," and some partners, children, and parents appear to accept transition in stride.

The stage model may also reflect some of the processes that parents and family members experience upon the birth of an intersexed child or becoming lovers or partners with an intersexed adult, although further exploration is needed to determine the relevance or accuracy of this stage model for families of intersexed people.

BOX 8.1.
Family Emergence Stages

Stage One: Discovery and Disclosure
The first stage for most family members involves the discovery and/or disclosure of gender variance in a loved one. They are often shocked by this revelation and experience betrayal and confusion. Even when they are aware of the gender issue, the realization of its importance can be emotionally devastating.

Stage Two: Turmoil
The second stage for family members is often filled with chaos and turmoil. Family members may become withdrawn or emotionally volatile. It is usually a time of intense stress and conflict within families that are struggling to accept the reality of gender variance.

Stage Three: Negotiation
The third stage is a time of negotiation for family members. Spouses and partners realize that the gender issues will not vanish and must be adjusted to in some manner. Partners and families begin to engage in a process of compromise, determining what they are comfortable living with regarding transition issues and what limits the family can set on gender expression.

Stage Four: Finding Balance
Balance does not necessarily infer transition nor does it infer permanent resolution of the gender issues. It means that transgenderism is no longer a secret, that the family is no longer in turmoil and has negotiated the larger issues involving transgenderism. The family has learned that there is a difference between secrecy and privacy and is now ready to integrate the transgendered person—*as* a transgendered person—back into the normative life of the family.

Stage One: Discovery and Disclosure

She is sitting on the edge of the couch, staring silently at the floor. "I don't know what to talk to you about. I'm so embarrassed to be here. Do I seem like the kind of person who would be on the *Jerry Springer* show?" This woman had made a therapy appointment after coming home early from work and finding her husband dressed in women's clothing, wearing a wig, makeup, and high heels. After a thirty-five-year marriage, she had never had any idea about her husband's cross-dressing. She is feeling shocked, bewildered, and emotionally overwhelmed.

The first stage for family members involves the discovery and disclosure of gender variance. When a partner or spouse discloses his or her transgenderism, there is often a sense of shock and betrayal experienced by the partner. Sometimes the disclosure is not intentional—the transgendered person is discovered dressing up or reading material is found that exposes the gender issue.

What does it mean for a wife to discover that a husband has been secretly cross-dressing for twenty years? Wives often feel betrayed, wondering what other secrets their husbands have kept from them. Overcoming issues of betrayal is often the most challenging hurdle for couples to address. Sometimes the cross-dressing is discovered in such a way that it appears that the person has "accidentally" left cues around and purposely been caught. The spouse may feel manipulated by this "purposeful" disclosure, although it may not have been a conscious process on the part of the cross-dresser. Sometimes wives have discovered "feminine" accoutrements (e.g., lipstick or perfume) and assumed these belonged to other women—never suspecting that the "other women" were actually their husbands.

Doctor (1988) outlined four basic areas of concern for spouses, including security issues ("what will the neighbors think?"), marital tension caused by the cross-dressing, concerns regarding children, and effects on couples' sex lives. Brown (1998) outlined twenty concerns expressed by women in relationships with cross-dressing men. Interestingly, the first question (which does not appear to be analyzed in the data) is "Am I a lesbian?" Other questions included, "What's wrong with *me* that he would have these wishes to dress as a woman?"; "Will this behavior progress to sex-change surgery?"; and "What should we tell the children?" Weinberg and Bullough (1988) found that two-thirds of the wives in their sample expressed fear that others would find out and 36 percent were concerned about how the cross-dressing would impact the children. Wives in traditional heterosexual marriages often express feeling inadequate. They are rarely knowledgeable about transgenderism and are fearful that it means that their partner is homosexual and/or mentally ill (Weinberg and Bullough, 1988). They do not have basic skills or support to cope with this level of upheaval in their social, sexual, and/or familial lives. The need for education is paramount, as well as finding social venues to talk with others going through similar experiences. Wise (1985) identified different coping styles for wives of cross-dressers, including rage and rejection, dysthymia and passivity, extracting punishment, alcoholism, hopes of cure, and acceptance and enjoyment.

The issues outlined earlier are more common for families in which a male partner is transitioning to female. When a female partner is transitioning, issues of discovery are often less pronounced, since the masculinity of the female partner was usually not as hidden or disguised. The shock of the word "transgendered" or the impact of transitioning can be devastating, but commonly the partner—male or female—is often aware of gender-variant behavior, appearance, and expression in their lover's presentation, even though they may be unaware of how "serious" it is or where it may lead. Very little is known about the male partners of male-to-female transsexuals, and even less about the male partners of female-to-male transsexuals, areas in need of clinical and scholarly attention.

As described previously, the earlier in the relationship a partner is informed about gender issues the more likely it is that they will be successfully resolved (Weinberg and Bullough, 1991; Peo, 1991). Transgendered people commonly disclose their cross-gender feelings when they are dating, but they also minimize the importance of these feelings and assure their potential future mate that this will not be an issue in their relationship. Although the disclosure can take place early in the relationship, the significance and meaning of gender issues are often downplayed so that when the feelings take greater prominence years into the partnership, the information is met with anger and betrayal. Transgendered people are often unaware of the salience of these issues or how they can change and manifest over time. Therapists can unwittingly contribute to this by underestimating the importance of the cross-dressing or cross-gender feelings and assuring the couple that it will be not be an issue.

Issues involving the discovery and disclosure of gender variance in young children will be covered in Chapter 9, but parents often have to contend with the discovery and disclosure of adult children's gender variance.

Larry and Jean Ramsey had no idea that their son Ricky had gender issues. Ricky was a college professor, a mostly shy and reserved man, who lived 500 miles away. On a trip home for Easter, Ricky was arrested for shoplifting a pair of women's earrings. His parents were shocked. He surely had the money to buy them, and yet he denied being involved with a woman for whom he might have stolen them. Ricky's arrest in their small town caused a minor scandal. Feeling confused and angry, his parents confronted him. Ricky told them that he was struggling with gender issues, had often cross-dressed as a woman, and belonged to a cross-dressing club in his hometown. He told them he was struggling with whether he was going to transition.

Overwhelmed and frightened, Ricky's parents sought therapy. They had had no indications that Ricky had any gender issues before this incident and were concerned for his future. They were able to not only learn more about transgenderism during the clinical process, but were also able to reach out more to Ricky—who had always been somewhat distant and isolated—and begin a more intimate and authentic relationship with him while he continued to examine his gender issues. In some ways Ricky's choice to shoplift in his hometown was a successful, though unconscious, plea for his parents' attention. All too often parents will not seek out professional help, and few places offer self-help groups for family members. Lesser (1999) documented the importance of a nonjudgmental empathic stance to assist aging parents in feeling validated by the therapist in their grieving process.

Timing of disclosure is rarely done consciously and directly, although a planned telling can enhance a successful reception. Disclosure should take place at a pace that is comfortable for the family member, and should be determined by the ability of the recipient to receive the information. This is often hard for people who have suppressed their gender concerns for many years, resulting in a self-disclosure that is often spontaneous and even explosive. Box 8.2 outlines some general guidelines for gender-variant people when disclosing to loved ones.

Stage Two: Turmoil

When Gina's husband said he needed to talk with her about something, she was completely surprised when he handed her a picture of himself dressed as a woman. It took her a minute to figure out what the picture was, or who it was, and her first reaction was to laugh. She thought Tom looked so funny, and was frightened and baffled by how dead serious he appeared. Tom stumbled over his words, trying to tell her that this was very important to him, that he was showing her a part of him he had kept hidden for a long time. Gina was shocked and appalled, even disgusted. She began crying, screaming, throwing things. It felt as if her life was falling apart around her.

After the disclosure has taken place, the family member will experience the second stage of family emergence, referred to here as *turmoil*. When the parent, child, spouse, or partner first learns that the loved one is experiencing gender-conflicting emotions, the initial response can resemble a post-traumatic stress reaction (Cole, 2000). This reaction is similar to the emergency stage experienced by people recognizing histories of sexual abuse, as described by Bass and Davis (1988), and mirrors the awareness stage that transgendered people often experience, as described in Chapter 7.

Spouses are often concerned about others' reactions (Weinberg and Bullough, 1991; Doctor, 1988). There is a sense of isolation as family members struggle with who to trust, coupled with an equally frightening fear of exposure that others will find out. In addition to their own shock of discovery, they soon realize that their loved one will be stigmatized and that being the family member of a gender-variant person will stigmatize them also. Roberts (1995) discussed the sense of "guilt by association" that family members experience, as if their gender and sexual selves are now in question because of their loved one's disclosure. There is nothing more important than supporting the partner in a full range of emotions. Miller (1996) suggested that one should be suspicious of a wife who appears totally delighted and

---

BOX 8.2.
Guidelines for Self-Disclosure

- Prepare carefully what you will say and practice with a friend, therapist, or in the mirror.
- Do not overwhelm loved ones with too much information.
- Do not show up cross-dressed, show pictures of yourself dressed, or show photos of successful surgical options when you are first disclosing.
- Be present for the other person and his or her issues. This is not about you; it is about supporting him or her.
- Prepare for others to be negative and ask foolish, judgmental, or even cruel questions.
- Keep reminding them who you have always been to them and that who you are has not changed with this disclosure.
- Do not act defensive or present yourself as mentally ill.
- Do not pretend to have answers that you do not yet have.
- Expect people to be inconsistent and labile in their emotional reactions.
- Develop a support network that will assist you through this process (therapist, peer group, electronic mailing list, etc.).
- Remember that it took you a long time to address your own gender issues. Do not expect your lover, spouse, partner, children, or parents to simply accept it all in one short talk. Coming to terms with transgenderism will take time.

---

supportive, and indeed many spouses become frozen and unable to let themselves feel as scared, angry, and confused as they really are. When a loved one discloses something that he or she has kept hidden, it often evokes questions about betrayal and trust. Has anything else been kept hidden? What else haven't you told me? This can provoke episodes of searching through papers, checking credit card receipts, and other expressions of distrust and jealousy on the part of family members. It is not unusual for loved ones to become withdrawn and cold, refusing to discuss the gender issues and, in some cases, pretending that nothing has been revealed, as if ignoring it will make it go away. On the other hand, some partners of both FTMs and MTFs tend to put their spouses' needs ahead of their own. Sometimes they are not even aware that they have needs. Cole (1998) suggested that partners should be encouraged to "strengthen recognition of their own sexuality, relationship needs, and personal health responsibilities" (p. 386).

Due to the confusion most people have about the relationship between sexual and gender identity, questions about sexual orientation and desire often surface for the gender-variant person as well as their family members.

Sometimes spouses will assume that the person is telling them he or she is gay or they will question their own sexual orientation and sexuality. Emotions run high during this stage. There is often an increase in familial tension, and words that are said in anger are not easily revoked. Threats to dissolve the marriage and sever parental rights are not uncommon. Partners can retreat to separate bedrooms, coerce their lovers to agree to not cross-dress, insist they stop attending support groups or seeing a therapist, threaten to "out" them, or refuse to allow them to tell significant others. In extreme cases, family members can become physically abusive (Blanchard et al., 1989; Courvant and Cooke-Daniels, 1998; Lev and Lev, 1999) and decide that the transgendered person is mentally ill and insist that the person find a therapist who will diagnose and prescribe medications for his or her psychopathology. Child custody and visitation issues can often become the proverbial carrot held out before the transgendered person who refuses this "treatment plan."

This is often a time of high stress filled with marital and familial conflict. Other unresolved issues in the family often begin to surface, including financial problems, health issues, past extramarital affairs, in-law problems, career conflicts, and parenting disagreements. Family members sometimes pick "sides," and subsystems form creating or reinforcing triangulated dynamics (McGoldrick, Gerson, and Shellenberger, 1999). Sometimes the turmoil stage is delayed, with family members appearing supportive, open, and even inviting of the transition. However, as the reality of body and lifestyle changes begin to become obvious, a sudden emotional explosion can result and previously undiscussed issues can surface.

The turmoil stage is possibly the most difficult stage to manage, and many people experience depression and anxiety at this point. People feel desperate and lonely while they struggle with fears of their own future, as well as their loved one's. It is during this time that families are most likely to reach out for therapeutic assistance. The presence of intense hopelessness and rage on the part of family members often leads therapists to prematurely decide that the family situation is irresolvable and to recommend separation, divorce, and restricted custody situations.

Stage Three: Negotiation

Melody knew about Larry's cross-dressing but had been assured that it was in the past when she agreed to marry him. After they were together for ten years, Larry tearfully revealed that he couldn't stop cross-dressing and that he thought he was a transsexual. Initially devastated, Melody decided that she wanted to make their marriage work and they began to negotiate and find compromises to accommodate both Larry's and Melody's needs. Some things were easy: They agreed on weekly "outings," as long as she did not see him dressed. They agreed that he would not keep his female clothing in the house. They agreed not to bring any cross-dressing into the bedroom and on how much money Larry could spend on clothing. They agreed Larry would not take hormones but that he could take herbal estrogen supplements. Their struggles involved issues of minor body modifications such as Larry shaving his legs or chest hair or wearing small stud earrings. The conflict focused on a minute level of detail regarding what Larry could wear which culminated in a screaming fight regarding the height of a pair of high heels (were they one and one-quarter inches, which was deemed acceptable, or one and one-half inches, which was not?).

As the crisis of gender disclosure and discovery, and the ensuing turmoil, begins to ease, the family enters a stage of negotiation. This stage is noted by the realization that the gender issue will not simply "go away" and will have to be adjusted to in some manner. In Weinberg and Bullough's (1988) research 48 percent of wives said that they "put limits" on their husband's cross-dressing, although they also expressed that they did not always successfully adhere to the guidelines. Depending on the family involved and the issues they are coping with, families will address this stage in myriad ways.

For spouses, the negotiation process often involves questions of whether they can "handle" their spouse having a sex change, and what level of change they feel they can live with. One study showed that few differences existed between transsexuals who completed sex reassignment surgery and those who chose not to go through with the surgery, except that those who did not go "all the way" were more often heterosexually married for a longer duration and had children (Kockott and Fahrner, 1987). These findings are supported by other studies (Blanchard, 1990; Walinder, Lundström, and Thuwe, 1978) and reveal that long-term commitment, marriage, and parenting responsibilities might serve as a boundary marker for some transsexuals. Having a spouse say, "I can go this far and no farther," might create a roadblock, whereas the person may agree to live within those boundaries. On the other hand it might make it blatantly clear for some people that they need to transition, even if it means losing their family.

Within certain segments of the transgender community, it has sometimes been viewed negatively for people to limit a transition process for the sake of maintaining their family. This is similar to the dilemma that many married gay people face when coming out, and has often been placed within an either/or paradigm, e.g., if you are gay and must leave a heterosexual marriage (Buxton, 1994; Dupwe, 2001). However, intimate relationships are far more complex than either/or paradigms, and many successful marriages exist between gay and heterosexual partners. Transgendered people and their spouses can make compromises that will enable both partners to remain in their marriages and this can be a healthy decision for some people. The process of weighing both persons' needs evokes what Osborne (2003) referred to as "relational ethics." She gives examples of the kinds of questions with which the transgendered person must grapple. "How do I balance my need for genuine self-expression against the fair consideration owed to loved ones sharing my life?" "To what extent have I been openly accountable to others for the loss of trust created by my failure to disclose the full extent of my lifelong gender conflict?" "If I do move forward with gender transition, what changes are necessary for me to fulfill my ongoing commitment to children and others who have relied on me?" Of course, spouses also need to engage in similar ethical questions as they contemplate whether they can remain in the relationship.

Part of Stages Four and Five of the emergence process is the soul-searching transgendered and transsexual people need to do in order to discover what physical or social modifications they desire so they can live at peace within their bodies. There are no right or wrong decisions. Each person must come to a place of comfort with their embodiment. However, for transgendered and transsexual people in long-term intimate relationships, this process is not simply an individual soul-searching process, but one that impacts both partners.

Some of the issues that often need to be negotiated in relationships include: Frequency of cross-dressing or "outings," how to leave or enter the home when dressed, public appearance, disclosure to significant others, how much money can be spent on clothing or medical treatments, revealing the gender issues to the children, and sexual accommodation including cross-dressing or cross-gender play in the bedroom. The scenario at the beginning of this section describes both the ease of certain compromises and the incredible difficulty of others. Melody and Larry's family anxiety became focused on what might be perceived as minutiae. The intense focus on detail becomes an attempt to control what is essentially uncontrollable—the loved one's transsexualism. Cole (1998) said that when the wife remains in the marriage, "She will usually assume the largest, most comprehensive responsibility from managing the 'secret' (his, hers, and theirs)" (p. 374).

For one client, the setting of limits was determined by noticing when certain issues made her feel "icky" inside. Icky became her barometer for her "bottom lines." Sometimes partners respond to limit setting by becoming anxious or feeling a compulsion to push against the boundary even in ways that might be dangerous to the well-being of their career or relationship. Negotiation is an ongoing process. Issues are often renegotiated again and again until the couple finds a comfortable place for themselves. Spouses and children may find that they have accepted more than they ever thought possible and transgendered people may find they are comfortable living in an "in-between" place. It is also true that sometimes the transgendered partner will not be satisfied "compromising" or willing to move slowly enough through the changes to accommodate the partner.

Wives often complain that there is a loss of intimacy because the "hobby" takes up all their husbands' time. Sometimes they feel resentful and competitive toward husbands who may dress more fashionably than they do, particularly if they have not bought new clothes for themselves in order to buy things for their children. In some families there has been a competitive edge between the partners in "feminizing." This can be especially challenging for female spouses who are not particularly interested in feminine accoutrements and whose husbands appear more feminine than they do.

Female partners of FTMs also struggle with negotiation issues. Female-to-male transgendered people are often less closeted than their male-to-female counterparts and have always presented in a masculine manner. Therefore, questions regarding secrecy or "discovering" cross-dressing are rarely present. However, the revelation that a lover is considering transition can be a shock to partners, evoking all of the issues raised earlier. Many couples who have lived as lesbians struggle with the impact that masculinizing will have on both their relationship and their social lives. Although women partners of FTMs are often attracted to their partner's masculinity, they are often resistant to imagining "living with a man." This is especially pronounced in some lesbian communities in which masculinity and maleness have been frowned on. Male partners also struggle with issues about having a wife transition and suddenly being viewed as a gay man. Sometimes health concerns arise regarding use of testosterone, decisions regarding chest surgery, and who will administer the hormone injections. Negotiations may also involve the use of male versus female pronouns, to whom to disclose, and attendance at lesbian and feminist gatherings.

The process of setting limits is fundamental to transitioning or even accepting transgenderism within families (Weinberg and Bullough, 1991). Some transgendered people believe that partners should be completely supportive or else the relationship is not worth keeping. However, partners need time to adjust to the idea of having a transgendered wife, husband, lover, or partner. They also need time to discover what they can comfortably live with. Each member of the partnership needs to examine what their "bottom lines" are, what they can and cannot compromise about, and what is and is not negotiable. Of course, not every couple is able to able to survive transition intact. An MTF might be able to restrict "his" cross-dressing for a period of time, but if his intention were to live full-time as a woman, eventually *she* would need the freedom to dress as she desired.

Janet came into therapy to discuss whether she wanted to leave her partner of seven years. Her partner, Eagle, had been dealing with issues of gender dysphoria for most of their relationship, but when he decided to begin testosterone and asked Janet to refer to him with male pronouns, she became increasingly depressed. As Eagle's body began to masculinize, Janet became further withdrawn, sullen, and weepy. Eagle was feeling good about his changes but extremely sad about how Janet was dealing with it. Janet felt clear that she didn't want to be involved with a man, and as much as she loved Eagle and felt as if they would always be "family," she began to recognize that the more she tried to accept his changes, the less whole she felt inside. She truly believed it was the right thing for Eagle, but she also knew that it wasn't right for her. Through a difficult process she came to accept that this was a journey she couldn't take with him. Deeply sad but at peace, she ended their partnership.

Stage Four: Finding Balance

A lesbian couple, Sari and Lyn, who had been lovers for a decade sought counseling because Lyn disclosed that she had always felt like a man, and that she felt ready to begin to live as one. Sari was devastated, caught between loving her partner and not wanting to be lovers with "a man." Each step toward transition that Lyn took was processed carefully with Sari, who was given space to grieve her partner's changes and accommodate to them. Sari openly rebeled against certain body modifications. Lyn was patient but insistent that she wanted to transition. Over a period of two years, Sari and Lyn moved through intense emotional periods adjusting to Lyn's bodily changes and the reality that they were now being perceived as a "heterosexual couple." They were saddened by the loss of some lesbian friends, but shared this grief together. They also recognized that many of their friends had come through the transition with them. Sari eventually came to see the positive effects of transitioning on Lyn and slowly began to feel more comfortable being lovers with a transman. They eventually came to a comfortable accommodation in their new lives.

Despite the negative pronouncements in the literature and the reality that not all couples survive transition, many families are able to negotiate transition issues successfully. For some people, balance might mean living with private cross-dressing. For instance, in Weinberg and Bullough's (1988) study, 81 percent of cross-dressing spouses dressed in front of their wives. In Brown's (1998) research, 94 percent of wives had seen their partners cross-dressed. For other families it might mean coping with a spouse who is transitioning. For many families it might mean living with the uncertainty of not knowing the trajectory of the gender variance and living with the "unknown." However, depending on the needs of transgendered persons, and their willingness to compromise and experiment for their spouses, couples can find a healthy balance in their lives. Families who are able to move through their fear, shame, and ignorance regarding gender variance are often able to find contentment and satisfaction in their daily lives.

Balance does not necessarily infer transition, nor does it infer permanent resolution of the gender issues. It means that transgenderism is no longer a secret, that the family is no longer in turmoil and has negotiated the larger issues involving transgenderism. The family has learned that there is a difference between secrecy and privacy. They will negotiate their own unique balance of revealing information if privacy is a concern, but they are not sworn to a painful secrecy. Balance means the family is now ready to integrate the transgendered person—*as* a transgendered person—back into the normative life of the family. Healing a relationship following the disclosure of gender variance requires, in the words of Wheeler and Schaefer (2000), "mutual education of the nature of transgenderism, the recognition that *both* members of the couple experience pain and unhappiness and disillusionment if the relationship disintegrates and discontinues and, very importantly that *both* members must share in the sacrifices required to achieve measures of equality."

It is important to remember that posttransition issues regarding transgenderism can arise even years after the actual transition. This may include a "postpartum/posttransition" type of depression for the transgendered person, or a post-traumatic stress reaction following the surgery on the part of a spouse. Friends and extended family members may become distressed by the apparent changes in lifestyles and identity that develop when a partner changes gender. "Are you a lesbian now?" a client's mother asked her when her husband transitioned. Sometimes it is not easy to answer questions like this, for negotiating questions of identity and sexuality are part of the emotionality of family emergence. Educating family members, schools, places of employment, and even new friends may be part of the ongoing work following a transition. Rosenfeld and Emerson (1998) suggested creating a ceremony to honor and ritualize the transition process, making it into a celebratory event.

Issues regarding gender will probably always be present. Most people who have lived closely with transgenderism know that it changes the way they see gender in all aspects of their lives. However, once the stage of balance has been achieved (and it is an achievement), the daily lives of family members will not revolve around cross-dressing, surgical decisions, and issues of disclosure. They will revolve around the family vacations, favorite TV shows, work-related successes, children's maturation, birthday celebrations, and all the other normative life-cycle events of families.

FAMILIES COPING WITH TRANSGENDERISM

[T]he types of relationships that gender dysphoric patients form are as varied as the colors on an artist's palette.

Betty Steiner
Gender Dysphoria, 1985

Numerous issues surface when partners, children, and parents are coping with gender variance and/or gender dysphoria in a loved one. Two issues will be outlined in this section that are often salient for families. The first issue is transgenderism as the "family secret" and the emotional cost of coming out. The second is the issue of sexual identity for partners and spouses.

Transgenderism As the "Family Secret"

Family therapists often talk about "family secrets." Students of systems therapy are taught to ask, "Does this family have a secret? What is this family hiding?" Families keep secrets as an act of self-preservation, a way to manage their pain (Imber-Black, 1998; Lerner, 1994). Some families maintain secrets about racial history, hiding any references to Black or Jewish family members (Ball, 1999; McBride, 1997; Pinderhughes, 1998). Sisters do not share the sexual abuse they both experienced from a parent or sibling, believing they are protecting each other and preserving the family (Forward and Buck, 1988; Wiehe, 1997). Often, issues of money—hoarding it, stealing it, banking it, spending it—are secrets kept from certain members of the family, exposed only when there is a death and a dispute over a will (Imber-Black, 1998). Certainly issues of mental illness become family secrets, and relatives get "put away" or disappear, becoming ghostlike figures within the family (Holley, 1997; Marsh, 1998).

The literature is replete with examples of how families sacrifice one member to maintain homeostasis (Boszormenyi-Nagy and Ulrich, 1981; Haley, 1963; Haley, 1979; Jackson, 1965; Minuchin and Fishman, 1981; Satir, 1967). Although the false balance they achieve is at the expense of wholeness and authenticity, it gives an illusion of functionality. The shame is kept underground where it permeates the entire system. Much like toxic waste in the groundwater, it is all too easy to ignore if it remains hidden. Alcoholism and substance abuse are often family secrets—hidden behind a veil of "social drinking," families conceal and protect their alcoholic relatives (Bepko and Krestan, 1985; Elkin, 1990). Weinberg and Bullough (1988) compared alcoholic and cross-dressing families and explored the similarities of how wives "collaborate" with concealing stigmatized information.

In the past few decades the issue of gay and lesbian identities has become another exposed secret (Eichberg, 1991; Isay, 1997a; Signorile, 1996). Although family members rarely react with the animosity that LGB people expect and are prepared for—often because they suspect anyway—occasionally people are ostracized, excommunicated, or treated with coldness after initially coming out. The parallels for transgendered people "coming out" are analogous and the impact on families is very similar. As Buxton (1994) said, "The liberation cry of gay, lesbian, and bisexual marriage partners became a sword that sundered the world of their spouses and children" (p. xviii).

Some transgendered people (like many LGB people) have never come out to anyone. It is unknown how many people harbor unresolved feelings and thoughts about their gender but remain completely reticent about these feelings, perhaps never acting on it, even in secret. Others might cross-dress, publicly or privately, and even have an active support system within the transgender community, and keep this information hidden from their significant other. In other cases, only the significant other knows and the secret is kept hidden from the rest of the world. The advent of the computer age and online communication has created a vast support network for people who might otherwise be isolated. Many people are only "out" online, or have opposite sex personas online, that have no other real-life existence.

The following are clinical vignettes of transgendered and transsexual individuals and their family members who presented in therapy to deal with their "family secret." In this section, people will be referred to in the sex/gender in which they presented at the time of the clinical encounter.

The Confessional—Teresa

Sometimes transgendered clients use therapy as a kind of priestly confessional. Unable or unwilling to come out, it is important that "someone" knows who they are, and the confidentiality of the therapeutic process creates an environment for safe disclosure without necessarily following through with any other life changes.

Teresa came to therapy wearing a man's shirt and a pair of slacks. Her face was stern, and she never made eye contact. She was an educated person who was married to a minister and had four children. She was also the daughter of a minister. She articulated clearly, without any obvious evidence of doubt or fear, that she was a transsexual. She said, "I have read all about it. I have known since I was a young child." She also stated that she would never leave her husband, her family, or her church. She said, "I just needed someone to know so I don't feel so alone." Teresa never made another appointment.

Perhaps Teresa will decide at some point in her life that she wants to pursue her gender issues, and perhaps she will decide to live her life as she always has. Teresa utilized therapy in the best way she saw fit, and if her confessional eased the dysphoria in her life, then it was a useful intervention.

The Double Life—Jonathon/Jill and Lucy

Male-to-female transsexuals often maintain a double existence, allowing their female personas a small range of freedom, but maintaining a traditional male existence, one that their families never know about.

Jonathon, a white male in his early fifties, came to therapy dressed in a traditional blue-collar manner. He wore mechanics' overalls and his hands were stained with grease. He had been married for more than twenty years to his high school sweetheart, and is very committed to his family, including an aging mother and five children. Jonathon has a typical transgendered trajectory. He first began cross-dressing when he was about five and continued to cross-dress into his adolescence, hiding clothes in the barn. Despite Jonathon's overt male physique, his female persona, Jill, is a stunning woman with long hair, immaculate nails, and a stylish and sexy dress. Jill is articulate where Jonathon is somewhat monosyllabic. Jill is poised and genteel, where Jonathon is somewhat gruff. He dresses as Jill in public as often as he can and is active in the transgender community, including attending conferences and some political activity within the LGBT community. He is motivated to transition and live full-time as a woman. He feels alien within his body and limited by his male gender role. Jonathon has been sneaking money for therapy and electrolysis for many years. Despite the nearly thirty years of cross-dressing, Jonathon and his wife, Lucy, have never discussed his cross-dressing. Jonathon does not believe that Lucy will ever accept Jill, and so he has chosen to remain with his wife and be an active "father" to his children. He is, however, a very believable male, and most people would be shocked to discover Jonathon's "secret" life.

Jill has lived "with" Jonathon his entire life, and is a strong, fully formed personality. Jonathon has also, however, internalized a sense of male responsibility. He will not hurt his wife and children by disclosing and making their lives more difficult. He has, however, paid off their house and saved a substantial amount of money for the children's college, as well as for Lucy's future, should she find out and decide to leave him. Rarely do people "care for" their families with Jonathon's diligence. When Jonathon first came to therapy, he had never cross-dressed outside of his home. Therapy became one of the first places Jill was able to be herself. Although Jonathon has been able to articulate some of Jill's plans and make arrangements for her future, he has been unable to find a way to communicate with Lucy. This is the only secret he has from Lucy and he claims they are extremely close and intimate except on this issue. Is it possible that Lucy really does not know? If they are as intimate as Jonathon says, would she actually leave him? How long can this double life continue? On one hand, it is hard to imagine this twenty-year marriage ending over this disclosure (it has survived large traumas and betrayals in the past). On the other hand, perhaps it will serve as a final straw for Lucy.

Jonathon, who is otherwise a very rational person, seems to be able to split his two lives with minimal dissonance. Although it is far from an ideal situation, he remains at a standstill. The thought of Lucy's potential rejection pains him, but he believes it is best to wait to disclose until the kids are grown so it will not interfere with their adolescent development. Jonathon has "researched" this question thoroughly within his transgender support group. He found that many wives who have remained with their cross-dressing husbands said that they would have left if they had found out when the children were still young, and this information has determined his position. Although he plans for a future in which Jill can live more freely, he is not sure when, if ever, this can happen. His preference, which he does not think is possible, is to live with Lucy as Jill. Jonathon is preparing to begin a more honest discussion with Lucy when the children are safely in college. He has been able to initiate some discussions with his wife and children about gay rights while watching television to begin to develop a sense of their reactions to alternative lifestyle issues.

Jonathon's willingness to live a double life in a long-term relationship is unusual. At the level of self-acceptance that Jonathon embodies, most clients are exploring options for transition. Advocating for honest communication is a comfortable position for a therapist, but in this case, Jonathon's caution might be more informed than common therapeutic wisdom.

The Exposure—Michael

Commonly, clients come into therapy when their cross-dressing impulses increase and they are on the verge of disclosing or have recently disclosed for the first time. Occasionally, they come into therapy following an unplanned exposure.

Michael presented in therapy in an extremely anxious state. His wife, Carla, had just discovered his cross-dressing and was threatening to end the marriage. She was outraged and disgusted and did not hesitate to express this to him. Michael had continued secretly cross-dressing, wearing his wife's and stepdaughter's clothing. He had never bought his own clothing or gone out dressed. Michael identified as a "cross-dresser" and assured me that he had researched transsexualism quite thoroughly and was not "one of them." He had been cross-

dressing with his sister's clothing since a very young age, and had also been interested in submissive sexual behavior since he was a teenager. Michael had
shared his cross-dressing fantasies with his wife before they had married; however, she was extremely judgmental and "forbade" these activities. After his
wife's discovery, Michael's cross-dressing behavior accelerated. He began to
buy his own clothes for the first time and hide them around the house, which of
course, his wife kept finding. He went out dressed for the first time, going to
neighborhoods and stores where he was well known and defying people to recognize him. Michael was cross-dressed one day when his stepdaughter came
home from school with friends. Carla asked him to move out and Michael began
to sleep in his office at the university where he was employed. Here too he cross-
dressed in the evening, until he was caught and subsequently laid off from his
job.

Within a few months of Carla's discovery, Michael had lost his wife, his
family, and his job. When he first came into therapy he was distraught, angry, and cross-dressing daily, placing himself in increasingly dangerous situations. Complicating his situation was his self-diagnosis, which involved a
rather complex medical analysis of the biochemical and neurological etiology of transsexualism. Michael had internalized his transgendered behavior
as "diseased," which he justified with quasimedical research.

Michael's cross-dressing behavior seemed linked to his sexual desires.
He said that he would often dress up and fantasize about getting caught and
being punished for his behavior. The DSM identifies "erotic transvestism"
as a paraphilia and also recognizes "forced cross-dressing" as one of the diagnostic indicators of "sexual masochism," another paraphilia. The pornographic literature is also replete with images of forced cross-dressing.
Carla's refusal to "allow" him to cross-dress, plus her berating him when
she found out, aroused Michael. In many ways, Carla's judgment served as
the foil to both limit the behavior and eroticize it further. He had found a
sexual partner who would enhance this double bind. Sadly, Michael's
eroticized humiliation was not confined to his sexual experience (i.e., within
the context of a consensual and loving sexual exchange with someone who
actually respected him) but was being played out in a real-life context.
Healthier avenues for sexual exploration were not available within his marriage.

It is not entirely clear why it took a decade for this situation to become a
crisis. Perhaps unresolved issues from Michael's own adolescence surfaced
when his step-daughter came into puberty. Many transgendered people find
that remaining closeted becomes increasingly uncomfortable in their forties. This might be related to the external shift in social mores and the
growth of the transgendered liberation movement as more viable options are
made visible, or it also might be a kind of mid-life crisis. Michael slowly be-

gan to admit that he was probably transsexual. The realization of his transsexualism had increased his anxiety, as well as his cross-dressing, and had triggered his "compulsive" behavior. Michael's presenting symptoms are common among transgendered people who are beginning to explore their gender issues. The intense anxiety, compulsive, and even dangerous behaviors, was an extreme, but typical response to accepting what initially felt unacceptable.

This case was complicated by the involvement of a cadre of professionals who were not well-educated about gender dysphoria. Michael was involved with a psychiatrist, two other therapists who were seeing his wife and step-daughter, attorneys, and a priest. Each of these professionals gave this family different advice and guided them in different directions. Michael agreed to a psychiatric hospitalization, which his wife insisted upon if he wanted to continue seeing his step-daughter. He was released with a diagnosis of obsessive-compulsive disorder and bipolar disorder. He was allowed supervised visitation with his step-daughter, if he remained on medication, since his behavior was perceived as dangerous to her. Michael's symptoms, although serious and troublesome, did not fit the DSM's criteria for either obsessive-compulsive disorder or bipolar disorder, but he was resigned to remaining on medication to appease his now ex-wife and remain in contact with his step-daughter. Michael's step-daughter was encouraged by the professionals treating the family to see him as a person with a mental illness, which was supported by the judicial decisions made about custody and visitation. The professionals who worked with Michael and his family persisted in seeing Michael's gender issues as a manifestation of his mental illness, instead of seeing his symptomatology as sequelae to the gender issues.

One can only speculate on how different Michael's life would be today if the professionals who worked with this case had normalized Michael's cross-dressing behavior. It was his good fortune that his sexual fantasies were never used as evidence for his mental illness within the judicial setting, although his wife often threatened to do so. How could Michael's descent into labile mood swings and emotional terror have been alleviated? Why did professionals never question his wife's harsh and judgmental behavior? Carla was allowed to humiliate, dominate, and denigrate Michael. She disempowered and dishonored him in front of his step-daughter. Clearly Carla needed support to negotiate Michael's breakdown, and most likely she could never have learned to live with his transgender emergence. However, at the time in his life when Michael most needed the support of his family, he was left alone to choose between his own needs and his family's, and ultimately he became the sacrificial lamb. Michael was left a broken "man," depressed, overmedicated, and impoverished, having lost his family and all that was dear to him. Despite being "outed" to his entire family and community, he had still not really begun to examine his own gender dysphoria.

The Disclosure—Alan/Alice and Sybil

The process of coming to accept a transsexual partner takes time, and both the partner exhibiting the gender dysphoria and the spouse need time to cope emotionally with all the changes.

Alan had been cross-dressing since he was a young child. He had told his wife about his cross-dressing, which had been a stable and consistent part of his life before they married, and had assured her that he had no interest in transitioning. Alan's desire to cross-dress had recently increased dramatically. He found himself wanting to do it four to five times a week, and longed for female clothing in the stores. He cried, expressing his desire to be "seen" as a woman. He knew that no matter how much his women friends appreciated his sensitivity and compassion, they still saw him as a man. He realized that he had been harboring fantasies of living full-time as a woman for many years. Alan surfed Internet chat rooms for transsexual sites, retreated from sexual relationships with his wife, and binged on food. He vacillated back and forth about whether this was, "OK, normal, just a feeling," or "really sick, weird, I can't believe I'm saying these things." Alan said that his marriage was wonderful, and that he and his wife were discussing having children. Alan wanted children but thought his wife would be opposed to his continuing to cross-dress with children in the house. He was terrified to share his feelings about transitioning with his wife. When Alan confessed to Sybil the increase in his gender-dysphoric feelings, she was shocked. She felt betrayed and accused Alan of having lied to her about his true intentions. Alan also felt that he had betrayed Sybil's trust.

Alan spent nearly two years in therapy exploring his thoughts, feelings, and behaviors about cross-dressing and gender dysphoria. He slowly came to understand that he had not lied to Sybil, but that something had truly changed or come into clearer consciousness within him. What had felt like "manageable" cross-dressing before had become an "unmanageable" desire for gender reassignment, and this was now affecting his marriage and his wife. Alan utilized therapy as a place to begin to explore his gender feelings. As with most transgendered people, talking about these feelings helped to decrease his isolation and feelings of disgust. The therapeutic environment became a safe place to investigate, explore, and examine his feelings with no pressure to make any decisions about them. He was encouraged to move slow and learn to trust the different moods and emotions that he experienced. Alan talked about how being raised in a dysfunctional family and working as a trial attorney had taught him to make emotionally charged, "correct" decisions quickly under pressure. The kind of struggles he was now facing demanded a different kind of skill and intellect. Alan took the time to sort through his many feelings, to not just make decisions in his head, but to utilize his heart also. Therapy gave Alan the space to fully examine his life as a series of possibilities, to really allow himself to think about his options.

The anxiety-driven, negative behaviors—surfing the Net, bingeing on food—were reframed as stress reactions, and not necessarily indicative of the "hidden truth" about who he was. Alan began to see that he was pushing Sybil away before she could push him away. As Alan explored his options in a safe environment, his anxiety began to subside. Alan began to allow Alice, his female persona, more freedom. Alan told good friends about Alice and she began to take more "outings." Sybil spent many months being extremely angry with Alan and refusing to have anything to do with Alice. Eventually though, they began to talk more and Sybil came to understand that Alan had not purposely deceived her. She began the long process of deciding whether she could support Alan in transitioning.

Sybil began to examine what it meant being married to a transsexual, how they could continue their marriage, and whether she was comfortable having children with Alan. Sybil became more comfortable with Alice and came to a resolution regarding being married to a transsexual. Gradually, Alice "replaced" Alan, as dress and hairstyles slowly changed into more feminine ones. Alice eventually had to come out professionally and publicly, and Sybil also had to cope with the professional fallout in her own work environment, which she was able to do with dignity. They made a decision to begin a family—which meant that Alice did not begin female hormones, although she was living full-time as a woman—and their family began to emerge in this new configuration. Sybil became so comfortable with Alice that she eventually stated, "I don't even remember her as a man. This is exactly how we were supposed to be."

The Announcement—Lois/Lou

Clients are also afraid to disclose to their families of origin. Disclosure of transgenderism can result in excommunication and ostracism from family, which can be especially traumatic if a person is close to his or her family, but can also be difficult to manage if someone is estranged from family.

Lois presented as a withdrawn and intelligent person who described a quiet, lonely life with few friends and few social or recreational interests. She wore flannel shirts and jeans with unstyled short hair. She presented no overt femininity, nor any typical male posturing. She spent her time with her beloved pets, worked as a computer programmer, and read science fiction novels. She had identified little sexual desire toward either men or women, and categorically refused any questions about whether she was a lesbian. Lois was the only daughter in a large family with six brothers. She was aware of having disappointed her mother at her resistance to frilly clothing, and described growing up in a family that was emotionally cold. On one hand she was distant from her family. On the other hand, she obsessed about them and their treatment of her, living in terror of telling them who she really was. Early on in treatment Lois accepted that she was transgendered and asked to be called Lou. Lou began a process of legally changing his name and telling a few acquaintances. He read information on transgenderism and joined electronic mailing lists, but remained somewhat isolated and alone. After months of discussing coming out to his parents, Lou announced his transsexualism, unplanned, at a family social event. The family's response was to pretend he hadn't said anything. Lou stood up and in a loud voice told his parents and siblings and their families that his name was now Lou. He repeated that he was a transsexual and told them that they would have to refer to him by his new name or else he would simply refuse to speak with them. With that said, Lou left. In therapy he discussed the years of silence he had endured from his family and how he had allowed that silence to shadow his life. He said, "It's over now. I feel free of their judgments."

In the weeks after coming out to his family, Lou's presence, manner, and demeanor dramatically changed. He held himself taller and laughed louder. His family attempted to telephone him a few times, calling him Lois, but he did not respond to their messages until they finally referred to him as Lou. They tried to criticize and belittle him, saying he had no idea what he was doing. He was able to succinctly explain exactly what he was doing and told them that he was not open to discussing this aspect of his life with them, since they had never had any previous interest in his life at all. He said, "I used to be afraid of what they would think if 'I became' a man, now I think it will make it easier for them to see me as I am." Lou began to increase his social contacts. He identified feeling less critical of others and less alien from them. After joining a local gay community center, Lou met—and fell deeply in love with—a gay man. The sense of coming home to himself was immediate. "How could I have known I was gay, till I knew I was a man?" he asked.

Lou's coming-out process to his family of origin was liberating in a deeply psychic way. He freed himself from a yoke he did not know he was carrying. His presence in his family sounded ghostlike and ethereal, and it became apparent that his invisibility in their eyes had left him invisible in his own. Stuck in a developmental lag since early puberty, Lou had frozen himself in a neutered latency pattern, appearing to be an independent adult in his work but living a withdrawn life, denying his own gender, and eschewing social and romantic involvements. For Lou, coming out opened the beginning of a new life. It also illustrates the complicated relationship between sexual and gender identities for people struggling with gender dysphoria.

Shifting Sexual Identities

The issue of living in a transgendered body becomes intensified when dealing with sexuality issues. Perhaps this is why the literature often refers to transsexuals as "asexual" people with little sex drive. This may not be a lack of sex drive, but the difficulty in finding partners who are compatible and understanding of body dysphoria and are able to negotiate the complex, interwoven worlds of gender identity, sexual orientation, and sexuality.

Sexual orientation and gender identity are distinct parts of each person's sense of self. However, sexual orientation and gender identity also impact each other in profound ways. Gender transition can have a tremendous impact on sexual orientation, sometimes affecting one's sexual interests and more often impacting how one is perceived by the outside world. For instance, in a heterosexual relationship a husband's transition would place the wife in a perceived "lesbian" relationship. For the average heterosexual woman, particularly one who has lived a privileged life within a socially acceptable lifestyle, this reality can be shattering.

Issues of sexual orientation (i.e., attraction or desire) and sexual identity (i.e., communities of association) exacerbate the family's struggles to cope with gender issues. Sexual orientation is not malleable and cannot be changed through force or will. Sometimes, however, people's sexual orientation appears to "spontaneously" change during or after their transition process (e.g., males that had once been exclusively attracted to women find themselves attracted to men once they are living as women). This can be emotionally difficult for the transgendered person but even more so for the spouse. Very little research has been conducted on the impact of sexual orientation confusion in relationships with a cross-dressing or transsexual partner, but one study revealed that wives of transsexuals struggle less with their own identity than do wives of cross-dressers (Hunt and Main, 1997). Clearly, this is an area in which greater clinical and research attention should be drawn.

Heterosexual to Lesbian, Not—Adam/Barbara and Crissy

When Adam began to explore transition, his marriage to Crissy was presented with a challenging dilemma. After the initial shock of Adam's disclosure had subsided, Crissy began to accept Adam's gender issues. She was able to explore with maturity and caring her feelings about the broken trust, her fears about her marriage, and even her concerns for their children. However, the issue of sexuality became difficult and painful.

Alan's sexual identity remained intact throughout his transition process, i.e., he had always been attracted to women, and when he transitioned to Barbara, his female self, he was still attracted to women. Barbara was aware that she was seen as a lesbian, although this did not upset her. However, this caused great conflict for Crissy, who was simply not interested in being involved with another woman, sexually or romantically. She acknowledged that "Barbara was the same person inside," but this presented an insurmountable challenge to her sexuality and her sexual expression. As Barbara moved along in her transition, Crissy became less and less sexually interested. Her attempts to "stretch" her own sexual expression met with failure and she was unable to be intimate with her partner's new body. She requested that they cease all sexual contact, which was extremely painful for Barbara, whose desire for Crissy remained the same. The couple began to examine whether they could stay together in a sexless marriage.

Crissy felt strongly that she needed a "man" and a "husband" for a sexual partner. As much as she loved and supported Barbara, she was unable to respond sexually to her transsexual woman partner. Barbara and Crissy were unable to resolve their sexual issues in a way that was satisfactory to both of them. For some people sexual desire and orientation have little flexibility, although others are able to overcome these obstacles with greater ease.

Feminine Man to Butch Lesbian—Leanne and Jose/Marissa

Transsexualism had never been a secret in this family. Jose had lived as a woman in his early twenties, but for reasons that are still unclear to him, he stopped taking female hormones and resumed living as a man, albeit a rather feminine man. When Leanne and Jose met, she knew all about his history. Except for occasional cross-dressing, which Leanne accepted, Jose felt his transsexualism was behind him. However, Jose's desire to live as a woman returned with a vengeance fifteen years into their marriage. Jose and Leanne were committed to making their marriage last. They had a loving and creative relationship and had weathered many storms before the gender issues surfaced.

Leanne was able to accept that Jose was indeed transsexual. She supported Jose's transition to Marissa by going clothes shopping with her, coming out to friends, parents, and children about the gender issues, and becoming involved with transgender politics. Similar to Crissy, however, Leanne simply could not see herself being sexual with a "woman." She did not think she was homophobic since her son was gay and she happily welcomed him and his lover into their home.

Before Jose disclosed to Leanne about Marissa's "resurfacing," Leanne and Jose had had an intense and passionate sex life. Once Marissa began to emerge in the marriage, Leanne became sexually withdrawn and cold. Leanne had always been attracted to Jose's "softness," but the farther Marissa moved into her transition, the more sexually turned off Leanne felt. Marissa deeply loved Leanne and wanted to find a compromise that would allow her to have some gender flexibility and yet remain in the marriage. At a social event, Leanne met a lesbian couple. In her words, "This woman was so butch, I didn't even know she was a woman. I was shocked at how much that turned me on." Laughing, she said, "I guess I like masculinity more than I realized." Marissa began to explore being more "masculine," a challenge for someone who was just learning to live as a woman. Marissa and Leanne discovered that within a sexual encounter, if Leanne "exaggerated" her femininity and Marissa "butched it up," they were able to enjoy something akin to the heterosexual passion they had once known without compromising either of their gender identities or sexual orientations. Marissa found that although she was very uncomfortable living as a man, she was comfortable expressing a more masculine gender within her female body. Leanne discovered that the butch/femme dynamic within a lesbian relationship was sexually appealing enough for her to remain sexually connected to Marissa.

Perhaps Marissa and Leanne found a unique adaptation to their unusual situation, but without focused research on families living with gender transitions, it is not known whether it is truly unique or a more common way to make sense of gender changes within already-established relationships.

Queer As a Three-Dollar Bill—Tom

Sometimes during the transition process people find their own sexuality shifting. Some MTFs suddenly find that although they had previously never considered being sexual with men (i.e., "as" a man) they become more sexually attracted to them after transition.

Tom, who was born female, had lived as a lesbian from his early teenage years until he transitioned in his early thirties. He had never been sexual with men, nor had he ever had the desire to do so. When his long-term relationship ended (unrelated to his gender transition), he found himself reluctant to date and somewhat aimless. One night, he went out with some friends, men and women, to a mostly gay male bar and was shocked to find himself deeply, sexually excited. He said, "If you had asked me a few years ago if I could ever imagine being in a relationship with a man, I would have unequivocally said, 'Never!' I have always been sexually attracted to women. To my surprise, I have found myself deeply attracted to men, longing for men in a way I'd never dreamed possible."

Sometimes the desire for "same-sex" (or "opposite-sex") relationships is more salient than the preference for a partner of a particular sex. It might be that for some people, the "gay" paradigm (or the heterosexual paradigm) is the core attraction in their sexuality, rather than the sex of their partner.

Under the Stone—Lise and Ronnie

Alcoholics Anonymous (AA) and sobriety were the central themes in Lise and Ronnie's lives. They had met in AA and had been living together for three years. Although they described their relationship as somewhat volatile, they had been successful at utilizing the skills they learned in AA to work through problems. Lise was twenty-eight years old and had been sober for four years. She had come out early in her recovery and was happy to finally "know who I am." She believed that she drank because of her denial about her sexual identity. Ronnie, who was thirty-five and lesbian-identified since her early teens, was only the second woman Lise had dated. Ronnie had a long history of alcohol abuse and a briefer period of cocaine and heroin abuse. Ronnie got clean and sober in a lesbian halfway house about five years earlier, and maintaining her sobriety has been difficult work.

Lise just about dragged Ronnie into therapy, and upon entering the therapy office blurted out, "I feel so frustrated because Ronnie won't let me touch her." Ronnie's stoic face gave little away, but after some gentle prodding she said, "I don't like how she wants to touch me. I've never liked having my breasts touched and I don't like her . . . going down there, you know what I mean." When asked what she did like to do in bed, Ronnie blushed and avoided the question. Lise burst out, "All she wants to do is fuck me, like she's a guy or something. I had enough of that when I was drunk, thank you!" As Ronnie shared her sexual history, it became clear that she had been sexually "stone" for most of her adult life. She did not enjoy any sexual contact to her genitals, which she said reminded her that she was a "woman," motioning to make quotation marks with her fingers around the word "woman." Lise said, "Well, you are a 'woman' and that is why I am with you. I like making love to women. Duh, that's why I came out as a lesbian." Ronnie, in a very quiet voice confessed, "I don't know if I'm a woman anymore." Her words reverberated in the room, and Lise sat shocked and confused while Ronnie came out to Lise as transgendered. Ronnie said that she had kept these feelings hidden her whole life and knew that it was affecting her relationship and her sobriety to continue to do so. Ronnie said she had been talking with her sponsor and spending some time on the Internet talking with other transgendered people. She said, "I think I am a guy, and that I've never really been a lesbian."

"Stone" sexuality has been perceived (when it has been seen at all) as a "dysfunctional rejection of womanhood by a self-hating subject who cannot bear her embodiment" (Halberstam, 1998a, p. 112). Seen as shut down, blocked, rigid, dysphoric, and frigid, stone butches have been labeled and judged by both sexologists and other lesbians. Halberstam suggested that stone butches have the only sexual identity that is described solely in terms of what practices they do *not* engage in. What other sexual identity descriptor has been seen only in the negative? By this definition, Halberstam suggested, males who reject penetration should be called "stone males." Halberstam offered an alternative view, which is to see stone butch as an adaptation, a way of resolving the paradox of butchness and female masculinity. She said, "It is a courageous and imaginative way of dealing with the contradictory demands and impulses of butch in a woman's body" (Halberstam, 1998a, p. 129).

Stone butch can be a comfortable identity for some people, one that demands a creativity in lovemaking since the stone butch is not comfortable having "her" body touched in ways that make her feel like a woman. Some lovers are able to develop innovative ways to ensure that both partners are sexually satisfied, and stone butches are often unusually loving and giving sexual partners. For Ronnie, however, being stone became unbearable, not only because of Lise's desire to touch her, but because she longed to be touched, but not, as she said, as a "woman." Ronnie struggled with what it meant to not be a "lesbian" anymore, and said she had avoided telling Lise. If Lise knew, she could no longer deny how important it was to address because it made it more real. She said that whenever she tried to talk with a therapist or her AA sponsor about these feelings, they blamed it on her childhood sexual abuse or "internalized homophobia." She said that the "lesbian" label had never felt quite right, and she had always suspected that she was a straight man.

Lise was flabbergasted to discover this about her lover. She said that she had no idea that Ronnie had struggled with her gender identity and had simply assumed Ronnie was butch with "issues" to work out. The disclosure of Ronnie's gender issues affected Lise's understanding of her own lesbianism. She loved being a lesbian, and the thought of Ronnie changing her body or identity terrified her. Clinicians who have not examined their own homophobic biases might assume that being perceived as heterosexual would be valued. However, being seen as heterosexual is not easily embraced by many transgendered people who have always identified as gay or lesbian. "Becoming" heterosexual may make them feel invisible and an outcast from the queer community that has always been their home. Unlike heterosexual relationships, lesbian and gay relationships have been built within a climate of hostility and homophobia. Many gay and lesbian people take pride in their "outlaw" status as queers. Their identity as homosexuals has given them a home and place where they have found acceptance and community, and they are reluctant to give up this security. They may have little desire to meld into heterosexual culture.

The partners of transitioning butches often feel as if they have been thrown into a crisis. They experience themselves as "still" lesbian or gay, despite their lovers' transition. Sadly, many lesbians and gay men have been forcibly exiled from the lesbian and gay community for addressing their transgenderism, and their partners are often exiled with them. As Rubin (1992) said, "Dealing with their sex-changing partners is difficult and confusing enough for the lovers of transsexuals without having to worry about being thrown out of their social universe" (p. 476). Lise and Ronnie were lucky because Ronnie began her transition within a supportive lesbian and the AA community. Ronnie began to take male hormones, adopted a male pronoun, and began passing in the world as a man. Lise needed to reevaluate her own sexual desires and identity in light of Ronnie's transition. She realized, as Leanne had, that she had a greater range of sexual expression available to her than she had originally suspected. Lise maintained her identity as a lesbian, and explained her relationship with Ronnie as "an exception." Her sexual desire and expression was still directed more toward women than men. Although it was a tumultuous time in their relationship, Lise was able to remain lovers with Ronnie because, as she said, "He is the same person he's always been inside."

Ronnie's social life remained mostly lesbian, although he fostered more relationships with biological men and other transmen. If pushed, he would say he was still "sort of" a lesbian, i.e., he was attracted to lesbian women, but said the label did not feel comfortable anymore. As his body changed through hormonal and surgical treatments, he became increasingly able to enjoy physical touch. This is not to suggest that all stone butches are really transmen. Many stone butches are able to find comfortable ways to live in their female bodies and still explore their sexuality. However, for Ronnie, sex reassignment was a positive step toward his own embodiment.

Bi Any Name—Sandy and Willow

Transition issues can often be easier to cope with when a partner is bisexually identified (Denny and Green, 1996). Although the issues of gender transition and being partnered with a transsexual may still be challenging, bisexual people may be better able to cope with transition than either heterosexually or homosexually identified people since gender is usually a less salient issue in their partner choice.

Sandy and Willow were a long-term heterosexual couple when they began therapy, though initially not for gender-related issues. In their late forties with their children nearly grown, they came to therapy dealing with typical marital issues of money, housework, and feeling stuck. Avowed hippies, Sandy and Willow had built their own home and homeschooled their children. Sandy wore his hair long, as did Willow, and both dressed in casually unisex clothing. Their marriage had few gender rules. Both cooked and cleaned, both gardened, both worked in their small flower store, and both identified as bisexual. Their marriage had been "open" at various times, both tending to be sexual with others in homosexual relationships, which had been minimally stressful on their relationship. They often joked in therapy that Sandy was the more sensitive and "womanly" of the two and that Willow was really the butch in the relationship.

After a few months in therapy, Sandy started talking about a friend of his from high school who he had just discovered had transitioned. Sandy appeared to be quite mesmerized by this news. He shared how much he had always felt like a woman, but living a counterculture lifestyle had always allowed him the freedom to dress in more feminine clothing. He was very uncomfortable with highly feminine clothing and believed it represented the worst kind of phoniness that women had to endure. He said, "I don't think I would appear that different in the world if I were to transition. I'd still wear flannel shirts and comfortable shoes, but I'd feel much happier in my body." Willow was comfortable with this in the beginning, though very concerned about the health risks of hormone treatment. She was mostly supportive, though she had experienced an "emergency stage" crisis about a year into transition. The crisis had lasted for about six months as she grew fearful of what it meant to be the wife of a transsexual. As the hormones began to change Sandy's body, she found she liked the changes they made. She confessed in therapy that she had always felt far more attracted to women, and if she had not loved Sandy so much she would have come out lesbian years ago. As Sandy's transition progressed, Sandy and Willow moved gracefully into a lesbian relationship, feeling few dramatic changes in their lives, and perhaps a greater intimacy.

For Sandy and Willow, the gender transition promoted greater closeness, and due to Willow's bisexuality (or perhaps lesbianism), Sandy's transition did not cause a conflict in this area of their lives. Sexuality and desire are, of course, complex, and bisexuality does not infer that any member of either sex is a potential sexual partner. As one male workshop participant whose wife was transitioning said, "I have always been bisexual, but I don't think that if I chose a male partner it would have necessarily been the type of guy that my partner has become." Sexual desire and sexual compatibility involve more than just issues of biological bodies and sexual preferences.

Sexual Styles—Sid and Marc

When individuals identify as transgendered they are expressing important things about how they see their bodies and how they want to be seen, even—or especially—if they are not utilizing medical treatments. This was evident in the description of stone butch sexuality, in which certain parts of the body may be off limits to touch or can only be touched in ways that honor the person's masculinity. The sexual arena can evoke many issues for transgendered people, because sexuality and desire are often experienced in very gendered ways.

Sid and Marc came to therapy able to clearly articulate the problems in their relationship. Sid was a gay man who had been out since his early adolescence and was very comfortable with his sexuality. He became involved with Marc, who was just coming out, and they fell deeply in love. When Marc began to withdraw, Sid assumed that it was related to school or work, but then began to suspect that it had to do with being gay. Marc confessed that he didn't think he was gay but thought he was transsexual. Although Marc was not seeking any bodily changes, this disclosure negatively impacted the couple's sexuality. Marc said, "I want him to make love to me as a woman. All he wants to do is have gay sex." Sid was very confused about "how" to have sex, since Marc's body was clearly male. Sid asked," How do I make love to him if he doesn't have those kinds of parts?" Sid and Marc's issues had to do more with sexual "style" than issues of sexual orientation. Marc began to explore how he wanted to be touched and made love to, and was able to tell Sid to use feminine words to describe his body parts. Sid was more than willing to do this, though he admitted that he still saw Marc as having a male body.

Sid and Marc were able to work out an erotic dance that validated each partner's sexuality. Sid did not seem to struggle with how Marc's transgendered identity affected his own sexual identity, but perhaps that would change if Marc decided to physically transition.

Transpositioned—Sally and Jean

Sometimes transgendered and transsexual people are sexually drawn to each other. This can involve heterosexual partnerships as well as homosexual ones. Although this can make transition issues easier—certainly the significant other is sensitive to the kinds of issues and feelings the transgendered partner is experiencing, having been there himself or herself—it does not necessarily mean that the partner embraces the transsexualism. Significant others who are transgendered themselves can react much in the same ways that nontransgendered people do, going through all of the stages of disclosure/discovery, turmoil, negotiation, and balance.

Sally and Jean had actually met through a transgendered support group ten years earlier. Sally had already been in the process of transition, which she completed during their first year together. Jean had identified as a cross-dresser and did not begin to talk about transitioning until they had been together for more than seven years and had been legally married as husband and wife. Sally voiced support for Jean, but it was couched in judgmental comments (e.g., "You really don't pass that well") and veiled threats (e.g., "I'm not sure if I want to be married to a woman"). Sally struggled with being honest with Jean about her feelings, since she was invested in having Jean see her as supportive. Jean waffled about transitioning, and struggled with insecurity and fears of how well she would pass and whether Sally would leave her. Sally was very resistant to being in a lesbian relationship, and her own transition had not made this process any easier.

Although Sally had chosen a partner who also struggled with issues of gender dysphoria, she was still resistant to being involved with a transgendered partner. There are other transgendered people who seek transgendered partners, being drawn to others who have traveled the same path or, in some cases, opposite path.

Since transgendered and transsexual people have been viewed as perverted, disordered, and disturbed, they have not been seen as potential lovers. Perceiving transgendered people as a desirable "catch" seems unimaginable to many. Historically, those who were attracted to transgendered people were labeled "fetishists," and could find no way to explore their desires except reading pornographic magazines. In an attempt to medicalize these "perversions," gender specialists have labeled men who are sexually attracted to transgendered males as gynandromorphophiles (Blanchard and Collins, 1993). Within the transgender community those who seek sexual gratification from transsexuals have been called "tranny chasers."

Transsensual Eroticism—Jack

Explicit sexual desire for transgendered people is neither a sexual perversion nor a fetish, and it does not make a person disordered or disturbed. It is simply another sexual style, and those who have tried to honor this sexual interest in transgender bodies have labeled this desire as "transsensual" (Bolus, n.d.)

The first time Jack saw a pornographic magazine about cross-dressing he was fascinated with the pictures. He was also embarrassed and disgusted with himself for having these feelings. He immediately threw out the magazine but found himself thinking about it all the time, until he finally ordered one through the mail. He looked through the pictures, read the stories, and found himself incredibly sexually excited. Jack had been married in the past, and had also had a few one-night stands with men, but nothing had turned him on as strongly as cross-dressed "women." Eventually, he got up enough courage to respond to some of the ads, and to his surprise discovered meeting with these "girls" to be even more sexually exciting in person. He also discovered that some of the cross-dressing women were interesting, intelligent, and fun. Jack came to ther-

apy confused about who he was ("Am I gay or straight?") and wanting to understand why he was so attracted to cross-dressers. After months of seeking answers by examining his childhood and analyzing his past sexual relationships,
Jack came to the conclusion that this was "just the way he was" and stopped trying to make sense of it. Eventually Jack settled down with Dawn, who worked as
a computer programmer as a man and spent a good deal of her free time as a
woman.

Jack was able to come to a sense of peace within himself as he and Dawn
worked out an intimate and domestic life together. For others, the awareness
of transsensual attraction comes long after the partnership is formed.

Transpassion—Denise and RJ

Often transgenderism is not revealed in a relationship for many years.
Couples may be able to negotiate the stages of emergence, but the transgendered status of one of the partners remains something tolerated rather than
embraced (particularly sexually). Cole (1998) discussed the surprise and
dissonance some wives experience, finding themselves erotically attracted
to their husbands' cross-dressing.

Denise had lived with RJ for fifteen years. They had started as a lesbian
couple until RJ began his gender transition almost a decade before. They
had remained together, had two children conceived through donor insemi-
nation, and both described their marriage as satisfying and happy.

Although she loved RJ, Denise still thought of herself as far more attracted to
women, and suspected that she would seek companionship within the lesbian
community if their relationship ever ended. Then the couple attended a conference for trans-identified people, and Denise found herself in a room with a number of other couples like her and RJ—female-to-male transsexuals and their female partners. Denise looked around the room, and to her surprise found herself
sexually attracted not to the women in the room, but to their male partners. This
was a revelation for Denise—one that made RJ very happy. She was very specifically attracted to these transmen, and discovered it was not simply a "fluke" that
she was with her husband. This realization brought Denise and RJ's long-term
partnership to a greater sense of intimacy and revitalized their sexual relationship.

The clinical vignettes described previously illustrate only a small sampling of some of the issues facing partners of transgendered and transsexual
people, and have focused primarily on issues of disclosure and sexual identity. Study of the developmental stages that family members negotiate, as
well as the impact on normative life-cycle processes that follow the emergence of a transgendered person within a family is a field in its infancy. The

age of the transgendered person when he or she first discloses, the length of time the partnership has endured, the presence and ages of children within the family, religious influences, as well as the levels of intimacy and resiliency previous to the disclosure will all impact the family's ability to navigate through the rough waters of transgender emergence.

Families that are coping with transition issues are often moving through myriad emotions, including rage, fear, loneliness, and feeling different. Like all people dealing with major life changes, transgendered and transsexual people can be self-centered, obsessed with their transition process, and oblivious to the impact of their behavior in their loved ones. Likewise, spouses can be selfish, avoidant, abusive, and controlling while they try to manage perceived cataclysmic life changes within what seems to be a vacuum of information and support. For children living in these families, it is often a time of confusion and disarray. Parents often attempt to "protect" children, unaware of how intensely tuned into family emotions children can be. Even when they are unaware of what exactly is happening, they are rarely naive to the fact that *something* is going on.

TRANSPARENTS SEE

When gender variance is expressed among an adult member of a family, family members are often concerned about how this will impact the children. Many people express concern for the gender development of children reared by transgendered or transsexual parents. The etiology of gender dysphoria, transgenderism, transsexualism, and even homosexuality has been rooted in psychoanalytic assumptions about parental psychopathology, particularly around gender issues (Coates, 1990; Lothstein, 1983, 1992; Rekers, 1995; Stoller, 1966, 1967a, 1975; Zucker and Bradley, 1995). Despite accusations of parental causation, most parents—transgendered or not—do not embrace gender variance in their children. It is usually "the last thing in the world a parent wants to hear" (Brown and Rounsley, 1996, p. 173). Although research on children growing up in families with a transitioning parent is rare, more extensive studies have been done on the children being raised in lesbian and gay families—families in which sexual and gender norms are often more varied and at least some of the individuals express nonnormative gender roles. These studies do not show any harm caused by children being raised in alternative family structures (Bailey et al., 1995; Bozett, 1987; Flaks et al., 1995; Golombok, Spencer, and Rutter, 1983; Patterson, 1994, 1995, 1996).

This is not to say being raised within an alternative family structure, or with a gender-variant parent, does not present unique opportunities, and that the children do not exhibit certain differences from a control group of children being raised within a heteronormative environment, or that these differences are not valuable to study. Indeed, at least one study has reviewed previous research and shown that children being raised in lesbian and gay families exhibit less rigid gender expressions and a greater sense of openness to dating members of the same sex. However, these are not necessarily negative outcomes (Stacey and Biblarz, 2001). The few studies and reports available specifically on children who are raised by transsexual parents have not shown negative effects for the children (Ettner and White, 2000; Green, 1978, 1998b). Significant numbers of children are growing up in homes with a transgendered or transsexual parent. In one study approximately 30 percent of the population seeking services for gender issues were parents (Valentine, 1998). No evidence exists to date that children being raised by a lesbian, gay, transgendered, or gender-variant parent have a greater chance of struggling with sexual or gender identity issues, or face difficulties with their gender development.

Families often question whether children can "catch" gender variance—either genetically or through social channels and modeling—and therapists often suggest that parents keep information about gender issues hidden from their children. One writer suggested, "If the patient has children, you must ascertain whether he ever allows the children to see him cross-dressed and counsel him against allowing this to happen" (Steiner, 1990, p. 101). However, this is obviously not possible if the parent is planning to transition. The concerns for children often border on the absurd. For instance, Steiner (1985c) wondered "what the future holds for this baby whose father is a 'penisless man'" (p. 356), as if a father's penis is a salient factor in family life. In many families, children have never even seen their parents naked.

Children raised in a home with a transgendered or transsexual parent will certainly have issues to face. When a parent transitions while their children are young, the children tend to have an easier time coping. As might be expected, adolescents often have a difficult time dealing with disclosure and transition issues (Cole, 1998); however, they have an even more difficult time finding out that information has been withheld (Ettner and White, 2000). Brown and Rounsley (1996) said, "It helps to recognize that children grow up with fairy tales and cartoons in which transformation occurs all the time. . . . Children accept transformation as normal, everyday fare" (p. 191). R. Green's (1998b) research showed that none of the children in his study exhibited signs of gender identity issues and all were accepting of their parents' transition. Cole (1998) reflected on her extensive clinical work with families with fathers who are openly transgendered. She said, "These families have raised their children in the presence of a transgendered father and have assimilated transgender into the family lifestyle. . . . Many of these families find comfort in creative, imaginative ways to cope with society's rigid reluctance to acknowledge persons who are transgendered" (p. 377).

Information should obviously be geared to the age of the child, with a focus on how the parent feels versus details involving surgery. Children should be reassured that the parent's gender issues are not caused by the child, nor will the child be likely to have similar issues. The transitioning parent should also be clear to reassure the child that even though the parent is unhappy with his or her sex, it does not mean that he or she dislikes other people of that sex. This is especially important to reinforce if the child and the parent are of the same biological sex, so the child does not feel "rejected" by the parent (i.e., "you don't like being a boy, so therefore you don't like me because I am also a boy").

Parents will need to make decisions regarding when to reveal transgenderism to children, evaluating their age, their maturity, and whether the gender transition will be noticeable. Parents will also need to examine their own comfort with the topic and their ability to adequately address children's needs during a time where they may be focused on their own issues regarding transition. Most important, parents will need to function as a team, working together and compromising and negotiating differences of opinion. This is probably the most important variable in the children's ability to manage this family crisis.

Therapists find that "factors within the parental relationship and family constellation [have] significantly more bearing on the outcome for the children than the transition itself" (Ettner and White, 2000). Some of these factors include abrupt separation from the transitioning parent, nonsupportive family members, parental conflict, and an inability for families to work together. As in all separation and divorce situations, how children manage their grief and loss is mediated through the way it is handled by the adults. Green (1998) cautioned against "terminated contact with a [transgendered] parent after divorce," and admonishes the legal system to not use the wife's anger at the gender transition to sever relationships between transsexual parents and children. Other writers, however, argue that, if the interests of the child are to be kept as a priority, contact with the transgendered parent may have to cease (Snaith, Tarsh, and Reid, as cited in Sales, 1995). It is hard to imagine how severing a relationship with a parental figure, even given the challenges posed by gender transitions, would be helpful for a child. Other writers (Sales, 1995) have developed successful family interventions to address the complex, and sometimes dysfunctional, issues involving the sex reassignment of a father, the divorce of the parents, and the subsequent remarriage of the custodial mother.

For many young people, issues regarding their parents' "sex-change" causes minimal crisis. One teenage daughter said, "I really don't care if my father lives as a woman or a man. That's his choice. How he treats me and my mother—that's what I care about. His gender issues are his business."

Families of gender-variant people have been offered a raw deal by the psychological community. Researchers, by the very questions they have asked, and clinicians, by the assumptions on which they have directed their interventions, have either ignored or pathologized the family members of gender- variant people, leaving them without adequate support during what could be viewed as a normative, but stressful, family life-cycle event (Carter and McGoldrick, 1999). What should appear obvious, but somehow has been hidden, is that family life is no less important or relevant to gender-variant people than it is to any other person. The families of gender-variant people are as healthy or dysfunctional as any other family, with strengths and weaknesses, religious and cultural concerns, and their own assorted gender biases, values, and stereotypes. Despite the difficulties and confusions of this soul-searching process that can lead to a transition process, there is no evidence that gender-variant people are uncommitted to their families. Rather, it might be more accurate to suggest that transgendered people are as invested and committed to their loved ones as are any other persons, but fear that knowledge of their authentic selves will alienate and destroy their familial bonds. Sadly, without social and systemic support, it often will.

Bolin (1988) said, "The family is the arena in which a transsexual drama is enacted, one in which transsexuals hope they will be accepted. Separation from families occurs as a last resort only if their families do the rejecting" (p. 93). It is precisely in this area that family therapists can offer hope and expertise that families can traverse the obstacles and struggles inherent in coping with gender issues without losing one another. It seems obvious that the more assistance families are offered during transition the better they will cope with the challenges unveiled in this process, and the more successful the transition will be for the transgendered person, as well as his or her loved ones.

Chapter 9

Transgendered Children and Youth

Who would you be if you had never been punished for gender-inappropriate behavior, or seen another child punished for deviations from masculine or feminine norms...?

Pat (now Patrick) Califia
Sex Changes, 1997

There is perhaps no area of transgendered health care that elicits as much controversy as the issues raised regarding the psychotherapeutic and medical needs of gender-variant and gender-dysphoric children and youth. Cross-gender behavior can be very anxiety provoking for parents, who may be embarrassed or frightened by a son's overt femininity or a daughter's masculine expression. Children and adolescents are powerless to access health care independent of their families, and they are often the unwilling participants in medical treatments that are sought by their parents and administered by medical staff who are trying to "treat" and "cure" the gender-variant expression. Clinical intervention is based on the belief that gender variance in children is associated with later gender dysphoria and sexual deviance, most commonly homosexuality and transsexualism. It is further believed that the earlier the intervention, the greater the likelihood of success, with success presumably defined as heterosexuality and gender-normative expression.

Underlying this treatment philosophy is the belief that gender identity should emanate, naturally and normally, from natal sex. Kohlberg's (1966) seminal theory on gender identity stated that the development of gender identity is a cognitive process. Children, according to Kohlberg, are active agents in cognitively recognizing the differences between males and females, and "correctly" identifying their own gender status as originating from their biological bodies. Kohlberg believed this was a "natural" ability of a child. If his theories are accurate, children who experience their gender at odds with their biological bodies are unable to move through a normative developmental process. Indeed, their gender dysphoria is, by definition, proof of their arrested developmental process. Children who do not move through the accepted stages of gender development are identified as having a "developmental lag" (Zucker et al., 1999). However, if gender identity was not automatically seen as an outgrowth of biological sex, it would be expected that those with cross-gender identities would exhibit a resistance to moving through the normative stages of gender stability and constancy. Gender-variant children, by definition, cannot have gender stability, since it is their experience that their gender identities do not emanate from their biological bodies. In order to reach a stage of gender consistency they must accept that their gender and sex are the same and unchanging through time and situations. However, their sincere hope is that gender can be malleable (and, of course, within a modern world, it is).

One aspect of traditional treatment strategies for childhood gender identity issues is to teach them that biological sex is unchangeable (Green, 1995). It is interesting to note that the very clinicians who have promulgated this intervention are also active in advocacy work for adult transsexuals. What would be the purpose of encouraging a child to feel trapped in his or her dysmorphic natal sex, when both the gender expert and possibly the child *know* that sex reassignment exists? Knowing that options are available in the future could serve to lessen some of their stress and confusion instead of reinforcing it. An understanding of gender identity acquisition not grounded in natal sex could allow for mature, healthy, and normative gender development for gender-variant children, including potential gender "constancy" and "gender stability," as well as a greater variation of gender expressions for all children. It is worth pondering whether small children actually have a more sophisticated understanding of the relationship of gender and sex than developmental psychologists whose biological determinism privileges the physical genitals, body parts that are rarely visible in social discourse. Kohlberg believed that children were active participants in their own gender acquisition but stopped short of acknowledging that this could be equally true for gender-variant children as well. Perhaps gender-variant children do not lack the cognitive development skills but rather social support and recognition of their authentic gender expression.

All experts in this field note that gender-variant children express the incongruence of their biological bodies and gender identities at remarkably young ages (P. Wilson, 1998). Florence Dillon (1999) described how her female child began to identify as a boy at three years old. She said, "In our neighborhood and on the playground at the park, Sarah began to introduce herself only as Steve. Within our family, she became more insistent that she was a boy. She never said 'I want to be a boy' or 'I wish I was a boy,' but always, 'I *am* a boy'" (Dillon, 1999, p. 5, italics mine). It is understandable, given the apartheid of sex in this society, why a parent would express concern for this "boy in a girl's body," worry about what would happen to "her," and seek treatment to help her accept being a girl. Parents witnessing a child developing along the "wrong" gender trajectory will experience fear, for regardless of one's educational background, parents recognize that the prognosis for this child is not good. If they are at all unsure of whether the child's gender expression is a problem, they need only to seek someone in the helping professions to reinforce their fears and be told how very serious their child's condition really is. Children with gender dysphoria are referred to as "gender disturbed." Benestad (2001) asked, "Should we rather say that some expressions of gender disturb?" (p. 61). Gerald Mallon (1999) asked, "Why are gender variant children so disturbing to people, especially parents?" (p. 55).

TREATMENT, PREVENTION, AND PARENTAL RIGHTS

Gender-variant children are commonly brought to the attention of clinicians through referrals by parents, schools, or medical professionals who are concerned about the child's gender-defiant behavior. Gender experts who specialize in children issues include professionals working within clinic settings and therapists in private practice who also work with gender-variant children. The treatment strategies currently used with gender-variant children are controversial and are outlined next.

Gender-variant children are diagnosed utilizing the DSM-IV's description of gender identity disorder (see Box 5.3). GID in children and adolescents is, however, considered a "rare phenomenon" (Meyer-Bahlburg, 1985). Green (1995) estimated the numbers of children with GID to be 1.5 to 3 percent for boys, which is double his estimates for girls. The DSM diagnostic criteria, which have a strong focus on childhood behavior, describe behaviors that are outside of what is considered normative gender roles for boys and girls. Two components are outlined in the DSM criteria that impact young children. The first is a "strong and persistent cross-gender identification" as evidenced by a

(1) repeatedly stated desire to be, or insistence that he or she is, the other sex
(2) in boys, preference for cross-dressing or simulating female attire; in girls, insistence on wearing only stereotypical masculine clothing
(3) strong and persistent preferences for cross-sex roles in make-believe play or persistent fantasies of being the other sex
(4) intense desire to participate in the stereotypical games and pastimes of the other sex

(5) strong preference for playmates of the other sex. (APA, 1994, p. 537. Reprinted with permission from the *Diagnostic and Statistical Manual of Mental Disorders,* Fourth Edition. Copyright 1994 American Psychiatric Association.)

The second component is a "persistent discomfort [about one's assigned] sex or sense of inappropriateness in the gender role of that sex." For boys this is noted by the

assertion that his penis or testes are disgusting or will disappear or assertion that it would be better to not have a penis, or aversion toward rough-and-tumble play and rejection of male stereotypical toys, games, and activities; and in girls [there is a] rejection of urinating in a sitting position, assertion that she has or will grow a penis, or assertion that she does not want to grow breasts or menstruate, or marked aversion toward normative feminine clothing. (APA, 1994, p. 537. Reprinted with permission from the *Diagnostic and Statistical Manual of Mental Disorders,* Fourth Edition. Copyright 1994 American Psychiatric Association.)

In adolescents (as well as adults) the DSM-IV incorporates additional symptomatology, including

a stated desire to be the other sex . . . desire to live or be treated as the other sex . . . the conviction that he or she has the typical feelings and reactions of the other sex . . . preoccupation with getting rid of primary and secondary sex characteristics (e.g., request for hormones, surgery, or other procedures to physically alter sexual characteristics to simulate the other sex) or belief that he or she was born the wrong sex. (APA, 1994, pp. 537-538. Reprinted with permission from the *Diagnostic and Statistical Manual of Mental Disorders,* Fourth Edition. Copyright 1994 American Psychiatric Association.)

The basic underlying issue for children and adolescents identified as having gender identity disorder, according to Zucker and Bradley (1995), is a "strong preference for sex-typed behaviors more characteristic of the opposite sex, and a rejection or avoidance of sex-typed behaviors more characteristic of one's own sex. There are also signs of distress and discomfort about one's status as a boy or a girl" (p. 11).

Despite the changes in social and cultural mores over the past forty years, including the shifting of role expectations for both women and men, the authors of the DSM assume clear-cut differences in proper male/female gender behavior, and experts in the field seem to universally accept that deviations from stereotypical male and female sex roles in young children are signs of pathology (Coates, Friedman, and Wolfe, 1991; Rekers and Kilgus, 1995; Zucker, 1990b; Zucker and Bradley, 1995). It is assumed that boys and girls should wear different clothes and that strong desires to wear the clothes of the opposite gender is pathological. The DSM also assumes that play is a gendered activity and cross-gendered play is a sign of dysfunction. Boys are held to rigid gender conformity in their dress and mannerisms and girls are punished for aggressive masculine behaviors and interest in "rough-and-tumble" play.

The number of boys referred for treatment far exceeds the number of girls—nine to one according to Green (1995) and seven to one according to Bradley and Zucker (1997)—which is clearly related to the more rigid societal gender expectations for males than females, as well as the greater psychosocial stressors placed on boys who deviate from proper gender behavior. For instance, girls must "insist" on male clothing to be diagnosed with GID, but boys can just "prefer" female clothing. Parents, schools, and medical personnel react to boys who transgress gender expectations with far greater concern and potential punishment than they do girls. Surely this is recognized by young boys and probably increases their discomfort and distress. Coates, Friedman, and Wolfe (1991) insisted that boys with GID are not simply androgynous, but their play is constricted, compulsive, rigid, and repetitive. Zucker, Bradley, and Sanikhani (1997) noted the differences in social expectations for boys and girls—which they refer to as the "social threshold hypothesis"—and concluded not that boys are overreferred for services based on outdated gender stereotypes but that girls are underreferred for treatment. It is interesting to note that many behaviors, traits, and expressions that have become normative for girls in the past twenty years would have been considered pathological only two generations ago.

One interesting theory presented in the literature is that boys with gender identity issues are often very "attractive" and have been described as pretty, beautiful, cute, and feminine. Stoller (1968a,b) was the first to recognize this "special beauty" in many gender-dysphoric boys. Green (1995) hypothesized that the "feminine appearance of these children stimulated a pattern of response in parents and others that induced or reinforced feminine behavior" (p. 2006). This is reminiscent of the comments that family and even strangers often make to new parents regarding a son's beautiful hair (which is "wasted" on a boy), or his lovely eyes or eyelashes that are "pretty enough to be a girl's," as if boys should somehow be naturally physically "plainer" than girls.

Some controversy exists in the literature on differentiating between children who feel they "are" the other sex and those who "want to be" the other sex, as well as between those who exhibit cross-gender behavior and desire to change sex and those who exhibit cross-gender expression but do not state any desire to change sex. Rekers (1996) referred to this as the difference between Gender Role Behavior Disturbance and the Cross Gender Identification Disturbance. In one of the most widely discussed cases, a male child named Kraig clearly stated that he knew he was a boy and that he would grow up to be a daddy, yet he was also described as one of the most severe cases of gender identity disorder yet assessed (Burke, 1996, p. 35). Zucker (1990a) described this continuum of behavior as an "ambiguous zone" in which some boys "do poorly in male peer groups, avoid rough-and-tumble play, are disinclined towards athletics, fail to show strongly masculine toy and play preferences, and appear generally uncomfortable about being male . . . [yet] do not wish to be girls or show an intense preoccupation with females or femininity" (pp. 10-11). He questioned whether this is a different syndrome or a mild case of gender identity disorder. He did not question whether it is just another way to be a boy.

Although the criteria used to determine appropriate boy and girl behaviors are based on an obviously stereotypical gender dichotomy, the DSM clearly states that children with this diagnosis are not merely androgynous in their behavior but have "intense," "strong," and "persistent" discomfort. Childhood gender specialists are careful to state that it is not minor deviations from social and gender expectations that are problematic, but severe divergences in which children are expressing extreme discomfort and whose behavior is isolating and targeting them for social abuse. For instance, Zucker and his colleagues are clear that they are not talking about children who are flexible in their gender-role behavior, but who actively reject prescribed and stereotypical sex roles (Zucker, 1990a,b; Zucker and Bradley, 1995). Richardson (1996, 1999) questioned whether those dedicated to treating gender-variant children are able to discern the difference between atypical gender expression and pathological and disturbed cross-gender behavior. He challenged Zucker (1999), who acknowledged the difficulty in discerning the difference, but insisted that only severely disturbed children should become the focus of treatment. Less severe forms of gender dysphoria are recognized in the literature. For example, Bradley (1998) examined how transvestic fetishism manifests in young boys who do not desire sex reassignment.

The literature is rich with descriptions of cross-gendered behavior that is described as pathological. One example concerns a seven-year-old girl who refused to wear dresses, enjoyed sports, played with darts and marbles, stood with her hands on her hips, did not like her more feminine younger sister, and displayed aggressive play behavior (Burke, 1996). Another author listed a checklist for "effeminate behaviors" in a treatment plan for a four-year-old boy, which included: "(a) plays with girls, (b) plays with female dolls, (c) feminine gestures, [including] limp wrist, swishy hand, arm or torso movements, sway of hips, etc., and (d) female role play, [including] impersonating or pretending to be a female (like actress, mother, female teacher) when playing games (like house, school, etc.)" (Burke, 1996, p. 39).

The criteria for establishing appropriate masculine and feminine behaviors are delineated in an almost bizarre minutia. Burke (1996) excerpted the work of David Barlow:

> Standing: If you stand with your feet apart you are masculine. If you stand with your feet together you are feminine. If you swing your arms from your shoulder, you are masculine; from the elbow, you are feminine. . . . If you have "two distinct arm or hand motions in a fifteen second period," you are feminine. . . . If the distance between the buttock and the back of the chair was four inches or more "away from the back of the chair" (keyed as masculine) was scored. Otherwise, "close to the back of the chair" (keyed as feminine) was scored. (Burke, pp. 7-8)

The prognosis for gender-variant boys without treatment is dismal. According to Fitzgibbons (2001),

> Boys who exhibit such symptoms before they enter school are more likely to be unhappy, lonely and isolated in elementary school; to suffer from separation anxiety, depression, and behavior problems; to be victimized by bullies and targeted by pedophiles; and to experience same-sex attraction in adolescence.

Sadly, this may be an accurate prognosis, but to not examine the reasons why gender-variant children have difficulty making friends and experience depression and behavior problems is to blame the victim for how he or she is treated. Gender-variant children and adolescents may indeed be more frequently targeted for abuse (Denny, 1995; Di Ceglie et al., 2002; James, 1998; Wilchins, 1997), which is all the more reason to protect them, not "fix" them.

Treatment of gender-variant children has been developed primarily by a handful of specialists including Rekers, Coates, Bradley, and Zucker. Treatment strategies consist of behavioral, psychodynamic, and pharmacological interventions, and range from group and family therapies to inpatient hospitalizations and hormonal and electroshock therapies. Although young children are often treated in day clinics, adolescents are often forcibly removed from their homes, hospitalized, and treated with behavior modification and psychotropic medications.

Most treatment programs are based on behavior modification techniques developed to socially reinforce "appropriate" behaviors and extinguish those deemed cross-gendered. They use behavior-shaping procedures and reward-and-punishment techniques that target cross-gender behaviors. Interventions include token economies, selective reinforcement, and self-regulating techniques such as the use of wrist monitors to target particular behaviors. Focusing particularly on boys, it is believed that by extinguishing or punishing specific feminine behaviors, such as playing with Barbie dolls, and rewarding masculine behaviors and encouraging what the DSM refers to as rough-and-tumble play, "skill deficits in athletic games in gender-disturbed boys can be remediated" (Rekers, 1995b, p. 283). These treatments are based on the belief that by praising "appropriate" behaviors and mannerisms, and ignoring or punishing cross-sex behavior, they will be able to modify not only the cross-gender behaviors but also gender dysphoria and cross-gender identity. The veracity of this assumption has not been proven, and it is unknown whether children revert back to their cross-gender behaviors when adults are not around.

Burke (1996) examined the literature on children and youth who were treated with behavioral protocols for gender identity disturbances. What she found appalled her. In one case cited by Burke, a teacher and a counselor treated a young boy, "Jerry," for gender inappropriate behavior at his elementary school. Jerry's parents were never notified of his treatment. Jerry was a nine-year-old boy who preferred to play with girls, was unskilled in sports, and was teased by other children for his gentle ways. Jerry was treated through behavioral interventions that manipulated his environment (e.g., seating him next to the boys, verbally encouraging rough-and-tumble play, and shunning him when he spent time with girls). In the words of his therapist, Jerry lacked "physical aggression. He wouldn't slug it out, or physically push people . . . people would view him as a gentle person" (Burke, 1996, p. 26). Clearly, this was unacceptable behavior for a boy, and one sign of Jerry's successful treatment was that he stopped sitting with girls and properly began to tease them. He was ranked as more popular by the researchers, although his self-esteem had plummeted. The therapist stated he would treat a child like Jerry "exactly" the same today, although he admitted that it is not as popular to study these treatments today as it once was. Burke stated that Jerry was treated for his nonconforming gender behavior, but "the children who are doing the teasing and name-calling are not assessed or treated for bullying behavior patterns, because these patterns are considered 'normal'" (Burke, 1996, p. 21). It is a sad statement about social values that a gentle child is considered a problem, but a boy teasing a girl is evidence of successful intervention.

In what is clearly one of the most disturbing narratives, Burke discussed the story of "Jamie," a six-year-old child who was essentially abandoned in a hospital where he stayed for the remainder of his childhood for treatment of his gender disorder! Jamie, who today identifies as a transsexual woman, was subjected to years of electroconvulsive therapy (ECT) during the 1950s and 1960s, described by Burke in frightening detail. It is easy to dismiss this horror story and assume that it could not happen in today's society. However, Scholinski's (1997) personal account of how she was treated in the 1980s proves such treatment is far from over. Scholinski was fourteen when she was institutionalized. She was an athletic girl and did not wear dresses. She was labeled with a gender disorder and oppositional defiant disorder. She was given psychiatric medication and had no contact with her family for three months. Her parents were told, "Girls in your daughter's condition usually spend the rest of their lives in mental institutions" (p. 86). Indeed, Scholinski remained at the institution, where she was given psychotropic medicines, taught to be more feminine, and counseled for her "sexual identity problems," until she was eighteen years old and could no longer be involuntarily committed.

Burke also outlined the story of another young woman, Lyn Duff, who was hospitalized at the Rivendell Psychiatric Center in Utah in the 1990s. She too was diagnosed with oppositional defiant disorder, gender identity disorder, and sexual identity disorder. She was treated by having children's stories read to her about how "furry animals need to accept that they do not have feathers, and feathered animals need to accept that they did not have scales" (Burke, 1996, p. 93). She was medicated with psychotropic medications and hormones, and participated in groups to discuss proper feminine attire. She was also placed in a special group for perpetrators because she had engaged in consensual lesbian sex before hospitalization.

The treatment strategies used in these examples are based in psychoanalytic thinking which postulates that cross-gender identity is caused by pathological early parenting strategies. Behavioral interventions are deemed appropriate because it is believed that the gender issues are induced by faulty environmental conditions, particularly the encouragement of cross-gender behavior by mothers and/or the absence of strong father figures in the daily life of the family. These theories suggest that femininity in males is caused by mothers who are excessively close to their sons (Stoller, 1966,1968a,b, 1975; Zuger, 1970) and/or the loss or absence of mothers, possibly through illness or death (Pruett and Dahl, 1982; Coates and Person, 1985). Spensley and Barter (1971) identified transvestite boys as having dominant aggressive mothers who, in addition to preferring their sisters, were hostile toward their sons' masculinity and rejoiced in their cross-dressing behavior. Coates, Friedman, and Wolfe (1991) identified boyhood cross-gender expression as "occurring in the context of a disturbance in the child's relational experience and experience of self" (p. 488). They perceived these boys to have separation anxiety and a trauma-induced attachment disorder that was expressed by appearing feminine. Coates and Person (1985) studied twenty-five "extremely" feminine boys with GID and determined that they exhibited pervasive psychological disturbances, including separation anxiety, difficulty with peers, and behavioral disturbances. Coates (1990) identified the mothers of gender-disturbed boys as having narcissistic, borderline, and dependent personality disorders as well as a high incidence of depression.

Stoller (1968b) inferred that mothers of feminine sons had gender identity conflicts themselves as children, or are bisexual, which led them to devalue men and masculinity. In order for their sons to maintain intimacy with their mothers they must avoid their own masculinity, hence relationships with male peers and fathers are encouraged as a treatment strategy. Rekers (1995a) postulated that boys with severe gender disturbances rarely had male role models. Lothstein (1992) said, "The [male] child's gender identity confusions and inner self structures were molded by the parents in an effort to control their son's body and mind and prohibit him from ever separating and individuating from mother and revealing of father's deficiencies as a caregiver, an intimate person, and a male" (p. 102).

Behavioral treatments have been justified on four grounds (Rekers and Kilgus, 1995; Zucker, 1990b; Zucker and Bradley, 1995). First is the need to eliminate peer ostracism, including alleviating short-term social distress and assisting children to mix more readily with same-sex peers. Second is the need to treat the underlying psychopathology in the families, including anxiety, depression, primitive object relations, and borderline traits found in the mothers of extremely feminine boys (Coates, 1990; Coates and Person, 1985; Marantz, 1984, as cited in Zucker, 1990b). Third is the need to prevent homosexuality, and fourth is the need to prevent gender identity disturbances in adults. Some researchers believe that GID in childhood and adolescence is indicative of later homosexuality or transsexualism. Zucker and Bradley (1995) noted that "homosexuality is the most common postpubertal psychosexual outcome" for children with GID (p. 53).

Although researchers state a concern for gender-variant children experiencing peer ostracism in childhood, they do not seem to focus their energies on sensitivity training in the school system or bias-related violence at a public policy level. In no other area in which children or youth are routinely taunted, battered, and abused (e.g., children with disabilities, racially motivated harassment) would clinicians intervene by modifying the abused child. With gender-variant children these treatments are justified because the child's behavior and expression is believed to emanate from pathological parenting. Very little attention is paid, outside of diagnostics, to treat these parents or intervene in their supposedly deviant behaviors. The clinical focus remains on eliminating the cross-gender expression of children. Some clinicians believe that parents should be seen in therapy because "individual therapy with the child will probably proceed more smoothly and quickly" and "because regular involvement . . . benefits the child's treatment" (Zucker and Bradley, 1995, p. 280). They suggest that the child would be more compliant with treatment when his or her parents are also involved. If these children are living in homes with severely psychopathological parents perhaps it would be best to consider interventions aimed at the parents or even alternative living arrangements for the children.

Despite the attempts to distract critics with issues regarding peer ostracism and parental pathology, it is clear from even a rudimentary overview of the treatment philosophies guiding intervention with gender-variant children that the clinician's primary concern and focus is on the elimination of adult homosexuality and transsexualism. Zucker (1990b) said that regardless of whether the focus of treatment is on the elimination of peer ostracism in childhood or the prevention of transsexualism in adulthood, they are both "so obviously clinically valid and consistent with the medical ethics of our time that either, by itself, would constitute sufficient justification for therapeutic intervention" (p. 30).

However, little evidence supports the thesis that children diagnosed with gender identity disorder in childhood or adolescence grow up to be transsexual, although Cohen-Kettenis (2001) suggested that her current data in the Netherlands may show GID in childhood leading to transsexualism outcomes in higher numbers than previous research. Treatment providers such as Rekers and his colleagues support clinical interventions to "prevent adult gender dysphoria and sexual deviation" (Rekers and Kilgus, 1995, p. 267), even though the etiological linkages between gender variance in childhood and adult transsexualism (as well as "sexual deviation") are still unclear. Research has, however, consistently shown that many children diagnosed with GID often grow up to be homosexual, not transsexual (Bailey and Zucker, 1995; Green, 1987; Zuger, 1984). Zuger's (1984) examination of the literature, as well as his own research, led to his conclusion that "all male homosexuality begins with early effeminate behavior" (p. 96). Indeed, many children who grow up to be lesbian, gay, or bisexual, acknowledge or remember cross-gender behavior in their own childhood (Bell, Weinberg, and Hammersmith, 1981; Saghir and Robins, 1973). Retrospective studies (see Bailey and Zucker, 1995) and anecdotal reports (Rottnek, 1999) of homosexual adults report gender nonconforming behavior to be common in children who grow up to be LGB identified, although this may, of course, present problems of selective recall.

It is interesting that clinics can receive funding to treat "prehomosexual" children when homosexuality is not considered pathological, although, of course, some clinicians still view homosexuality as a treatable condition (Nicolosi, 1991; Socarides, 1999). Corbett (1998) noted that there is no "homosexual boyhood," only a theory of adult homosexuality that is "infused with a pathologized gendered past" (p. 352). Paul (1993) said theories that link cross-gender expression in childhood with "prehomosexual" boyhood are overly biologically deterministic. Homosexuality and transgenderism are sometimes seen as hierarchical disorders, with transsexualism seen as a more severe type of homosexuality. In one reported intervention, a seventeen-year-old boy diagnosed with gender dysphoria was treated with behavioral modification. As his treatment progressed, he went from being transsexual to homosexual, until he was finally and completely cured, i.e., he became heterosexual without gender dysphoria (Barlow, Reynolds, and Agras, 1973).

Bartlett, Vasey, and Bukowski (2000) said, "It would be naive to believe that prevention of homosexuality is not a motivating factor for at least some of the clinicians who work with children referred for gender-atypicality." Zucker (1990b) justified attempts to cure prehomosexual children by saying that "a homosexual lifestyle, in a basically unaccepting culture, simply creates social difficulties" (pp. 29-30). The distaste that many clinicians have for homosexuality is visceral. Irvine (1990) said, "The literature on homosexuality, transsexualism, and sissy boys reveals that mannerisms perceived as feminine are intolerable to researchers" (p. 241). This is most obvious in Rekers' writings, in which his disdain for homosexual behavior on religious and moral grounds is blatant (see Lundy and Rekers, 1995a,b). Rekers even wrote a book called *Shaping Your Child's Sexual Identity* (Rekers, 1982). Rekers and his colleagues are critical of those who advocate for the liberalism of sexual mores, including homosexuality, stating that such advocates have a political agenda (Lundy and Rekers, 1995a; Rekers and Kilgus, 1995). Rekers and colleagues forget that they also have a political agenda, albeit a more conservative one. There is little question about Rekers' (1996) homophobia or his agenda. Rekers goes as far as to suggest that homosexuality should be reexamined as a mental disorder, since its etiology rests in childhood cross-gender identity. As evidence for a connection between childhood gender variance and homosexuality mounts, some activists are critical of clinicians treating GID in prehomosexual boys (Morin and Schultz, 1978) and have accused such clinicians of "homosexual genocide" (Green, 1987, p. 260).

Rekers is the "most vehement and forthright proponent of the view that treatment of GID in children can prevent homosexuality" (Minter, 1999, p. 13), and many clinicians want to distance themselves from his blatant, religiously based homophobia. However, these other clinicians still advocate for interventions to eliminate cross-gender expression employing the same type of behavior modification intervention, stating that they can be "justified on other grounds, including parental taste and parental morality" (Zucker, 1990b, p. 29). Clinical intervention as a response to parental requests is a stance Rekers takes also. He said, "It is appropriate to intervene for a child with cross-gender behavior upon the request of concerned parents who possess the legal rights to grant informed consent for clinical interventions for their children" (Rekers and Kilgus, 1995, p. 267).

Green (1987) believed that "the rights of parents to oversee the development of children is [a] long-established principle. Who is to dictate that parents may not try to raise their children in a manner that maximizes the possibility of a heterosexual outcome?" (p. 260). Green thought that parents have a right to insist on treatment even if treatment will not alter the outcome. He said, "Parents have the legal right to seek treatment to modify their child's cross-gender behavior to standard boy and girl behavior even if their only motivation is to prevent homosexuality" (Green, 1995, p. 2007), although he also stated that there is "no convincing data that anything the therapist does can modify the direction of sexual orientation" (p. 2014). It is important to note that the child need not be disturbed by his or her own behavior—it needs only to be disturbing to adults. All of the writers are clear that cross-gender behavior is profoundly disturbing for parents, and indeed this is enough of a reason to justify intervention.

It is true that parents' rights to raise children as they see fit is a long-established principle in a democratic country, as well it should be. It is also true that these rights have always been limited by social mores. As our society has developed an understanding of child physical and sexual abuse, it has set clearly defined limits regarding a parent's right to "discipline" or punish a child. The sexual rules of conduct allowed between parent and child are also determined by public scrutiny. A parent who allows his or her teenage child to have sex with an adult can be deemed negligent by child protective services. Social mores determine that children must attend school, and parents who homeschool are held to certain educational guidelines. The rights of parents to raise their children as they see fit has always had numerous caveats determining expectations for acceptable behavior. As social mores have changed, previous limitations have also shifted. In many states it is no longer considered in the best interests of the children to be removed from gay or lesbian parents' homes in child custody disputes. It has also become possible for gay couples to adopt children jointly in many states.

The issue here is not simply parents' rights to raise their children to "maximize a heterosexual outcome"—consciously or unconsciously most parents do this anyway, including perhaps gay and lesbian parents. It is rare parents who, in raising their infants and toddlers, do not "assume" and even "assign" heterosexuality through their daily interactions. The issue at stake here is not parental whim but clinical responsibility. It is one thing for a parent to support heterosexuality or even punish gender-deviant behavior. It is another thing entirely for professional researchers and psychotherapists to develop treatment programs to support this ideology. That these programs have not raised the hackles of ethicists surely speaks to an underlying sentiment that having a cross-gender expression is truly deplorable, and that even if we do not know how to fix it, clinicians should do everything they can to try anyway.

Try as they may, little evidence has supported the efficacy of these treatments. Green (1987) completed an extensive longitudinal study on gender-variant boys—whom he referred to as "sissy boys"—and lamented on the "apparent powerlessness of treatment to interrupt the progression from 'feminine' boy to homosexual or bisexual man" (p. 318). Although most parents in his study did not seek therapy for their children even when it was offered, the longitudinal results of those who were treated show a high incidence of adult homosexuality. Nearly three-quarters of those who were available for follow-up interviews as adults identified as homosexual or bisexual. Of the twelve boys who received treatment for GID, nine later identified as gay. In Zuger's (1984) research of fifty-five boys over a twenty-seven-year period, he found that (excluding seven who were lost to follow-up) 72.9 percent were homosexual and 20.8 percent were undecided. Zuger expressed difficulty retaining the boys in therapy because they stated there was "nothing wrong with them and they didn't need it" (p. 91). The evidence points to a connection between feminine behavior in boyhood and adult gay identity, as well as the failure to effectively impact the adult sexual orientation of young feminine boys by manipulating their gender expression, disputing the value of these "treatments."

Rekers (1995) suggested that his team saw "positive results" from behavioral therapy techniques in reducing cross-gender behavior, which according to Zucker (1990b) inferred a reduction in a desire to change sex. Although Zucker believed that short-term benefits to behavioral treatments exist, he expressed reservations about Rekers' methodology and conclusions. Zucker also stated that the short-term results of psychotherapy appeared to show "success," although these children were also in other therapeutic treatments and it would be difficult to sort out the meaning or the results. Mallon (1999) reminded clinicians that, "Since most children desire to please parental figures, it is no wonder that many gender variant children go to great extremes to make adaptations to their 'gender non-conforming' behaviors once they are pointed out" (p. 53), including modifying their behaviors following therapeutic intervention. Whether this infers a resolution of the issues or a reduction of gender dysphoria has not been established. Although no evidence of long-term success of any treatment methods exists, Zucker and Bradley (1995) admitted they are still advocates for the value of these treatments.

Green has recommended the treatment of boys with gender dysphoria since early in his career (Green, 1971), and it is his conviction that stigma and conflict are reduced by these treatments, even if they do not succeed in making these boys heterosexual in adulthood. He has failed, however, to mention the potential negative effects of these treatments and whether "sissy boys" are harmed by treatment. What happens to children who are studied, interviewed, analyzed for their gender deviance? Very little research has been conducted into the impact of these behavioral treatment programs on the self-esteem and identity development of those who are "treated" as though their gender expression is a psychiatric problem. It is possible that the pressures on gender-dysphoric young people to live in the sex role they abhor prevents them from a normative adolescent development, and that some of the mental health disturbances witnessed in adults are related not to the gender issues but to developmental maladjustment in youth (Wren, 2000).

The diagnosis of socially determined gender variances has come under the scrutiny of numerous writers who are critical of the implicit value judgments that underlie these therapeutic interventions. MacKenzie (1994) referred to "so-called treatment for 'feminine' boys" as "nothing more than scare tactics, threats, and physical punishment" (p. 94). As Corbett (1998) remarked, "Within the sissy-boy discourse, femininity becomes a symptom" (p. 355). Given the fact that social expectations about gender have shifted in the past thirty years and that the treatment protocols have shown little success—if success is defined as curing or lessening the gender-variant behavior and expression—these treatments may be more accurately a part of the problem than valid clinical solutions.

FAMILIES WITH GENDER-VARIANT CHILDREN

Many children are brought into treatment by well-meaning and frightened parents who are experiencing fear, worry, anger, confusion, and concern about their child's gender identity and sexual orientation. They often minimize the gender variance, seeing it as normative experimentation or "just a phase," and seek services only when they fear the child will not grow out of it (Stoller, 1967a; Zucker and Bradley, 1995). Even when faced with sex reassignment and transsexualism in their children, it is surprising "how accepting some family members, particularly mothers, can be of their off-springs' change in gender identity" (Steiner, 1990, p. 103).

Zucker and Bradley (1995) identified four salient questions for parents, although they do not directly answer them. These questions are: "(1) Is their child's behavior really a problem? (2) How do they broach the topic with their child? (3) Does their child need to participate in an assessment? [and] (4) Will the assessment damage their child?" (pp. 72-73). It appears that the answers to these questions rest on the answer to question number one: Is the child's behavior really a problem? Treating gender identity disorders in childhood rests on the clinical belief that nonnormative gender behavior is definitely a problem, as evidenced by Robert Stoller's (1968a) comment that the first step in treatment is to "convince the family that the condition is pathological" (p. 253).

If Stoller's position is accurate and the "condition is pathological," then once any caring family is fully convinced of the pathology, they would of course embrace treatment. However, parents have continued to be ambiva-lent about these treatments. Zucker and Bradley (1995) thought that in re-cent years parents were increasingly more ambivalent about the assessment process and less willing to follow through on treatment recommendations. They suggested that the most ambivalent parents probably never initiated calling, and that the parental ambivalence was "part of the problem." They said the ambivalence signaled a poor prognosis for the family's ability to en-ter treatment (pp. 72-73).

Zucker and Bradley (1995) outlined a treatment plan utilized within their clinic and the difficulties with compliance they experienced from parents. Their treatment recommendations for parents included the following guide-lines:

> not allow cross-dressing, discourage cross-gender role play and fan-tasy play, restrict play with cross-sex toys, tell the child they value *him as a boy or her as a girl,* encourage same sex peer relations, and help the child engage in more sex-appropriate or neutral activities. Many parents, however, require ongoing support in implementing the rec-ommendations, perhaps because of their own ambivalence and reser-vations about gender identity issues . . . some of these parents find it difficult to believe that their child has a gender identity problem; oth-ers are reluctant to restrict their child's favorite fantasies or activities. (p. 95, italics mine)

Perhaps parents are noncompliant or resistant because they also see how painful these treatments are for their child. Perhaps they value their child as he or she is and suspect nothing is "wrong" with their child outside of how they are treated in the social milieu. Those who treat GID in children minimize the value of a parent's ambivalence—the natural protective instinct of a parent to question an invasive treatment strategy—and seem unaware of their own influence as "experts" on the assessment process and the damage they can cause. Parents, however, have a right to question whether the assessment or treatment process will be harmful for their children.

Zucker and Bradley (1995) described one case of a four-year-old boy exhibiting GID. Using a semistructured gender identity interview schedule developed in their clinic, they asked the child a series of questions about "his" gender identity (e.g., "Are you a boy or girl?" "Do you think it's better to be a boy or girl?"). The male child consistently stated that he was a girl, which the interviewer challenged. The child eventually ran out of the room to his mother. The clinical assessment stated, "The distress experienced by this youngster appears quite palpable" (Zucker and Bradley, 1995, pp. 56-57). "Distress" is always important to examine when looking at mental health issues; however, Zucker and Bradley did not discuss whether the distress could have been caused by the experience of being "interrogated" by an authority figure in a gender clinic. Instead, they attributed his reaction to their questions to be indicative of the child's level of gender dysphoria and did not consider that their invasive assessment processes were the iatrogenic cause. Given the lack of "successful" treatments for gender issues, these assessment processes seem to be needlessly intrusive lab tests. If the concerns were actually about the child's dysphoria and discomfort, assessment protocols would be less invasive and treatment more focused on addressing the child's emotional pain (instead of increasing it), as well as changing the social conditions that reinforce the discomfort.

It is interesting to note that parental "rights" have been used by these experts to defend the need for treatment, yet much of their treatment is about convincing the parents why the treatment is necessary. Perhaps the researchers are actually treating neither the child's distress nor the parents' distress, but their own. This is important since "distress" is one of the primary reasons for a diagnosis. However, the child's distress is most notable for its absence (Bartlett, Vasey, and Bukowski, 2000).

Sadly, Zucker and Bradley did not address the second question they raised regarding how to initiate discussion within the family system about gender and gender variation, for it is perhaps the salient issue for families with gender-variant children. It is common knowledge that parents "know" their children, and often notice cross-gender behavior in their children at very young ages and suspect they are struggling with sexual or gender identity issues, although they are rarely skilled in how to appropriately address the issues. It seems this is an area of treatment in need of development—

how can family therapists advocate, support, and assist families dealing with childhood gender variance? This issue was addressed by Pleak (1999) who said, "We often find it necessary to intervene in the parents' extremely negative responses and overreactions to their child's cross-gender behavior, which draw inordinate attention to these behaviors and are a set-up for increased gender-atypical behaviors due more to the child's oppositionalism than to gender identification" (p. 44).

Families will need support to grieve their assumptions and hopes as to who their child would become, skill development to address extended family members, siblings, and school officials, and assistance in incorporating their child's needs into the daily flow of family life so that the child does not become the focal point of family "pathology." When a child is dealing with gender variance, sometimes parents will prefer that the child is gay. Parents often say to the therapist, "It's okay with us if he or she is gay, but not 'transsexual'." This illustrates how far society has come in accepting the messages of gay liberation over the past few decades, as well as how gender issues are still intensely stigmatized. Parents also wonder whether they have somehow caused their children's gender issues. They will need reassurance that their children's sex or gender development is not "caused" by their parenting, although their children's self-esteem will be impacted by their reactions. It is hoped that developing therapeutic family interventions that support gender-variant children will become a fertile area of inquiry, study, and professional discourse, for both specialists in child development and family systems theorists.

Let us return to Zucker and Bradley's (1995) first question one last time—"Is this child's behavior really a problem?" If clinicians were to decide that the child's behavior is actually not a problem it would change the entire focus of treatment. If the problem is societal discomfort regarding cross-gender behavior, particularly extreme transgressions, then treatment strategies will focus on education and social advocacy, interpersonal support, and assisting the child and family in emotional adaptation. This does not mean the child will not face problems; it means the problems are not defined as originating within the child, but as existing within a social matrix. Most likely the child will have social problems, interpersonal problems, and potential medical concerns that will need to be addressed. The child's family will face certain parenting dilemmas, including the challenge of rearing a gender-variant child within a dimorphic social structure. Many of these issues are similar to the questions raised in Chapter 10 regarding intersexed children.

GENDER VARIANCE AND PROGRESSIVE TREATMENTS

The Harry Benjamin International Gender Dysphoria Association has addressed the issue of gender-variant children and significantly modified the standards of care for children and adolescents, allowing for earlier medical interventions. The SOC are clear that gender identity disorder as it manifests in children is not necessarily equivalent to adult GID, nor does childhood gender dysphoria necessarily lead to adult transsexualism. It states, "Gender identity disorders in children and adolescents are different from those seen in adults. . . . There is greater fluidity and variability in outcomes, especially in pre-pubertal children" (Meyer et al., 2001, pp. 14-15).

Bartlett, Vasey, and Bukowski (2000), after a careful analysis of the DSM's criteria for GID and the definition for "mental disorder" as outlined in the DSM-IV, concluded that gender-variant children who "do not experience discomfort with their biological sex should not be considered to have GID." They feel that if gender-variant children do not have discomfort with their bodies, they should not be diagnosed with GID. They recommended that in its current form GID should not be in the DSM. They found numerous difficulties with the diagnostic criteria, including the fact that criterion A equates having a preference for other-sex playmates with the stated desire to be a member of the other sex. Because one has to meet only four of five criterion, a child can be diagnosed with GID who does not have any stated desire to be the other sex. Furthermore, criterion B conflates issues of gender and sex and compares issues regarding the child experiencing disgust with his or her genitals to a child preferring other sex clothing and play. Many children may be unhappy with socially proscribed gender roles without necessarily having issues with their biological sex. However, these concerns are not delineated within the current diagnostic criteria.

The DSM's diagnostic criteria conflate three issues that confound the treatment of gender-variant children. These issues are gender variance as an expression of gender diversity and its potentiality in all children, gender variance as an early expression of homosexuality or bisexuality, and gender variance as an early expression of transgenderism with or without gender dysphoria. These issues are described here as natural developmental processes.

Gender Variance As Gender Diversity

The first issue is reflective of the changing social mores regarding gender roles and the sexism that is inherent in the DSM's criteria for GID and consequently sanctioned by treatment programs based on this medical model.

The model reproduces and reinforces a strict polarized gender schema that is no longer necessary in contemporary society. Treating children for gender disorders in a society that is moving toward greater equality in gender-role expression becomes hypocritical.

Many specialists who treat gender identity disorder insist that it is not the clinician's role to change culture, but to help children adapt to culture as it is. Clinicians are, however, agents of social change. Clinicians do not (nor should they) help children adapt to the violence in our culture by accepting it or teaching them to become more violent in order to protect themselves. Clinicians do not encourage young girls to give up their career goals in order to become housewives, even when their goals include professions normally exclusive of women. They do not encourage young black men to forgo their educations and become unemployed and imprisoned. Instead, clinicians work to reduce domestic violence in families, assist families in becoming more intimate and less reliant on consumerism, and encourage parents to become involved with their children in hope of circumventing substance abuse and teenage pregnancy. Indeed, clinicians *should be* agents of change when it comes to helping families rear differently gendered children and assisting schools to integrate such children and prevent peer aggression.

If we are to create a world in which both men and women are productive wage earners and equally responsible for housework and child rearing, then we cannot punish feminine boys and masculine girls who express or experience cross-gender behavior. Gender-role traits such as artistic interest, athletic prowess, tending to the needs of small children, or self-beautifying techniques—even when extremely divergent from the norm—should not be indicative of any "problems," but part of human potentiality for all people, and should be celebrated as such.

Parents, especially mothers, have been blamed for their children's gender variance, and feminism in particular has been indicted. Lothstein (1988, as cited by Zucker, 1990b) asserted that one mother "inadvertently induced a gender identity disorder in her four-year-old son by allowing him to overhear her anti-male speeches to her feminist discussion group" (p. 35). The message here is very clear. Feminism is damaging to small boys, instead of being a valuable philosophy to guide the raising of both girls and boys to respect one another, as well as teaching them sensitivity to power dynamics preexisting in male/female relationships. This, of course, should not imply that "antimale" speeches are healthy for young boys or girls to overhear. Attributing this to feminism is an inadequate representation. It is also true that many women who would disavow the term *feminist* express extremely anti-male sentiment, and even more men who are blatantly antifeminist express antifemale "speeches" as part of daily interactions. However, the damage caused by normative societal sexism does not seem to be a concern for these clinicians.

Feminist authors have spoken eloquently about how these "mother-blame" theories have negatively impacted mothering by encouraging women to emotionally "abandon" their sons to a masculine world of emotional disconnection because they fear feminizing them (Silverstein and Rashbaum, 1995; Luepnitz, 1992). As much as this has been damaging to normatively masculine boys, it has been emotionally devastating for "sissy boys." It disempowers mothers from being supportive and effective allies for their gender-variant children, for their protectiveness and unconditional love becomes translated into causal theories.

However, it is also true that given the sexist assumptions which still abound in the world, many children may be confused by role expectations. For example, a boy who was treated for gender dysphoria during the Vietnam War said that he did not want to "go to the army and be killed, so then I wanted to be a girl 'cause I didn't want to go get killed" (quoted in Burke, 1996, p. 35). Can this honestly be considered a gender identity dysphoria, or is this a young child trying to find an escape clause when faced with an untenable social role? Irvine (1990) asked, "Is it a success for a boy to stop wearing a dress and pick up a gun?" (p. 277).

Treatment for gender-variant children should, first and foremost, normalize the children's gender expression, and educate social service and school systems to celebrate the diversity of human gender expression. Parents need support from therapists to advocate for their children and assist them in developing appropriate self-esteem. Instead of "convincing the family that the condition is pathological," as Stoller (1968a) recommended, concerned clinicians need to do the opposite—they need to assist parents in understanding that their children's gender variance is a normal and natural human variation. Mothers and fathers need to learn to love their children as they are and not send messages of disappointment to their feminine sons and masculine daughters that they are less deserving of love or more deserving of treatment. Parents need assistance to work through their feelings of disappointment, confusion, anger, and fear for the future, so they can be the best advocates for their children. Their children will need them—for although the world is changing, it is changing slowly.

Gender Variance As Early Expression of Same-Sex Sexuality

The second issue that confounds the treatment of gender-variant children is that, according to the extant research, many of these children grow up to be homosexual or bisexual. Since homosexuality is no longer viewed as a pathology within the diagnostic manuals, the only interventions necessary for gender-variant people who may grow up to be gay, lesbian, and bisexual are to assist parents and school systems to accept their children's budding sexuality as it develops and ensure their safety in a homophobic world.

Matilda and Peter Roberts sought counseling for help dealing with their sixteen-year-old son, Kurt. Kurt had recently come out to them as gay, although Matilda said, "I always suspected it." Peter admitted that when Kurt resisted playing sports—Peter's major social interest—he was deeply disappointed. He said, "At some point I realized that if I kept holding my son up to my expectations, I was going to lose him." Kurt was, according to his parents, very flamboyant and feminine in appearance. He was involved in the theater and had a large circle of friends, mostly girls. He had told his parents he had been involved with one boy sexually during summer theater camp. Peter described how he began to attend theatrical productions with Kurt, and even worked with his son on dance routines. He laughingly said, "The son I always wanted has sure changed me." The Robertses were trying to accept their son, realizing that he couldn't "change." They were often brought to tears by their concerns for his future and his risks of contracting HIV. Matilda and Peter worked hard on grieving their own fantasies for who their son should be, as well as figuring out how to be good parents to a young gay man. They realized that they needed to talk with Kurt about safer sex in the same way they had discussed birth control with his older sister. They had come to therapy afraid that they did not know "how" to parent a gay son, but once they accepted his sexual orientation and grew less intimidated by the ways he was "different" from them, they were able to utilize the excellent parenting skills they already possessed to set firm appropriate limits for Kurt, as well as educate him about safety issues.

Gender Variance As an Early Expression of Transgenderism

Normalizing gender-variant behavior for all children and supporting the youthful expression of gay, lesbian, and bisexual identities does not minimize the issues inherent in cross-gender identity for children with gender dysphoria or early transgender expression. Much of what is described in this section might be equally true for all gender-variant children, and is familiar to those who later identify as lesbian, gay, or bisexual. For transgendered children and youth, however, these experiences can be profoundly intense, particularly when gender variance is experienced in a dysphoric way and/or their social world is rigidly gendered.

Young children experiencing gender dysphoria are often confused and in pain. They often do not have words to describe what they are feeling, or in many cases are not cognizant that it is their "gender" that is causing them to feel different. They may be aware that adults are uncomfortable with certain mannerisms or behaviors, but they might not know why. A child experiencing a cross-gender identity may begin manifesting distress and discomfort in the preschool years, when gender-dimorphic behavior becomes institutionalized. Toys, games, dress, and behavior become markedly gender-polarized at this age, and children who deviate become noticeable.

Often this age is more difficult for boys since the clothing restrictions are so much more severe and cross-dressing often begins before or during early puberty. Boys experiencing cross-gender desires often suffer tremendous shame and develop many strategies to hide their behavior. Girls, at least in contemporary culture, can wear pants and, at worst, be considered a "tomboy." However, some girls growing up in more strict environments describe the same kind of secrecy that boys exhibit. One girl, who was raised in an Orthodox Jewish home, used to sneak into the basement and put on not only her brother's clothes but also his prayer shawl. The dysphoria may be profoundly physical, with marked distress regarding genitalia, but is often "only" experienced as a social discomfort, since others do not see them as they see themselves. This was beautifully described in the film *Ma Vie en Rose* (My Life in Pink), the story of a young male child who knows himself to be a girl. His pain is not focused on the fact that he has a male body but rather that his parents, siblings, and peers do not see that he is "really" a girl.

In families in which gender is rigidly defined and the gender expectations for boys and girls is markedly disparate and strictly adhered to, young children expressing gender-variant behavior might experience their gender discomfort more acutely at an earlier age. Sometimes parents can be very direct in their disapproval, even to the point of abusive behavior. For example, a woman in a shoe store screamed loudly at her seven-year-old son when he took the purple snow boots off the shelf: "No son of mine is going to wear those girl shoes!" In other families, the disapproval might be more subtle. Boys may be pushed into sports or girls may be forced to grow their hair or pierce their ears. Gilbert (2000) described the psychological and social process that young boys who are gender variant experience and how adults often carefully scrutinize their gender behavior. He said a boy "learns very quickly not to make these desires public. . . . He learns to sublimate the feelings of wrong-ness, and, often, though he watches little girls and, at least partially, identifies with them, envies them, wants to be with them."

Children who are aware that they are not gender normative may consciously avoid expressing it, and life then becomes a challenge of concealment. For others, the awareness remains hidden, denied, and often dissociated from their conscious life. Some children are pegged or marked as being differently gendered and are often labeled homosexual or "queer," while others express no outer signs of their dysphoria and are spared the social stigma, but not necessarily the psychological dissonance. Miller (1996) said, "Either the child acts out by taking on the social role of the opposite gender and trying everyone's patience and expertise, or the child learns to pretend and lie about [his or her] perceived identity . . . in order to fit in" (p. 40). The price for "acting out" is often to be treated for their "condition" in the programs described earlier, which reinforces the idea that gender differences are pathological for both the child and his or her parents. The price for pretending and lying about one's authentic gender identity is the construction of a false self and the corollary psychological dysfunction. Sadly, the psychosocial problems that result are blamed on the gender issues instead of the process of repressing them.

In families in which gender is not as rigidly defined and both boys and girls are allowed to play in traditional male and female gendered activities, these distinctions, and the inherent turmoil that ensues, might not become obvious until bodily changes manifest in puberty. Many young people are hopeful that their bodies will miraculously "change" once they begin puberty, and they experience great confusion and pain having to face adolescence and adulthood in the "wrong" body. One biological female described her profound surprise in puberty when she realized that she was developing breasts. She had assumed she would begin to mature into a man when she grew up, as her brother had. Burgess (1999) said, "Physically, transgender youth may become repelled or ashamed of their developing sexual characteristics. They may begin to wear bulky clothing year-round to mask physical changes, and to use tight undergarments or bandages to bind breasts or genitals" (p. 41).

Adolescents struggling with gender dysphoria are in a difficult and potentially volatile position. Youth are especially leery of telling their parents, and many adolescents do not disclose their cross-dressing, but are instead discovered. In Di Ceglie and colleagues' (2002) clinic in London, 80 percent of the youth over twelve were self-referred for treatment, seeking assistance and solace from professionals. Adolescents experiencing gender dysphoria are often confused about their sexual identity, unsure whether they are gay. Unfortunately, friends, parents and even helping professionals are often confused about this too. One client discussed how she had told her mother that she thought she was a boy at age fifteen, and her mother found a social worker who specialized in working with gay adolescents. This client came out as lesbian at fifteen with the support of her social worker and mother. In her early twenties she realized that she still felt profound discomfort around her gender, and didn't see herself as a lesbian, but as a "guy." Unfortunately, this had never been addressed in therapy (Lev, 1998).

Due to their age, it is often hard for youth to access therapeutic help, and they find the doors closed to most medical assistance until they are at least sixteen years old, and perhaps eighteen. One young transgendered woman, desperate for someone to listen to her, tried to cut off her penis and nearly bled to death. In the hospital emergency room four medical personnel asked the young woman, "What were you thinking?" Although they were shocked by her behavior, none of them sat down to actually hear the answer. Young people struggling with gender identity issues often feel alienated from their parents, isolated from their peers, and make up a large percentage of young people who are living on the streets, turning to drugs, or attempting to end their lives. Gender-variant, gay, lesbian, and bisexual youth are at potential risk for numerous mental health problems, violence, sexual assault, suicidality, homelessness, and substance abuse (Herrell et al., 1999; Garofalo et al., 1998, 1999; Gibson, 1994; Klein, 1999; Lev and Lev, 1999; Pazos, 1999; Remafedi et al., 1991, 1998; Sadowski and Gaffney, 1998; SAMHSA:CAT, 2001; Savin-Williams, 1994). Although statistics are more readily available for LGB youth than transgendered youth, most studies acknowledge that gender-nonconforming expression is a major risk factor in becoming the victim of violence. It is also unclear how many youth identified in studies as LGB are gender variant, gender nonconforming, transgendered, and/or transsexual.

A brief overview of the literature reveals startling statistics about the quality of life for LGBT youth. According to a 1989 report of the Secretary of Health and Human Services' Task Force on Youth Suicide, "gay" youth account for 30 percent of completed suicides and forty percent of LGBT youth have attempted or seriously contemplated suicide (Garofalo et al., 1999; McDaniel, Purcell, and D'Augelli, 2001; Remafedi, Farrow, and Deisher, 1991). Almost half of gay male youth and 20 percent of lesbian youth are verbally or physically assaulted in school (Gibson, 1994), and LGBT youth are four times more likely to be threatened with a weapon on school property than heterosexual peers (Garofalo et al., 1998). Youth, particularly males, who report same-sex romantic attractions are more likely to experience extreme forms of violence than those who report exclusively other-sex attractions. They are more likely to witness violence as well as to be perpetrators of violence (Russell and Joyner, 2001). Many LGBT youth leave home or are forced to leave their homes because of homophobic or transphobic family situations or family violence, and turn to prostitution in order to survive (Klein, 1999; Kruks, 1991; Savin-Williams, 1994). LGBT youth often feel isolated, and the weaker their family relationships are, the less likely they are to come out to their parents, which can further isolate them. Finally, research has shown that a high incidence of substance use and misuse exists among LGBT youth (Kreiss and Patterson, 1997; Lombardi and van Servellen, 2000; McDaniel, Purcell, and D'Augelli, 2001; Remafedi et al., 1991; Savin-Williams, 1994). That gender-variant youth experience violence and peer ostracism is undeniable. Whether their struggles are greater than other children who are "different" (e.g., children of color, disabled children, overweight children) is not yet known (Bartlett, Vasey, and Bukowski, 2000).

Savin-Williams (2001) also questioned how researchers have defined sexual minority youth as well as the act, meaning, or seriousness of the suicide attempt. He asked whether the hardships of identity development in youth have been exaggerated and whether LGBT youth feel that suidicality is a necessary part of their emerging identity and community affiliation due to intense focus on the issue by professionals.

The information that specifically addresses transgendered youth is sparse. However, evidence suggests that they suffer from all of the previously discussed mental health difficulties in addition to being at a higher risk of violence (Denny, 1995; Di Ceglie et al., 2002; James, 1998; Wilchins, 1997). Many transgender youth also experience medical problems related to self-administering hormones obtained through the black market and without medical guidance. They are at potential risk for self-harm and self-mutilation as they attempt to deal with gender dysphoria and body dysmorphia that increases with puberty (Lothstein, 1992; Swann and Herbert, 1999). Burgess (1999) said, "In extreme cases, young people may also make attempts at removing unwanted sex organs through auto-castration or constant repeated pounding of breasts" (p. 41). That this population is in need of services is undeniable. Sadly, sometimes services are sought, but quickly minimized by the family.

Casey, a ten-year-old female, was brought to therapy because of her tomboyish behavior and insistence that she wanted to be a boy. After a few sessions, which confirmed the child's persistent gender dysphoria, her parents discontinued therapy when she expressed romantic interest in a boy at school and agreed to grow her hair longer.

Clinicians have used three main approaches to treating children and youth with gender issues (Swann and Herbert, 1999). The first approach is to alter the gender identity to match the biological sex. This is still the standard approach, despite the lack of evidence supporting this as a successful intervention. The second approach is to use supportive psychotherapy with the hope of lessening distress. This approach appears to be a necessary component of any treatment program working with transgendered populations. The final approach is to utilize a treatment strategy that views transgender identification as a viable outcome. This treatment approach stands in opposition to the current wisdom and has raised significant ethical dilemmas.

The most glaring issue that arises in contemplating progressive treatment strategies for transgendered youth, i.e., those that do not pathologize or attempt to "cure" the gender variance, involves the ethical dilemmas inherent in prescribing hormonal and surgical interventions to underage and immature persons versus their autonomy and ability to make informed decisions (Swann and Herbert, 1999). As Cohen-Kettenis and van Goozen (1997) said, "The chance of making the wrong diagnosis and the consequent risk of postoperative regret is therefore felt to be higher in adolescents than in adults, as a consequence of the developmental phase itself" (p. 263). Assisting adolescents in making permanent and irreversible body changes evokes for the medical community the specter of adolescent identity crises and youthful "phases" that in maturity can lead to legal battles with adults who later "change their minds" and cite medical incompetence. Youth are still legally under their parents' guardianship, and few physicians will contradict parental wishes; few parents will advocate for permanent body changes for their children.

Since we do not yet have evidence that gender variance in childhood will yield a transsexual trajectory—indeed, we have evidence that it often does not—a cautious, measured approach seems ethical and reasonable (Meyerburg, 1999; Smith, van Goozen, and Cohen-Kettenis, 2001). It may also protect those who resolve their gender identities with maturity. However, these protective strategies may also become paternalistic and impede the ability for transsexual youth to make adaptive sex reassignments early in life.

Earlier sex reassignment may yield some benefits. First, the earlier in puberty reassignment is established the less physical bodily changes would develop in the direction of their biological sex (Cohen-Kettenis, van Goozen, and Cohen, 1998; Cohen-Kettenis and Gooren, 1999). This would mean they would develop fewer secondary sex characteristics, some of which cause irreversible manifestations that would hinder their ability to pass after sex reassignment. Some of the difficulties for those born male in presenting as females often involve height, body hair growth, deepening of the voice, and male balding patterns—all of which can be prevented by delaying puberty. In those born female, halting physical maturation will delay the growth of breasts, allow for potential increased height, and delay the roundedness of the hips caused by the surge of female hormones at menarche. Halting the progression of these sex-linked biological characteristics will allow these adolescents to mature without developing physically in their natal sex. Gooren and Delemarre-van de Waal (1996) said, "A large number of adult transsexuals . . . remember puberty with abhorrence, since the hormones of puberty precisely induced the body characteristics they perceived as improper in relation to their gender identity. . . . They all agree that this period in their lives has been a vexation." Brown and Rounsley (1996) referred to puberty as "nature's cruel trick." Research has shown that people who transition in adolescence show improved postsurgical psychological adjustment as compared to transsexuals who transition later in life (Cohen-Kettenis, van Goozen, and Cohen, 1998; Cohen-Kettenis and van Goozen, 2002).

If development is not halted and sex-linked characteristics are allowed to develop, it will, in some cases, make successful passing in adulthood nearly impossible, which can interfere with social acceptability, self-esteem, and work opportunities. No one can deny that, for example, an extremely tall female with a deep voice might be the focus of questions about her transsexualism. Reversing the effects of physical maturation will also require expensive and painful cosmetic and surgical interventions to assist passing, such as breast removal for females and electrolysis of facial hair for males. Although there is certainly a great diversity of human sex-linked characteristics in both males and females in terms of height, body-fat distribution, hair growth patterns, and even breast development, for those who are transsexual successful transition often rests on the success of their ability to pass. Passing is often dependent on the cues of gender attribution, making what might appear to be minor gender discrepancies for others into details that foil acceptable presentation.

The second benefit of earlier sex reassignment is that these youth would not need to develop a false self in a gender identity and expression that does not feel authentic to them. Their socialization as women or men would happen naturally during their pubescent years, avoiding the need to "unlearn" their original gender socialization and learn a new one. This developmental process would take place during the proper life-cycle stage for exploration of sexual and gender identity, and would assist these adolescents in a more integrated synthesis of all of the various issues of identity that are normatively examined during youth. Many partners of adult transsexuals comment that during transition their spouses act like "teenagers" and appear to go through a second maturation. Indeed, because a salient part of the self involving core gender identity has been submerged, denied, ignored, or repressed throughout their teenage years and adulthood, it would make sense they would have to "go back" and reclaim and integrate developmental processes. Stating that earlier sex reassignment would assist youth in an easier gender socialization does not deny the feminist position that the socialization of children needs to be less rigid, nor does it infer a support of "men" and "women" as living in two separate spheres. However, it does acknowledge that these dualities exist in the world, and that transgendered and transsexual youth will have easier lives if they are allowed to mature within a social gender that is congruent with their core gender identity. This will not protect them from all the inherent complications of adolescent gender development available to their peers. Hopefully, it will alleviate some of the additional stressors of gender dysphoria during the turbulence of adolescence.

The third benefit of earlier sex reassignment is that the struggles of coping with gender dysphoria can impact psychosocial development and increase various mental-health-related issues, what Cohen-Kettenis and van Goozen (2002) refer to as "iatrogenic damage" caused by withholding treatment. As cited earlier, youth dealing with sexual and gender identity struggles have higher suicidality, homelessness, depression, acting-out, and substance abuse issues. Feeling "stuck" until adulthood in a gender identity expression that does not feel authentic "engenders feelings of hopelessness and slows down their social, psychological, and intellectual development" (Cohen-Kettenis and van Goozen, 1997, p. 264). These youth watch their bodies develop while they tick off the days until they are mature enough to be seen as adults by the medico-therapeutic establishment and judged competent to make their own medical decisions. Zucker and Bradley (1995) said, "When adolescents . . . are significantly stressed and the process of achieving sex reassignment surgery . . . is delayed, their anxiety increases; this may lead to a variety of acting-out behaviors" (p. 309), including various attempts at self-harm. It is unclear how many of the mental health issues that are cited in the literature to be present in adult transsexuals seeking treatment are the result not of their transsexualism per se, but of the need to develop a false self and repress an authentic gender identity during the crucial years of their adolescent development.

Examining the obvious benefits of early sex reassignment does not solve the ethical dilemmas associated with assessing and approving young people for irreversible medical procedures. If anything it highlights the need to develop criteria to distinguish those gender-variant youth who are transsexual from those who are homosexual, bisexual, confused, or struggling with other issues that are manifesting with gender dysphoria (e.g., trauma related to sexual abuse, body dysmorphic disorders). Cohen-Kettenis and van Goozen (1997) outlined a complex protocol for considering sex reassignment surgery for teenagers. This is a valuable and useful document for the consideration of medical and surgical intervention, but progressive treatment protocols are also necessary to assist children and youth in cross-gender behavior and expression that may or may not include a surgical progression.

TRANSGENDER EMERGENCE—
STEP-BY-STEP MATURATION

Do I contradict myself?
Very well then I contradict myself,
(I am large, I contain multitudes.)

Walt Whitman

Children and youth experiencing their own emergence go through similar stages as adults, except that they have often not "submerged" their gender variance. The differences between adults and children coping with transgenderism are perhaps more a matter of conscious awareness and ability to put into language their experience. Youth are also impacted by adults who can control their access to information. Often young people who are aware of their gender issues do not go through a period of denial, avoidance, or repression, but are living in an awareness stage from early consciousness. How this is dealt with depends on the reactions of family when they become attuned to their child's gender-variant expression. The more the gender behavior is repressed externally (through punishment or ostracism), the more intense the discomfort will be for the child, and generally the less information (or the less accurate the information) they will be able to access.

Supporting Cross-Gender Expression

Although it is still rare, children today are being raised in homes in which they are not being taught to repress their unique gender expressions and therefore not experiencing their emergence within a hostile environment (Boenke, 1999; Just Evelyn, 1998). Perhaps this will help them construct a functional gender identity within a more graceful developmental process, eliminating the need for self-hating defense structures. However, these children need to be taught coping skills to deal with an oppressive social system. It is hoped that because the family is respecting and honoring their unique gender expression, that they will not grow up with shame and denial.

The first issue for gender-variant children is the question of "allowing" them to dress or behave as they desire, even when it goes against social prescriptions of proper boy/girl expression. Conventional wisdom suggests that allowing children to do this would encourage the behavior and, in essence, promote it. The alternative, of course, is to refuse to allow the cross-dressing, and attempt to alleviate the behaviors through behavior modification and punishment. Allowing children to cross-dress may incur the wrath of social service agencies and legal authorities, who then step in to judge whether the child's normative behavior is caused by a parental pathology, highlighting the double-bind for these parents, who are blamed for inducing the behavior and then punished for advocating for the children.

For parents, choosing to advocate and support children who present with cross-gender expression can present many challenges, and potentially puts them into an adversarial relationship with social services agencies and the educational system. Simply allowing a child to cross-dress or respecting his or her desire to be referred to by a different name can be viewed as child abuse. In August 2000, an Ohio court removed a six-year-old child from her home after her parents tried to enroll her in school as a girl. Aurora Lipscomb was born physically a boy, but had been identifying as a girl since she was two years old. After years of counseling, her parents were following the guidelines of the child's therapist by accepting the child's cross-gender identity, yet she was forcibly removed from her home by child protective services (GenderPAC, 2000). In another case, a transgendered teen in Boston took her school to court in order to win the right to dress in female clothing (GenderPAC, 2001).

It seems that the first step in developing more progressive treatment protocols for gender-dysphoric, transgendered, transsexual, cross-dressing, LGB, and questioning children and youth, is simply to support a greater diversity of gender expression for all children. The assumption has been that it will be harmful to these children to "allow" cross-dressing expression. The actuality is that it has proved harmful to try to control it. This should, of course, be part of an overall treatment plan that assists the child and his or her family in supportive psychotherapy. Community services that create supportive environments for sexual-minority youth are a necessary addition to existing social services (James, 1998).

Supportive Psychotherapy and Family Therapy

Supportive psychotherapy for gender-variant children and youth should include:

- information and education about gender diversity for parents, the child, and his or her siblings (as age appropriate);
- referral and resource information for support groups and e-mail lists to alleviate isolation;
- advocacy for addressing schools and legal authorities; and
- appropriate boundary and limit setting.

Clinicians serving this population need to be informed about gender diversity issues and child development, and have access to resource information and educational sources. It is not enough to provide competent psychotherapeutic services, but is incumbent on the clinicians to serve as an advocate in addressing systemic and macrolevel policies that interfere with the child's safety. Group therapy can be a valuable tool, particularly for transgendered youth who are living without parental supports (Klein, 1999).

Clinicians need to be savvy to the manipulation used by some gender-variant children who have learned to "use" their gender differences to intimidate authority figures. Sometimes parents grow frustrated by their children's acting-out behaviors and throw their hands up in exasperation, allowing their children to engage in risk-taking behavior. For instance, a female child with small but newly visible breasts should not be encouraged to go swimming topless—even when she insists on this. Instead, camp personnel can be educated about her situation and can perhaps be encouraged to stretch their pool rules to allow her to swim with trunks and a T-shirt.

Depending on the nature of the child's needs, the safety issues inherent in the community, as well as the parents' ability to assimilate the necessary information to be supportive to their child, children can be encouraged to only cross-dress at home, wear unisex clothing, be monitored in their use of transgendered resources on the Internet, change their name to a more gender-neutral one, or explore their cross-gender identity while on vacation. In some situations children might need to attend a more supportive school, particularly if the school system is highly gendered in its daily programs. The parents of the child's friends might need to be educated about the issues, especially if the child is "passing" as someone of the other sex in the schoolyard or while dating. One transgendered teenager dated numerous girls across town at another high school, passing the entire time as a boy. However, when his cover was blown by a neighborhood child, he was severely beaten by other kids, and faced with police action for "impersonating" a boy.

Supportive psychotherapy, coupled with advocacy for children and their families, can address many of the same issues clinicians have already identified (peer ostracism, social isolation). However, the focus is not on changing the child, but helping him or her adapt to the constraints of a gendered culture, while simultaneously working to change the social system that encourages the abuse. Despite the social stigma of transgenderism, many children and youth are actually quite accepting of peer difference, especially when it is not penalized within school and social systems. In one school, when a boy was suspended from school for wearing a dress because he found it more comfortable, eight other boys responded by also wearing skirts to class (GenderPac, 1998). Peers, despite the potential for abuse and violence, can also be incredibly solid supports, and can serve a protective role in assisting friends through gender transitions.

The strategies related earlier may be enough for many children, at least until puberty. Puberty brings with it many complications, including bodily changes, an increase in social peer pressure, as well as a growing independence from parental authority. For many gender-variant youth, adolescence is a time of intense pressure and fear. The realization that their body is maturing in the "wrong" direction coupled with societal pressure to conform can increase anxiety, depression, and other acting-out behaviors.

Linda Williams, a single working mother, sought therapy because her eleven-year-old daughter, Lakisha, refused to wear dresses and had given herself a boy's haircut. Lakisha had always been a "tomboy," but her behavior was becoming increasingly frightening for her mother, particularly since Lakisha became more aggressive toward any attempt to feminize her. Lakisha was assessed and labeled with gender identity disorder and oppositional defiant disorder and was treated with behavior modification intervention. The clinician explained that some of Lakisha's behavior might be related to not having a father in the home. Lakisha's behavior became increasingly hostile and, after a suicide attempt, she was referred to a psychiatric hospital and placed on psychotropic medication for bipolar disorder. It was never suggested that Lakisha's behavior could be a normative response for an adolescent entering puberty and struggling with issues related to her sexual or gender identity exploration. It was never suggested that her masculine appearance could be a developmentally appropriate expression of Lakisha's authentic emergent self and that her aggressiveness was a survival strategy.

Situations such as Lakisha's are all too familiar to gender specialists. Unfortunately the gender issues are often seen as sequelae to other more "serious" psychological problems. When Lakisha began to address her gender issues with a supportive therapist, she revealed that she saw herself as more of a "guy" than a girl and that her sexual attraction was to other girls. It is likely that Lakisha's aggressive behaviors were treated more harshly by previous professionals because she was a large black female. Lakisha was struggling with her developing body, was terrified to be "gay," and described feeling like an "alien" in her body. Lakisha's behavior significantly improved once she was able to talk about these issues, first with a therapist, then with her closest friend, and eventually with her mother. Lakisha spent much of her early adolescence "trying on" various social identities in her attempts to feel comfortable with herself. She identified as "gay," "butch," and "boi," and experimented with various clothing styles as she struggled with how to integrate her masculine identity. By the age of sixteen, she was involved in a "lesbian" relationship in which she was comfortable being butch identified but would not allow her partner to touch her body. She was no longer angry or impulsive and was not taking any psychotropic medication. She explored in therapy whether she was interested in taking hormones or "becoming" a man. Her process of examining her gender dysphoria was mature—an intellectual and emotional process—but one that owned and embraced her masculinity and exploration as part of her normative adolescent gender development.

Reversible Treatments—Real-Life Experience and Partial Hormonal Treatment

Supportive psychotherapy has its limits for many transgendered teens, particularly those with a transsexual trajectory. As described earlier, when puberty begins to transform their bodies, transgendered teens are often thrown into a deep psychological crisis that includes acting-out and self-harm behaviors, substance misuse, depression, anxiety, and suicidality. It is a frightening time for parents, as well as therapists, and of course, a terrifying time for the transgendered child. The following case describes a natal male child.

Maxie spent much of her early puberty in and out of psychiatric hospitals. At fifteen, she arrived in therapy with a case file four inches thick, all carefully organized and copied by her mother. Maxie had been exhibiting classic gender issues since early childhood, expressed in her dress, her choice of toys and playthings, and her preference for female friends. She had been articulate since her early toddler years about wanting to be a girl, which was severely discouraged by her traditional father but more tolerated by her mother. In early puberty, Maxie began running away from home, getting into legal trouble, and was caught stealing and ingesting her mother's hormones. She felt disgusted in the few attempts she made to be sexual—with both boys as well as girls—and began binding her genitals. She was repeatedly hospitalized and diagnosed with numerous mental health disorders, including bipolar disorder, depression, impulse disorder, somatization disorder, and psychotic episodes, as well as numerous personality disorders (narcissistic, borderline, histrionic). Her mother had even taken her to see nationally recognized gender specialists, all of whom recognized Maxie's severe gender dysphoria. However, few recommendations were made for her treatment (outside of psychotropic medications to alleviate her symptoms), nor did any clinicians ever offer family counseling to assist the family. Maxie was enrolled in an "alternative" school, in which she was doing poorly and trying to "get away" with whatever feminizing the school and her family would allow.

Maxie presented with a clear gender identity disorder trajectory, but as often happens in cases such as this, professionals were unwilling to recommend transition, particularly given her extensive history of mental health problems. When it was recommended that Maxie begin living full-time as a female, her family, school officials, and a handful of clinical experts breathed a near audible sigh of relief. Although the professional team was unsure "where" to begin, Maxie had no reservations. She transitioned immediately, changing her hairstyle, adapting her already feminine clothing, asking people to use female pronouns, and making plans for hormonal and surgical treatments. Within weeks she was literally a changed person. Although still intense, immature, and impulsive, her behavior modified to a more typical moody adolescent behavior. Her acting out, risk taking, and dramatic presentation decreased significantly, and her suicidality disappeared. She became somewhat more engaged in her schooling and talked about dating, careers, and her future. At sixteen Maxie began a hormonal regimen. The transition did not alleviate all of Maxie's problems. Indeed, it created new ones (changing her working papers to a female gender involved legally changing her name; taunting from kids in the neighborhood, including getting beaten up; a growing distance with her father; and having to face her school-related difficulties, including testing for learning disabilities). However, the severity of her psychopathology was lessened dramatically as Maxie was able to live authentically without having to "force" the authority figures in her life to see her as she is. A recent research study of adolescents who are seeking sex reassignment surgery does not show an elevated level of psychopathology or mental health problems (Cohen-Kettenis and van Goozen, 2002).

Transgendered youth develop many adaptive ways to present in their desired gender, altering their clothing styles, haircuts, mannerisms, creating false breasts (MTFs), and packing their crotch with socks to look as if they have a penis (FTMs) (Pazos, 1999). For many youth, however, this is not enough to assist them in effectively passing, and medical treatments become necessary for their mental stability. Developing treatment protocols to begin youth on hormonal regimens is a complex process involving an intensive assessment, including information from family, clinicians, and school systems, and real-life experience. Medically prescribed partial hormone treatments serve to halt the progression of puberty, leaving the child in a suspended latency. Partial hormone treatments are commonly in the form of luteinizing hormone-releasing hormone (LHRH) agonists, as well as other hormones that impact the endrocinological system such as progestins or antiandrogens to suppress estrogen or testosterone production (Cohen-Kettenis and van Goozen, 1997; Gooren and Delemarre-van de Waal, 1996; Meyer et al., 2001). The benefits of these treatments are that they block the action of sex steroids and stop the masculinzation/feminization of the body along the normative natal pathway.

The effects of LHRH agonists are fully reversible, and if the medication is stopped, the hormonal activity of puberty is resumed. As Gooren and Delemarre-van de Waal (1996) said, "Treatment with LHRH agonists buys time . . . [and] can be used when there are clear signs of sexual maturation to delay pubertal development until an age that a balanced and responsible decision can be made" (p. 73).

These treatment regimens are dependent on the ability of the adolescent to make informed and educated decisions, as well as the support and approval of his or her parents. Swann and Herbert (1999) suggested, "The ability to make informed decisions is one of the hallmarks of a mature adolescent" (p. 21). Certainly, some people believe that adolescents are too young to make decisions for their future—despite the historical reality that in most epochs throughout the world people were marrying and having children in what we now call "adolescence." Not all teenagers are capable of making these decisions, and many are coping with other developmental issues that may confuse and mask the gender issues. However, some young transsexuals are clearly competent to make decisions about their bodies and identities and should be encouraged to do so with emotional and medical supports. Gooren and Delemarre-van de Waal (1996) said, "It is to be remembered that giving, *but also withholding* endocrine treatment is a momentous and responsible decision from the side of the therapist with important implications for the person in question" (p. 69).

Irreversible Treatments—Virilizing/Feminizing Hormones and Surgical Treatments

The treatments listed earlier are all reversible. However, once virilizing and feminizing hormonal treatments are begun, their effects are not totally reversible. The SOC and the Royal College of Psychiatrists' (1998) guidelines for care refer to hormonal treatments as "partially reversible." However, once breast growth begins on a natal male or facial hair growth and voice depth commences for a natal female, "reversibility" becomes a questionable term. Certainly, natal males can have breast tissue removed and natal females can have facial hair electrolyzed, but these are extensive medical interventions for treatments that are originally medically induced. It seems best to treat hormonal treatments as "irreversible" for the purposes of psychological decision making. The SOC recommend that partially reversible hormonal treatments not commence until the adolescent is at least sixteen years old.

Surgical intervention, because of its irreversible nature, is rarely performed and usually discouraged until age eighteen (Meyer et al., 2001). Transsexual transition in youth has been treated delicately and conservatively. However, at least one clinic has performed these surgeries, and postoperative follow-up studies have shown that sexual reassignment surgery has been "therapeutic and beneficial" (Cohen-Kettenis and van Goozen, 1997, p. 269; Cohen-Kettenis and van Goozen, 2002). The gender dysphoria was resolved and "socially and psychologically these adolescents do not seem to function very differently from nontranssexual peers" (Cohen-Kettenis and van Goozen, 1997, p. 269). For the adolescent who has desired surgery his or her whole life, the transition can sometimes be rather smooth, which is not to deny the difficulties coping with socialization and the judgments of others.

Regardless of the trajectory of treatment, general therapeutic guidelines for working with children and youth with GID exist. Di Ceglie (1995, 1998) outlined treatment aims, some of which include: fostering recognition and nonjudgmental acceptance of the gender identity problem; ameliorating associated emotional, behavioral, and relationship difficulties; breaking the cycle of secrecy; encouraging exploration of mind-body relationships by promoting close collaboration among professionals; allowing mourning processes to occur; and enabling the child or adolescent and the family to tolerate uncertainty in the area of gender identity development. Guidance in the treatment of children and young people with gender identity problems has recently been published by the Royal College of Psychiatrists (1998). These guidelines advocate a cautious approach, with reversible and partially reversible physical interventions being delayed as long as it is clinically appropriate.

Clearly, the decision to transition in youth is a decision that must be made carefully by the adolescent, his or her family, and with competent and skilled professional assistance. Personal stories of transition also offer successful outcomes (Just Evelyn, 1998) as do follow-up studies of those who have successfully transitioned (Smith, van Goozen, and Cohen-Kettenis, 2001). Gender dysphoria is emotionally painful, and few youth are able to access supportive services. Most are being treated in behavioral treatment programs or psychiatric settings, or have run away from home and are making their own way on the streets. Mallon (1999) said, "Although some transgendered children are healthy and resilient, many gender variant children are at great risk within their family system and within institutional structures" (p. 57). It is this lack of services that must be addressed—the violence that transgendered youth experience at the hands of family, school systems, peers, and treatment programs that are geared toward breaking their spirit. The literature has been mostly silent on these issues.

The spectrum of treatment for transgendered children and youth must include supportive individual and family therapy, social work advocacy in schools and other societal institution, as well as access to medical treatment. The need to treat gender-dysphoric children and their families together is essential for effective resolution and/or transition. Parents will struggle with letting go of previous dreams for their children and worry about the future. Parents essentially need to transition with their children (TSON-PFLAG, 1999). As Cooper (1999) said, when someone is coming out as trans and changing their gender identity they are not just "expressing their innermost sense of self but are re-establishing their relationship to the world" (p. 113). For youth this includes re-creating relationships with their families. Although assisting a child through a gender transition or helping them integrate a nonnormative gender expression may not have been on most parents' agenda when they planned on beginning a family, all parents know that the nature of parenting is endless surprise at whom their children actually become. Therapists can help families to cease from seeing their gender-variant children as disordered and disturbed and embrace their differently gendered children as life's precious and unique, albeit unexpected, gifts.

Chapter 10

The Treatment of Intersexed People: Time for a New Paradigm

[G]enital ambiguity is "corrected" not because it is threatening to the infant's life but because it is threatening to the infant's culture.

Suzanne J. Kessler
The Medical Construction of Gender, 1990

The term *intersex* refers to congenital anomalies of the reproductive system, which can sometimes involve genital ambiguity. These conditions happen frequently enough to be referred to by the American Association of Pediatrics as "common childhood problems." Approximately one child in every 2,000 will be born with ambiguous genitalia that make the determination of his or her natal sex difficult (see Preves, 2003). Almost 2 percent of the population is born with biological or physical conditions that can be considered intersexed (Fausto-Sterling, 2000)—an enormous amount of people given the virtual silence on this subject and the medical bioethical issues it raises. The number of people whose lives are strongly affected by an intersex condition is about 0.1 percent (Blackless et al., 2000), and estimates range from 1 to 4 percent of the population are impacted by genital ambiguity (Preves, 2003).

When a child is born in a modern medical facility, the first pronouncement in the delivery room is the child's sex. Literally, the first words spoken are often "It's a boy" or "It's a girl." This announcement, and all the ramifications that follow, is based on the initial visible examination of the child's genitalia. Chromosomal abnormalities are not identified because no indications for karyotyping exist if the genitals appear normal (Abramsky et al., 2001). The presence or absence of a penis becomes the determining mark of sex identification. In humans the physical distinction at birth between males and females is easily determined, unlike, for example, newborn cats. Many families have funny stories attesting to this ambiguity when their male cat has kittens.

With the recent advancement of pelvic sonograms, parents and medical professionals are able to obtain information about their baby's sex in utero. The inconvenient placement of a finger, of course, has been responsible for numerous erroneous "sex sightings." Some obstetricians refuse to reveal the sex of the fetus, protecting themselves from lawsuits when parents claim they have experienced "psychological distress" by preparing the nursery and buying clothing in the "wrong" colors. Recent research shows that when information regarding chromosomal anomalies is discovered during prenatal testing, health care professionals are ill prepared to counsel parents. In many cases no protocol was in place to utilize when informing parents, no one on staff was knowledgeable about sex chromosome anomalies or had training in counseling parents, and in some cases staff were misinformed about the impact of these conditions and therefore offered faulty advice to parents (Abramsky et al., 2001). Preves (2003) warned that prenatal screening, depending on how it is used by medical professionals, could lead to an increase in selective abortion to prevent intersexed births.

ASSIGNING SEX AND THE MODERN MEDICAL PROTOCOLS

> The demands put on the hermaphroditic body therefore are many, as many agendas—scientific, medical, personal, national, professional, moral, and political—meet. This is perhaps inevitable, for in any human culture, a body is never a body unto itself, and bodies that openly challenge significant boundaries are particularly prone to being caught in the struggles over those boundaries.
>
> Alice Domurat Dreger
> *Hermaphrodites and the Medical Invention of Sex,* 1998

Although the sex of the embryo is determined at the time of conception, the anatomical differences between males and females do not develop until about six weeks into gestation (see Figure 3.1). The gonads are the undifferentiated organs that will later become either testes or ovaries. In an XY fetus, the presence of male hormones triggers the development of male testes. In an XX fetus, without the influence of male hormones, the gonads develop into ovaries. The primitive duct systems are identical, and the reproductive organs of each sex have an analog, or counterpart, in the other sex. The male and female gonads produce various hormones that further differentiate male from female and eventually stimulate the development of internal and external genitalia (Carroll and Wolpe, 1996; Money, 1993).

Although the term *hermaphrodite* is frowned up among intersexed people today, harkening back to nineteenth-century sexologists' attempts to discover or dissect the "true sex" of those born with ambiguous genitalia, it is still commonly used in the medical literature. In Victorian taxonomy, *hermaphrodite* included three groups of people. The first group is those who possess some ovarian and some testicular cells, which can be one testis and one ovary, one ovary and an ovotestis, one testis and an ovotestis, or two ovotestes, and who exhibit some mixture of male and female characteristics, traditionally referred to as "true hermaphrodites." The second group is those who have testes as well as some aspects of female genitalia, traditionally referred to as "male pseudohermaphrodites." The third group is those who have ovaries and some aspects of male genitalia, traditionally referred to as "female pseudohermaphrodites." Fausto-Sterling (1993) once suggested that these three intersexes "deserve to be considered additional sexes in their own right" (p. 21). Although it is an idea she no longer promulgates, it was a step toward the reevaluation of the two-sex binary. The term *intersex*—which is the term currently preferred—refers to congenital anomalies of the reproductive system and includes more than seventy different atypical chromosomal and hormonal conditions, some of which may involve ambiguous genitalia (see Appendix B, Common Intersexed Conditions).

When a child is born with ambiguous genitalia, which signals a potential intersexed condition, a "medical and psychosocial emergency" (Parker, 1998, p. 15) is heralded. The American Academy of Pediatrics' policy statement for the "Evaluation of the Newborn with Developmental Anomalies of the External Genitalia" begins with the sentence, "The birth of a child with ambiguous genitalia constitutes a social emergency" (AAP, 2000). The treatment for this psychosocial emergency is to immediately assign a male or female sex to the child and perform surgery to make the appearance of the genitals mirror the assigned sex.

Ambiguous genitalia can alert physicians to potential medical problems. However, the only time-sensitive medical emergency for intersexed children involves the need for a careful evaluation for congenital adrenal hyperplasia (CAH), which can cause a life-threatening electrolyte imbalance within the early weeks of life. Children with androgen insensitivity syndrome (AIS) can develop testicular cancer in their undescended testes if they are not removed before adulthood, but certainly this does not involve the need for emergency surgeries at birth. Severe hypospadias can also require surgery, but rarely immediately following birth.

Kessler (1998) distinguished among three categories of genital surgery: surgeries that are lifesaving, those that improve the quality of life, and those that are aesthetic. CAH is the only condition that could fall in the lifesaving category, and the treatment would not involve genital surgeries. Surgical correction of severe hypospadias could potentially enhance the quality of life for some men; however, there is no "emergency" involved in this decision. As difficult as it is for surgeons to admit, nearly all of the surgeries performed on the genitalia of intersexed babies are for aesthetic purposes.

Despite the fact that, excluding the conditions listed previously, no medical emergency exists in the majority of intersexed births, the presence of a human being who cannot be easily assigned a sex classification is considered a crisis needing immediate intervention. Decisions are made quickly, within days or hours of the child's birth, to assign the child to an official sex. Unlike the sexologists of the late nineteenth century, physicians do not search for the "true" sex of the baby (Dreger, 1998; Meyer-Bahlburg, 1999; Wilson and Reiner, 1999) but instead work within parameters created for what is hoped to be the best psychosocial outcome. The nineteenth-century search for true sex, which was believed to lie within the gonads, was a biologically based theory. The theory that replaced it is thoroughly immersed in the power of the environment to manipulate biological underpinnings.

Based on the established theories of gender development advanced by Money and his colleagues in the 1950s and 1960s (Diamond, 1996; Money, 1961; Money and Ehrhardt, 1972; Money, Hampson, and Hampson, 1955a,b, 1956, 1957; Money and Tucker, 1975), the human infant is psychosexually neutral at birth and can develop along either gender trajectory regardless of their biological sex, as long as the child's rearing is in the same direction as the sex assignment. As Green (1987) reported, early studies done by Albert Ellis in 1945 and a literature review of eighty cases dating back as early as 1767 supported the idea of a critical period of intervention in which the direction of gender could best be nurtured. Money asserted that since the human species is sexually dimorphic, children with visibly intersexed anatomy could not develop into healthy adults without being "assigned" to one sex or the other. Therefore policy decisions were guided by attempts to determine the "optimal" gender, which is defined by the hopes for the child's future reproductive and sexual functioning, a minimum of surgical procedures, overall gender appearance, and projected stable gender identity (Meyer-Bahlburg, 1999).

Emergency surgical "correction" of ambiguous genitalia based on the sex assignment assessed by pediatric endocrinologists and urologists became the routine and recommended treatment protocol. This treatment strategy has been endorsed by the American Academy of Pediatrics (AAP) and prominent physicians for the past thirty years (AAP, 1996a,b, 2000; Donahoe and Schnitzer, 1996; Federman and Donahoe, 1995; Grumbrach and Conte, 1998; Lerman, McAleer, and Kaplan, 2000; Migeon, Berkovitz, and Brown, 1994; Witchel and Lee, 1996), and is based on two postulates. The first is that individuals are psychosexually neutral at birth, and the second is that healthy psychosexual development is dependent upon the appearance of the genitals (Diamond and Sigmundson, 1997b).

The theory of psychosexual neutrality is consistent with a perspective that gender is socially constructed. However, to deny any biological influence on the sexual differentiation or gender identity development of children is surely an oversimplification (Diamond, 1996). When a nonintersexed child is born, physicians do not feel compelled to assure parents that gender assignment is arbitrary and will be determined more by the rearing of the child than any biological imperatives. It would seem logical that there might be increased flexibility in gender development for children who are intersexed. However, Money did not limit his beliefs to intersexed children, but felt that all human development has a window of psychosexual neutrality that could be manipulated in the direction of surgically constructed genitals. As early as 1965, Diamond argued that research on intersexed people was unrepresentative of how gender identity is established in nonintersexed people because—by the very nature of being intersexed—these children were more malleable. Since the exposé of the John/Joan case and David Reimer's public admittance of his botched circumcision and failed female sex reassignment (see Chapter 4), the theory of the psychosexual neutrality of newborns is finally being reexamined. The literature is replete with examples of "failed" sex assignments (Birnbacker et al., 1999; Meyer-Bahlburg et al., 1996; Reiner, 1996; Phornphutkul, Fausto-Sterling, and Gruppuso, 2000; Wilson and Reiner, 1999), including examples from Money's own research (Money, 1987; Money, Devore, and Norman, 1986).

The second postulate—that healthy psychosexual development is dependent upon the appearance of genitalia—is at the crux of the modern treatment of intersexed babies. Medical, surgical, and sexological experts have assumed that gender identity emanates as the logical outcome of physiological sex, and that the creation of a morphologically correct body can determine the internal experience of gender. When physicians assign sex to a child, they "endorse the view that the perception of the child's genitals is more influential than anything else in terms of gender identity formation" (Crouch, 1999, p. 31).

There is, of course, a natural range of genital formation, variation, and distinction even within the two established sexes. The genitalia of intersexed infants becomes scrutinized by medical professionals even though it is a part of the human anatomy rarely seen by others (Kessler, 1997/1998). Questions immediately arise regarding how "ambiguous" genitals must be before they come under the scrutiny of the medical experts, and how physicians determine the "correct" size of the male/female genitalia. Kessler (1998) suggested using the word *variability* instead of *ambiguity,* since variability does not assume a "norm" with which all else is compared. Who is to determine what is outside of the acceptable range of variability? Ambiguity, however, becomes something that is measurable within the medical domain. Dreger (1998a), a medical historian and ethicist, asked, "How small must a baby's penis be before it counts as 'ambiguous'?" The answer is that microphallus (i.e., small penis) and clitoromegaly (i.e., large clitoris) are determined, literally measured, by the ruler (see Figure 10.1). A penis "should" not measure less than 2.5 centimeters at birth, or a clitoris more than 0.9 centimeters or else it needs to be altered—or the sex of the child re-assigned—regardless of the health or functionality of the organs involved. Medical doctors also measure labial lengths, vaginal depths, degree of scrotal fusion, and testicular mass (Kessler, 1997/1998).

In order to determine the correct sex assignment for newborns with ambiguous genitalia, phallic and clitoral sizes are among the important considerations physicians rely upon. Children with ambiguous genitalia are most commonly assigned as females (Schober, 1999a), however, many XY babies are also virilized to appear more masculine. The size of the penis and the depth of vagina at birth are examined to determine if the genitalia fit the correct dimensions and will be "adequate." Genetic male babies (XY) that have an "adequate" phallus are assigned to be male, as defined by the estimation of how large the adult penis will be, whether he will be able to stand while urinating, and whether his penis can penetrate a woman. If his phallus is not large enough, he will be reassigned as a female. Enlarged clitorises are made smaller and short vaginas are enlarged. "Adequacy" for a functional vagina is defined as one that can accommodate a "normal"-sized penis. Cli-

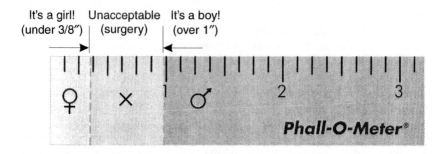

FIGURE 10.1. This ruler (not to scale) was developed by ISNA to graphically illustrate how surgical decisions are made based on the size of the child's genitalia. Please note that on the actual ruler, the "girl's" section is colored pink, the "boy's" secion is blue, and the middle is purple—a mixing of the two colors. Permission to reprint courtesy of the Intersex Society of North America.

torises that are considered too large are removed or "recessed" so they will not appear "penislike."

By far the most important criterion regarding sexual reassignment is the preservation of reproductive functioning or what the AAP (2000) referred to as "fertility potential." Genetic females (XX), regardless of the masculinization of their genitalia, are assigned as females if their reproductive capacities can be preserved (Dreger, 1998). The doctors have privileged the ability to reproduce rather than the preservation of female sexual desire and functionality. Donahoe and colleagues said, "Genetic females should always be raised as females, preserving reproductive potential, regardless of how severely the patients are virilized. In the genetic male, however, the gender of assignment is based on the infant's anatomy, predominately the size of the phallus" (as quoted in Fausto-Sterling, 2000, p. 57). Clearly, the worth of a woman is in her ability to bear children and the worth of a man in his ability to penetrate a woman. Even for cases in which fertility cannot be salvaged, motherhood and marriage (i.e., heterosexuality) are inferred for the female's psychosocial adjustment. Money and Ehrhardt (1972) said that the child should be informed "she *would* become a mother by adoption, one day, *when* she married and wanted to have a family" (p. 110, emphasis mine).

Surgical skill for reconstructive genital surgery is far more advanced in the creation of female genitalia, so males with small penises, even those with no discernible medical problems, are often surgically altered and assigned as females. Cromwell (1997) said, "The attitude that prevails is that without male genitalia a person cannot be a man" (1997, p. 131). P. J. Mears, a transgender activist and trainer, noted, "The measure of my manhood is always based on five questions, and if they don't ask them, they are more than likely thinking them." These questions are: Do you have a penis? How big is it? Does it work? Do you stand up to pee? In which bathroom do you do that? (Mears, 2001, personal communication). Indeed, the questions that laypeople ask Mears in trying to understand transgenderism are not that different from the questions medical experts raise in making permanent surgical decisions about the future gender identity of newborns.

Gayle Rubin (1975) looked beyond the mere functionality of the penis to the symbol of the phallus and said, "The phallus is more than a feature which distinguishes the sexes: it is the embodiment of the male status, to which men accede, and in which certain rights inhere—among them, the right to a woman. It is an expression of the transmission of male dominance" (p. 47). It is inconceivable for most male physicians to define their own manhood without the symbol of the phallus, a kind of physiological coat of arms that serves as both a shield and a sign of their inherited status.

Hawbecker (1999), in a beautifully written article, described what it was like to be a man with a small penis. His parents, in their wisdom, refused to surgically "reassign" him as an infant, although, sadly, he was unnecessarily castrated to avoid his testicles becoming cancerous before his actual condition was understood (he is consequently infertile). He said,

> Although doctors tried to convince my parents that I would be miserable living as a man with such small genitals, their fears have not been my life story. . . . I do not spend a lot of time concerned about my genitalia. My penis, although small, especially when it is not erect, does everything that I want it to do. It allows me to urinate standing up. It brings me and my partner a great deal of pleasure. It grows erect, it penetrates her vagina, it ejaculates. I don't know what else I need it to do. . . . I am a very good life partner. I am faithful, long-term. I write poetry and am very funny. . . . I am a successful attorney with a good salary. I identify as a man, and do not have a difficult time playing the part. As a matter of fact, I am actually glad that I was born the way that I was. I view it as a secret challenge that I have overcome, like climbing Everest; it has given me a lot of self-esteem. (pp. 112-113)

Increased self-esteem is not one of the sequelae of having a micropenis that is usually cited in the literature. Surgical reassignment for micropenis is currently being reexamined by medical professionals (van Seters and Slob, 1988; Bin-Abbas et al., 1999).

Micropenis is not, however, the only reason for genital sex reassignment surgery on newborn males. A condition called hypospadias occurs in one of 200 to 300 births and refers to the urethral meatus (the hole at the end of the penis through which the urine is evacuated and at which the urethra terminates) being located along the underside, rather than at the tip of the penis, and is a common reason for surgical intervention. Hypospadias can range from a minor misplacement of the urethra to more pronounced cases in wich the opening may be along the shaft of the penis or even be absent entirely. Minor hypospadias is essentially a cosmetic difference and may involve the man needing to urinate sitting, rather than standing. Kessler (1998) emphasized that the issue is not performing surgery so that males *can* urinate—which would be a bona fide emergency—but to "allow him to urinate in a culturally sanctioned position" (p. 70). In more severe cases hypospadias can cause repeated urinary tract infection and may require surgical intervention. Drawbacks of surgery can include constriction of the constructed urethra requiring dilation, scarring, damage to sexual function, and a greater risk of urinary tract infections—the very condition the surgery was meant to alleviate. A hypospadiac penis is entirely capable of pleasurable sexual sensation and orgasm. Whether routine surgery on mild hypospadias is necessary is questionable. In one study of 500 "normal" men, 45 percent displayed hypospadias to some degree and most men were unaware of having any problems with appearance or sexual or reproductive functioning, and were able to urinate in a standing position (Fichtner et al., 1995).

Vaginoplasty surgery, the process of building or extending the vaginal canal, can be problematic (Alizai et al., 1999; Creighton, Minto, and Steele, 2001; Schober, 1999a), and even women who identify general satisfaction with their treatments suggest that vaginoplasty surgeries be postponed till adolescence or adulthood (Wisniewski et al., 2000). In genetic (XX) females who have ambiguous genitalia, the second priority after preservation of reproductive capacity is to surgically create a vagina that is deep enough for penetration, presumably by a male penis. Vaginoplasty surgery increases the size of the vagina, though not without surgical complications, and often requires repeated dilation of the vaginal opening so that it remains open. This is often a painful procedure that is performed on infants and small children. The parent, presumably the mother, carries out this procedure.

The medical experts have not investigated the impact on the child's sexual development in having a parent perform this invasive procedure. Even though the intent is not abusive, it is hard to imagine that the child does not experience the effect as abusive, and that both parent and child are not traumatized by the need to repeat these dilations on a daily basis. As Foley and Morley (1992) said, "Ironically, procedures designed to promote adjustment and normalcy for these patients can instead result in psychosexual problems" (p. 74). The underlying values determining genital surgeries in females is that "women are passive recipients during sex, simply there to please their sexual partners" (Crouch, 1999, p. 33), which, it is assumed, will be accomplished as long as she has an "adequate" vagina. This says as much about the medical experts' opinions of men as their opinions of women.

Female infants with clitoromegaly have their clitorises shaved smaller, or receded, although in previous generations the clitoris was commonly removed. In the past, the surgery was openly termed *clitorectomy*. As Chase (2001, personal communication) said, "Today, though surgeons have changed the names they give to operations on the clitoris ('clitoroplasty,' 'clitoral recession'), they are still removing clitoral tissue, as well as extensively dissecting the female genitals." Decisions to alter the infant's genitals rarely take into consideration issues of sexual arousal or the child's future sexual functioning but are more concerned that the child appears "normal," trading what Kessler (1998) called "function" for "appearance." Is the appearance of a woman's genitals more important than her ability to experience sexual pleasure? The literature often states that surgical procedures are improving and the impact on sexual functioning is minimal, a point Chase (1999b) is critical of, particularly when increased surgical skill is heralded as the "solution" to fix intersexed people. Plastic surgery on the genitals, by its nature, damages rather than improves erotic sensation. The problems associated with clitoral recession are mentioned in the literature (Barrett and Gonzales, 1980; Baskin et al., 1999; Newman, Randolph, and Parson, 1992) and Meyer-Bahlburg (1998) said, "Sexual sensitivity of the clitoris *or its remnant* may be markedly reduced" (p. 12, emphasis mine). Newman, Randolph, and Anderson (1992) said, "The cosmetic effect is excellent. Late studies with assessment of sexual gratification, orgasm, and general psychologic adjustment are unavailable . . . and remain in question" (p. 651).

Many questions are raised about the current system of "corrective" surgeries. Reconstructive surgeries for infant genitalia are still experimental, and much is still unknown. These surgeries include a high rate of complication and reduced sensation, and some children are left without any sexually functioning tissue. Complications include repeated surgeries, lifelong hormonal treatments, and psychosocial difficulties, including shame, sexual dysfunction, gender dysphoria, and feeling betrayed by their bodies (Schober, 1999a). Results of the surgeries often damage fertility, and patients are left feeling misled by trusted adults, including parents and physicians. Feelings of betrayal and humiliation often lead to highly negative feelings about all helping professions, so that many intersexed adults avoid medical care and resist seeking counseling. Few follow-up studies have tested the success of these surgeries and sometimes the child has no knowledge of having been surgically altered. The foundation that these surgeries are based on, i.e., that having ambiguous genitalia will lead to psychological harm and that surgical alteration will alleviate this trauma, has not been proved. The question remains whether these surgeries actually succeed in either making the child look more normal or even feel more normal. Dreger (1997) asked, "Are the genitals shaped by the scalpel necessarily less traumatic than those shaped by the womb?" (p. 21).

The literature is replete with examples of intersexed patients who are angry at physicians for their invasive treatment (Dittmann, 1998). One woman wrote to her medical doctor: "In my teens, when I first realized exactly what had been done to me, my reaction was that I must have been truly repulsive to my parents and doctors if the result of the surgery performed on me could be considered an improvement. The assurances of my therapist that my doctors considered my surgery to be a success only strengthened that conviction" (Joan W., 2001). Dreger (2000) and Preves (2003) discussed the way that intersexed bodies have been examined—and displayed—by medical specialists with little regard to how those who inhabit intersexed bodies may feel. Body parts are photographed with eyes properly blocked out, furthering the sense of objectification and alienation. Preves' (2003) research subjects discussed the feeling of being young children and having hundreds of physicians parading before their hospital beds, each examining their genitalia and commenting on the "unusual" case.

The voices of intersexed people who have had surgeries (see Alexander, 1999; Caldera, 1999; Cameron, 1999; Devore, 1999; Holmes, 1997/1998; McClintock, 1997/1998; Triea, 1999) seem to suggest that the surgeries themselves might be causing the very trauma they have been designed to eliminate. Some writers have brought attention to the discrepancy between Western society's shock at female genital mutilation in non-Western (mostly Arab and African) cultures, and our routine acceptance of intersexed surgeries within our own culture (Coventry, 2000; Holmes, 1995). Chase (1998) in particular noted the discrepancy between feminist concern over clitorectomies in third world countries and their virtual silence on "medical intersex management as another form of violence against women" (p. 207).

According to Fausto-Sterling (1993), "Scientific dogma has held fast to the assumption that without medical care hermaphrodites are doomed to a life of misery" (p. 23). However, evidence is proving this incorrect. Reilly and Woodhouse (1989) studied twenty adult male patients who were born with micropenises, and all stated that they were sexually active and functioned normally. The group reported long-term, close, and intimate (heterosexual) relationships, as well as an experimental attitude toward sexual positions and methods that contributed to their partners' sexual satisfaction using nonpenetrative techniques. They concluded that a microphallus alone "should not dictate a female gender assignment in infancy" (p. 571). In another study of males with ambiguous genitalia and hypospadias due to 46, XY condition, 76 percent of the participants who were reared as males were "mainly satisfied" with their sex of rearing (Migeon, Wisniewski, Gearhart, et al., 2002). Stoller (1968b) said, "The male external genitalia are a sign to the individual and to society that this is a male, but they are not essential to producing a sense of maleness" (p. 47).

What is perhaps the most surprising evidence regarding the need to reexamine surgical protocols for intersexed babies is an unpublished dissertation, available only through Harvard University's Widener Library, written in 1951. The monograph reviewed more than 250 cases on intersexed children who received no surgical intervention. It shows that, "Far from manifesting psychological traumas and mental illnesses . . . [they] not only made an 'adequate adjustment' to life, but lived in a way virtually indistinguishable from people without genital differences" (Colapinto, 2000, p. 233). These results seemed to amaze the study's author—doctoral candidate John Money! How the man who completed this dissertation in the early 1950s became a world renowned proponent of genital surgery on newborn intersexed infants by the late 1950s, when his own research clearly showed that it was unnecessary, is still a professional mystery. Money, now in his eighties, has remained silent while this controversy has raged around him.

Dr. Bruce Wilson, director of pediatric endocrinology at Michigan State University, said, "It makes a lot of sense to go back to the primary rule in medicine: Do no harm. If we don't have data proving that the risky surgeries being performed are better than no surgeries, why are we doing them?" (ISNA, 1998, p. 4). Surgical attempts to "fix" what is not broken and "correct" what is not damaged by identifying what is intact as "deformed" (Kessler, 1997/1998, p. 34) so that infants' bodies appear "normal" even though they are no longer functioning is surely a medical protocol begging for revision.

CREATING PSYCHOSOCIAL EMERGENCY

When we stop thinking of our children born with atypical genitals as monsters, we will no longer risk their adult sexualities with non-consensual, medically unnecessary genital surgeries.

Cheryl Chase
Intersex in the Age of Ethics, 1999

The underlying assumption guiding the medical experts treating intersexed babies with surgery is that following the surgery "these individuals will cease to be intersexed—that the social problem will be forestalled or eliminated" (Dreger, 1998, p. 186). Of course, no evidence exists that surgery can simply eliminate, or even alleviate, the challenges of being intersexed within a gender-polarized social system. Surgically altered and sex-reassigned babies often face physical complications that need medical attention, hormonal treatments to reinforce the sex assignment, and repeated visits to medical doctors for follow-up examinations. Groveman (1999) said, "Doctors behave as though the 'problem' has been cured ('you used to be intersexed, but we fixed it') as though being intersexed was an historical detail of the patient's life" (p. 27). This is precisely the issue—that being intersexed is not a historical problem to be "fixed," but an ongoing life experience that must be integrated and incorporated into the whole of a person's life.

In addition to the many medical and ethical issues raised by the current medical treatment paradigm, a number of problems exist from a psychological perspective. Identifying each of these problem areas will offer some insight into the lack of therapeutic attention to certain areas of intersexed treatment strategies, particularly those that most directly impact healthy psychosocial adjustment.

It is clear, first of all, that the debate cannot be resolved without research, particularly follow-up studies that examine the benefits and problems associated with intersexed surgeries. However, it is difficult to conduct these studies, precisely because the whole point of the surgeries is to "disappear" the problem. In order to conduct longitudinal research, those who have undergone surgery have to be able to talk about these issues, and yet the nature of the treatment strategies ensures that the "the condition is often shrouded in silence and lies" (Dreger, 1998, p. 190). Medical experts believe that talking about these issues will undermine the purpose of the technological interventions themselves, i.e., to avoid psychological suffering. Kipnis and Diamond (1998) referred to this as an "epistemological black hole," in which the very people who have the knowledge the researchers need have been silenced and shamed by the researchers' own theoretical paradigms into not talking about being intersexed. This is a catch-22, or what family therapists refer to as a double bind (Bateson et al., 1968).

Despite the difficulties that intersexed surgeries appear to cause, no one—not even the surgically altered survivors themselves—"blame" the medical profession for acting out of malice, sadism, or a desire to cause harm. The medical experts who specialize in intersexed treatment have created protocols that they believe will cause the least psychosocial trauma and assist in the best quality of life. Chase said, "Surgeons are not trained to deal with patients who are upset. They are trained to 'fix' things. When people like me grow up and say, 'This hurt me', they don't want to hear it, because they would have to see how they had hurt their patients, and they would have to admit their impotence in addressing this by surgery" (as quoted in Yronwode, 1999).

That some patients have been hurt is undisputed. How many patients have been hurt is unknown. Intersexed people are mostly a hidden population that receive "little psychological support" for either themselves or their families (Dreger, 1998b, p. 190). The following three areas in which psychosocial support has been absent or, in some cases, misdirected will be examined: psychotherapeutic services offered to (1) parents of newborn intersexed babies, (2) intersexed children and adolescents, and (3) adults who are beginning to recognize that they were surgically altered as children.

Parents of Newborn Intersexed Babies

For most parents the birth of a child with atypical sex anatomy is a frightening event, received at a vulnerable time of anticipated joy and great stress.

Although all parents entertain frightening "what ifs" during pregnancy and labor, few parents anticipate dealing with an intersexed child. Books directed at new parents (i.e., mothers) do not mention these issues as possibilities, although sometimes other potentially challenging situations are discussed. Medical experts usually step in quickly when a child is born with ambiguous genitalia, sometimes whisking the child away from the mother for examination immediately after birth. Although these medical questions may be necessary for evaluation purposes, they sometimes leave a mother feeling responsible and blamed for her child's condition.

Children who are intersexed with no immediately visible differences are not recognized unless a physical condition is manifested, which sometimes does not occur until puberty.

Parents of intersexed newborns are often told that their children have a "birth defect" and that, given some time, they will be able to identify the "true" sex. They never admit, said Fausto-Sterling (2000), that the children do not have a "true" sex (p. 50). Parents are told that the "trouble lies in the doctor's ability to determine the gender, not in the baby's gender per se" (Kessler, 1990, p. 16). The medical team avoids using words such as *hermaphroditism* or *intersexuality,* and use only benign terms such as *improperly formed gonads* (Laurent, 1996/1997), so that once sex assignment is determined/decided, parents will not feel any confusion over the "real" sex of their babies. The AAP (2000) suggested, "The infant should be referred to as 'your baby' or 'your child'—not 'it,' 'he,' or 'she.'" The AAP (2000) also recommended that parents avoid naming the child or registering the birth until the sex of rearing is "established." The underlying presentation to the parents is that the physicians need time to determine the accurate sex of the child, not that the child is outside of common sex categorization and that the physicians are making educated guesses regarding assigning the infant to one of the two available categories based on unproved theories of the child's best psychosocial adjustment.

Parents, usually frightened and confused over the birth of their "imperfect" infants, assume that these recommended surgeries are medically necessary. They are vulnerable to medical interventions that they may have been ill prepared for. Parents have historically been left out of the decision-making process and care providers have been encouraged to be less than honest with parents about their children's true status. Laurence Baskin, an associate professor of urology and pediatrics at the University of California at San Francisco, said it can be "very disturbing to *parents*" to have an intersexed child (Yronwode, 1999, emphasis mine). There is no doubt that "Intersexed genitalia make almost everyone—doctors, parents, and society as a whole uncomfortable" (Ford, 2001). Indeed, it is the physicians' compassion for the parents that directs them to encourage the family to maintain the medical procedures as a secret from family and friends (Howe, 1999; Wilson and Reiner, 1999).

The lack of informed education parents are given regarding what it means to have an intersexed child, medically or psychologically, are based on the early postulates of John Money. Money (Money and Ehrhardt, 1972) believed, "If the parents are consistently unequivocal in their rearing of their child as a girl (regardless of natal sex), then the chances are high that the child will differentiate a girl's gender identity" (p. 16). It was believed that nothing was more important for a successful outcome than the parents' complete and total belief that the gender of rearing was the child's proper sex identity.

Since so much rested on how the parents reared the child, it was assumed that the best way to ensure parents' unequivocal support and unflinching belief in the child's assigned gender—with no reservations or questions—was to keep them uninformed as to the actual medical conditions and potential psychological issues that might develop. The medical reasoning for this veil of secrecy is that the surgical procedures will make the child look "normal," and the lack of detailed information will keep the parents naive and untroubled, ensuring their complete belief in the sex assignment and, therefore, a successful outcome. Although it is assumed that parents will accept their children more easily if they look "normal," it is not clear that surgically altered genitalia look "normal." As Kessler (1998) said, "Parenting a female with clitoral insensitivity and vaginal complications is seen as preferable to parenting a female with a larger-than-typical clitoris and smaller-than-typical vagina. Parenting a male with a scarred and insensitive penis is seen as preferable to parenting a male with a normally functioning (but small) one" (p. 76). As Wilson and Reiner (1999) noted, "No data [showed] that surgery has any positive psychological impact on the parents, let alone the child" (p. 128). Preves (2003) said, "Surgery is just one of the many possible responses to sexual variation, and medical sex assignment is a product of specific cultural and historical factors" (p. 22).

Following these protocols, very little support, education, counseling, or therapy is offered to the parents, for it is thought that the more information they have, the more ambivalence they will have in rearing their child. Certainly, whatever "preoperative counseling" is offered is not sufficient to address the multiple issues that the family faces dealing with what surely might be perceived as—given the level of medical involvement and concern—a "defective" child. The parents do not receive any counseling for the trauma of having a child who "needs" surgery, nor do they receive any education regarding the multiple physical and health issues that might face the child and how to best address the child's actual concerns as she or he ages.

It has been suggested that perhaps the child's body should be left intact, and that skilled therapeutic counseling, coupled with education regarding the child's actual condition, would best serve the family. Laurent (1996/1997) suggested that providing the family with support for having a child who is "different" might be a superior treatment strategy. Certainly, the family could be encouraged to engage in therapy, and any medical decisions (assuming there is no need for medical expediency) could be postponed for weeks or even years, when the family was able to make an informed and conscious decision about what would best serve their child.

Some medical experts see the value of therapeutic intervention and education. Reilly and Woodhouse (1989) concurred with other experts in the field about the importance of parental attitude in determining the adjustment of intersexed children. Their research of adult men with micropenises showed that parents who fostered open communication and support within a framework of normalcy "produced more confident and well-adjusted boys" (p. 571). It was, however, not secrecy, but its opposite—open communication—that allowed for superior adjustment. Schober (1998a) said, "Surgery makes parents and doctors more comfortable, but counseling makes people comfortable too, and [it] is not irreversible" (p. 547).

Instead of surgically operating on children to make their parents more comfortable, experts can acknowledge that when parents feel ambivalence toward their intersexed infant, it is indeed a problem. However, it is not the child's problem, it is the adults' responsibility to address the issues. Howe (1999) suggested that parental ambivalence which prevents parents from loving their infant is a "pathological response, and [the parents] should seek therapy" (p. 216). Although perhaps too harshly stated, it is indeed accurate that the focus should not be on adjusting the child's genitals to external views of normalcy, but supporting the family to deal with a difficult and challenging situation.

Surgical alteration of a child with ambiguous genitalia is an established treatment protocol, and for parents to refuse these surgeries has been perceived by some members of the medical establishment as akin to child abuse. These same members have recommended using the legal system to force parents to surgically alter their children (Rossiter and Diehi, 1998). Consequently, it has been difficult for parents to speak out against a medical team of "experts." Those who attempt to advocate for their children's rights are often thwarted in the process. Perhaps, as the following vignette shows, it is the surgeons who should be on tenuous legal grounds.

One mother tried to resist surgically altering her infant son and rearing him as a girl after she had seen him have an erection. The doctors (all twenty of them!) reluctantly agreed. However, two and one-half months later, one of the doctors insisted that the child's ovotestis (the male gonad that contained ovarian tissue) was probably cancerous and the mother agreed to a biopsy. Following surgery the surgeon stated that it had indeed been malignant and had been removed. The mother insisted on obtaining a pathology report, which, when she finally received it after repeated requests, stated, "normal, healthy testicle." The child was now castrated and unable to produce sperm. The mother had been lied to not only about the reasons for the surgery but also about its actual results (Lehrman, 1999).

Coping with the birth of an intersexed child, particularly in a culture that has silenced this discussion, can be an emotionally devastating experience for most parents. Parents are forced to think prematurely about their intersexed child as potentially sexual beings at a time when few other parents are forced to think of the later developmental stages of their children's lives (Sutton and Whittaker, 1998). Parents are entitled to have time to understand what they are faced with, obtain information to make educated decisions, and identify supportive caregivers who will nurture them through the range of normative emotions they will experience. Most of all they should be protected from a medical team that is pressuring them to make premature decisions about their child's future.

The time following the birth of a baby is a sacred time, and the first task of new parents is to bond with their child. To this end, medical experts should support parents in welcoming home, with joy, their newborn child. The medical paradigm has postulated that when parents are not ambivalent about their child's gender, they will pass that confidence along to their child. Does it not follow that when the medical experts believe that the intersexed child is a healthy, normal newborn—an expression of the human diversity that medical experts surely routinely see—they will pass *that confidence* along to the parents? Instead of being met by a concerned, worried, and anxious team of medical experts who are poking and prodding their newborn baby's body, they could be met by a caring birth team who, as an alternative to creating medical and psychosocial emergencies, would forestall crises through compassionate caregiving and education. Advocates for the intersexed child and his or her family would, as their first task, ensure that the baby entered the family feeling warmly welcomed and fully accepted. The birth of a healthy, albeit differently gendered, child is not the time for medical decisions or anxious experts. It is the time for parent/child bonding.

Issues Facing Children and Adolescents

Since the primary treatment strategy has been to maintain secrecy and silence regarding the truth about their bodies, most children and adolescents who are intersexed or born with ambiguous genitalia have little or no information regarding their bodies. In all fairness, most children and adolescents grow up in a virtual silence about issues regarding their bodies, their reproductive capabilities, and most of all their sexuality. However, for children who have been surgically altered, who appear "different" than other children, who are forced to see medical specialists and take hormonal medications, or who have further corrective or cosmetic surgeries, the impact of this silence is surely devastating.

Chase (1999b) suggested that the greatest harm for intersexed people is caused by the "underlying attitude that intersexuality is so shameful that it must be erased before the child can have any say what will be done to his or her body" (p. 147). In one study, thirty-seven intersexed adults were interviewed, and Preves (1999) found that "being encouraged to keep silent about their differences and surgical alterations only served to enforce feelings of isolation, stigma, and shame—the very feelings that such procedures are attempting to alleviate" (pp. 55-56). In contrast, those intersexed adults who did not undergo medical treatments did not express the same negative self-view (Preves, 2003).

To date, few stories have been told by children and adolescents, although many intersexed adults have reflected back on their experiences. Coventry (1999) said, "When the surgeon cut out most of my half-inch clitoris, it was as if he had cut out my tongue" (p. 71), a dramatic expression of how the surgery itself reinforces a complete silencing of young children. Many adults have described their attempts to talk with their parents and how their parents literally change the subject or humiliate them in an effort to silence them. The information they have been given is veiled. Their own memories about their body are denied, and questions about why they have had surgery, or why doctors are examining their genitals, or any questions they have about sexuality are carefully silenced. Even children who are given rudimentary information are never told that they were born with "intersexed" parts or, as is common in cases in which intersexed children are assigned as females, that they once had male sex gonads. They are sometimes told they had "twisted" ovaries or even cancer, which can create fear of a reoccurrence. These parents were, of course, sworn to secrecy by doctors who had assured them that if they told their children the truth it would damage the children psychologically.

However, the consequences of denial, avoidance, and outright lying also have a cost. Coventry (1999) said, "To be lied to as a child about your own body, to have your life as a sexual being so ignored that you are not even given answers to your questions is to have your heart and soul relentlessly undermined" (p. 72). Some children continue to have surgeries through their latency, yet the reasons for these hospitalizations are rarely fully explained and are described in vague terms. Holmes (1997/1998) said, "What [surgery] actually did was change a perfectly healthy seven-year-old girl into a woman who feared her own body and her past and who hated herself for being different" (p. 9).

The philosophy that has guided intersex surgeries has also guided medical opinion for boys that have experienced traumatic injury to their penises during infancy or early toddlerhood. The most famous case was, of course, the John/Joan case (i.e., David Reimer), but many more are noted in the literature. In one clinical evaluation, Westman and Zarwell (1975) discussed a case in which a psychotic mother intentionally severed her infant son's penis at five and one-half weeks of age. The report is noteworthy for its in-depth analysis of many psychosocial issues, including the available adoptive possibilities for the child and the traumatic impact of his birth mother's violence. After a thorough assessment the decision was made to retain his male sex; however, the philosophy of deception still guides the treatment team. At the article's conclusion Westman and Zarwell said, "[the boy] was placed with an adoptive family elsewhere [i.e., one who did not know his history], with his medical record indicating *a congenital phallic defect* which would require subsequent surgical management" (p. 63, emphasis mine). It was presumed that being lied to would best protect the child, and having his adoptive parents unaware of the situation was the best way to re-inforce the artifice so common in both intersexuality and adoption decisions.

Intersexuality, by its very nature, raises concerns about not only gender identification but also sexual orientation. It is not only difficult to know "for sure" someone's sex when they are technically a mix of both sexes; it is also difficult to determine the nature, direction, or meaning of sexual orientation. Is the child who was born with both male and female gonads and was surgically assigned as a female and grew up to be a lesbian *really* in an opposite-sex relationship, or is she acting on a "heterosexual" desire as someone with an internal core male biology or identity? Of course, this becomes a "concern" only when homosexuality is defined as a less optimal outcome for an adult sexual being than heterosexuality. Homosexuality is still not considered an "acceptable" or "successful" outcome, and researchers often stress that their adult, surgically altered patients are heterosexual to demonstrate successful treatment. Since heterosexual development (i.e., opposites attract) is thought to flow directly from stable gender identity (i.e., being a man or a woman), the silence and denial pertaining to intersexuality is reinforced precisely with the hopes of stabilizing gender identity within the assigned sex and therefore controlling the direction of sexual desire. Despite the depathologization of homosexuality within the psychiatric nosology, heterosexist values are still guiding many of the medical protocols regarding "mixed-sex" children (Holmes, 1995).

It would seem logical that intersexed children would struggle with some gender-related issues, whether the struggles are rooted in biology, in socialization, or simply in coping with a sexually dimorphic cultural environment. Some of the challenges for the gender development of intersexed children include:

> marked gender atypical interests and behaviors *that may elicit the parents' concern;* body image problems associated with ambiguous genitalia or with the beginning development of gender-contrary secondary sex characteristics in puberty; questions about sexual orientation; gender insecurity or doubts about correct gender assignment; frank requests for sex change. (Meyer-Bahlburg, 1994, p. 22, emphasis mine)

In all fairness, parental concerns regarding their children's sexual development are valid issues, as are the questions about further gender identity and sexual orientation. Some researchers have seen high levels of psychopathology in intersexed people (Meyer-Bahlberg, 1993; Slijper et al., 1998). Although the intersexed people studied have usually been surgically altered, the definition of psychopathology includes concerns about their gender identity! Diamond (1998) questioned whether the high incidence of psychopathology "might, in part, be due to the lack of support for the individual desirous of sex reassignment or cross-gender identification."

For the record, no one is suggesting the children should be raised without a sex assignment as a solution to the flexibility of gender potentiality, rather that they should not be surgically altered to match that assignment. Those in support of early sex reassignment surgeries (see Slijper et al., 1998) often infer that those who recommend a more conservative approach are suggesting children be raised "ambiguously." This is a misreading of the literature (see Diamond, 1998). The recommendation is that surgery be halted until the child is old enough to identify his or her own gender identity and request surgery. The reality is that the nature of being intersexed evokes questions about gender for both children and parents. Surgical alteration does not eliminate the psychosocial challenge; it simply complicates it.

Children who are intersexed or have ambiguous or surgically altered genitalia have a right to accurate information about their bodies, as is appropriate for their age and level of development. It should seem obvious that children and adolescents would need assistance sorting through feelings about their bodies, their sexuality, their identity—as all children and teenagers do. Intersexed children would especially need space to mourn and grieve their situation (Groveman, 1999) in order to develop a sense of comfort in their bodies. This is especially true for adolescents that are beginning to date, explore their bodies, develop sexual feelings, and reach out to others to begin intimate relationships. Social and sexual development for intersexed people may be delayed (and sometimes it is severely delayed or does not occur at all). They may not begin to address issues of sexuality until they are in their late teens or early adulthood, and this developmental lag may isolate them from peers and create an awkwardness regarding the awakening of sexuality and intimacy issues.

The taboo surrounding honest discussion with children and adolescents about their bodies is akin to a kind of child abuse. It will disrupt their normative emotional and sexual development as well as create and reinforce tension within the family system. Walcutt (1995/1996) described some of the impact of this secrecy:

> I've spent my whole life with my feelings so bottled up, it's really hard to change now. . . . I can't tell you what my diagnosis was—because no one ever told me. . . . No one explained anything to me before or immediately after the surgery [to "fix" her enlarged clitoris]. . . . Around age 14 or 15, they told me that I would need surgery "if you ever wanted to have normal sex with your husband." . . . At age 17, they told me to take birth control pills . . . but the pills put me on an emotional roller coaster, up one day and suicidally depressed the next. . . . I knew I was different . . . but I couldn't talk about this with my parents . . . and I couldn't talk about this with the counselors [who] just told me what was going to happen to me, but I really couldn't talk about how I felt, or ask them questions. I was always uncomfortable in the counseling sessions. I would tell them almost anything so that I could just get out of there. (pp. 10-11)

Children and adolescents often act out hidden and shameful issues within families, even when they are unsure what the actual issues are. Family therapist Imber-Black (1998) discussed the way people develop unusual and unexplainable behaviors that are actually metaphors for "the unimaginable maze of secrecy in which such actions are embedded" (p. 12). She said that adolescence is "a powerful season in family relationships" and that "revelation of a long-standing secret *whose essence belongs to a child* will have reverberations across all family relationships" (p. 259, italics mine). Intersexuality is clearly a secret whose essence belongs to the child. If the secrecy has not been revealed by adolescence, it should definitely be shared while the child is still within the family home, so the child can deal with his or her feelings while still in a loving family environment. It is possible that when the child finds out as an adult, he or she will feel so betrayed that it causes a permanent rift in the parent-child relationship.

The research on children born with ambiguous genitalia reveals numerous cases in which gender assignment was incorrect and children later choose sex reassignment. In one interesting case, a child born with ambiguous genitalia was raised as a boy until age four, then reassigned as a female, and then lived from late puberty onward as a man (Dittmann, 1998). Although the author discussed many issues of patient management that were problematic, including the patient's "late" reassignment as a female (i.e., past the window of psychosocial neutrality), the fact that the child was wrongly assigned at birth does not seem to be an issue of clinical self-evaluation. If the child had not been surgically assigned at birth, the need to arbitrarily reassign him would not have existed, and he would have been free to make a choice about his sex and gender designation in puberty, as he had done anyway, without the need for repeated surgeries. Some children and teenagers are verbal at a young age that they have been assigned incorrectly and request corrective sex reassignment.

In one case, an adolescent Hmong immigrant who had been raised as a girl presented for sex reassignment. "She" had lived socially in a masculine role since puberty, and when she sought out medical assistance, was discovered to have an intersex condition. Sexual reassignment was initiated and, after some initial disappointment in the surgical results and a need for resocialization in the male role, he successfully transitioned into a stable male gender identity (Reiner, 1996).

Some children adapt well to the original assignment (Bradley et al., 1998), while others do not. Similarly, some children who reassign themselves as teenagers also adapt well to their new gender, while others do not. This reflects the complex variables associated with the development and establishment of a stable gender identity. However, all people, whether they are adapting well or poorly—including children and adolescents—deserve accurate information to assist them in making informed choices about their lives and bodies.

Intersexed Adults Naming Their Pain

As the issue of intersexuality becomes part of the public discourse, more and more adults are beginning to recognize themselves in the stories that they see on television and read about in magazines and books. Adults who have wondered about their genitalia being "different" or lived with the secrecy surrounding surgeries as children are slowly beginning to talk with their physicians, significant others, or perhaps their therapists about these fears. Perhaps physicians and mental health experts have been too quick to dismiss clients' concerns over "odd-looking genitalia" or questions about surgeries and need to pay more attention to the difficulty clients have in even raising these issues.

To discover at thirty or forty years old that one was surgically operated on as an infant or was "made into" a girl, even though one was born as a boy, can be shocking and is an area of clinical expertise that few are trained for. One woman said, "One of the things about being born with genitals that challenge what is considered normal is that no one ever tells you that there is anyone like you. You feel completely and totally alone" (Coventry, 1999, p. 75). As gynecologists and women's health advocates have always known, women often worry whether their genitals look "normal," and manhood has long been measured by the size of a man's phallus. It is important that the raising of these questions on a social level does not increase the body anxiety that people already experience or feed the obsessive narcissism regarding looks and perfectionism that is already a socially prevalent fixation.

Healing is a process that is significantly increased with the support of others who have been through the same experiences. The Intersex Society of North America (ISNA) is a peer support, education, and advocacy group founded and operated by intersexed pioneer Cheryl Chase. As part of her own psychological healing from "years of secrecy, unexplained surgeries, and sexual dysfunction caused by the removal of her clitoris" (Yronwode, 1999), Chase founded ISNA in 1994 after she published a letter to the editor in *The Sciences,* responding to Anne Fausto-Sterling's article, "The Five Sexes." In her letter, in which she came out as an intersexual, she said she was the president of a group called the Intersex Society of North America. ISNA did not yet exist, but soon the post office box she listed was filled with mail from other intersexed people who wanted to join, and ISNA was born (Preves, 2003). Now with more than 3,000 subscribers to the ISNA newsletter, under the leadership of Monica Casper, ISNA serves as an educational resource, a support group for intersexed people and their families, and is at the forefront of the organizing and advocacy work dedicated to assisting physicians to reexamine their position on genital surgery for intersexed infants.

Adult intersexed clients may have carried the knowledge of their intersex condition their whole lives in secrecy, or they may have literally been "the last to know." Perhaps they have wondered about secrecy in the family, or why their sexual response did not seem as full of fireworks as descriptions they had heard or read about. If they are infertile but unable to find reasons why they could not conceive, or their genitals seemed different looking than others, they may have wondered in silence. Questioning whether one has been the unknowing victim of genital surgery in infancy, or coming to a realization that being intersexed is an "explanation" for much of what has been previously confusing, evokes many feelings.

Although issues of transsexualism and issues of intersexuality are etiologically and functionally different, many overlapping developmental and emotional similarities exist that are related to treatment concerns. The six stages outlined for transgender emergence, with some modifications, are similar to the process that adult intersexed people experience as they come to terms with their sexual and gender identities. For example, the process of coming into awareness, seeking information, reaching out, and disclosing to significant others are all part of a normative process for adult intersexed clients that are realizing or coming to accept that they are intersexed. Intersexed people also move through a process of exploration regarding their identity and body configuration and ultimately come to a place of integration and synthesis.

Although transgendered people often have anger to resolve regarding the price they paid for living in a binary system, intersexed people have the additional rage of knowing that they were surgically altered to fit into the binary system, often losing their sexual functioning and fertility in the process. The literature clearly distinguishes between transsexuals and intersexed people—having an intersexed condition actually precludes a person from having a diagnosis of gender identity disorder. It is interesting to note that people who are transgendered often request karyotype and hormonal testing in hopes that science can explain their transgender experience (although most transgender people are not anatomically intersexed and some intersexed people do identify as transgendered).

Meyer-Bahlburg (1994; Meyer-Bahlburg et al., 1996) examined the relationship of intersexuality with gender identity disorder (GID), since intersexed people often struggle with issues related to gender identity development (he viewed these as separate phenomena). Meyer-Bahlburg concluded that significant differences in how gender issues manifest among intersexed people make GID a less than appropriate diagnosis. These issues include a later age of onset and higher prevalence of gender identity concerns among intersexed people than the nonintersexed population. The sex ratio is also reversed. Historically, more natal males have requested SRS than natal females among the transsexual population. However, many more intersexed children raised as girls are requesting surgery than those raised as boys. Meyer-Bahlburg did not acknowledge the irony of this situation, that more intersexed children have been surgically altered and "made into" girls.

The issues facing adult intersexed people are only now becoming an area of therapeutic concern. Clients will often need assistance tracking down records of their own genital surgeries, records that are often "closed" to even the clients themselves (Preves, 2003). They will need to learn the medical language necessary to understand their condition and the purposes of the surgeries that were performed on them, so that they can converse intelligently with physicians. Couples who are dealing with an intersexed partner may need help coping with the aftermath of the trauma, as well as (re)learning about their bodies and sexuality. When intersexed people begin dating, or form partnerships with others, issues regarding their physical differences may need to be addressed, and lovers and spouses will need to learn about their partners' bodies. The partner may feel confused and betrayed by this information, and the intersexed person may cope with issues of shame and self-hatred, as well as rage, at their partner's reaction.

When Kevin had first started dating Patricia she had told him that she was infertile. This had disturbed him at first, since he very much wanted to be a father, but he began to explore the issue of adoption or surrogacy and realized that he loved Patricia more than he cared about whether or not she could physically birth a child. As the couple became more intimate and began to talk about marriage, Patricia disclosed to Kevin the circumstances of her birth and the details of her medically intersexed condition. Kevin was shocked. He pulled back from Patricia, suddenly imagining her as a man. He began to notice the traits and mannerisms that he used to find endearing now appeared frighteningly masculine to him. His reaction was very painful for Patricia, and they both withdrew from each other, feeling betrayed. Both committed themselves to a therapy process, and Kevin was able to learn more about intersexuality. He eventually grew comfortable and understanding of Patricia's medical condition, as well as the unique physical and emotional issues she was facing. In this process, Patricia began to educate herself more about intersexed issues and discovered that having a partner in this process decreased some of her shame and confusion.

As the issue of intersexuality comes out of the proverbial closet, many clients will need assistance making sense of their medical conditions. They will need to address the impact of medical treatments on their bodies, their relationship to their sexuality and gender, as well as initiating communication with family members. The need for qualified therapists, knowledgeable about medical issues, human sexuality, and family dynamics will be of great importance to these families.

STANDARDS OF HUMANE TREATMENT
FOR INTERSEXED PEOPLE

Imagine . . . a new ethic of medical treatment, one that would permit ambiguity in a culture that has overcome sexual division.

Anne Fausto-Sterling
"The Five Sexes," 1993

In examining the current treatment protocols for intersexed treatment it becomes blatantly clear that simply not enough research has been done to establish routine genital surgery and sex reassignment of intersexed infants and children. Numerous medical professionals, as well as legal experts, ethicists, and researchers, are reexamining traditional protocols for early surgeries and how decisions are made about initial sex assignment (Beh and Diamond, 2000; Berenbaum, 2003; Lewis, 2000; Melton, 2001; Reiner, 1997, 1999; Scannell, 2001; Schober, 1999c), and all, even those committed to surgical treatments, are in agreement about the need for more follow-up research as well as quality-of-life studies (Meyer-Bahlburg et al., 1996; Newman, Randolph, and Anderson, 1992; Schober, 1999b; Wisniewski et al., 2000).

Chase (1999a) stated that there are three arguments against early genital cosmetic surgery. These are: (1) damage to potential sexual function, (2) establishing that the baby is "not acceptable as he or she was born" (p. 453), and (3) that some people are reassigned incorrectly. ISNA (1994) has been at the forefront of developing a new treatment paradigm for intersexed people. The model is based on the "avoidance of harmful or unnecessary surgery, qualified professional mental health care for the intersexual child and his/her family, and empowering the intersexual to understand his/her own status and to choose (or reject) any medical intervention." ISNA says that all surgery which is not "absolutely necessary" should be "deferred until the intersexual child is able to understand the risks and benefits of the proposed surgery and is able to provide appropriately informed consent." This sentiment is echoed by the United Kingdom Intersex Association's (UKIA) Web site, which states the importance of, "Any life-saving intervention procedures to be undertaken with due regard to preserving, where possible, the fundamental physical/ chromosomal sex of the infant, until such time as the child can demonstrate some gender-identifying behavioural features for themselves" (UKIA, n.d.).

Although Chase, the ISNA, and UKIA represent a minority voice, some physicians have recently come out against the standard protocols and have decided that surgery and hormonal treatments should be performed only with the informed consent of the intersexed person (Ford, 2001; Kipnis and Diamond, 1998; Howe, 1999; Schober, 1999a,c; Wilson and Reiner, 1999). Kipnis and Diamond (1998) recommended that a general moratorium be placed on surgeries done without the consent of the patient and that the moratorium should remain in place until comprehensive "look-back" studies and a review of outcomes are conducted. Schober (1998c) advocated a position of "watchful waiting." Most practitioners, however, do not advocate such a "radical" position although all are in agreement that long-term outcome studies of the current treatment protocols are necessary (Lerman, McAleer, and Kaplan, 2000). Meyer-Bahlburg has acquiesced that he would advocate for "less surgery for 'minor' cases of genital abnormalities" (Laurent, 1995/1996, p. 13).

Some researchers are beginning to study adults who were diagnosed with intersexed conditions at birth, and are finding that most patients were satisfied with their physical appearance, gender assignment, and medical treatments (Migeon, Wisniewski, Brown, et al., 2002; Migeon, Wisniewski, Gearhart, et al., 2002; Wisniewski et al., 2000). However, those reared as women who were not born with ambiguous genitalia were less often told about their condition. In one study 64 percent stated that they did not fully understand their diagnosis as adults and still desired more information about their condition (Wisniewski et al., 2000), and in another study about 50 percent of the patients, reared both as males and females, stated they were not well informed about their medical and surgical history and were not satisfied with their knowledge about their condition (Migeon, Wisniewski, Brown, et al., 2002). This research was conducted in response to critical outcries from surgically altered intersexed adults for retrospective studies (which proves that the medical community is listening). Therefore, it seems scientifically appropriate to raise questions about the ability for individuals to determine "satisfaction" when they are unaware of their own medical condition. Another study concluded that "either male or female sex of rearing can lead to successful long-term outcome for the majority of cases," despite the fact that five men and four women, 23 percent of participants, were dissatisfied with their sex of rearing, with two participants (one reared male and the other reared female) choosing sex reassignment in adulthood (Migeon, 2002b). Terms such as *success* and *satisfaction* clearly need to be further operationalized.

The one area that activists and medical professionals seem to agree is that more psychosocial support is necessary in the form of counseling or psychotherapy for parents who birth intersexed children and intersexed people themselves, either as children or as adults (Yronwode, 1999). Outside of the rare intersex condition that needs immediate medical intervention, most intersexed births are considered "psychosocial" emergencies, despite the fact that clinical interventions have not been psychosocial, but medical.

Many providers may recommend therapy or counseling—and certainly few would oppose it—however, no guidelines are available to assist the therapist working with intersexed children or their families. Generally, no programs or protocols are in place for professional counseling at clinics that specialize in treating intersexual children. The intersex literature often suggests the benefits of psychotherapy, but no psychotherapeutic guidelines for the clinical treatment of intersexed people currently exist. (For example, a PubMed search on "intersex and psychotherapy" produced only two citations—one of which actually discusses transsexuality rather than intersexuality—and neither is a guide for therapists. In contrast, a search for "diabetes and psychotherapy" produced 420 citations.)

Diamond (1996) said that theoretical thinking regarding the significance of "nurture" in the nature-versus-nurture controversy has ebbed somewhat in the past few years, in part because of the exposé of the John/Joan case. However, that has not impacted the *surgical treatment* of intersexed children, despite evidence suggesting the role of nature and nurture to be far more complex than previously thought. This may not be that surprising, given that the theoretical examination of gender development and the relationship of nature to nurture is often a discussion that takes place in the social science texts, not the medical journals. The perceived medical needs of intersexed people are managed by physicians, who also determine the direction of psychosocial treatments. Groveman (2001) noted that parents are often looking toward the physicians for emotional assistance, but that they would be best served seeking counseling outside of the medical arena.

Schober (1999a) suggested that "the role of counsellor should not be left to an endocrinologist, urologist, geneticist, or surgeon, nor a genetic counsellor" (p. 47). However, Meyer-Bahlburg (1994) said, "In most cases, the psychosocial issues of intersex patients are managed, *if at all,* by the physicians who provide the medical care" (p. 22, emphasis mine). While pediatric endocrinologists and surgeons have received extensive medical training, they have rarely been trained in mental health issues or psychotherapeutic counseling skills. As the ISNA said, "Non-psychiatrically trained physicians should no more practice psychotherapy than psychiatrists or non-medically trained psychotherapists should perform surgery or prescribe hormones" (ISNA, 1994, p. 2).

Curran and Chase (2001) surveyed fifty pediatric endocrinology fellowship programs in the United States and Canada and received responses from twenty-seven. Sixteen said they have a mental health worker available, however, of these only five offered counseling following the initial diagnosis. Eleven said they would offer referrals for adults who are intersexed, but only four could offer the names of actual referral sources. Many commented that they were unable to find qualified mental health professionals. Lightfoot-Klein and colleagues (2000) suggested, "With some specialized training, mental health professions would be well-equipped to address the emotional distress of the parents and the child as he or she grows up" (p. 458). In reality, few psychotherapists are currently trained in working with intersexed clients or their families. Therapeutic treatment paradigms can, indeed must, be developed that will move beyond merely serving as educators to parents about surgical protocols developed by physicians.

It is interesting that when transsexuals desire surgical treatment they must be approved by gatekeepers who determine who can get *in* to receive medical treatment, but intersexed children are not allowed to opt *out* of treatment. Just as psychotherapists must become more than assessment gatherers, diagnosticians, and gatekeepers for the transgendered community, clinicians working with the intersexed community must also become educators, advocates, and psychotherapists prepared to assist their clients through complex issues involving grief, anger, intimacy, and sexuality.

Therapeutic trust cannot be established in a relationship that is based in maintaining secrecy, securing closed patient files, utilizing semantics to distort medical descriptions, and a predetermined stance as to the preferred outcome of human development. Howe (1999) said, "The trust between patients and care providers may be more important to intersexuals' welfare than any other goal that is immediately achievable" (p. 213). In order to develop trust, intersexed people and their families must first establish a relationship of mutual respect and a sense that the clinician is not just a puppet for the medical doctors, but an integral part of the treatment team.

Zucker (1996) suggested that a professional organization similar to HBIGDA should be developed for intersex treatment issues, and in 2000 a new independent and self-governing organization was developed. The North American Task Force on Intersex (NATFI) brings together an interdisciplinary group of physicians and intersex advocacy groups, including, for the first time, intersex patient advocates. They are a progressive body dedicated to establishing standards for informed consent, developing a retrospective review of the long-term psychosexual status of patients treated for intersex conditions, establishing guidelines for the management of children born with ambiguous sex anatomy, initiating a prospective registry, and revising medical nomenclature (ISNA, 2000). There is, however, a notable lack of involvement among social workers, psychologists, and family system therapists.

Even physicians who are supportive of involving mental health providers on the interdisciplinary team serving intersexed persons still ignore the mental health providers who are experts in family treatment—marital and family therapists and social workers, who are the prime providers of services (U.S. Department of Labor, 2000/2001). For example, Wilson and Reiner (1999) proposed a progressive treatment paradigm that includes the parents as part of the team. They are compassionately aware that the parents may not be able to function effectively as part of a team of medical "experts," particularly at the same time they are coping with the reality of their child's condition, so they recommended the addition of a child psychiatrist, noting their specialized training in working with children with medical problems. They also noted that child psychologists and social workers usually lack this expertise. In reality, many psychologists and social workers are trained in medical and psychiatric conditions and work with children facing chronic and acute health problems in hospital settings as well as child development settings, whereas few child psychiatrists are trained in family systems or family dynamics. Wilson and Reiner, although perhaps well-meaning, seem to reinforce an established medical hierarchy that empowers physicians, in this case psychiatrists, and disempowers social workers and other therapeutically skilled counselors.

The recommendations listed in Box 10.1 place therapeutic evaluation and education at the center of clinical and medical decisions regarding the pregnancy, birth, and rearing of intersexed children. Trained mental health providers must be encouraged to be on medical boards that currently make decisions regarding the protocols for intersexed children.

Examining the standard protocols for intersex treatment, particularly the lack of therapeutic services now offered to intersexed people, seems to be an issue whose time has arrived. Crouch (1999) said, "Our ideas about inter-sexuality are just that—ideas—and thus open to scrutiny and revision" (p. 41). Medicine has a long history of revising its protocols, instituting increasingly progressive and innovative techniques, and discontinuing outdated modalities. Indeed many physicians who are open-minded to the voices of ISNA nonetheless defend their treatment protocols as necessary because the culture is the way it is, ignoring the fact that it is the way it is because medical protocol has assisted in its creation. It may not be as intellectually challenging to take a medical stance of "do nothing," but it may prove to be the best treatment strategy with the most successful long-term results. According to Lightfoot-Klein and colleagues (2000),

> Medical practices that were once professionally respectable but have now been eliminated because of social condemnation include forced sterilization for eugenic purposes; hysterectomy and oopherectomy for psychological disorders in women . . . ; lobotomy, electroshock, and aversion therapy for treatment of homosexuality . . . ; clitoral excision or cauterization for elimination of masturbation . . . ; radiation experiments on institutionalized handicapped children; and syphilis experiments on impoverished African American men. "Genital reconstruction" of intersex infants should finally be added to the list. (p. 458)

"Intersexuality," in Schober's (1999a) words, is a "naturally dimorphic condition" (p. 45), and intersexed people are a small but consistent percentage of the human population. They deserve the right to make their own decisions about their bodies. Advocates for the rights of children, therapists concerned about the impact of trauma and betrayal in families, compassionate physicians, and activists who support the expression of sexual and gender diversity must all come together to develop effective protocols for the "management" of intersexed conditions that places intersexed people and their empowerment at the center of all treatment strategies.

BOX 10.1.
Guidelines for Therapeutic Treatment
of People Born with Intersexed Conditions
or Ambiguous Genitalia and Their Families

- Protocols should be developed within gynecological and obstetric offices and departments to provide or refer clients for genetic and prenatal testing for sex chromosomal-related anomalies. Staff must be trained and competent about the existence of intersex conditions, and be able to convey potential outcomes in a nonjudgmental manner.
- When a child is born with ambiguous genitalia, the child should be examined to determine whether any medical conditions exist that need immediate attention. The medical team should attend to any medical emergencies and delay any non-life-threatening medical interventions.
- The child's birth should be celebrated as would any other birth. The medical staff should emphasize positives and refer to the baby as a "whole" child, not just a set of genitals. Parents should be reminded that sexual ambiguity is a minor anomaly compared with many other congenital conditions. The child should not be needlessly isolated in the neonatal intensive care unit for the convenience of medical access to the child, or to spare the family from having visitors see their newborn child.
- The child's condition should be evaluated by a team of experts, which should include such medical specialists as pediatric endocrinologists, urologists, and geneticists, as well as qualified mental health professionals who are trained in understanding both family dynamics and issues related to sex and gender development. This could include a family therapist, social worker, and/or child psychologist.
- The family should be an integral part of the entire treatment process, receiving adequate attention, education, and time to understand complex medical issues.
- Based on the information available, the best "educated guess" of the medical staff, and the agreement of the family, the child should be assigned a sex, with the understanding that genital anatomy and biological underpinnings are "signals," not determiners of gender identity. All sex assignments should be assumed preliminary.
- The family should be sent home to bond with their newborn.
- Surgical alteration of the child's genitalia should be avoided, except when there is a definite medical need. Cosmetic surgeries should be avoided until the child is of age to consent and is capable of a realistic understanding of the possible risks and benefits of the surgery. The intersexed person must have autonomy and desire to undergo the surgery.

(continued)

(continued)

- When surgeries are performed, the family and child should be informed about potential problems with sexual sensation, less-than-perfect cosmetics, and the need for further or ongoing treatments. It should be made clear to the family that surgery does not "cure" the intersexed condition, although it can make the child appear more like others. Surgery may not alleviate any of the other psychosocial issues related to having an intersexed condition.
- Through the process of therapeutic follow-up, families should be informed of the many choices available for treatment, including cosmetic surgeries. Parents should be encouraged to seek out additional information, speak with family and friends, and seek counseling before making any surgical decisions.
- Therapeutic support should continue to be available to the family, including offering medical information, education about sex and gender development, and assistance in making informed medical decisions. Linkages with other families and adults with intersexed conditions should be encouraged.
- Therapy should be made available to the family throughout the life cycle of the family, as different stages of development may reveal different struggles with body image, feeling "different," or questions about intimacy and identity, including issues related to sex, gender, or sexual orientation.

Appendix A

The *International Classification of Diseases,* Tenth Revision, Definition of Transsexualism

The *International Classification of Diseases,* Tenth Revision, (ICD-10) (WHO, 1992) now provides five diagnoses for gender identity disorders (F64), including one for children and two categories that are unspecified but can be used for intersexed people struggling with gender identity issues. Below are the criteria for transsexualism and dual-role transvestism.

Transsexualism (F64.0) has three criteria:

1. The desire to live and be accepted as a member of the opposite sex, usually accompanied by the wish to make his or her body as congruent as possible with the preferred sex through surgery and hormone treatment;
2. The transsexual identity has been present persistently for at least two years;
3. The disorder is not a symptom of another mental disorder or a chromosomal abnormality.

Dual-role transvestism (F64.1) has three criteria:

1. The individual wears clothes of the opposite sex in order to experience temporary membership in the opposite sex;
2. There is no sexual motivation for the cross-dressing;
3. The individual has no desire for a permanent change to the opposite sex.

Appendix B

Common Intersexed Conditions

There are more than 70 different atypical chromosomal and hormonal conditions that can cause intersexed syndromes or ambiguous genitalia.

Complete androgen insensitivity syndrome (CAIS) and **partial androgen insensitivity syndrome** (PAIS) are genetic syndromes (46 XY karyotype), often inherited, occurring in approximately one in 20,000 individuals. These syndromes are also known as testicular feminization syndrome. CAIS and PAIS are examples of an intersexed condition in which the internal reproductive organs differ from the person's chromosomal sex due to a defect located on the X chromosome. In androgen insensitivity syndrome (AIS) conditions, the fetus develops testes but is unable to respond to androgens and the genitals differentiate into the female rather than the male pattern. AIS babies are raised as females. In PAIS, the insensitivity is not complete and the external genitalia can appear typically male, typically female, or intermediate in structure between male and female. AIS is not a disorder of the sex chromosomes (e.g., Klinefelter's and Turner's syndromes), because the sex chromosomes in an AIS baby are those of an XY male whose cellular receptors do not work properly, causing an irregularity in the development of the genitals. The newborn AIS infant has genitals of normal female appearance, undescended or partially descended testes instead of ovaries, an absent uterus and cervix, and a vagina that is usually short or absent. The undescended testes can result in an inguinal hernia in infancy, which is when AIS is often diagnosed. Sometimes AIS is not discovered until puberty when the girl does not begin to menstruate. Tumors may develop in the testes after the onset of puberty, with a lifetime risk of about 1:3; the medical establishment has recommended that they be removed, although the timing of this has been open to debate. At puberty the testes produce high levels of testosterone, some of which naturally converts back to its precursor, estrogen. Although estrogen may produce relatively typical female development, the girl will not menstruate and is infertile. The appearance of nipples, facial oil, and pubic and underarm hair in women are controlled by testosterone, so women with AIS always have somewhat immature nipples and genitals, an absence of underarm and pubic hair, and do not have facial oil or acne. People with PAIS raised as males usually have masculinizing genital surgery (urethroplasty of the hypospadiac penis to make urination in a standing position possible). Hormone replacement with androgens may not result in full development of male secondary sex characteristics such as beard growth or deepening of the voice. People with PAIS who are raised as females are castrated, and various genital surgeries are performed to create a vagina and possibly to alter the size of the clitoris. As a genetic anomaly, AIS runs in families, and some people with AIS have been able to locate other siblings or relatives with AIS, although it can also occur as a spontaneous genetic change.

Congenital adrenal hyperplasia (CAH) is the most prevalent cause of intersexuality among XX people with a frequency of about one in 10,000 births. It is an inherited recessive disorder in females caused when an anomaly of adrenal function disrupts the synthesis of cortisone and causes the secretion of an androgen precursor, initiating virilization of an XX person in utero. Androgens are introduced too late to affect the differentiation of the internal structures; however, they can affect the external genitalia. Depending on the extent of the masculinization, the clitoris may appear slightly enlarged, quite ambiguous (with labial fusion), or may have the appearance of a typical penis and scrotum (but with testes absent). The vagina may be smaller than typical, or it may connect internally to the urethra, having no exit to the perineum. Because the virilization originates metabolically, masculinizing effects continue after birth with the possible added complication of metabolic problems that upset serum sodium balance (salt losing form). The metabolic effects of CAH can be counteracted with cortisone, though not without side effects, and many people with CAH experience lifelong medical issues.

Klinefelter's syndrome is a common chromosomal condition that affects approximately one in every 800 live male births. People with Klinefelter's syndrome have an extra X chromosome (47 XXY karyotype) inherited either from their mother or father. This condition can produce a range of physical effects. The testes are small and firm and their ejaculate does not usually contain any sperm, causing infertility. Some males with Klinefelter's syndrome are never diagnosed since the penis is average size at birth. Their testosterone production, however, is often low, which affects their development in puberty. Compared to other men, they do not virilize as strongly (e.g., they have less facial or body hair, a smaller penis, and their voice does not become as deep, and some experience gynecomastia—breast growth— or more rounded body contours). They tend to have lower sex drives and are often described as passive with a lack of ambition. Treatment has consisted of lifelong testosterone beginning at puberty that may increase sexual interest and enhance the development of secondary sex characteristics. It is possible that more males with Klinefelter's syndrome are homosexual or transsexual, but there is controversy in the literature regarding this.

Turner's syndrome is a chromosomal condition that occurs in approximately one out of 2,500 female births and is caused by a 45 XO karyotype, in which an ovum is fertilized without any sex chromosomes or in which an error occurs early in cell division. People with Turner's syndrome have a female body type, nonfunctional streak ovaries, and lack secondary sex characteristics unless hormone replacement is provided during puberty. In addition, most females with Turner's syndrome are short statured, and can have webbed skin on the neck with swelling on the back of the hands and feet. The condition sometimes has an impact on certain aspects of cognitive processing. Individuals with Turner's syndrome are also prone to cardiovascular problems, kidney and thyroid problems, skeletal disorders such as scoliosis or dislocated hips, and hearing and ear disturbances. Since estrogen replacement treatment will often decrease the girl's ultimate height, replacement is often delayed until late puberty.

Source: Carroll and Wolpe, 1996; Chase, 2001, personal communication; Migeon, Wisniewski, and Gearhart, 2001.

Appendix C

Letters of Recommendation for Hormones

When a clinician has assessed a client and feels that the eligibility criteria (outlined below) have been met and the client is ready to begin hormone treatment, he or she writes a letter of recommendation to an endocrinologist or physician trained in trans-medicine. The letter should follow the form of a general psychosocial recommendation that would be used in any mental health setting, with an emphasis on the person's history of gender dysphoria. When working with a physician for the first time, a letter of introduction from the referring clinician can help establish the relationship. Depending on the extent of the client's history or psychosocial issues, a letter can be anywhere from one to four pages. The purpose of the letter is to introduce the client to the endocrinologist and establish a clinical team approach between the referring clinician and medical expert, so they can work together for the benefit of the client.

The Harry Benjamin International Gender Dysphoria Association has developed requirements for hormone therapy that include criteria for eligibility and readiness. These criteria are paraphrased below.

Eligibility criteria include:

1. The person requesting hormone treatment must be 18 years old, although provisions are made for adolescents with parental permission who are 16 years old.
2. The person understands what the hormones can and cannot do, and also their social risks and benefits.
3. A documented real-life experience of at least three months prior to the administration of hormones,

   Or

   A period of psychotherapy that follows the initial evaluation—the time frames for both of these processes are specified by the mental health specialist, but three months is recommended. It is acceptable to make exceptions for this third category, for example as an alternative to black-market hormones.

Readiness criteria include:

1. A consolidation of gender identity during the real-life experience or psychotherapy.
2. Any other identified problems have been addressed sufficiently so the person is improving or continuing stable mental health, including substance abuse, or mental health issues.
3. The patient is likely to use hormones in a responsible manner.

Eligibility and readiness for surgery are outlined in the HGIBDA standards of care, but the letter for recommendation can follow a similar format.

1. *Client identification:* This should include client's legal name as well as other names they may use, address, phone number, e-mail, and any other contact information. In addition, information on the client's birth date/age, relational and family status, employment and/or educational situation should be briefly outlined. The client should be referred to in his or her preferred pronoun, except when he or she is still living in his or her natal sex. It is acceptable to use natal pronouns when discussing his or her childhood and history. Race/ethnicity, religion, disability, or any other pertinent information about the client's identity should be mentioned, as appropriate.
2. *Reason for referral:* This section should include information about the length of evaluation and/or psychotherapy, and the results of any psychological testing, ecomaps, or genograms. The reason the client is seeking medical treatment at this time should be noted.
3. *Familial history:* Information regarding the client's family of origin should be described, including parent and sibling relationships, past and current. A basic outline of the client's upbringing should be described including information on familial deaths, divorces, the functioning of the family as a whole, salience of any cultural themes in the family, values expressed within family, and characteristics of communication style. Any pertinent information regarding the client's childhood (poverty, health issues, family member's disability, involvement in the military, frequent moving, living in multiple households, adoption or fostering, additional members living in the home, etc.) should also be listed here. When possible, the therapist is basing this knowledge on information attained through contact with family members.
4. *Current living situation:* Information regarding the client's current living situation should be described. If the client is in a significant intimate relationship, and/or is parenting children this should be noted, as

well as any past marriages or committed relationships. Identify who is living in the current household, and the quality of the client's relationship with his or her child/children, whether or not they are currently living with the client. Describe the quality, duration, and communication patterns of any intimate relationships, including issues of power and decision making.

5. *Work and education:* Discuss the client's educational background or current schooling. Identify any history of learning problems, or developmental challenges that have impacted schooling or work life. The client's current work and career goals should be outlined, including the likelihood of maintaining employment through transition and his or her plans for transition at work.

6. *Gender issues:* The client's relationship to his or her gender, from early childhood through the present, should be thoroughly outlined. This establishes the history of gender-related issues. Examples of cross-dressing discomfort in his or her gender role, body dysphoria, and family reaction to the gender issues should be discussed. Information about the client's current gender expression and trajectory regarding transition should be outlined.

7. *Social support:* This section should identify the clients' social supports, including hobbies, community involvement, friends, and social activities. Relationship to transgendered community resources and access to information (including Internet access) is also important to note. Familial support or resistance for transition should be noted. If the client is living at home with parents, or living on a college campus, or in a work situation that is problematic, education and counseling should be offered, as appropriate, to those in an ongoing relationship with a person person beginning hormones.

8. *Psychosocial stressors:* Any mental health or medical issues, criminal history, pending legal problems or probation should be outlined, as well as the client's current status. A thorough drug and alcohol evaluation should be part of the assessment. Any history of domestic violence, sexual assault, childhood sexual or physical abuse or neglect, or being the victim of a bias-related crime should be thoroughly evaluated. Previous therapy should be noted, including in- or outpatient mental health or substance abuse treatment, or psychiatric hospitalization. Clients should be evaluated for anxiety, depression, characterological disturbances, and suicidality. Skills of daily living, including basic hygiene, eating and sleeping patterns, and relationship to social service agencies should also be noted. Approval for hormones depends on the client's stability, and issues that may prove stressing should be addressed, so that the treatment team (i.e., the mental health

counselor making the referral and the endocrinologist receiving the referral) can work together to support the client through any difficulties.

9. *Summary:* A description of the client's behavioral characteristics, attitudes, affect, maturational level, attitudes toward self, ability to cope with stress, familial and social supports, and general outlook on life should be outlined. In the final section, the clinician shares his or her observations of the client, including any concerns about transition issues that might require continuing psychotherapy. Diagnostic eligibility is established—including an appropriate diagnosis—and the recommendation for medical treatment is clearly stated.

Glossary

bi-gender: Some gender-variant people reject the choices of male/female, man/woman and feel their gender encompasses "both" genders. Some feel that they are androgynous, simultaneously exhibiting masculine and feminine traits, and others feel they are neutral or without gender. This steps outside of a "changing sex" paradigm and allows for more flexibility of gender expression and identity. Bi-gendered people often identify as being of both genders. Transsexual people do not commonly consider themselves to be bi-gendered. Within some American Indian cultures, expressing both genders is referred to as "Two-Spirited." Within contemporary urban life bi-gendered people often refer to themselves as "gender queers," "gender benders," "third sex," and "gender perverts" with pride.

bisexual: A woman or man who is, or feels she or he has the potential to be, sexually and emotionally attracted to members of either the same or other sex. Bisexuality can be viewed as a continuum in that degrees of attraction can vary. Some bisexual people feel equally attracted to members of either sex, while others express a preference. Bisexual people can be in long-term monogamous relationships with members of either sex. Some are strongly identified with the gay political movement, whereas others are not. Bisexual people can also be transgendered.

butch: *Butch* is commonly used in the lesbian and gay communities to identify masculine females or sometimes masculine gay men. The spectrum of identity within the lesbian community can include "soft" butches who identify as masculine women, transgender butches who often do not identify as "women" and are somewhat bi-gendered in their identity, and those who identify as transmen/FTMs but still retain an identity as "butch." *Stone butch* refers to butches who prefer to be sexually pleasured in ways that are not feminizing. Commonly, they prefer to pleasure their partners and avoid having their own (female) body parts touched.

coming out: The process, often lifelong, in which LGBT people become aware of, acknowledge, accept, appreciate, and let others know about their sexual identity. Coming out can involve self-knowledge, or sharing this information with friends, family, and employers. An LGB person must "come out" of other people's assumptions that they are heterosexual, whereas a transgendered person must come out of other people's assumptions regarding his or her gender identity.

cross-dressers (CDs): Cross-dressers are people who wear clothing usually assigned to the opposite sex. They have been referred to in the clinical literature as "transvestites" (TVs), but most prefer the term cross-dresser. Some cross-dress for erotic fulfillment, some for social fun (e.g., doing "drag"), and still others just for comfort. Since women have more freedom of dress in American culture, cross-dressers are, by clinical definition, males who dress in women's clothing. Most are heterosexually identified. Many cross-dressers purge their female clothing periodically as a way to try to cure themselves of their behavior. The length of time a person cross-dresses can vary from infrequent to full-time. Drag queens are males, often gay men, who dress as women in an extreme feminine manner, for fun, or "camp." Drag kings are females who dress as men in an extremely masculine manner, often for entertainment. Some drag queens and drag kings might live full-time in these identities. Female impersonators are men who work in the entertainment industry and dress as women as part of their job. They may be cross-dressers or be transgendered, but not necessarily. Male impersonators are their female counterparts.

emergence: The process of becoming aware of, acknowledging, accepting, appreciating, and letting others know about one's (trans)gender identity. It is similar to the "coming-out" experience for lesbian, gay, and bisexual people, but can also involve body modification and changes in pronoun use. It is, therefore, less easily hidden socially or vocationally. Emergence is normative within a culture that allows only dimorphic, immutable gender expressions. It describes an adaptive process that is necessary within a confining social system.

female-to-male transsexuals (FTMs): Female-to-male transsexuals are natal females who live as men. This includes a broad range of experience from those who identify as "male" or "men" to those who identify as transsexual, "transmen," "female men," or FTM as their gender identity. FTMs are often contrasted with "biomen" or biologically born men. Some transsexuals are comfortable being included in the category of transgender and others are not.

femme: *Femme* is commonly used in the lesbian community to identify feminine lesbians. These include women who are lesbian-identified and are often, although not exclusively, attracted to masculine females or butches. Femmes often feel invisible as lesbians, since they pass in the world appearing as normal heterosexual women. Femme is not an identity of passivity, but one of strength and power.

gay: Men who are sexually and emotionally attracted to other men and form their primary loving and sexual relationships with other men. The term "gay" is sometimes used generically to include both men and women, but many women prefer to identify as "lesbian." A female-to-male transsexual can also be a gay man.

gender community: This is a colloquial term for the transgender community or people who are dealing with issues of gender identity. It often includes the significant others of transgendered people, referred to as SOFFA (significant others, family, friends, and allies) and pronounced "softa."

gender identity: Gender is a social construct that divides people into "natural" categories of men and women that are assumed to derive from their physiological male and female bodies. Gender attributes vary from culture to culture, and are arbitrarily imposed, denying individuality. Most people's gender identity is congruent with their assigned sex, but many people experience their gender identity to be discordant with their natal sex. A person's self concept of their gender (regardless of their biological sex) is called their gender identity.

gender role: Gender roles are the expression of masculinity and femininity and has often been referred to as "sex roles." Gender roles are a reflection of one's gender identity and are socially dictated and reinforced. Gender roles describe how gender is enacted or "performed" (consciously or unconsciously) and may or may not be related to gender identity or natal sex.

heterosexism: The institutionalized set of beliefs that heterosexuality—opposite-sex sexuality—is normal, natural, and superior to homosexuality. Homophobia (a fear and hatred of gays and lesbians) is an outgrowth of heterosexism that confers certain privileges such as legal protection, the right to marry, and freedom to be publicly affectionate on people who are heterosexual (or appear to be). Biphobia—a fear and hatred of bisexuals—and transphobia—a fear and hatred of transgendered people—are also institutionalized and further reinforce sexual and gender norms.

intersex: Intersex refers to people who are not easily classified into the binary of male and female categories. They have physical sex characteristics, often including ambiguous genitalia, of both males and females, and are not easily differentiated into established sex divisions. Intersexed people are assigned to either male or female categories at birth and many have been surgically altered. Intersexuality and surgical alteration is often a secret, sometimes even to those who have been altered. Intersexed people can be heterosexual, gay, lesbian, bisexual, transgendered, or transsexual from the perspective of the sex and gender identity that they have been assigned. Approximately 2 percent of the population are intersexed.

lesbian: Lesbians are women who are sexually and emotionally attracted to other women, and who form their primary loving and sexual relationships with other women. Lesbians can also refer to themselves as gay women or "dykes." Some lesbians identify with feminist politics, whereas others do not. A male-to-female transsexual can also be a lesbian.

LGBT: An acronym for "lesbian, gay, bisexual, and transgender." Also referred to as queer. Sometimes a "Q" is added (LGBTQ) for those "questioning" their sexual and gender identities.

male-to-female transsexuals (MTF): Male-to-female transsexuals are natal males who live as women. This includes a broad range of experience, including those who identify as "female" or "women" and those who identify as transsexual women. Some words used to refer to transsexual women are "Tgirl" and "new women," which is contrasted with "GGs" or genetic women. Some transsexual people are comfortable being included in the category of transgender, while others are not.

passing: To pass is to be able to successfully assume the gender role of the opposite sex when interacting with society and being able to function in public situations as a member of that gender. When someone does not pass well, or is "read" as a member of his or her assigned sex, it can invite public ridicule and violence. Some transgender activists reject the idea of trying to pass, seeing it as playing into a dual-gender system. However, for many transsexual people passing well is seen as affirming their reintegration into society.

sex: Sex is the physiological makeup of a human being, referred to as the biological or natal sex. Sex is usually thought of in a bipolar way, dividing the world into males and females. In reality, sex is a complex relationship of genetic, hormonal, morphological, biochemical, and anatomical determinates that impact the physiology of the body and the sexual differentiation of the brain. Although everyone is assigned a sex at birth, approximately 2 percent of the population are intersexed and do not easily fit into a dimorphic division of two sexes that are "opposite."

sexual identity: An overall term that describes an individual's sense of their own sexuality, including the complex relationship of sex and gender as components of identity. Sexual identity includes a biopsychosocial integration of biological sex, gender identity, gender-role expression and sexual orientation. This term is sometimes used in a more narrow sense to mean sexual orientation or preference, particularly for gay people who not only "behave" homosexually, but have pride or "identify" with that aspect of themselves.

sexual orientation: Sexual orientation is the self-perception of the direction of sexual desire. It describes sexual preference and emotional attraction. Some people experience their sexual orientation as an unchanging essential part of their nature, whereas others experience it in a more fluid way. Sexual orientation can be directed toward members of the same sex (homosexual), opposite sex (heterosexual), both sexes (bisexual), and neither sex (nonsexual). Sexual orientation is not merely "same-sex" attraction, but is experienced through the person's gender identity regardless of his or her biology.

SRS (sex reassignment surgery): SRS, also referred to as GRS (gender reassignment surgery), is the surgical process involved in changing one's sex. This most often refers to genital reconstruction, but also can include mastectomy and chest reconstruction for female-to-male transsexuals, as well as a variety of cosmetic surgeries to enhance one's gender presentation. Genital surgeries for male-to-females are currently more advanced than those available for female-to-males.

transgender: *Transgender* is an umbrella term including many categories of people who are gender variant. This can include people who identify as transsexuals, cross-dressers, masculine-identified females, feminine-identified males, MTFs, FTMs, transmen, transgendered women, intersexed, and other differently gendered people. Transgendered people can be heterosexual, homosexual, bisexual, or nonsexual. *Transgenderist* is a term used by some cross-dressers who feel they are more than cross-dressers, but not quite transsexuals.

transition: The process that transgendered people move through in accepting their gender identity, particularly the physical, legal, and psychological experience of moving from one gender identity to another or allowing others to see their authentic identity. Transition is similar to a rebirthing experience, in which the person reemerges with a social identity that is the best expression of their internal core gender identity. Part of this process involves cross-living as the other gender or going through the real-life experience—or real-life test—to experience what living as the other gender is like before being referred for sex reassignment surgery. Transition often implies hormonal and surgical treatments and the physical changes that accompany them.

transsexuals (TS or **Ts):** Transsexuals are people who believe that their physiological bodies do not represent their true sex. Although most transsexuals desire sex reassignment surgery, transsexual people may be preoperative, postoperative, or nonoperative (i.e., choosing to not have surgical modification). Some transsexuals prefer to not have their birth sex known and attempt to "pass," whereas others are comfortable being known as transsexual and take pride in this identity. Most transsexuals prefer to be referred to simply as men or women according to their gender identity and gender presentation, regardless of their surgical status.

References

Abramowitz, S.I. (1986). Psychosocial outcomes of sex reassignment surgery. *Journal of Consulting and Clinical Psychology, 54* (2), 183-189.

Abramsky, L., Hall, S., Levitan, J., and Marteau, T.M. (2001). What parents are told after prenatal diagnosis of a sex chromosome abnormality: Interview and questionnaire study. *BMJ,* 322, 463-466. Available: <http://www.bmj.com/cgi/content/full/322/7284/463>.

Ako, T. (2001). Beginnings of sex reassignment surgery in Japan. *International Journal of Transgenderism, 1* (5). Available: <http://www.symposion.com/ijt/ijtvo05no01_02.htm>.

Alexander, T. (1999). Silence=death. In A.D. Dreger (ed.), *Intersex in the age of ethics* (pp. 103-110). Hagerstown, MD: University Publishing Group.

Alizai, N.K., Thomas, D.F., Lilford, R.J, Batchelor, A.G., and Johnson, N. (1999). Feminizing genitoplasty for congenital adrenal hyperplasia: What happens at puberty? *Journal of Urology, 161* (5), 1588-1591.

Allison, B. (1998). Janice Raymond and autogynephilia. Available: <http://www.drbecky.com/raymond.html>.

Altman, D. (1971). *Homosexual: Oppression and liberation* (New edition). London: AllenLane.

American Academy of Pediatrics (AAP) (1996a). Policy statement newborn screening fact sheets (RE9632). *Pediatrics, 98* (3), 473-501. Available: <http://www.aap.org/policy/01565.html>.

American Academy of Pediatrics (AAP) (1996b). Policy statement timing of elective surgery on the genitalia of male children with particular reference to the risks, benefits, and psychological effects of surgery and anesthesia (RE9610). *Pediatrics, 97* (4), 590-594. Available: <http://www.aap.org/policy/01306.html>.

American Academy of Pediatrics (AAP) (2000). Policy statement on evaluation of the newborn with developmental anomalies of the external genitalia (RE9958). *Pediatrics, 106* (1), 138-142. Available: <http://www.aap.org/policy/re9958.html>.

American Boyz (n.d.). Available: <http://www.amboyz.org>.

American Psychiatric Association (APA) (1952). *Diagnostic and statistical manual of mental disorders.* Washington, DC: American Psychiatric Association.

American Psychiatric Association (APA) (1968). *Diagnostic and statistical manual of mental disorders* (Second edition). Washington, DC: American Psychiatric Association.

American Psychiatric Association (APA) (1980). *Diagnostic and statistical manual of mental disorders* (Third edition). Washington, DC: American Psychiatric Association.

American Psychiatric Association (APA) (1987). *Diagnostic and statistical manual of mental disorders* (Third edition, Revised). Washington, DC: American Psychiatric Association.

American Psychiatric Association (APA) (1994). *Diagnostic and statistical manual of mental disorders* (Fourth edition). Washington, DC: American Psychiatric Association.

American Psychiatric Association (APA) (1999). *Diagnostic and statistical manual of mental disorders* (Fourth edition). Washington, DC: American Psychiatric Association.

American Psychiatric Association (APA) (2000). *Diagnostic and statistical manual of mental disorders* (Fourth edition, Text revision). Washington, DC: American Psychiatric Association.

The American Public Health Association (APHA) (1999). Policy statements adopted by the governing council of the American Public Health Association, November 19. Available: <http://www.apha.org/legislative/policy/99policy.pdf>.

The American Public Health Association (APHA) (2001). Lesbian, Gay, Bisexual, and Transgender Health. *The American Journal of Public Health, 91* (6).

Anderson, B. (1998). Therapeutic issues in working with transgendered clients. In D. Dallas (ed.), *Current concepts in transgender identity* (pp. 215-226). New York: Garland.

Anderson, H. and Goolishian, H. (1992). The client is the expert: A not-knowing approach to therapy. In S. McNamee and K.J. Gergen (eds.), *Therapy as social construction* (pp. 7-24). Thousand Oaks, CA: Sage.

Anzaldua, G.E. and Keating, A. (2002). *This bridge we call home: Radical visions for transformation.* New York: Routledge.

Asscheman, H., Gooren, L., and Eklund, P.L. (1989). Mortality and morbidity in transsexual patients with cross gender hormone treatment. *Metabolism: Clinical and experimental, 38* (9), 869-873.

Bailey, J.M. (2003). *The man who would be queen: The science of gender-bending and transsexualism.* Washington, DC: Joseph Henry Press.

Bailey, J.M., Bobrow, D., Wolfe, M., and Mikach, S. (1995). Sexual orientation of adult sons of gay fathers. *Developmental Psychology, 31,* 124-129.

Bailey, J.M. and Zucker, K.J. (1995). Childhood sex-typed behavior and sexual orientation: A conceptual analysis and quantitative review. *Developmental Psychology, 31* (1), 43-55.

Bakker, A., Van Kesteren, P.J., Gooren, L.G.J., and Bezemer, P.D. (1993). The prevalence of transsexualism in the Netherlands. *Acta Psychiatrica Scandinavica, 87* (4), 237-238.

Ball, E. (1999). *Slaves in the family.* New York: Random House.

Balwin, J. and Giovanni, N. (1973). *A dialogue.* London: Penguin Books.

Baptiste, D.A. (1990). Night terrors as a defense against feelings of homosexual panic: A case report. *Journal of Gay and Lesbian Psychotherapy, 1* (3), 121-131.

Barlow, D.H., Reynolds, E.J., and Agras, W.S. (1973). Gender identity change in a transsexual. *Archives of General Psychiatry, 28,* 569-576.

Barrett, T.M. and Gonzales, E.T. (1980). Reconstruction of the female external genitalia. *Urologic Clinics of North America, 7,* 455-463.

Bartlett, N.H., Vasey, P.L., and Bukowski, W.M. (2000). Is gender identity disorder in children a mental disorder? *Sex Roles: A Journal of Research.* Available: <http://www.findarticles.com/cf_0/m2294/2000_Dec/75959827/print.jhtml>.

Baskin, L.S., Erol, A., Li, Y.W., Liu, W.H., Kurzrock, E., and Cunha, G.R. (1999). Anatomical studies of the human clitoris. *Journal of Urology, 162* (3 Part 2), 1015-1020.

Bass, E. and Davis, L. (1988). *The courage to heal: A guide for women survivors of child sexual abuse.* New York: Harper & Row.

Bateson, G., Jackson, D., Haley, J., and Weakland, J. (1956). Towards a theory of schizophrenia. *Behavioural Science, 1,* 251-264.

Baumbach, J. and Turner, L.A. (1992). Female gender disorder: A new model and clinical applications. In W.O. Bockting and E. Coleman (eds.), *Gender dysphoria: Interdisciplinary approaches in clinical management* (pp. 107-129). Binghamton, NY: The Haworth Press.

Bayer, R. (1981). *Homosexuality and American psychiatry: The politics of diagnosis.* Princeton, NJ: Princeton University Press.

Becker, J.V. and Kavoussi, R.J. (1996). Sexual and gender disorders. In R.E. Hales and S.C. Yudofsy (eds.), *The American Psychiatric Press: Synopsis of psychiatry* (pp. 605-623). Washington, DC: American Psychiatric Press.

Beh, H.G. and Diamond, M. (2000). An emerging ethical and medical dilemma: Should physicians perform sex assignment surgery on infants with ambiguous genitalia? *Michigan Journal of Gender and Law, 7* (1), 1-65.

Bell, L.V. (1980). *Treating the mentally ill: From colonial times to the present.* New York: Praeger.

Belotti, E.G. (1975). *Little girls: Social conditioning and its effects on the stereotyped role of women during infancy.* New York: Schocken Books.

Bem, S.L. (1974). The measurement of psychological androgyny. *Journal of Consulting and Clinical Psychology, 42,* 155-162.

Bem, S.L. (1993). *The lenses of gender: Transforming the debate on sexual inequality.* New Haven, CT: Yale University Press.

Bem, S.L. (1995). Dismantling gender polarization and compulsory heterosexuality: Should we turn the volume down or up? *Journal of Sex Research, 32* (4), 329-333.

Benestad, E.E.P. (2001). Gender belonging: Children, adolescents, adults and the role of the therapist. *Gecko: A Journal of Deconstruction and Narrative Ideas in Therapeutic Practice, 1* (8), 58-80.

Benjamin, H. (1966). *The transsexual phenomenon.* New York: Julian Press.

Benjamin, H. (1967). *Christine Jorgensen: A personal autobiography.* New York: Paul S. Eriksson Publisher.

Benkov, L. (1994). *Reinventing the family: The emerging story of lesbian and gay parents.* New York: Crown.

Bentler, P.M. (1976). A typology of transsexualism: Gender identity theory and data. *Archives of Sexual Behavior, 5,* 567-584.

Bentler, P.M. and Prince, C. (1970). Psychiatric symptomatology in transvestites. *Journal of Clinical Psychology, 26,* 434-435.

Bepko, C. and Krestan, J.-A. (1985). *The responsibility trap: A blueprint for treating the alcoholic family.* New York: Free Press.

Berenbaum, S.A. (2003). Management of children with intersex conditions: Psychological and methodological perspectives. *Growth, Genetics & Hormones, 19* (1). Available: <http://www.gghjournal.com>.

Besnier, N. (1994). Polynesian gender liminality through time and space. In G. Herdt (ed.), *Third sex, third gender: Beyond sexual dimorphism in culture and history* (pp. 285-328). New York: Zone Books.

Bieber, I., Dain, H.J., Dince, P.R., Drellich, M.G., Grand, H.G., Gundlach, R.H., Kremer, M.W., Rifkin, A.H., Wilbur, C.B., and Bieber, T.B. (1962). *Homosexuality: A psychoanalytic study of male homosexuals.* New York: Basic Books.

Billings, D.B. and Urban, T. (1982). The socio-medical construction of transsexualism: An interpretation and critique. *Social Problems, 29* (3), 266-282.

Bin-Abbas, B.S., Conte, F.A., Grumbach, M.M., and Kaplan, S.L. (1999). Congenital hypogonadotropic hypogonadism and micropenis: Why sex reversal is not indicated. *Journal of Pediatrics, 134* (5), 579-583.

Birnbacher, R., Marberger, M., Weissenbacher, G., Schober, E., and Frisch, H. (1999). Gender identity reversal in an adolescent with mixed gonadal dysgenesis. *Journal of Pediatric Endocrinology and Metabolism, 12* (5), 687-690.

Blackless, M., Charuvastra, A., Derryck, A., Fausto-Sterling, A., Lauzanne, K., and Lee, E. (2000). How sexually dimorphic are we? Review and synthesis. *American Journal of Human Biology, 12* (2), 151-166.

Blackwood, E. (1999). Tombois in West Sumatra: Constructing masculinity and erotic desire. In E. Blackwood and S.E. Wieringa (eds.), *Same-sex relations and female desires: Transgender practices across cultures* (pp.181-205). New York: Columbia University Press.

Blackwood, E. and Wieringa, S.E. (eds.) (1999a). *Same-sex relations and female desires: Transgender practices across cultures.* New York: Columbia University Press.

Blackwood, E. and Wieringa, S.E. (1999b). Sapphic shadows: Challenging the silence in the study of sexuality. In E. Blackwood and S.E. Wieringa (eds.), *Same-sex relations and female desires: Transgender practices across cultures* (pp. 39-63). New York: Columbia University Press.

Blanchard, R. (1985). Research methods for the typological study of gender disorders in males. In B.W. Steiner (ed.), *Gender dysphoria: Development, research, management* (pp. 227-257). New York: Plenum.

Blanchard, R. (1989a). The classification and labeling of nonhomosexual gender dysphorias. *Archives of Sexual Behavior, 18,* 315-334.

Blanchard, R. (1989b). The concept of autogynephilia and the typology of male gender dysphoria. *Journal of Nervous and Mental Disease, 177,* 616-623.

Blanchard, R. (1990). Gender identity disorders in men. In R. Blanchard and B.W. Steiner (ed.), *Clinical management of gender identity disorders in children and adults* (pp. 49-76). Washington, DC: APA.

Blanchard, R. (1991). Clinical observation and systematic studies of autogynephilia. *Journal of Sex and Marital Therapy, 17* (4), 235-251.

Blanchard, R. (1993a). The she-male phenomenon and the concept of partial autogynephilia. *Journal of Sex and Marital Therapy, 19* (1), 69-76.

Blanchard, R. (1993b). Varieties of autogynephilia and their relationship to gender dysphoria. *Archives of Sexual Behavior, 22* (3), 241-251.

Blanchard, R., Clemmensen, L., and Steiner, B. (1987). Heterosexual and homosexual gender dysphoria. *Archives of Sexual Behavior, 16* (2), 139-152.

Blanchard, R. and Collins, P.L. (1993). Men with sexual interest in transvestites, transsexuals, and she-males. *The Journal of Nervous and Mental Disorders, 181,* (9), 570-575.

Blanchard, R. and Sheridan, P.M. (1990). Gender reorientation and psychosocial adjustment. In R. Blanchard and B.W. Steiner (eds.), *Clinical management of gender identity disorders in children and adults* (pp. 159-189). Washington, DC: APA.

Blanchard, R. and Steiner, B.W. (1983). Gender reorientation, psychological adjustment, and involvement with female partners in female-to-male transsexuals. *Archives of Sexual Behavior, 12* (2), 149-157.

Blanchard, R. and Steiner, B.W. (eds.) (1990). *Clinical management of gender identity disorders in children and adults.* Washington, DC: APA.

Blanchard, R., Steiner, B.W., Clemmensen, L.H., and Dickey, R. (1989). Prediction of regrets in postoperative transsexuals. *Canadian Journal of Psychiatry, 34,* 43-45.

Bleier, R. (1984). *Science and gender: A critique of biology and its theories on women.* New York: Pergamon Press.

Block, S.R. and Fisher, W.P. (1979). Problems in the evaluation of persons who request sex-change surgery. *Clinical Social Work Journal, 7* (2), 115-122.

Blumstein, P.W. and Schwartz, P. (1993). Bisexuality: Some social psychological issues. In L.D. Garnets and D.C. Kimmel (eds.), *Psychological perspectives on lesbian and gay male experiences* (pp. 168-183). New York: Columbia University Press.

Bockting, W.O. (1997). Transgender coming out: Implications for the clinical management of gender dysphoria. In B. Bullough, V.L. Bullough, and J. Elias (eds.), *Gender blending* (pp. 48-52). Amherst, NY: Prometheus Books.

Bockting, W.O. and Coleman, E. (1992). A comprehensive approach to the treatment of gender dysphoria. In W.O. Bockting and E. Coleman (eds.), *Gender dysphoria: Interdisciplinary approaches in clinical management* (pp. 131-155). Binghamton, NY: The Haworth Press.

Bockting, W.O. and Kirk, S. (eds.) (2001). *Transgender and HIV: Risks, prevention, and care.* Binghamton, NY: The Haworth Press.

Bockting, W.O., Rosser, B.R.S., and Coleman, E. (1999). Transgender HIV prevention: Community involvement and empowerment. *International Journal of Transgenderism, 3* (1, 2). Available: <http://www.symposion.com/ijt/hiv_risk/bockting.htm>.

Boenke, M. (ed.) (1999). *Transforming families: Real stories about transgendered loved ones.* Imperial Beach, CA: Walter Trook.

Bohan, J.S. and Russell, G.M. (1999). Implications for psychological research and theory building. In J.S. Bohan and G.M. Russell (eds.), *Conversations about psychology and sexual orientation* (pp. 85-105). New York: New York University Press.

Bolin, A. (1988). *In search of Eve: Transsexual rites of passage.* New York: Bergin & Garvey.

Bolin, A. (1992). Coming of age among transsexuals. In T.L. Whitehead and B.V. Reid (eds.), *Gender constructs and social issues* (pp. 13-39). Chicago: University of Illinois.

Bolin, A. (1997). Transforming tranvestism and transsexualism: Polarity, politics, and gender. In B. Bullough, V. L. Bullough, and J. Elias (eds.), *Gender blending* (pp. 25-31). Amherst, NY: Prometheus Press.

Bolus, S. (n.d.). Transgendered butches and FTMs: A uniquely femme perspective. *Femme: The Magazine.* Available: <http://www.stonefemme.com/FemmeMagazine/cover.htm>.

Bolus, S. (2000). *Transensual femme website.* Available: <http://www.geocities.com/WestHollywood/Cafe/6603/about/theory.html>.

Bornstein, K. (1994). *Gender outlaw: On men, women, and the rest of us.* New York: Routledge.

Boswell, H. (1991). The transgender alternative. *Chrysalis: The Journal of Transgressive Gender Identities, 1* (2), 29-31.

Boswell, H. (1998). The transgender paradigm shift toward free expression. In D. Denny (ed.), *Current concepts in transgender identity* (pp. 55-56). New York: Garland.

Boswell, J. (1980). *Christianity, social tolerance, and homosexuality: Gay people in Western Europe from the beginning of the Christian era to the fourteenth century.* University of Chicago Press.

Boszormenyi-Nagy, I. and Ulrich, D. (1981). Contextual family therapy. In A. Gurman and D. Kniskern (eds.), *Handbook of family therapy.* New York: Brunner/Mazel.

Bowen, G. (1998). The entire rainbow of possibilities. In L. Feinberg (ed.), *Trans Liberation: Beyond pink and blue* (pp. 63-66). Boston: Beacon Press.

Bower, H. (2001). The gender identity disorder in the DSM: A critical evaluation. *Australian and New Zealand Journal of Psychiatry, 35* (1), 1-8.

Bozett, F.W. (ed.) (1987). *Gay and lesbian parents.* New York: Praeger.

Bozett, F.W. and Sussman, M.B. (eds.) (1990). *Homosexuality and family relationships.* Binghamton, NY: Harrington Park Press.

Bradley, S.J. (1985). Gender disorders in children: A formulation. In B.W. Steiner (ed.), *Gender dysphoria: Development, research, management* (pp. 175-188). New York: Plenum.

Bradley, S.J. (1998). Transvestism during adolescence. In D. Di Ceglie (ed.), *A stranger in my own body: Atypical gender identity development and mental health* (pp. 109-117). London: Karnac Books.

Bradley, S.J., Oliver, G.D., Chernick, A.B., and Zucker, K.J. (1998). Experiment of nurture: Ablatio penis at 2 months, sex reassignment at 7 months, and a psychosexual follow-up in young adulthood. *Pediatrics, 102,* (1). Available: <http://www.pediatrics.org/cgi/content/full/102/1/e9>.

Bradley, S.J. and Zucker, K.J. (1997). Gender identity disorder: A review of the past 10 years. *Journal of the American Academy of Child and Adolescent Psychiatry, 36* (7), 872-880.

Bradley, S.J. and Zucker, K.J. (1998). Drs. Bradley and Zucker reply to Menvielle: Letter to the editor. *Journal of the American Academy of Child and Adolescent Psychiatry, 37* (3), 244-245.

Bradshaw, J. (1988). *Healing the shame that binds you.* Edison, NJ: Health Communications.

Briere, J. (1989). *Therapy for adults molested as children.* New York: Springer.

Broverman, I.K., Broverman, D.M., Clarkson, D.E., Rosenkrantz, P.S., and Vogel, S.R. (1970). Sex-role stereotypes and clinical judgments of mental health. *Journal of Counseling and Clinical Psychology, 34,* 1-7.

Brown, G.R. (1994). Women in relationships with cross-dressing men: A descriptive study from a nonclinical setting. *Archives of Sexual Behavior, 23* (5), 515-530.

Brown, G.R. (1998). Women in the closet: Relationships with transgendered men. In D. Dallas (ed.), *Current concepts in transgender identity* (pp. 353-372). New York: Garland.

Brown, G.R. (1990). A review of clinical approaches to gender dysphoria. *Journal of Clinical Psychiatry, 51* (2), 57-64.

Brown, G.R. and Collier, L. (1989). Transvestites' women revisited: A nonpatient sample. *Archives of Sexual Behavior, 18* (1), 73-83.

Brown, J.C. (1989). Lesbian sexuality in medieval and early modern Europe. In M.B. Duberman, M. Vicinus, and G. Chauncey (eds.), *Hidden from history: Reclaiming the gay and lesbian past* (pp. 67-75). New York: New American Library/Penguin.

Brown, L.A. (2001). Fractured masks: Voices from the shards of language. In F. Haynes and T. McKenna (eds.), *Unseen genders: Beyond the binaries* (pp. 193-201). New York: Peter Lang.

Brown, L.S. (1994). *Subversive dialogues: Theory in feminist therapy.* New York: Basic Books.

Brown, M.L. and Rounsley, C.A. (1996). *True selves understand transsexualism—for families, friends, coworkers, and helping professionals.* San Francisco: Jossey-Bass.

Brownmiller, S. (1975). *Against our will: Men, women, and rape.* New York: Simon and Schuster.

Bruner, J. (1986). *Actual minds, possible worlds.* Cambridge, MA: Harvard University Press.

Bruner, J. (1987). Life as narrative. *Social Research, 54* (1), 1-15.

Bruner, J. (1994). The "remembered" self. In U. Neisser and R. Fivush (eds.), *The remembered self: Construction and accuracy in the self-narrative* (pp. 41-54). Boston: Cambridge University Press.

Buhrich, N. and McConaghy, N. (1977a). Can fetishism occur in transsexualism? *Archives of Sexual Behavior, 6* (3), 223-235.

Buhrich, N. and McConaghy, N. (1977b). The discrete syndromes of transvestism and transsexualism. *Archives of Sexual Behavior, 6* (3), 483-495.

Buhrich, N. and McConaghy, N. (1979). Three clinically discrete categories of fetishistic transvestism. *Archives of Sexual Behavior, 8,* 151-157.

Bullough, B. and Bullough,V.L. (1993). *Crossdressing, sex, and gender.* Philadelphia: University of Pennsylvania Press.

Bullough, B. and Bullough, V.L. (1997). Are transvestites necessarily heterosexual? *Archives of Sexual Behavior, 26* (1), 1-12.

Bullough, B. and Bullough, V.L. (1998). Transsexualism historical perspectives 1952 to present. In D. Dallas (ed.), *Current concepts in transgender identity* (pp. 15-34). New York: Garland.

Bullough, V.L. (1999). Medicine and gender dysphoria: A brief overview. *Journal of Sex Education and Therapy, 24* (3), 110-116.

Bullough, V.L. (2000). Transgenderism and the concept of gender. *The International Journal of Transgenderism, 4* (3). Available: <http://www.symposion.com/ijt/gilbert/bullough.htm>.

Burana, L., Roxxie, and Due, L. (eds.) (1994). *Dagger: On butch women.* Pittsburgh: Cleis.

Burch, B. (1995). Gender identities, lesbianism, and potential space. In J.M. Glassgold and S. Iasenza (eds.), *Lesbians and psychoanalysis: Revolutions in theory and practice* (pp. 287-307). New York: Free Press.

Burgess, C. (1999). Internal and external stress factors associated with the identity development of transgendered youth. In G. P. Mallon (ed.), *Social services with transgendered youth* (pp. 35-48). Binghamton, NY: The Haworth Press.

Burke, P. (1996). *Gender shock: Exploding the myths of male and female.* New York: Anchor Books/Doubleday.

Butler, J. (1990). *Gender trouble: Feminism and the subversion of gender.* New York: Routledge.

Butler, J. (1993). *Bodies that matter: On the discursive limits of sex.* New York: Routledge.

Buxton, A.P. (1994). *The other side of the closet: The coming-out crisis for straight spouses and families* (revised edition). New York: John Wiley & Sons.

Caldera, R.B. (1999). Mythical beast. *Transgendered Tapestry, 88,* 16-17, 31.

Califia, P. (1997). *Sex changes: The politics of transgenderism.* San Francisco: Cleis.

Califia-Rice, P. (2000). The queer issue: Two dads with a difference—neither of us were born male. *Village Voice.* Available: <http://www.villagevoice.com/issues/0025/califia-rice.php>.

Cameron, D. (1999). Caught between: An essay on intersexuality. In A.D. Dreger (eds.), *Intersex in the age of ethics* (pp. 91-98). Hagerstown, MD: University Publishing Group.

Cantor, C. (2002). Transsexualism—Need it always be a DSM-IV disorder? *Australian and New Zealand Journal of Psychiatry, 36* (1), 141-142.

Caplan, P.J. (1995). *They say you're crazy.* New York: Addison-Wesley.

Caplan, P.J. and Caplan, J.B. (1994). *Thinking critically about research on sex and gender.* New York: HarperCollins.

Caplan, P.J. and Hall-McCorquodale, I. (1985). The scapegoating of mothers: A call for change. *American Journal of Orthopsychiatry, 55,* 345-353.

Carrier, J. and Murray, S.O. (1998). Woman-woman marriage in Africa. In S.O. Murray and W. Roscoe (eds.), *Boy-wives and female husbands: Studies of African homosexualities* (pp. 255-266). New York: St. Martin's.

Carroll, J.L. and Wolpe, P.R. (1996). *Sexuality and gender in society.* New York: HarperCollins.

Carroll, L., Gilroy, P.J., and Ryan, J. (2002). Counseling transgendered, transsexual, and gender-variant clients. *Journal of Counseling and Development, 80,* 131-139.

Carroll, M.P. (1998). But fingerprints don't lie, eh?: Prevailing gender ideologies and scientific knowledge. *Psychology of Women Quarterly, 22,* 739-749.

Carroll, R. (1999). Outcomes of treatment for gender dysphoria. *Journal of Sex Education and Therapy, 24,* 128-136.

Carter, B. and McGoldrick, M. (eds.) (1999). *The expanded family life cycle: Individual, family and social perspectives* (third edition). Needham Heights, MA: Allyn & Bacon.

Carter, J.P. (1997). Normality, whiteness, authorship: Evolutionary sexology and primitive pervert. In V.A. Rosario (ed.), *Science and homosexualities* (pp. 155-176). London: Routledge.

Cass, V.C. (1979). Homosexuality identity formation: A theoretical model. *Journal of Homosexuality, 4* (3), 219-235.

Cass, V.C. (1998). Sexual orientation identity formation: A western phenomenon. In R.J. Cabaj and T.S. Stein (eds.), *Textbook of homosexuality and mental health* (pp. 227-251). Washington, DC: APA.

Chase, C. (1998). Hermaphrodites with attitude. *GLQ, 4* (2), 189-212.

Chase, C. (1999a). Rethinking treatment for ambiguous genitalia. *Pediatric Nursing, 25* (4), 451-455.

Chase, C. (1999b). Surgical progress is not the answer to intersexuality. In A. D. Dreger (ed.), *Intersex in the age of ethics* (pp. 147-160). Hagerstown, MD: University Publishing Group.

Chauncey, G. (1982). From sexual inversion to homosexuality: Medicine and the changing conceptualization of female deviance. *Salmagundi, 58-59,* 114-146.

Chauncey, G. (1994). *Gay New York: Gender, urban culture, and the making of the gay male world 1890-1940.* New York: Basic Books.

Chesler, P. (1972). *Women and madness.* Garden City, NY: Avon Books.

Chodorow, N. (1978). *The reproduction of mothering.* Berkeley: University of California Press.

Chong, J.M.L. (1990). Social assessment of transsexuals who apply for sex reassignment therapy. *Social Work in Health Care, 14* (3), 87-105.

Clare, D. and Tully, B. (1989). Transhomosexuality, or the dissociation of sexual orientation and sex object choice. *Archives of Sexual Behavior, 18,* 531-536.

Clements-Nolle, K., Marx, R., Guzman, R., and Katz, M. (2001). HIV prevalence, risk behaviors, health care use, and mental health status of transgender persons: Implications for public health intervention. *American Journal of Public Health, 91* (6), 915-921.

Clemmensen, L.H. (1990). The "real-life" test for surgical candidates. In R. Blanchard and B.W. Steiner (eds.), *Clinical management of gender identity disorders in children and adults* (pp. 121-135). Washington, DC: APA.

Coates, S. (1990). Ontogenesis of boyhood gender identity disorder. *Journal of the American Academy of Psychoanalysis, 18* (3), 414-438.

Coates, S., Friedman, R.C., and Wolfe, S. (1991). The etiology of boyhood gender identity disorder: A model for integrating temperament, development, and psychodynamics. *Psychoanalytic Dialogues, 1* (4), 481-523.

Coates, S. and Person, E.S. (1985). Extreme boyhood femininity: Isolated behavior or pervasive disorder? *Journal of the American Academy of Child Psychiatry, 24* (6), 702-709.

Cohen, K.M. and Savin-Williams, R.C. (1996). Developmental perspectives on coming out to self and others. In R.C. Savin-Williams and K.M. Cohen (eds.), *The lives of lesbians, gays, and bisexuals: Children to adults* (pp. 113-151). Fort Worth, TX: Harcourt Brace.

Cohen-Kettenis, P. (2001). Gender identity disorder in DSM? *Journal of the American Academy of Child and Adolescent Psychiatry, 40* (4), 391.

Cohen-Kettenis, P. and Gooren, L.J.G. (1992). The influence of hormone treatment on psychological functioning of transsexuals. In W.O. Bockting and E. Coleman (eds.), *Gender dysphoria: Interdisciplinary approaches in clinical management* (pp. 55-67). Binghamton, NY: The Haworth Press.

Cohen-Kettenis, P. and Gooren, L.J.G. (1999). Transsexualism: A review of etiology, diagnosis, and treatment. *Journal of Psychosomatic Research, 46* (4), 315-333.

Cohen-Kettenis, P. and van Goozen, S. (1997). Sex reassignment of adolescent transsexuals: A follow-up study. *Journal of the American Academy of Child and Adolescent Psychiatry, 36* (2), 263-271.

Cohen-Kettenis, P. and van Goozen, S.H.M. (2002). Adolescents who are eligible for sex reassignment surgery: Parental reports of emotional and behavioral problems. *Clinical Child Psychology and Psychiatry, 7* (3), 412-422.

Cohen-Kettenis, P., van Goozen, S., and Cohen, L. (1998). Transsexualism during adolescence. In D. Di Ceglie (ed.), *A stranger in my own body: Atypical gender identity development and mental health* (pp. 118-125). London: Karnac Books.

Colapinto, J. (1997). The true story of John/Joan. *Rolling Stone, 11,* 54-97. Available: <http://infocirc.org/rollston.htm>.

Colapinto, J. (2000). *As nature made him: The boy who was raised as a girl.* New York: HarperCollins.

Cole, C., O'Boyle, M., Emory, L., and Meyer, W. (1997). Comorbidity of gender dysphoria, and other major psychiatric disorders. *Archives of Sexual Behavior, 26,* 13-26.

Cole, S. (2000). A transgendered dilemma: The forgotten journey of the partners and families. Paper presented at the XVI Harry Benjamin International Gender Dysphoria Association Symposium. August 17-21, 1999, London, UK. Abstract at *The International Journal of Transgenderism, 4* (1). Available: <http://www.symposion.com/ijt/greenpresidental/green10.htm>.

Cole, S.S. (1998). The female experience of the femme: A transgender challenge. In D. Dallas (ed.), *Current concepts in transgender identity* (pp. 373-390). New York: Garland.

Cole, S.S., Denny, D., Eyler, A.E., and Samons, S.L. (2000). Issues of transgender. In L.T. Szuchman and F. Muscarella (eds.), *Psychological perspectives of human sexuality* (pp. 149-195). New York: John Wiley & Sons.

Coleman, E. (1982). Developmental stages of the coming out process. *Journal of Homosexuality, 7,* 1-9.

Coleman, E. (1987). Assessment of sexual orientation. *Journal of Homosexuality, 14* (1/2), 9-24.

Coleman, E. and Bockting, W. (1988). "Heterosexual" prior to sex reassignment, "homosexual" afterward: A case study of female-to-male transsexual. *Journal of Psychology and Human Sexuality, 12,* 69-82.

Coleman, E., Bockting, W.O., and Gooren, L. (1993). Homosexual and bisexual identity in sex-reassigned female-to-male transsexuals. *Archives of Sexual Behavior, 22,* 37-50.

Coleman, E., Colgan, P., and Gooren, L. (1992). Male cross-gender behavior in Myanmar (Burma): A description of the Acault. *Archives of Sexual Behavior, 21* (3), 313-321.

Conover, P. (2002). *Transgender good news.* Silver Spring, MD: New Wineskins Press.

Constantinople, A. (1973). Masculinity-femininity: An exception to a famous dictum? *Psychological Bulletin, 80,* 389-407.

Conway, J.K. (1998). *When memory speaks: Exploring the art of autobiography,* New York: Vintage Books.

Conway, L. (2001). Basic TG/TS/IS Information. Available: <http://ai.eecs.umich.edu/people/conway/TS/TS.html>.

Cook-Daniels, L. (1998). Trans-positioned (First published in *Circles Magazine,* pp. 16-22). Available: <http://www.forge=forward.org/handouts/Transpositioned.html>.

Cooper, K. (1999). Practice with transgendered youth and their families. In G.P. Mallon (ed.), *Social services with transgendered youth* (pp. 111-130). Binghamton, NY: The Haworth Press.

Corbett, K. (1998). Cross-gendered identifications and homosexual boyhood: Toward a more complex theory of gender. *American Journal of Orthopsychiatry, 68* (3), 352-360.

Corbett, S. (2001). When Debbie met Christina, who then became Chris. *The New York Times Magazine,* October 14, 84-87.

Courvant, D. and Cook-Daniels, L. (1998). Transgender and intersex survivors of domestic violence: Defining terms, barriers, and responsibilities. In National Coalition Against Domestic Violence (NCADV), *Conference manual.* Denver, CO: NCADV.

Coventry, M. (1999). Finding the words. In A.D. Dreger (ed.), *Intersex in the age of ethics* (pp. 71-78). Hagerstown, MD: University Publishing Group.

Coventry, M. (2000). Making the cut. *Ms. Magazine.* Available: <http://www.msmagazine.com/oct00/makingthecut.html>.

Creighton, S.M., Minto, C.L., and Steele, S.J. (2001). Objective cosmetic and anatomical outcomes at adolescence of feminising surgery for ambiguous genitalia done in childhood. *The Lancet, 358* (9276), 124-125.

Cromwell, J. (1997). Traditions of gender diversity and sexualities: A female-to-male transgendered perspective. In S.-E. Jacobs, W. Thomas, and S. Lang (eds.), *Two-spirit people: Native American gender identity, sexuality, and spirituality* (pp. 119-142). Chicago: University of Illinois.

Cromwell, J. (1999). *Transmen and FTMs: Identities, bodies, genders, and sexualities.* Champaign, IL: University of Illinois.

Crouch, R.A. (1999). Betwixt and between: The past and future of intersexuality. In A.D. Dreger (ed.), *Intersex in the age of ethics* (pp. 29-49). Hagerstown, MD: University Publishing Group.

Cullen, J. (1997). Transgenderism and social work: An experiential journey. *The Social Worker, 65* (3), 46-54.

Curran, M. and Chase, C. (2001). Survey of mental health services for intersex in pediatric endocrinology fellowship programs (unpublished study). Intersex Society of North America.

Daskalos, C.T. (1998). Changes in sexual orientation of six heterosexual male-to-female transsexuals. *Archives of Sexual Behavior, 27* (6), 605-614.

D'Augelli, A.R. and C.J. Patterson (eds.) (1995). *Lesbian, gay, bisexual identities over the lifespan: Psychological perspectives.* New York: Oxford Press.

Davies, B. (1989). *Frogs and snails and feminist tales: Preschool children and gender.* St. Leonards, NSW, Australia: Allen and Unwin.

Davis, D.L. (1998). The sexual and gender identity disorders. *Transcultural Psychiatry, 35* (3), 401-412.

de Beauvoir, S. (1952). *The second sex.* New York: Bantham.

De Cecco, J.P. and Elia, J.P. (1993). A critique and synthesis of biological essentialism and social constructionist views of sexuality and gender. In J.P. De Cecco and J.P. Elia (eds.), *If you seduce a straight person can you make them gay? Issues in biological essentialism versus social constructionism in gay and lesbian identities* (pp. 1-26). Binghamton, NY: The Haworth Press.

D'Emilio, J. (1983). *Sexual politics, sexual communities: The making of the homosexual minority in the United States, 1940-1970.* Chicago: University of Chicago Press.

deMonteflores, C. (1993). Notes on the management of difference. In L.D. Garnets and D.C. Kimmel (eds.), *Psychological perspectives on lesbian and gay male experiences* (pp. 218-247). New York: Columbia University Press.

deMonteflores, C. and Schultz, S.J. (1978). Coming out. *Journal of Social Issues, 34* (3), 59-72.

Denny, D. (1992). The politics of diagnosis and a diagnosis of politics: The university-affiliated gender clinics and how they failed to meet the needs of transsexual people. *Chrysalis: The Journal of Transgressive Gender Identities, 1* (3), 9-20.

Denny, D. (1993). The Benjamin Standards of Care: A safeguard for consumers and caregivers. *Cross-Talk, 49,* 19-22.

Denny, D. (1995). *Transgendered youth at risk for exploitation, HIV, hate crimes.* Available: <http://www.aidsinfonyc.org/Q-zone/youth.html>.

Denny, D. (1996). In search of the "true" transsexual. *Chrysalis: The Journal of Transgressive Gender Identities, 2* (3), 39-48.

Denny, D. (1997). Transgender: Some historical, cross-cultural, and contemporary models and methods of coping and treatment. In B. Bullough, V.L. Bullough, and J. Elias (eds.), *Gender blending* (pp. 33-47). Amherst, NY: Prometheus Books.

Denny, D. (1998). Black telephones and white refrigerators: Rethinking Christine Jorgensen. In D. Denny (ed.), *Current concepts in transgender identity* (pp. 35-44). New York: Garland.

Denny, D. and Green, J. (1996). Gender identity and bisexuality. In B. Firestein (ed.), *Bisexuality: The psychology and politics of an invisible minority* (pp. 84-102). Thousand Oaks, CA: Sage.

Denny, D. and Miller, C. (1994). The counseling needs of transgendered persons. *AEGIS.*

Denny, D. and Roberts, J. (1997). Results of a questionnaire on the standards of care of the Harry Benjamin International Dysphoria Association. In B. Bullough, V.L. Bullough, and J. Elias (eds.), *Gender blending* (pp. 320-336). Amherst, NY: Prometheus Books.

Devor, H. (1989). *Gender blending: Confronting the limits of duality.* Bloomington, IN: Indiana University Press.

Devor, H. (1997a). Female Gender Dysphoria: Personal Problem or Social Problem? *Annual Review of Sex Research, 7,* 44-89. Available: <http://web.uvic. ca/~hdevor/FEMDYS.html>.

Devor, H. (1997b). *FTM: Female-to-male transsexuals in society.* Bloomington, IN: Indiana University Press.

Devor, H. (1997c). More than manly women: How female-to-male transsexuals reject lesbian identities. In B. Bullough, V.L. Bullough, and J. Elias (eds.), *Gender blending* (pp. 87-102). Amherst, NY: Prometheus Books.

Devor, H. (1998). Sexual orientation identities, attractions, and practices of female-to-male transsexuals. In D. Denny (ed.), *Current concepts in transgender identity* (pp. 249-275). New York: Garland.

Devor, H. (2000). Reed Erickson and the beginnings of the Harry Benjamin International Gender Dysphoria Association. Paper presented at the 16th Harry Benjamin International Gender Dysphoria Association Symposium August 17-21, 1999, London. *International Journal of Transgenderism, 4* (3). Available: <http:// www.symposion.com/ijt/greenpresidental/green11.htm>.

Devore, H. (1999). Growing up in a surgical maelstrom. In A.D. Dreger (ed.), *Intersex in the age of ethics* (pp. 79-82). Hagerstown, MD: University Publishing Group.

Di Ceglie, D. (1995). Gender identity disorders in children and adolescents. *The British Journal of Hospital Medicine, 53* (6). Available: <http://www.mermaids. freeuk.com/journal.html>.

Di Ceglie, D. (1998). Reflections on the nature of the "atypical gender identity organization." In D. Di Ceglie (ed.), *A stranger in my own body: Atypical gender identity development and mental health* (pp. 9-25). London: Karnac Books.

Di Ceglie, D., Freedman, D., Mc Pherson, S., and Richardson, P. (2002). Children and adolescents referred to a specialist gender identity development service: Clinical features and demographic characteristics. *International Journal of Transgenderism, 6,* 1. Available: <http://www.symposion.com/ijt/ijtvo06no01_01.htm>.

Diamond, M. (1965). The critical evaluation of the ontogeny of human sexual behavior. *Quarterly Review of Biology, 40,* 147-175.

Diamond, M. (1996). Prenatal predisposition and the clinical management of some pediatric conditions. *Journal of Sex and Marital Therapy, 22* (3), 139-147.

Diamond, M. (1998). Intersexuality: Recommendations for management. *Archives of Sexual Behavior, 27* (6), 634-652.

Diamond, M. (2002). Sex and gender are different: Sexual identity and gender identity are different. *Clinical Child Psychology & Psychiatry, 7* (3), 320-334. Available: <http://www.hawaii.edu/PCSS/online_artcls/intersex/sexual_I_G_web.html>.

Diamond, M. and Sigmundson, H.K. (1997a). Management of intersexuality: Guidelines for dealing with individuals with ambiguous genitalia. *Archives of Pediatrics and Adolescent Medicine, 151,* 1046-1050. Available: <http://www.healthyplace2.com/Communities/Gender/intersexuals/article_management_guidelines.htm>.

Diamond, M. and Sigmundson, H.K. (1997b). Sex reassignment at birth: Long-term review and clinical implications. *Archives of Pediatrics and Adolescent Medicine, 151,* 298-304.

Dickey, R. and Stephens, J. (1995). Female-to-male transsexualism, heterosexual type: Two cases. *Archives of Sexual Behavior, 24* (4), 439-445.

Dillard, A. (1974). *Pilgrim at Tinker Creek.* New York: Harper's Magazine Press.

Dillon, F. (1999). Tell grandma I'm a boy. In M. Boenke (ed.), *Transforming families: Real stories about transgendered loved ones.* Imperial Beach, CA: Walter Trook Publishing.

Dinnerstein, D. (1977). *The mermaid and the minotaur: Sexual arrangements and human malaise.* New York: Harper & Row.

Dittmann, R.W. (1998). Ambiguous genitalia, gender-identity problems, and sex reassignment. *Journal of Sex and Marital Therapy, 24,* 255-271.

Dobkin, A. (2000). The emperor's new gender. *Off Our Backs,* April. Available: <http://www.rapereliefshelter.bc.ca/issues/newgender.html>.

Doctor, R.F. (1988). *Transvestites and transsexuals: Toward a theory of cross-gender behavior.* New York: Plenum.

Doctor, R.F. and Prince, V. (1997). Transvestism: A survey of 1032 cross-dressers. *Archives of Sexual Behavior, 26* (6), 589-605.

Donahoe, P.K. and Schnitzer, J.J. (1996). Evaluation of the infant who has ambiguous genitalia and principles of operative management. *Seminars in Pediatric Surgery, 5,* 30-40.

Doorn, C.D., Poortinga, J., and Verschoor, A.M. (1994). Cross-gender identity in transvestites and male transsexuals. *Archives of Sexual Behavior, 23* (2), 85-201.

Dorner, G., Poppe, L., Stahl, F., Kolzsch, J., and Uebelhack, R. (1991). Gene and environment-dependent neuroendocrine etiogenesis of homosexuality and transsexuality. *Experimental and Clinical Endocrinology, 98* (2), 141-150.

Dreger, A.D. (1997/1998). Doctors containing hermaphrodites: The Victorian legacy. *Chrysalis: The Journal of Transgressive Gender Identities, 2* (7), 15-22.

Dreger, A.D. (1998a). "Ambiguous sex"—or ambivalent medicine? *The Hastings Center Report, 28* (3), 24-35. Available: <http://isna.org/library/dreger-ambivalent.html>.

Dreger, A.D. (1998b). *Hermaphrodites and the medical invention of sex.* Harvard University Press.

Dreger, A.D. (ed.) (1999). *Intersex in the age of ethics.* Hagerstown, MD: University Publishing Group.

Dreger, A.D. (2000). Jarring bodies: Thoughts on the display of unusual anatomies. *Perspectives in Biology and Medicine, 43* (2), 161-172.

Duberman, M.B. (1993). *Stonewall.* New York: Plume.

Duberman, M.B., Vicinus, M., and Chauncey, G. (eds.) (1989). *Hidden from history: Reclaiming the gay and lesbian past.* New York: New American Library/Penguin.

Dupwe, B. (2001). Living contradictions: Married and gay. *In the Family, 6* (4), 6-12.

Ebershoff, D. (2001). *The Danish girl.* New York: Penguin.

Ehrenreich, B. and English, D. (1973). *Complaints and disorders: The sexual politics of sickness.* New York: The Feminist Press at the City University of New York.

Ehrenreich, B. and English, D. (1978). *For her own good: 150 years of the experts' advice to women.* Garden City, NY: Anchor Press/Doubleday.

Eichberg, R. (1991). *Coming out: An act of love.* Santa Cruz, CA: Plume.

Eisenberg, L. (1988). The social construction of mental illness. *Psychological Medicine, 18,* 1-9.

Ekins, R. and King, D. (1996). *Blending genders: Social aspects of cross-dressing and sex-changing.* New York: Routledge.

Ekins, R. and King, D. (1998). Blending genders: Contributions to the emerging field of transgender studies. In D. Denny (ed.), *Current concepts in transgender identity* (pp. 97-115). New York: Garland.

Ekins, R. and King, D. (1999). Towards a sociology of transgendered bodies. *Sociological Review, 47,* 580-602.

Ekins, R. and King, D. (2001). Pioneers of transgendering: The popular sexology of David O. Cauldwell. *International Journal of Transgenderism, 5* (2). Available: <http://www.symposion.com/ijt/cauldwell/cauldwell_01.htm>.

Elkin, M. (1990). *Families under the influence: Changing alcoholic patterns.* New York: W.W. Norton.

Ellis, H. and Symonds, J.A. ([1897] 1975). *Sexual inversion.* New York: Arno Press.

Ellis, K.M. and Erikson, K. (2001). Transsexual and transgenderist experiences and treatment options. *The Family Journal, 10* (3), 289-299.

Elliston, D.A. (1999). Negotiating transnational sexual economies: Female Mahu and same-sex sexuality in Tahiti and her islands. In E. Blackwood and S.E. Wieringa (eds.), *Same-sex relations and female desires: Transgender practices across cultures* (pp. 232-252). New York: Columbia University Press.

Epston, D., White, M., and Murray, K. (1992). A proposal for a re-authoring therapy: Rose's revisioning of her life and commentary. In S. McNamee and K.J.

Gergen (eds.), *Therapy as social construction* (pp. 96-115). Thousand Oaks, CA: Sage.

Erickson Educational Foundation (1973). *An outline of medical management of the transexual.* Brochure.

Etaugh, C. and Liss, M.B. (1992). Home, school, and playroom: Training grounds for adult gender roles. *Sex Roles, 26,* 273-280.

Ettner, R. (1996). *Confessions of a gender defender.* Evanston, IL: Chicago Spectrum Press.

Ettner, R. and Brown, G.R. (1999). *Gender loving care: A guide to counseling gender-variant clients.* New York: W.W. Norton.

Ettner, R.I. and White, T.J.H. (2000). Children of a parent undergoing a gender transition: Disclosure, risk, and protective factors. Paper presented at the XVI Harry Benjamin International Gender Dysphoria Association Symposium August 17-21, 1999, London, *International Journal of Transgenderism, 4* (3). Available: <http://www.symposion.com/ijt/greenpresidental/green17.htm>.

Evans, A. (1978). *Witchcraft and the gay counterculture.* Boston: Fag Rag Books.

Eyler, A.E. and Wright, K. (1997). Gender identification and sexual orientation among genetic females with gender-blended self-perception in childhood and adolescence. *International Journal of Transgenderism, 1* (1). Available: <http://www.symposium.com/ijt/ijtc0102.htm>.

Faderman, L. (1981). *Surpassing the love of men: Romantic friendships and love between women from the renaissance to the present.* New York: Quill/William Morrow.

Faderman, L. (1991). *Odd girls and twilight lovers: A history of lesbian life in twentieth-century America.* New York: Columbia University Press.

Fagot, B.I., Hagen, R., Leinbach, M.D., and Kronsberg, S. (1985). Differential reactions to assertive and communicative acts of toddler boys and girls. *Child development, 56,* 1499-1505.

Faraday, A. (1981). Liberating lesbian research. In K. Plummer (ed.), *The making of the modern homosexual* (pp. 112-129). London: Hutchinson.

Fast, I. (1984). *Gender identity: A differentiation model.* Mahwah, NJ: The Analytic Press.

Fausto-Sterling, A. (1993). The five sexes: Why male and female are not enough. *The Sciences, 33* (2), 20-25.

Fausto-Sterling, A. (2000). *Sexing the body: Gender politics and the construction of sexuality.* New York: Basic Books.

Federman, D.D. and Donahoe, P.K. (1995). Ambiguous genitalia—etiology, diagnosis, and therapy. *Advancement in Endocrinological Metabolism, 6,* 91-111.

Feinberg, L. (1993). *Stone butch blues.* Ithaca, NY: Firebrand Books.

Feinberg, L. (1996). *Transgendered warriors.* Boston: Beacon Press.

Feinberg, L. (1998). *Trans Liberation: Beyond pink or blue.* Boston: Beacon Press.

Feinberg, L. (2001). Trans health crisis: For us it's life or death. *American Journal of Public Health, 91* (6), 897-900.

Feinbloom, D. (1976). *Transvestites and transsexuals.* New York: Dell.

Fernández-Aranda, F., Peri, J.M., Navarro, V., Badía-Casanovas, A., Turón-Gil, V., and Vallejo-Ruiloba, J. (2000). Transsexualism and anorexia nervosa: A case report. *Eating Disorders, 8,* 63-66.

Fichtner, J., Filipas, D., Mottrie, A.M., Voges, G.E., and Hohenfellner, R. (1995). Analysis of meatal location in 500 men: Wide variation questions need for meatal advancement in all pediatric anterior hypospadias cases. *Journal of Urology, 154,* 833-834.

Finkelhor, D. (1979). *Sexually victimized children.* New York: The Free Press.

Finnegan, D.G. and McNally, E.B. (2002). *Counseling lesbian, gay, bisexual, and transgender substance abusers: Dual identities.* Binghamton, NY: The Haworth Press.

Fisk, N. (1973). Gender dysphoria syndrome. In D. Laub and P. Gandy (eds.), *Proceedings of the second interdisciplinary symposium on gender dysphoria syndrome* (pp. 7-14). Stanford, CA: Stanford University Medical Center.

Fitzgibbons, R.P. (2001). Gender identity disorder in children. *National Associations for the Research and Treatment of Homosexuality* (NARTH). Available: <http://www.narth.com/docs/fitz.html>.

Fivush, R. (1994). Constructing narrative, emotion, and self in parent-child conversations about the past. In U. Neisser and R. Fivush (eds.), *The remembered self: Construction and accuracy in the self-narrative* (pp. 136-157). Cambridge, MA: Cambridge University Press.

Flaks, D.K., Ficher, I., Masterpasqua, F., and Joseph, G. (1995). Lesbians choosing motherhood. A comparative study of lesbian and heterosexual parents and their children. *Developmental Psychology, 31,* 105-114.

Fleming, M., MacGowan, B., and Costos, D. (1985). The dyadic adjustment of female-to-male transsexuals. *Archives of Sexual Behavior, 14* (1), 47-55.

Fleming, M., Steinman, C., and Bocknek, G. (1980). Methodological problems in assessing sex-reassignment surgery: A reply to Meyer and Reter. *Archives of Sexual Behavior, 9,* 451-456.

Foley, S. and Morley, G.W. (1992). Care and counseling of the patient with vaginal agenesis. *The Female Patient, 17,* 73-80. Available: <http://www.isna.org/articles/foley-morley.html>.

Ford, K.-K. (2001). "First, do no harm"—the fiction of legal parental consent to genital-normalizing surgery on intersexed infants. *Yale Law and Policy Review, 19* (469), 73-80.

Forward, S. and Buck, C. (1988). *Betrayal of innocence: Incest and its devastation.* New York: Penguin.

Foucault, M. (1978). *The history of sexuality: An introduction (vol. 1).* New York: Pantheon Books.

Foucault, M. (1990). *The history of sexuality: The use of pleasure (vol. 2).* New York: Vintage Books.

Freedman, E.B. (1995). The historical construction of homosexuality. *Socialist Review, 25* (1), 31-46.

Freedman, J. and Coombs, G. (1996). *Narrative therapy: The social construction of preferred realities.* New York: W.W. Norton.

Freire, P. (1971). *Pedagogy of the oppressed.* Translated by Myra Bergman Ramos. New York: Herder & Herder.

Freud, S. ([1905] 1962). *Three essays on the theory of sexuality.* Translated and edited by J. Stachey. New York: Basic Books.

Freud, S. ([1923] 1962). The infantile genital organization: An interpolation into the theory of sexuality. In J. Stachey (trans. and ed.) *Standard edition,* volume 19 (pp. 141-148). London: The Hogarth Press.

Freud, S. ([1925] 1962). Some psychical consequences of the anatomical distinction between the sexes. In J. Stachey (trans. and ed.) *Standard edition,* volume 19 (pp. 243-260). London: The Hogarth Press.

Freud, S. ([1931] 1962). Female sexuality. In J. Stachey (trans. and ed.) *Standard edition,* volume 21 (pp. 223-243). London: The Hogarth Press.

Freud, S. ([1933] 1962). Femininity. In J. Stachey (trans. and ed.) *Standard edition,* volume 22 (pp. 173-182). London: The Hogarth Press.

Freund, K. and Blanchard, R. (1983). Is the distant relationship of fathers and homosexual sons related to the sons' erotic preference for male partners, or to the sons' atypical gender identity, or to both? *Journal of Homosexuality, 9,* 7-25.

Freund, K., Steiner, B.W., and Chan, S. (1982). Two types of cross-gender identity. *Archives of Sexual Behavior, 8,* 527-558.

Friedman, R.M., Katz-Levy, J., Manderscheid, R., and Sondheimer, D. (1996). Prevalence of serious emotional disturbance in children and adolescents. In R.W. Manderscheid and M.A. Sonnenschein (eds.), *Mental Health, United States* (pp. 71-89). Rockville, MD: U.S. Department of Health and Human Services, Center for Mental Health Services.

Gagné, P., Tewksbury, R., and McGaughey, D. (1997). Coming out and crossing over: Identity formation and proclamation in a transgender community. *Gender and Society, 11* (4), 478-508.

Gagnon, J.H. and Simon, W. (1973). *Sexual conduct: The social sources of human sexuality.* Chicago: Aldine.

Gainor, K.A. (2000). Including transgender issues in lesbian, gay, and bisexual psychology: Implications for clinical practice and training. In B. Greene and G.L. Croom (eds.), *Education, research, and practice in lesbian, gay, bisexual, and transgendered psychology: A resource manual* (pp.131-160). Thousand Oaks, CA: Sage.

Galford, E. (1985). *Moll Cutpurse: Her true history.* Ithaca, NY: Firebrand.

Garber, M. (1992). *Vested interests: Cross-dressing and cultural anxiety.* New York: HarperPerennial.

Garofalo, R., Wolf, R.C., Kessel, S., Palfrey, J., and DuRant, R.H. (1998). The association between health risk behaviors and sexual orientations among a school-based sample of adolescents. *Pediatric, 101* (5), 895-902.

Garofalo, R., Wolf, R.C., Wissow, L.S., Woods, E.R., and Goodman, E. (1999). Sexual orientation and risk of suicide attempts among a representative sample of youth. *Archives of Pediatric and Adolescent Medicine, 153,* 487-493.

Gay and Lesbian Medical Association and LGBT health experts (2001). *Healthy People 2010 companion document for lesbian, gay, bisexual, and transgender (LGBT) health.* San Francisco, CA: Gay and Lesbian Medical Association.

Geller, J.L. and Harris, M. (1994). *Women of the asylum: Voices from behind the walls 1840-1945.* New York: Anchor Books/Doubleday.

GenderPAC (1998). Connecticut school boy wearing dress suspended. *National News,* April 2. Available: <http://www.gpac.org/archive/news/index.html?cmd=view&archive=news&msgnum=0003>.

GenderPAC (2000). Ohio court removes child from parents because of her gender. *National News,* August 29. Available: <http://www.gpac.org/archive/action/?cmd=view&archive=action&msgnum =0009>.

GenderPAC (2001). Appeals court upholds right to express gender: Backs transgender student. *National News,* January 18. Available: <http://www.gpac.org/archive/news/index.html?cmd=view&archive=news&msgnum=0267>.

Gergen, K.J. (1991). *The saturated self.* New York: Basic Books.

Gergen, K.J. (1994). Mind, text, and society: Self-memory in social context. In U. Neisser and R. Fivush (ed.), *The remembered self: Construction and accuracy in the self-narrative* (pp. 78-104). Cambridge, MA: Cambridge University Press.

Gergen, K.J. (2000). *An invitation to social construction.* Thousand Oaks, CA: Sage.

Gergen, K.J. and Gergen, M.M. (1984). The social construction of narrative accounts. In K.J. Gergen and M.M. Gergen (eds.), *Historical social psychology* (pp. 173-190). Hillsdale, NJ: Lawrence Erlbaum Associates.

Gergen, K.J. and Gergen, M.M. (1986). Narrative form and construction of psychological science. In T.R. Sarbin (ed.), *Narrative psychology: The storied nature of human conduct* (pp. 22-44). New York: Praeger.

Germain, C.B. and Bloom, M. (1999). *Human behavior in the social environment: An ecological view* (second edition). New York: Columbia University Press.

Gibson, P. (1994). Gay male and lesbian youth suicide. In G. Remafedi (ed.), *Death by denial: Studies of suicide in gay and lesbian teens* (pp. 15-88). Boston: Alyson.

Gilbert, M. (Miqqi Alicia) (2000). Special issue: What is transgender? The transgendered philosopher. *International Journal of Transgenderism, 4* (3). Available: <http://www.symposion.com/ijt/gilbert/gilbert.htm>.

Gilbert, P. and Taylor, S. (1991). *Fashioning the feminine: Girls' popular culture and schooling.* St. Leonards, NSW, Australia: Allen and Unwin.

Gilligan, C. (1982). *In a different voice: Psychological theory and women's development.* Cambridge, MA: Harvard University Press.

Goffman, E. (1963). *Stigma: Notes on the management of spoiled identity.* Englewood Cliffs, NJ: Prentice Hall.

Goldner, V. (1988). Generation and gender: Normative and covert hierarchies. *Family process, 27,* 17-31.

Golombok, S. and Fivush, R. (1994). *Gender development.* Melbourne, Australia: Cambridge University Press.

Gooren, L.J.G. (1990). The endocrinology of transsexualism: A review and commentary. *Psychoneuroendocrinology, 15* (1), 3-14.

Gooren, L.J.G. (1999). Hormonal sex reassignment. *International Journal of Transgenderism, 3* (3). Available: <http://www.symposion.com/ijt/ijt990301.htm>.

Gooren, L.J.G. and Delemarre-van de Waal, H. (1996). The feasibility of endocrine interventions in juvenile transsexuals. *Journal of Psychology and Human Sexuality, 8* (4), 69-74.

Gosselin, C. and Wilson, G. (1980). *Sexual variations.* New York: Simon and Schuster.

Green, J. (1994a). Getting real about FTM surgery. *Chrysalis: The Journal of Transgressive Gender Identities, 2* (2), 27-32.

Green, J. (1994b). A report by the Human Rights Commission City and County of San Francisco. Available: <http://www.ci.sf.ca.us/sfhumanrights/tgreport.pdf>.

Green, J. (1998). FTM: An emerging voice. In D. Denny (ed.), *Current concepts in transgender identity* (pp.145-161). New York: Garland.

Green, J. (1999). Look! No, don't! The visibility dilemma for transsexual men. In K. More and S. Whittle (eds.), *Reclaiming genders: Transsexual grammars at the fin de siècle* (pp. 117-131). London: Cassell.

Green, J. (2001). The art and nature of gender. In F. Haynes and T. McKenna (eds.), *Unseen genders: Beyond the binaries* (pp. 59-70). New York: Peter Lang.

Green, R. (1971). Diagnosis and treatment of gender identity disorders during childhood. *Archives of Sexual Behavior, 1* (2), 167-173.

Green, R. (1974). *Sexual identity conflict in children and adults.* New York: Basic Books.

Green, R. (1978). Sexual identity of 37 children raised by homosexual or transsexual parents. *American Journal of Psychiatry, 135* (6), 692-697.

Green, R. (1987). *The "sissy boy syndrome" and the development of homosexuality.* New Haven, CT: Yale University Press.

Green, R. (1995). Gender identity disorder in children. In G.O. Gabbard (ed.), *Treatments of psychiatric disorders* (second edition, pp. 2001-2014). Washington, DC: American Psychiatric Press.

Green, R. (1998a). Mythological, historical, and cross-cultural aspects of transsexualism. In D. Denny (ed.), *Current concepts in transgender identity* (pp. 3-14). New York: Garland.

Green, R. (1998b). Transsexuals' children. *International Journal of Transgenderism 2* (4). Available: <http://www.symposion.com/ijt/ijtc0601.htm>.

Green, R. (2000a). The family cooccurrence of "gender dysphoria": Ten siblings of parent-child pairs. *Archives of Sexual Behavior, 29* (5), 499-507.

Green, R. (2000b). Reflections on "transsexualism and sex reassignment" 1969-1999: Presidential address, 16th Harry Benjamin International Gender Dysphoria Association Symposium, August 17-21, 1999, London. *International Journal of Transgenderism, 4* (3). Available: <http://www.symposion.com/ijt/greenpresidental/green00.htm>.

Green, R. and Fleming, D. (1990). Transsexual surgery follow-up: Status in the 1990s. *Annual Review of Sex Research, 7,* 351-369.

Green, R. and Money, J. (eds.) (1969). *Transsexualism and sex reassignment.* Baltimore, MD: The Johns Hopkins Press.

Green, R. and Schiavi, R.C. (1995). Sexual and gender identity disorders. In G.O. Gabbard (ed.), *Treatments of psychiatric disorders* (second edition, pp. 1837-2079). Washington, DC: American Psychiatric Press.

Greenberg, D.F. (1988). *The construction of homosexuality*. Chicago: University of Chicago Press.

Greer, G. (2000). *The whole woman*. New York: Anchor Books.

Grimm, D.E. (1987). Toward a theory of gender. *American Behavioral Scientists, 31* (1), 66-85.

Grobs, G.N. (1991). Origins of DSM-I: A study in appearance and reality. *American Journal of Psychiatry, 148* (4), 421-430.

Grof, C. and Grof, G. (1990). *The stormy search of self.* CA: Jeremy P. Tarcher.

Groveman, S. (1999). The Hanukkah bush: An ethical implication in the clinical management of intersex. In A.D. Dreger (ed.), *Intersex in the age of ethics* (pp. 23-28). Hagerstown, MD: University Publishing Group.

Groveman, S. (2001). Ethics primer for clinical management of intersex. *Kaiser Permanente Ethics Rounds, 10* (1), 3-5. Available: <http://www.isna.org/articles/kaiserethicsrounds.pdf>.

Grumbrach, M.M. and Conte, F. (1998). Disorder of sex differentiation. In J.W. Wilson and D.W. Foster (eds.), *Williams Textbook of Endocrinology* (ninth edition, pp. 1400-1405). Philadelphia, PA: W.B. Saunders.

Gurvich, S.E. (1991). *The transsexual husband: The wife's experience*. PhD thesis, Texas Woman's University, DAI, vol. 52-08A, 3089-3248.

Gutierrez, R.A. (1989). Must we deracinate Indians to find gay roots? *Outlook Magazine, 1* (4), 61-67.

Halberstam, J. (1998a). *Female masculinity*. Durham, NC: Duke University Press.

Halberstam, J. (1998b). Transgender butch: Butch/FTM border wars and the masculine continuum. *GLQ, 4* (2), 287-310.

Hale, C.J. (1997). Suggested rules for non-transsexuals writing about transsexuals, transsexuality, transsexualism, or trans____. Available: <http://sandystone.com/hale.rules.html>.

Hale, C.J. (1998). Consuming the living, dis(re)memebering the dead in the butch/ftm borderlands. *GLQ, 4* (2), 311-348.

Haley, J. (1963). *Strategies of psychotherapy*. New York: Grune & Stratton.

Haley, J. (1979). *Leaving home: Therapy with disturbed young people*. New York: McGraw-Hill.

Hall, R. (1928). *The well of loneliness*. New York: Covici Friede.

Halperin, D.M. (2000). How to do the history of male homosexuality. *The Journal of Lesbian and Gay Studies, 1* (6), 87-123.

Hamilton, J.A. and Jensvold, M. (1992). Personality, psychopathology, and depressions in women. In L.S. Brown and M. Balou (eds.), *Personality and psychopathology: Feminist reappraisals* (pp. 116-143). New York: Guilford Press.

Hanley-Hackenbruck, P. (1988). Psychotherapy and the "coming out" process. *Journal of Gay and Lesbian Psychotherapy, 1* (1), 21-39.

Haraldsen, I.R. and Dahl, A.A. (2000). Symptom profile of gender dysphoric patients of transsexual type compared to patients with personality disorders and healthy adults. *Acta Psychiatrica Scandinavica, 102*, 276-281.

Harding, E.U. (1993). *Kali: The black goddess of Dakshineswar*. York Beach, ME : Nicolas-Hays.

Hardy, K.V. (1995). *The psychological residuals of slavery* [videotape]. Steve Lerner Production (Producer). New York: Guilford.

Hare-Mustin, R. (1978). A feminist approach to family therapy. *Family Process, 17* (2), 181-194.

Hare-Mustin, R. (1991). The problem of gender in family therapy. In M. McGoldrick, C.M. Anderson, and F. Walsh (eds.), *Women in families: A framework for family therapy* (pp. 61-77). New York: W.W. Norton.

Hare-Mustin, R. and Broderick, P.C. (1979). The myth of motherhood: A study of attitudes toward motherhood. *Psychology of Women Quarterly, 4* (1), 114-128.

Harne, L. and Miller, E. (eds.) (1996). *All the rage: Reasserting radical lesbian feminism.* London: The Women's Press.

Hartmann, U., Becker, H., and Rueffer-Hesse, C. (1997). Self and gender: Narcissistic pathology and personality factors in gender dysphoric patients. Preliminary results of a prospective study. *International Journal of Transgenderism, 1* (1). Available: <http://www.symposion.com/ijt/ijtc0103.htm>.

Hausman, B. (2000). Do boys have to be boys? Gender, narrative, and the John/Joan case. *NWSA Journal, 12* (3), 114-138.

Hausman, B.L. (1995). *Changing sex: Transsexualism, technology, and idea of gender.* Durham, NC: Duke University Press.

Hawbecker, H. (1999). "Who did this to you?" In A.D. Dreger (ed.), *Intersex in the age of ethics* (pp. 111-113). Hagerstown, MD: University Publishing Group.

Hekma, G. (1994). A female soul in a male body: Sexual inversion as gender inversion in nineteenth-century sexology. In G. Herdt (ed.), *Third sex third gender: Beyond sexual dimorphism in culture and history* (pp. 213-240). New York: Zone Books.

Herdt, G. (1994). Introduction: Third sex third gender. In G. Herdt (ed.), *Third sex third gender: Beyond sexual dimorphism in culture and history* (pp. 21-81). New York: Zone Books.

Herman, J.L. (1992). *Trauma and recovery: The aftermath of violence—from domestic abuse to political terror.* New York: Basic Books.

Herrell, R., Goldberg, J., True, W.R., Ramakrishnan, V., Lyons, M., Eisen, S., and Tsuang, M.T. (1999). Sexual orientation and suicidality. *Archives of General Psychiatry, 56,* 867-874.

Herrnstein, R.J. and Murray, C. (1994). *The bell curve: Intelligence and class structure in American life.* New York: The Free Press/Simon and Schuster.

Hirschauer, S. (1997). The medicalization of gender migration. *International Journal of Transgenderism, 1* (1). Available: <http://www.symposion.com/ijt/ijtc0104.htm>.

Hixon, L. (1992). *Great swan: Meetings with Ramakrishna.* Boston: Shambhala.

Hoenig, J. and Kenna, J.C. (1974). The nosological position of transsexualism. *Archives of Sexual Behavior, 3,* 273-287.

Hoffman, I. (1977). Changes in family roles, socialization, and sex differences. *American Psychologist, 32,* 644-657.

Holley, T.E. (1997). *My mother's keeper—A daughter's memoir of growing up in the shadow of schizophrenia.* New York: William Morrow.

Holmes, C.A. and Warelow, P. (1999). Implementing psychiatry as risk management: DSM-IV as a postmodern taxonomy. *Health, Risk and Society, 1* (2), 167-178.

Holmes, M. (1995). *Queer cut bodies: Intersexuality and homophobia in medical practice.* Available: <http://www.usc.edu/isd/archives/queerfrontiers/queer/papers/holmes.long.html>.

Holmes, M. (1997-1998). Is growing up in silence better than growing up different? *Chrysalis: The Journal of Transgressive Gender Identities, 2* (5), 7-9.

Holtzman, W.H., Thorpe, J.S., Swartz, J.D., and Herron, E.W. (1961). *Inkblot perception and personality.* Austin, TX: University of Texas Press.

hooks, b. (1989). *Talking back: Thinking feminist, thinking black.* Boston: South End.

hooks, b. (1996). *Killing rage: Ending racism.* New York: Henry Holt.

Hooley, J. (1997). Transgender politics, medicine, and representation: Off our backs, off our bodies. *Social Alternatives, 16* (1), 31-34.

Horney, K. (1967). *Feminine psychology.* New York: W.W. Norton.

Howe, E.G. (1999). Intersexuality: What should care providers do now? In A.D. Dreger (ed.), *Intersex in the Age of Ethics* (pp. 210-220). Hagerstown, MD: University Publishing Group.

Hubbard, R. (1998). Gender and genitals: Constructs of sex and gender. In D. Dallas (ed.), *Current concepts in transgender identity* (pp. 45-54). New York: Garland.

Hunt, S. and Main, T.L. (1997). Sexual orientation confusion among spouses of transvestites and transsexuals following disclosure of spouse's gender dysphoria. *Journal of Psychology and Human Sexuality, 9* (2), 39-51.

Huxley, P.J., Kenna, J.C., and Brandon, S. (1981a). Partnership in transsexualism: Part I—Paired and non-paired groups. *Archives of Sexual Behavior, 10* (2), 133-141.

Huxley, P.J., Kenna, J.C., and Brandon, S. (1981b). Partnership in transsexualism: Part II—the nature of the partnership, *Archives of Sexual Behavior, 10* (2), 143-160.

Imber-Black, E. (1998). *The secret life of families: Truth-telling, privacy, and reconciliation in a tell-all society.* New York: Bantam Books.

Imperato-McGinley, J., Peterson, R.E., Gautier, T., and Sturla, E. (1979). Androgens and the evolution of male-gender identity among male pseudohermaphrodites with 5-alpha-reductase deficiency. *Obstetrical and Gynecological Survey, 34,* 769-770.

Inness, S.A. and Lloyd, M.E. (1996). GI Joes in Barbie land: Recontextualizing butch in twentieth-century lesbian-culture. In B. Beemyn and M. Eliason (eds.), *Queer studies: A lesbian, gay, bisexual and transgender anthology* (pp. 10-34). New York: New York University Press.

Intersex Society of North America (ISNA) (1994). Recommendations for treatment. Available: <http://isna.org/library/recommendations.html>.

Intersex Society of North America (ISNA) (1998). Physician challenges the status quo. *Hermaphrodites With Attitude,* summer, 4-5. Available: <http://isna.org/newsletter/summer98/summer98.html>.

Intersex Society of North America (ISNA) (2000). North American Task Force on Intersex (NAFTI) formed: Seeks broad interdisciplinary consensus on treatment (press release). Available: <http://www.isna.org/pr/pr02-23-00.html>.

Irvine, J.M. (1990). *Disorders of desire: Sex and gender in modern American sexology.* Philadelphia: Temple University Press.

Isay, R.A. (1987). Fathers and their homosexually inclined sons. *Psychoanalytic Study of Children, 42,* 275-294.

Isay, R.A. (1989). *Being homosexual: Gay men and their development.* New York: Farrar Straus Giroux.

Isay, R.A. (1997a). *Becoming gay: The journey to self-acceptance.* New York: Henry Holt.

Isay, R.A. (1997b). Remove gender identity disorder from the DSM. *Psychiatric News/Viewpoints,* November 21. Available: <http://www.psych.org/pnews/97-11-21/isay.html>.

Israel, G.E. and Tarver, D.E. (1997). *Transgender care: Recommended guidelines, practical information, and personal accounts.* Philadelphia: Temple University Press.

Jackson, D.D. (1957). The question of family homeostasis. *Psychiatric Quarterly, 31* (supplement), 79-80.

Jackson, D.D. (1965). The study of the family. *Family Process, 4* (1), 1-20.

Jacobs, S.E., Thomas, W., and Lang, S. (1997). *Two-spirit people: Native American gender identity, sexuality, and spirituality.* Urbana, IL: University of Illinois.

James, S.E. (1998). Fulfilling the promise: Community response to the needs of sexual minority youth and families. *American Orthopsychiatric Association, 68* (3), 447-454.

Jeffreys, S. (1994). *The lesbian heresy: A feminist perspective on the lesbian sexual revolution.* London: The Women's Press.

Jeffreys, S. (1997). Transgender activism: A lesbian-feminist perspective. *Journal of lesbian studies, 1* (3-4), 55-74.

Jensen, P.S. and Hoagwood, K., (1997). *The book of names: DSM-IV in context development and psychopathology, 9,* 231-249.

Joan, W. (2001). Dear Dr. M. *ISNA News.* Available: <http://www.isna.org/newsletter/may2001/may2001.html>.

Johnson, S. and Hunt, D. (1990). The relationship of male transsexual typology to psychosocial adjustment. *Archives of Sexual Behavior, 19* (4), 349-360.

Jones, E.E. (1982). Psychotherapist's impressions of treatment outcome as a function of race. *Journal of Clinical Psychology, 38,* 722-731.

JSI Research and Training Institute (2000). *Access to health care for transgendered persons in Greater Boston.* Boston: Gay, Lesbian, Bisexual and Transgender Health Access Project.

Just Evelyn (1998). *Mom, I need to be a girl.* Imperial Beach, CA: Walter Trook.

Kameya, Y. and Narita, Y. (2000). A clinical and psycho-sociological case study on gender identity disorder in Japan. *Journal of Sex and Marital Therapy, (26),* 345-350.

Kaplan, A. (trans.) (1981). *The living Torah: The five books of Moses.* Brooklyn, New York: Maznaim.

Kates, G. (1991). d'Éon returns to France: Gender and power in 1777. In J. Epstein and K. Straub (eds), *Body guards: The cultural politics of gender ambiguity.* New York: Routledge.

Katz, J. (1976). *Gay American history: Lesbians and gay men in the USA.* New York: Thomas Y. Crowell.

Katz, J.N. (1995). *The invention of heterosexuality.* New York: Dutton.

Keller, E.F. (1985). *Reflections of gender and science.* New Haven, CT: Yale University Press.

Kelley, T. (1991). Stages of resolution with spouses. In J. Dixon and D. Dixon (eds.), *Wives, partners, and others* (pp.126-133). Waltham, MA: International Foundation for Gender Education (IFGE).

Kenen, S.H. (1997). Who counts when you're counting homosexuals? Hormones and homosexuality in mid-twentieth-century America. In V.A. Rosario (ed.), *Science and homosexualities* (pp. 197-218). London: Routledge.

Kennedy, E.J. and Davis, M.D. (1993). *Boots of leather, slippers of gold: The history of a lesbian community.* New York: Penguin Books.

Kennedy, H. (1997). Karl Heinrich Ulrichs: First theorist of homosexuality. In V.A. Rosario (ed.), *Science and homosexualities* (pp. 26-45). London: Routledge.

Kessler, S.J. (1990). The medical construction of gender: Case management of intersexed infants. *Signs, 16,* 3-26.

Kessler, S.J. (1997-1998). Meaning of gender variability: Constructs of sex and gender. *Chrysalis: The Journal of Transgressive Gender Identities, 2* (5), 33-37.

Kessler, S.J. (1998). *Lessons from the intersexed.* New Brunswick, NJ: Rutgers University Press.

Kessler, S.J. and McKenna, W. (1978). *Gender: An ethnomethodological approach.* New York: John Wiley & Sons.

King, D. (1987). Social constructionism and medical knowledge: The case of transsexualism. *Sociology of Health and Illness, 9* (4), 351-377.

King, D. (1993). *The transvestite and the transsexual: Public categories and private identities.* Brookfield, VT: Avebury/Ashgate.

King, D. (1996). Gender blending: Medical perspectives. In R. Ekins and D. King (eds.), *Blending genders: Social aspects of cross-dressing and sex-changing* (pp. 79-98). New York: Routledge.

Kinsey, A. (1948). *Sexual behavior in the human male.* Philadelphia: W.B. Saunders.

Kinsey, A. (1953). *Sexual behavior in the human female.* Philadelphia: W.B. Saunders.

Kinsley, D. (1987). *Hindu goddesses: Visions of the divine feminine in the Hindu religious tradition.* Delhi, India: Motilal Banarsidass.

Kipnis, K. and Diamond, M. (1998). Pediatric ethics and the surgical assignment of sex. *Journal of Clinical Ethics, 9* (4), 398-410.

Kirk, S. and Kutchins, H. (1997). *Making us crazy: DSM, the psychiatric bible and the creation of mental disorders.* New York: Free Press.

Kitzinger, C. (1987). *Social construction of lesbianism.* Thousand Oaks, CA: Sage.

Kleeman, J.A. (1971). The establishment of core gender identity in normal girls. *Archives of Sexual Behavior, 2,* 103-116.

Klein, F. (1993). *The bisexual option.* Binghamton, NY: The Haworth Press.

Klein, F. (1999). Psychology of sexual orientation. In J.S. Bohan and G.M. Russell (eds.), *Conversations about psychology and sexual identities* (pp. 129-138). New York: University Press.

Klein, F., Sepekoff, B., and Wolfe, T.J. (1985). Sexual orientation: A multi-variable dynamic process. *Journal of Homosexuality, 11* (1/2), 35-50.

Klein, R. (1999). Group work practice with transgendered male to female sex workers. In G.P. Mallon (ed.), *Social services with transgendered youth* (pp. 95-109). Binghamton, NY: The Haworth Press.

Kockott, G. and Fahrner, E.-M. (1987). Transsexuals who have not undergone surgery: Follow-up study. *Archives of Sexual Behavior, 16* (6), 511-522.

Kohlberg, L. (1966). A cognitive-developmental analysis of children's sex role concepts and attitudes. In E.E. Maccoby (ed.), *The development of sex differences* (pp. 82-173). Stanford, CA: Stanford University Press.

Koyama, E. (1999). *The transfeminism manifesto.* Available: <http://www.transfeminism.org/pdf/tfmanifesto.pdf>.

Kreiss, J.L. and Patterson, D. (1997). Psychosocial issues in primary care of lesbian, gay, bisexual, and transgender youth. *Journal of Pediatric Health Care, 11,* 266-274.

Kremer, J. and den Daas, H.P. (1990). Case report: A man with breast dysphoria. *Archives of Sexual Behavior, 19* (2), 179-181.

Kruijver, F.P.M., Zhou, J.-N., Pool, C.W., Hofman, M.A., Gooren, L.J.G., and Swaab, D.F. (2000). Male-to-female transsexuals have female neuron numbers in a limbic nucleus. *Journal of Clinical Endocrinology and Metabolism, 85* (5), 2034-2041.

Kruks, G. (1991). Gay and lesbian homelessness: Street youth special issues and concerns. *Journal of Adolescent Health, 12,* 515-518.

Kus, R.J. (1995). Addiction and recovery in gay and lesbian persons. *Journal of Gay and Lesbian Social Services, 2* (1).

Laird, J. (1999). Gender and sexuality in lesbian relationships. In J. Laird (ed.), *Lesbians and lesbian families: Reflections on theory and practice* (pp. 47-90). New York: Columbia University Press.

Laird, J. and Green, R.-J. (eds.) (1996). *Lesbians and gays in couples and families: A handbook for therapists.* San Francisco: Jossey-Bass.

Landén, M., Wålinder, J., Hambert, G., and Lundström, B. (1998). Factors predictive of regret in sex reassignment. *Acta Psychiatrica Scandinavica 97,* 284-289.

Lang, S. (1997). Various kinds of two-spirit people: Gender variance and homosexuality in Native American communities. In S.-E. Jacobs, W. Thomas, and S. Lang (eds.), *Two-spirit people: Native American gender identity, sexuality, and spirituality* (pp. 100-118). Chicago: University of Illinois.

Langevin, R. (1985). The meaning of cross-dressing. In R. Blanchard and B.W. Steiner (eds.), *Clinical management of gender identity disorders in children and adults* (pp. 207-225). Washington, DC: APA.

Laqueur, T. (1990). *Making sex: Body and gender from the Greeks to Freud.* Boston: Harvard University Press.

Laurent, B. (1995). Intersexuality—A plea for honesty and emotional support. *Association for Humanistic Psychology*. Available: <http://www.ahpweb.org/pub/perspective/intersex.html>.

Laurent, B. (1995-1996). Sexual scientists question treatment. *Hermaphrodites with Attitude, 16,* 11-13. Available: <http://songweaver.com/gender/intersex.html>.

Laurent, B. (1999). Medical intersex management and the emergence of intersex advocacy. *Transgendered Tapestry, 88,* 33.

Lawrence, A. (2000). Men trapped in men's bodies: An introduction to the concept of autogynephilia. Available: <http://www.annelawrence.com/autogynephilia.html>.

Lax, W.D. (1992). Postmodern thinking in a clinical practice. In S. McNamee and K.J. Gergen (eds.), *Therapy as social construction* (pp. 69-85). Thousand Oaks, CA: Sage.

Lehrman, S. (1999). *Sex police*. Available: <http://www.salon.com/health/feature/1999/04/05/sex_police/>.

Leone, C. and Robertson, K. (1989). Some effects of sex-linked clothing and gender schema on the stereotyping of infants. *Journal of Social Psychology, 129,* 609-619.

Lerman, S.E., McAleer, I.M., and Kaplan, G.W. (2000). Sex assignment in cases of ambiguous genitalia and its outcome. *Urology, 55* (1), 8-12.

Lerner, H. (1994). *The dance of deception: Pretending and truth-telling in women's lives*. New York: HarperCollins.

Leshko, I. (1996). Minnie Bruce Pratt: Femme, Poet, Activist. *Sojourner, 21* (6).

Lesser, J.G. (1999). When your son becomes your daughter: A mother's adjustment to a transgender child. *Families in Society: The Journal of Contemporary Human Services, 80* (2), 182-190.

Lev, A.I. (1998). Invisible gender. *In the Family, 4* (2), 8-11.

Lev, A.I. (in press). *How queer: Lesbian, gay, bisexual, and transgendered parenting*. New York: Penguin Press.

Lev, A.I. and Lev, S.S. (1999). Sexual assault in the lesbian, gay, bisexual, and transgendered communities. In C. McClennen and J. Gunther (eds.), *A professional guide to understanding gay and lesbian domestic violence: Understanding practice interventions* (pp. 35-62). Lewiston, NY: Edwin Mellen Press.

Levine, S. (1993). Gender-disturbed males. *Journal of Sex and Marital Therapy, 19* (2), 131-141.

Levine, S. and Lothstein, L. (1981). Transsexualism or the gender dysphoria syndromes. *Journal of Sex and Marital Therapy, 7* (2), 85-113.

Levine, S.B. and Shumaker, R.E. (1983). Increasingly Ruth: Toward understanding sex reassignment. *Archives of Sexual Behavior, 12* (3), 247-261.

Lewins, F. (1995). *Transsexualism in society: A sociology of male-to-female transsexuals*. South Melbourne, Australia: MacMillan.

Lewis, L. (2000). Reevaluating sex reassignment: Evidence supports nature over nurture in establishing gender identity. *The Scientist, 14* (14), 6. Available: <http://www.the-scientist.com/yr2000/jul/lewis_p6_000710.html>.

Lightfoot-Klein, H., Chase, C., Hammon, T., and Goldman, R. (2000). Genital surgery on children below the age of consent. In L.T. Szuchman and F. Muscarella (eds.), *Psychological perspectives of human sexuality* (pp. 440-479). New York: John Wiley & Sons.

Litwoman, J. (1990). Some thoughts on bisexuality. *Lesbian Contradiction, 29,* 2-6.

Lombardi, E. (2001). Enhancing transgender health care. *American Journal of Public Health, 91* (6), 869-872.

Lombardi, E.L. and van Servellen, G. (2000). Building culturally sensitive substance use prevention and treatment programs for transgendered populations. *Journal of Substance Abuse Treatment, 19,* 291-296.

Lorde, A. (1984a). The master's tools will never dismantle the master's house. In A. Lorde, *Sister outsider: Essays and speeches* (pp. 110-113). Trumansburg, NY: The Crossing Press.

Lorde, A. (1984b). The transformation of silence into language and action. In A. Lorde, *Sister outsider: Essays and speeches* (pp. 40-45). Trumansburg, NY: The Crossing Press.

Loring, M. and Powell, B. (1988). Gender, race, and DSM-III: A study of the objectivity of psychiatric diagnostic behavior. *Journal of Health and Social Behavior, 29,* 1-22.

Lothstein, L. (1979). Psychodynamics and sociodynamics of gender-dysphoric states. *American Journal of Psychotherapy, 33,* 214-238.

Lothstein, L. (1983). *Female-to-male transsexualism: Historical, clinical, and theoretical issues.* Boston: Routledge and Kegan Paul.

Lothstein, L. (1992). Clinical management of gender dysphoria in young boys: Genital mutilation and DSM-IV implications. In W.O. Bockting and E. Coleman (eds.), *Gender dysphoria: Interdisciplinary approaches in clinical management* (pp. 87-106). Binghamton, NY: The Haworth Press.

Lothstein, L.M. and Roback, H. (1984). Black female transsexuals and schizophrenia: A serendipitous finding? *Archives of Sexual Behavior, 13* (4), 371-386.

Loulan, J. (1990). *The lesbian erotic dance: Butch, femme, androgyne, and other rhythms.* San Francisco: Spinsters, Ink.

Luepnitz, D.A. (1992). *The family interpreted: Psychoanalysis, feminism, and family therapy.* New York: Basic Books.

Lukoff, D., Lu, F., and Turner, R. (1992). Toward a more culturally sensitive DSM-IV: Psychoreligious and psychospiritual problems. *Journal of Nervous and Mental Disease, 180,* 11.

Lundsrom, B., Pauly, I., and Walinder, J. (1984). Outcome of sex reassignment surgery. *Acta Psychiatrica Scandinavica, 70,* 289-294.

Lundy, M.S. and Rekers, G.A. (1995a). Homosexuality: Development, risks, parental values, and controversies. In G.A. Rekers (ed.), *Handbook of child and adolescent sexual problems* (pp. 290-312). New York: Lexington Books.

Lundy, M.S. and Rekers, G.A. (1995b). Homosexuality: Presentation, evaluation and clinical decision making. In G.A. Rekers (ed.), *Handbook of child and adolescent sexual problems* (pp. 313-340). New York: Lexington Books.

Ma, J.L.C. (1997). A systems approach to the social difficulties of transsexuals in Hong Kong. *Journal of Family Therapy, 19* (1), 71-88.

MacKenzie, G.O. (1994). *Transgender nation.* Bowling Green State University, OH: Popular Press.

Mallon, G.P. (1999). *Social services with transgendered youth.* Binghamton, NY: The Haworth Press.

Marcel, A.D. (1998). *Determining barriers to treatment for transsexuals and transgenders in substance abuse programs.* Boston: Transgender Education Network, Justice Resource Institute of Health.

Markowitz, L. (1995). Bisexuality: Challenging our either/or thinking. *In the Family, 1* (1).

Marsh, D.T. (1998). *Serious mental illness and the family: The practitioner's guide.* New York: John Wiley & Sons.

Martin, D. (1989). *Battered wives.* Volcano, CA: Volcano Press.

Masson, J.M. (1984). *The assault on truth: Freud's suppression of the seduction theory* (revision). New York: Pocket Books.

Matzner, A. (2001). *'O Au No Keia—Voices from Hawaii's Mahu and transgender communities.* Philadelphia, PA: Xlibris Corporation.

McAdams, D.P. (1993). *The stories we live by: Personal myths and the making of the self.* New York: William Morrow.

McBride, J. (1997). *The color of water: A black man's tribute to his white mother.* New York: Riverhead Books.

McClintock, J. (1997-1998). Growing up in a surgical maelstrom. *Chrysalis: The Journal of Transgressive Gender Identities, 2* (5), 53-54.

McCloskey, D.N. (2000). *Crossing: A memoir.* Chicago: University of Chicago Press.

McConaghy, N. (1997). Sexual and gender identity disorders. In S.M. Turner and M. Hersen (eds.), *Adult psychopathology and diagnosis* (Third edition, pp. 409-464). New York: John Wiley & Sons.

McDaniel, J.S., Purcell, D., and D'Augelli, A.R. (2001). The relationship between sexual orientation and risk for suicide: Research findings and future directions for research and prevention. *Suicide and Life-Threatening Behavior, 31* (1 [supplement]), 84-105.

McGoldrick, M. (1998). *Revisioning family therapy.* New York: Guilford Press.

McGoldrick, M., Anderson, C.M., and Walsh, F. (eds.) (1991). *Women in families: A framework for family therapy.* New York: W.W. Norton.

McGoldrick, M., Gerson, R., and Shellenberger, S. (1999). *Genograms: Assessment and intervention.* New York: W.W Norton.

McGoldrick, M., Giordano, J., and Pearce, J.K. (1996). *Ethnicity and family therapy* (second edition). New York: Guilford.

McGowan, C.K. (1999). *Transgender needs assessment (for the HIV Prevention Planning Unit).* New York: New York City Department of Health.

McKain, T.L. (1996). Acknowledging mixed-sex people. *Journal of Sex and Marital Therapy, 22* (4), 265-279.

Mears, P.J. (2001). *A view from the edge. A hero's journey through the labyrinth of gender identity.* Unpublished thesis. Montpelier, VT: Vermont College.

Melton, L. (2001). New perspectives on the management of intersex. *The Lancet, 357* (9274), 2110.

Menvielle, E.J. (1998). Gender identity disorder: Letter to the editor. *Journal of the American Academy of Child and Adolescent Psychiatry, 37* (3), 243-244.

Merriam-Webster Online (2000). *Merriam-Webster Dictionary.* Available: <http://www.m-w.com/dictionary>.

Meyer, J.K. (1974). Clinical variants among applicants for sex reassignment. *Archives of Sexual Behavior, 3,* 527-558.

Meyer, J.K. and Reter, D. (1979). Sex reassignment: Follow-up. *Archives of General Psychiatry, 36* (9), 1010-1015.

Meyer, W., Bockting, W., Cohen-Kettenis, P., Coleman, E., Di Ceglie, D., Devor, H., Gooren, L., Joris Hage, J., Kirk, S., Kuiper, B., Laub, D., Lawrence, A., Menard, Y., Patton, J., Schaefer, L., Webb, A., and Wheeler, C. (2001). The standards of care for gender identity disorder—sixth version. *International Journal of Transgenderism, 5,* 1. Available: <http://www.symposion.com/ijt/soc_2001/index.htm>.

Meyer-Bahlburg, H. (1985). Gender identity disorder of childhood: Introduction. *Journal of the American Academy of Child and Adolescent Psychiatry, 24,* 681-883.

Meyer-Bahlburg, H.F.L. (1993). Gender identity development in intersex patients. *Child and Adolescent Psychiatric Clinics of North America, 2* (3), 501-512.

Meyer-Bahlburg, H.F.L. (1994). Intersexuality and the diagnosis of gender identity disorder. *Archives of Sexual Behavior, 23* (1), 21-40.

Meyer-Bahlburg, H.F.L. (1998). Gender assignment in intersexuality. *Journal of Psychology and Human Sexuality, 10,* 1-21.

Meyer-Bahlburg, H.F.L. (1999). Gender assignment and reassignment in 46, XY pseudohermaphroditism and related conditions. *Journal of Clinical Endocrinological Metabolism, 84* (10), 3455-3458.

Meyer-Bahlburg, H.F.L., Rhoda, S., Gruen, R.S., New, M.I., Bell, J.J., Morishima, A., Shimshi, M., Bueno, Y., Vargas, I., and Baker, S.W. (1996). Gender change from female to male in classical congenital adrenal hyperplasia. *Hormones and Behavior, 30,* 319-322.

Meyerburg, B. (1999). Gender identity disorder in adolescence: Outcomes of psychotherapy. *Adolescence, 34* (134), 305-313.

Meyerowitz, J. (1998). Sex change and the popular press: Historical notes on transsexuality in the United States, 1930-1955. *GLQ, 4* (2), 159-187.

Meyerowitz, J. (2002). *How sex changed: A history of transsexuality in the United States.* Cambridge, MA: Harvard University Press.

Miach, P.P., Berah, E.F., Butcher, J.N., and Rouse, S. (2000). Utility of the MMPI-2 in assessing gender dysphoric patients. *Journal of Personality Assessment, 75* (2), 268-279.

Michel, A., Mormont, C., and Legros, J.J. (2001). A psycho-endocrinological overview of transsexualism. *European Journal of Endocrinology, 145,* 365-376.

Migeon, C.J., Berkovitz, G.D., and Brown, T.R. (1994). Sexual differentiation and ambiguity. In M.S. Kappy, R.M. Blizzard, and C.J. Migeon (eds.), *The diagnosis and treatment of endocrine disorders in childhood and adolescence* (fourth edition, pp. 664-670). Springfield, MA: Charles Thomas.

Migeon, C.J., Wisniewski, A.B., Brown, T.R., Rock, J.A., Meyer-Bahlburg, H.F.L., Money, M., and Berkovitz, G.D. (2002). 46,XY intersex individuals: Phenotypic and etiologic classification, knowledge of condition, and satisfaction with knowledge in adulthood. *Pediatrics, 10* (3), e32. Available: <http://www.pediatrics. org/cgi/content/full/110/3/e32>.

Migeon, C.J., Wisniewski, A.B., and Gearhart, J.P. (2001). *Syndromes of abnormal sex differentiation.* Baltimore: Johns Hopkins Children's Center. Available: <http://www.med.jhu.edu/pedendo/intersex/sd4.html>.

Migeon, C.J., Wisniewski, A.B., Gearhart, J.P., Meyer-Bahlburg, H.F.L., Rock, J.A., Brown, T.R., Casella, S.J., Maret, A., Ngai, K.M., Money, J., and Berkovitz, G.D. (2002). Ambiguous genitalia with perineoscrotal hypospadias in 46,XY individuals: Long-term medical, surgical, and psychosexual outcome. *Pediatrics, 110* (3), e31. Available: <http://www.pediatrics.org/cgi/content/full/110/3/e31>.

Miller, C.L. (1987). Qualitative differences among gender-stereotyped toys: Implications for cognitive and social development in girls and boys. *Sex Roles, 16,* 473-487.

Miller, D. (1995). *Women who hurt themselves: A book of hope and understanding.* New York: Basic Books.

Miller, J.B. (1976). *Toward a new psychology of women.* Boston: Beacon Press.

Miller, N. (1996). *Counseling in genderland: A guide for you and your transgendered client.* Boston: Different Path Press.

Minter, S. (1999). Diagnosis and treatment of gender identity disorder in children. In M. Rottnek (ed.), *Sissies and tomboys: Gender nonconformity and homosexual childhoods* (pp. 9-33). New York: University Press.

Minuchin, S. and Fishman, H.C. (1981). *Family therapy techniques.* Cambridge, MA: Harvard University Press.

Mitchell, S. (2000). *Influence and autonomy in psychoanalysis.* Hillsdale, NJ: Jason Aronson.

Moane, G. and Campling, J. (1999). *Gender and colonialism: A psychological analysis of oppression and liberation.* New York: Palgrave Macmillan.

Money, J. (1961). Sex hormones and other variables in human eroticism. In W.C. Young (ed.), *Sex and internal secretions* (third edition, pp. 383-1400). Baltimore: Williams & Wilkins.

Money, J. (1971). Prefatory remarks on outcome of sex reassignment in 24 cases of transsexualism. *Archives of Sexual Behavior, 1* (2), 163-165.

Money, J. (1975). Ablatio penis: Normal male infant sex-reassigned as a girl. *Archives of Sexual Behavior, 4* (1), 65-71.

Money, J. (1987). Gender identity and gender transposition: Longitudinal outcome study of 24 male hermaphrodites assigned as boys. *Journal of Sex and Marital Therapy, 13* (2), 75-92.

Money, J. (1993). Sin, sickness, or status? Homosexual gender identity and psychoneuroendocrinology. In L.D. Garnets and D.C. Kimmel (eds.), *Psychological perspectives on lesbian and gay male experiences* (pp. 131-167). New York: Columbia University Press.

Money, J. (1995). *Gendermaps: Social constructionism, feminism, and sexosophical history.* New York: Continuum.

Money, J. (1998). *Sin, science, and sex police.* New York: Prometheus Books.

Money, J. (1999). *Principles of developmental sexology.* New York: Continuum.

Money, J., Devore, H., and Norman, B.F. (1986). Gender identity and gender transposition: Longitudinal outcome study of 32 male hermaphrodites assigned as girls. *Journal of Sex and Marital Therapy, 12* (3), 165-181.

Money, J. and Ehrhardt, A. (1972). *Man and woman: Boy and girl.* Baltimore: Johns Hopkins Press.

Money, J., Hampson, J., and Hampson, J. (1955a). An examination of some basic sexual concepts: The evidence of human hermaphroditism. *Bulletin of Johns Hopkins Hospital, 97* (4), 301-319.

Money, J., Hampson, J., and Hampson, J. (1955b). Hermaphroditism: Recommendations concerning assignments of sex, change of sex, and psychological management. *Bulletin of Johns Hopkins Hospital, 97,* 284-300.

Money, J., Hampson, J., and Hampson, J. (1956). Sexual incongruities and psychopathology: The evidence of human. *Bulletin of Johns Hopkins Hospital, 98* (1), 43-57.

Money, J., Hampson, J., and Hampson, J. (1957). Imprinting and the establishment of gender role. *Archives of Neurology and Psychiatry, 77,* 333-336.

Money, J. and Lamacz, M. (1984). Genital examination and exposure experienced as nosocomial sexual abuse in childhood. *Journal of Nervous and Mental Disease, 175* (12), 713-721.

Money, J. and Lehne, G.K. (1999). Gender identity disorders. In R.T. Ammerman, M. Hersen, and C.G. Last (eds.), *Handbook of prescriptive treatments for children and adolescents* (second edition, pp. 214-228). Needham Heights, MA: Allyn and Bacon.

Money, J. and Tucker, P. (1975). *Sexual signatures: On being a man or a woman.* Boston: Little Brown.

Moraga, C. and Anzaldua, G. (1984). *This bridge called my back: Writings by radical women of color.* New York: Kitchen Table/Women of Color Press.

More, S.D. (1998). The pregnant man—an oxymoron ? *Journal of Gender Studies, 7* (3), 319-325.

Morin, S. and Schultz, P. (1978). The gay movement and rights of children. *Journal of Social Issues, 34,* 137-148.

Morris, J. (1974). *Conundrum.* New York: New America Library.

Mowbray, C.T., Lanir, S., and Hulce, M. (eds.) (1985). *Women and mental health: New directions for change.* Binghamton, NY: Harrington Park Press.

Munt, S. (ed.) (1998). *Butch/femme: Inside lesbian gender.* London: Cassell.

Murray, S.O. and Roscoe, W. (eds.) (1998). *Boy-wives and female husbands: Studies of African homosexualities.* New York: St. Martin's.

Nakamura, K. (1997). Narrating ourselves: Duped or duplicitous? In B. Bullough, V.L. Bullough, and J. Elias (eds.), *Gender blending* (pp. 74-86). Amherst, NY: Prometheus Books.

Nanda, S. (1994). Hijira: An alternative sex and gender role in India. In G. Herdt (ed.), *Third sex third gender: Beyond sexual dimorphism in culture and history* (pp. 373-417). New York: Zone Books.

Nangeroni, N. (n.d.). *Revised standards of care: Perpetuating pathology?* Transgender comment. Available: <http://www.ifge.org/comment/nrnsoc.htm>.

National Association of Social Workers (NASW) (2000). Transgender and gender identity issues, National Association of Social Workers policy statements 2000-2003. *Social work speaks* (fifth edition). Washington, DC: NASW Press.

National Institute for Alcohol Abuse and Alcoholism (NIAAA) (1994). NIAAA's Epidemiological Bulletin No. 35. *Alcohol Health and Research World, 18* (3), 243, 245.

Nelson, J.L. (1998). The silence of the bioethicists: Ethical and political aspects of managing gender dysphoria, *GLQ, 4* (2), 213-230.

Nemoto, T., Keatley, J., Cauley, V., Fernandez, A., Rivera, M., Mathew, A., Operario, D., Tamar-Mattis, S., and Tran, J. (1998). *MTF transgender of color study: Preliminary summary from focus groups.* San Francisco: Health Studies for People of Color, Center for AIDS Prevention Studies, UCSF.

Nestle, J. ([1981] 1987). Butch-fem roles: Sexual courage in the 1950s. Reprinted in J. Nestle (ed.), *A Restricted Country* (pp. 100-109). Ithaca, NY: Firebrand.

Nestle, J. (1992). *The persistent desire: A femme-butch reader.* Los Angeles: Alyson.

Nestle, J. (1998). On rereading "Esther's story." *In a fragile union* (pp. 107-114). San Francisco: Cleis.

Nestle, J., Wilchins, R.A., and Howell, C. (2002). *Genderqueer: Voices from beyond the sexual binary.* Los Angeles: Alyson.

Newman, K., Randolph, J., and Anderson, K. (1992). The surgical management of infants and children with ambiguous genitalia: Lessons learned from 25 years. *Annals of Surgery, 215* (6), 644-653.

Newman, K., Randolph, J., and Parson, S. (1992). Functional results in young women having clitoral reconstruction as infants. *Journal of Pediatric Surgery, 27,* 180-184.

Newman, L.E. and Stoller, R. J. (1973). Nontranssexual men who seek sex reassignment. *American Journal of Psychiatry, 131,* 437-441.

Newton, E. (2000). My butch career. In E. Newton (ed.), *Margaret Mead made me gay: Personal essays, public ideas* (pp. 195-212). Durham, NC: Duke University Press.

Newton, E. (with S. Walton) (2000). The misunderstanding: Toward a more precise sexual vocabulary. In E. Newton (ed.), *Margaret Mead made me gay: Personal essays, public ideas* (pp.167-175). Durham, NC: Duke University Press.

Nickel-Dubin, A. (1998). The effects on a family system when one member is transgender: A case study. *Progress: Family Systems Research and Therapy, 7,* 163-172.

Nicolosi, J. (1991). *Reparative therapy of male homosexuality: A new clinical approach.* Northvale, NJ: Jason Aronson.

Oboler, R. (1980). Is the female husband a man? Woman/woman marriage among the Nandi of Kenya. *Ethnology, 19* (1), 69-88.

O'Brien, D. (1977). Female husbands in southern Bantu societies. In A. Schlegel (ed.), *Sexual stratification: A cross-cultural view* (pp. 109-126). New York: Columbia University Press.

Oggins, J. and Eichenbaum, J. (2002). Engaging transgender substance users in substance use treatment. *International Journal of Transgenderism, 6, 2*. Available: <http://www.symposion.com/ijt/ijtvo06no02_03.htm>.

O'Hartigan, M.D. (1997). The GID controversy: Transsexuals need the gender identity disorder diagnosis. *Transgender Tapestry, 79*, 30, 46.

O'Keefe, T. (1999). *Sex, gender and sexuality: 21st century transformation*. London: Extraordinary People Press.

Okun, B.F. (1992). Object relations and self psychology: Overview and feminist persepectives. In L.S. Brown and M. Balou (eds.), *Personality and psychopathology: Feminist reappraisals* (pp. 20-45). New York: Guilford.

Oles, M.N. (1977). The transsexual client: A discussion of transsexualism and issues in psychotherapy. *American Journal of Orthopsychiatry, 46* (1), 66-74.

Oosterhuis, H. (1997). Richard von Krafft-Ebing's "step-children of nature": Psychiatry and the making of homosexual identity. In V.A. Rosario (ed.), *Science and homosexualities* (pp. 67-88). London: Routledge.

Osborne, C. and Wise, T.N. (2002). Split gender identity: Problem or solution? Proposed parameters for addressing the gender dysphoric patient. *Journal of Sex and Marital Therapy, 28* (2), 165-173.

Osborne, M. (2003). Beyond gatekeeping: Truth and trust in therapy with transsexuals. Paper presented at the 2003 International Foundation for Gender Education conference, Philadelphia, PA. Available: <http://www.antijen.org/osbo1.html>.

Otis, M.D. and W.F. Skinner (1996). The prevalence of victimization and its effect on mental well-being among lesbian and gay people. *Journal of Homosexuality, 30* (3), 93-121.

Padgug, R. (1989). Sexual matters: Rethinking sexuality in history. In M.B. Duberman, M. Vicinus, and G. Chauncey (eds.), *Hidden from history: Reclaiming the gay and lesbian past* (pp. 54-64). New York: New American Library/Penguin.

Paludi, M.A. (1998). *The psychology of women*. Upper Saddle River, NJ: Prentice Hall.

Paoletti, J.B. (1987). Clothing and gender in America: Children's fashions. 1890-1920. *Signs, 13*, 136-143.

Parker, L.A. (1998). Ambiguous genitalia: Etiology, treatment, and nursing implications. *Journal of Obstetric, Gynecologic, and Neonatal Nursing, 27*, 15-22.

Patterson, C. (1994). Children of the lesbian baby boom: Behavioral adjustment, self-concepts, and sex-role identity. In B. Greene and G. Herek (eds.), *Contemporary perspectives of gay and lesbian psychology: Theory, research, and applications* (pp. 156-175). Beverly Hills, CA: Sage.

Patterson, C.J. (1995). Lesbian mothers, gay fathers, and their children. In A.R. D'Augelli and C.J. Patterson (eds.), *Lesbian, gay, bisexual identities over the lifespan: Psychological perspectives* (pp. 262-290). New York: Oxford Press.

Patterson, C.J. (1996). Lesbian mothers and their children: Findings from the bay area families study. In J. Laird and R.-J. Green (eds.), *Lesbians and gays in cou-*

ples and families: A handbook for therapists (pp. 420-437). San Francisco: Jossey-Bass.

Paul, J.P. (1993). Childhood cross-gender behavior and adult homosexuality: The resurgence of biologic models of sexuality. In J.P. De Cecco and J.P. Elia (eds.), *If you seduce a straight person can you make them gay? Issues in biological essentialism versus social constructionism in gay and lesbian identities* (pp. 41-54). Binghamton, NY: The Haworth Press.

Pauly, I. (1968). The current status of the change of sex operation. *Journal of Nervous and Mental Disease, 147,* 460-471.

Pauly, I. (1974). Female transsexualism I and II. *Archives of Sexual Behavior, 3,* 487-526.

Pauly, I. (1981). Outcome of sex reassignment surgery for transsexuals. *Australian and New Zealand Journal of Psychiatry, 15,* 5-51.

Pauly, I. (1990). Gender identity disorders: Evaluation and treatment. *Journal of Sex Education and Therapy, 16,* 2-24.

Pauly, I. and Edgerton, M.T. (1986). The gender identity movement: A growing surgical-psychiatric liaison. *Archives of Sexual Behavior, 15,* 315-329.

Pauly, I.B. (1992). Terminology and classification of gender identity disorders. In W.O. Bockting and E. Coleman (eds.), *Gender dysphoria: Interdisciplinary approaches in clinical management* (pp. 1-14). Binghamton, NY: The Haworth Press.

Pauly, I.B. (1998). Gender identity and sexual orientation. In D. Denny (ed.), *Current concepts in transgender identity* (pp. 237-248). New York: Garland.

Pazos, S. (1999). Practice with female-to-male transgendered youth. In G.P. Mallon (ed.), *Social services with transgendered youth* (pp. 65-82). Binghamton, NY: The Haworth Press.

Peo, R. (1988). Tranvestism. *Journal of Social Work and Human Sexuality, 7* (1), 57-75.

Peo, R. (1991). To have and to hold. In J. Dixon and D. Dixon (eds.), *Wives, partners, and others* (pp. 134-140). Waltham, MA: IFGE.

Person, E. and Ovesey, L. (1974a). The transsexual syndrome in males I: Primary transsexualism. *American Journal of Psychotherapy, 28,* 4-20.

Person, E. and Ovesey, L. (1974b). The transsexual syndrome in males II: Secondary transsexuality. *American Journal of Psychotherapy, 28,* 174-193.

Person, E. and Ovesey, L. (1976). Transvestism: A disorder of the sense of self. *International Journal of Psychoanalytic Psychotherapy, 5,* 221-235.

Person, E. and Ovesey, L. (1984). Homosexual cross-dressers. *Journal of the American Academy of Psychoanalysis, 12,* 167-186.

Petersen, M.E. and Dickey, R. (1995). Surgical sex reassignment: A comparative survey of international centers. *Archives of Sexual Behavior 24* (2), 135-156.

Pfäefflin, F. and Colemann, E. (1997). Introduction. *International Journal of Transgenderism, 1,*1. Available: <http://www.symposion.com/ijt/ijtintro.htm>.

Pfäefflin, F. and Junge, A. (1998). Sex reassignment: Thirty years of international follow-up studies after sex reassignment surgery: A comprehensive review, 1961-1991. Translated by R.B. Jacobson and A.B. Meier. Dusseldorf, Germany:

Symposion Books. Available: <http://209.143.139.183/ijtbooks/pfaefflin/1000. asp>.

Pharr, S. (1997). *Homophobia: A weapon of sexism,* revised edition. Little Rock: Chardon Press.

Phornphutkul, C., Fausto-Sterling, A., Gruppuso, P.A. (2000). Gender self-reassignment in an XY adolescent female born with ambiguous genitalia. *Pediatrics, 106* (1), 135-137.

Pinderhughes, E. (1998). Black genealogy revisited: Restorying an African American family. In M. McGoldrick (ed.), *Re-visioning family therapy* (pp. 179-1990). New York: Guilford.

Pleak, R.R. (1999). Ethical issues in diagnosing and treating gender-dysphoric children and adolescents. In M. Rottnek (ed.), *Sissies and tomboys: Gender noncomfority and homosexual childhoods* (pp. 34-51). New York: University Press.

Plummer, K. (ed.) (1981). *The making of the modern homosexual.* London: Hutchinson.

Plummer, K. (1995). *Telling sexual stories: Power, change, and social worlds.* London: Routledge.

Pomerleau, A., Bolduc, D., Malcutt, G., and Cossette, L. (1990). Pink or blue: Environmental gender stereotypes in the first two years of life. *Sex Roles, 22,* 359-367.

Preves, S. (2002). Intersex and identity: The contested self. New Brunswick, NJ: Rutgers University Press.

Preves, S.E. (1999). For the sake of the children: Destigmatizing intersexuality. In A.D. Dreger (ed.), *Intersex in the age of ethics* (pp. 51-65). Hagerstown, MD: University Publishing Group.

Prince, C. and Bentler, P.M. (1972). Survey of 504 cases of transvestism. *Journal of Psychological Report, 31,* 903-917.

Prince, V. (1967). *The transvestite and his wife.* Los Angeles: Argyle Books.

Prince, V. (1976). *Understanding crossdressing.* Los Angeles: Chevalier.

Prince, V. (1978). Transsexuals and pseudotranssexuals. *Archives of Sexual Behavior, 7,* 263-272.

Prosser, J. (1998). *Second skins: The body narratives of transsexuality.* New York: Columbia University Press.

Prosser, J. (1999). Exceptional locations: Transsexual travelogues. In K. More and S. Whittle (eds.), *Reclaiming genders: Transsexual grammars at the fin de siècle* (pp. 83-114). London: Cassell.

Pruett, K.D. and Dahl, E.K. (1982). Psychotherapy of gender identity conflict in young boys. *Journal of the American Academy of Child and Adolescent Psychiatry, 21,* 65-67.

Quinodoz, D. (1998). A fe/male transsexual patient in psychoanalysis. *Journal of Psychoanalysis, 79,* 95-111.

Rachlin, K. (1997). *Partners in the journey: Psychotherapy and six stages of gender revelation.* Paper presented at the Second Congress on Sex and Gender, June, King of Prussia, PA.

Rachlin, K. (1999). Individual's decisions when considering female-to-male genital reconstructive surgery. *International Journal of Transgenderism, 3* (3). Available: <http://www.symposion.com/ijt/ijtvo06no01_03.htm>.

Rachlin, K. (2001). *Transgendered individuals' experiences of psychotherapy.* Paper presented at the American Psychological Association 109th Annual Convention, August 24-28, San Francisco, CA.

Raj, R. (2001). Towards a transpositive therapeutic model: Developing clinical sensitivity and cultural competence in the effective support of transsexual and transgendered clients. *The International Journal of Transgenderism, 6* (2). Available: <http://www.symposion.com/ijt/ijtvo06no02_04.htm>.

Raj, R. (2002). Towards a transpositive therapeutic model: Developing clinical sensitivity and cultural competence in the effective support of transsexual and transgendered clients. *The International Journal of Transgenderism, 6* (2). Available: <http://www.symposion.com/ijt/ijtvo06no02_04.htm>.

Rakie, Z., Starcevic, V., Marie, J., and Kelin, K. (1996). The outcome of sex reassignment surgery in Belgrade: 32 patients of both sexes. *Archives of Sexual Behavior, 25* (5), 515-525.

Randell, J. (1971). Indications for sex reassignment surgery. *Archives of Sexual Behavior, 1* (2), 153-161.

Ratner, E. (1993). Treatment for chemically dependent lesbian and gay men. In L.D. Garnets and D.C. Kimmel (eds.), *Psychological perspectives on lesbian and gay male experience* (pp. 567-578). New York: Columbia University Press.

Raymond, J. (1979). *The transsexual empire: The making of the she-male.* Boston: Beacon Press.

Raymond, J. (1996). The politics of transgenderism. In R. Ekins and D. King (eds.), *Blending genders: Social aspects of cross-dressing and sex-changing* (pp. 215-223). New York: Routledge.

Regier, D.A., Narrow, W.E., Rae, D.S., Manderscheid, R.W., Locke, B.Z., and Goodwin, F.K. (1993). The de facto mental and addictive disorders service system. Epidemiologic catchment area prospective 1-year prevalence rates of disorders and services. *Archives of General Psychiatry, 50* (2), 85-94.

Reilly, J.M. and Woodhouse, C.R.J. (1989). Small penis and the male sexual role. *Journal of Urology, 142,* 569-571.

Reiner, W.G. (1996). Case study: Sex reassignment in a teenage girl. *Journal of the American Academy Child and Adolescent Psychiatry, 35,* 799-803.

Reiner, W.G. (1997). Sex assignment in the neonate with intersex or inadequate genitalia. *Archives of Pediatric Adolescent Medicine, 151* (10), 1044-1045.

Reiner, W.G. (1999). Assignment in neonates with ambiguous genitalia. *Current Opinions in Pediatrics, 11,* 363-365.

Rekers, G.A. (1982). *Shaping your child's sexual identity.* Grand Rapids, MI: Baker Book House.

Rekers, G.A. (1995a). Assessment and treatment methods for gender identity disorder and transvestism. In G.A. Rekers (ed.), *Handbook of child and adolescent sexual problems* (pp. 272-289). New York: Lexington Books.

Rekers, G.A. (ed.) (1995b). *Handbook of child and adolescent sexual problems.* New York: Lexington Books.

Rekers, G.A. (1996). Gender identity disorder. *The Journal of Human Sexuality, 2* (3). Available: <http://www.leaderu.com/jhs/rekers.html>.

Rekers, G.A. and Jurich, A.P. (1983). Development of problems of puberty and sex roles in adolescence. In C.E. Walker and M.C. Roberts (eds.), *Handbook of Clinical Child Psychology* (pp. 785-812). New York: John Wiley and Sons.

Rekers, G.A. and Kilgus, M.D. (1995). Differential diagnosis and rationale for treatment of gender identity disorders and transvestism. In G.A. Rekers (ed.), *Handbook of child and adolescent sexual problems* (pp. 255-271). New York: Lexington Books.

Remafedi, G., Farrow, J.A., and Deisher, R.W. (1991). Risk factors for attempted suicide in gay and bisexual youth. *Pediatrics, 87,* 869-875.

Remafedi, G., French, S., Story, M., Resnick, M.D., and Blum, R. (1998). The relationship between suicide risk and sexual orientation: Results of a population-based study. *American Journal of Public Health, 88,* 57-60.

Rich, A. (1980). Compulsory heterosexuality and lesbian existence. *Signs: Journal of Women in Culture and Society, 5* (4), 631-660.

Richards, R. (1983). *Second serve: The Renee Richards story.* New York: Stein & Day.

Richardson, J. (1996). Setting limits on gender health. *Harvard Review of Psychiatry, 4,* 49-53.

Richardson, J. (1999). Response: Finding the disorder in gender identity disorder. *Harvard Review of Psychiatry, 7,* 43-50.

Roback, H.B. and Lothstein, L.M. (1986). The female mid-life sex change applicant: A comparison with younger female transsexuals and older male sex change applicants. *Archives of Sexual Behavior, 15* (5), 401-415.

Roberts, J. (1995). *Coping with crossdressing: Tools and strategies for partners in committed relationships* (third edition). King of Prussia, PA: Creative Design Services.

Rosario, V.A. (1996). Trans (homo) sexuality? Double inversion, psychiatric confusion, and hetero-hegemony. In B. Beemyn and M. Eliason (eds.), *Queer studies: A lesbian, gay, bisexual and transgender anthology* (pp. 35-55). New York: New York University Press.

Roscoe, W. (1994). How to become a berdache: Toward a unified analysis of gender diversity. In G. Herdt (ed.), *Third sex third gender: Beyond sexual dimorphism in culture and history* (pp. 329-372). New York: Zone Books.

Roscoe, W. (1998). *Changing ones: Third and fourth genders in native North America.* New York: St. Martin's.

Rosenfeld, C. and Emerson, S. (1998). A process model of supportive therapy for families of transgender individuals. In D. Denny (ed.), *Current concepts in transgender identity* (pp. 391-400). New York: Garland.

Ross, M.W. (1986). Causes of gender dysphoria: How does transsexualism develop and why? In W.A.W. Walters and M.W. Ross (eds.), *Transsexualism and sex reassignment* (pp. 16-25). Melbourne, Australia: Oxford University.

Ross, M.W. and Need, J.A. (1989). Effects of adequacy of gender reassignment surgery on psychological adjustment: A follow-up of fourteen male-to-female patients. *Archives of Sexual Behavior, 18* (2), 145-153.

Ross, M.W., Walinder, J., Lundstrom, B., and Thuwe, I. (1981). Cross-cultural approaches to transsexualism: A comparison between Sweden and Australia. *Acta Psychiatrica Scandinavica, 63,* 75-82.

Rossiter, K. and Diehi, S. (1998). Gender reassignment in children: Ethical conflicts in surrogate decision making. *Pediatric Nursing, 24* (1), 59-62.

Rothblatt, M. (1995). *The apartheid of sex: A manifesto on the freedom of gender.* New York: Crown Publications.

Rothblum, E.D. and Brehony, K.A. (1993). *Boston marriages: Romantic but asexual relationships among contemporary lesbians.* Amherst: University of Massachusetts Press.

Rottnek, M. (ed.) (1999). *Sissies and tomboys: Gender noncomfority and homosexual childhoods.* New York: New York University Press.

Royal College of Psychiatrists (1998). Gender identity disorders in children and adolescents: Guidance for management, Council report CR 63. London: Royal College of Psychiatrists. In D. Di Ceglie (ed.), *A stranger in my own body: Atypical gender identity development and mental health* (pp. 297-394). London: Karnac Books.

Rubin, G. (1975). The traffic in women: Notes on the political economy of sex. In R.R. Reiter (ed.), *Toward an anthropology of women* (pp. 157-210). New York: Monthly Review Press.

Rubin, G. (1984). Thinking sex: Notes for a radical theory of the politics of sexuality. In C.S. Vance (ed.), *Pleasure and danger: Exploring female sexuality* (pp. 267-319). Boston: Routledge and Kegan Paul.

Rubin, G. (1992). Of catamites and kings: Reflections on butch gender and boundaries. In J. Nestle (ed.), *The persistent desire: A femme-butch reader.* Los Angeles: Alyson.

Rubin, H.S. (1996). *Transformations: Emerging female to male transsexual identities.* UMI dissertation services. Ann Arbor, MI: Bell and Howell.

Rubin, J.Z., Provenzano, F.J., and Luria, Z. (1974). The eye of the beholder: Parents' views on sex of newborns. *American Journal of Orthopsychiatry, 44,* 512-519.

Russell, D.E.H. (1986). *The secret trauma: Incest in the lives of girls and women.* New York: Basic Books.

Russell, S.T. and Joyner, K. (2001). Adolescent sexual orientation and suicide risk: Evidence from a national study. *American Journal of Public Health, 91* (8), 276-281.

Sadowski, H. and Gaffney, B. (1998). Gender identity disorder, depression, and suicidal risk. In D. Di Ceglie (ed.), *A stranger in my own body: Atypical gender identity development and mental health* (pp. 126-136). London: Karnac Books.

Saghir, M.T. and Robins, E. (1973). *Male and female homosexuality: A comprehensive investigation.* Baltimore, MD: Williams and Wilkins.

Saks, B.M. (1998). Transgenderism and dissociative identity disorder: A case study. *International Journal of Transgenderism, 2* (2). Available: <http://www.symposion.com/ijt/ijtc0404.htm>.

Sales, J. (1995). Children of a transsexual father: A successful intervention. *European Child and Adolescent Psychiatry, 4* (2), 136-139.

The San Francisco Lesbian and Gay History Project (1989). She even chewed tobacco: A pictorial narrative of passing women. In M.B. Duberman, M. Vicinus, and G. Chauncey (eds.), *Hidden from history: Reclaiming the gay and lesbian past* (pp. 183-194). New York: New American Library/Penguin.

Sarbin, T.R. (1986). The narrative as a root metaphor for psychology. In T.R. Sarbin (ed.), *Narrative psychology: The storied nature of human conduct* (pp. 3-21). New York: Praeger.

Satir, V.M. (1967). *Conjoint family therapy.* Palo Alto, CA: Science & Behavior Books.

Satterfield, S.B. (1988). Transsexualism. *Journal of Social Work and Human Sexuality, 7* (1), 77-87.

Savin-Williams, R.C. (1994). Verbal and physical abuse as stressors in the lives of lesbian, gay male, and bisexual youths: Associations with school problems, running away, substance abuse, prostitution, and suicide. *Journal of Consulting and Clinical Psychology, 62,* 261-269.

Savin-Williams, R.C. (2001). Suicide attempts among sexual-minority youths: Population and measurement issues. *Journal of Consulting and Clinical Psychology, 69* (6), 983-991.

Scannell, K. (2001). Engendered differences: Ethical issues about intersex. *Kaiser Permanente Ethics Rounds, 10* (1), 1-8. Available: <http://www.isna.org/articles/kaiserethicsrounds.pdf>.

Schaefer, L.C., Lazer, S., Wheeler, C.C., and Melman, A. (2000). The reported sexual and surgery satisfactions of 27 postoperative male-to-female transsexual patients. Paper presented at the XVI Harry Benjamin International Gender Dysphoria Association Symposium, August 17-21, 1999, London, UK. Abstract at *The International Journal of Transgenderism, 4* (1). Available: <http://www.symposion.com/ijt/greenpresidental/green46.htm>.

Schaefer, L.C. and Wheeler, C.C. (1995). Harry Benjamin's first 10 cases (1938-1953): A clinical historical note. *Archives of Sexual Behavior, 24* (1), 73-93.

Schaefer, L.C., Wheeler, C.C., Futterweit, W. (1995). Gender identity disorders (transsexualism). In G.O. Gabbard (ed.), *Treatment of psychiatric disorders.* Washington, DC: APA.

Schechter, S. (1982). *Women and male violence: The visions and struggles of the battered women's movement.* Cambridge, MA: South End Press.

Scheman, N. (1999). Queering the center by centering the queer: Reflections on transsexuals and secular Jews. In M. Rottnek (ed.), *Sissies and tomboys: Gender noncomformity and homosexual childhoods* (pp. 58-103). New York: New York University Press.

Schober, J.M. (1998a). Early feminizing genitoplasty or watchful waiting. *Journal of Pediatric and Adolescent Gynecology, 11* (3), 154-156.

Schober, J.M. (1998b). Feminizing genitoplasty for intersex. In M.D. Stringer, K.T. Oldham, P.D.E. Mouriquand, and E.R. Howard (eds.), *Pediatric surgery and urology: Long term outcomes* (pp. 549-558). London: W.W. Saunders.

Schober, J.M. (1999a). Long-term outcomes and changing attitudes to intersexuality. *BJU International, 83* (3[supplement]), 39-50.

Schober, J.M. (1999b). Quality-of-life studies in patients with ambiguous genitalia. *World Journal of Urology, 17* (4), 249-252.

Schober, J.M. (1999c). A surgeon's response to the intersex controversy. In A.D. Dreger (ed.), *Intersex in the age of ethics* (pp.161-168). Hagerstown, MD: University Publishing Group.

Scholinski, D. (with J.M. Adams) (1997). *The last time I wore a dress: A memoir.* New York: Riverhead Books.

Schwartz, L.A. and Markham, W.T. (1985). Sex stereotyping in children's toy advertisements. *Sex Roles: A Journal of Research, 12,* 157-170.

Schwartz, P.G. (1988). A case of concurrent multiple personality disorder and transsexualism. *Dissociation, 1* (2), 48-57.

Seavey, C.A., Katz, P.A., and Zalk, S.R. (1975). Baby X: The effect of gender labels on adult responses to infants. *Sex Roles, 1,* 104-109.

Sedgwick, E.K. (1990). *Epistemology of the closet.* Berkeley: University of California Press.

Seil, D. (1997). Dissociation as a defense against ego-dystonic transsexualism. In B. Bullough, V.L. Bullough, and J. Elias (eds.), *Gender blending* (pp. 137-145). Amherst, NY: Prometheus Books.

Seligman, M.E.P. (1972). *Annual Review of Medicine, 23,* 407-412.

Sell, I. (2001). Not man, not woman: Psychospiritual characteristics of a western third gender. *Journal of Transpersonal Psychology, 33* (1), 16-36.

Sexuality Information and Education Council of the United States (SIECUS) (1999). *The Construction of Gender, 28* (1). Available: <http://www.siecus. org/pubs/srpt/srpt0023.html>.

Shapiro, J. (1991). Transsexualism: Reflections of the persistence of gender and the mutability of sex. In J. Epstein and J. Straub (eds.), *Body guards: The cultural politics of gender ambiguity* (pp. 248-279). New York: Routledge.

Shively, M.G. and De Cecco, J.P. (1993). Components of sexual identity. In L.D. Garnets and D.C. Kimmel (eds.), *Psychological perspectives on lesbian and gay male experiences* (pp. 80-88). New York: Columbia University Press.

Signorile, M. (1996). *Outing yourself: How to come out as lesbian or gay to your family, friends, and coworkers.* New York: Fireside Books.

Silverstein, O. and Rashbaum, B. (1995). *The courage to raise good men.* New York: Penguin Books.

Slater, S. (1995). *The lesbian family lifecycle.* New York: Free Press.

Slijper, F.M.E., Drop, S.I.S., Molenaar, J.C., and Keizer-Schrama, S.M. (1998). Long-term psychological evaluation of intersex children. *Archives of Sexual Behavior, 27,* 125-144.

Smith, J. (1988). Psychopathology, homosexuality, and homophobia. In M.W. Ross (ed.), *The treatment of homosexuals with mental health disorders* (pp. 59-74). Binghamton, NY: The Haworth Press.

Smith, Y.L., van Goozen, S.H.M., and Cohen-Kettenis, P.T. (2001). Adolescents with gender identity disorder who were accepted or rejected for sex reassignment surgery: A prospective follow-up study. *Journal of the American Academy of Child and Adolescent Psychiatry, 40* (4), 472-481.

Smith-Rosenberg, C. (1975). The female world of love and ritual: Relations between women in nineteenth-century America. *Signs: A journal of women in culture and society, 1,* 1-29.

Socarides, C.W. (1969). The desire for sexual transformation: A psychiatric evaluation of transsexualism. *American Journal of Psychiatry, 125* (10), 1419-1425.

Socarides, C.W. (1982). Abdicating father, homosexual sons: Psychoanalytic observations of the contribution of the father to the development of male homosexuality. In S.H. Cath (ed.), *Father and child: Developmental and clinical perspectives* (pp. 509-521). Boston: Little Brown.

Socarides, C.W. (1999). Thought reform and the psychology of homosexual advocacy. *National Association for Research and Therapy of Homosexuality.* Available: <http://www.leaderu.com/orgs/narth/1995papers/socarides.html>.

Somerville, S.B. (2000). *Queering the color line: Race and the invention of homosexuality in American culture.* Durham, NC: Duke University Press.

Sophie, J. (1985-1986). A critical examination of stage theories of lesbian identity development. *Journal of Homosexuality, 12* (2), 39-51.

Spensley, J. and Barter, J.T. (1971). The adolescent transvestite on a psychiatric service: Family patterns. *Archives of Sexual Behavior, 1* (4), 347-356.

Sperber, M.A. (1973). The "as if" personality and transvestism. *Psychoanalytic Review, 60,* 605-612.

Stacey, J. and Biblarz, T.J. (2001). (How) does the sexual orientation of parents matter? *American Sociological Review, 66,* 159-183.

Steakley, J.D. (1997). Per scientiam ad justitiam: Magnus Hirschfeld and the sexual politics of innate homosexuality. In V.A. Rosario (ed.), *Science and homosexualities* (pp. 133-154). London: Routledge.

Steiner, B.W. (ed.) (1985a). Gender dysphoria: Development, research, management. New York: Plenum.

Steiner, B.W. (1985b). The management of patients with gender disorders. In B.W. Steiner (ed.), *Gender dysphoria: Development, research, management* (pp. 325-350). New York: Plenum.

Steiner, B.W. (1985c). Transsexual, transvestites, and their partners. In B.W. Steiner (ed.), *Gender dysphoria: Development, research, management* (pp. 351-364). New York: Plenum.

Steiner, B.W. (1990). Intake assessment of gender-dysphoric patients. In R. Blanchard and B.W. Steiner (eds.), *Clinical management of gender identity disorders in children and adults* (pp. 95-117). Washington, DC: APA.

Steiner, B.W. and Bernstein, S.M. (1981). Female-to-male transsexuals and their partners. *Canadian Journal of Psychiatry, 26,* 178-182.

Stermac, L., Blanchard, R., Clemmensen, L.H., and Dickey, R. (1991). Group therapy for gender-dysphoric heterosexual men. *Journal of Sex and Marital Therapy, 17* (4), 252-258.

Stevens, L., Freedman, E.B., and Bérubé, A. (1983). *She even chewed tobacco, she drank, she swore, she even courted girls: Passing women in 19th century America.* New York: Women Make Movies, videocassette.

Stoller, R.J. (1966). The mother's contribution to infantile transvestic behavior. *International Journal of Psychoanalysis, 47,* 384-395.

Stoller, R.J. (1967a), "It's only a phase": Femininity in boys. *Journal of the American Medical Association, 201,* 314-315.

Stoller, R.J. (1967b). Transvestites' women. *American Journal of Psychiatry, 124,* 89-95.

Stoller, R.J. (1968a). Male childhood transsexualism. *Journal of the American Academy of Child Psychiatry, 7,* 193-209.

Stoller, R.J. (1968b). *Sex and gender (vol. 1): The development of masculinity and femininity.* New York: Jason Aronson.

Stoller, R.J. (1972). Etiological factors in female transsexualism: A first approximation. *Archives of Sexual Behavior, 12* (1), 47-64.

Stoller, R.J. (1973). *Splitting: A case of female masculinity.* New York Times Book.

Stoller, R.J. (1974). *The transsexual experiment (vol 2). Sex and gender.* New York: Jason Aronson.

Stoller, R.J. (1975). *Perversion: An erotic form of hatred.* New York: Pantheon Books/Random House.

Stoller, R.J. (1982). Transvestism in women. *Archives of Sexual Behavior, 11* (2), 99-115.

Stoller, R.J., Marmor, J., Beiber, I., Gold, R., Socarides, C.W., Green, R., and Spitzer, R.L. (1973). A symposium: Should homosexuality be in the APA nomenclature? *American Journal of Psychiatry, 130,* 1207-1216.

Stoller, R.J. and Newman, L.E. (1971). The bisexual identity of transsexuals: Two case examples. *Archives of Sexual Behavior, 1* (1), 17-28.

Stone, S. (1991). The empire strikes back: A posttranssexual manifesto. In J. Epstein and K. Straub (eds.), *Body guards: The cultural politics of gender ambiguity* (pp. 280-304). New York: Routledge.

Substance Abuse Mental Health Services Administration: Center for Substance Abuse Treatment (SAMHSA: CSAT) (ed.) (2001). *A provider's introduction to substance abuse treatment for lesbian, gay, bisexual, and transgender individuals.* Washington, DC: SAMHSA: CSAT.

Suchet, M. (1995). Having it both ways: Rethinking female sexuality. In J.M. Glassgold and S. Iasenza (eds.), *Lesbians and psychoanalysis: Revolutions in theory and practice* (pp. 39-61). New York: Free Press.

Sullivan, L. (1990a). *From female to male: The life of Jack Bee Garland.* Boston: Alyson.

Sullivan, L. (1990b). *Information for the female to male cross dresser and transsexual.* Seattle: Ingersoll Gender Center.

Sutton, A. and Whittaker, J. (1998). Intersex disorder in childhood and adolescence: Gender identity, gender role, sex assignment, and general mental health. In D. Di Ceglie (ed.), *Stranger in my own body: Atypical gender identity development and mental health* (pp. 173-184). London: Karnac Books.

Swann, S. and Herbert, S.E. (1999). Ethical issues in the mental health treatment of gender dysphoric adolescents. In G.P. Mallon (ed.), *Social services with transgendered youth* (pp. 19-34). Binghamton, NY: The Haworth Press.

Szasz, T. (1970). *The myth of mental illness.* New York: Doubleday.

Szasz, T. (1973) *The second sin.* Garden City, NY: Anchor Doubleday.

Szkrybalo, J. and Ruble, D.N. (1999). "God made me a girl": Sex-category constancy judgments and explanations revisited. *Developmental Psychology, 35* (2), 392-402.

Tafoya, T. (1992). Native gay and lesbian issues: The two-spirited. In B. Berzon (ed.), *Positively Gay* (pp. 253-259). Berkeley: Celestial Arts.

Tafoya, T. and Wirth, D.A. (1996). Native American two-spirit men. In J.F. Longres (ed.), *Men of color: A context for service to homosexually active men* (pp. 51-67). New York: Harrington Park Press.

Talamini, J.T. (1982). *Boys will be girls.* Washington, DC: University Press of America.

Tarver, D. (2002). Transgender mental health: The intersection of race, sexual orientation, and gender identity. In B.E. Jones and M.J. Hill (eds.), *Mental health issues in lesbian, gay, bisexual, and transgender communities* (pp. 93-108). Washington, DC: American Psychiatric Publishing.

Tauchert, A. (2001). Beyond the binary: Fuzzy gender and the radical center. In F. Haynes and T. McKenna (eds.), *Unseen genders: Beyond the binaries* (pp. 181-191). New York: Peter Lang.

Tayleur, C. (1994). Transsexuals and addiction: The unacknowledged crisis. *Chrysalis: The Journal of Transgressive Gender Identities, 1* (7), 11-14.

Teh, Y.K. (2001). Mak Nyahs (male transsexuals) in Malaysia: The influence of culture and religion on their identity. *International Journal of Transgenderism, 5* (3), Available: <http://www.symposion.com/ijt/ijtvo05no03_04.htm>.

Terry, J. (1999). *An American obsession: Science, medicine, and homosexuality in modern society.* Chicago: University of Chicago Press.

Thomas, W. (1997). Navajo cultural constructions of gender and sexuality. In S.-E. Jacobs, W. Thomas, and S. Lang (eds.), *Two-spirit people: Native American gender identity, sexuality, and spirituality* (pp. 156-173). Chicago: University of Illinois Press.

Thompson, M. (1991). *Leatherfolk: Radical sex, people, politics, and practice.* Los Angeles: Alyson.

Thorne, B. (1993). *Gender play: Girls and boys in school.* New Brunswick, NJ: Rutgers University Press.

Tracy, D.M. (1987). Toys, spatial ability, and science and mathematics achievements: Are they related? *Sex Roles, 8,* 375-380.

Transgender Community Health Project (1999). *Descriptive Results.* San Francisco: San Francisco Department of Public Health.

Transgender Special Outreach Network of Parents, Families, and Friends of Lesbians and Gays (TSON-PFLAG) (1999). *Our trans children.* Washington, DC: TSON-PFLAG.

The Transgender Substance Abuse Treatment Policy Group (1995). *Transgender protocol: Treatment services guidelines for substance abuse treatment providers.* San Francisco: TSATPG, San Francisco Lesbian, Gay, Bisexual, and Transgender Substance Abuse Task Force.

Triea, K. (1999). Power, orgasm, and the psychohormonal unit. In A.D. Dreger (ed.), *Intersex in the age of ethics* (pp. 141-146). Hagerstown, MD: University Publishing Group.

Troiden, R.R. (1993). The formation of homosexual identities. In L.D. Garnets and D.C. Kimmel (eds.), *Psychological perspectives on lesbian and gay male experiences* (pp. 191-217). New York: Columbia University Press.

Trumbach, R. (1994). London's sapphists: From three sexes to four genders in the making of modern culture. In G. Herdt (ed.), *Third sex third gender: Beyond sexual dimorphism in culture and history* (pp. 111-136). New York: Zone Books.

Tsoi, W.F. (1988). The prevalence of transsexualism in Singapore. *Acta Psychiatrica Scandinavica, 78,* 501-514.

Udry, J.R. (2000). Biological limits of gender construction. *American Sociological Review, 65,* 443-457.

United Kingdom Intersex Association (n.d.). *Recommendations for the assessment and treatment of intersex conditions.* Available: <http://www.ukia.co.uk/ukiaguid.htm>.

United States Department of Labor, Bureau of Labor Statistics (2000-2001). *Occupational Outlook Handbook.* Available: <http://stats.bls.gov/oco/ocos060.htm#employment>.

Valentine, D. (1998). *Gender identity project: Report on intake statistics, 1989-April, 1997.* New York: Lesbian and Gay Community Services Center.

Van der Kolk, B.A., McFarlane, A.C., and Weisaeth, L. (eds.) (1996). *Traumatic stress: The effects of overwhelming experience on mind, body, and society.* New York: Guilford.

Van Kesteren, P.J., Gooren, L.G.J., and Megens, J.A. (1996). An epidemiological and demographic study of transsexuals in the Netherlands. *Archives of Sexual Behavior, 25* (6), 598-600.

Van Kesteren, P.J., Megens, J.A., Asscheman, H., and Gooren, L.G.J. (1997). Side effects of cross-sex hormone administration in transsexuals. *Clinical Endocrinology, 47,* 337-342.

Van Seters, A.P. and Slob, A.K. (1988). Mutually gratifying heterosexual relationship with micropenis of husband. *Journal of Sex and Marital Therapy, 14* (2), 98-107.

Vanderburgh, R. (2001). Gender dissonance: A new paradigm. Master's thesis in counseling psychology (transpersonal psychology). Orinda, CA: Graduate School for Holistic Studies, John F. Kennedy University.

Vigykian, P.D. (1978). *Triangles.* Philadelphia: Dorrance.

Vitale, A. (1996). *Client/therapist conflict: How it started and some thoughts on how to resolve it.* Available: <http://www.avitale.com/TvsClient.html>.

Vyras, P. (1996). Neglected defender of homosexuality: A commemoration. *Journal of Sex and Marital Therapy, 22* (2), 121-129.

Wade, J.C. (1993). Institutional racism: An analysis of the mental health system. *American Journal of Orthopsychiatry, 63* (4), 536-544.

Wakefield, J.C. (1997). Diagnosing DSM-IV—Part 1: DSM-IV and the concept of mental disorder. *Behavior Research and Therapy, 35* (7), 633-649.

Walcutt, H. (1995-1996). Counterpoint—physically screwed by the cultural myth: The story of a Buffalo Children's Hospital survivor. *Hermaphrodites with Attitude* (fall/winter), 10-11.

Walinder, J. ([1967] 1997). *Transsexualism: A study of forty-three cases.* (Originally published by Akademiförlaget-Gumperts, Göteborg, 1967). Available: <http://www.symposion.com/ijt/walinder/index.htm>.

Walinder, J. (1971). Incidence and sex ratio of transsexualism in Sweden. *British Journal of Psychiatry, 119* (549), 195-196.

Walinder, J.B., Lundström, B., and Thuwe, L. (1978). Prognostic factors in the assessment of male transsexuals for sex reassignment. *British Journal of Psychiatry, 132,* 16-20.

Walker, L. (1984). *The battered woman syndrome.* Focus on women 6. New York: Springer.

Walters, M., Carter, B., and Silverstein, O. (1992). *The invisible web: Gender patterns in family relationships.* Guilford Family Therapy Series. New York: Guilford.

Walters, W. (1997). The transgender phenomenon: An overview of Australian perspective. *Venereology, 10* (3), 147-149.

Walters, W.A.W., Kennedy, T., and Ross, M.W. (1986). Results of gender reassignment. In W.A.W. Walters and M.W. Ross (eds.), *Transsexualism and sex reassignment* (pp. 145-151). Melbourne, Australia: Oxford University.

Walters, W.A.W. and Ross, M.W. (1986) (eds.). *Transsexualism and sex reassignment.* Melbourne, Australia: Oxford University.

Walworth, J. (1997). Sex reassignment surgery in male-to-female transsexuals: Client satisfaction in relation to selection criteria. In B. Bullough, V.L. Bullough, and J. Elias (eds.), *Gender blending* (pp. 352-373). Amherst, NY: Prometheus Books.

Wasserman, G.A. and Lewis, M. (1985). Infant sex differences: Ecological effects. *Sex Roles, 12,* 91-95.

Weeks, J. (1981). Discourse, desire and sexual deviance: Some problems in a history of homosexuality. In K. Plummer (ed.), *The making of the modern homosexual* (pp. 76-111). London: Hutchinson.

Weinberg, M.S., Williams, C.J., and Pryor, D.W. (1994). *Dual attraction: Understanding bisexuality.* New York: Oxford University Press.

Weinberg, T. and Bullough, V.L. (1988). Alienation, self-image, and the importance of support groups for wives of TV's. *Journal of Sex Research, 24,* 262-268.

Weinberg, T. and Bullough, V.L. (1991). Women married to transvestites: Problems with adjustment. In J. Dixon and D. Dixon (eds.), *Wives, partners and others: Living with cross-dressing* (pp. 114-125). Waltham, MA: International Foundation for Gender Education (IFGE).

Weitze, C. and Osburg S. (1996). Transsexualism in Germany: Empirical data on epidemiology and application of the German transsexuals' act during its first ten years. *Archives of Sexual Behavior, 25,* 409-425.

Westman, J.C. and Zarwell, D.H. (1975). Traumatic phallic amputation during infancy. *Archives of Sexual Behavior, 4* (1), 53-63.

Wheeler, C.C. and Schaefer, L.C. (2000). *Anatomy of gender relationships: Can this 'marriage' be saved?* Paper presented at the XVI Harry Benjamin International Gender Dysphoria Association Symposium, August 17–21, 1999, London, UK. Abstract at *The International Journal of Transgenderism, 4* (1). Available: <http://www.symposion.com/ijt/greenpresidental/green51.htm>.

White, M. (1993). Deconstruction and therapy. In S. Gilligan and R. Price (eds.), *Therapeutic conversations* (pp. 22-61). New York: W.W. Norton.

White, M. (1995). *Re-authoring lives: Interviews and essays.* Adelaide, South Australia: Dulwich Centre Publications.

White, M. and Epston, D. (1990). *Narrative means to therapeutic ends.* New York: W.W. Norton.

Whitman, W. (1950). Song of myself. In W. Whitman, *Leaves of grass and selected prose.* New York: The Modern Library.

Whittle, S. (1993). The history of a psychiatric diagnostic category: Transsexualism. *Chrysalis: The Journal of Transgressive Gender Identities, 1* (5), 25-32, 49.

Whittle, S. (1995). *Transsexuals and the law.* Doctoral thesis. Manchester, England: Manchester Metropolitan University.

Whittle, S. (1999). Introduction. In K. More and S. Whittle (eds.), *Reclaiming genders: Transsexual grammars at the fin de siècle* (pp. 6-11). London: Cassell.

Whittle, S. (2000). Where did we go wrong? Feminism and trans theory—two teams on the same side. Speech given at the True Spirit Conference, Alexandria, VA, February. Available: <http://www.execpc.com/~dmmunson/tsc2k/Stephen Whittle.htm>.

Wicks, L.K. (1977). Transsexualism: A social work approach. *Health and Social Work, 2* (1), 179-193.

Wiehe, V.R. (1997). *Sibling abuse: Hidden physical, emotional, and sexual trauma.* Thousand Oaks. CA: Sage.

Wieringa, S.E. and Blackwood, E. (1999). Introduction. In E. Blackwood and S.E. Wieringa (eds.), *Same-sex relations and female desires: Transgender practices across cultures* (pp. 1-38). New York: Columbia University Press.

Wilchins, R.A. (1997a). The GID controversy: Gender identity disorder diagnosis harms transsexuals. *Transgender Tapestry, 79,* 31, 44-45.

Wilchins, R.A. (1997b). *Read my lips: Sexual subversion and the end of gender.* Ithaca, NY: Firebrand.

Wilchins, R. A. (1999). *InYourFace* interview with Riki Anne Wilchins. Available: <http://www.camptrans.com/archive/1999/stories/interview.html>.

Williams, N. (2002). The imposition of gender: Psychoanalytic encounters with genital atypicality. *Psychoanalytic Psychology, 19* (3), 455-474. Available: <http://www.bodieslikeours.org/research/williams_2002_apa.html>.

Williams, W. (1992). *The spirit and the flesh: Sexual diversity in American Indian culture.* Boston: Beacon Press.

Wilson, B.E. and Reiner, W.G. (1999). Management of intersex: A shifting paradigm. In A.D. Dreger (ed.), *Intersex in the age of ethics* (pp. 119-136). Hagerstown, MD: University Publishing Group.

Wilson, K. (1997). Gender as illness: Issues of psychiatric classification. Sixth annual International Conference on Transgender Law and Employment Policy (ICTLEP), Houston Texas. Available: <http://www.transgender.org/tg/gic/ictltext.html>.

Wilson, K. (1998). The disparate classification of gender and sexual orientation in American psychiatry. Available: <http://www.priory.com/psych/disparat.htm>.

Wilson, K. (2000). Autogynephilia: New medical thinking or old stereotype? *Transgender Forum Magazine.* Available: <http://www.transgender.org/tg/gidr/kwauto 00.html>.

Wilson, K. (2002). DSM-IV-TR: Gender identity disorder in adolescents and adults, 302.85. *GIDreform.org: Challenging psychiatric stereotypes of gender diversity.* Available: <http://www.gidreform.org/gid30285.html>.

Wilson, K. and Lev, A.I. (2003). Gender identity disorder in adults: Issues of diagnostic reform. Annual meeting of the American Psychiatric Association, May 19, San Francisco, CA.

Wilson, P. (1998). Development and mental health: The issue of difference in atypical gender identity development. In D. Di Ceglie (ed.), *A stranger in my own body: Atypical gender identity development and mental health* (pp. 1-8). London: Karnac Books.

Wilson, P., Sharp, C., and Carr, S. (1999). The prevalence of gender dysphoria in Scotland: A primary care study. *British Journal of General Practice, 49,* 991-992.

Winnicott, D.W. (1957). *Mother and child. A primer of first relationships.* New York: Basic Books.

Winnicott, D.W. (1965). *The family and individual development.* London: Tavistock Publications.

Wise, T.N. (1985). Coping with a transvestic mate: Clinical implications. *Journal of Sex and Marital Therapy, 11* (4), 293-300.

Wise, T.N., Dupkin, C., and Meyer, J.K. (1981). Partners of distressed transvestites. *American Journal of Psychiatry, 138,* 1221-1224.

Wise, T.N. and Meyer, J.K. (1980). The border area between transvestism and gender dysphoria: Tranvestite applicants for sex reassignment. *Archives of Sexual Behavior, 9* (4), 327-342.

Wisniewski, A.B., Migeon, C.J., Meyer-Bahlburg, H.F.L., Gearheart, J.P., Berkovitz, G.D., Brown, T.R., and Money, J. (2000). Complete androgen insensitivity syndrome: Long-term medical, surgical, and psychosexual outcome. *The Journal of Clinical Endocrinology and Medicine, 85* (8), 2664-2669.

Witchel, S.S. and Lee, P.A. (1996). Ambiguous genitalia. In M.A. Sperling (ed.), *Pediatric Endocrinology* (first edition, pp. 41-45). Philadelphia, PA: W.B. Saunders.

Wittig, M. (1982). The category of sex. *Feminist Issues, 2,* 63-68.

Woodhouse, C.R.J. (1994). The sexual and reproductive consequences of congenital genitourinary anomalies. *The Journal of Urology, 152,* 645-651.

Wren, B. (2000). Early physical intervention for young people with atypical gender identity development. *Clinical Child Psychology and Psychiatry, 5* (2), 220-231.

Wright, R. (1966). *Native son.* New York: Harper & Row.

Wylie, M.S. (1995). Diagnosing for dollars. *Family Therapy Networker,* May/June, 23-33.

Wylie, P. (1942). *Generation of vipers.* New York: Rinehart and Winston.

Xavier, J.M. (2000). *The Washington, DC, transgender needs assessment survey: Final report for phase two.* Washington, DC: Administration for HIV/AIDS, Department of Health of the District of Columbia Government.

Yalom, I. D. (1995). *Theory and practice of group psychotherapy.* New York: Basic Books.

Yronwode, A. (1999). Intersex individuals dispute wisdom of surgery on infants. *Synapse* (UCSF campus weekly), March 11, 1. Available: <http://www.luckymojo.com/tkintersex.html>.

Zhaoji, X. and Chuanmin, W. (reported by V.L. Bullough) (1997). Transsexualism in China in 1995. In B. Bullough, V.L. Bullough, and J. Elias (eds.), *Gender blending* (pp. 377-382). Amherst, New York: Prometheus Books.

Zhou, J.-N., Hofman, M.A., Gooren, L.J., and Swaab, D.F. (1995). A sex difference in the human brain and its relation to transsexuality. *Nature, 378* (6552), 68-70.

Zucker, K.J. (1990a). Gender identity disorders in children: Clinical descriptions and natural history. In R. Blanchard and B.W. Steiner (eds.), *Clinical management of gender identity disorders in children and adults* (pp. 3-23). Washington, DC: APA.

Zucker K.J. (1990b). Treatment of gender identity disorder in children. In R. Blanchard and B.W. Steiner (eds.), *Clinical management of gender identity disorders in children and adults* (pp. 24-45). Washington, DC: APA.

Zucker, K.J. (1996). Commentary on Diamond's prenatal predisposition and the clinical management of some pediatric conditions. *Journal of Sex and Marital Therapy, 22* (3), 148-160.

Zucker, K.J. (1999a). Controversies on Richardson's (1996) "Setting the limits on gender health." *Harvard Review of Psychiatry, 7,* 37-42.

Zucker, K.J. (1999b). Gender identity disorder in the DSM-IV: Letter to the editor. *Journal of Sex and Marital Therapy, 25* (1), 5-9.

Zucker, K. (2000). Gender identity disorder. In A.J. Sameroff, M. Lewis, and S.M. Miller (eds.), *Handbook of developmental psychopathology* (second edition, pp. 671-686). New York: Kluwer Academic/Plenum Publishing.

Zucker, K. and Bradley, S. (1995). *Gender identity disorder and psychosexual problems in children and adolescents.* New York: Guilford.

Zucker, K.J., Bradley, S.J., Kuksis, M., Pecore, K., Birkenfeld-Adams, A., Doering, R.W., Mitchell, J.N., and Wild, J. (1999). Gender constancy judgments in children with gender identity disorder: Evidence for a developmental lag. *Archives of Sexual Behavior, 28* (6), 475-502.

Zucker, K.J., Bradley, S.J., and Sanikhani, M. (1997). Sex differences in referral rates of children with gender identity disorder: Some hypotheses. *Journal of Abnormal Child Psychology, 25* (3), 217-227.

Zuger, B. (1970). The role of familial factors in persistent effeminate behaviors in boys. *American Journal of Psychiatry, 126,* 1167-1170.

Zuger, B. (1984). Early effeminate behaviors in boys: Outcome and significance for homosexuality. *Journal of Nervous and Mental Disease, 32,* 449-463.

Index

('b' indicates boxed material; 'i' indicates an illustration)